THE
SCIENCE FICTION FILM SOURCE BOOK

THE
SCIENCE FICTION FILM
SOURCE BOOK

edited by
David Wingrove

Longman

For my parents, Rose and George Wingrove

Longman Group Limited,
Longman House, Burnt Mill, Harlow,
Essex CM20 2JE, England
and Associated Companies throughout the world.

Produced by Shuckburgh Reynolds Limited,
289 Westbourne Grove,
London W11 2QA

First published in 1985

British Library Cataloguing in Publication Data

Science fiction film source book.
  1. Science fiction films—Dictionaries
  I. Wingrove, David
  791.43'09'0915   PN1995.9.S26

  ISBN 0-582-89239-2
  ISBN 0-582-89310-0 Pbk

Typeset by Tradespools Ltd, Frome, Somerset
Printed and bound in Spain by Printer Industria Grafica SA
DLB 23188/85
Design by Bill Mason
Photographs supplied by Joel Finler Collection and John Brosnan.

Contents

Foreword
Brian W. Aldiss   1

Contributors   6

Introduction: Picturing the Impossible   7

The Science Fiction Cinema: A Brief History
David Wingrove   10

Chronology of Important Films   19

Science Fiction Films: A–Z   20

The Sf Serials 1913–1956   271

Creators of Sf on Screen   272

The Literary Sources: Books Into Film   295

Special Effects in Science Fiction Cinema
John Brosnan   301

Glossary of Special Effects Terms   309

All-Time Rental Figures for Sf Films   311

Select Bibliography   312

Foreword
Brian W. Aldiss

The Cinema goes by different popular names in the United States and Britain. In the U.S.A., films are familiarly "the movies", a term which has replaced "the talkies". In Britain, we say we are going to "the pictures". The English have a static concept of many things, never more clearly seen than in this instance. While the phrase "the pictures" of course tells us something obvious and essential about Cinema, "the movies" leaps right to the heart of the matter. The pictures move. Action is the name of the game.

The way we perceive the movement of the pictures is a trick. The frames go by at the rate of 48 per second; owing to the limitations of our optical equipment, we translate this progression of stills into movement. The motion picture is not only a composite of advanced technology: it is an illusion in the human brain. No wonder that cinema and science fiction came together so early this century.

George Méliès is one of the first honoured names in cinematograph history. His extraordinary productions are almost all science fiction, as in the case of his famous *Le Voyage dans la Lune* (1902), based on the stories of Jules Verne and H.G. Wells. Here at once is an emphasis on the voyage, on action, the built-in principle of much SF. Together with the art of illusion.

Quite apart from entertaining, the viewing of motion pictures must do something highly pleasurable to the neurotransmitters in the brain, since cinema-going proved habit-forming from the start. The great movie palaces of the twenties and thirties were places of worship where a good percentage of the population went twice a week to have their neurotransmitters activated. Now television has a similarly captive audience.

Films remain, by and large, directed towards the emotive self rather than the thinking self in us. Action remains the chief name of the game although not the only one, particularly since audiences fragmented. An early refinement on pure action was something that Cinema took over from the pantomime, the transformation scene. Transformation scenes could be better done in the cinema than elsewhere; they took place before your very eyes. Of all transformation scenes, the most famous is probably that in which Dr Jekyll, having swallowed his potion, turns into Mr Hyde.

R.L. Stevenson's story, *Dr Jekyll and Mr Hyde*, has been filmed many times, more because film-makers and viewers enjoy the transformation, I'd guess, than because they wish to be reminded that good and evil exists in all of us, or that – to take an alternative reading – class distinctions breed sexual repression. The transformation of the poor Wolf Man at the time of the full moon – from Lon Chaney to the wolf-teenager of Michael Jackson – comes trailing fewer moral questions – and is a lesser creation for that reason. The transformation of dead tissue into a living Frankenstein's monster, or of the bat that enters by the moonlit castle window into Count Dracula, are other potent images which occur throughout the history of the movies. Most of them are horrific and, at least in part, science fictional.

The pumpkin, the golden coach. Transformations set cheek-by-jowl two disparate items, thereby creating a new thing, a wonder.

Their ambitions vary in sophistication. Susan Cabot's change into Wasp Woman, in Roger Corman's awful flick of that name, was a cliché even in 1960. Soon we were treated to more bizarre transactions. A submarine shrank and was injected into a human being via hyperdermic. A moron was transformed into a genius and then relapsed back into semi-imbecility again. Ralph Richardson mutated into a bed-sitting-room. The world was ready to believe anything, provided the special effects were good enough.

I remember with pleasure the early Hammer film, *The Quatermass Experiment* (1955) in which the returned astronaut struggles out of his hospital bed and staggers over to the window, on the sill of which stands a cactus in a pot. The man brings his fist down on the cactus. When he lifts it again, the cactus is growing on him. He is not man but alien. The transformation is metaphysical.

Perhaps the greatest transformation scene in the history of the cinema occurs in a science fiction film. It is the moment in *2001 – A Space Odyssey* when the bone, tossed into the air in triumph by the ape-man who has used it as a murder weapon, becomes the "Discovery", floating in space. This profound connection distills the texts of many learned studies. The juxtaposed shots contain a history of Homo Faber.

After *2001*, science fiction in the cinema could never be the same. A new generation of artists and craftsmen learnt from Kubrick on the sound stage at Pinewood, and changed the movie industry's attitude to science fiction. The earlier philosophy of "Put a monster in it and we'll at least break even" has disappeared. Indeed, in *2001*, and in the later *2010* from another Clarke novel, the aliens do not appear on the screen at all. The SF movie itself has been transformed.

After lingering in the grass roots for a while, science fiction suddenly upped and took over the world – or at least the world of entertainment – just as we had always anticipated. Blockbusting films and best-selling novels now proliferate. It's true that respectability has yet to descend, but that can wait for another few centuries; the Elizabethan dramatists, Shakespeare included, were regarded as the hacks of their day. With big and small screen, we can now have wall-to-wall science fiction.

There's an interesting paradox involved in this situation. David Wingrove puts his finger on it. The gap between written SF and movie SF remains wide. So, I believe, does the gap between the audiences. For the great movie-going audience, your diet of Spielberg and Lucas falls out of the blue, the way manna descended on the Israelites. SF literature, by contrast, is quarried out of the ground. It requires more

The spaceship Discovery *and pod, in Kubrick's* 2001

effort, more empathy, more imagination, from the reader.

The gulf between the two media is demonstrated in the case of Frank Herbert's *Dune* vs. David Lynch's *Dune*. The great deserts of Arakis comprise the presiding image in the novel, lending it a kind of majesty; one may have one's quibbles with *Dune*, but it is not easily forgotten. The film reduces the desert; it becomes merely one item in a menu of special effects. It is dominated by the giggling-silly-evil antics of the baddies. Instead of trying to come to terms with Arakis, the viewer is left struggling to figure out the tiresome entanglements of plot. Frank Herbert's novels are thoughtful if ponderous. Thoughtful the film is not.

And this has always been the complaint of SF readers regarding SF films. They remove the ideas and inject melodrama. Yet *Dune* is, as Wingrove points out, the first major SF novel to be filmed. There is every reason to suspect that the future will bring more novels to the screen, filmed with some feeling for the originals (as I believe was the case in 1974 with Jack Gold's under-esteemed movie version of Algis Budrys' novel *Who?*).

Wingrove points to the damage that film companies have done to great originals, most notably in the case of Mary Shelley's *Frankenstein*, whose highly articulate monster is reduced on celluloid to a maniacal destroyer, trailing wires and rubber tubing as it bashes through doors. However, the balance is not all on one side. Stanley Kubrick vastly improved Peter George's dim novel *Red Alert* when translating it into *Dr Strangelove* – just as later he was to improve Thackeray's laboured costume drama, *Henry Esmond*, by dint of his superb photography. Tarkovsky's *Solaris* has a mystery and poignance on film denied the book.

The Millenium Falcon avoids an Imperial fighter in Star Wars

Strangelove is by no means the only evil doctor to stalk the screen. The power-crazed Dr Mabuse was alive and well in the twenties, together with Dr Jekyll. We'll forget about Dr Who's disastrous appearance on the wide screen. I became an addict of SF films – often trying to shake my addiction – with the appearance of the formidable *Dr Cyclops*, who lives in the heart of the Peruvian jungle and shrinks those who oppose him in his radium mine, until they are fifteen inches high. They get him in the end. This remarkable movie was a precursor of the equally enjoyable *The Incredible Shrinking Man* (with its great line at the close, "For Gard there is no Zeero") in which another tiny hero also has to confront a domestic cat bigger than he is.

Some of the silliness which seemed necessarily to stigmatise the old low-grade SF movies has not vanished over-night. The goodies are still seen to shoot more accurately than the baddies. But the SF film has taken vast steps forward, and this volume celebrates the fact.

The old need for action remains. It is often the driving force behind the amazing sceneries to which the SF cinema has treated us. The shattered and fog-shrouded planet in *Alien*, the deserts of Luke Skywalker's home planet, the sub-molecular world of *Tron*. . . It will be a long while before we run out of backdrops. And the dazzling photography . . . so seductive nowadays that the tritest subject comes dressed in riches.

Even a trite-seeming film can secrete interesting ideas. *Star Trek: The*

Motion Picture, despite its pomposities and a silly ending, offered magnificent spectacle and a consideration of the possibility of sex between man and machine – doubtless a social problem stored up in all our futures.

In fact, the possibility of such couplings has been around for some while, starting possibly with the telemovie *A for Andromeda*, in which Julie Christie is a synthetic woman created by coded messages from the distant nebula (script by Fred Hoyle). Later, Christie has trouble of a sexual nature with a computer in *Demon Seed*. Is it conceivable – and I use the term advisedly – that such things have genuine predictive power? Whether that is so or not, they certainly point to a closer rapport between humanity and its machines, a rapport which the SF film itself represents.

Of course, I do not always agree with Wingrove's assessments of films. That is hardly to be expected. I found *Deathwatch*, like the novel from which it derived, grey and without energy; I prefer *Star Wars* to *Return of the Jedi*; I think better of George Pal's *War of the Worlds* – and of George Pal in general – than he does; I believe that Ray Harryhausen carried dimensional stop-action animation photography – a method superceded by computer controlled cameras – to an artistic climax in the delectably odd *Valley of the Gwangi* and that lovely fantasy *The Golden Voyage of Sinbad*. And so on. There is no accounting for tastes.

Of course, it would have been easier for Wingrove if he could have discussed *Star Wars* and *Close Encounters* in the context of Lucas's and Spielberg's earlier films, particularly *American Graffiti* and *Duel*, or have contrasted Boorman's *Zardoz* with his previous and more compelling film *Deliverance*, where isolated communities are considerably nastier than the Eternals in his fantasy. And so on. But this is not that sort of book.

What it is is a generous and stimulating assessment of scence fiction cinema, with wise emphasis on its development. Where I did not agree with David Wingrove, his judgement is generally kinder and – face the fact – more thoughtful than mine might have been. He has changed my mind on a number of points. He has certainly made me long to see again some of those visions we sat through when we went in all innocence to "the pictures".

Contributors

Contributions by: John Brosnan, Tony Crawley, Garry Kilworth, Tony Richards, Ritchie Smith and David Wingrove.

The initials of the appropriate contributor appear at the end of each entry in the A–Z listing. Entries with no initials are written by David Wingrove.

In the introduction to this volume I've commented on my reasons for selection and omission, but something needs to be added concerning the star-ratings given to the 1,300 films listed in this section. For most films of the silent era – that is, prior to 1928 – I've decided not to award any stars, primarily because there's little chance, unless it's a major presentation like *Metropolis*, that you'll get to see the film. Likewise, with some non-English-speaking films which I haven't been able to see and feel it unlikely will be made available on video or as TV features, I've merely made comment. With most of such films it's important to establish their existence, if only to give a context to those other films which are shown more regularly. As for the star-ratings themselves, they're a fun element, and provide a quick, personal appraisal of four different (and, admittedly, overlapping) aspects of each film: Plot (P); Technical Merit (T); Enjoyment (E); Artistic Merit (A). Credits given in the entries are not repeated in the credit listing that follows.

EDITOR

David Wingrove is a full-time writer and editor and was formerly editor of *Vector*, the critical journal of the British Science Fiction Association. His books include *The Immortals Of Science Fiction, Apertures: A Study Of The Writings Of Brian W. Aldiss* and *The Science Fiction Source Book*. He has contributed to a variety of newspapers and periodicals, including *The Sunday Tribune* and *London Magazine*, and is editor of "SF Alternatives", a series of science fiction reprints. He has just completed a science fiction novel, *A Perfect Art*, and is working on a full-length study of Philip K. Dick (with Brian Griffin) and a doctoral thesis in English Literature on Thomas Hardy, D. H. Lawrence and William Golding. In his spare time he looks after his young daughter, Jessica.

CONTRIBUTORS TO SCIENCE FICTION FILMS: A CONSUMER'S GUIDE

John Brosnan is a freelance journalist who contributes regularly to *Starburst* magazine. He is also the author of two fine books on the history and development of the science fiction cinema, *Movie Magic: The Story Of Special Effects* (1976) and *Future Tense: The Cinema Of Science Fiction* (1978).

Tony Crawley is a freelance film journalist and author, and contributes to most of the major film magazines. He is author of *The Steven Spielberg Story* (1983) and contributes the popular "Things To Come" section for *Starburst* magazine.

Garry Kilworth is author of five science fiction novels and one collection of science fiction stories, *The Songbirds Of Pain* (1984). He has contributed stories to *Omni* and to *Isaac Asimov's Science Fiction Magazine*. His most recent novel was *A Theatre Of Timesmiths* (1984).

Tony Richards is a freelance writer in the science fiction, fantasy and horror genres. He has contributed to magazines like *Fantasy And Science Fiction* and *Isaac Asimov's Science Fiction Magazine*.

Ritchie Smith is a teacher and freelance writer. His short stories (co-authored with Tom Penman) have appeared in *New Writings In Sf*. He is currently collaborating with Penman on a novel.

Introduction: Picturing the Impossible
David Wingrove

Images. My first thought is of images – the reason for watching rather than reading.

In silent monochrome, drab, careworn figures tend the vast, unceasing wheels of giant mechanisms. Elsewhere the lightning flashes in a dark and cluttered lab where that first Promethean sin of theft is re-enacted ... and the creature wakes. Footprints appear from nowhere in the snow and a peal of laughter sounds in an empty street. A giant telescope peers outward at the vastness of the star-filled night, while frail and tiny men discuss the fate of Man. Time passes.

It is years later in the realm of real events, and in the timeless realm of image we (sometimes) see in colour. Alien warships, inimical to Man, scorch across Earth's sky like comets and crash-land, biding their time of conquest. From the depths of a dark, forbidding lake crawls something from our nightmare past, gilled and scaled, while down in the storm-drains of Los Angeles, frightened but determined men walk into the darkness of the tunnels, where wait the giant ants. Far across space itself, the crew of a human spaceship watch in terror as something huge suggests its invisible form, flashing and sparking as it tries to breach the force-shield. In a cellar of a small American town a pod is ripening, arms splitting from the trunk, its unformed caricature of a face slowly evolving its perfect mimicry of Man. And, in another cellar, another town, the tiny figure of a man, smaller with each moment, battles against a spider as big as himself, armed only with a needle.

Again time passes. And so to now, the "future" so many of science fiction's visionaries dreamed of and guessed about so wrongly. More images. Subtler, more complex images. Images so perfectly achieved that they fool the eye and seduce the sense, making us believe in their reality. A new age of illusion. A new generation of images.

A mile-long spaceship thunders overhead, lasers flashing as it closes on a smaller craft that seeks the safety of the planet below. In the dark corridors of a space-freighter a man turns suddenly, a giant alien head – salivating, teeth glinting like sharpened knives – briefly illuminated in his flashlight. The giant head of a god floats above the outlands; guns pour from its mouth like rain. In a room of bronze and amber light an owl watches as a man questions a beautiful girl to see whether she is human or android, while in the parched desert of some otherwise-envisaged world of the near future, spiked and vicious cars – the mechanosauri of the future – carry their cargoes of barbarian malice towards their certain fates. Blood vessels swell and muscles contort as two men with special powers duel to the death, eyeballs bursting, skin igniting. Another, different spacecraft moves silently, scientifically, towards a giant wheel of girdered metal while the *Blue Danube* fills our ears. Ape faces bark their laughter as they deny intelligence in Man, while in a tank of orange gas a hideously distorted creature – once human floats before the Emperor of known space and makes a treaty.

We pause a moment, look at old images now renewed – of giant apes and super-heroes, of pods and Things and further re-awakenings of the creature – then turn to see, amongst the multitude of furry toys piled in a child's toy cupboard, a small, long-necked alien, club-headed and ugly, yet with beautifully expressive eyes.

Images ...

There are many more, of course, and that, essentially, is what this book – this gathering of a wide range of films under the vague heading of "science fiction" – is about. This is a guide to those images and to the creators of those images; images which attempt, as the literature of science fiction attempted before them, to create pictures of the impossible. This volume attempts to be no more than an opening into that world of science fiction imagery which is, through the medium of cinema, immediately open to us. We need do nothing; we need only sit before the screen and attend. Yet we might – through the medium of a book such as this – gain an idea of what kind of experience we are letting ourselves in for before we take that seat. So, there's an attempt, especially in the large, central A–Z section, to comment upon each picture and ascertain its qualities (or absence of them). That attempt is, necessarily, personal and thus subjective. I can guarantee that no-one will agree with all the judgements and that some of you may well disagree strongly over specific films, yet even in that disagreement (which, I must say, sometimes existed between my contributors and I) there's a lot of fun. If this book gets you talking about the merits or de-merits of certain films then part of its intention – to involve the reader – will have been achieved.

It is necessary, I believe, to make some sort of comment on my criteria for selection of films. There isn't, as far as I'm aware, an adequate definition for science fiction, and so to further attempt to define what is and what is not a science fiction film presents problems. I found that it wasn't enough to demand that there was a scientific idea behind the tale, though that proved a good starting point: most of the films listed have, at least as a pretext, the idea that something is different, that somehow things have changed. I ruled out what was overtly fantastic (*The Never-Ending Story, Conan* and *The Wizard of Oz*, for instance – films sometimes claimed for the genre) or horror-oriented (the Dracula, Wolfman and Mummy films, except where they overlapped with the Frankenstein films with their tenuous but existent link to Mary Shelley's original novel, itself a pure example of science fiction). Elsewhere I've tried to distinguish where to draw the line. Films about animated cars (*Herbie* and its German equivalent, *Dudu*) were omitted on the grounds that they were pure fantasy, included were "Lost World" stories (long related to sf through the pulp magazines) and tales of Pre-History (again, long annexed as a part of science fiction's realm, even if the juxtaposition of man and dinosaur is an impossible-to-swallow anachro-nism).

These, the many faces of science fiction, make it the most interesting and most exciting of film's genres, as well as the most abused by the producers and directors who've exploited it, many of whom are listed in the section, Creators Of Sf On Screen.

This book is designed for practical use, for fun, and – because we are so rapidly entering a time when most films are becoming available on video – as a guide to the sf films now available on video. Rather more space has been taken up in dealing with those than in earlier (usually pre-1950) films, because those are the films which you are likely to be seeing, but no film of importance in the history of sf film (such as *Things To Come*, for instance) has been neglected in the commentary, and if we've been dismissive, there's usually good reason.

Welcome to *The Science Fiction Film Source Book*. May it open the way, not merely to many pleasant hours of reading, but to many hours of fascinating viewing.

David Wingrove
April 1985

The Science Fiction Cinema: A Brief History
David Wingrove

1968 was an important year for the science fiction cinema. It was a year in which three different trends within the cinematic genre each produced a single film of some degree of excellence. For 70 years, film-makers had worked at presenting images of the fantastic, with limited success, and then, suddenly, in a single year, all that had gone before seemed only a preface, a proto-form of the real thing: a true cinema of science fiction seemed possible at last. Which is not to say that science fiction films had not been made prior to 1968, merely to identify that before those three films science fiction (at least in cinematic terms) had been an adjunct to the horror film and was often dealt with as such. The genres overlapped extensively, with *Frankenstein* (1931) at the focal point. Mad scientists, part-Moreau, part-Frankenstein, part-Hyde, did devilish things to their fellow men (or to apes) in their hissing, gurgling laboratories; fading beauties sought the secret of eternal youth, criminals stole the secret, deadly inventions of unwitting and naïve scientists, while out in the jungle explorers were discovering fantastic left-overs from our prehistoric past.

When the Bomb came along the genre merely adapted itself to the (then unknown) possible consequences of radioactive fall-out and produced a whole succession of enlarged and distorted creatures that would have graced the nightmares of Hieronymus Bosch. It was the genre parodied so perfectly in Richard O'Brien's *The Rocky Horror Picture Show* (1975), a genre neglected by the men who held Hollywood's purse-strings and ignored by most of those (and, it must be said, they were rare in those days) with any artistic feeling for the cinema. It suffered on all counts: was ridiculed by the critics, exploited by the unscrupulous and (perhaps its greatest liability) was home for the inept. But the fans loved it, much as the fans of the written form of science fiction uncritically loved the garish *schlock* they were presented with in the pulp magazines of the 1920s and 1930s.

Why? Well, maybe it was because what was so evidently lacking in terms of artistic achievement was compensated for by the genre's over-abundant enthusiasm for outrageous ideas – for presenting concepts (however ineptly) that made you think, made you wonder. Concepts that the "straight" cinema scorned to consider. It was an age of innocence, when it was still possible to believe that Eddie Parker in a rubber suit really *was* the hideous creature he was meant to be; when the mind could ignore the tell-tale wires and believe that the space-suited actors really *were* in space. And yet, somehow, it was never quite enough to persuade the multitudes who weren't quite so fanatical and yet were predisposed to like the fantastic imagery of science fiction *if presented well*. It was in that area of presentation that science fiction cinema consistently let itself down: the make-up, however good, never quite disguised the human form beneath; the special effects, however well achieved, never did quite convince you of their reality.

Which returns me to 1968 and my three films, my three trends. Science fiction cinema, prior to 1968 was – with notable exceptions – oriented towards projects where the talents of a make-up artist were valuable if not indispensable. The Golem, Frankenstein, Dr Jekyll, the Creature From The Black Lagoon, the Monster From Outer Space, Godzilla, the Invaders From Mars, various ape-men and numerous dinosaurs and enlarged creepy-crawlies (these last courtesy of animation experts and cinematographers): these fantastic

A scene from Beneath The Planet Of The Apes

creations crowded the screens, particularly in the 1950s, which were the
heyday of the "Creature-feature". It
was this trend of science fiction
movie-making that the 1968 film
Planet Of The Apes seems, at first
glance, to be part of. The film brought
make-up to a fine art. It was possible,
at last, to believe that the chimpanzees, orang-utangs and gorillas really
were what they purported to be.
Hollywood itself recognized this
much in giving John Chambers, the film's make-up expert, an Oscar for his
work. It was, undoubtedly, the high-point of this tradition (even if used to tell a
story which was, in the first two of the "Ape" films at least, pure social satire
and not borderline horror) and set a new standard, a new set of expectations in
the audience. From then on make-up would have to be as good as if not better
than that of the "Ape" movies to satisfy filmgoers.

Something similar happened in another area of the cinematic genre in 1968.
The film was *2001: A Space Odyssey*, and its special effects works ushered in a
revolution in techniques which is still going on in the science fiction cinema.
2001 was in the tradition of earlier films like *By Rocket To The Moon* (1929),
Destination Moon (1950), *When Worlds Collide* (1951), *This Island Earth* (1955),
and *Forbidden Planet* (1956), films which were expressions of a purer, hard-
tech-oriented form of science fiction. Generally – and this was something *2001*
shared with these earlier films – the huge effort put into creating effective and
believable special effects created an imbalance within the film. Story –
characterization, particularly – suffered, and we might easily criticize these
films for their stilted, awkward "feel". To their credit we might say that their
brave attempts at creating a sense of scientific spectacle were, once again,
adding to cinema, the best medium for illusion we currently have, something
that the "straight" cinema shied away from. Something which has, in the last
decade, become the most important growth area in modern cinema, satisfying
Hollywood's unchanging criterion: "Does it make money?".

Kubrick's special effects work on *2001* was laborious and thorough, and
modern computer techniques have made the whole job much easier, but the
discoveries made in making the film, and the subsequent critical and popular
reception of the film, again changed attitudes. Of course, low-budget movies
with lousy special effects would still be made, but the public's taste – their
expectations; always a shaper of developments in any medium – had been
whetted. In time that hunger for science fiction spectacle would need to be
satisfied.

The third of the films made in 1968 which seem to me to have changed
attitudes towards the genre is one which many may not even have heard of, and
yet it won an Oscar for Cliff Robertson, its leading actor. *Charly*, adapted from
Daniel Keyes's deeply moving novel, *Flowers For Algernon*, had nothing
spectacular in the way of make-up or special effects – in fact it made no use of
either. What it did have was an intelligent script, a sensitive cast and a director
who knew how to make an excellent film: all demands of the "straight" cinema.
And yet it was – quite definitely was – science fiction. Not sci-fi, as much of the

science fiction cinema prior to 1968 can justly be termed, but the intelligent, ordered working-out of a science-fictional idea. For once the visual medium gave an accurate reflection of the literature from which it derived.

It's difficult, perhaps even irrelevant, to compare written science fiction with its cinematic equivalent. The short length of a film argues against it being able to provide too deep an exposition of a science fiction idea, and literary science fiction would seem to have an advantage in that area, yet the written form sometimes suffers from the heavy burden of having to describe the look and feel of a different, future society, something that film (especially a modern film like *Blade Runner* (1982)) can infer through its settings within minutes. The science fiction cinema has also, for the main part, seen itself as a medium for adventure, which again gives it advantages (in terms of pure excitement – its condensed images piled on in breathless succession) and disadvantages (it can seem trite, even stupid, through its paper-thin plot). But when it ignores the demand to be slick and showily spectacular, the science fiction cinema is capable of producing something possessing the strengths of both written and visual forms. There were few instances of this marriage of forms before *Charly*, yet they were memorable – perhaps the finest of the pre-1968 sf films – for making you leave the cinema not merely with the sense of having enjoyed a movie, but with having somehow grown through having to consider a novel idea. *Invasion Of The Bodysnatchers* (1956), ostensibly just a "scare" movie, is one such film, with its subtle, understated argument about differences in the quality of life. *Dr Strangelove* (1963) is another, its dark comedy revealing a genuine fear about "those in control". Truffaut's 1966 film, *Fahrenheit 451*, is almost such a film, but allowed its visual poetry to swamp Bradbury's elegant plea for literacy. Rarities. Yet *Charly*, lacking the "sensational" aspect of the earlier films, pointed the way towards a more thoughtful attitude towards plot, towards the all-important literary input which could transform a flashy confection into a classic of the genre.

To me these three 1968 films seem to reflect different attributes of good science fiction cinema; the two kinds of technical mastery and the additional quality, less rarely found now but still the last consideration of the money-men, of intelligence. Bearing this in mind, I'd like to quickly trace how the science fiction cinema capitalized upon its 1968 discoveries and how it changed into a true, multi-expressive genre, no longer a haven just for sf fanatics, but for tens of millions of cinema-goers. Oh, and one last factor needs a moment's consideration before launching out on the post-1968 journey of discovery: the changing nature of the cinema audience. Between 1968 and 1984 cinema has become a medium for the young; under-25s now comprise the vast majority of the cinema-going public. The same age-group are reading science fiction, playing science-fiction-oriented computer games and generally coming to terms with a world where change, not stability, is the norm. As a result the men in Hollywood who make the financial decisions now have to face the fact that their young audience *like* science fiction. But, of course, there's also the consoling fact for them that the science fiction cinema is now the most lucrative field to work in.

But back to 1968. Innovation, unlike financial success, takes its time to stir the imaginations of those who fund the huge projects that Hollywood (and its lesser imitations worldwide) produces. None of the 1968 films were run-away successes, and those with long memories could cite films like *Metropolis* (1926), *Just Imagine* (1930) and *Things To Come* (1936) as spectacular, well-intentioned financial dodos. In the circles that mattered, then, there was no confidence that science fiction was the next big thing, and so it was little wonder that in the

Peter Sellers as President Muffley and Peter Bull as Ambassador de Sadesky in a scene from Dr Strangelove

five years that followed the more memorable science fiction offerings came from independent sources; medium-budget films for the main part by directors who had some kind of commitment to science fiction. 1970 found Robert Wise (who had already made *The Day The Earth Stood Still* in 1951) filming Michael Crichton's *The Andromeda Strain*, an intelligent medical thriller, while George Lucas (later of *Star Wars* fame) was cutting his cinematic teeth on *THX 1138*, encouraged by Francis Ford Coppola. 1971 found Stanley Kubrick filming Anthony Burgess's *A Clockwork Orange* (he had already shown his interest in sf cinema with *Dr Strangelove*), and Douglas Trumbull, part of the *2001* special effects team, making his own use of his discoveries in *Silent Running*. Distinct from all that was happening in Western cinema, and yet just as significant, Andrei Tarkovsky, the Russian director, made *Solaris*, perhaps the first true hybrid of the three elements I've discussed.

1972 was a quiet year for the sf cinema, producing the flawed but interesting *Slaughterhouse Five*, but in 1973 four films were made which suggested that science fiction cinema had come of age, even if it had yet to earn more than pocket-money rates. Least of these, if the most enjoyable, was *Westworld*, perhaps the first film to present androids as perfect imitations of humans. More whimsical, more complex and – because it was even filmed – more surprising, was *The Final Programme*, a cinematic rendering of Michael Moorcock's 1960s anti-hero, Jerry Cornelius. The two gems of the year, however, were *Phase IV*, the first science fiction film to make us consider a non-Anthropocentric view – we learned to empathize with the ants – and John Boorman's intriguing puzzle of a film, *Zardoz*, which so casually accepted modern science-fictional ideas and so immaculately presented them.

1974 brought two items of eccentric interest from directors who were to return to the genre with more polished work. John Carpenter's *Dark Star*, made on a shoestring budget but with a lot of loving care, drifts rather aimlessly in places (imitating its spaceship, one might say), but its vocabulary is, for once, 1970s science fiction (most sf films lag a good 20 years or so behind trends in the written genre), and its talking bomb – a machine nurtured on philosophy – and dead captain make it a rather disconcerting experience for those who like their science fiction in the Star Trek mould. The second item was Peter Weir's *The Cars That Ate Paris*, which single-handedly spawned a whole sub-genre of "Road" movies, with the later *Mad Max II* perhaps the best of them. 1974 also saw Ira Levin's novel, *The Stepford Wives*, come to the screen. He was a mainstream writer and his film was dealt with as a mainstream film: but its subject matter was science-fictional; the production of subservient female android duplicates in a small American town.

Amongst the more interesting sf films released in 1975 were *The Ultimate Warrior, A Boy And His Dog* and *Death Race 2000*, the last from Roger Corman's exploitation stable, New World. Corman had been active in the 1950s and 1960s, mimicking the trends of the science fiction cinema in his own low-budget productions; in the 1970s and 1980s he merely upped his budget – and gave us the same old sick *schlock*. The film of the year, however, was the critically under-rated movie, *Rollerball*, with its mixture of violence and future sociology.

1976 was a far from golden year for the science fiction cinema. Films like *Futureworld, The Food Of The Gods, At The Earth's Core* and *Rollerbabies* seemed to return the genre to its pre-1968 state, and even the two best films of the year were far from classics, particularly *Logan's Run*, which was disowned by its original authors. *The Man Who Fell To Earth* was better, admittedly, and its choice of David Bowie as the alien was inspired, yet even that film seemed to peter out at the end, as if science fiction cinema had petered out along with it. It would have been a very brave man who would have placed his money on two science fiction films becoming, in the next 12 months, the biggest-grossing films of all time.

1977, as much as 1968, was a crucial year for the science fiction cinema, if for different reasons. If 1968's harvest of movies had shown *how* the genre could progress, 1977's crop demonstrated to the men controlling the purse-strings that it was in their interest to help the genre progress.

Let's deal with the second-rate productions of the year first – though in pre-1968 terms we might consider them important movies. *Capricorn One* was writer/director Peter Hyams's first encounter with the sf cinema, and he sacrificed the realism he seemed to be striving for to the demands of a slick thriller plot. A mission to Mars is faked and the cover-up job is deadly. It could have been a good film, and remains a good entertainment, but somewhere along the line Hyams stopped thinking about what he was doing. The same could be said for *Demon Seed*, which again fell between two stools. Was it to be a serious film based on a good science fiction idea, or was it to be a sensationalized piece of entertainment? In each case a film which demanded intelligent appreciation on the part of its audience fell apart because of lapses in its own logic.

Logic was the last thing on the minds of George Lucas and Steven Spielberg when they were making their films. Cohesion, yes, and a concern for slick, fast-action storytelling, but not logic. Both directors wanted us to feel again that "sense of wonder" science fiction fans had long claimed had vanished from the written genre back in the 1950s: the sense of a teeming universe of possibility. First into the cinemas was George Lucas with *Star Wars* – Part Four, Lucas told us, of a nine-part epic adventure set in the far distant past in a far distant part of the universe. It was greeted with open-mouthed adulation. Here was what *2001* had promised but, in its struggle to perfect the special effects, had failed to deliver. Perhaps it lacked intelligence, but who cared? Look at the spaceships! the robots! the aliens! The future (albeit in the past) was suddenly here. It was pure fairy story, of course – a young hopeful, a princess to be rescued, a lovable rogue mercenary and his "walking carpet" wookie pal, an evil Emperor and his wizard-like servant. Fairy story with the best-looking sf gloss anyone had ever managed to create. The movie moguls, no longer cautious when they saw how many bums Lucas had managed to put on seats, realized its significance at once. And in the meantime Steven Spielberg released his own little sf movie, *Close Encounters Of The Third Kind*, and sat back to witness the cash registers ring and the fans again heap praise on its creator. A well-told UFO story had, through the loving care of its director, some superb acting by Richard Dreyfuss and special effects that matched those of *Star Wars* in every department – especially in the Mother Ship sequence at the end – become what some, Ray Bradbury amongst them, equated with a religious experience. Both films are stirring experiences with a sense of mythic depth, and if they lack some element of intelligence in their storylines (for the concepts behind *Close Encounters* are the usual, tedious UFO-nut rubbish), they greatly compensate in visual splendour. Nothing could be the same in the science fiction cinema after 1977 – if only because the moguls saw the glint of pure gold.

The immediate effect of the *Star Wars/Close Encounters* success story was that money was invested heavily (and for the first time ever) in special effects. Companies like Industrial Light and Magic, Apogee Inc., and Digital Productions were set up with no other purpose than to create and develop special effects techniques. The result was to come in the 1980s with a whole glut of beautiful-looking films that were vehicles for unbelievably good special effects. In the years between, however, the sf cinema had a bout of nostalgia and began to look towards its comic-book origins for inspiration.

The first super-hero to be resurrected was Superman, played by Christopher Reeve. The claim "You'll really believe a man can fly" emphasized once again the advance in special effects, but the film fortunately did not hinge on such dazzling pyrotechnics and, to its credit, evoked a sense of innocent epic. Like *Close Encounters* its lack of realism didn't matter; it had a big heart. Less successful were the semi-spoofs of *Buck Rogers In The 25th Century* (1979) and *Flash Gordon* (1980). 1978 saw also the re-make of *Invasion Of The Body Snatchers*, but the new version, again benefiting from the amazing advances in special effects, yet sacrificed something of the original's atmosphere: we were too busy watching the garish happenings to be deeply involved in the paranoid vision. And if we're talking of re-makes, one might consider *Battlestar Galactica*, rushed out in the wake of *Star Wars* to exploit the sudden market for space opera. Like Roger Corman's 1980 film, *Battle Beyond The Stars*, however, it was only visually similar to the Lucas original. Something had gone missing in the wash, so to speak. What was myth in *Star Wars* became mere event in the lesser films: we didn't really care what happened to the heroes, even if we did really rather like the special effects.

And so we come to 1979 and another exceptionally good year for the science fiction cinema. It had its dodos, of course, including what must be the worst of the post-1969 mega-budget movies, *The Black Hole*, but it also had *Stalker*, Andrei Tarkovsky's three-hour work of art – possibly the finest film in the science fiction cinema. The former demonstrated what happens when the money-men alone have their say, the latter what can be achieved with a minimum of special effects and a sense of the sheer potentiality of cinema as an art form. The two films which shared the highest media profile that year, however, were *Alien* and *Star Trek: The Motion Picture*.

Alien took a good old-fashioned 1940s-style science fiction novella and gave it the high-gloss horror treatment. Despite the hype that preceded it, it *was* worth venturing into the dark of a cinema to see, even if, at moments, you wished you were elsewhere. And what the film stressed once more – as if it needed stressing – was that science fiction *had* come of age, and that anything could be filmed.

If you're a fan of the TV series of *Star Trek* (and I'll admit that I once was) then the movie could not help but be a must. But the film of *Star Trek* proved a rather slow, cumbersome beast, lavishly produced but ultimately without much more to offer than an average weekly episode padded out to feature length. Captain Kirk had been promoted, but otherwise nothing had changed in the *Enterprise*'s cosy bridge.

Three such good films might have been enough for a whole decade prior to 1969, but also on offer that year were three more films which deserve comment. The first, *Mad Max*, is the road movie that introduced George Miller's mythical anti-hero, and is an entertaining, roughly-made B-movie which did not for a moment suggest how good its sequel would be. *Deathwatch* was a different kind of sf film again, its perfect transformation of D. G. Compton's novel into Bernard Tavernier's film evidence of a growing acceptance of science fiction as an art form by certain directors. A film in the tradition of *Charly*, it is full of resounding images that remain with you long after the film has ended. *Quintet*, another medium-budget science fiction film, starred Paul Newman and was directed by Robert Altman (both signs of a change in attitude – science fiction was no longer crank fodder!). Like *Alien* it was pure science fiction, but of a different kind altogether. It was as modern as the written genre, assuming a high degree of intelligence in its audience, yet repaying such careful attention as it was given. Spectacle and adventure had been replaced, in these last two films, by more demanding artistic criteria. The seeds of *Charly*, long sown, were at last bearing fruit.

1980 saw the release of the second film in the Star Wars sequence, a film every bit as exciting and delightful to the eye as its prequel. That Christmas every home with a young child or two in it was cluttered with *Star Wars* toys. The boom was definitely on. Every film that appeared had what seemed to be ever-subtler improvements in special effects. David Cronenberg's *Scanners* depicted duelling telepaths, exploding heads and, to its credit, an intelligent storyline. *Altered States* again played with the concept of mind-games and showed William Hurt regressing back to an ape-man: an old theme from the 1930s was thus given new life.

While everyone was waiting for Spielberg to follow up *Close Encounters*, 1981 arrived, and with it *Mad Max II*, father and mother to innumerable bastard children (most of them Italian, it seems). Peter Hyams's second science fiction venture, *Outland*, for all its *High Noon* reverberations, really looked as it were set on the distant moon of Jupiter, Io. Again, images familiar to sf fans from the written form had been given a stunning visual representation. And, as if to emphasize that really everyone was in on the science fiction act, the Monty Python team, under Terry Gilliam, were present in *Time Bandits*, a remarkable, funny, intelligent and brilliantly visual film.

Fourteen years on from 1968, years in which computer technology had transformed numerous aspects of our world, found science fiction at its high-water mark. It was no longer possible, as it had been in the 1950s, to single out one film as the good science fiction film of the year because the year produced eight films which, in their own ways, were all superior to anything that had been produced way back then. *Android, Big Meat Eater, Blade Runner, E.T., Firefox, The Thing, Tron* and *Videodrome*. And this is to neglect *Star Trek II* and *Xtro!* Biggest film of the year – of the century? – was *E.T. The Extra-Terrestrial*, Steven Spielberg's homage to the heart and its ability to empathize with even the ugliest-looking alien with big soft eyes. I admit I cried when Elliott cried, laughed when E.T. got drunk, did all the things Spielberg intended me to do . . . and didn't begrudge him for doing it to me.

And while Spielberg was manipulating us, Ridley Scott was tinkering with a Philip K. Dick novel to produce the visually magnificent *Blade Runner*, my own favourite for that year, if only because it reflects some aspects of science fiction's most remarkable writer. *Blade Runner* called its androids "Replicants" and hunted them down, but *Android* called a spade a spade and showed the "thing" in all its uncertain, almost-human, not-quite-natural state. For sheer charm, *Android* excels, paying its dues along the way to Fritz Lang's *Metropolis* (1926), the film which could be said to have started it all.

John Carpenter's *The Thing* – a re-make of *The Thing (From Another World)* (1951) – succeeds in ways that his earlier, self-scripted *Escape From New York* failed. With *The Thing*, Carpenter relied on John Campbell's original story, "Who Goes There?" to give him his science fiction framework, adding to that work of imagination the technical abilities of his special effects crew, who proved capable of mimicking absolutely anything Campbell could dream up. The result was a piece of pure cinematic nightmare, for "The Thing" is a re-awakened alien predator with the ability of mimicking absolutely anything and a drive to survive at the expense of anything else that comes in its way.

Videodrome was another film that dealt with plasticity and the horror of mutated, distorted shapes. From Canadian director David Cronenberg there's always something gory to be expected, but *Videodrome* proved exceptional even for him. Less bloodthirsty, yet in its own way, every bit as distinctive as a Cronenberg film, was *Big Meat Eater*, the fevered imaginings of another young Canadian director, Chris Windsor. A low-budget "parody" of 1950s science fiction, it is really too much a child of its age – the confused and malleable 1980s – to be seen *merely* as parody. Its eccentricity and pure style mark it out as one of a new kind of sf film, drawing upon science fiction cinema for its images but unconcerned with telling a traditional sf story. *Repo Man* (1984) is another film in this vein and doubtless we'll see many more in the next few years.

The range and sophistication of science fiction cinema was again displayed in 1983. Another Star Wars episode came from Lucas Films, *Return Of The Jedi*, completing the central trilogy of tales. And if the critics were bored, the fans certainly weren't. *Superman III* played it for laughs and proved the most enjoyable of that trilogy. Douglas Trumbull, special effects doyen of *2001*, *Close Encounters* and *Blade Runner* fame, produced another of his own projects, *Brainstorm*, despite the tragedy of actress Natalie Wood's death in the midst of shooting. Like *Altered States* it attempted to portray events happening in the mind and, like the other film, only partly achieved its aims. *Krull*, one of the most beautiful-looking films yet made in the genre, was flawed for a different reason: the ineptness of scriptwriters and actors. What good were such settings when the story was so poor, the acting so indifferent? Too much energy was, it seemed, going into the production of visual spectacle. Even so, another film, *Spacehunter: Adventures In The Forbidden Zone*, seemed to strike the perfect balance to transcend its medium-budget origins.

And so, finally, to 1984, Orwell's ominous year. Predictably, yet surprisingly with a great deal of haste, a film was made of Orwell's classic dystopian novel, starring John Hurt and Richard Burton. It was one of Burton's finest performances, but unfortunately the film was *too* faithful, too unremittingly bleak, to make good cinema. It was, to summarize, worthily unenjoyable. Better by far was *Ghostbusters*, not so worthy but oh so much more enjoyable than anything we'd seen on our screens for a long, long time. It has a creaky old science fiction idea straight out of the pages of H. P. Lovecraft or Clarke Ashton Smith, yet its irreverence was simply delightful.

Dreamscape, another "tinkering with the mind" film, gave a high-tech special effects gloss to a rather weak story, yet not so weak, nor so high gloss as *The Last Starfighter*, which might be identified as the first of a whole new generation of big-budget, mindless B-movies, sons and daughters of *The Black Hole* (to where they all should be consigned) created by idiots for idiots. And yet even as I say that I'm aware that I enjoyed something of the spectacle, the special effects – was impressed despite myself by the film's computer simulations, by its aliens

Spaceship modelling on 2010

and spaceships. Much the same could be said of *Dune*, the incomprehensible film of an unfilmable novel, which promised so much and, sad to say, delivered so little. Of course, had *Dune* been made in 1964 it would have been *the* classic of science fiction cinema, but standards are higher, expectations greater. The larger, less patrician audience we now have for sf film demands much more. That's not to say that they want art films, simply that they're not content with melodrama disguised as myth. A simpler, much more direct film that was a success in 1984 was *Firestarter*, which, like *The Dead Zone* (1983), came from a Stephen King novel. It was *Carrie* with an sf rationale, but it worked, whereas *Dune* didn't.

And so to 1985, to now. What's happening to the cinema of science fiction? What trends might be discerned? Certainly the existence of *2010* bodes well for the future of the genre. It's one of those few films that has built upon the discoveries of 1968 and learned the lessons that subsequent films have made – whether to the good *or* bad. But set against that is a sense that big-budget films like *Morons From Outer Space* and *Starman* are signs of decline rather than health. Will Lucas Films continue on their dogged path and present us, ultimately (by 2001, ironically enough, at the present rate!) with all nine films in the envisaged Star Wars saga? Will Spielberg film *E.T. II* when Henry Thomas is old enough? After long consideration, I believe that the science fiction cinema will continue to thrive for at least another decade – if only because there's so much untapped written material, so many unfilmed themes and ideas, and because all those special effects companies will be out there bullying the movie moguls to give them work! – but will begin to diversify between slick entertainments and intelligent art films even more than it does at present. The lesson of *2001* and *Planet Of The Apes* was well learned, but the more crucial lesson of *Charly* has still to be learned. Somewhere, in the next ten years, I hope to watch the science fiction film I've always dreamed about – perhaps someone will film LeGuin's *The Dispossessed*, Aldiss's *Hothouse*, or even a version of *Frankenstein* which is true to Mary Shelley's original. Whatever happens, the possibility is there and has been there since 1968, the year when it all changed.

Chronology of Important Films

1926	*Metropolis*
1929	*By Rocket To The Moon*
1931	*Frankenstein*
1933	*The Invisible Man*
1936	*Things To Come*
	Flash Gordon (Serial)
1939	*Buck Rogers* (Serial)
1950	*Destination Moon*
1951	*The Day The Earth Stood Still*
	When Worlds Collide
1953	*War Of The Worlds*
1954	*The Creature From The Black Lagoon*
	Godzilla, King Of The Monsters
	Them!
1955	*This Island Earth*
1956	*Forbidden Planet*
	Invasion Of The Body Snatchers
1957	*The Curse Of Frankenstein*
	The Incredible Shrinking Man
1958	*I Married A Monster From Outer Space*
1960	*The Time Machine*
1961	*The Day The Earth Caught Fire*
1962	*Dr No*
1963	*Children Of The Damned*
1964	*Dr Strangelove*
1965	*Alphaville*
1966	*Fahrenheit 451*
	Fantastic Voyage
1967	*Barbarella*
	The Power
1968	*Charly*
	Planet Of The Apes
	2001: A Space Odyssey
1970	*The Andromeda Strain*
	THX 1138
1971	*A Clockwork Orange*
	Silent Running
	Solaris
1972	*Slaughterhouse Five*
1973	*The Final Programme*
	Phase IV
	Westworld
	Zardoz

1974	*The Cars That Ate Paris*
	Dark Star
	The Stepford Wives
1975	*Rollerball*
1976	*Logan's Run*
	The Man Who Fell To Earth
1977	*Capricorn One*
	Close Encounters Of The Third Kind
	Demon Seed
	Star Wars
1978	*Battlestar Galactica*
	Invasion Of The Body Snatchers
	Superman: The Movie
1979	*Alien*
	The Black Hole
	Deathwatch
	Mad Max
	Quintet
	Stalker
	Star Trek – The Motion Picture
1980	*Altered States*
	The Empire Strikes Back
	Saturn 3
	Scanners
1981	*Mad Max II*
	Outland
	Time Bandits
1982	*Android*
	Big Meat Eater
	Blade Runner
	E.T. The Extra-Terrestrial
	Firefox
	The Thing
	Tron
	Videodrome
1983	*Brainstorm*
	Krull
	Return of the Jedi
	Spacehunter: Adventures In The Forbidden Zone
	Superman III
	War Games
1984	*Dreamscape*
	Dune
	Firestarter
	Ghostbusters
	The Last Starfighter
	1984
	Star Trek III

Science Fiction Films: A–Z

ABBOTT AND COSTELLO GO TO MARS (1953) For once the comedy duo's routines fall flat, as their rocket misdirects and lands on Venus. A tribe of semi-eternal Amazonian aliens (Miss Universe contestants all!) fluff and preen to little avail. Queen Allura, a man-hater, chases them off the planet. Tiresome rather than entertaining, but look out for a young (22) Anita Ekberg in one of her earliest roles.

P★	T★	E★	A

Directed by Charles Lamont. Written by John Grant and D. D. Beauchamp. Special Effects by David S. Horsley. With Robert Paige and Martha Hyer.

ABBOTT AND COSTELLO MEET DR JEKYLL AND MR HYDE (1953) Boris Karloff's fine performance as Jekyll (Eddie Parker was Hyde) doesn't quite save this from being fairly formulaic. The comedy duo play American detectives sent to Edwardian London to solve the murders.

P★	T★★	E★	A

Directed by Charles Lamont. Written by Leo Loels and John Grant. Special Effects by David S. Horsley. Make-up by Bud Westmore. With Bud Abbott, Lou Costello, Helen Westcott, Craig Stevens, John Dierkes, and Reginald Denny.

ABBOTT AND COSTELLO MEET FRANKENSTEIN (1948) Potty script wherein Dracula is seeking a new brain for Frankenstein and the comedy duo get involved. Lots of scary fun.

P★	T★★	E★★★	A

Directed by Charles T. Barton. Written by John Grant, Frederic I. Rinaldo, and Robert Lees. Special Effects by David S. Horsley and Jerome H. Ash. Make-up by Bud Westmore. With Bud Abbott, Lou Costello, Bela Lugosi, Lon Chaney Jr, Glenn Strange and Vincent Price (voice only).

ABBOTT AND COSTELLO MEET THE INVISIBLE MAN (1951) A rather limp comedy offering with a gimmicky use of Wells's idea to perk up a rather mundane murder mystery surrounding a boxer.

P★	T★	E★	A

Directed by Charles Lamont. Written by Frederic I. Rinaldo, John Grant and Robert Lees. Special Effects by David S. Horsley. Make-up by Bud Westmore. With Bud Abbott, Lou Costello, Nancy Guild, Adele Jergens and Arthur Franz.

THE ABOMINABLE SNOWMAN OF THE HIMALAYAS (1957) Ageing "star" (Forest Tucker) and botanist, (Peter Cushing), hunt the Yeti on a set resembling a Himalayan peak. The Yeti proves the hero of this slow-paced Hammer feature, directed by *Quatermass* man, Val Guest, and scripted by Nigel Kneale from his own play, "The Creature".

P★★	T★★★	E★	A★

Set Design by Ted Marshall. Cinematography by Arthur Grant. With Maureen Connell and Richard Wattis.

THE ABSENT-MINDED PROFESSOR (1961) Based on Samuel Taylor's short story, "A Situation Of Gravity", Fred MacMurray is the professor who invents a flying rubber, Flubber, which defies gravity. His exploits – including a flying Model T Ford, one of the quaintest UFOs in screen history – make a highly amusing film which reflects American sf's love of idiosyncratic and anti-authoritarian inventors. See also the sequel, *Son Of Flubber* (q.v.).

| P★★★ | T★★ | E★★★★ | A★ |

Directed by Robert Stevenson. Special Effects by Peter Ellenshaw and Eustace Lycett. With Nancy Olson, Keenan Wynn, Ed Wynn and Tommy Kirk.

ACH JODEL MIR NOCH EINEN – STOSZTRUPP VENUS BLAEST ZUM ANGRIFF (1973) *see* 2069: A SEX ODYSSEY (1973)

THE ADVENTURES OF BARON MUNCHHAUSEN (1927) One of several films based on the stories by Rudolph Erich Raspe, in this animation Munchhausen blows up Earth and then travels to the Moon. Paul Peroff directed this brief silent offering.

THE ADVENTURES OF BARON MUNCHHAUSEN (1943) A delightful adventure story, far superior to its Hollywood equivalent of the time. Josef von Baky, one of the directors who stayed under the Nazi regime, carefully sidesteps immediate political issues whilst conjuring up marvellous visual images of an ageless pastoral Germany. The tale itself is of Munchhausen, granted immortality by a sorcerer, and telling the story of his long (250-year) life to a group of contemporary (i.e. 1940s) friends. With exploits in the Russia of Catherine the Great, encounters with a messenger who can run at 200 mph, his ability to make himself invisible, and, finally, a trip to the Moon with its headless plant people, this is marvellous science fantasy, colourful, enjoyable and with elements of true originality of thought.

| P★★ | T★★★ | E★★★★ | A★★ |

Written by Erich Kastner. Special Effects by Konstantin Irmen-Tschet. With Hans Albers, Brigitte Horney, Ferdinand Marian and Kathe Haack.

THE ADVENTURES OF QUIQUE AND ARTHUR THE ROBOT (1965) *see* THE DISINTEGRATING RAY (1965)

ADVENTURE UNLIMITED (1945) *see* WHITE PONGO (1945)

AELITA (1924) Only damaged, shortened prints remain of what many consider one of the classics of the silent sf cinema. Its overtly propagandist plot – Soviet astronauts spark off a revolution on oppressed Mars – makes one think that there is an unintentional irony in the film's subtitle, "The Revolt of the Robots", but the comedy of Alexei Tolstoy's original play still comes through, more in the interplanetary romance between the young cosmonaut/inventor (Nikolai Tseretelli) and Aelita, Queen of Mars (Yulia Solnzeva), than in its pokes at Western decadence. The film is, however, most striking for its Cubist/Expressionist settings and costumes, designed by Isaac Rabonovitch and Alexandra Exter of the Kamerny Theatre, Moscow. The spiky, futuristic visual textures were highly influential (if not always tastefully so) on American sf serials throughout the 1930s. The film proves – in its ending – fantasy; it's all a dream. Nonetheless, it remains one of the earliest pure examples of space opera, parodied by the now untraceable *Mezhplanetnaya Revolutsiya* (Interplanetary Revolution) that same year.

| P★★ | T★★ | E★ | A★★ |

Directed by Yakov A. Protazanov. Written by Fyodor Otsep and Alexei Faiko. With Igor Ilinski, Konstantin Eggert and Nikolai Batalov.

AERIAL ANARCHISTS (1911) Director Walter Booth's predictions of terror from the air probably did seem fantastic at the time – especially the bombing of St Paul's from a giant airship – yet also captured a strong pre-War sense of paranoia. Its 11 minutes are crammed with action-adventure.

AERIAL TORPEDO (1909) *see* THE AIRSHIP DESTROYER (1909)

AERIAL WARFARE (1909) *see* THE AIRSHIP DESTROYER (1909)

THE AFTERMATH (1980) A surprisingly professional venture from what seems almost a family concern (Steve Barkett writes, directs, produces, stars and has half his family in the cast, making models, editing or doing other tasks). A rocket ship returns to Earth and finds it devastated after the Holocaust. Parallels to Stewart's *Earth Abides* see Barkett as the misanthropic Newman take on the amoral crazies (led by Cutter) in the ruins of Los Angeles. He wins a new family to replace the one lost five years before then has that new balance destroyed. As a survivalist tract it's better than most and its values less dubious.

P★★	T★★	E★★	A★

Cinematography by Dennis Skotak and Tom Denove. With Lynn Margulies, Sid Haig, Christopher Barkett and Alfie Martin.

AGENTE LEMMY CAUTION MISSIONE ALPHAVILLE: TARZAN VS IBM (1965) *see* ALPHAVILLE (1965)

AGENT FOR HARM (1965) One of a crop of spy thrillers with an sf element, this has deadly spores (from meteorites) turning people into fungoid messes. Of course, it's all a Russky plot to spoil the US harvest ...

P★	T★★	E★★	A

Directed by Gerd Oswald. Written by Blair Robertson. With Mark Richman, Wendell Corey, Carl Esmond and Barbara Bouchet.

THE AIRSHIP DESTROYER (1909) H. G. Wells wrote his *War In The Air* in 1908. It was a popular theme and this brief adventure played upon fears of bombs from the air which were later to be made into a reality.

Directed by Walter Booth.

A LA CONQUETE DE L'AIR (1901) *see* THE FLYING MACHINE (1901)

A LA CONQUETE DU POLE (1912) *see* CONQUEST OF THE POLE (1912)

ALARM IN WELTALL (1967) *see* PERRY RHODAN – SOS IN WELTALL (1967)

ALGOL (1920) Poet-architect Paul Scheerbart constructed the sets for this now missing film about an evil female spirit from the planet Algol who gives a human a machine which will enable him to rule the world.

Directed by Hans Werkmeister. Written by Hans Brenert. With Emil Jennings, John Gottowt, Kathe Haack and Hanna Ralph.

ALIEN (1979) The commercial space freighter, *Nostromo*, carrying 20 million tons of mineral ore, is on its way back to Earth. Its crew of seven are woken from cryogenic sleep by "Mother", the ship's computer, long before they have reached the solar system and in response to a regular signal from a planet close to their route. There is a clause in their contracts which says they must investigate or lose their share of the contract monies due, and so they go down on to the surface of a storm-wreathed, primordial planet where they discover a strange alien spacecraft (like a giant rounded horseshoe – designed by H. R. Giger). Within the alien ship they discover a long-dead giant alien, his skeleton betraying that he somehow exploded from within, his rib-cage being shattered outward. Exploring further they discover a hatchery of sorts, containing thousands of small pod-like, plant-like growths. Crew member Kane (John Hurt) slips into this and, touching one of the pods, wakes it. It responds quickly, opening up and, as he looks into the open pod, it strikes, penetrating his helmet and wrapping itself about his head. From this point on the film is a well-crafted if not brilliantly choreographed horror-thriller. Unlike other monster movies, however, the sf element is meticulously explored. What is the creature? What are its properties? Why does the Company want it? Why does Ash (Ian Holm), the science officer, work so hard to protect it and study it? Ridley Scott directs with a real feeling for the sudden horror of the beast. This is the ultimate predator, molecular acid for blood, ferocious and cunning in nature, and, or so it seems until the very end of the movie, utterly unstoppable. The moments of horror are sharp, explosive, almost unbearable, even on a second and third viewing: the alien ripping its way out of Kane's stomach; the science officer, Ash, going beserk, and proving to be an android, fighting on even after Parker (Yaphet Kotto) decapitates it; the alien appearing in ship captain Dallas's torch-light as he turns; and the final turn of the screw when Ripley (Sigourney Weaver) finds that the alien has entered the escape pod with her. These moments aren't the to-be-expected vicarious gory-horrific scenes that are the staple of spatter movies these days but the working out of what seems an inexorable fate. The creature is truly alien in that it is inimical – utterly hostile – to human life. This primary level of the plot is supported by a sub-plot, about the Company and its priorities, which serves to accentuate the distance between human values (values captured in the closing moments when Ripley and her cat settle down for well-deserved respite) and the life-diminishing abstract values which the Company, the robot Ash, and the alien life-form all seem to serve. The Company have put Ash on board presum-ably because they knew about the signal; their concern was with getting the alien for study – perhaps as a super-weapon? – and they have devised rules which negate humanity. When Ripley questions "Mother" as to what Special Order 937 is, it prints out: PRIORITY ONE: INSURE RETURN OF ORGANISM FOR ANALYSIS. ... CREW EXPENDABLE. This much is also inimical, is *alien*. The purity that science officer Ash admires in the alien is the same kind of quality that the Nazis admired so much, and this single comment, as much as anything in the film, helps remind us that this is more than a gratuitous horror movie. Much adverse criticism of the film resulted from the advertising campaign prior to its re-lease – "In space no one can hear you scream" was the slogan – but it would be wrong to condemn the movie for the hype which surrounded it. It is one of the finest sf movies yet committed to celluloid, prov-ing that a simple storyline – what would, in print, be no more than a short story – provides the best material for sf film.

Sigourney Weaver as the surviving crew-member in Alien

Another accusation was that Scott and writer Dan O'Bannon had "stolen" the storyline from A. E. Van Vogt's 1939 *Astounding* story, "Black Destroyer", but, apart from both tales having to do with large, nasty alien predators, there is little in common between them. Van Vogt's Coeurl is a creature who can manipulate vibrations and thus energy, and who builds himself a spaceship, planning to lead his race on a conquest of the galaxy. Scott's alien is simply a super-efficient shark; a shark with the ability to adapt to almost any conditions. It can be seen that there is little *real* resemblance and it seems to me simply another attempt to take credit away from *Alien* for being what it is – one of the best ten sf movies made. There's a need to comment on the realism of *Alien*; on the technical look and feel of the film; on the superb special effects; on the psychologi-cal accuracy of its vision of what crew life on a freighter like *Nostromo* would be like. All of these things add to the film's richness – for this is one of the best-looking sf films, a visual treat which prefi-gures Scott's *Blade Runner* (q.v.).

P★★★   T★★★★★   E★★★★★   A★★★

Produced by Gordon Carroll, David Giler and Walter Hill. Special Effects by Filmfex Animation Services, Carlo Rambaldi, Clinton Cavers, Nick Allder, Brian Johnson, Bernard Lodge, Allan Bryce. Cinematography by Derek Vanlint and Denys Ayling. With Tom Skerritt, Veronica Cartwright, Harry Dean Stanton and Bohaji Badejo (monster).

ALIEN ATTACK (1979) Feature-length adaptation of several episodes from the British TV series *Space 1999*, wherein the build-up of "magnetic radiation" in a Nuclear Waste dumping site on the Moon results in an explosion which fires the Moon (and Moon-Base Alpha with 300-plus staff) out from Earth's orbit, and off on a journey towards the distant stars. The first half of the film deals with this, the second with an encounter with a wandering planet, Meta, a veritable Utopia of perfect harmony. Man meets and is dismissed by superior beings as being "a contaminating organism", not yet fit for Utopia. The special effects are as good as anything *Star Trek* ever offered, though there's less glamour and more pseudo-science in this space-opera, set – unlike the series – in 2100.

P★★	T★★★	E★★★	A★

Directed by Lee H. Katzin, Charles Crichton and Bill Lenny. Written by Dennis Spooner, George Bellack and Christopher Penfold. Special Effects by Brian Johnson and Nick Allder. With Martin Landau, Barbara Bain, Barry Morse, Roy Dotrice, Anthony Valentine and Isla Blair.

ALIEN CONTAMINATION (1981) Rather second-rate alien invasion tale, involving cyclops from Mars seeding the Earth with their eggs. They fail, but then they deserved to.

P★	T★★	E★	A

Directed by Lewis Coates. Written by Coates. With Ian McCulloch, Louise Monroe and Siegfried Rauch.

ALIEN ENCOUNTER (1977) *see* STARSHIP INVASIONS (1977)

THE ALIEN ENCOUNTERS (1979) Deathly dull B-movie UFO story with dire effects and no real encounters at all. Aliens from Barnard's Star pass on the secrets of a rejuvenating machine, a Beta-tron. Endless desert scenes and interminable talk-overs disguise crank concerns of writer/director James T. Flocker.

P	T★	E	A

Special Effects by Holger Kasper. With Augie Tribach, Matt Boston and Phil Catalli.

THE ALIEN TERROR (1982) A dull *Alien* (q.v.) rip-off made by caving enthusiast Sam Cromwell (who produced, directed and wrote). Most 1950s B-movies seem classics by comparison.

P	T	E	A

Special Effects by Donald Patterly. With Belinda Mayne, Marc Bodin and Robert Barrese.

ALLIGATOR (1980) A baby alligator is flushed down the toilet in a Chicago household and, 12 years later, owing to the dumping of chemical wastes from a pharmaceutical company's experiments, grows into a 30-foot monster. A policeman, David Madison (Robert Forster), and a female alligator expert, Dr Kendall (Robin Piker), go after it and eventually destroy it, but not until after we've had lots of gory deaths, plenty of *THEM!*-style drain-storm tension, and a deal of City Hall corruption. There are two coincidences too many (the drug company's boss being killed by the 'gator, and the alligator expert having been the young girl whose alligator baby it originally was), but all in all it's a thoroughly entertaining and strangely intelligent movie. One of the better creature-features.

P★★★	T★★★	E★★★★	A★

Directed by Lewis Teague. Written by John Sayles (from a story by Sayles and Frank Ray Perilli). Special Effects by William F. Shourt. With Michael Gazzo, Dean Jagger, Sidney Lassick, Jack Carter and Perry Lang.

THE ALLIGATOR PEOPLE (1959) Silly cheap budget movie about a singular Alligator person created when alligator-based serum has side effects.

P	T	E★	A

Directed by Roy Del Ruth. Written by Orville Hampton. With Beverly Garland, Bruce Bennett, Lon Chaney Jr and George Macready.

ALMOST HUMAN (1970) *see* SHOCK WAVES (1970)

ALPHAVILLE (1965) Jean-Luc Godard here utilizes the plot-trappings and metaphors of science fiction to talk about the disjointed, increasingly mecha-

A scene from Jean-Luc Godard's experimental Alphaville

nized modern world. Ostensibly it's about Alphaville, a city-state in an alternate universe ruled by the computer Alpha 60 and its creator Dr von Braun. Agent Lemmy Caution "drives" to Alphaville and, in a plot about as obscure as Godard could make it, he kills the tyrant and his computer, and escapes with his daughter Natasha. If you love Godard's work, you'll enjoy this potpourri of influences and styles, if not – and I can't say that I do – then it simply irritates as just another artsy 1960s film with a juvenile streak to its supposed intelligence.

P★	T★★	E★★	A★★

Written by Godard. With Howard Vernon, Eddie Constantine, Anna Karina and Akim Tamiroff.

ALPHAVILLE, UNE ETRANGE AVENTURE DE LEMMY CAUTION (1965) *see* ALPHAVILLE (1965)

ALRAUNE (1918) Eugen Illes's film, the first of Hanns Heinz Ewers's dark and haunting novel, is now lost, and unfortunately little is known of it.

With Hilde Wolter and Gustav Adolf Semler.

ALRAUNE (1928) British viewers, confused by the censor's cuts, would not have understood that Alraune (the beautiful Brigitte Helm) was created by artificially inseminating a prostitute with the semen of a hanged murderer – making her a kind of homunculus because of the legend of

the mandrake root grown from such diseased seed. Paul Wegener plays the scientist/father in director Heinrich Galeen's excellent version of the Hanns Heinz Ewers novel. Her symbiosis with the "root" – a sexual connection – causes her to kill all human men who fall for her. It is a frightening, erotic and highly emotional film with fine cinematography by Franz Planer. (Silent)

P★★★	T★★	E★★★	A★★★

With Ivan Petrovich and Mia Pankau.

ALRAUNE (1930) This was Brigitte Helm's second portrayal of the coldly erotic Alraune. Director Richard Oswald's briefer version (103 minutes against Galeen's 125) is less potent in attempting a greater realism.

P★★★	T★★	E★★	A★★

Written by Charlie Roellinghoff and Richard Weisbach. With Albert Bassermann, Agnes Straub and Kathe Haack.

ALRAUNE (1952) The soul-less, loveless Alraune in this rather soul-less version of the Ewers classic is played by Hildegard Knef. The attempt to make this gothic myth topical – artificial insemination was by that time considered feasible – reduces the story to a B-Horror format.

P★★	T★★	E★	A★

Directed by Arthur Maria Rabenalt. Written by Fritz Rotter. With Erich Von Stroheim, Karl Boehm and Trude Hesterberg.

ALTERED STATES (1980) Eddie Jessop's experiments with "altered states of consciousness" lead him into taking a Mexican Indian drug whilst undergoing sensory deprivation in an isolation chamber. Obsessed with religious experiences, schizophrenia and with tracing the racial memory in mankind, he ultimately makes a breakthrough and regresses evolutionarily, becoming one of the earliest, part-Simian men. (All this however, isn't very good for his marriage, which is on the verge of breaking up.) After one final, mind-blitzing "white-light" experience in the tank, he goes back to the first cause of life and finds the terrifying fact that in the beginning there was "simple, hideous nothing" and not *meaning*, as he was searching for. The regression involves becoming a blob-like creature with a screaming mouth, he can return to this blob-like state at any moment, unless ... he accepts his wife's love and defies the encoded message in his genetic structure which beckons him back to the blob-likeness. Of course, *amor vincit omnia*, but in the meantime there's some Jekyll and Hyde fun as his body occasionally turns into Simian form. It's all a good idea with some nice visuals, but lacking any real scientific understanding. The scene with the Indians is a typical Ken Russell demonic orgy scene, and I found it rather hard to believe in the ever-youthful-looking William Hurt as a professor at Harvard. But it was very handy indeed to make his wife an anthropologist studying ape-language ; too neat, perhaps, but that was in Paddy Chayefsky's original novel, so don't blame Russell. Interesting, even entertaining, but ultimately *deeply* flawed and unconvincing.

| P★★ | T★★★★ | E★★★ | A★★ |

Written by Sidney Aaron. Special Visual Effects by Bran Ferren. Special Effects by Chuck Gaspar. Special Optical Effects by Robbie Blalack and Jamie Shourt. Make-up by Dick Smith, Craig Reardon and Carl Fullerton. With Blair Brown, Bob Balaban and Charles Haid.

AMANTI D'OLTRETOMBA (1965)
see THE FACELESS MONSTER (1965)

THE AMAZING CAPTAIN NEMO
(1977) Amazingly silly update of Verne's tale, with Nemo (Jose Ferrer) brought back to life from suspended animation and set against a villain with a super-sub.

| P★ | T★★ | E★ | A |

Written by Norman Katkov, Preston Wood, Robert C. Dennis, William Keys, Mann Rubin, Robert Bloch and Larry Alexander (!). Special Effects by L. B. Abbott, Van Der Veer Photo Effects. With Burgess Meredith, Tom Hallick, Burr DeBenning and Lynda Day George.

THE AMAZING COLOSSAL MAN
(1957) Another Bert I. Gordon spectacular, this presents the 60-foot mutant man,

the product of an atomic accident. This ludicrous farrago of other people's ideas (*King Kong* perhaps foremost amongst them) ends with the giant (Glenn Langan) falling to his death off the Hoover Dam (presumably the Empire State Building was closed for the day!).

| P | T★ | E★ | A |

Written by Bert Gordon and Mark Hanna. With Cathy Downs, William Hudson, James Seay, Russ Bender and Judd Holdren.

THE AMAZING MR H (1963) *see*
MADMEN OF MANDORAS (1963)

THE AMAZING TRANSPARENT MAN
(1959) One of two sf films shot back-to-back by director Edgar G. Ulmer (with *Beyond The Time Barrier*, q.v.), its cheap-budget origins show throughout. "Amazing" claims too much for what is essentially a thriller involving an escaped criminal using an invisibility serum.

| P★ | T★ | E★★ | A★ |

With Marguerite Chapman, Douglas Kennedy and James Griffith.

THE AMBUSHERS
(1967) Dean Martin starred as Matt Helm, that James Bond spoof (Connery with songs and an alcohol problem?), in an adventure which involves flying saucers and ray-guns. Donald Hamilton's novel was the lacklustre inspiration.

| P★ | T★★ | E★★ | A |

Directed by Henry Levin. Written by Herbert Baker. Special Effects by Danny Lee. With Senta Berger, Janice Rule and James Gregory.

AMERICATHON
(1978) Fantasy about a bankrupt future America which holds a telethon to raise funds ...

| P★ | T★★ | E★★ | A |

Directed by Neil Israel. Written by Israel, Michael Mislove and Monica Johnson. With Peter Reigert, Harvey Korman, Fred Willard and John Ritter.

AMID THE WORKINGS OF THE DEEP
(1905) *see* TWENTY THOUSAND LEAGUES UNDER THE SEA (1905)

AMMUNITINAMENTO NELLO SPAZIO (1964) *see* MUTINY IN OUTER SPACE (1964)

UN AMOUR DE POCHE (1957) *see* GIRL IN HIS POCKET (1957)

THE AMPHIBIAN MAN (1961) An almost fabular Russian story (based on Alexander Belyayev's novel) tells of Dr Salvator's son, a boy genetically altered to make him capable of surviving in the sea. Love won and lost is the film's theme – much more than a dry investigation of the sf idea.

P★★   T★★   E★★★   A★★

Directed by Gennadi Kazansky and Vladimir Chebotaryov. Written by Alexander Xenofontov, Alexei Kapler and Akiba Golburt. With Vladimir Korenev, Anastasia Vertinskaya, Mikhail Kozakov and Anatoli Smiranin.

AM RANDE DER VELT (1927) *see* AT THE EDGE OF THE WORLD (1927)

ANDROID (1982) If-I-were-a-carpenter time . . . *Android* is Son of *Dark Star* (q.v.). Difficult, now, to talk of one without reference to the other. They share much: low-cost inventiveness, impact and, although not an asset usually found in gritty sf – charm. There are, perhaps, more direct connecting threads with *Assault On Precinct 13*. Whichever way you view it, John Carpenter remains this film's surrogate father. What we have here is the neatest, shortest, most imaginative genre film made since Carpenter and O'Bannon re-tooled their collegiate fun 'n games aboard the *Dark Star* in the 1970s. *Android* and its effects look far better than they should, given the paltry million-dollar budget (lunch-money for a Spielberg unit). But you can't buy or budget love. When money is sparse, invention is all. Not always; look at other Corman quickies. Scorning the sets of one (or all) of those, Lipstadt and his admirable team breezed along, shot the film in four weeks, ran their first cut for the boss three weeks later – and at 80 minutes, there was nothing for him to cut and/or ruin. He let it be and is probably shaken still by its success – in Europe, that is.

Euro-critics love discovering films. Americans have to be frog-marched to them, with champagne launches thrown in. Hence, the witless *Cinéfantastique* review saying not much more than "a typical New World production that opens nice, but soon shortcircuits with all the cliches of the genre". Rot! *Android* stays firmly nice from start to finish. For all its allusions to most movies listed in this book, the major influence proves to be Jimmy Stewart in *It's A Wonderful Life* (1946). Capra's film, like Lang's *Metropolis* (q.v.), is constantly watched by Max 404, android assistant to a space-lab scientist in ad 2036. The Doc (Klaus Kinski), who could be called Victor not Daniel, is busy building a better future: a blonde android, Cassandra One. Max, then, has time aplenty to play old rock tapes, older movies and settle on Jimmy Stewart as his human role-model. He saves a damaged space-craft's crew and is tickled pink and Stewart-tongue-tied at meeting his first real woman. Sparks actually do fly. Cassandra is activated. And that's the end of Daniel, an android himself, of course. Claiming to be Daniel and his aide, Max and Cassandra are taken back to Earth where androids are banned since their Munich revolution. Nice one. All round. From Lipstadt, perfectly controlled behind camera, to Klaus Kinski on, and, particularly, co-writer Don Opper's Max, a wonderfully envisaged and etched character. But what if he'd only had Jimmy Cagney movies? Or Clint Eastwood's?

P★★★★   T★★★★★   E★★★★★   A★★★★

Directed by Aaron Lipstadt. Written by James Reigle and Don Opper, from a Will Reigle story. With Brie Howard, Norbert Weisser, Crofton Hardester and Kendra Kirchner. (TC)

THE ANDROMEDA NEBULA (1967) A rather dull interpretation of Russian author Ivan Efremov's novel about a journey to a far star. Russian polemicism swamps the fragile, introspective plot.

P★★   T★★   E★   A★

Directed by Eudgen Sherstobitov. Written by Sherstobitov and Vladimir Dimitriyevski. With Viya Artmane and Sergey Stolyarov.

THE ANDROMEDA STRAIN

(1971) Michael Crichton's intelligent sf thriller, recounting the effects of an alien virus brought back from space on a small, isolated US community, was given a respectful treatment by producer/director Robert Wise. The mixture of science fiction and science fact, and the deliberate playing upon people's fears of some unknown retribution for our ventures into space, gives the film a real dramatic tension. Douglas Trumbull and James Shourt worked on the special effects and Nelson Gidding adapted the novel for the screen, while Wise chose to make the film seem more documentary than fiction and it's a ploy that worked very well. The cast of little known actors who play the scientists (Arthur Hill, David Wayne and James Olson) give convincing performances.

P★★★   T★★★   E★★★   A★★

Cinematography by Richard H. Kline. With Kate Reid, Paula Kelly and George Mitchell.

ANGEL OF H.E.A.T. (1981) see THE PROTECTORS: BOOK 1 (1981)

THE ANGRY RED PLANET (1959)

A rather late Burroughsian vision of Mars (long after popular consciousness had accepted that Mars was a fairly lifeless desert world) as a lush world of exotic forests, ancient civilizations and giant monsters. A harmless travelogue from director Ib Melchior.

P★   T★   E★★   A

Written by S. Pink. Special Effects by Herman Townsley. With Gerald Mohr, Nora Hayden, Les Tremayne, Jack Kruschen and Paul Han.

ANIMAL FARM (1954) Long animated version of Orwell's novel about a group of farm animals who effect a revolution against Man. Visually impressive and satirically ferocious, it's a film that hasn't been given the recognition it deserves.

P★★★★   T★★★   E★★★   A★★

Directed and animated by John Halas and Joy Batchelor. Written by Lothar Wolff, Bordan Mace, Phillip Stace, Halas and Batchelor. Narrator Gordon Heath. Voices by Maurice Denham.

Kate Reid as the epileptic scientist in The Andromeda Strain.

L'ANNEE DERNIERE A MARIENBAD (1961) see LAST YEAR IN MARIENBAD (1961)

ANOTHER WILD IDEA (1934) Hal Roach produced and directed this Charley Chase comedy about a ray gun which releases all inhibitions. With Betty Mack and Frank Austin in support this is a rather pleasing gimmick story.

P★   T★   E★★   A

ANY DAY NOW (1977) Dutch dystopian view of near-future world split into three, with the Third World, owners of all the raw materials, holding the United States of Europe to ransom.

P★★   T★★   E★★   A★

Produced and directed by Roeland Kerbosch. Written by Kerbosch and Ton Van Duinhoven. With Ton van Duinhoven, Wim de Haas, Cees Linnebank and Huib Roos.

THE APE MAN (1943) Mundane man-turned-partly-into-ape tale starring Bela Lugosi. An injection of ape spinal-fluid causes the transformation here.

P★   T★   E★   A

Directed by William Beaudine. Written by Barney Sarecky. With Wallace Ford and Louise Currie.

A PIED, A CHEVAL ET PAR SPOUTNIK (1958) see A DOG, A MOUSE AND A SPUTNIK (1958)

THE APPLE (1980) Rather poor rock musical set in 1994. The usual conformity vs. rebellion stuff, with sf flavouring.

P★	T	E★	A

Directed by Menahem Golan. Written by Golan and Yoram Globus. With Catherine Mary Stuart, Joss Ackland, George Gilmour, Grace Kennedy and Allan Love.

APRIL 1, 2000 (1952) Rudolf Brunn-graber and Ernst Maboe apparently wrote this script at the Austrian government's request, the film depicting a future harmonious Austria. There's little action in this piece of propaganda designed to get the Allied Occupation Forces off Austrian territory.

P★	T★	E★	A

Directed by Wolfgang Liebeneiner. With Curt Jurgens, Peter Gerhard, Elizabeth Sternberger, Hilder Krahl, Josef Meinrad, Paul Horbiger and Waltraut Haas.

ARAÑAS INFERNALES (1966) *see* HELLISH SPIDERS (1966)

THE ARC (1919) Two-part German epic based on the novel by Werner Scheff in which civilization is destroyed in the near future.

Directed by Richard Oswald. Cinematography by Karl Freund. With Eugen Klopfer.

ARENA (1969) Hungarian short by Judit Vas based vaguely on Frederic Brown's short story, where people are captured and tested by aliens.

Written by Lajos Matos.

AROUND A STAR (1906) *see* A VOYAGE AROUND A STAR (1906)

AROUND THE WORLD UNDER THE SEA (1966) Jules Verne isn't credited here, but his influence is writ large in this uninspired attempt to cross-breed the disaster movie with sf. Lloyd Bridges leads an all-wooden cast of scientists to discover why the Earth is falling apart. The obligatory sea monster (a giant eel) adds a frisson to the submarine's exploits.

P★	T★★	E★	A

Produced and directed by Andrew Marton. Written by Arthur Weiss and Art Arthur. Special Effects by Project Unlimited Inc. Cinematography by Clifford Poland. With Shirley Eaton, Brian Kelly, David McCallum, Keenan Wynn and Marshall Thompson.

L'ASSASSINO HA LE ORE CONTATE (1967) *see* COPLAN SAVES HIS SKIN (1967)

ASSIGNMENT OUTER SPACE (1960) Director Antonio Margheriti's first sf venture was a story about a malfunctioning computer which controls a spaceship and threatens to destroy Earth. Good special effects by Caesar Peace, but a poor script from Vassily Petrov makes this an effort to watch.

P★	T★★	E★	A

With Rik von Nutter, Gaby Farinon, David Montressor, Archie Savage and Alain Dijon.

ASSIGNMENT TERROR (1971) *see* DRACULA VS. FRANKENSTEIN (1971)

THE ASTOUNDING SHE MONSTER (1958) Frank Hall's script would win itself a pink pig for chauvinism these days as he disposes of an invading alien female (who could kill with a touch).

P	T	E★	A

Produced and directed by Ronnie Ashcroft. With Robert Clarke, Keene Duncan, Marilyn Harvey, Jeanne Tatum and Shirley Kirkpatrick (the alien).

THE ASTRONAUT (1971) Made for TV movie about a man who impersonates the first man on Mars (who has died for unknown reasons) to get government funding for the continuation of the space programme.

P★★	T★★	E★★	A

Directed by Robert Michael Lewis. Written by Robert S. Biheller, Charles R. Keunstle and Gerald DiPego. With Jackie Cooper, Monte Markham, Susan Clark, Robert Lansing and Richard Anderson.

LOS ASTRONAUTAS (1960) *see* INTERPLANETARY TOURISTS (1960)

ASTRONAUTS (1959) *see* FIRST SPACESHIP ON VENUS (1959)

THE ASTRO ZOMBIES (1968) The mad doctor's artificial men need a constant supply of blood and organs in this pointless Ted V. Mikels production (he also wrote the script and directed.

P	T	E	A

With John Carradine, Wendell Corey, Wally Moon, Rafael Campos and Tom Pace.

ATARAGON (1963) *see* ATRAGON (1963)

ATARANGON, THE FLYING SUPERSUB (1963) *see* ATRAGON (1963)

L'ATLANTIDE (1921) *see* LOST ATLANTIS (1921)

L'ATLANTIDE (1932) *see* LOST ATLANTIS (1932)

L'ATLANTIDE – ANTINEE L'AMANTE DELLA CITTA SEPOLTA (1961) *see* JOURNEY BENEATH THE DESERT (1961)

ATLANTIS (1947) *see* SIREN OF ATLANTIS (1947)

THE ATLANTIS INTERCEPTORS (1982) Mike and Washington are adventurers who get involved in the sudden re-surfacing of Atlantis, just off Miami, Florida, in 1994. Mad-Max-style leather loonies decimate a town, die by the thousands at the hands of our intrepid heroes. All-action mindless adventure results in them sending Atlantis back to the sea bed. Not so much suspension of disbelief as total suspension of all brain activity.

P	T★★	E★	A

Directed by Roger Franklin. Written by Vincent Mannino and Robert Gold. With Christopher Connelly, Marie Fields, Tony King, Mike Miller.

ATLANTIS, THE LOST CONTINENT (1960) George Pal always brought the true tradition of Hollywood to bear on his sf ventures, and this is no exception. Sir Gerald Hargreaves's play *Atlanta* was the raw material here given the Pal schlock treatment with Lost Atlantis, death rays, a Nemo-like submarine and a mad scientist all thrown in. No expense was spared in buying up footage from *Quo Vadis* to give it true period flavour. Avoid.

P	T★	E	A

Directed by Pal. Written (partly) by Daniel Mainwaring. Special Effects by A. Arnold Gillespie, Lee LeBlanc and Robert R. Hoag. With Anthony Hall, Joyce Taylor, Ed Platt and John Dall.

ATOM AGE VAMPIRE (1960) A facially disfigured singer has a face graft – her beauty kept by injections of a serum from dead women. In theme similar to *The Man Who Could Cheat Death* (q.v.), it has little indeed to do with the Atom Age.

P★	T★	E★	A

Directed by Anton Guilio Majano and Richard McNamara. Written by Piero Monviso, Gino de Sanctis, Alberto Bevilacqua, A. G. Majano and John Hart. Special Effects by Ugo Amadoro. With Alberto Lupo and Susanne Loret.

THE ATOMIC MAN (1956) *see* TIMESLIP (1956)

THE ATOMIC BRAIN (1963) *see* MONSTROSITY (1963)

THE ATOMIC KID (1954) Blake Edwards wrote the original story from which director Leslie H. Martinson made an amusing sf comedy. Mickey Rooney is the boy who lives through an atomic blast and becomes radioactive. In scientific terms it's fantasy, but a charming one.

P★★	T★★	E★★	A

Written by Benedict Freeman and John Fenton Murphy. Special Effects by Howard and Theodore Lydecker. With Robert Strauss, Elaine Davis, Bill Goodwin, Whit Bissell and Hal March.

THE ATOMIC MONSTER (1941) *see* MAN MADE MONSTER (1941)

THE ATOMIC SUBMARINE (1959) One of the very few UFO flicks where the flying saucer is to be found under the sea at the North Pole.

P★	T★	E★	A

Directed by Spencer G. Bennet. Written by O. H. Hampton from an idea by J. Rabin and I. Block. Special Effects by Rabin, Block and Louis De Witt. With Arthur Franz, Dick Foran, Brett Halsey, Tom Conway and Paul Dubov.

ATORAGON (1963) *see* ATRAGON (1963)

ATRAGON (1963) The Japanese commander of this atomic-powered submarine must have been hiding out in the underwater jungles for 20 years before returning here to fight off (without nuking) the inhabitants of lost Mu. A curiously nationalistic piece from the Toho studio.

| P★ | T★ | E★ | A |

Directed by Inoshiro Honda. Written by Shinidi Sekizawa. Special Effects by Eiji Tsuburaya. With Tadao Takashima, Yoko Fujiyama, Yu Fujiki, Hiroshi Koizumi, Ken Uchara and Jim Tazaki.

ATTACK FROM OUTER SPACE (1964) *see* MUTINY IN OUTER SPACE (1964)

ATTACK OF THE BLOOD LEECHES (1959) *see* THE GIANT LEECHES (1959)

ATTACK OF THE CRAB MONSTERS (1956) A terse film which is almost a classic of the B-movie formula. Roger Corman's direction of a rather trite script (atomically mutated crabs, 25 feet in size and mind-absorbing, undermine – literally – a tiny island) gives it a surprisingly lively touch.

| P★ | T★ | E★★ | A |

Written by Charles Griffith. With Richard Garland, Pamela Duncan and Russell Johnson.

ATTACK OF THE FIFTY FOOT WOMAN (1957) Allison Hayes is the woman of the title who encounters a giant bald alien, and is changed by him to suit his size. A thoroughly silly film which utilizes one giant hand and a succession of dolls' houses for its special effects.

| P | T | E★ | A |

Directed by Nathan Hertz. Written by Mark Hanna. With William Hudson and Yvette Vickers.

ATTACK OF THE GIANT LEECHES (1959) *see* THE GIANT LEECHES (1959)

ATTACK OF THE KILLER TOMATOES (1978) John De Bello has a hand in producing, directing and writing this spoof of the 1950s B-format creature-feature. Giant tomatoes ravage San Diego. Not quite so funny as it could have been.

| P★ | T★★ | E★★ | A |

Co-written by Steve Peace and Costa Dillon. Special Effects by Greg Auer. With David Miller, George Wilson, Sharon Taylor and Jack Riley.

ATTACK OF THE MARCHING MONSTERS (1968) *see* DESTROY ALL MONSTERS (1968)

ATTACK OF THE MONSTERS (1969) Gamera the giant turtle here battles with Guiron to save the world and various Japanese children. Beautiful brain-eating space girls are defeated in this, Gamera's fifth professional bout.

| P | T★ | E★ | A |

Directed by Noriaki Yuasa. Written by Fumi Takahashi. With Nobuhiro Najima, Miyuki Akiyama, Christopher Murphy, Yuko Hamada, Eiji Funakoshi and Ken Omura.

ATTACK OF THE MUSHROOM PEOPLE (1963) From the costumes of the mushroom people (who become such after eating strange mushrooms on an island they're shipwrecked upon) this might have had a far lewder title. A Japanese Toho (Godzilla) production, its supposed seriousness is swamped by its silliness.

| P★ | T★ | E★★ | A |

Directed by Inoshiro Honda and Eiji Tsuburaya. Written by Takeshi Kimura. Special Effects by Tsuburaya. With Akiro Kubo, Yoshio Tsuchiya, Hiroshi Koizumi and Hiroshi Tachikawa.

ATTACK OF THE PUPPET PEOPLE (1958) An evil dollmaker reduces people to 6-inch-tall "puppets" and places them in marionette shows (one of which is, ironically, Jekyll and Hyde).

| P★ | T★ | E★ | A |

Produced, directed, written and special effects by Bert I. Gordon. Written by George W. Yates from Gordon's story. Cinematography by Ernest Laszlo. With John Agar, John Hoyt, June Kenney, Michael Mark and Marlene Willis.

ATTACK OF THE ROBOTS (1962)
Best-forgotten French-Spanish production where men become killer robots.

P	T★	E	A

Directed by Jesus Franco. Written by Jean-Claude Carrière. With Eddie Constantine, Sophie Hardy, Fernando Rey and Alfredo Mayo.

AT THE EARTH'S CORE (1976)
This rather silly journey to E. R. Burroughs's Pellucidar at the centre of the Earth is, for once, not as good as the (mediocre) novel. The usual prehistoric creatures and neolithic races abound.

P★	T★★	E★	A

Directed by Kevin Connor. Written by Milton Subotsky. Special Effects by Ian Wingrove. With Doug McClure, Peter Cushing, Caroline Munro, Cy Grant, Keith Barron and Godfrey James.

AT THE EDGE OF THE WORLD
(1927) German film about future warfare, starring Brigitte Helm (later made famous for her female lead in *Metropolis* (q.v.)).

Directed by Karl Grume. With Imre Raday, Viktor Janson and Max Schreck.

AT 3.25 (1923) *see* THE CRAZY RAY
(1923)

THE AUTOMATIC MOTORIST
(1911) An inventor creates a clockwork man as chauffeur, but this machine-man malfunctions. Walter Booth emulates Méliès in having his car shoot off and visit the Moon and Saturn. A fantasy with this one sf touch.

AUTOMAT NA PRANI (1967) *see*
THE WISHING MACHINE (1967)

AVENTURAS DE QUIQUE Y ARTURO EL ROBOT (1965) *see*
THE DISINTEGRATING RAY (1965)

THE AWFUL DR ORLOFF (1961) A
sadistic mad doctor movie, taken from the novel by David Kuhne. A borderline hor-

ror-medical film involving skin grafts. There was a sequel, *Dr Orloff's Monster* (1964).

P★★	T★★	E★★	A★

Directed and written by Jesus Franco. With Howard Vernon and Conrado San Martin.

A 077, SFIDA AI KILLERS (1965) *see*
KILLERS ARE CHALLENGED (1965)

THE AZTEC MUMMY VERSUS THE HUMAN ROBOT (1957) *see*
THE ROBOT VS. THE AZTEC MUMMY (1957)

AZ OSEMBER (1917) *see* THE PRE-
HISTORIC MAN (1917)

B

BAMBOO SAUCER (1967) A UFO is
discovered in China. Russian and American teams race to trace it and have to cooperate.

P★★	T★★	E★★	A

Directed and written by Frank Telford. Special Effects by J. Fulton and Glen Robinson. With Dan Duryea, John Ericson and Lois Nettleton.

THE BANG BANG KID (1968)
Amusing Spanish-Italian production about a gunslinging robot (five years before *Westworld*).

P★★	T★★	E★★	A

Directed by Luciano Lelly. Written by José L. Bayonas. With Guy Madison, Tom Bosley, Sandra Milo and José Maria Caffarell.

BANG, YOU'RE DEAD (1965) *see*
SPY IN YOUR EYE (1965)

BARBARELLA (1967) A rather light-
weight, tongue-in-cheek space romance which, in its gaudy trappings, is a precursor to producer Dino De Laurentiis's later *Flash Gordon* (q.v.). Director Roger Vadim presented his (then) wife, Jane Fonda, in the title role as the woman who everyone in the galaxy (male and female) seems to

David Hemmings and Jane Fonda in Barbarella.

want to make love to. In a pacified future universe, where love is the norm and violence a regression to savagery, Barbarella is sent out into the uncharted regions of Tau Ceti in search of Duran Duran, a scientist who has disappeared there. She sets forth in her pink, fur-lined spacecraft and eventually finds herself in the labyrinth of Sogo, City of the Night, where all that are good are banished. Sogo itself is an evil place, set above the Matmos, a lake of liquid, living energy that feeds on "negative pyschic vibrations" (evil). Barbarella makes love with a blind angel Pygar (John Phillip Law) (giving him back the power of flight), meets revolutionary Dildano (David Hemmings) and makes love by means of pill and fingertips, spurns the black queen (Anita Pallenberg), encounters Duran Duran (Milo O'Shea) and overloads his pleasure organ, the Senses Machine, and, finally, is trapped in the Chamber of Dreams, while Matmos blows its fuse. It is all over-the-top enjoyment with Duran Duran out to be master of the universe and Barbarella out for fun, perfectly reflecting its comic-strip origins. Only the music is genuinely dated. Claude Renoir's lavish cinematography and set designer Mario Garbuglia's imaginative backdrops make it all a visual delight.

P★   T★★★   E★★★★   A★★

Written by Terry Southern, Claude Brule, Vittorio Bonicelli, Brian Degas, Roger Vadim, Tudor Gates and Clement Biddle Wood. Special Effects by Augie Lohman. With Marcel Marceau, Ugo Tognazzi and Romolo Valli.

BATMAN (1966) Film version of the popular TV series starring Adam West

(Batman) and Burt Ward (Robin). The sf element is provided here by a machine which turns people to dust, and all the stock villains – The Penguin (Burgess Meredith), The Joker (Cesar Romero), The Riddler (Frank Gorshin) and CatWoman (Lee Meriwether) – are here in top comic-book form. Director Leslie H. Martinson plays it for laughs in what is an almost surreal visual experience.

P★★   T★★   E★★★   A★

Special Effects by L. B. Abbott. Cinematography by Howard Schwartz. With Stafford Repp, Reginald Denny and Milton Frome.

BATTLE BENEATH THE EARTH (1967) Fairly dreadful movie about a Chinese attempt to tunnel under the Pacific using laser beams and attack the US of A. Reds under the bedrock.

P★   T★★   E★   A

Directed by Montgomery Tully. Written by L. Z. Hargreaves. Special Effects by Sidney Stone. With Kerwin Matthews and Viviane Ventura.

BATTLE BEYOND THE STARS (1968) *see* THE GREEN SLIME (1968)

BATTLE BEYOND THE STARS (1980) A thoughtless, enjoyable adventure with special effects the equal of *Star Wars* (q.v.). What distinguishes it from its predecessor (and there's not a doubt that executive producer Roger Corman had Lucas's space opera in mind when he conceived this film) is not so much the lack of a coherent storyline, because both plots are fairly thin when examined, but the absence of a mythic depth to the story. *Star Wars* was an allegorical battle between the good and evil sides of the force; *Battle Beyond The Stars* is a power struggle for survival, with references to a code of living, the "Vada", thrown in now and then when the inhabitants of Akir, the peaceful planet threatened by the warlord Sador of the Malmori, forget why they're doing things. Roger Corman may be wondering why, when his film looks as good as, is as exciting as, and is as seemingly facile as *Star Wars*, it hasn't made the mega-bucks that Lucas's brainchild has. This absence of mythic depth explains all.

Battle . . . keeps you riveted, impresses you with its spacecraft hardware, its planetary landscapes, its androids, aliens and lobotomized mutants, but ultimately you don't feel moved by it as you do by *Star Wars*, nor do you want to see it again after a while, as you do *Star Wars*. It's a good film, but it's somehow only an entertainment whereas *Star Wars* touched something deeper in us – that "sense of wonder", perhaps, that sf fans so treasure.

P★★   T★★★★★   E★★★★   A★★

Directed by Jimmy T. Murakami. Written by John Sayles (from a story by Sayles and Anne Dyer). With Richard Thomas, Robert Vaughn, John Saxon, George Peppard, Darlanne Fluegel, Sybil Danning, Sam Jaffe and Jeff Corey.

BATTLE BEYOND THE SUN
(1963) Roger Corman plunders Russian cinema, this time *The Heavens Call* (1959). Ignore the title; this is about the space race of Russia and America to get to Mars, featuring all the best footage from Kozyr's film.

P★   T★★   E★   A★

Produced and directed by Thomas Colchart. Written by Nicholas Colbert and Edwin Palmer. With Ed Perry, Arla Powell and Andy Stewart.

BATTLE FOR THE PLANET OF THE APES
(1973) Last of the five Ape movies this proves a kind of prequel to the first. A battle between apes, gorillas and mutant humans results in the apes at the top of the social heap.

P★   T★★★   E★★   A

Directed by J. Lee Thompson. Written by John William Corrington and Joyce Hooper Corrington. With Roddy McDowall, Claude Akins, Severn Darden, Lew Ayres, Natalie Trundy and John Huston.

BATTLE IN OUTER SPACE
(1959) Space opera from the Toho studios with Earth under attack from aliens in 1965. The model sets are illogically futuristic and the ray-gun battles in space just silly.

P★   T★   E★   A

Directed by Inoshiro Honda. Written by Shinichi Sekizawa. Special Effects by Eiji Tsuburaya. With Ryo Ikebe, Kyoko Anzai and Minoru Takada.

THE BATTLE IN THE CLOUDS
(1909)   *see*   THE   AIRSHIP   DESTROYERS (1909)

BATTLE OF THE ASTROS (1965)
see MONSTER ZERO (1965)

BATTLE OF THE GIANTS (1940)
see ONE MILLION B.C. (1940)

BATTLE OF THE STARS (1979)
Aliens from Gona have deposited their Supreme Entity, a huge computer, on Earth, are slowly taking over humans and plan – after 300 years of study – to invade and take over Earth. Aliens from Ganeymede give us a hand (immortals with robot boy companion) and though the Gonian UFOs penetrate the outer defence ring, they didn't know about the inner one and so – haha! – are blasted. Earth is saved. Not that we care a jot by the end of this tedious farrago of confused ideas. Come on the Gonians! This is credited to Picturemedia, New York, but has the look and feel of a 1960s spaghetti-sf Italian venture, updated for the post-*Star Wars* (q.v.) market. Avoid.

P★   T★★   E★   A

Directed by Al Bradley. Written by Maxim Lo Jacono and Jacob Macchi. Special Effects by Al Frollini. With Gisella Hahn and West Buchanan.

BATTLE OF THE WORLDS (1960)
Meteor proves to be a controlled planet which sends out saucers to invade Earth. The alien masters, however, have died, and a computer is waging the war. Some nice visual effects but ultimately a disappointing Italian B-movie.

P★★   T★★   E★   A

Directed by Antonio Margheriti. Written by Vassily Petrov. Cinematography by Cesare Allion. With Claude Rains and Maya Brent.

BATTLESTAR GALACTICA
(1977) A *Star Wars* (q.v.) bandwagon film with good special effects, but without the necessary touch of fantastical humour of *SW*. Human colonies and their protective battleships are all but wiped out by an attack of the Cylons, who hate the human race because it believes in freedom and

democracy. A single space battleship, the *Battlestar Galactica*, escapes destruction and, along with survivors from its home planet, forms the core of a space Dunkirk fleet searching for a new world. The sentiment and dramatically delivered banality cloy a reasonable adventure story with plenty of action, though that action depends much on World War Two tactics, such as strafing streets with fighter craft and clearing paths through mine fields. The gullibility and stupidity of its human politicians, who seem to give the Cylons every opportunity to annihilate their race, is frankly less credible than the warfare.

| P★★ | T★★★★ | E★★★ | A★ |

Directed by Richard A Colla. Written by Glen A. Larson. Special Effects by John Dykstra, Richard Edlund, Dennis Muren, Karl Miller and Joe Goss. With Richard Hatch, Dirk Benedict, Lorne Greene and Ray Milland. (GDK)

BATTLETRUCK (1981) Following the Oil Wars of the early twenty-first century, the 60-foot battletruck ravages the countryside gobbling up any spare oil it can find, at whatever cost to the locals. *Mad Max* (q.v.) New Zealand-style, yet without the eventual sense of myth the Mel Gibson character accumulates. James Wainwright plays the amoral trucker and Michael Beck the goodie biker.

| P★ | T★★★ | E★★ | A★ |

Directed by Harley Cockliss. Written by Cockliss, Irving Austin and John Beech. With Annie McEnroe, John Ratzenberger and Bruno Lawrence.

BEAST FROM HAUNTED CAVE (1959) Roger Corman produced this slight monster movie, where a spider-like creature preys on gangsters and wraps them in its man-sized cocoons.

| P★ | T★ | E★ | A |

Directed by Monte Hellman. Written by Charles Griffith. With Michael Forest, Sheila Carol, Frank Wolff, Wally Campo and Chris Robinson.

BEAST FROM 20,000 FATHOMS (1953) Based very loosely on Ray Bradbury's short story, "The Foghorn", and adapted by Bradbury himself, this was one of the seminal monster movies. A nuclear explosion thaws out a dinosaur beast which then returns to its place of birth – New York. Despite a tired screenplay, an enjoyable film which paved the way for a few better and many lesser imitations.

| P★★ | T★★ | E★★★ | A★ |

Directed by Eugene Lourie. Written by Lou Morheim and Fred Freiberger. Special Effects by Ray Harryhausen and Willis Cook. With Paul Christian, Paula Raymond, Cecil Kellaway, Kenneth Tobey, Lee Van Cleef and King Donovan.

THE BEAST OF YUCCA FLATS (1961) A scientist is forced into an A-bomb test area after defecting from Russia, and is turned into a monster by the bomb's radiation. Films like this did little to help an understanding of the real dangers a lot of servicemen had undergone in chillingly similar circumstances.

| P★ | T | E★ | A |

Directed and Written by Coleman Francis. With Douglas Mellor, Barbara Francis, Bing Stanford, Tony Cardoza and Tor Johnson.

THE BEAST WITH A MILLION EYES (1955) A strangely atmospheric film about an alien which can control insentient living things. Hostile to Man, it sets animals against a small American community who fight back, and win.

| P★★ | T★ | E★★★ | A★ |

Produced by Roger Corman. Directed by David Kramarsky (also Executive Producer). Written by Tom Filer. Special Effects by Paul Blaisdell. With Paul Birch, Lorna Thayer and Chester Conklin.

BEAST WITH TWO HEADS (1972) *see* THE THING WITH TWO HEADS (1972)

BEAUTIFUL WOMEN AND THE HYDROGEN MAN (1958) *see* THE H-MAN (1958)

BEAUTY AND THE ROBOT (1960) *see* SEX KITTENS GO TO COLLEGE (1960)

THE BEDSITTING ROOM (1969) A film very much grounded in its own time, of Goon Shows on the radio and

Michael Hordern and Ralph Richardson in The Bedsitting Room.

Aldermaston marches on the streets – the John Antrobus script, based on the stage play by Antrobus and Spike Milligan, is founded on the idea that, if the Bomb is an insane concept, then it will spread on detonation not just death but total lunacy. When most of the era's avant-garde comics are here, and Ralph Richardson puts in an appearance too, the sense of protest is complete – it's not so much a movie as a signed petition with jokes. Around half a dozen vignettes jostle for our attention: Arthur Lowe, a city gent complete with bowler hat, lives in the place where he spent half his pre-nuclear life anyway – a tube train, trundling perpetually and aimlessly around the Circle Line; Ralph Richardson is slowly transmuting into the bedsitting room of the title; Michael Hordern and Rita Tushingham as the young lovers get married just in time for Tushingham to give birth to something we never see, which gives off a frightening, feline mewling noise as its baby-carriage is wheeled across the blasted landscape. The hand of Milligan shows heavily throughout the film – there are the same send-ups of petty officialdom we came to recognize in his radio shows, and a parody of the British attachment to the Royal Family which is one of the movie's funniest skits. He's picked up on the old sf idea that we'll repeat our usual mistakes even after the

holocaust, but instead of translating that idea into a violence and barbarism that's purely physical he has tossed us back our own stupidity, stripped to the bare bones by the radioactive blast.

P★★	T★★★	E★★★★	A★★

Directed by Richard Lester. Special Effects by Phil Stokes. With Mona Washbourne, Peter Cook, Dudley Moore, Harry Secombe, Marty Feldman, Spike Milligan, Jim Dale and Dandy Nichols. (TR)

THE BEES (1978) Quickie exploitation of *The Swarm*'s (q.v.) advertising campaign, with experimentally developed killer bees ravaging the USA and Brazil. The angle here is that the Corporation are marketing huge amounts of honey and bee sperm (in perfume). John Carradine plays a berserk German scientist.

P	T★	E★	A

Produced, directed, and written by Alfredo Zacharias. With John Saxon.

BEES IN PARADISE (1964) Slight film about an island colony of women which is run like a bee hive. A rather comic Utopian vision.

P★	T★	E★★	A

Directed by Val Guest. Written by Guest and Marriott Edgar. With Arthur Askey, Anne Shelton, Jean Kent and Peter Graves.

BEHEMOTH, THE SEA MONSTER (1958) *see* THE GIANT BEHEMOTH (1958)

BELA LUGOSI MEETS A BROOKLYN GORILLA (1952) Lugosi plays Dr Zagor, a Moreau-like figure who has a gorilla serum. Impersonators Sammy Petrillo and Duke Mitchell are his victims in this abysmally dull film.

P★	T★	E	A

Directed by William Beaudine. Written by Tim Ryan. With Muriel Landers.

THE BELLS (1981) An old idea brushed off and given an uninspired update, with a murder mystery involving killing by phone.

P★	T★★	E★	A

Directed by Michael Anderson. Written by Dennis Shryack, Michael Butler and John Kent Harrison. With Richard Chamberlain, John Houseman, Sara Botsford and Barry Morse.

BEN (1972) Further adventure of the super-rats from *Willard* (1971) (q.v.). Most of the horror is of a phobic kind.

| P★★ | T★★ | E★★ | A★ |

Directed by Phil Karlson. Written by Gilbert Ralston. With Lee Harcourt Montgomery, Joseph Campanella and Arthur O'Connell.

BENEATH THE PLANET OF THE APES (1969) Not so much an Ape movie as an anti-Bomb film. Brent (James Franciscus), another astronaut from 20th-Century Earth, arrives in ad 3955, in pursuit of Taylor (Charlton Heston). What he finds are the bickering factions of apes (Orang Utangs, Chimpanzees and Gorillas), a colony of mutant, telepathic humans in the underground system beneath old New York (in the "forbidden zone") and a Doomsday Bomb – which Taylor sets off with his last breath. This, the direct sequel to *Planet Of The Apes* (1968) (q.v.), might have been the last of the Ape films but for the prequels that followed.

| P★★★ | T★★★ | E★★★ | A★★ |

Directed by Ted Post. Written by Paul Dehn. Special Photographic Effects by L. B. Abbott and Art Cruikshank. Cinematography by Milton Krasner. With Kim Hunter, Maurice Evans, Linda Harrison, Paul Richards, Victor Burns, James Gregory, Jeff Corey and Natalie Trundy.

BERLINO, APPUNTAMENTO PRE LE SPIE (1965) *see* SPY IN YOUR EYE (1965)

BEWARE! THE BLOB! (1971) The sequel to *The Blob* (1958) is, if anything, worse than the original. An in-joke, directed by Larry "J.R." Hagman.

| P★ | T★★ | E★ | A |

Written by Jack Woods and Anthony Harris. Special Effects by Tim Barr. With Robert Walker, Gwynne Gilford and Richard Stahl.

BEYOND THE TIME BARRIER (1960) Shot back-to-back with *The Amazing Transparent Man* (q.v.), this B-feature

by director Edgar G. Ulmer transcends its limitations (mainly financial) in depicting a subterranean city populated by mutant humans following World War Three. Robert Clarke plays the pilot rocketed into the future by his hypersonic aircraft.

| P★★ | T★★ | E★★★ | A★ |

Written by Arthur C. Pierce. Special Effects by Roger George. With Darlene Tompkins, Arianne Arden, Vladimir Sokoloff and John Van Dreelen.

BEYOND THE VEIL (1928) *see* THE SECRET KINGDOM (1928)

BEZLUDA PLANETA (1962) *see* UNINHABITED PLANET (1962)

BIG DUEL IN THE NORTH SEA (1966) *see* GODZILLA VERSUS THE SEA MONSTER (1966)

THE BIGGEST FIGHT ON EARTH (1965) *see* GHIDRAH, THE THREE-HEADED MONSTER (1965)

A BIG GREY-BLUE BIRD (1970) Lyrical film about an old man's formula which can change the basic structure of the universe. He donates his formula to a poet who turns it into a poem.

| P★★ | T★★ | E★ | A★ |

Produced and directed by Thomas Schamoni. Written by Schamoni, Uwe Brandner, Hans Noever and Max Zichlmann. With Klaus Leenke, Olivera Vuco, Sylvia Winter and Lukas Ammann.

BIG MEAT EATER (1980) Imagine a slick B-movie feature with a distinct 1950s look about it, with at least five sf elements too many and a plot that makes the TV spoof, *Soap*, seem sane. This absurd alien invasion tale, set in a small Canadian town, is, like *Repo Man* (q.v.), one of a new generation of genuinely eccentric sf films. Its director and co-writer, Chris Windsor, admits to having gone out to make a really good bad movie, and for once aim and achievement coincide. *Big Meat Eater* was made for $150,000 Canadian, ignores stunning special effects technology and yet, through its irreverent approach to the genre, works beautifully. The re-animated corpse of the mayor is at the heart of the plot, of course, but then there are also the dime-store robots (in fictional reality the invading aliens), a genius tinkering with baloneum to make his car into a rocket-ship, belly dancers and fortune tellers, Abdullah the Big Meat Eater himself, and plenty of songs along the way.

| P★★★ | T★★ | E★★★★★ | A★★ |

Written by Laurence Keane and Phil Savath. Special Effects by Michael Dorsey, Iain Best and Jim Bridge. With George Dawson, Big Miller, Andrew Gillies and Georgina Hedegos.

THE BIG MESS (1971) A satirical future comedy, based on *The Monopole Capitalism* by Baran and Sweezy, depicting the ramshackle, economically messed-up society of 2034 – bureaucracy bogging down the romance of space. In the midst of this two astronauts are attempting to wreck spaceships and then salvage their remains for the insurance claims.

| P★★ | T★★ | E★★★ | A★ |

Directed and written by Alexander Kluge. Special Effects by Guenther Hoermann. With Vinzenz Sterr, Maria Sterr, Sigi Grane and Silvia Fors-thofer.

BIJYO TO EXITAININGEN (1958) *see* THE H-MAN (1958)

BILA NEMOC (1937) *see* SKELETON ON HORSEBACK (1937)

BILLION DOLLAR BRAIN (1967) Last in the series of Harry Palmer films, adapted from the novels by Len Deighton. Where *The Ipcress File* was excellently moody and *Funeral in Berlin* comic and macabre, this tale of seedy agent Palmer (Michael Caine) uncovering a plot by a crazed Texan oil millionaire to invade the Soviet Union is simply an overblown James Bond spoof. The "Brain" of the title is a talking computer which oversees the whole doomed operation. It's notable for being the second film directed by Ken Russell, and, while he sticks to the beaten track of conventional movie-making for the most part, he cannot resist bubbling over, near the end, into that aggressively phillistinic style we have mostly come to

hate. There are some beautiful shots of Helsinki in winter, while Oscar Homolka is mesmerizing as the sanguine, brutish Colonel Stok.

| P | T★★★★ | E | A |

Written by John McGrath. With Karl Malden, Françoise Dorléac and Ed Begley. (TR)

THE BIONIC BOY (1977) Rather sick exploitation of the bionic man theme. A boy victim of a car crash which kills his family (a crash caused by gangsters) is given bionic limbs and goes out for ven-geance. He's an 11-year-old Singapore martial arts champion – a display of which occupies most of this film.

| P★ | T★★ | E★ | A |

Directed by Leody M. Diaz. Written by Romeo N. Galang. With Johnson Yap, Ron Rogers, Susan Beacher, Carole King and Clem Parsons.

THE BIRDS (1963) Perhaps Hitch-cock's most famous movie next to *Psycho*, this film does for the open sky and sea what the abovementioned did for that "dark old creepy house". A young woman arrives on the Californian coastline (it was Cornwall in the original Daphne du Maurier story) with a pair of tropical lovebirds in a gilded cage, and it is around these tiny creatures that the horror centres. Untypically, Hitchcock, usually so obsessive about tying up his loose ends, never explains quite what influence the caged birds have that makes all their wild cousins in the vicinity gang up and attack humans – but attack they do, and it is the humans who become caged in. The sight of the open coastal sky becomes, by a stroke of the Master's genius, a claustro-phobic one. In any other hands, *The Birds* might have become but one in that legion of films about ants, rats or whatever that conspire to destroy the human race. But Hitchcock uses what tropes he needs from the disaster movie genre, and no more, to the full extent of his blackly melodramatic style. He divides his time between the actual attacks – some, like the one where the cast, sealed up in a house against the larger birds, finds a host of tinier ones pouring like animate soot down the chim-

ney, are stunning – and building the suspense to an eerie pitch as no one else can. The action is infinitely more disjointed than the average Hitchock movie, and the acting is so frequently wooden we find it hard to sympathize with the victims – but we're not watching them, we're watching Hitchcock as he lines crows up on the telephone wires to stare down at their victims, shows us a glimpse so fleeting it's practically subliminal of a dead man with his eyes plucked out by the birds, and uses the camera lens as a direct hotline to our subconscious in the style which has made him one of the finest of populist movie-makers.

P★	T★★★★	E★★★★★	A★★★

Written by Evan Hunter. Special Effects by Lawrence A. Hampton and Ub Iwerks. With Rod Taylor, Tippi Hedren, Jessica Tandy and Suzanne Pleshette. (TR).

BLACK FRIDAY (1940) Brain transplant story starring Boris Karloff and Bela Lugosi (who else?) which has Stanley Ridges suffering from a Jekyll–Hyde existence as his donor's personality takes occasional possession of him.

P★★	T★	E★★	A★

Directed by Arthur Lubin. Written by Curt Siodmak and Eric Taylor. With Anne Nagel, Anne Gwynne, James Craig, Jack Mulhall and Paul Fix.

THE BLACK HOLE (1979) This Walt Disney effort deserves some kind of accolade for being the science fiction film with the least real science in it. Its inanity is unlimited as a probe crew discover a lost ship stationary beside a black (really red!) hole. The red whirlpool (sometimes blue) obviously isn't a black hole as any modern physicist would know it, sharing none of the properties of one, but who cares anyway as the all-star cast (complete with obligatory twee robots – Vincent I.F. 396 this time!) display their total lack of scientific knowledge. Maximilian Schell plays the villainous Dr Hans Reinhardt, while the goodies are Anthony Perkins, Ernest Borgnine, Robert Forster, Yvette Mimieux and Joseph Bottoms. The mad scientist movie meets with *Star Wars* (q.v.). The meteorite storm is the highlight

of the film's scientific ludicrousness, the mighty orange meteors entering the ship, rolling along the central corridor and not – somehow – decompressurizing the whole ship. There's no real ending either, only a light show reminiscent of *2001*. Even Disney would turn in his grave.

P	T★★★	E★	A

Produced by Ron Miller. Directed by Gary Nelson. Written by Jeb Rosebrook and Gerry Day. Special Effects by Peter Ellenshaw, Art Cruikshank, Joe Hale and Danny Lee.

BLACK MOON (1975) Part dystopian, part fantasy, this curious film exaggerates both the desire of young women to escape from their present sex roles and their participation in the male fantasy. In this future, the sexes are at war in a more literal sense than we normally expect.

P★	T★★	E★★	A★★

Directed by Louis Malle. Written by Malle, Joyce Buñuel and Ghislain Uhry. With Cathryn Harrison, Thérèse Hiehse and Joe Dallesandro.

BLACK OXEN (1923) This rejuvenation and perpetual youth story was based on Gertrude Atherton's novel, and Frank Lloyd's direction avoids the usual clichés (serums, glands, etc.). X-rays return the heroine 30 years in personal time and make her 28 again. The film examines the psychological and social effects.

P★★	T★	E★★★	A★

Written by Mary O'Hara. With Corinne Griffith, Conway Tearle and Clara Bow.

THE BLACK SCORPION (1957) Uninspired giant insect movie using the best special effects sequences from an unfinished Willis O'Brien movie, *Gwangi*.

P★	T★★	E★	A

Directed by Edward Ludwig. Written by David Duncan and Robert Blees. Special Effects by O'Brien and Peter Peterson. With Richard Denning, Mara Corday and Carlos Rivas.

THE BLACK SLEEP (1956) Scientist develops a cure for catalepsy (from which his wife suffers) but his technique leaves malformed, brain-damaged victims. Basil

Rathbone plays the mad scientist, while Lon Chaney Jr and Bela Lugosi, John Carradine and Herbert Rudley give good support.

P★	T★	E★★	A

Produced by Howard W. Koch. Directed by Reginald LeBorg. Special Effects by Jack Rabin and Louis De Witt. Make-up by George Bau. With Akim Tamiroff, Tor Johnson and John Sheffield.

BLACK SUN (1979)

Re-make of Karel Capek's story *Krakatit* (see film version of 1948) about a controllable super-explosive. A lengthy thriller, this falters in places and fails to make any coherent statement on technological developments or human nature.

P★	T★★	E★	A★

Directed by Otakar Varvra. Written by Jiri Sotala and Otakar Varvra. With Radoslav Hrzobohaty, Jiri Thomas and Magda Vasaryova.

BLADE RUNNER (1982)

As is so often the case when sf novels are turned into movies the director of this version of Philip K. Dick's *Do Androids Dream of Electric Sheep?* omitted the central theme of the book. But even so, he – Ridley Scott – *did* succeed in making one of the more interesting and richly textured sf movies in a period when most of them have all the thematic substance of a video game. The novel is set in a future where the majority of the people have emigrated to the colony planets after an atomic war has poisoned the earth and killed off almost all the animals. The few animals that survive are worshipped by the remaining human inhabitants. Those who can't afford to own a genuine animal make do with robot replicas. The novel's protagonist, Decard (called Deckard in the film), is a policeman who spends his time hunting down renegade androids. He's eager to own a real animal but knows he'll never be able to afford one on his salary. Then he's assigned to pursue and eliminate six special androids who have escaped from the grimness of the Martian colony. The bounty on the six will make Decard rich and he'll be able to buy his heart's desire – a real, live sheep. But as the hunt progresses, with many twists and turns and typical Dickian reality shifts (at one point the androids convince Decard that they are the police and he's an android with an artificially implanted memory) he starts to have second thoughts about what he's doing. He becomes disgusted at the killing of beings who seem indistinguishable from humans, and then he's seduced by a female android called Rachel who's one of the six. She believes that after making love to her he'll be unable to kill any more of her companions but to their mutual surprise he continues on with his assignment and eliminates them all. The film differs in many ways. Firstly, the setting is no longer a sparsely populated one but a future Los Angeles teeming with people (mainly orientals), and the androids, called Replicants, have a much more substantial motive for coming to Earth; they want to discover how to override their genetic programming that limits them to a short life of only a few years. Deckard is also different. The typically idiosyncratic and all-too-fallible Dick character of the novel has been transformed into a tough man-of-action; a futuristic Sam Spade or Philip Marlowe (the Chandleresque element is further enhanced by a Marlowe-style voice-over). Admittedly the character has his weaknesses but the movie Deckard is nearer to the usual Hollywood hero than a Philip K. Dick creation (the casting of Harrison Ford in the part, though he gives a good performance, reinforces this impression). But the main difference, and the one that subverts the central theme of the novel, is in the treatment of the androids. Dick makes it clear that his androids, no matter how sympathetic some of them appear, are basically *evil* because they lack souls. The movie, ironically, takes a more *humanistic* approach to the androids, or Replicants, and presents them as victims of human evil. The Replicants are capable of murder but even so they emerge, by the end of the film, as *morally*, as well as physically, superior to their human hunters. Another, less important, difference is the lack of any explanation in the script for the film's oblique references to the robot animals. Unless you've read the book you wouldn't know

Harrison Ford in Blade Runner.

that real animals had become extremely scarce. Nor would you understand clearly why all the questions in the empathy test designed to detect Replicants relate to animals. It may be that this explanation was another casualty of the severe recutting the film underwent after disappointing preview reactions in America. One definite casualty was a sub-plot in which it's suggested that Deckard is a Replicant too but doesn't know it. (This might explain why the number of renegade Replicants supposedly on the loose seems to vary as the film progresses.) And apart from the recutting, and the added, unnecessary voice-over, a new ending was inserted. In the original version it ended on an ambiguous note with Deckard and Rachel entering the elevator; the revised ending is much more up-beat with them flying off over the countryside while Deckard's voice-over informs us that Rachel (Sean Young) isn't doomed to die prematurely after all – which is totally at odds with everything we've been told about the Replicant's physiology. But for all its flaws *Blade Runner* is a superior sf film. Its chief strength lies in its overall look and it's clear that Scott – a former graphic designer – concentrated most of his artistic energies on this aspect of the production. Just as one critic rightly said of *Star Wars* (q.v.) that it was like seeing the first Western to use real exteriors so you feel with *Blade Runner* that you are seeing for the first time in a movie a *real* city of the future. The opening shots are breathtaking. With the huge pyramids and skyscrapers, and the towers belching fire and smoke, it's like an aerial view of hell after the property developers have moved in. Then, at street level, the viewer is overwhelmed with a barrage of visual information; the strange and the unfamiliar is mingled bizarrely with familiar images from our own time, such as the Coca-Cola adverts, all of which creates a future world of convincing reality that no other sf film has yet managed to achieve.

P★★★	T★★★★★	E★★★★	A★★★

Produced by Michael Deeley. Directed by Ridley Scott. Written by Hampton Fancher and David Peoples. Special Effects by Douglas Trumbull, Richard Yuricich and David Dryer. With Rutger Hauer, Daryl Hannah, Joanna Cassidy and William Sanderson. (JB)

BLAST OFF! (1954) Pedestrian and drearily comic rendering of a Jules Verne P. T. Barnum adventure – Barnum wishes to send a rocket containing a midget to the Moon, but due to tinkering it lands in Tsarist Russia.

P★	T★★	E★	A

Directed by Don Sharp. Written by Dave Freeman. Special Effects by Les Bowie and Pat Moore. With Burl Ives, Troy Donahue, Gert Frobe, Terry Thomas, Lionel Jeffries, Hermione Gingold, Daliah Lavi, Dennis Price, Edward De Souza, Klaus Kinski, Joan Sterndale Bennett, Jimmy Clitheroe and Derek Francis.

THE BLOB (1958) Steve McQueen's inauspicious debut had him fighting off the ever-growing, people-devouring red blob brought to Earth on a meteorite. Irwin Yeaworth, who did so well a year later with *The 4-D Man*, was here uninspired in his direction. A Middle American town here is the target of terror.

P★	T★	E★★	A

Written by Theodore Simonson and Kate Phillips. Special Effects by Barton Sloane. With Aneta Corseaut, Earl Rowe and Olin Holin.

BLOND GORILLA (1945) *see* WHITE PONGO (1945)

BLOOD BEAST FROM HELL (1967) *see* THE VAMPIRE-BEAST CRAVES BLOOD (1967)

BLOOD BEAST FROM OUTER SPACE (1965) An alien from Ganymede has come to Earth to seek girls for his experiments – a kind of white slave trade. The police are on to him, however, in this borderline horror story.

P★★	T★	E★★	A

Directed by John Gilling. Written by Jim O'Connolly. With John Saxon, Maurice Denham, Patricia Haynes, Alfred Burke, John Carson and Robert Crewdson.

THE BLOOD BEAST TERROR (1967) *see* THE VAMPIRE-BEAST CRAVES BLOOD (1967)

BLOOD CREATURE (1959) *see* TERROR IS A MAN (1959)

BLOOD OF FRANKENSTEIN (1970) A spritely dark comedy, more funny than sinister with its use of various horror elements. The twist here is that Dracula (Zandor Vorkov) and Frankenstein's monster (John Bloom) are pitted against the mad scientist and his moronic, bloodthirsty assistant (Lon Chaney Jr).

P★★	T★★★	E★★★	A★

Directed by Al Adamson. Written by William Pugsley and Samuel M. Sherman. Make-up by George Barr. Special Effects by Ken Strickfaden. With J. Carrol Naish, Anthony Eisley, Regina Carol, Russ Tamblyn and Forrest J. Ackerman.

BLOOD OF THE WEREWOLF (1957) *see* I WAS A TEENAGE WEREWOLF (1957)

BLOOD ON HIS LIPS (1959) *see* THE HIDEOUS SUN DEMON (1959)

THE BLOOD SEEKERS (1970) *see* BLOOD OF FRANKENSTEIN (1970)

THE BLOOD SUCKERS (1966) *see* ISLAND OF THE DOOMED (1966)

BLUE SUNSHINE (1977) You'll either love this or loathe it. Blue Sunshine is a new form of hallucinogenic drug which has strange delayed side-effects – sudden hair loss and a psychotic desire to kill. The bizarre mixture of the comic and nasty that is a property of the drug is likewise a property of the film, which teeters between the two.

P★★	T★★	E★★★	A★

Directed and written by Jeff Lieberman. With Zalman King and Deborah Winters.

BLUE THUNDER (1983) A new-technology near-future story about helicopter police in LA, street riots, berserk Vietnam veterans. The focus is the super-copter *Blue Thunder*, with which the right-wing police chief might impose martial law on the city.

P★★	T★★★	E★★★	A★

Directed by John Badham. Written by Dan O'Bannon and Don Jakoby. With Roy Scheider, Warren Oates, Daniel Stern, Malcolm McDowell, Candy Clark and Joe Santos.

BLUMEN FUER DEN MANN IM MOND (1975) *see* FLOWERS FOR THE MAN IN THE MOON (1975)

THE BODY DISAPPEARS (1941) A serum devised to revive the dead instead makes the corpse vanish. The living start vanishing too in this lukewarm comedy.

P★	T★	E★	A

Directed by D. Ross Lederman. Written by Erna Lazarus (!) and Scott Darling. Special Effects by Edwin B. Draper. With Jeffery Lynn, Jane Wyman and Edward Everett Horton.

THE BODY STEALERS (1969) *see* INVASION OF THE BODY STEALERS (1969)

UN BON LIT (1899) *see* A MIDNIGHT EPISODE (1899)

THE BOOGIE MAN WILL GET YOU (1942) Boris Karloff and Peter Lorre share starring roles in this surprisingly silly comedy about a doctor who is building supermen from spare parts to help the war effort. His failure is a comic twist on the Frankenstein myth.

P★★	T★★	E★★★	A

Directed by Lew Landers. Written by Edwin Blum. With Jeff Donnell, Maxie Rosenblum, Larry Parks and Maude Eburne.

BORMAN (1966) Old Nazis never die, they simply keep on trying to create the Ubermensch and wipe out the rest. Here they're led by Martin Borman.

P★   T★   E★   A

Directed by Bruno Paolinelli. Written by Jack Savyam. With Sandro Moretti, Liana Orfei, Dominiqui Boschero and Moa Thai.

BORN IN FLAMES (1983) Near-future American feminist tale of a Utopian future which decidedly isn't Utopian – the revolution has come and gone, the democratic "Party" reigns and ... well, nothing radically has altered. The answer? Perpetual revolution. Ah, well...

P★★   T★   E★★   A★

Produced, directed and written by Lizzie Borden. Special Effects by Hisa Tayo. With Adele Bertei, Honey, Jeanne Satterfield and Flo Kennedy.

A BOY AND HIS DOG (1975) Harlan Ellison's award-winning story (it won the Nebula in 1969) of Vic, a 15-year-old, and his dog, Blood, is one of the finest depictions of post-Holocaust existence in sf's written corpus. Director L. Q. Jones's film (he also wrote the screenplay) is reasonably faithful to the original, but, in the manner of the cinematic genre, exaggerates the more sensational aspects of the tale. In both versions the world of 2024 is a ruined, desolate, run-down world of "solos" and their dogs – telepathically connected – within which the priorities of life are survive, eat, fuck, in that order. Love, as we discover, is of a boy for his dog. Other channels are stifled. Blood seeks out women (rare) for Vic to rape; in this one instance a girl from the "downunder" of Topeka, Quilla June (Susanne Benton), who has – we learn later – been sent out to attract a fertile male down into the underground town. Vic (Don Johnson) defends her from a street gang, is seduced by her, knocked out by her and – when he goes in pursuit into the "downunder" – is captured by the inhabitants. Here the film differs radically from Ellison's original. What was a marvellous parody of the small town, pre-World War One society in the story, here becomes a grotesque, with a

robot policeman disguised as a yokel and all of the inhabitants made up to seem clown-like. And, rather than becoming the town's stud, as he is to be in the story, he is to be mechanically milked for his sperm. This exaggeration blunts what is Ellison's satire on middle-American values (especially religious values) and makes it simply another piece of sensationalism. The same urge shapes the ending of the film where Vic and Blood eat Quilla June (remember the priorities). Blood's comment "She had marvellously good taste" twists what was a subtle commentary on life priorities into an act of vicious, rather sexist humour. This said, it remains a good film, plausible despite its exaggerations and memorable for its desolate landscapes.

P★★★★   T★★★   E★★★   A★★★

Special Effects by Frank Rowe. With Tim McIntyre (Blood's voice), Alvy Moore, Jason Robards, Helen Winston and Charles McGraw. Tiger played Blood the dog.

THE BOYS FROM BRAZIL (1978) A faithful adaptation by screenwriter Heywood Gould of the bestselling thriller by Ira Levin, with a plot which people tend to find either ingenious or ludicrous, depending on their taste. Ageing Nazi-hunter Yakov Lieberman (Laurence Olivier) finds himself on the track of a group of similarly ageing Nazis who, operating out of South America, are mysteriously killing minor civil servants 65 years of age. Almost a hundred of them in fact, scattered all over Europe and the United States. Why? Well, it won't be giving too much away to say the science-fictional idea is that of cloning Hitler. It all worked briskly and well in the novel, which makes it puzzling that a script which stuck so closely to Levin's original should end up as the basis for a movie as slow and disjointed as this one. Like most of the characters, it dodders along. We end up with a series of vignettes, and the feeling that director Franklin J. Schaffner expected us to be enthralled, not by the action and ideas, but by the frequently changing location shots; and by the movie's climax we are treated to not so much a zenith of suspense but a macho display of superstarmanship as, surrounded by a pack of dobermans whose mannerisms seem infectious, Olivier and Gregory Peck (in a villainous role for a change as Josef Mengele) snarl, glare, and curl their lips at each other. Both major actors perform as though they were playing out cameo roles, rather than lead and support. They wind up, in observance of the golden law of screen acting, being totally upstaged by the doggies. What *Boys from Brazil* should have been was a dark, swift, rather chilling sf thriller – what audiences ended up with is a movie which is barely competent, bizarre enough in plot to hold the attention for the requisite time, but that is all; and that's a shame.

P★★★	T★	E★★	A

With James Mason, Rosemary Harris, Bruno Gantz, Uta Hagen, Lilli Palmer, Jeremy Black, Steven Guttenberg, Denholm Elliot, John Dehner, John Rubinstein, David Hurst, Michael Gough, Anne Meara and Prunella Scales. (TR)

THE BOYS FROM BROOKLYN
(1952) *see* BELA LUGOSI MEETS A BROOKLYN GORILLA (1952)

THE BOY WHO TURNED YELLOW
(1972) Rather silly fantasy enacting the film's title. The Children's Film Foundation in the UK produced this, the sole purpose of which seems to be to teach kids that light travels at 186,000 miles per second, in waves and through TV sets!

P	T★	E	A

Directed by Michael Powell. Written by Emeric Pressburger. With Mark Dightman and Robert Eddison.

THE BRAIN
(1962) Based on Curt Siodmak's novel, *Donovan's Brain*, this is the third film version of the story. A scientist keeps the brain of an industrialist alive, but the brain begins to control him.

P★★	T★★	E★★	A★

Directed by Freddie Francis. Written by Robert Stewart and Phil Mackie. With Peter Van Eyck, Anne Heywood and Cecil Parker.

THE BRAIN EATERS
(1958) Alien parasites take over and control the bodies of Earthmen. Edwin Nelson produces and stars in this mediocre rendition of Robert A. Heinlein's *The Puppet Masters*.

P★	T★	E★	A

Directed by Bruno Ve Sota. With Alan Frost, Jack Hill, Jody Fair, Joanna Lee and Leonard Nimoy.

THE BRAIN FROM PLANET AROUS
(1958) Gor, an alien brain, enters a human's body (John Agar) and controls him. Vol, a good brain from the same place, pursues Gor to Earth and, with Agar's girlfriend's help, destroys it. Nathan Hertz directed and Ray Buffum wrote the inane script.

P	T★	E★	A

With Joyce Meadows, Robert Fuller, Thomas B. Henry and Ken Terrell.

THE BRAIN OF FRANKENSTEIN
(1948) *see* ABBOTT AND COSTELLO MEET FRANKENSTEIN (1948)

THE BRAINSNATCHER
(1936) *see* THE MAN WHO LIVED AGAIN (1936)

BRAINSTORM
(1983) We've never really seen this one. Doug Trumbull designed it for his brave new world cinematics, Showscan. "But it's impossible to make substantial changes in technology with Hollywood studios run by agents and attorneys. They don't even know that most movies are 35 mm, running at 24 frames per second!" His theme (most personal: "determination, integrity, human values, not effects") forms a perplexed plot about head-sets to share/possess another's existence. Yet this interior odyssey is the core and the brain-transference effects, crucially those of death and beyond, are not what they should be. (Could they ever be?) What's so tame on MGM screens would have engulfed us in the Showscan. So, we're left with half a movie, the remainder damaged by Natalie Wood's drowning before the 1981 shooting concluded. For Trumbull the director, see *Silent Running*. Better still, see *New Magic*. That *is* in Showscan – 70 mm at 60 frames per second!

P★	T★★	E★	A★★

Directed by Douglas Trumbull. Written by Robert Stitzell and Philip Frank Massina from a story by Bruce Joel Rubin. With Louise Fletcher, Cliff Robertson, Jordan Christopher, Joe Dorsey and Alan Fudge. (TC)

THE BRAIN THAT WOULDN'T DIE (1959)

A mad scientist brain (or, rather, head) transplant story with a strong love interest. The mad doctor's girlfriend is decapitated and he finds a stripper with a disfigured face to make a perfect match. His fiancée's head, however, wants to die and frees the scientist's spare-part monster to set the lab on fire. Byron Baer's special effects are grotesquely gory.

P★	T★★	E★★	A

Directed and written by Joseph Green. With Virginia Leith, Herb Evers, Adele Lamont and Bruce Brighton.

BRAIN TRANSPLANT (1970) see THE SECRET OF DR CHALMERS (1970)

BRAINWAVES (1982)

A murder-thriller involving an sf device – brain transplants. Brain movies were a staple of the 1950s and 1960s; this Ulli Lommel film (he wrote, produced and directed) resurrects the theme with intelligence. It begins with the murder of a girl in her bath. Something of her personality is used by a computer to return a road accident victim to normalcy from coma but the memory of the murder is also transferred. Husband of accident victim tracks down murder victim, eventually traces murderer and justice is – accidentally – served. But the murderer is then, at the film's end, to be used for the next brain transplant.

P★★	T★★	E★★★	A★

Special Effects by N.H.P. Inc. Cinematography by Ulli Lommel (!). With Tony Curtis, Vera Miles, Percy Rodrigues, Paul Willson and Keir Dullea.

BRIDE OF FRANKENSTEIN (1935)

Sequel to director James Whale's almost definitive *Frankenstein* (1931) (q.v.), this has Elsa Lanchester join Boris Karloff as the monster's bride. The plot, involving miniaturized people (homunculi), is even further from Mary Shelley's novel, yet the gothic flavouring of the film evokes some-

thing of Shelley's haunting work. Dr Pretorius builds the monster (saved from the fire that supposedly engulfed him in *Frankenstein*) a mate. Almost laughably, a further sequel, *Son Of Frankenstein*, had the monster revived yet again.

P★★	T★★	E★★★★	A★★

Written by John Balderston. Special Effects by John P. Fulton. Make-up by Jack Pierce. With Colin Clive, Ernest Thesiger, Valerie Hobson, Dwight Frye, Una O'Connor and Lucien Prival.

BRIDE OF THE ATOM (1955) see BRIDE OF THE MONSTER (1955)

BRIDE OF THE MONSTER (1955)

Yet another mad scientist with atomic ray in a swamp movie. Starring Bela Lugosi!

P	T	E	A

Produced and directed by Edward D. Wood. Written by Wood and Alex Gordon. Special Effects by Pat Dinga. With Tor Johnson, Tony McCoy, Loretta King and William Benedict.

BRIDES OF BLOOD (1968)

A close encounter of the fifth kind – sex with a radiation monster. But this nasty eats the girls, too.

P	T★	E★	A

Directed by Gerardo de Leon and Eddie Romero. With John Ashley, Kent Taylor, Beverly Hills, Eva Darren, Mario Montenegro and Oscar Keesee.

BRIDES OF DEATH (1968) see BRIDES OF BLOOD (1968)

THE BRIDGE OF TIME (1915)

A lighthearted dream fantasy where, in a fever, a man returns to the body of his evil ancestor back in Elizabethan times.

Directed by Frank Beal. Written by Roy L. McCardell. With Harry Mestayer, Guy Oliver, Virginia Kirtley and Bert Grassby.

DAS BRILLANTENSCHIFF (1920) see THE BRILLIANT SHIP (1920)

THE BRILLIANT SHIP (1920)

Fritz Lang's fast-action adventure story is the great-grandfather to *Raiders Of The Lost Ark* (q.v.) with Carl de Vogt as Kay Hoog, an American adventurer who fights against supercriminals out to take over the world. Like its Spielberg/Lucas descendant, its events and effects are spectacularly *Boys Own* stuff. This is Part Two of *The Spiders* (q.v.), the first part of which, *Der Goldene See*, was a more straightforward adventure yarn.

P★★	T★★	E★★★★	A★★

Cinematography by Karl Freund. With Ressel Orla, Lil Dagover, Paul Morgan, Friedrich Kühne, Georg John and Meinhardt Maur.

THE BROOD (1979)

THE BROOD (1979) No film written and directed by David Cronenberg can be considered easy viewing, and *The Brood* seems almost to demand that you have seen Cronenberg's earlier films to appreciate the full range of what is going on. On the surface it's a gore movie about a psychoplasmatist (Oliver Reed) who is dealing in physical manifestations of psychological trauma. In Cronenberg's world the evil is not external to us, but within us, literally, in our distorting, changing, mutating bodies – in the things we spawn. Samantha Eggar plays the utterly neurotic wife whose "brood" are, in fact, physical manifestations of her neuroses. In cinematic terms this is the bringing to life of a metaphor; that we visit our own fears, traumas and psychological garbage upon our children. David Cronenberg but takes that idea one step further (what good sf always does) and makes those neuroses-made-flesh into vengeful killers.

P★★★	T★★★	E★★★	A★★★

Special Effects by Jack Young and Dennis Pike. With Art Hindle and Cindy Hinds.

THE BROTHER FROM ANOTHER PLANET (1984)

A subtle use of sf to provide an outsider's view of black street life in modern-day America. The Brother (Joe Morton) is a black extraterrestrial being pursued by bounty hunters from outer space. He has a few super powers/abilities, but mainly this is about drugs, music and love. Runaway slaves in space . . .

P★★	T★★	E★★★	A★★

Directed and written by John Sayles. With Dee Dee Bridgewater, Ed Baran, Tom Wright, John Sayles and David Strathairn.

BROTHER JOHN (1971)

An alien (Sidney Poitier) born of human parents is checking out the Earth to see whether or not it ought to be destroyed.

P★★	T★★	E★★	A★

Directed by James Goldstone. Written by Ernest Kinoy. With Will Geer, Bradford Dillman and Beverly Todd.

BRUTE FORCE (1913)

Long ago science fiction annexed prehistoric times as part of its domain. This early look at Prehistory, wars and all, is in the form of a dream-fantasia, with dinosaurs and alligator monsters.

Directed and written by D. W. Griffith. Special Effects by Howard Gaye. With Robert Harron, Mae Marsh and Wilfred Lucas.

THE BUBBLE (1966)

Aliens have placed a force "bubble" over an American small town and turned the inhabitants into zombies. A strong example of sf as metaphor, if not itself a strong film. In 3-D.

P★	T★	E★★	A★

Produced, directed and written by Arch Oboler. With Johnny Desmond, Michael Cole and Deborah Walley.

BUCK ROGERS IN THE 25TH CENTURY (1979)

Yet another in the plethora of *Star-Wars*-type movies which appeared around the end of the 1970s, and the second from the inauspicious but commercially successful Glen A. Larson stables (the other was *Battlestar Galactica* (q.v.) – both wound up as television series). Fortunately, writer Leslie Stevens saw the perfect opportunity to lampoon the George Lucas hit, and he's placed his tongue so firmly in his cheek it would take a team of surgeons to get it out. Buck (Gil Gerard), space-age hero from the pre-War comic strips, is on a NASA mission when he and his ship get frozen in outer space. He's thawed out half a millennium later to discover that a very different Earth from the one he knew is under threat from an evil intergalactic Princess (Pamela Hensley). She's the perfect vamp, lounging on leopard skins and contriving to seduce our all-American hero. Aiding Buck are a blonde girlfriend, a computer which he hangs around his neck like a singles-bar medallion, and the most vicious take-off of the *Star Wars'* androids you could ever dream for. "Twiki" is three foot tall, metallic and yet cuddly-looking, and stands to represent every cute robot who's ever, inexplicably, won the hearts of millions in an sf movie – his stuttering little walk and a voice with all the coyness of a hormonally deficient child are calculated to nauseate on impact. "My warranty doesn't cover this!" he exclaims as the action gets hotter. The final scenes take place inside a vast invading spacecraft bearing an alarming resemblance to the "Death Star"; Buck saves universe, gets girl. The humour often descends to the crudest kind of parody, and the fun you derive from this movie is a silly, giggling type, but for those who were never entirely sold on the Lucas original, it's a tonic. Inexplicably, when the film was translated into a small screen series, with many of the original cast, they decided to play it straight.

P★   T★★★★   E★★★★★   A

Directed by Daniel Haller. Special Effects by Bud Ewing. With Erin Gray, Henry Silva, Tim O'Connor, Joseph Wiseman and Felix Silla. (TR)

BUG (1975) A fire-eating insect is crossed with a cockroach in this silly mad scientist movie.

P★   T★★   E★   A

Directed by Jeannot Szwarc. Written by William Castle and Thomas Page. With Bradford Dillman, Joanne Miles and Richard Gilliland.

BURIED ALIVE (1942) *see* DOCTOR RENAULT'S SECRET (1942)

BY FOOT, BY HORSE, AND BY SPUTNIK (1958) *see* A DOG, A MOUSE AND A SPUTNIK (1958)

BY ROCKET TO THE MOON (1929) Three years after making his classic *Metropolis* (q.v.), Fritz Lang again teamed up with his wife and screenwriter Thea Von Harbou to produce and direct the first realistic film about a journey to the Moon. Lang used rocket experts Willy

Ley and Hermann Oberth (the former became a science writer for the American sf magazine *Galaxy*, the latter a rocket propulsions expert for the Nazis) as his technical advisers – a step which gave the film a degree of technological authority unsurpassed until *Destination Moon* (q.v.) some 20 years later. The plot was a rather straightforward interplanetary romance, with the Moon as a source of ore, to be mined by those who can stake their claims, and suffers from a pedestrian unravelling of ideas. The Moon, in this version, has an unscientifically breathable atmosphere, but the film was otherwise accurate enough to make the Nazis destroy every print of it they could lay their hands on in an attempt to protect their V-1 and V-2 rocket secrets. New prints have subsequently been pieced together.

P★   T★★   E★   A★

Special Effects by Konstantin Tschetwerikoff. With **Gerda Marus, Willy Fitsch, Fritz Rasp, Klaus Pohl and Gustav von Waggenheim.**

THE CABINET OF DR CALIGARI
(1919) Whilst strictly not science fiction – the story is about a mad doctor who controls a somnambulistic killer – the use of stark Expressionist/Cubist sets, Robert Wiene's direction and Fritz Lang's appar-

Conrad Veidt and Lil Dagover in The Cabinet of Dr Caligari

ent involvement in doctoring the script give the film an important role in influencing the cinematic genre.

P★   T★★   E★   A★★

Written by Carl Mayer and Hans Janowitz. Designed and Art Directed by Walter Reimann, Hermann Warn and Walter Röhrig. With Conrad Veidt, Werner Krauss, Lil Dagover, Hans Heinrich Von Tvardorvsky, Rudolph Lettinger, Rudolf Kleine-Rogge and Frederich Feher.

CAGE OF DOOM (1958) see TERROR FROM THE YEAR 5000 (1958)

THE CALLING (1981) see BELLS (1981)

CALL ME ROBERT (1967) A humanoid robot replica (of its master) encounters a few difficulties in trying to cope with everyday life.

P★★   T★★   E★★   A★

Directed by George Ungvald-Hilkevich. Written by Yuri Cherniavsky. With Oleg Strizhenov, Marianna Vertinskaya and Vladimir Pobol.

CALTIKI, THE IMMORTAL MONSTER (1959) Co-director Mario Bava was later to enter the spaghetti-sf field in a big way; here he rivals Japan's Toho studios with their blob-like monster which goes on the rampage. A thoroughly uninteresting outing.

P★   T★★   E★   A

Co-directed by Robert Hampton. Written by Philip Just. Special Effects by Mario Bava. With John Merivale, Didi Sullivan, Gerard Herter, Daniela Rocca and Giacomo Rossi-Stuart.

THE CAPE CANAVERAL MONSTERS (1960) The space race is jeopardized by alien life forces which take over the bodies of important personnel, turning them into zombie-like creatures.

P★   T★   E★   A

Directed and written by Phil Tucker. With Scott Peters, Linda Connell and Katherine Victor.

CAPRICORN ONE (1978) The first manned space mission to Mars is due to be launched – the budget of the space programme depends on its success. But when it is discovered that some of the equipment on board the ship is lethally faulty, the NASA authorities decide to fake the whole mission. And then something goes horribly wrong. It's little more than a movie version of that hoary old chestnut, expounded in a thousand late-night bars, that men never really did land on the Moon, that the whole thing was done with trick photography and special effects. But this Lew Grade production managed to capture the attention of audiences and critics alike with the tightness of its plot, the swiftness of its action. Elliot Gould is droll and convincing as the shabby reporter who stumbles across the cover-up in this tense, hugely entertaining science fiction thriller.

P★★★★   T★★★   E★★★★★   A★

Directed and written by Peter Hyams. Special Effects by Henry Millar Snr and Henry Millar Jr. With James Brolin, O. J. Simpson, Sam Waterstone, Brenda Vaccaro and Telly Savalas. (TR)

CAPTAIN KRONOS — VAMPIRE HUNTER (1957) see KRONOS (1957)

CAPTAIN NEMO AND THE UNDERWATER CITY (1969) A passenger liner carrying a US Senator (Chuck Connors) sinks in mid-Atlantic, but Nemo and the *Nautilus* pick up some survivors and take them to the underwater city of Templemer. There's adventure with a giant monster and a rebellion in the city, but Nemo gets the survivors home.

P★★   T★★   E★★   A★

Directed by James Hill. Written by Pip Barker, Jane Barker and R. Wright Campbell. With Robert Ryan, Nanette Newman, Luciana Paluzzi, Bill Fraser and Kenneth Connor.

CAPTIVE WILD WOMEN (1943) Jekyll–Hyde story of gorilla who is changed into a woman and reverts whenever she gets jealous. Unbelievably it had two sequels.

P   T★   E★   A

Directed by Edward Dmytryk. Written by Henry Sucher and Griffin Jay. Make-up by Jack Pierce. With John Carradine, Evelyn Ankers, Milburn Stone, Lloyd Corrigan, Fay Helm and Paul Fix.

CAPTIVE WOMEN (1952) Set in a Post-Atom War New York, this is a complex but entertaining story about the Mutates and the Norms and their struggles against the evil Upriver people. Its avoidance of the normal monster/brain formulae is to be applauded, if not its production values.

P★★   T★   E★★   A

Directed by Stuart Gilmore. Written by Aubrey Wisberg and Jack Pollexfen. With Robert Clarke, Margaret Field and Gloria Saunders.

LA CARA DEL TERROR (1962) *see* FACE OF TERROR (1962)

CARNE PER FRANKENSTEIN (1973) *see* FLESH FOR FRANKENSTEIN (1973)

THE CARS THAT ATE PARIS (1974) Pre-empting *Death Race 2000* in its concerns, Peter Weir's film debut (he wrote and directed) was a nasty little story about a small town in the Australian outback, Paris (actually Sofala, NSW), which survives economically on salvaging crashed cars. That is, it diverts cars into its environs and then makes them crash. From this premise Weir develops a story of young car maniacs (who build spiky death machines from the remnants of the crashed cars) and their clash with the older inhabitants of the town. Made for only Aus. $220,000, it's a surprisingly polished film, exciting, frightening and – unlike so many of the spiky-car films that followed – thoughtful.

One of the sinister-looking cars from The Cars That Ate Paris

P★★★   T★★★   E★★★   A★★

Written by Weir, Keith Gow and Piers Davis. Cinematography by John McLean. With Terry Camilleri, John Meillon, Melissa Jaffer, Kevin Miles and Max Gillies.

CARTAS BOCA ARRIBA (1962) *see* ATTACK OF THE ROBOTS (1962)

CARTES SUR TABLE (1962) *see* ATTACK OF THE ROBOTS (1962)

THE CASE OF THE MISSING BRIDES (1942) *see* THE CORPSE VANISHES (1942)

CASINO ROYALE (1967) A rarity, a Bond film not produced by Broccoli and Saltzman, since the rights to Ian Fleming's novel were bought long before 007 fever set in. It got turned into a self-indulgent all-star spoof – Frankenstein, flying saucers and all – with the kind of 1960s humour which flaps around like a fish out of water, and only Woody Allen, as 007's inept nephew, seems to be working at all hard to amuse.

P   T★★   E★   A

Directed by John Huston. Written by Wolf Mankowitz, John Law and Michael Sayers. With David Niven, Deborah Kerr, Orson Welles, Peter Sellers, Ursula Andress, Peter O'Toole, William Holden, Charles Boyer and Jean-Paul Belmondo. (TR)

CASTLE OF EVIL (1966) The robot double of a deceased mad scientist's heirs.

P★   T★   E★   A

Directed by Francis D. Lyon. Written by Charles A. Wallace. Special Effects by Roger George. Make-up by Bob Dawn. With Scott Brady, Virginia Mayo, Lisa Gaye and David Brian.

THE CAT FROM OUTER SPACE (1978) The Walt Disney approach to sf used to be a fairly simple one (it changed somewhat with *Tron* (q.v.)): take an ordinary UFO, an extraordinary animal (in this case a cat), a few caricature Americans, and mix them together in a story which has plenty of gimmicks (of the simplistic cinematic kind – beer pouring back into the can from the glass), no sex, no real threat (only a mild sense of bumbling authority trying to assert itself – here the military), a few comic-book baddies, a mild love interest and a great deal of sentimentalized patriotism. Add, in this case, a mindless plot and a ridiculous rationale (this cat is from a parallel evolution in a different galaxy – in their case they didn't need to develop into man-like creatures because they concentrated on things of the mind; even so they have huge, non-mental spacecraft to contradict this!). The cat's UFO has broken down and needs $125,000 of pure gold to be fixed. He has to rendezvous with the mother ship by 5.30 on Sunday, too, or be left stranded on Earth. Of course, to save the human hero's girlfriend and her female cat, he misses his rendezvous and stays on – as an American citizen. Some juveniles are bad, this is simply *awful*, a poor parody of earlier films like *The Absent-minded Professor*.

| P | T★★ | E★ | A |

Directed by Norman Tokar. Written by Ted Key. Special Effects by Eustace Lycett, Art Cruickshank and Danny Lee. With Ken Berry, Sandy Duncan, Harry Morgan and Roddy McDowall.

CAT PEOPLE (1942) Re-made in 1982, this classic of a woman who, when sexually aroused or jealous, becomes a cat-like creature, is an atmospheric, stunningly subtle movie, tense rather than horrific. Its modern-day (then) setting and love-triangle concerns make it *sui generis*; a tale of a young girl alienated from herself by what she is.

| P★★★ | T★★★ | E★★★★ | A★★★ |

Directed by Jacques Tourneur. Written by De-Witt Bodeen. With Simone Simon, Tom Conway, Kent Smith, Jack Holt and Jane Randolph.

CAT PEOPLE (1982) An under-rated remake of the 1942 Val Lewton classic. Natassja Kinski discovers that she is descended from an ancient race who, when they make love, are transformed into panthers and devour their lovers. Hauntingly shot against the old quarter of New Orleans, where the orchid scent of decadence seems to hang in every shadowed corner, the film verges into silliness on a

couple of occasions, but that is because it's taking risks, and for the large part director Paul Schrader manages to maintain a brooding depth and an intelligence light years away from the puerility of the *Star Wars* (q.v.) dopplegangers which were every other film-maker's idea of science fiction in the early 1980s. The transmutations are superb – a clever variation on the technique John Landis used in *An American Werewolf in London*. Malcolm MacDowell's slightly flabby performance is the only real disappointment. Schrader was pilloried – for allegedly representing a hostile view of female sexuality – by critics who seemed to have little understanding of the subconsciously derived nature of the horror-fantasy genre.

| P★★★ | T★★★★★ | E★★★★★ | A★★★ |

Written by Alan Armsby. Special Effects by Albert Whitlock, Robert Blalack. Make-up by Tom Burman. With John Heard, Annette O'Toole, Ruby Dee and Ed Begley Jnr. (TR)

CAT WOMEN OF THE MOON
(1953) Sonny Tufts and Marie Windsor stumble through an inept story of telepathic cat women at the Moon's core. The cat women look about as alien as Nancy Reagan in a leotard. Battles with giant spiders and a 3-D presentation make this instantly forgettable.

| P | T | E | A |

Directed by Arthur Hilton. Written by Roy Hamilton. Special Effects by Jack Rabin and Al Zimbalist. With Victor Jory and Susan Morrow.

LE CAUCHEMAR FRANCO-ANGLAIS (1907) see TUNNELLING THE ENGLISH CHANNEL (1907)

CAVE MAN (1940) see ONE MILLION B.C. (1940)

CAVES OF STEEL (1967) Peter Sasdy and Peter Cushing starred in this BBC adaptation of Isaac Asimov's sf detective thriller about a murder mystery in a super-city of the future.

| P★★★ | T★ | E★★ | A |

Directed by Eric Taylor.

CELOVEK ANFIBJAN (1961) *see* THE AMPHIBIAN MAN (1961)

CERNE SLUNCE (1979) *see* THE BLACK SUN (1979)

CESTA DO PRAVEKU (1954) *see* JOURNEY TO THE BEGINNING OF TIME (1954)

THE CHAIN REACTION (1980) Nuclear waste leaks and converts nearby people into psychopathic crazies. But all the while the authorities are sponsoring a massive cover-up.

P★	T★★	E★	A

Directed and written by Ian Barry. With Steve Bisley and Arna-Maria Winchester.

THE CHAIRMAN (1969) Gregory Peck starred in this often-sedentary sf thriller about a scientist assigned to purloin from the Red Chinese the formula of an enzyme which causes fantastic growth rate in crop plants. Peck has a radio-mike installed inside his skull, to aid him in his espionage – what the CIA have neglected to inform him is that the gizmo includes a small bomb, in case they feel it necessary for him to self-destruct. The high-spot, an attempted escape across the border into Russia, helps to make up for an absurd scene in which Peck confronts Chairman Mao over a game of ping-pong, in a movie which seemed naive at the time of its release but, in the light of revelations by the post-Mao government, seems far closer to the truth than we suspected.

P★★	T★★	E★★★	A

Directed by J. Lee Thompson. Written by Ben Maddow, from the novel by Jay Richard. With Anne Heywood, Arthur Hill, Conrad Yama and Keye Luke. (TR)

THE CHALLENGE (1970) A simple little allegory of World War Three, with two men fighting on an island to settle the result of the war.

P★	T★★	E★★	A★

Directed by Allen Smithee. Written by Marc Norman. Special Effects by L. B. Abbott. With Darren McGavin and Broderick Crawford.

THE CHALLENGE OF KING KONG (1945) *see* WHITE PONGO (1945)

CHANDU, THE MAGICIAN (1932) Based on a radio serial, Edmund Lowe plays Chandu against Bela Lugosi's mad scientist act. Chandu foils a fiendish world domination plot involving death rays and miniaturized men. In the sequel, *The Return of Chandu* (q.v.), Lugosi took Lowe's role for a less-than-inspired performance.

P★	T★	E★	A

Directed by Marcel Varnel and William Cameron Menzies. Written by Barry Conners and Philip Klein. With Irene Ware, Herbert Mundin and Henry B. Walthall.

CHANGE OF MIND (1969) Another sf variant on the racial problem, with a white man's brain being transplanted into a black man's body.

P★★	T★★	E★★	A★

Directed by Robert Stevens. Written by Seeleg Lester and Richard Wesson. With Raymond St Jacques, Susan Oliver and Janet MacLachlan.

CHARLESTON (1926) In a post-Apocalypse Earth of 2028 a scientist encounters a surviving woman and communicates through dance. He also finds white aborigines dancing the Charleston. This light-hearted jazz short (25 minutes) was produced and directed by Jean Renoir from an idea by André Cerf.

Written by Pierre Lestringuez. With Johnny Higgins, Catherine Hessling and Pierre Braunberger.

CHARLESTON PARADE (1926) *see* CHARLESTON (1926)

CHARLY (1968) I'm not alone in believing "Flowers For Algernon" to be one of the finest science fiction short stories ever written – one of the few with the power to move you deeply and genuinely. *Charly* is a film of the novel version of Daniel Keyes's original story, and won lead actor Cliff Robertson not merely the praise of the sf community but an Oscar for Best Actor. The story is about a mind-improving experimental drug which is first tested on a mouse named Algernon, and then upon a floor sweeper from a bakery, the mentally deficient but amiable Charly Gordon (Cliff Robertson). His progression from dyslexic idiocy to super-genius is brilliantly charted, as is the pathos of his decline (and the death of his friend, the mouse). It might be accused of being sentimental, but I'd view this not as sentiment but as genuine tragedy: Charly must live on knowing what he once was, but unable to be it any longer. The film, with its occasional didactic tone does not quite match up to the story, but then there's little on the screen or in the pages of sf's literature that does.

P★★★★   T★★★   E★★★★★   A★★★

Produced and directed by Ralph Nelson. Written by Stirling Silliphant. Make-up by Vincent Kehoe. With Claire Bloom, Lilia Skala, Leon Janney, Dick Van Patten and Ruth White.

DER CHEF WUNSCHT KEINE ZEUGEN (1963) see NO SURVIVORS, PLEASE (1963)

CHELOVIEK AMPHIBIA (1961) see THE AMPHIBIAN MAN (1961)

THE CHEMIST (1936) A brief Buster Keaton skit involving a potion developed by the Chemist which can shrink and enlarge.

P★   T★   E★★   A

Written by David Freedman. With Marlyn Stuart and Earl Gilbert.

CHEREZ TERNII K ZVEZDAM (1981) see PER ASPERA AD ASTRA (1981)

THE CHIEF WANTS NO SURVIVORS (1963) see NO SURVIVORS, PLEASE (1963)

CHIKYU BOEIGUN (1957) see THE MYSTERIANS (1957)

CHIKYU SAIDA NO KESSAN (1965) see GHIDRAH, THE THREE-HEADED MONSTER (1965)

CHILDREN OF THE DAMNED (1963) Second 1960s version of John Wyndham's novel, *The Midwich Cuckoos*. Ian Hendry and Alan Badel play UNESCO investigators attempting to communicate with six children brought from various countries, who possess strange, super-human powers. Unlike the children in *Village Of The Damned* (q.v.) they are benevolent rather than distant and threatening, and a certain pathos is derived from their ultimate accidental death. While it is more sophisticated than the previous version it lacks the impact.

P★★   T★★   E★★★   A★

Directed by Anton M. Leader. Written by Jack Briley. Special Effects by Tom Howard. With Barbara Ferris, Alfred Burke, Clive Powell, Frank Summerscales and Bessie Love.

CHIRURGIEN AMERICAIN (1897) see A TWENTIETH CENTURY SURGEON (1897)

THE CHOSEN (1978) see HOLOCAUST 2000 (1978)

CHRONOPOLIS (1982) Clever stop-motion animated feature by Polish filmmaker Piotr Kamler which demonstrates an understanding of science fiction and its games with abstract notions that few sf films possess. Chronopolis is a far-future city, lost in space, run by immortals who enliven their days through a manipulation of the substance or fabric of time.

P★★★   T★★★★★   E★★★   A★★★

Graphics by Diane Chretien, Maria Tatarczuk and Babette Vimenet.

IL CIELO SULLA TESTA (1964) see SKY ABOVE HEAVEN (1964)

LE CIEL SUR LA TETE (1964) see SKY ABOVE HEAVEN (1964)

CINDERELLA 2000 (1977) Sex comedy set in the year 2047 where love has been banned. A rather uninspired sexploitation movie that capitalized on the success of *Star Wars (q.v.)* earlier in the year.

P★   T★★   E★★   A★

Directed by Al Adamson, Written by Bud Donnelly. With Catherine Erhardt, Jay B. Larson,
Vaughn Armstrong and Erwin Fuller.

LA CITE FOUDROYEE (1922) *see* THE CITY DESTROYED (1922)

CITY BENEATH THE SEA (1970)

The city in question holds America's gold
reserves, and criminals plan to remove
them. Amphibious men, explosive isotopes
and heading-for-collision-with-Earth asteroids confuse a tired plot.

P★	T★★	E★★	A

Produced and directed by Irwin Allen. Written by
John Meredyth Lucas. Special Effects by L. B.
Abbott & Art Cruikshank. With Stuart Whitman,
Robert Wagner, Rosemary Forsyth, Richard
Basehart, Paul Stewart, Joseph Cotten, James
Darren, Whit Bissell and Sugar Ray Robinson.

THE CITY DESTROYED (1922) A

mad scientist, seeking to rule the world,
destroys Paris with his ray gun.

Produced and directed by Luitz Marat. Written
by Jean-Louis Bouquet. With Daniel Mendille,
Jeanne Maguenat and Armand Morins.

CITY OF THE WALKING DEAD
(1980) *see* NIGHTMARE CITY (1980)

THE CITY UNDER THE SEA
(1965) *see* WAR-GODS OF THE DEEP
(1965)

A CLOCKWORK ORANGE (1971)

Adapted from Anthony Burgess's superb
novel this film by Stanley Kubrick is
perhaps the most frightening of the near-
future scenarios in the sf pantheon, basically because it is so recognizably and
realistically extrapolated from our own
world. The landscape of England has
changed only in that it has further decayed
– decent life seems possible only in the
countryside, and even that is threatened by
rampaging thugs from the cities – like
Alex and his gang of droogs. Gone is
Burgess's clever semi-Russian/English
argot, yet retained intact is the central
moral concern of the novel – should man
be allowed free will, even if the exercise of
that free will results in harm to his fellow
beings? It's quite rare for such an intelli-

A scene from A Clockwork Orange

gent polemic to survive the translation
from book to film, but Kubrick (helped by
the publicity centring around the rape
scene and the stark violence of the film)
managed to convey Burgess's argument to
several million people in an unadulterated
form. Alex (Malcolm MacDowell) is captured, rehabilitated (by electric shock
therapy) and becomes an obedient, well-
behaved citizen. But in the process something is lost – his appreciation of Beetho-
ven is lost, symptomatic of his loss of
vitality. But when this outcome is publicized in the popular press the outcry
causes the government to reverse his
treatment and return Alex to his old violent, music-loving self. It is not a comfort-
able message and, unless you revel in
violence and enjoy the sense of decadence
the film conveys, the film is a discomfiting
experience. But excellent cinema, no
doubt about that.

P★★★★	T★★★★	E★★★★	A★★★★

Produced, directed and written by Stanley
Kubrick. With Patrick Magee, Michael Bates,
Adrienne Corri, Miriam Karlin and John Clive.

THE CLONES (1973) Unsure whether

it's a serious thriller or a comedy, this
scientist - duplicates - others - in - plan - to -
take-over-the-World story doesn't ever
truly approach either the sinister possibili-
ties nor the comic potential.

P★	T★★	E★	A

Directed by Paul Hunt and Lamar Card. Written
by Steve Fisher. With Michael Greene, Otis
Young and Gregory Sierra.

CLONUS (1979) see PARTS: THE CLONUS HORROR (1979)

CLOSE ENCOUNTERS OF THE THIRD KIND (1977) We are not alone

... By 1977, 15 million Americans had reported seeing UFOs. Georgia's Governor, peanut farmer Jimmy Carter, was among them. Spielberg, therefore, is watching the skies. Again. Or, the 90-foot-high ceiling of the 450 ft × 250ft dirigible hangar in Mobile, Alabama, where his most mobile magic was made, behind as tight a security blackout as the US Government (and others) is said to place on all records of UFO sightings. By the time he reached the White House, Carter never kept his promise to break that ban – if there is one. This is Spielberg's dream movie. The one he wanted to make (again) for ten years or more. "I would have gone to great (not, any?) lengths to make it, whether I did it in America or elsewhere. Somehow, I would have found the money." Columbia did; and he did it in America and India, with a record eleven cameraces. He still maintains it's not science fiction, that he's agnostic about UFOs until achieving that other big dream – of spotting one for himself. (He has a telescope in his Amblin office.) He does, though, tend to believe that we've been under galactic scrutiny for eons and not necessarily by BEMs hell-bent on obliterating mankind. At base, CE3K is a gargantuan re-make of the teenage Spielberg's 8 mm Firelight (1963). He dropped fire for a real furnace of light but the setting remains as typical a signature as the lightshow. Mid-America, mid-class, mid-surburbia. Where the people, or some, are determinedly, frenetically (one damn near crazily) preparing for visitation from the universe, while the Army, the Government or Some Typically Spoilsport Adult Establishment (it turned out to be film critics in the main) aim to ruin the event by keeping it under wraps in case Wyoming does an Orson Welles on the turnpike. Spielberg borrows two (more) of Hitchcock's Ordinary People for decidedly far from Hitchcockian Extraordinary Circumstances, once they slip the security net

(rather easily). Richard Dreyfuss as an Indiana hard-hat, an electrical worker who's blown a fuse, and Melinda Dillon, mother of an infant whisked away by Them. They're drawn, among others, to the conical-shaped Devil's Tower mountain in Wyoming. Once here, the movie really ignites. Hitchcock is dropped. Spielberg takes over. He, we, are starstruck. The careful, often careless building of character and suspense, the inspiration in casting (and the playing) of the late François Truffaut as the UFOlogist is but an overture to the almost religious experience of the shining arrival and landing of the visitors' mother ship and the primordial five-tone musical conversation between us and Them. (Truffaut said it first, acting in his script of L'Enfant sauvage (1970), "Language is also music."). Doug Trumbull said that creating an UFO was like photographing God. They sure got close in a blaze of let-there-be-Spielbergian-light! Doug's ship, based on the director's view of an oil refinery lit up at night, is the biggest mother ship of them all. A dazzling, incandescent "city of light", touching down with John Williams's backing and screen-searing majesty. It makes all its predecessors – the Enterprise, Discovery, Nostromo, whatever – look like skateboards. That Carlo Rambaldi aliens skip out of it, with endearing smiles above pipecleaner limbs, that they return pilots missing since The Bermuda Triangle (hah!) swallowed their planes from 1945 onwards, that Dreyfuss goes off with them, is but a mini-encore. Nothing quite matches the sheer power of the Spielberg-Trumbull dream ship. Even Paul Schrader, who wrote the first script, ditched with a certain acrimony, agreed that the young maestro (29) had pulled off the impossible. British critic Richard Combs suggested the film was really about its own illusionism. Mais quelle illusion, alors? Almost alone among critics, Time's Frank Rich caught the true essence of the film (and its maker): "a celebration not only of children's dreams but also of the movies that help fuel those dreams." Other reviews defy belief, now as then. Such writers should never be allowed to forget ... They ranged from scribes too concerned with being prophets of doom ("The picture will be a colossal flop," William Flanagan, *New York* magazine; "a chaotic, often absurd, utterly unengaging mish-mash," David Cobb, *MacLean's*) to more established critics, strangely removed (by age?) from their times. "A monumentally silly bit of film-making," judged Alexander Walker, *London Evening Standard*. While Andrew Sarris, dean of Greenwich Village's *Voice*, felt that Spielberg "would have made a competent second-unit director in the days when movies still contained drama and narrative and recognizable human feelings"! Movies still do. But drama, comedy, sf entertainment, even human feelings as understood in the Village (preferring Redford's to Spielberg's ordinary people?) take on fresh formats, the way painting, photography, music, soccer, sex, all the arts, adapt to an era. It took a real believer to appreciate all this. Ray Bradbury named Spielberg as probably H. G. Wells's son, certainly Jules Verne's grandson, for finally making – *2001* or no *2001* – the sf film we'd been waiting for since before we were born ... "in all probability, the most important film of our time". Okay, certain questions were dodged, other issues skirted, the script wasn't as hot as the visuals. But hell, did it *work*? Did the earth move for you, too? You betcha!

CLOSE ENCOUNTERS OF THE THIRD KIND – *THE SPECIAL EDITION* (1980) Spielberg dreams never end. He's loath to see films die after their release period. "They're ongoing situations." He was still filming *CE3K* three weeks before the 1977 previews and never got all he wanted into it. Nor in his later tinkering – which pleased him, not us. He cut 16 minutes, added 13; seven of old, alternate takes; six of fresh footage. This allowed Dreyfuss into Puck's blindingly lit mother ship, but no longer going berserk with his neighbours' garbage; more Truffaut in Bombay; a badly spliced-in glimpse of a ship beached in the desert, like the opening Grumman TBF Avenger planes; and ... oh, is that all? Alas, yes. Allen

Daviau, who shot *Amblin'* (1964), was the twelfth camerace aboard and stuck around for the next dream once Spielberg pondered, what if one of Puck's aliens got caught short and missed the bus home ...?

(for both editions)

| P★★★ | T★★★★★ | E★★★★★ | A★★★★★ |

Produced by Julia Phillips and Michael Phillips. Directed and written by Steven Spielberg. With Teri Garr, Bob Balaban, Cary Guffey, Lance Hendriksen, Warren Kemmerling, Roberts Blossom, Philip Dodds, Shawn Bishop, Adrienne Campbell, Justin Dreyfuss, Merrill Connally, George DiCenzo and Carl Weathers. (TC)

CLOUDS OVER EUROPE (1937) A curious mixture of spy thriller and pre-War technological prediction, with Laurence Olivier and Ralph Richardson foiling the plans of spies to destroy Britain's experimental bombers with a death ray.

| P★ | T★ | E★ | A |

Directed by Tim Whelan and Arthur Woods. Written by Brock Williams, Jack Whitingham and Arthur Wimperis, adapted by Ian Dalrymple. With Valerie Hobson and George Curzon.

THE CLOWN AND THE AUTO-MATON (1897) Lost film by George Méliès, showing a clown's reaction to a mechanical man.

CLOWN FERDINAND AND THE ROCKET (1962) Intelligent juvenile by Czech director Jindrich Polak about a friendly robot who rescues Clown Ferdinand and some children from the ruins of an Earth city.

| P★★ | T★★ | E★★ | A★ |

Written by Ota Hofman and Polak. With Jiri Vrstala, E. Hrabetova, V. Horka and Hanus Bor.

CODE OF THE AIR (1928) Stereotyped thriller with "kappa rays" which destroy aeroplanes, invented by an evil Professor. The hero and his dog are in pursuit.

| P | T | E★ | A |

Directed by James P. Hogan. Written by Barry Barenger. With Kenneth Harlan, June Marlow, William V. Mong, Arthur Rankin and Silverstreak (the dog).

COLOSSUS, 1980 (1967) see COLOSSUS, THE FORBIN PROJECT (1967)

THE COLOSSUS OF NEW YORK
(1958) The Colossus is a giant mechanical monster containing the brain of a dead scientist. It has death rays which can shoot from its eyes (making it the superior of Frankenstein) and runs amok until it encounters the scientist's son.

P★★	T★★	E★★	A

Directed by Eugene Lourie. Written by Thelma Schnee. Special Effects by John P. Fulton. Make-up by Wally Westmore. With John Baragrey, Mala Powers, Otto Kruger and Charles Herbert.

COLOSSUS, THE FORBIN PROJECT (1967) James Bridges's adaptation of D. F. Jones's novel, Colossus, made for a taut, highly enjoyable thriller about the linking up of the two super-intelligent computers which run the US and Russian defence systems. It believes, of course, that it can run the world better than Man.

P★★	T★★	E★★★	A★★

Directed by Joseph Sargent. Special Effects by Albert Whitlock. With Eric Braeden, Susan Clark, Gordon Pinsent and William Schallert.

COMA (1978) Hollywood tried countless times to bring to the screen a living, breathing characterization of the New Woman (they finally succeeded, at very long last, in 1983 with Joanna Cassidy's astonishing performance in Under Fire) – but Geneviève Bujold, in this adaptation of the Robin Cook bestseller, is simply irritating. Some Beverly Hills dowager might have thought up this paranoiac fantasy in her spare time – that the doctors, those nice men in clean white coats, are out to get you. Bujold plays an intern at a Boston Hospital; she notices that perfectly healthy young patients are going into coma after minor operations, being shipped off to the impenetrable confines of the Jefferson Institute. What happens to them there (they become storage fodder for illicit organ transplants) – combined with a scene where the head of the hospital reveals himself as an elitist maniac with God-delusions – serves to make this one of the silliest movies of its year.

P★	T★★	E★	A

Directed and written by Michael Crichton. Special Effects by Joe Day and Ernie Smith. With Lois Chiles, Michael Douglas, Richard Widmark, Rip Torn and Elizabeth Ashley. (TR)

COMEDIA FANTASTICA (1975) see A FANTASTIC COMEDY (1975)

THE COMET'S COMEBACK
(1916) A mysterious comet approaches the Earth and produces lethargy-inducing gases which slow everything and everyone down. A nice mixture of apocalypse and comedy.

With John Steppling, John Sheehan, Carol Halloway and Dick Rosson.

COMME MARS EN CAREME
(1967) see DON'T PLAY WITH THE MARTIANS (1967)

THE COMPUTER WORE TENNIS SHOES (1969) Disney practice run for Tron (q.v.). A young boy (Kurt Russell) has all the knowledge in a computer fired into his brain, with comic results.

P★	T★★	E★★	A

Directed by Robert Butler. Written by Joseph L. McEveety. With Cesar Romero, Joe Flynn and William Schallert.

CONGO PONGO (1945) see WHITE PONGO (1945)

A CONNECTICUT YANKEE (1931)
David Butler's film was a perfect escapist fantasy for the Depression years, more faithful to the Twain original than the other versions, with Will Rogers and Maureen O'Sullivan heading the cast.

P★★	T★	E★★	A

Written by Owen Davis and William Conselman. With William Farnum, Frank Albertson, Myrna Loy and Brandon Hurst.

THE CONNECTICUT YANKEE AT KING ARTHUR'S COURT
(1920) Director Emmett J. Flynn's version of Mark Twain's novel is the earliest adaptation (by Bernard McConville) of this future-in-the-past tale, with tele-

phones, plumbing and other modern conveniences being introduced, with comic effect, into the England of Arthur's time.

P★★	T★	E★★	A

With Harry C. Myers, Pauline Starke, Rosemary Theby, William V. Mong, and Charles Clary.

A CONNECTICUT YANKEE IN KING ARTHUR'S COURT (1948)

The most lightweight adaptation of Twain's classic is also the most enjoyable, with Bing Crosby "busy doing nothing" along with Rhonda Fleming. Gordon Jennings was scarcely called upon to use his Special Effects talents.

P★	T★★	E★★★	A★

Directed by Tay Garnett. Written by Edmund Beloin. With William Bendix, Cedric Hardwicke, Murvyn Vye, Henry Wilcoxon and Richard Webb.

THE CONQUEST OF SPACE

(1955) Any film based on a coffee table book (by Chesley Bonestell and Willy Ley) and a technical tract by Wernher von Braun (*The Mars Project*) has a head start in the handicap stakes, but James O'Hanlon's script sunk this George Pal production before it began. The psychology of the spacecraft's crew and its (almost lifeless) adventures break the back of this dull, almost unwatchable film and – so most critics agree – killed realism in space movies until *2001* (q.v.).

P	T★★	E	A

Directed by Byron Haskin. Special Effects by John P. Fulton, Irmin Roberts, Paul Lerpae, Ivyl Burks and Jan Domela. With Walter Brooke, Eric Fleming and Mickey Shaughnessy.

CONQUEST OF THE EARTH

(1980) Third and last of the *Battlestar Galactica* (q.v.) sequence. Here the straggle of surviving human ships finally reach Earth and attempt to defend it against a forthcoming Cylon attack. The weakest of these rather thoughtless offerings.

P★	T★★★	E★★	A★

Directed by Sidney Hayers, Sigmund Neufeld Jr and Barry Crane. Written by Glen A. Larson. Special Effects by David M. Garber, Wayne Smith. With Kent McCord, Barry Van Dyke, Robyn Douglas and Lorne Greene.

CONQUEST OF THE PLANET OF THE APES

(1972) Fourth film in the Apes series and a prequel to the first, this is a disappointing (particularly in so far as plot explanations go) addition which tries and fails to explain how the apes became intelligent.

P★	T★★	E★	A

Directed by J. Lee Thompson. Written by Paul Dehn. Make-up by John Chalmers and Don Striepeke. With Roddy McDowall, Don Murray, Ricardo Montalban and Natalie Trundy

CONQUEST OF THE POLE (1912)

A late example of George Méliès one-man cinematographic fantasies involves an aerobus and an expedition to the North Pole. On the way they encounter a snow giant.

With Fernande Albany.

COPLAN FX 18 CASSE TOUT

(1965) *see* THE EXTERMINATORS (1965)

COPLAN SAUVE SA PEAU (1967)

see COPLAN SAVES HIS SKIN (1967)

COPLAN SAVES HIS SKIN (1967)

A film which isn't quite sure whether it's spoof or not. A mad scientist (named Hugo Gernsbach, after the editor of the sf magazine *Amazing* in the 1920s) sets out to destroy the world. Klaus Kinski, later to star in *Android* (q.v.), plays a small role.

P★	T★★	E★	A

Directed by Yves Boisset. Written by Boisset and Claude Veillot from the novel *Coplan Paie le Cercueil* by Paul Kenny. With Caludio Brook, Margaret Lee, Bernard Blier and Jean Topart.

THE CORPSE VANISHES (1942)

Eternal-youth stories are usually tediously similar, and this is no exception. Bela Lugosi stars in this story about an 80-year-old wife kept alive and young by glandular injections. The serum, as ever, can only be obtained from healthy, living young girls.

P★	T★	E★	A

Directed and written by Harvey Gates. With Luana Walters, Tristram Coffin, Minerva Urecal and Elizabeth Russell.

THE COSMIC MAN (1958) Strange mixture of the benign alien and Christ myths in a story where the Cosmic Man (who has a negative image) comes to Earth to preach peace before it's too late, curing a crippled boy to prove his goodness.

P★★   T★   E★★   A

Directed by Herbert Greene. Written by Arthur C. Pierce. Special Effects by Charles Duncan. With Bruce Bennett, John Carradine, Angela Greene, Paul Langton and Lyn Osborn.

THE COSMIC MAN APPEARS IN TOKYO (1956) see MYSTERIOUS SATELLITE (1956)

THE COSMIC MONSTER (1957) see THE STRANGE WORLD OF PLANET X (1957)

COSMIC MONSTERS (1957) see THE STRANGE WORLD OF PLANET X (1957)

COSMONAUTS ON VENUS (1962) see PLANET OF STORMS (1962)

COUNTDOWN (1967) In the light of subsequent developments in the space race, and by comparison to *The Right Stuff* (1983), this is almost unwatchable in terms of its premise – that the first Moonshot would be a solo flight – but keeps attention through its character portrayals. Based on the novel, *The Pilgrim Project*, by Hank Searles.

P★   T★★   E★   A

Directed by Robert Altman. Written by Loring Mandel. With Robert Duvall, James Caan, Steve Ihnat, Charles Aidman and Joanna Moore.

COUNTER-ATTACK OF THE MONSTER (1955) see GIGANTIS, THE FIRE MONSTER (1955)

COUNTERBLAST (1948) An escaped Nazi scientist (mad, what else?) is working on an antidote to a nerve gas – not for everyone, but for the Nazis who have developed the original. World domination remains the (then not so incredible) underlying threat. A nice twist here is that

the scientist (Mervyn Johns) is both baddie and, ultimately, goodie, dying an ironic death (by poisonous gas in a ship's hold).

P★★★   T★★   E★★   A★

Directed by Paul L. Stein. Written by Jack Whittingham. With Nora Pilbeam, Karel Stepanek, Robert Beatty and Margaretta Scott.

COZ TAKHLE DAT SI SPENAT (1976) see WHAT WOULD YOU SAY TO SOME SPINACH? (1976)

CRACK IN THE WORLD (1965) Any event severe enough to split the Earth open and give us a second Moon would in all probability end life on Earth, but we struggle by in this unconvincing disaster epic, as an experiment to tap energy from the Earth's core goes badly wrong.

P★   T★★   E★   A

Directed by Andrew Marton. Written by Jon Manchip White and Julian Halevy. Special Effects by Alec Weldon. With Dana Andrews, Janette Scott, Kieron Moore and Alexander Knox.

THE CRAWLING EYE (1958) see THE TROLLENBERG TERROR (1958)

THE CRAWLING HAND (1963) When an astronaut's craft explodes on its return to Earth, only a hand survives, infused with alien life. Possession of the hand turns a boy into a killer.

P★   T★   E★   A

Directed by Herbert L. Strock. Written by William Edelson and Herbert L. Strock. With Peter Brook, Kent Taylor, Rod Lauren, Arline Judge, Richard Arlen, Allison Hayes and Alan Hale.

THE CRAWLING MONSTER (1964) see THE CREEPING TERROR (1964)

THE CRAWLING TERROR (1957) see THE STRANGE WORLD OF PLANET X (1957)

THE CRAZIES (1973) A zombie horror film with a science fiction rationale – a special, government-developed virus which is let loose on a small town population when a government plane crashes.

P★★   T★★★   E★★   A★

Directed and written by George Romero. Special Effects by Regis Survinski and Tony Pantanello. With Lane Carroll, W. G. McMillan and Harold Wayne Jones.

THE CRAZY RAY (1923) One of the most inventive of the early, silent movies, with the first genuine mad scientist, whose ray petrifies Paris at 3.25 in the morning. Most of the inaction is seen through the eyes of the watchman on the Eiffel Tower who has escaped the ray's effects. Director/writer France René Clair had fun with cinematic tricks, of course, but also gave a decent storyline, as a result of which this remains one of the few sf films of the period of more than historical interest.

P★★   T★★   E★★   A★

With Henri Rollan, Albert Préjean, Madeleine Rodrigue, Marcel Vallée and Charles Martinelli.

CREATION OF THE HUMANOIDS (1962) Jay Simms wrote the screenplay of this highly intelligent, if static film about a post-nuclear Earth where Mankind – almost sterile, its numbers depleted by 92 per cent by the War – is dying out, yet has created, as its helpers, a race of humanoid robots. The Luddite-like Brotherhood, the Order of Flesh and Blood, oppose the proliferation of these androids – "clickers" in common parlance – and one of their members, Kenneth Craigus (Don Megowan) is vehement in his dislike of them. But Craigus, as it turns out, is himself a robot – an R96; 96 per cent human. The sets are period, looking like sketches from a 1960s sf magazine, and there is practically no action or plot tension, but the arguments for and against a caring, human-like robot form (which has all the memories and emotions of the dead human it has replaced) are beautifully rehearsed in this much-underrated film. Wesley E. Barry's direction and wooden acting by Megowan, Frances McCann (as Maxine Megan), Erica Elliot (as Craigus's sister) and Don Dolittle (as Dr Raven) doesn't help, but Simms's arguments are marvellous science fiction.

P★★★★   T★★   E★★★   A★

CREATURE FROM ANOTHER WORLD (1958) see THE TROLLENBERG TERROR (1958)

CREATURE FROM BLOOD ISLAND (1959) see TERROR IS A MAN (1959)

THE CREATURE FROM GALAXY 27 (1958) Fear of parasitism lies behind this alien-impregnates-astronaut story from Roger Corman's production stable.

P★   T★   E★   A

Directed by Bernard Kowalski. Written by Martin Varno. With Michael Emmet, Angela Greene, John Baer and Ed Nelson.

THE CREATURE FROM THE BLACK LAGOON (1953) More a crude exploitation of phobia than the atmospheric work of art some sf fans claim it is. In spite of its popularity and the fondness with which the creature itself is held by many, this is not by any means a major sf film, though its more gothic elements have a strange charm. The creature is the last survivor of a species of man, aquatic and semi-reptilian, that developed parallel to Mankind proper. It's a swamp dweller and takes a fancy to a human female (wouldn't it find her grotesquely ugly?) which it wants as its mate. This is, in one sense, merely the animation of one of those scary alien-grabs-human-woman covers that adorned the science fiction magazines throughout the 1930s, 1940s

Julia Adams, Richard Carlson and "The Creature" in Creature From The Black Lagoon

and 1950s. Two sequels followed, *Revenge Of The Creature* (1955) (q.v.) and *The Creature Walks Among Us* (1956) (q.v.), only going to prove that taste and originality counted for little back in the 1950s.

P★	T★★	E★★★	A★

Directed by Jack Arnold. Written by Harry Essex and Arthur Ross. Special Effects by Charles S. Welbourne. With Richard Carlson, Julie Adams, Richard Denning, Ricou Browning, Whit Bissell and Nestor Paiva.

CREATURE FROM THE HAUNTED SEA (1961) Roger Corman produced and directed this essentially silly film about a monster that threatens a group of idiots.

P	T	E	A

Written by Charles Griffith. With Anthony Carbone, Betsy Jones-Moreland and Edward Wain.

LES CREATURES (1966) *see* THE CREATURES (1966)

THE CREATURES (1966) Self-conscious film (French/Swedish) where an sf writer discovers a man with a machine that can make other people obey him.

P★★	T★★	E★	A★

Directed and written by Agnes Varda. With Catherine Deneuve and Michel Piccoli.

CREATURES OF THE PREHISTORIC PLANET (1970) *see* THE HORROR OF THE BLOOD MONSTERS (1970)

CREATURES OF THE RED PLANET (1970) *see* HORROR OF THE BLOOD MONSTERS (1970)

THE CREATURE WALKS AMONG US (1956) Ricou Browning was once again the adorably threatening creature (a gilled man) in this sequel to *The Creature From The Black Lagoon* (q.v.). John Sherwood directed this one. The gill-man is trapped, burned (he loses his gills), taken to San Francisco and finally escapes. Does he drown? We don't know, but this was the third and last of the creature's cinematic exploits.

P★★	T★★	E★★	A★

Written by Arthur Ross. Special Effects by Clifford Stine. With Jeff Morrow, Rex Reason, Leigh Snowden, Gregg Palmer and Don Megowan.

THE CREATURE WASN'T NICE (1981) *see* SPACESHIP (1981)

THE CREATURE WITH THE ATOM BRAIN (1955) A curiously bad film in view of Curt Siodmak's involvement as writer, even by "brain" movie standards. These robot-like zombies have been created by a scientist's experiments, replacing their brains with atom-powered units which make them as strong as several men.

P	T★	E★	A

Directed by Edward L. Cahn. With Richard Denning, Angela Stevens, Harry Lanter, Tristram Coffin, John Launer and Gregory Gay.

THE CREEPER (1948) Formula film in which a serum changes a man into a cat-like monster.

P★	T★	E★	A

Directed by Jean Yarbrough. Written by Maurice Tombragel. With Eduardo Ciannelli, June Vincent, Onslow Stevens and Ralph Morgan.

THE CREEPERS (1966) *see* THE ISLAND OF TERROR (1966)

THE CREEPING TERROR (1964) Eight grown men shift 600 lb of polyurethane foam about the countryside, attempting to swallow unsuspecting victims. Art J. Nelson directed this tale of an alien carpet attempting to work out mankind's chemical composition by swallowing several specimens. Clifford Stine and John Lackey deserve some kind of award for producing what must be some of the direst special effects on celluloid. It's entertaining only because it's so bad.

P	T	E★★	A

With Vic Savage and Shannon O'Neil.

THE CREEPING UNKNOWN (1955) *see* THE QUATERMASS EXPERIMENT (1955)

THE CREMATORS (1972) An intelligent meteor falls to Earth 300 years ago, and is somehow woken when a scientist finds fragments and tests them. When agitated the pieces glow and summon a giant rolling fireball which incinerates the offending agitator. Pathetic script, acting and special effects. Dull, too.

P	T	E	A

Produced, directed and written by Harry Essex. Special Effects by Doug Beswick. With Maria de Aragon and Marvin Howard.

CRIMES OF DR MABUSE (1933) see THE TESTAMENT OF DR MABUSE (1933)

CRIMES OF THE FUTURE (1970) A savage vision of the results of man's tinkering with his genetic heritage, from David Cronenberg. A cosmetic product has succeeded in wiping out all women of child-bearing age, and paedophilia (with the intent of impregnating female children) has become *the* crime of the future (though various other forms of sexual deviancy are also criminal). A disturbing yet thoughtful film, prefiguring much of Cronenberg's later work.

P★★★	T★★	E★★★	A★

Directed, written, filmed and edited by David Cronenberg. With Ronald Mlodzik, Tania Zolty, John Lidolt, Jack Messinger and Paul Mulholland.

I CRIMINALI DELLA GALASSIA (1965) see WILD WILD PLANET (1965)

CROISIÈRES SIDERALES (1941) see SIDEREAL CRUISES (1941)

CROSSTALK (1982) Mildly interesting but scarcely ingenious tale of a computerized home (looking after its crippled inventor) and its moral response to the question of its own fate. Avoiding the garishness of *Demon Seed* (q.v.), this deals with several of the problems involving advanced technology with intelligence.

P★★★	T★★	E★★	A★

Directed by Mark Egerton. Written by Egerton, Linda Lane and Denis Whitburn. With Gary Day, Penny Downie, Brian McDermott and Peter Collingwood.

THE CULT OF VIOLENCE (1965) see SPY IN YOUR EYE (1965)

THE CURIOUS DR HUMPP (1967) A strong sexual twist upon the mad scientist caper, with a controlling brain in the lab ultimately responsible for the city's large number of kidnappings and disappearances. An Argentinian offering with a little more style than usual.

P★★	T★★	E★★	A★

Directed and written by Emilio Vieyra. With Richard Bauleo, Gloria Prat and Aldo Barbero.

THE CURIOUS FEMALE (1969) In the super-computer-controlled age of 2177 sexual permissiveness is the norm and romance is censored – so romance becomes the pornography of the age.

P★★	T★★	E★★	A★

Produced and directed by Paul Rapp. Written by Winston R. Paul. With Angelique Pettyjohn, Charlene Jones, Bunny Allister and David Westberg.

A CURIOUS WAY TO LOVE (1967) see PLUCKED (1967)

THE CURSE OF FRANKENSTEIN (1957) A Hammer Horror movie which perverts Mary Shelley's original conception, making Victor Frankenstein (Peter Cushing) a homicidal maniac in pursuit of pure knowledge and his monster (Christopher Lee) a brain-damaged, super-strong zombie. Visually it's a treat, however, with a gothic picture-book look.

P★	T★★	E★★★	A★

Directed by Terence Fisher. Written by Jimmy Sangster. Make-up by Phil Leakey. Cinematography by Jack Asher. With Hazel Court, Robert Urquhart and Melvyn Hayes.

THE CURSE OF THE FLY (1965) The only connection between this and the earlier Fly films is the matter-transmitter (which bungles things usually – why do they keep on experimenting with it when the failure rate is so high?), which here creates a few more monsters and one rapidly ageing man.

P★	T★★	E★	A

Directed by Don Sharp. Written by Harry Spalding. Special Effects by Harold Fletcher. Make-up by Eleanor Jones. With Brian Donlevy, George Baker, Carole Gray and Michael Graham.

CURSE OF THE SWAMP CREATURE (1966) Typical mad-scientist-in-a-swamp movie, with John Agar as the doctor working on the creation of a half-human, half-reptilian creature.

P★	T★	E★	A

Directed by Larry Buchanan. Written by Tony Huston. With Francine York, Shirley McLine, Bill Thurman and Jeff Alexander.

CYBERNETIC GRANDMOTHER (1962) Czech animated puppet film (20 minutes); an anti-machine comedy involving robots.

Directed, written and designed by Jiri Trnka, based on a story by Ivan Klima.

CYBORG 009 – UNDERGROUND DUEL (1967) Japanese animated film involving giant robots and sea monsters battling with the plucky cyborg.

P★	T★	E★	A

Directed by Yugo Serikawa. Written by Kei Iijima, Y. Serikawa and Daisaku Shirakawa.

CYBORG 2087 (1966) A pleasing and modest film from the pen of Arthur C. Pierce. A cyborg travels back in time to prevent the creation of cyborgs, hoping to prevent the sterile, controlled world of 2087.

P★★★	T★★	E★★★	A★

Directed by Franklin Adreon. With Michael Rennie, Karen Steele, Wendell Grey, Warren Stevens and Edward Franz.

THE CYCLOPS (1957) Radiation in a Central American valley mutates people and animals, the Cyclops being a huge (20-foot plus) one-eyed mutant. A cheapo production from the reliably bad Bert I. Gordon stable (he produced, directed, wrote and did the special effects!).

P★	T	E★	A

With James Craig, Gloria Talbott, Lon Chaney Jr.

DAGORA, THE SPACE MONSTER (1964) The dogora (yes, not dagora) are radiation-mutated cells that look like flying jellyfish or octopi. They're greedy devils, too, gobbling up lots of riches everywhere they float. Japanese ingenuity and wasp venom stops them from eating all the diamonds in Japan.

P	T★	E	A

Directed by Inoshiro Honda. Written by Shinichi Sekizawa. Special Effects by Eiji Tsuburaya. With Yosuke Natsuki and Yoko Fujiyama.

DAIKAIJU BARAN (1958) see VARAN THE UNBELIEVABLE (1958)

DAIKAIJU GAMERA (1966) see GAMERA (1966)

DAIKYAJU GAPPA (1967) see MONSTER FROM A PREHISTORIC PLANET (1967)

DAI KOESU YONGKARI (1967) see YONGKARI, MONSTER FROM THE DEEP (1967)

DAI SANJI SEKAI TAISEN – YONJU ICHI JIKAN NO KYOFU (1960) see THE FINAL WAR (1960)

DALEKS – INVASION EARTH 2150 AD (1966) They may seem silly now, but I can remember how the Daleks, with their threatening, electronically treated voices ("Exter-minate!") and their shell-like metal bodies, utterly inhuman, with alien blobs inside, used to petrify me as a youngster. Here Peter Cushing plays the time-travelling Time Lord, Dr Who, who, helped by a London policeman (Bernard Cribbins), prevents the Daleks from destroying the Earth.

P★★	T★★	E★★★	A★

Produced by Max J. Rosenberg and Milton Subotsky. Directed by Gordon Flemyng. Written by Subotsky. Special Effects by Ted Samuels. Make-up by Bunty Phillips. With Ray Brooks, Andrew Keir, Jill Curzon and Eddie Powell.

DAMNATION ALLEY (1977) Author Roger Zelazny disowned this Jack Smight adaptation of his cult novel – mild stuff, Zelazny, you should have shot Jack Smight. The scene is post-Holocaust America, the hero is "Hell" Tanner (Jan Michael Vincent), a one-time soldier turned biking wide-boy (the only "wide" thing about Vincent here is his smile, certainly not the range of his talent). He and his friends live in the middle of a radioactive desert, believing themselves to be the last men alive. When they pick up a radio message from Canada, they build a super-armoured car to carry them across the devastated States to this last outpost of civilization. Post-war America is a place of giant scorpions, demented hillbillies, and the worst plastic cockroaches ever to be tugged by a piece of string across a movie set by an equally demented special effects man. But the last outpost of civilization, when Tanner and Co. finally reach it, has you baying for someone to bring the roaches back – it's a place of white picket fences, clean porches and blond, smiling children. Unless you're very young or very old, the tweeness leaves you horrified, smell of antiseptic nauseates in seconds. "Hell" has travelled all that way to end up in a Coca-Cola ad. Oh, there's also a portion of the plot which explains how Earth is going through an ecological disaster because the nuclear war has tipped it off its axis. At the end of the movie, the Earth tips back, the sky turns blue in the time it takes you to mutter Norman Rockwell, and the sun shines down just in time to catch on the mane of a white horse gambling along the inexplicably verdant roadside. It might have made a good spoof, but everyone seems to be playing it straight. The audience went comatose.

P	T	E	A

Written by Alan Sharpe and Lukas Heller. Special Effects by Milt Rice. With George Peppard, Dominique Sanda, Kip Niven, Paul Winfield and Jackie Earle Haley. (TR)

THE DAMNED (1961) Based on the novel, *The Children of Light*, by H. L. Lawrence, this is one of the more memorable British films of the early 1960s. A secret project is being undertaken in the cave system beneath a military establishment in England, children being raised in isolation to make them immune to radioactivity. However, when a couple stumble upon them and attempt to free them, they discover that the children are themselves highly radioactive and the couple are contaminated. Not so much an anti-science tale as a dark irony.

P★★	T★★	E★★★	A★★

Directed by Joseph Losey. Written by Evan Jones. With MacDonald Carey, Shirley Ann Field, Oliver Reed and Viveca Lindfors.

DANGER: DIABOLIK (1967) Arch criminal come alternate super-hero, Diabolik (John Phillip Law) systematically and contemptuously plunders the world's riches. An all-action adventure concerned with power and its symbols, its master touch is to have Diabolik encased in molten gold at the end – an accident from which he emerges as a piece of rich, living sculpture.

P★★	T★★	E★★	A★★

Produced by Dino De Laurentiis. Directed by Mario Bava. Written by Mario Bava, Dino Mauri and Adriano Baracco. With Marisa Mell, Michel Piccoli, Adolfo Celi and Terry Thomas.

LE DANGER VIENT DE L'ES-PACE (1958) *see* THE DAY THE SKY EXPLODED (1958)

DANS LES GRIFFES DU MANIA-QUE (1965) *see* THE DIABOLICAL DR Z (1965)

THE DARK (1979) The alien as ourselves? Another modern variation on the idea that aliens might be just like us, yet think and act differently – though not that differently from psychopathic killers. This is a better-than-average feature, considering it comes from director John "Bud" Cardos.

P★★	T★★	E★★	A★

Written by Standford Whitmore. With William Devane, Cathy Lee Crosby, Richard Jaeckel and Keenan Wynn.

THE DARK CRYSTAL (1982) Extra-ordinary! Not simply in terms of the marathon effort of puppeteers, mimes, designers, sculptors and hunters after taxidermist eyes – but the on-screen vistas. Here's genuine sf. The creation of another universe. A Tolkienesque mix of Jim Henson's land of Gorch and Brian Froud's Faeries, peopled by bizarre shapes, sizes and sounds. The contrived plot is a quest as in all good movies. The *mise-en-scène* is absolutely dazzling. That it never clocked is a box-office-land mystery.

P★	T★★★★★	E★★	A★★★★★

Directed by Jim Henson and Frank Oz. Written by David Odell, from a story by Henson. With voices of Stephen Garlick, Lisa Maxwell, Billie Whitelaw, Percy Edwards, Barry Dennen, Brian Muehl, David Buck, Sean Barrett and Joseph O'Connor. (TC)

DARK ENEMY (1984) The British Children's Film Unit were responsible for this After-The-Holocaust tale with telepathic Moonchildren, valley people and "the dark enemy in all of us" (our vices). Unfortunately it's not merely juvenile but clichéd, and lacks any real dramatic impact.

P★	T★	E★	A

Directed by Colin Finbow. With Rory MacFarquar, David Haig, Douglas Storm.

DARK STAR (1974) A curiosity, a genre landmark, and a good movie – probably in that order. It was John Carpenter's first film, made as a 16 mm student movie at UCLA and later expanded, as its cult status grew, to 35 mm for theatre release. Co-scripted by Dan O'Bannon, who also appeared in the cast, it was one of the first attempts to assimilate the hippie youth culture of the late 1960s and early 1970s into the science fiction movie. The faster-than-light ship *Dark Star* has been in outer space for 19 years, its crew are faced with the routine, dreary task of identifying and destroying planets which might shift orbit and spiral into their sun, causing a supernova which might damage Earth. Adding to their problems are a troublesome alien beast they have taken aboard as a mascot, a sentient talking bomb which seems intent on killing them, and the dead captain of the ship, who is being kept on ice in the ship's hold and can still talk to his subordinates through an electronic device. All the preoccupations and in-jokes of the Flower Power scene are present in this macabre black comedy: the crew are bearded longhairs, each caught in their individual symptoms of psychosis and paranoia; authority is sent up both through the computer which controls the ship and through the dead but still influential captain, and the theme seems to be in part that of the Vietnam War – the reason the planets are destroyed seems a parody of the domino theory. As for in-jokes, there were never monsters like the one in *Dark Star* before, but then few previous film-makers had emerged from a college scene where LSD and the art-work it inspired were in vogue. For the most part it works extraordinarily well – there's an uneasy strangeness about the movie you find it hard to imagine more experienced film-makers achieving. But, because it was made with such a rarefied audience in mind, the film does tend to assume that its jokes and motifs will be instantly understood – they are probably lost on audiences over 30. There also seems to be an assumption, at points, that that rarefied audience is going to show up stoned – if you're not stoned, a couple of the sequences drag to an incredible degree. Scenes which should have been superb become a little uneven ... for instance, the sometimes very funny scene where O'Bannon is harassed by the freaky monster is a good few minutes overlength, and since there's hardly any dialogue throughout you're left with the nasty impression of a silent movie slapstick routine with added sound effects. A good movie thirdmost, then, one that has become over-rated through the years, but one that continues to draw attention because of its essential *differentness*.

P★★	T★★★	E★★★	A★★

Produced by Jack H. Harris. Special Effects by Dan O'Bannon. With Brian Narelle, Dre Pahich and Cal Kumiholm. (TR)

A crew member consults the "dead" captain in Dark Star

THE DAY AFTER TOMORROW
(1942) Based on Arch Oboler's radio play, "This Precious Freedom". A US businessman returns from a holiday in the wilderness to discover that the USA is being run by a Fascist dictatorship.

P★★	T★★	E★★	A★

Directed and written by Arch Oboler. Special Effects by Howard Anderson and Ray Mercer. With Claude Rains, Barbara Bates, Paul Hilton, Gloria Holden, Milton Kibbee, Bobbie Stebbins and Martin Kosleck.

THE DAY MARS INVADED
EARTH (1962) The Martians duplicate Earth people and slowly take over the world. For once they aren't stopped, but then, who cares in this lacklustre film?

P★	T★	E★	A

Produced and directed by Maury Dexter. Written by Harry Spalding. With Kent Taylor, Marie Windsor, William Muns and Betty Beal.

THE DAY OF THE DOLPHIN
(1973) Scriptwriter Buck Henry's adaptation of Robert Merle's novel captures something of the uneasiness of the original: should it be an examination of sentience – what makes a species intelligent – or should it be a political thriller? The film, divided between the two urges, actually switches from the former to the latter at its halfway stage – once the marine biologist (George C. Scott) has taught the dolphins to speak English we are then caught up in the power struggle to *use* the dolphins.

P★★	T★★	E★★	A★

Directed by Mike Nichols. Special Effects by Albert Whitlock and Jim White. With Trish Van Devere, Paul Sorvino and Fritz Weaver.

DAY OF THE TRIFFIDS (1963) A
stultifyingly bad adaptation of John Wyndham's famous novel about the strange man-killing plants which start to become the world's dominant species once humankind has been blinded wholesale by a meteorite storm. Wyndham produced a minor masterpiece, bridging the chasm between sf and mainstream so thoroughly you would not even notice the rift was there – only the shell of his idea remains, and as for the basic integrity of the novel, well, it has been translated into pure, if that's the word, B-movie exploitativeness. Howard Keel is the sailor who awakes in a London hospital to find himself one of the chosen few who have retained their sight. Others are the adolescent girl and the wily petty criminal he picks up on his way to Spain, and the scenes of dissolution and societal collapse they encounter, far from horrifying audiences, bring out smirks – they remind you of the orchestrated scenes of doom and debauchery in a bad Biblical epic. What we have here is *Sodom and Gomorrah* with rampaging rutabagas. When you realize that Wyndham's most pertinent suggestion has been omitted – that the meteorites did not make people blind, but, rather, triggered off a battery of weapons *mankind* had put in orbit – you wonder what on earth writer-producer Phillip Yordan and director Steve Sekeley thought they were doing. A movie about vegetables, by and for.

P	T★★	E	A

Special Effects by Wally Veevers. With Nicole Maurey, Kieron Moore, Janette Scott.

THE DAY THE EARTH CAUGHT
FIRE (1961) No massive budget was behind this effective sf thriller, just a tight script, some good location shooting, and a few excellent actors. Edward Judd plays

Peter Stenning, a cynical, alcoholic *Daily Express* journalist who relates the story of how simultaneous nuclear tests at the world's poles, by the USA and USSR, have shifted the Earth's axis and sent it tumbling off course towards the sun. The splendid Leo McKern is his colleague, and Janet Munro the girl he becomes involved with in the last doomed days. Director Val Guest – a journalist himself (who co-wrote the script with Wolf Mankowitz, and produced the movie) – starts us on the final day, with the world waiting for the outcome of a further nuclear blast calculated to send the planet back into its proper orbit. The London we see has become reminiscent of Sydney in *On The Beach (1959)* – a hollow shell of a city, the sun so close the tarmac on the streets is melting. Stenning backtracks to the start of it all, as he begins with the hint of an alarming scoop, and then finds himself on the edges of a maelstrom as the populace go through all the stages of terror and despair in a city where the Thames has evaporated. The *Daily Express* offices were used in the filming, and the screen editor is Arthur Christiansen, former editor in real life of the Beaverbrook paper. For all its sun-blinded quality, there are strong touches of *noir* to the movie and its central character which lend the film a quiet strength where otherwise it might have become bogged under with hysteria. It's a near perfect example of how science fiction movies often succeed best when elements of other genres are added – *The Day The Earth Caught Fire* shares part of its genesis with the pessimistic thrillers of pre-War Hollywood, and is, like many of those films, a minor classic in its field.

P★★★   T★★   E★★★★★   A★★

Special Effects by Les Bowie. With Michael Goodlife. (TR)

THE DAY THE EARTH STOOD STILL (1951) Based on Harry Bates's story "Farewell To The Master" (*Astounding*, October 1940), Robert Wise directed one of the seminal sf movies of the 1950s, changing only the final irony of Bates's story (where the robot, not the

humanoid, proves to be "the Master") which described the arrival on Earth of Klaatu (Michael Rennie) and his robot, Gort (Lock Martin) and their attempts to prevent Mankind from blowing itself away in a nuclear war. That message underlies the film and gives it its potency, yet the charm of the film lies in Klaatu's relationship with an American widow (Patricia Neal). The final scene – with Gort carrying the dead Klaatu back into the saucer – is amongst the most memorable in sf cinema. The Earth "stands still" when Klaatu demonstrates his power by shutting down all of Earth's electrically-powered machinery. Not quite a classic, but in the midst of the monster boom which followed its sanity was welcome.

P★★★   T★★   E★★★   A★

Written by Edmund H. North. With Sam Jaffe, Hugh Marlow, Billy Gray and James Seay.

THE DAY THE FISH CAME OUT
(1967) Dark comedy with a nasty conclusion as the doomsday weapon, a virus, is amongst the load on a plane that crashes into the sea near a Greek island.

P★★   T★★   E★★   A★

Produced, directed and written by Michael Cacoyannis. With Tom Courtenay, Sam Wanamaker, Colin Blakely, Candice Bergen and Ian Ogilvy.

THE DAY THE SKY EXPLODED
(1958) An international rocket expedition goes wrong, aborts and smashes into the sun, causing several asteroids to go astray and hurtle towards the Earth. The Russians and Americans fire A-bombs at the asteroids to save the world.

P★   T★   E★   A

Directed by Paolo Hensch. Written by Marcello Coscia and Alessandro Continenza. With Paul Hubschmid and Madeleine Fischer.

THE DAY THE WORLD CHANGED HANDS (1967) *see* COLOSSUS, THE FORBIN PROJECT (1967)

THE DAY THE WORLD ENDED
(1956) Awful clichéd post-Holocaust movie – the survivors of the War

encounter three-eyed telepathic man-eating mutants – notable only for being Roger Corman's debut in sf cinema, as producer and director.

P★	T★	E★	A

Written by Lou Rusoff. Special Effects by Paul Blaisdell. With Richard Denning, Adele Jergens, Lori Nelson, Touch Connors and Paul Blaisdell.

THE DAY TIME ENDED (1979)

Shoddy working of the alien invasion theme, featuring a family who are warned when they move into their new house. Avoid.

P★	T★★	E★	A

Directed by John Cardos. Written by Wayne Schmidt, J. Larry Carroll and David Schmoeller. Special Effects by Paul W. Gentry, Pete Kuran and Rich Bennette. With Jim Davis, Chris Mitchum, Dorothy Malone and Marcey Lafferty.

THE DEADLY BEES (1966)

Mad bee-keeper Frank Finlay is breeding killer bees on a remote island. Based on a novel by H. F. Heard, *A Taste For Honey*.

P★	T★★	E★	A

Directed by Freddie Francis. Written by Robert Bloch and Anthony Marriott. Special Effects by Michael Collins and John Mackie. With Suzanna Leigh, Guy Doleman and John Harvey.

THE DEADLY DIAPHANOIDS (1965) *see* WAR OF THE PLANETS (1965)

DEADLY HARVEST (1972)

Unlikely story of the collapse of America after two disastrous harvests and the sale of food reserves to "Asia". While it serves as a good reminder that all economic wealth is ultimately based on agricultural stability, it fails to show how bad such a collapse would really be, and depicts the catastrophe in the terms of one farming community defending itself against black market raiders from the city.

P★★	T★★	E★★	A★

Directed by Timothy Bond. Written by Martin Lager. With Clint Walker, Nehemiah Persoff, Gary Davies and Kim Cattrall.

THE DEADLY INVENTION (1958) *see* THE FABULOUS WORLD OF JULES VERNE (1958)

THE DEADLY MANTIS (1957)

A giant insect movie of little note. The huge preying mantis ravages New York.

P	T★	E★	A

Directed by Nathan Juran. Written by Martin Berkeley from a story by William Alland. Special Effects by Clifford Stine. With Craig Stevens, Alix Talton, William Hopper and Florenz Ames.

A scene from The Deadly Mantis

A DEAD MAN SEEKS HIS MURDERER (1962) *see* THE BRAIN (1962)

THE DEAD MOUNTAINEER HOTEL (1979)

Developed from a short story by Arkadi and Boris Strugatski, the Russian sf writers, this excellent Russian film is of a different order of intelligence from the usual wide-screen offering like *Star Wars* (q.v.). A detective murder mystery without a murder, it might be called; the real mystery lies in the fact that all of the guests in the isolated hotel high in the mountains of Kazakhstan are alien, with alien mores, social customs and thought processes. As in Tarkovsky's *Stalker* (q.v.), the dimension of alienness relies not on special effects but on forms of behaviour we would consider strange.

P★★★★	T★★★	E★★★★	A★★★

Directed by Grigori Kromarov. Written by Arkadi and Boris Strugatski. With Uldis Putsitis, Yuri Yarvet, Lembit Peterson and Mikk Mikiver.

THE DEAD ZONE (1983)

Johnny Smith (Christopher Walken) kisses his teacher girlfriend, Sarah, goodnight then, driving home, smashes into an overturned milk lorry. For five years he lies in a coma, and when he wakes his beloved is married. Not only that, he discovers he has second sight: by touching someone he can see moments of crisis or disaster in their pasts, presents and futures. For once the Stephen King "formula" does not run to the whole gamut of horror clichés but instead depicts the curse of such a "gift" on an ordinary man. Smith is not himself evil, but can discern (by a touch) the evil potential in others. After solving a murder case, saving a little girl from death in a fire, and saving the life of a tutee, he is finally brought to confront the "morality" of his gift when he shakes the hand of Senator-delegate Greg Stilson (Martin Sheen) and sees a future where, as President, Stilson, obsessed with a Hitler-like belief in his own "destiny", pushes the button that begins the Holocaust. What is impressive about this film is the careful psychology of its characterization and that final moral dilemma: is it right to attempt to kill a man who you *know* will be responsible for millions of deaths if you do not? This is couched by Smith to his doctor, Weizak (Herbert Lom), in the terms, would it be right to kill Hitler if you could go back in time and do it before he rose to power? It's a central sf idea which is intelligently handled (with a nice twist – though I'll not spoil it by revealing it here). A convincing, thoughtful and thoroughly entertaining movie.

| P★★★ | T★★★ | E★★★★★ | A★★ |

Directed by David Cronenberg. Written by Jeffrey Boam. With Brooke Adams, Tom Skerrit, Anthony Zerbe and Colleen Dewhurst.

DEATH COMES FROM OUTER SPACE (1958) *see* THE DAY THE SKY EXPLODED (1958)

DEATH CORPS (1970) *see* SHOCK WAVES (1970)

DEATH HAS LAID AN EGG (1967) *see* PLUCKED (1967)

DEATH IN THE AIR (1909) *see* THE AIRSHIP DESTROYED (1909)

DEATHLINE (1972) An interesting film which takes the "submerged nation" theme pretty literally. Building work on a tube station beneath the British Museum in the 1890s results in a cave-in and the burial alive of a group of workers; the last survivor, his wife dying of a horrible leprous disease down below, comes to get aid for her. If you can ignore questions like What were their families doing down there at the time of the cave-in? then this is an excellent B-feature with a genuine sense of pathos.

| P★★ | T★★ | E★★★ | A★ |

Directed by Gary Sherman. Written by Ceri Jones. Special Effects by John Horton. With Donald Pleasance, Norman Rossington, Hugh Armstrong, Christopher Lee and Sharon Gurney.

THE DEATH PREDICTER (1939) *see* THE WORLD WILL SHAKE (1939)

DEATH RACE 2000 (1975) At the turn of the next century, hit-and-run accidents have become, logically, a spectator sport in America. Points are scored for every pedestrian killed; the combatants in this annual event tear from coast to coast in garish, evil sports cars – so customized with hooks, blades, spikes and armour plating they resemble dinosaurs on wheels – mowing down bystanders of widely differing degrees of innocence. The movie is one of the best from the Roger Corman schlock stable, and for once the unabashed exploitativeness of the man's productions has found a theme to match them – a send-up of every car-chase/car-smash movie ever to fill an auditorium with the rank odour of crushed beer cans and bloodlust. It's Gorman sending up both Corman and his audience. The result is a neat black comedy, with David Carradine playing the ace driver Frankenstein, and Sylvester Stallone putting in a blubbery, block-headed, extremely funny performance as his arch rival; for all that muscle, Stallone is an intelligent actor, and he complements the movie's spoof tone by sending *himself* up. Carradine comes across as distant and impassive as though he were operating on a different plane, the perfect hero for a movie which, like all the best black comedies, lapses over into downright strangeness – on the evening of the race, he is visited by a girl elected from his Fan Club to bear the honour of being run down by his car: they dance, the next morning she stands in a translucent white robe in the middle of the road, spreads her arms to greet the oncoming bonnet of his car, and dies. Otherwise, the humour ranges between the Goonish and the grotesque with careless ease. There are laughs to be gained, too, from the terrible special effects in the futuristic-city scene, but whether they are intentional, or a result of the low budget, is anybody's guess.

| P★★ | T★★ | E★★★★★ | A★ |

Directed by Paul Bartel. Written by Robert Thom and Charles B. Griffith. Special Effects by Jack Rabin (& Associates). With Louisa Moritz and Simone Griffith. (TR)

THE DEATH RAY (1925) Not to be confused with *Luchi Smerti (The Death Ray)*, this was a quasi-documentary by H. Grindell-Matthews, based on his supposed invention of a searchlight-like device which destroys planes.

THE DEATH RAY (1925) Revolutionaries and reactionaries try to gain control of the death ray in this fast-action adventure from director Lev Kuleshov.

Written by Vsevolod Pudovkin. With Porfiri Podobed and Vsevolod Pudovkin.

THE DEATH RAY (1932) *see* MURDER AT DAWN (1932)

THE DEATH RAYS OF DR MABUSE (1964) *see* SECRET OF DR MABUSE (1964)

DEATHSHEAD VAMPIRE (1967) *see* THE VAMPIRE-BEAST CRAVES BLOOD (1967)

DEATHSPORT (1978) Roger Corman produces, David Carradine stars in another *Deathrace 2000* (q.v.) style movie, this time on motorbikes a thousand years in the future (why motorbikes? surely they'd have developed something better!).

Fast-paced, humourless and mindless, with quasi-mystical passages owing more to Carradine's participation in *Kung Fu* than any future world.

| P★ | T★★ | E★★ | A★ |

Directed by Henry Suso and Allan Arkush. Written by Suso and Donald Stewart. Special Effects by Hank Stickert, Philip Huff and Jack Rabin. With Claudia Jennings, Richard Lynch, William Smithers and David McLean.

DEATH, THE GREEN SLIME (1968) *see* THE GREEN SLIME (1968)

DEATHWATCH (1979) Katherine Mortenhoe is a writer – or, rather, Harriet, her computer, actually *writes* the trite, simplistic books, Katherine programmes and monitors the process. And Katherine Mortenhoe is, we learn, dying from an incurable disease in a near future where such an event is rare. She has two months to live, and "the word is out"; the media pursue her for her story as she becomes an unwilling celebrity. NTV, a company who televise the last months of such dying people, attempt to persuade her to let them film her, but she refuses. They do so anyway, by having their man, Roddy (Harvey Keitel) befriend her, seemingly by accident. Roddy has had cameras planted behind his eyes and what he sees is seen by the voracious voyeuristic millions who swell NTV's ratings. The absence of morality and the invasion of privacy involved in this subterfuge (it also turns out that Katherine wasn't dying but has been given so-called painkiller drugs to make her think she is – all part of NTV's plan) are chillingly explored. Where this proves a superior tale is in the way it sees the cameraman as being as much a victim of the process as his subject; he cannot even make love to his own wife because millions will share the experience, a poignant moment. Filmed in Glasgow, the cinematography (by Pierre-William Glenn) is exceptional, utilizing glass/lenses as a motif throughout, emphasizing this one aspect of the story. Director Bertrand Tavernier, by chance or otherwise, captures the precise mood of the original novel, *The Continuous Katherine Mortenhoe*, by D. G.

Compton; a sense that life in the West is crumbling despite technological advances. If there's a flaw in all of this it is in the portrayal of the future society, which is sketchy at best; everything about the world through which the fleeing Katherine travels is glimpsed peripherally. But that's a small gripe in the face of an excellent script and marvellous visuals. It all ends at Land's End, with Katherine, now aware of the duplicity of all concerned, cheating them all by taking her own life; a scene which, like the whole film, is effective because understated. Romy Schneider, as Katherine, gives an authoritative performance.

P★★★★   T★★★   E★★★   A★★★★

Written by Bertrand Tavernier and David Rayfield. With Harry Dean Stanton, Max Von Sydow, Thérèse Liotard and Caroline Langrishe.

LA DECIMA VITTIMA (1965) *see* THE TENTH VICTIM (1965)

LE DEJEUNER SUR L'HERBE (1966) *see* PICNIC ON THE GRASS (1966)

DELUGE (1933) One of the first epic disaster movies, with tidal waves and earthquakes destroying New York after an eclipse of the sun. Its special effects sequences were used in countless films thereafter. Based on the novel by Sydney Fowler Wright.

P★   T★★★   E★★   A★

Directed by Felix E. Feist. Written by John Goodrich and Warren B. Duff. Special Effects by Ned Mann. Special Effects Cinematography by William B. Williams. With Sidney Blackmer, Peggy Shannon, Matt Moore and Lois Wilson.

THE DEMON DOCTOR (1961) *see* THE AWFUL DR ORLOFF (1961)

THE DEMON PLANET (1965) *see* PLANET OF THE VAMPIRES (1965)

DEMON SEED (1976) Sf cinema is littered with squandered opportunities, and *Demon Seed* is one of the worst cases. A modern-day exploration of the Frankenstein theme – the development of an artificial intelligence system that then wishes to take on flesh and become, in a sense, a man – the film allows itself to be side-tracked into the then popular ecology theme: the result, an unscrupulous computer which worries about what Man is doing to the environment, is too great a paradox to swallow. Nonetheless, aspects of the film remain gripping – especially those scenes when Dr Susan Harris (Julie Christie) is trapped in her own super-computerized home by Proteus IV, the brainchild of her husband Alex (Fritz Weaver). Time and again, however, the film betrays its rather tenuous logic – the computer, Proteus, can produce a gamete of itself by modifying Dr Harris's genetic material but, or so it claims, it doesn't have the facilities to reconstruct a human womb (allowing a machine-rapes-woman scene!). A case rather similar to God stopping at one miracle... And, whenever threatened, the machine uses incredible, clumsy force. This mixture of B-movie frisson and sf intellectualizing is, as the film progresses, more and more irritating, and the film's conclusion – where Proteus's child proves to be a rapidly gestated, rapidly matured perfect reproduction of the child Susan Harris lost to leukaemia (which Proteus provided the cure for earlier in the film) years before – is simply baffling. Is Proteus a threat, a bonus for Mankind, what?

P★   T★★★   E★★   A★

Directed by Donald Cammell. Written by Robert Jaffe and Roger O. Hirson. Special Effects by Tom Fisher. With Gerrit Graham, Berry Kroeger, Lisa Lu, Larry J. Blake, John O'Leary and Alfred Dennis. Felix Silla animated the shell-like baby.

DEMONS OF THE SWAMP (1959) *see* THE GIANT LEECHES (1959)

DENSO NINGEN (1960) *see* SECRET OF THE TELEGIAN (1960)

LE DERNIER HOMME (1968) *see* THE LAST MAN (1968)

EL DESCUARTIZADOR DE BINBROOK (1971) *see* NECROPHAGUS (1971)

DESTINATION INNER SPACE
(1966) A belated homage to *The Creature From The Black Lagoon* (q.v.), with aliens at the bottom of the ocean.

P★	T★	E★	A

Directed by Francis Lyon. Written by Arthur C. Pierce. Special Effects by Roger George. Make-up by Bob Dawn. With Scott Brady, Sheree North, Gary Merrill and Mike Road.

DESTINATION MARS (1968) *see* MISSION MARS (1968)

DESTINATION MOON (1950) Producer George Pal spent $586,000 to make this version of Robert Heinlein's *Rocket-ship Galileo*, and, as ever with Pal, he ignored the original just enough to make a rather dull hash of the job. Heinlein had a hand in the script (along with Rip Van Ronkel and James O'Hanlon) and ensured that the science was as good and as correct as they could make it (not very good and not very correct, as it happened). For its time it was a lovely-looking film, and one of the first to accurately reflect what space travel *might* be like, but the documentary effect robs the story of any real dramatic tension. The race to get to the Moon before the Russians perverts the original inventor-and-sons-find-Nazi-base-on-Moon story, but reflects the growing Cold War fears of the time. In these days of military shuttle flights it's ironical to think that back then the Americans feared that space would be militarized!

P★★	T★★★	E★	A★

Directed by Irving Pichel. Astronomical art by Chesley Bonestell. Special Effects by Lee Zavitz. With John Archer, Warner Anderson, Tom Powers, Dick Wesson and Erin O'Brien-Moore.

DESTROY ALL MONSTERS (1968)
All of Toho's resident monsters (Godzilla, Son of Godzilla, Mothra, Varan, Angrous, Manda, Rodan, Gorosaurus, Skree and Barugon) take on aliens who want to conquer Japan.

P	T★	E	A

Directed by Ishiro Honda. Written by Kaoru Mabuchi and Ishiro Honda. Special Effects by Eiji Tsuburaya and Sadamasa Arikawa. With Akira Kubo, Jun Tazaki and Yoshio Tsuchiya.

DESTROY ALL PLANETS (1968)
Juvenile from Japan's Daiei studios, with Gamera, the hero, taking on Viras, a squid-like alien invader who can control minds.

P	T★	E★	A

Directed by Noriaki Yuasa. Written by Fumi Takahashi. Special Effects by Kazafumi Fujii and Yuzo Kaneko. With Kajiro Hongo, Toru Takatsuka and Peter Williams.

THE DESTRUCTORS (1966) Run-of-the-mill spy thriller involving a super laser called the Cyclops.

P★	T★	E★	A

Directed by Francis D. Lyon. Written by Arthur C. Pierce and Larry E. Jackson. With Richard Egan, Patricia Owen and John Ericson.

THE DEVIL COMMANDS (1941)
This memorable film is an unusual twist on the mad scientist tale, with Boris Karloff as the scientist mad with grief at his wife's death who will do anything to communicate with her. In one sinister, futuristic scene, he forms a ring of dead bodies, each sealed within a metal suit and linked to a live subject (Amanda Duff) in an attempt to penetrate the final barrier, between the living and the dead. His machines work upon brain impulses. Based on the novel *The Edge Of Running Water* by William Sloane.

P★★	T★★★	E★★★	A★★

Directed by Edward Dmytryk. Written by Robert D. Andrews and Milton Gunzburg. Special Effects by Phil Faulkner. With Richard Fiske, Anne Revere, Ralph Penney and Dorothy Adams.

THE DEVIL-DOLL (1936) Director and adapter Tod Browning mixed elements of his own story "The Witch of Timbuktoo" with Abraham Merritt's "Burn, Witch, Burn!" to create a story of a mad scientist who discovers how to miniaturize people and control them; using them for various crimes of revenge.

P★★	T★★	E★★	A★

Written by Garrett Ford, Guy Endore and Erich Von Stroheim. With Lionel Barrymore, Maureen O'Sullivan and Lucy Beaumont.

DEVIL GIRL FROM MARS (1954)
With a seriousness which is quite laughable, the cast stumble through one of the silliest scripts of all time for an sf movie, as a representative of the Martian matriarchy and her robot come to a Scottish inn (why there?) looking for good male breeding stock to take back to Mars.

P	T★	E★★	A

Directed by David MacDonald. Written by John C. Mather and James Eastwood. Special Effects by Jack Whitehead. With Patricia Laffen, Hazel Court, Hugh McDermott, Adrienne Corri and John Laurie.

DEVILMAN STORY (1967) Devilman wants a super brain in his head, so gets a mad scientist to help find one.

P★	T★★	E★	A

Directed by Paolo Bianchini. With Guy Madison, Luisa Baratto, Luciano Picozzi, Diana Lorys, Aldo Sambrell and Giovanni Cianfriglia.

THE DEVIL MEN FROM SPACE (1965) *see* SNOW DEVILS (1965)

THE DEVIL'S BROOD (1944) *see* HOUSE OF FRANKENSTEIN (1944)

THE DEVILS FROM SPACE (1965) *see* SNOW DEVILS (1965)

DEVIL'S GARDEN (1967) *see* COPLAN SAVES HIS SKIN (1967)

THE DEVIL'S MAN (1967) *see* DEVILMAN STORY (1967)

THE DEVIL'S PLOT (1948) *see* COUNTERBLAST (1948)

THE DEVIL TO PAY (1920) The theme of the wrongly executed man brought back to life and determined to avenge himself upon those who framed him became a cliché in later years, but here it's treated as new. Ray Stewart is the revivee who "haunts" wealthy banker Robert McKim until the guilty one hangs himself. As a working of conscience the idea is as old as the theatre itself, but the scientific explanation – the doctor's operation – gives it a modern twist.

P★★	T★	E★★	A★

Directed by Ernest C. Warde. Written by Jack Cunningham. With Fritzi Brunette, George Fisher and Evelyn Selbie.

THE DIABOLICAL DR Z (1965) A further sequel to *The Awful Dr Orloff* (1961) (q.v.) and *Dr Orloff's Monster* (1964) (q.v.), this introduces a personality-changing device and human robots to the mixture of mad doctor and mutilations.

P★	T★	E★	A

Directed by Jesus Franco. Written by Jesus Franco and Jean-Claude Carrière. With Mabel Karr, Fernando Montes and Estella Blain.

THE DIABOLIC INVENTION (1958) *see* THE FABULOUS WORLD OF JULES VERNE (1958)

IL DIABOLICO DOTTORE MABUSE (1960) *see* THE THOUSAND EYES OF DR MABUSE (1960)

DIABOLIK (1967) *see* DANGER: DIABOLIK (1967)

I DIAFANOIDI PORTANO LA MORT (1965) *see* WAR OF THE PLANETS (1965)

DIAMONDS ARE FOREVER (1971) Sean Connery returned, after Lazenby's brief sojourn, for this opulent Bond adventure, with Blofeld (Charles Gray) holding a gun to the world's head in the form of a giant outer-space laser. Much of the movie is based in Las Vegas, and what better setting for the playboy myth-figure of the twentieth century. The action never slows, and Connery, showing more than a little grey now, is such a cool and elegant Bond – this was his last appearance save for his own 1983 effort – that any sensible producer would have realized it impossible to continue the series without him.

P★★	T★★★★	E★★★★★	A

Directed by Guy Hamilton. Written by Richard Maibaum and Tom Mankiewicz, from the novel by Ian Fleming. Special Effects by Albert Whitlock, Wally Veevers, Leslie Hillman and Whitey McMahon. With Jill St-John, Bruce Cabot, Jimmy Dean and Lana Wood. (TR)

I DIAVOLI DELLO SPAZIO (1965) *see* SNOW DEVILS (1965)

DID YOU HEAR THE ONE ABOUT THE TRAVELLING SALESLADY? (1968) Mild-mannered comedy starring Phyllis Diller about a small-town community in 1900 and its eccentric inventor (of, amongst other things, a wood-burning car and an aphrodisiac machine).

| P★★ | T★★ | E★★ | A★ |

Directed by Don Weiss. Written by John Fenton Murray. With Bob Denver, Joe Flynn, Eileen Wesson, Jeanette Nolan and Bob Hastings.

DIE! MONSTER DIE! (1965) The garish beauty of H. P. Lovecraft's *The Color Out Of Space* is captured in this film. Boris Karloff is the scientist faced with a radioactive meteorite which causes plants to grow huge and mutates humans and animals into ghastly shapes.

| P★★ | T★★★ | E★★★ | A★★ |

Directed by Daniel Haller. Written by Jerry Sohl. with Nick Adams, Freda Jackson, Suzan Farmer, Terence de Marney and Patrick Magee.

DIGBY – THE BIGGEST DOG IN THE WORLD (1973) A soft-hearted giant animal movie which is only partly successful as a comedy. Digby, the dog, is mistakenly fed on a super-growth chemical developed for growing vegetables during space flight and grows to massive proportions.

| P★★ | T★★ | E★★★ | A★ |

Directed by Joseph McGrath. Written by Michael Pertwee. Special Effects by Tom Howard. With Jim Dale, Spike Milligan, Angela Douglas, Richard Beaumont and Milo O'Shea.

DIMENSION FIVE (1966) This time it's not the Russians but the Chinese who are planning to blow up a chunk of the United States. But US time-travel agents can't fail to stop them setting off their A-bomb in LA.

| P★★ | T★★ | E★★ | A |

Directed by Franklin Adreon. Written by Arthur C. Pierce. Special Effects by Roger George. With Jeffrey Hunter and France Nuyen.

DIMENSION FOUR (1966) *see* DIMENSION FIVE (1966)

DINOSAUR ISLAND (1966) *see* THE ISLAND OF THE DINOSAURS (1966)

DIOS ELIGIO SUS VIAJEROS (1964) *see* THE UNKNOWN HOUR (1964)

LE DIRIGEABLE FANTASTIQUE OU LE CAUCHEMAR D'UN INVENTEUR (1906) *see* THE FANTASTICAL AIRSHIP (1906)

DIRTY WORK (1933) Laurel and Hardy present a comic twist on an even-then clichéd idea. Cleaning a house, they discover a youth serum, but when Ollie takes it he's turned into a monkey.

| P★ | T★ | E★★★ | A★ |

Directed by Lloyd French. With Stan Laurel, Oliver Hardy, Lucien Littlefield and Sam Adams.

IL DISCO VOLANTE (1964) *see* THE FLYING SAUCER (1964)

THE DISINTEGRATING RAY (1965) A Spanish juvenile, where a boy and his robot go after a group of criminals who have stolen the deadly ray.

| P★ | T★ | E★ | A |

Directed by Pascual Cervera. Written by Cervera and José E. Aranguren. With Peter Solis, Maria Jesus Balenciaza and Joaquin Nieto.

THE DISMEMBERER OF BIN-BROOK (1971) *see* NECROPHAGUS (1971)

LA DIXIÈME VICTIME (1965) *see* THE TENTH VICTIM (1965)

DR BLACK AND MR HYDE (1976) Predictable and, in some senses, dreadful version of the Stevenson story, updated to 1976 and set in Watts, Los Angeles. A rather senseless black exploitation movie.

| P★ | T★★ | E★ | A |

Directed by William Crain. Written by Larry LeBron. With Bernie Casey, Rosalind Cash, Marie O'Henry, Ji-Tu Combuka and Milt Kogan.

DR BREEDLOVE (1964) Capitalizing upon Kubrick's success with *Dr Strangelove* (q.v.), this has little to do with atomic war and focuses rather on an alien's quest for fertile women – a quest satisfied by Sellers look-alike Breedlove, who creates artificial women. A soft porn comedy.

| P★★ | T★★ | E★★★ | A★ |

Produced, directed and written by Russ Meyer. With Jackie De Witt, Fred Coe and Althea Currier.

DR BROMPTON-WATT'S AGE-ADJUSTER (1912) Fun and games with a serum that removes the years from old men and regresses babies into the ape stage of evolution.

Produced and directed by Thomas Edison. With John Sturgeon, Edward Boulden and Mrs Wallace Erskine.

DR CADMAN'S SECRET (1956) *see* THE BLACK SLEEP (1956)

DR CRIMEN (1953) A Mexican reworking of the Frankenstein myth. Here a doctor disinters a corpse, places a savage's brain into its cranium and brings it back to life. The twist here is that the mad doctor wants to use the creature to kill his indifferent love but the monster falls for her and has his love reciprocated.

| P★★★ | T★★ | E★★★ | A★ |

Directed and written by Chano Urueta. Special Effects by Jorge Benavides. With Miroslava, Carlos Navarro and José Maria Linares Rivas.

DR CYCLOPS (1939) In the heart of the South American jungle, Dr Cyclops, a thoroughly mad scientist, is reducing humans to one foot tall. From there on in it's a battle with seemingly monster-sized animals, prefiguring *The Incredible Shrinking Man* 18 years later.

| P★★ | T★★★ | E★★★ | A★ |

Directed by Ernest B. Schoedsack. Written by Tom Kilpatrick. Special Effects by Farciot Edouard and Wallace Kelly. With Albert Dekker, Janice Logan and Thomas Coley.

DR FRANKENSTEIN ON CAMPUS (1967) Robin Ward plays a humanoid creation of a university professor, given the unlikely name of Viktor Frankenstein IV, in a film more concerned with contemporary attitudes than with the Frankenstein myth.

| P★ | T★★ | E★ | A |

Directed by Gil Taylor. Written by David Cobb, Bill Marshall and Gil Taylor. With Kathleen Sawyer, Austin Willis and Sean Sullivan.

DR GOLDFOOT AND THE BIKINI MACHINE (1965) Vincent Price starred in this sf comedy about a mad doctor who builds a series of girl robots, intending to use them to seduce powerful figures and take over the world.

| P★ | T★★ | E★ | A |

Directed by Norman Taurog. Written by Elwood Ullman and Robert Kaufman. Special Effects by Roger George. With Frankie Avalon, Dwayne Hickman, Susan Hart, Jack Mullaney, Fred Clark, Annette Funicello and Harvey Lembeck.

DR GOLDFOOT AND THE GIRL BOMBS (1966) In this sequel to *Dr Goldfoot And The Bikini Machine* (1966) (q.v.), Goldfoot (Vincent Price) is creating beautiful robot girls with the aim of seducing generals and blowing them up during intercourse. This would – naturally – ferment trouble between the USA and Russia. Goldfoot is foiled, but there's a good deal of fun on the way to his fall.

| P★ | T★★ | E★★ | A★ |

Directed by Mario Bava. Written by Louis M. Heyward, Robert Kaufman and Castellano Pipolo. With Fabian, Franco Franchi, Ciccio Ingrassia, Laura Antonelli and Moana Tahi.

DR HECKYL AND MR HYPE (1980) Oliver Reed stars as the suicidal chiropodist who, after attempting to end it all with a bottle of slimming potion, becomes Mr Hype, a real ladykiller. Played with tongues firmly in cheeks by all concerned, this is an enjoyable romp.

| P★★ | T★★★ | E★★★ | A★ |

Directed and written by Charles B. Griffith. With Sunny Johnson, Mel Welles and Jackie Coogan.

DR JEKYLL AND MR BLOOD (1971) *see* THE MAN WITH TWO HEADS (1971)

DR JEKYLL AND MR HYDE (1912)

Surprisingly, this was the fourth version of Robert Louis Stevenson's classic good/evil chemical schizophrenia story. Here it's played very straight, with Hyde battling with the evil creature his experiments have released within him.

Directed by Lucius Henderson. With James Cruze, Marguerite Snow and Harry Benham.

DR JEKYLL AND MR HYDE (1913)

Orthodox version of the tale, featuring King Baggott as the chemically transforming doctor. He *almost* gets to the antidote in this version.

Directed and written by Herbert Brenon. With Jane Gail, Matt Snyder and Howard Crampton.

DR JEKYLL AND MR HYDE (1920)

John Barrymore starred in this rather melodramatic rendering of Stevenson's tale. It superficially follows Stevenson's story without ever really understanding it (in the way, for example, that the 1931 version does). It has atmosphere, but is, to my mind, unjustifiably famous.

P★★   T★★   E★   A★

Directed by John S. Robertson. Written by Clara S. Beranger. With Nita Naldi, Brandon Hurst, Louis Wolheim and Charles Lane.

DR JEKYLL AND MR HYDE (1920)

Contemporary update of the story, not to be confused with the mediocre but better Barrymore version of the same year.

With Sheldon Lewis, Alexander Shannon, Dora Mills Adams and Gladys Field.

DR JEKYLL AND MR HYDE (1931)

Probably the best and, surprisingly, most sophisticated of the numerous versions of this story, Jekyll's frustrated sexuality as well as his innate evil is channelled into Hyde's dark, sinister figure. As such the film becomes a fable of psychological repression, more in keeping with Stevenson's (unconscious?) aim. A much-edited version was released, but Frederic March still won an Oscar for Best Actor. Hyde's regression to ape-like, sensual creature is also an aspect emphasized more in this version than in others.

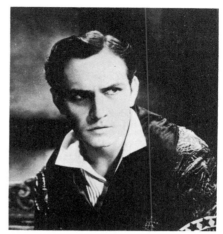

Frederic March in the 1931 version of Dr Jekyll and Mr Hyde

P★★★   T★★★   E★★★★★★   A★★★

Produced and directed by Rouben Mamoulian. Written by Samuel Hoffenstein and Percy Heath. Make-up by Wally Westmore. With Miriam Hopkins, Rose Hobart and Holmes Herbert.

DR JEKYLL AND MR HYDE (1941)

A rather disappointing re-make of the 1931 Paramount version of Stevenson's classic story, starring Spencer Tracy as the artificially schizophrenic doctor and Ingrid Bergman as his loved one. It lacks the dramatic edge of other versions.

P★★   T★★   E★★   A★

Produced and directed by Victor Fleming. Written by John Lee Malin. Make-up by Jack Dawn. Special Effects by Warren Newcombe. With Lana Turner, Donald Crisp and Ian Hunter.

DR JEKYLL AND SISTER HYDE

(1971) Unremarkable re-working of the Stevenson tale such that in his quest for perpetual youth, Jekyll frees another, murderous female self. Hammer studios' period London is as effective as ever, but this plotline is rather stereotyped.

P★   T★★   E★★   A★

Directed by Roy Ward Baker. Written by Brian Clemens. With Ralph Bates, Martine Beswick, Gerald Sim and Lewis Flander.

DR MABUSE (1971) A rather disappointing addition to the film history of

Norbert Jacques's powerful criminal doctor, and based on a novel by David Kuhne. In this instance Mabuse is after some intelligent Moon rocks that have been discovered – a long way from the evil genius of Lang's 1922 film.

P★	T★	E	A

Directed by Jesus Franco. Written by Franco and Art Bernd. With Fred Williams, Ewa Stromberg, Roberto Camardiel and Ewa Garden.

EL DR MABUSE (1971) see DR MABUSE (1971)

DR MABUSE, THE GAMBLER

(1922) The idea of the world-conquering evil-genius did not entirely begin with either Norbert Jacques's novel about Mabuse, nor with Lang's film, but both developed the idea to the point where all that followed had, intentionally or otherwise, to refer back to Mabuse. The fictional world James Bond inhabits, with its world-encompassing web of criminal activity, is merely an update of the world Fritz Lang created for Mabuse in this first and finest of the Mabuse films. The dystopic world of this film (originally issued in two parts, *The Great Gambler* and *Inferno*) is, of course, that of between-Wars Germany, and Mabuse (Rudolf Klein-Rogge) is, in true villainous manner, exploiting his "friends" and amassing a vast fortune from manipulating Germany's misfortunes. Mabuse's control seems absolute – a reign of terror no less potent than the real one that followed under Hitler. This use of others has its price and turns Mabuse mad, but not before he is able to demonstrate his hypnotic control of all those about him. It's a film which depicts raw, naked power – power for its own sake – and is a vital precursor of that part of the sf cinema which was to deal specifically with the misuse of technology and science for evil means (usually without as memorable a result as this).

P★★★	T★★	E★★★	A★★

Directed by Fritz Lang. Written by Lang and Thea von Harbou. With Aud Egede Nissen, Alfred Abel, Gertrud Welcker, Bernhardt Goetze, Paul Richter, Hans Von Schlettow, Forster Larrinaga and Georg John.

DR MABUSE'S RAYS OF DEATH (1964) see SECRET OF DR MABUSE (1964)

DR MABUSE VS. SCOTLAND YARD (1963) see SCOTLAND YARD HUNTS DR MABUSE (1963)

DR MANIAC (1936) see THE MAN WHO LIVED AGAIN (1936)

DR NO (1962) The first movie featuring Ian Fleming's super-spy James Bond, and the film which set the template for a routine as rigidly formulated, and commercially successful, as a Barbara Cartland romance: the beautiful, treacherous women; the car chases; the gadgetry; the exotic locations; Bond's capture by the villains halfway through the picture; the final showdown in a vast cavern, with all of its Freudian overtones. The plot has SMERSH, headed by Joseph Wiseman, diverting Cape Canaveral rockets off course from his Bahamian hideaway. But for all its violence and 'Playboy' philosophy, there's a certain naïve innocence about the 23-year-old movie – *that* white bikini Ursula Andress emerges from the waves in would barely twitch an eyebrow these days. And Sean Connery in his first attempt at the role seems awkward, as though he were worrying, even then, that he was getting himself into something he'd have trouble getting out of.

P★	T★★★	E★★★	A

Directed by Terence Young. Written by Richard Maibaum, Joanna Harwood and Berkely Mather. Special Effects by Frank George. With Jack Lord, Bernard Lee, Lois Maxwell, John Kitzmuller, Zena Marshall and Eunice Gayson. (TR)

DOCTOR OF DOOM (1962) Standard Mexican sf fare; mad doctors, brain transplants and the inevitable wrestling.

P	T	E	A

Directed by Rene Cardona. Written by Alfred Salazar. With Armando Silvestre, Lorena Velazquez, Roberto Canedo and Martha Solis.

DR ORLOFF'S MONSTER (1964) Sequel to *The Awful Dr Orloff* (1961) (q.v.), this is much more science-fictional,

with a human robot guided by a controlling beam towards its victims. Not as darkly atmospheric as the earlier film.

P★	T★★	E★	A

Directed by Jesus Franco. Written by Franco and Nick Frank. With José Rubio, Agnes Spaak, Perla Cristal, Pastor Serrador and Hugo Blanco.

DOCTOR RENAULT'S SECRET
(1942) A mad scientist working on accelerated evolution transforms an ape into an ape-man in this rather tired offering.

P★	T★	E★	A

Directed by Harry Lachman. Written by William Bruckner and Robert F. Metzler. With J. Carroll Naish, George Zucco and Lynne Roberts.

THE DOCTOR'S EXPERIMENT
(1908) Monkey serum changes men into apes, thereby proving Darwin was right, but leaving the poor victims as apes.

DR SMITH'S AUTOMATON
(1910) A mildly humorous short about a robot of canvas and springs who, once activated, cannot stop until he collides with a wall.

DR STRANGELOVE, OR: HOW I LEARNED TO STOP WORRYING AND LOVE THE BOMB
(1963) One means of approaching the unthinkable is by way of humour. How, for instance, deal with the possibility of total world destruction resultant from nuclear war? It's an absurd yet ever more likely concept, and, though the Cuba missile crisis had come and gone when Stanley Kubrick made *Dr Strangelove*, and the world was feeling somewhat more secure, the exaggerated notions of the film were still a valid satirical vision of that possibility. We need to laugh at our deepest fears, and Kubrick presented the ultimate vehicle for our laughter. It's a brilliant film, as effective now, 22 years on, as it was on the day of release, and its dark, savage view of paranoia, buck-passing and ineffectual leadership remains as cuttingly apt. Kubrick's starting point was an inoffensive little novel by Peter George, *Red Alert*, a thriller without humour, a tale of nuclear war caused through inadvertence, ironical

Peter Sellers, playing one of his many roles in Dr Strangelove

rather than satirical. Kubrick recognized potentials in the story that the author had missed and radically re-constructed its elements, distorting them into grotesque parodies and caricatures. And, curiously enough, this distortion creates a sense that what happens in the film is a chilling possibility; that what we are seeing is a cartoon of an actuality. The actuality of human foibles, of the wrong men being in charge, of poor decisions being made for the wrong reasons. Base Commander General Jack D. Ripper (Sterling Hayden) is convinced that water fluoridation is a Commie plot to poison his precious bodily fluids and has decided to give the command for his bombers to attack Soviet Russia. Such eccentric insanity is beautifully portrayed by Hayden, as is the response of the President Murphy Muffley (Peter Sellers) and his German adviser, Dr Strangelove (Peter Sellers, again, reprising the mad scientist Rotwang from *Metropolis* (q.v.)). The President tries to get Ripper to recall his bombers, and fails, so orders Ripper's second in command, Mandrake (again Sellers, this time as an RAF type) to take the base, force Ripper to give the recall signal and save the world. Meanwhile, the President tries to contact and reassure the Russian Premier Kissoff and keep order in his own War Room ("No fighting in the War Room!" is the order at one stage). George C. Scott, as Airforce Commander General "Buck" Turgidson, is busy covering his butt and passing the buck, while Strangelove (the name, like all the others, denoting an essential quality in him – here, perhaps, the strange love he has for the abstract notion of total annihilation) reveals his Nazi origins in an over-the-top comic performance from Sellers. The airforce base is taken, but Ripper has killed himself rather than give the recall code away. Mandrake, however, works it out and recalls the bombers. All, that is, except for one: that of Major T. J. "King" Kong (Slim Pickens), which fails to receive the signal. As the film draws to its close we see Kong riding one of his A-bombs down into the heart of Russia, yi-haing in best cowboy style. And we know that as soon as that bomb hits the Russian "Doomsday Weapon" will be activated and the world of Man will end. Over stock footage of atomic explosions Kubrick plays his last dark card of humour: Vera Lynn singing "We'll Meet Again . . .". The film's excellence lies in its terse dialogue and its telling exaggerations. Its weaknesses are those of so many pre-*2001* sf films: limited sets (Kubrick used three), poor visuals and little to impress in the way of special effects. But *Dr Strangelove* suffers less than most because of Kubrick's instinctive sense of timing and the enthusiasm (if not relish) of the cast. Yes, 22 years on, *Dr Strangelove* remains the last word on nuclear war scenarios.

| P★★★★ | T★★★ | E★★★★★ | A★★★ |

Written by Stanley Kubrick, Terry Southern and Peter George. Special Effects by Wally Veevers. With Keenan Wynn and Peter Bull.

DR WHO AND THE DALEKS

(1965) First cinematic tussle between the Time Lord, Dr Who, and the alien Daleks on their home planet of Skaro. It's easy to forget that the Daleks were cyborg adaptations of a mutated species. Here they're fighting the good Thals and using neutron bombs to achieve their end. Lacking the humour of the later TV episodes, this is a standard piece of scary adventure.

| P★★ | T★★ | E★★ | A★ |

Directed by Gordon Flemyng. Written by Milton Subotsky. With Peter Cushing, Roy Castle, Jennie Linden, Roberta Tovey and Michael Coles.

DOCTOR X (1932) A gruesome little story about cannibalistic murders. Doctor Xavier (Lionel Atwill) runs a clinic, scene of dubious goings-on. Dr Wells (Preston Foster), his partner, is busy creating synthetic flesh; replacing lost arms with new, stronger ones. As ever, the moral is that Man, in toying with the darker side, unleashes powers he cannot control.

| P★★ | T★★ | E★★ | A★ |

Directed by Michael Curtiz. Written by Robert Tasker and Earl Baldwin. With Fay Wray, Lee Tracy, Arthur Edmund Carew and Mae Busch.

A DOG, A MOUSE, AND A SPUTNIK

(1958) A mild comedy with a scant sf element – as a man is accidentally launched into space after discovering the dog and mouse of the title, creatures lost from a Russian satellite.

| P★ | T★★ | E★★ | A |

Directed by Jean Dreville. Written by Jean-Jacques Vital. With Noel-Noel, Denise Gray, Mischa Auer, Darry Cowl and Noel Roquevert.

DOGORA 1964) *see* DAGORA, THE SPACE MONSTER (1964)

DER DOKTOR MABUSE (1971) *see* DR MABUSE (1971)

DONOVAN'S BRAIN (1953) Second of three adaptations of Curt Siodmak's novel, *Donovan's Brain* (the others are *The Lady And The Monster* (q.v.) and *Vengeance* (q.v.)). This is a fairly straightforward version where a millionaire, Donovan, dies, but has his brain saved by a scientist. The brain slowly takes over the scientist and uses him for its evil ends.

| P★★ | T★★ | E★★ | A★ |

Directed and written by Felix Feist. Special Effects by Harry Redmond Jr. With Lew Ayres, Steve Brodie and Michael Colgan.

DON'T CRY WOLF (1963) *see* THE CRAWLING HAND (1963)

DON'T LOOK NOW (1973) Nicolas Roeg's movie of precognition. Set in a Venice as decayed as a rotting log, as shadowed as a cavern, the film is perfect material for Roeg's distorted time-sense, his overlaying of imagery. There are blind old women, strange and frightening dwarfs, funeral gondolas plying the stagnant, dark canals like lost ships out of legend. Julie Christie and Donald Sutherland play a couple who have already suffered one death, that of their daughter – she seems to be trying to contact them from the other side – and they both look stunned as though by the hammer, cold and distant towards each other until they re-unite in a sex scene which probably became so controversial because it was purely, unexploitatively erotic, about as far from pornography as you can get. It is violence which Roeg tends to overdo – a shame he could not restrain himself towards the end, in this otherwise powerful and eerie movie.

P★★★   T★★★★   E★★★★   A★★★★

Written by Allan Scott and Chris Bryant, from a story by Daphne du Maurier. Cinematography by Anthony Richmond (TR)

DON'T PLAY WITH THE MARTIANS (1967) Silly rather than charming tale of the birth of sextuplets to Martians on an island off Brittany. The aliens return to claim the children. Based on Michel Labry's *Les Sextuplets de Locqmaria*.

P★   T★   E★   A

Directed by Henri Lanoe. Written by Lanoe and Johanne Harwood. With Jean Rochefort, Macha Meril, Andre Vallardy, Haydee Politoff and Pierre Dac.

DOOM OF DRACULA (1944) *see* HOUSE OF FRANKENSTEIN (1944)

DOOMWATCH (1972) A spin-off movie from the successful BBC television series with, as heroes, a team of scientists briefed to combat ecological disasters. Dangerous chemicals have been dumped off an isolated Scottish island – the cannisters have leaked, their contents have got into the fish, and thereby into the islanders with frightening consequences. Real problems arise when the simple crofters, not understanding the reasons for their tragedy, try to cover up to the

point of attacking those who poke their noses in. The Doomwatch crew, however, are relentless nose-pokers, and it's this humourless do-gooder stance which results in the stillbirth of what might have been a chilling little film. When you're presented with a piece of polemic as deadpan as this, you begin to wonder whether it is not only the *islanders*' brains the chemical has affected.

P★★★   T★   E★★   A

Directed by Peter Sasdy. Written by Clive Exton. With Judy Geeson, Ian Bannen, John Paul, Simon Oates, George Sanders and Percy Herbert. (TR)

DOPPELGANGER (1969) *see* JOURNEY TO THE FAR SIDE OF THE SUN (1969)

DOS COSMONAUTAS A LA FUERZA (1967) *see* TWO COSMONAUTS AGAINST THEIR WILL (1967)

DOTTOR YEKYLL (1951) *see* THE MAN AND THE BEAST (1951)

DOZNANIYE PILOTA PIRSKA (1978) *see* THE TEST OF PILOT PIRIX (1978)

DRACULA VS. FRANKENSTEIN (1970) *see* BLOOD OF FRANKENSTEIN (1970)

DRACULA VS. FRANKENSTEIN (1971) Well, for a start Dracula never gets to fight Frankenstein, but that's a ploy to get bums on cinema seats. Michael Rennie (who came to Earth peacefully in *The Day The Earth Stood Still* (q.v.)) leads an alien invasion here. The aliens take on monster forms to frighten any humans they encounter. A good idea pathetically presented.

P★   T★★   E★   A

Directed by Tulio Demichelli. Written by Jacinto Molina Alvarez. With Karin Dor and Craig Hill.

A DREAM (1914) *see* HIS PREH˹˼ TORIC PAST (1914)

A DREAM COME TRUE (196 Soviet film more notable for its desig sense than for its plot. Aliens from Cen

turus are attracted by Earth's music and
come to investigate.

| P★ | T★★ | E★ | A★ |

Directed by Mikhail Karyukov. Written by Karyukov, Alexander Berdink, Ivan Bondin. With
Larissa Gordiechik and Otar Koberidze.

THE DREAM MACHINE (1957) see
THE ELECTRONIC MONSTER (1957)

DREAM ONE (1984) The Frenchman
màking it (twice; first in Super-8) calls it
Nemo, which ruins the obvious comment:
this Dream is a nightmare. While the
fairy-tale of a (Spielbergian) lad's Verne-
imaginings has a certain (nursery) charm,
John Boorman's backing of an ex-aide's
first feature is a soul-less hybrid of global
casting, all-American dubbing, perfunc-
tory effects. Best sf aspect remains
unseen: the plastic bubble studio it was
shot (reared?) in. Bond's coolest babe,
Carole Bouquet, is the most impressive
(alien) of a unit mostly numbering Boorman's offspring. And so they should –
back to Super-8.

| P | T★ | E | A★ |

Directed by Arnaud Selignac. Written by Selignac, Jean-Pierre Esquenazi and Telsche Boorman. With Seth Kibel, Jason Connery, Harvey
Keitel and Michel Blanc. (TC)

DREAMSCAPE (1983) *Dreamscape* is a
neatly crafted, occasionally stylish film,
with interesting sf-sourced ideas that are
handled somewhat banally. The US President, played by Eddie Albert, is tormented
by dreams of the world after nuclear
Armageddon – such symbolic "dream-
scapes" feature heavily in this film – and,
awakening, puts détente firmly on the
political agenda again. Inside his government, however, there are men using and
misusing psychics – playing with forces
that are eerily powerful. They are being
used for good ends, helping to cure the
psychiatrically disturbed, while Bob Blair
(played by Christopher Plummer) is misusing them for very bad ends indeed. The
characterization here is really derived
from television stereotypes, but the fine
cast carry off the script's clichés well.

Many of the visual effects are impressive –
there is a sexual dreamscape that is quite
effective, and the post-atomic reddish
gloom is really very gloomy indeed – and
these help to make Joe Ruben's *Dreamscape* more memorable than the run-of-
the-mill conspiracy thriller, and the film
culminates effectively in a spectacular
showdown between two duelling psychics.
The spectator sees Good battle Evil in a
dream landscape that exists only in the
mind of the President of the United
States.

| P★★ | T★★★★ | E★★★ | A★★ |

Directed by Joe Ruben. Written by Ruben, David
Loughery and Chuck Russell. Special Effects by
Peter Kuran. Make-up by Craig Reardon. With
Dennis Quaid, Max Von Sydow, Kate Capshaw,
David Patrick Kelly and George Wendt. (RS)

DREAM TOWN (1973) Dream Town
is an isolated place where you can go and
live out your wishes. Such an idea seems
promising but, like the dreams of most of
those who make the journey, proves tedious and at times simply nasty. This overlong, meandering film is also tedious,
though not too nasty.

| P★★ | T★★ | E★ | A★ |

Directed and written by Johannes Schaaf. With
Per Oscarsson, Rosemarie Fendel, Eva Maria
Meineke and Alexander May.

DROPS OF BLOOD (1960) *see* MILL
OF THE STONE WOMEN (1960)

**DUEL OF THE SPACE MON-
STERS** (1965) *see* FRANKENSTEIN
MEETS THE SPACEMONSTER (1965)

I DUE MAFIOSI DELL FBI (1966)
see
DR GOLDFOOT AND THE GIRL
BOMBS (1966)

DUNE (1984) While elements of *Dune*,
the novel, are commonplace, the totality of
the book far exceeds the parts; it stands up
to re-reading. The film, on the other
hand, impressive enough on a first viewing, begins to fall apart with each new
viewing, simply because it *has no totality*.
The thing that tied the pages and chapters
of the book together – Arrakis, the desert

world – is barely present in the film. It is consistently glimpsed, but it isn't omni-present. It doesn't *shape* the events of the film as it does those of the book. This wasn't the first attempt to film *Dune* – several brave directors have tried. David Lynch's successes with *Eraserhead* (q.v.) and *The Elephant Man* made it seem that he might succeed where others failed. It seems, on viewing the results of his work, that he too has failed. And it isn't even a glorious failure. This is not to say that the film doesn't have its moments, simply that overall what has emerged is a caricature of the novel, and the caricature is pure Victorian Melodrama, right down to the heavy rococo sets and the breathless lines of dialogue, the Dickensian goodies and the over-theatrical baddies. These last are the principal disappointment. How are we to believe that this is an adult sf film when the villains are patently juvenile creations? There's no subtlety in Baron Harkonnen and his henchmen. This is comic-book evil, not the invidious reality. Similarly, the ambiguous nature of Paul Atreides's Jihad, stressed by Herbert in his novel(s) is here glossed over. Paul is simply good, even though he is a killer, and the ending perverts Herbert's original not merely by having it rain, but by having Paul bring peace to the galaxy. In the book his accession to the Emperor's throne brings in years of slaughter that make Auschwitz look like a tea party. The film was weak in specifics, too. Anyone with a knowledge of the book would realize that this is set after the Butlerian Jihad which rid the galaxy of all machines – hence the Mentats, the human computers. But here we have Paul playing with a teaching computer. We have a guild report which uses computer print-out techniques. We have spacecraft which, unless I'm seriously mistaken, must use some computer guidance system to get to and from the big guild freighters. So, the one reason for Mentats is made redundant. This future *has* computers. Then again (and these are weaknesses shared with the book) why did only the guildsmen mutate from eating the spice? Why not the Fremen? Why can't they see the future and fold space? And why aren't

Kyle MacLachlan as Paul Atreides in Dune

the guildsmen's eyes blue from the spice? The film also made me ask one question I'd never bothered to ask myself when reading the book: what do the worms eat? Sand? In any case, anyone watching the film without a knowledge of the book must be a genius if they can discern what the precise link *is* between worms and spice, because it's never explained. Generally it's best to ignore the claims for this as the first genuine adult sf movie, because it's really much in the *Star Wars* (q.v.) vein, even if some are going to claim that *Star Wars* borrowed much from *Dune* in the first place. The different environments, the Emperor's planet, Caladan (home of the Atreides) and Giedi Prime (home of the Harkonnens), are nicely created, par-ticularly the scene when the Guild Navi-gator comes to visit the Emperor at the film's beginning. But Arrakis (Dune) itself is a grave disappointment. And if it's to be argued that you can't capture the spirit of the desert on film, then just think back to *Lawrence of Arabia*. Good also are the Guild Navigators themselves – super-mutated humans like Queen ants given super-powers – and the worms. But good special effects do not make a classic sf movie, particularly when it's all delivered so straight-faced and serious as it is here. Herbert's book is devoid of humour, too, but he gets away with it there, able to present his complex story through subtle shadings. Film is a more demanding medium as far as pacing goes, and Lynch's attempt to be true to the spirit of the book lumbered him with a ponderous storyline which no amount of talk-overs, expository dialogue and graphics could make sense of. I only followed the story because I knew it already. In places it drags, and, strangely enough, one such place is in the overlong battle sequence at the end, which is every bit as unconvincing as a 1950s B-movie. My list of disappointments is not complete, however, without mentioning what the film does to the novel's mystical level, turning what was fictionally credible into just another power fantasy. Paul "MuadDib" Atreides becomes a god, but in the film he has machines (weirding modules) to do it. And unlike the book we're never wholly convinced that it wasn't all a sham anyway; Kyle MacLachlan as Paul isn't bad in the part, it's simply that the way the part is written for the film he never gets a chance to convince us he has god-like powers – just a few super-being tricks *à la* Superman. In the end, then, I'd prefer to see this $45 million "epic" as a tolerable allegory of good and evil, an sf cartoon of kinds, commonplace enough in the genre. It's also the first *major* sf novel to be filmed – my excuse for dwelling upon all these comparisons – though by no means the best choice for filming. It's a good illustration that little remains that cannot be filmed; few ideas remain for which special effects cannot be devised; and in that sense alone it's a good, hopeful sign for the future of the film genre, if not a very good film itself.

P★★★	T★★★★★	E★★★	A★★

Produced by Raffaella De Laurentiis. Special Effects by Ron Miller, Carlo Rambaldi, Anthony Masters and Tony Masters. Written by David Lynch. With Francesca Annis, Virginia Madsen, Jose Ferrer, Kenneth McMillan, Sting, Sean Young, Alicia Roanne Witt, Jurgen Prochnow, Freddie Jones, Dean Stockwell, Paul Smith, Brad Dourif, Jack Nance, Max Von Sydow, Linda Hunt and Patrick Stewart.

THE DUNE ROLLER (1972) *see* THE CREMATORS (1972)

DYNAMITE JOHNSON (1978) The nauseatingly proficient martial arts boy is back in a sequel to *The Bionic Boy* (1977) (q.v.), facing a mad Nazi. Even more dreadful than the first film.

P★	T★	E	A

Directed by Bobby A. Suarez. Written by Ken Metcalf and Joseph Zucchero. With Johnson Yap, Marie Lee, Jonny Wilson and Ken Metcalf.

E

EARTHBOUND (1981) Very human aliens break down, land on Earth to service their spacecraft and help Burl Ives to save his hotel while finding the element Storine for their repairs. Tedious. They decide to stay and become the Robinson family of Kansas.

P★	T★	E★	A

Directed by James L. Conway. Written and produced by Michael Fisher. With Joseph Campanella and Christopher Connelly.

EARTH DEFENCE FORCES (1957) *see* THE MYSTERIANS (1957)

THE EARTH DIES SCREAMING (1964) Confused alien invasion story. Alien robots have destroyed England and are taking over people, making zombies of their corpses.

P★	T★★	E★	A

Directed by Terence Fisher. Written by Henry Cross. With Willard Parker, Virginia Field, Dennis Price and Thorley Walters.

THE EARTHQUAKE ALARM (1909) Long before seismographs could (within reason) predict forthcoming earthquakes, this short comedy anticipated such an alarm, using a "cry wolf" plot-line to induce humour.

EARTH II (1971) Even if you can accept the unlikely notion of the USA launching an orbiting Earth satellite-station which they wish to be neutral – 71 per cent of their citizens vote for this on the rocket's fly-over early in the film! – this dull story of international intrigue and the rights and wrongs of pacifism in space merely demonstrates how sterile this school of space "realism" can be. It all looks highly convincing – and as interesting as a game of bowls.

P★	T★★★	E	A

Directed by Tom Gries. Written by William Read Woodfield and Allan Balter. Special Effects by Howard Anderson Jr., Art Cruikshank, Robert Ryder and J. McMillan Johnson. With Gary Lockwood, Scott Hylands and Hari Rhodes.

EARTH VS. THE FLYING SAUCERS (1956) A re-working of *War Of The Worlds* with the more credible notion that the aliens began by being friendly and were shot at. They die of mysterious diseases at the end, of course. Suggested by *Flying Saucers From Outer Space* by Donald E. Keyhoe.

P★	T★★	E★	A★

Directed by Fred F. Sears. Written by George Worthing Yates and Raymond T. Marcus from a story by Curt Siodmak. Special Effects by Ray Harryhausen and Russ Kelley. With Joan Taylor, Hugh Marlowe and Harry Lauter.

EARTH VS. THE GIANT SPIDER (1958) Another case of producer/director Bert I. Gordon borrowing heavily from someone else's film, this time *Tarantula* (q.v.), and re-hashing it as a decidedly worse creature-feature.

P	T	E	A

Written by Laszlo Gorog and George Worthing Yates. Special Effects by Bert and Flora Gordon. With Ed Kemmer, June Kenney, Gene Persson, Gene Roth, Hal Torey and Mickey Finn.

EBIRAH, HORROR OF THE DEEP (1966) *see* GODZILLA VERSUS THE SEA MONSTER (1966)

EDICT (1971) *see* ZERO POPULATION GROWTH (1971)

EGGHEAD'S ROBOT (1970) A charming little comedy from the Chil-

dren's Film Foundation, with Keith Chegwin as the boy who has a robot duplicate of himself. Fun at school and with the local park-keeper (Roy Kinnear) results.

P★★	T★★	E★★	A★

Directed by Milo Lewis. Written by Leif Saxon. With Jeffrey Chegwin, Kathryn Dawe and Richard Wattis.

THE ELECTRIC DOLL (1914) An English professor invents a life-like robot.

Directed by Edwin Collins.

ELECTRIC DREAMS (1984) Here science fiction gives "the eternal triangle" a whole new dimension – in this case, the boy meets girl by way of a musical computer. But what happens when the computer gets jealous? Nothing particularly dramatic. This is one of the pleasant technically accomplished films the new Hollywood makes for its audience of adolescents; it has the vivid colours and the sweet taste and entire lack of substance of marshmallow. The hero, Miles, is a clean-cut, naïve computer freak, using his talkative computer Edgar to compose neat little melodies he hopes will impress the lady cellist upstairs. She – following the conventions of romantic comedy – of course begins to respond. Edgar begins to resent this ... There is, of course, a happy ending. The film is skilfully done, but lacks all real depth and passion, taking place in a middle-class and air-conditioned Never-Never Land. Virgin Films put money into this production, and one of their artists sings Giorgio Moroder's title song; luckily, this *very* electric music fits the film well, so there is no question of the kind of controversy that raged over the re-done soundtrack to *1984*. Here the principals Lenny Von Dohlen and Virginia Madsen play their parts slickly enough, and the script is not as unintelligent as some of its equivalents, but for me Phil Oakey's voice on the title song is probably the most memorable thing about this film.

P★★	T★★★	E★★★	A★★

Directed by Steve Barron. Written by Rusty Lemorande. With Maxwell Caulfied and Bud Cort. (RS)

THE ELECTRIC GOOSE (1905)
Gimmicky short where electricity restores
life to the Christmas dinner. A model for
Eraserhead? (q.v.)

Directed by Alf Collins.

THE ELECTRIC HOTEL (1905)
Perhaps the first appearance of an idea
that Chaplin was to utilize to comic per-
fection in *Modern Times* (1936). Here the
fully automated hotel goes haywire.

Directed and written by Segundo de Chomon.

THE ELECTRIC LEG (1912) Or, the
adventures of a one-legged man, Hoppit,
who gets an uncontrollable electric leg and
is led, literally, into trouble by it.

Directed by Percy Stow.

THE ELECTRIC VITALISER
(1910) A delightful short comedy about a
machine which, by electricity, can return
life to the dead and animate the previously
inanimate.

Directed and written by Walter Booth.

THE ELECTRONIC MONSTER
(1957) Prefiguring *Brainstorm* (q.v.) by at
least two decades, this flawed but interesting film, based on Charles Eric Maine's
novel, *Escapement*, describes the effect of a
machine which can induce hallucinations
upon the patients of a special clinic. Instead of curing psychoses, the inductor
gives its doctor operator power over his
patients.

P★★	T★★	E★★	A★

Directed by Montgomery Tully. Written by
Charles Eric Maine and J. MacLaren-Ross. With
Rod Cameron and Mary Murphy.

THE ELIXIR OF LIFE (1907) Trick
comedy about an elixir which gives its user
vigour and strength, making him not
merely super-strong, but master in his
own home again.

THE ELIXIR OF STRENGTH
(1907) *see* THE ELIXIR OF LIFE (1907)

EMBRYO (1976) In the mould of "it
could happen now" medical science fic-

tion films, *Embryo* plods slowly to its central story, that of a foetus brought to
maturity outside the womb (its mother
suicided at 14 weeks) by means of rapid
growth techniques. The rapid growth,
however, results in an imbalance. The
"baby", when it wakes, is a 25-year-old
woman of extreme intelligence and beauty
(Barbara Carrera). For a time she seems
the perfect complement to the doctor
(Rock Hudson) who created her, but then
the rapid ageing process begins again and
she is forced to kill to save herself. This
oversimplifies what is a subtle, skilful plot
with some nice touches, particularly the
final birth of a child to the now grotesquely old woman as she dies, and the
death (as if by a curse of association) of all
the doctor's immediate family.

P★★★	T★★	E★★★	A★★

Directed by Ralph Nelson. Written by Anita
Doohan and Jack W. Thomas. With Diane Ladd,
Roddy McDowall and Anne Schedeen.

EMPIRE OF THE ANTS (1977) Pos-
sibly the only giant insect film of the 1970s
sillier and more inept than *Food Of The
Gods* (1976) (q.v.), which was also made by
Bert I. Gordon (director/producer and
special effects here, along with Roy Dow-
ney). Large ants, property developers and
radioactive waste are the elements in this
charmless, talentless plot.

P	T★	E	A

Written by Jack Turley. With Joan Collins, Robert
Lansing, John David Carson and Albert Salmi.

THE EMPIRE STRIKES BACK
(1980) A direct sequel to *Star Wars* (q.v.),
this is Episode V of Lucas's planned nine-
part future (or far past) history. It begins
much like *Star Wars*, with an Imperial
space cruiser hurtling through space, this
time sending out probe droids in search of
the rebel base. One of these droids, looking much like the illustrations for H. G.
Wells's Martian invaders, lands on the ice
planet Hoth where the rebel base is. After
a moment's danger – when Luke Skywalker (Mark Hamill) is captured by a
Wampa Ice Creature, escapes by using
"the force" and is found and saved by Han

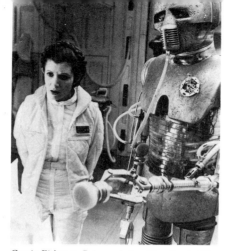

Carrie Fisher as Princess Leia with robot in The Empire Strikes Back

Solo (who keeps him, for warmth, in the guts of a tauntaun – an ice lizard used as a mount) – we get back to the battle of good versus evil, Jedi-Republic against evil-Empire. The evil fleet comes to Hoth and lands its armoured assault vehicles (ingeniously designed "Walkers") and the battle commences. In *Star Wars* the humour was deftly handled; here it's more overt. C-3PO is constantly quoting the odds of survival – like a robotic parody of Dr Spock in *Star Trek* – until Princess Leia (Carrie Fisher) finally puts her hand over his mouth to shut him up. And between Han Solo (Harrison Ford) and Leia there's a deliberate escalation of their love–hate relationship, which provides almost a sub-plot throughout the film. The battle goes the Empire's way, as it must, though the rebels for the main part escape (to fight another day). Luke, told by the spirit of Obi-Wan Kenobi (Alec Guinness) to go to the Dagobah System and find a Jedi "Master", Yoda, sets off on this task while the *Millennium Falcon* (Solo's starship) with everyone else aboard hides from the Empire's fleet by actually attaching itself to Darth Vader's flagship. The pursuit of the *Falcon* into the middle of a meteor storm, and their exploits inside a tunnelled asteroid (they find themselves in the stomach of a giant space-worm; what did *that* eat?) take up a good amount of screen time while Luke learns humility and power from the wizened and comic

Yoda (whose voice, that of Frank Oz, is rather too much like the Muppets' Fozzie Bear for comfort!). These counterpointed plot-lines prevent the story from dragging too much (as it otherwise would have). We leave Luke learning his mental disciplines while Solo, Chewbacca, Leia and the robots fly to Bespin, where Solo's old roguish friend, Lando, runs a mining concern. The Empire, however, have already got to Bespin and the *Falcon* and its crew fall into Vader's hands. In what is almost a reprise of the rescue-Leia-from-the-Death-Star sequence in *Star Wars*, Luke rushes to Bespin to save her. Which is exactly what Vader wanted. While Lando (Billy Dee Williams) proves that he's not as traitorous as he seemed by freeing the Princess, Luke battles with Vader, who, it is revealed, is in fact his father. A few cliff-hanging moments follow, before Luke is in his turn rescued by the *Falcon* (piloted by Lando, who used to own the ship before he lost it to Solo). Though the storyline of *The Empire Strikes Back* is as slight as that of its predecessor, the special effects and visual scenarios are even more spectacular than in *Star Wars* and in some respects this is a better film. It shares the same faults, of course, particularly in the final duel scene between Luke and Vader – the fall Luke has into the rubbish chutes is utterly unbelievable; he could not have survived it – but once again the accent is not so much on realism as on spectacle and story-telling. For this first sequel George Lucas stepped into the background, letting Irvin Kershner direct under Gary Kurtz's production. Leigh Brackett, an sf writer from the 1940s and 1950s and a good screenwriter, shared writing credits with Lawrence Kasdan. But in spite of these changes there is a homogeneity to these films which gives the impression that Lucas was overseeing every scene and every aspect of this movie. Indeed, the storyline was his.

P★★   T★★★★★   E★★★★★   A★★

Special Effects by Brian Johnson, Richard Edlund. Cinematography by Peter Suschitzky. With Anthony Daniels, Kenny Baker, Peter Mayhew and David Prowse.

END OF AUGUST AT THE HOTEL OZONE (1965) Czech film, set 15 years after the Holocaust. A gang of female scavengers descends on a small, isolated hotel and menace the ageing male owner.

P★★	T★★	E★★	A★★

Directed by Jan Schmidt. Written by Pavel Juracek. With Ondrej Janabek, Beta Ponicanova, Magda Seidlerova and Hana Votkova.

THE END OF THE WORLD (1916) Danish vision of how society would react to the news of a comet on collision course with Earth. Here the poor rise up and battle with the rich as Earth's atmosphere begins to change violently.

Directed by August Blom. Written by Otto Rung. With Olaf Foenss and Ebba Thomsen.

THE END OF THE WORLD (1930) Hard-edged semi-erotic version of Camille Flammarion's book *La Fin du Monde* (1894), mercifully cut from an original length of 105 minutes to a terser 54. A comet approaches Earth on collision course, and society falls apart.

P★★	T★	E★	A★★

Directed and written by Abel Gance. With Abel Gance, Colette Darfeuil and Sylvia Grenade.

END OF THE WORLD (1958) *see* THE WORLD, THE FLESH AND THE DEVIL (1958)

END OF THE WORLD (1962) *see* PANIC IN THE YEAR ZERO (1962)

THE END OF THE WORLD (1977) For once it's not collision with a meteor, but being blown apart by a group of nuns and priests who are really aliens from the planet Utopia. Perversely silly and laughably inept, yet some strange quality of eccentric genius shines through.

P★	T★	E★★★	A

Directed by John Hayes. Written by Frank Ray Perilli. Special Effects by Harry Woolman. With Christopher Lee, Sue Lyon and Kirk Scott.

ENEMY FROM SPACE (1957) *see* QUATERMASS II (1957)

ENERGIZER (1908) Unremarkable spoof on advertising claims re products; here a breakfast food gives a man amazing, super-human strength.

Directed by Wallace McGutcheon.

ENGINEER GARIN'S DEATH RAY (1965) *see* THE HYPERBOLOID OF ENGINEER GARIN (1965)

EPITAPH FOR A SPY (1965) *see* SPY IN YOUR EYE (1965)

ERASERHEAD (1979) This surreal, horrific film has become a cult classic. It was director/*auteur* David Lynch's third film – his first of any length – and told a simple little story about Henry and his baby. Set in a post-Industrial wasteland it presents a surreal, frightening landscape wherein Henry lives and tries to love. I'm not going to attempt to unravel more than a single thread of its multivalent imagery – it might, for instance, be a kind of perverse Second-Coming story, with Mary X as the mother – and even to do that is to lose some of the film's intensely interwoven richness. Henry (Jack Nance) and his girlfriend have an inhuman, monstrous child who, when fully unravelled from his swaddling clothes, looks like nothing so much as a giant sperm: perhaps the ultimate in sterile re-creation of the self. Filmed on a low budget in black and white and containing numerous fantastic sequences, it is ultimately a dream; perhaps the most potent dream yet placed on film. A disturbing, nightmarish, illogical dream, with one of the most fearful, frightening final scenes. A long way from the predictable formulae of *Dune* (q.v.).

P★★★	T★★★★	E★★★★	A★★★★

Cinematography by Frederick Elmes and Herbert Cardwell. Special Effects by David Lynch. With Charlotte Stewart, Allen Joseph, Jeanne Bates, Judith Anne Roberts and Laurel Near.

AZ EROD (1979) *see* THE FORTRESS (1979)

ESCAPE FROM NEW YORK (1981) Science fiction, more than any other form, depends upon the reader's/viewer's suspension of disbelief. The future may *be* incredible, but it must *seem* credible. John Carpenter's *Escape From New York* begins with the totally incredible and unacceptable idea that within seven years New York will have become a walled-in high-security prison. The film, set some nine years further on, in 1997, goes downhill from that dubious starting point. The President of the United States, on his way to a crucial summit meeting of the super-powers, and with a vital, irreplaceable tape in his possession, is kidnapped by terrorists (in Airforce One) and crashes in the heart of Manhattan Island. One Snake Plissken, ex-Special Forces and captured criminal, is reprieved his term inside New York if he rescues the President. Despite the mind-bending illogicality of all this it might still have been a reasonable film given some imaginative input, but Carpenter (and co-writer Nick Castle) plump for cliché after cliché – punk gangs, a black Duke (Isaac Hayes) running the criminal city, a gladiatorial contest with spiked clubs, a car chase across a mined bridge. It's all comic-book stuff with a minimal regard for psychological or social realism. Donald Pleasance makes a suitably cowering and frightened President, but Kurt Russell's mindless and rather uninspired portrayal of Snake (mind you, he wasn't given much to start with!), a man compelled to go through the motions because he's got bombs planted in his major arteries (pity they weren't elsewhere!), is endemic of the whole extremely poor show. Oh, and one last jibe before I finish: despite staged scenarios like the drive down Broadway, this New York was a whole lot less threatening than that Scorsese gave us in *Taxi Driver*. Now that *was* credible.

P	T★★	E★	A

Cinematography by Dean Cundey. With Lee Van Cleef, Ernest Borgnine, Adrienne Barbeau, Harry Dean Stanton, Tom Atkins and Charles Cyphers.

ESCAPE FROM THE PLANET OF THE APES (1971) Somehow, two of the apes from the exploding world of AD 3955 (see *Beneath The Planet Of The Apes* (1969)) escape through a time-warp to the human-run Earth of 1973 and there become objects of curiosity and pursuit.

P★	T★★	E★	A★

Directed by Don Taylor. Written by Paul Dehn. Make-up by John Chambers and Dan Striepeke. With Roddy McDowall, Kim Hunter, Bradford Dillman and Natalie Trundy.

ESCAPEMENT (1957) see THE ELECTRONIC MONSTER (1957)

THE ESCAPE OF MEGAGODZILLA (1975) see MONSTERS FROM THE UNKNOWN PLANET (1975)

ESCAPE TO WITCH MOUNTAIN (1974) A typical Disney sf production of its time with two absent-minded teenagers from space, the usual stock villains and a heavy dose of corn and sentimentality. As ever, a sequel followed, *Return From Witch Mountain* (q.v.), though not until 1978.

P★	T★	E★	A

Directed by John Hough. Written by Robert Malcolm Young. Special Effects by Art Cruickshank and Danny Lee. With Eddie Albert, Ray Milland, Donald Pleasance and Kim Richards.

E.T. THE EXTRA-TERRESTRIAL (1982) "A little film," Spielberg kept saying. "A happily pacifistic film, made according to how I think children behave today, what they dream and wish for at night. About best friends, relationships and letting go. I wanted people to believe in something. Because I don't believe in a lot of things that are current and considered to be of immediate global importance, I always dream and think about what I haven't experienced, as opposed to what I can experience by turning on my TV." Just another film, then. Another dream. Another ten years in the mind's melting-pot that has since become Amblin's conveyor-belt – brought to the boil by scenarist Melissa Mathison – a.k.a. Mrs Harrison Ford. ("We've a lot of experience with young American kids," said the director. Yeah, Ben and Willard Harrison, in particular.) And so ... just another mega-hit. The biggest! Still No. 1. in *Variety*'s form of world box-office history and staying there with 1985's re-issue. If

E.T. The Extra-Terrestrial

they don't make films like they used to,
they still make producers like the old days:
Selznick was also prone to taking holidays
in Hawaii ... *CE3K* (q.v.) can be (and has
been) described as the film of our times.
E.T., therefore, is the film of our lifetime,
whatever our age. Because we feel we're
directing it. Everything we, or the kid
Spielberg uncannily unlocks within us,
wants to happen – happens! Let's fly,
E.T.! So we fly. Don't die, E.T.! So he
doesn't. Come back, E.T...? Well, Melissa
wrote the sequel in 1983. It's simply
awaiting the right (financial) moment, or
Henry Thomas to reach around 20 for it
to start Amblin into history. So, of course,
it's one helluva good movie. We're making
it! It's *Peter Pan* and it's *Wizard of Oz*. It's
Bambi. A bit of *Dumbo*, for good measure.
It's *Snow White And The One Dwarf*. It's *A
Closer Encounter*. It's *Huck Finn Meets The
Alien*. Its influences and roots are as many
and varied as treasured in the director's
skull. Above all, it's literally magic. One of
those rare movies – whatever the genre –
that offers and delivers a memorable time.
(I was there at Cannes, 1982, when hard-
boiled critics, who spurned *CE3K*, wept
and cheered like the rest of us mortals.
That was some moving experience, soon
enough repeated at every friendly neigh-
bourhood cinema from Roanoke to Reyk-
javik.) Oddly enough, what it isn't (much)
about is what Spielberg insisted it was: a
film about modern American kids. (The
movie François Truffaut kept pushing him
to make, "because you are a keed!") Apart
from Elliott calling his brother penis-
breath, these kids could be in *The Little
House on the Prairie*, among the *Swiss
Family Robinson* or even *The Jetsons*. Not
modern, just ... kids. Modernity is part of
their lives, more than of their story. Where
modernity really comes into it is that this is
a Disney film, but the kind of *modern*
Disney film that Walt's studio couldn't
match in the 1980s – nor the 1970s, for
that matter. It's about childhood, sure;
yesterday's, today's and tomorrow's. A
fairy-tale set in the remarkably cloistered
childhood that Spielberg was raised in.
All-American Suburbia. That's his house
in the movie. That's his sisters, wrapped
up in little Gertie. That's him as Elliott.
Well, not quite. That's his fantasy of
himself, how he wished he'd been, with
the friend he wished he'd had. (Except
that with such a close chum, he might
never have turned to 8 mm movie-making.
Loneliness can be a great spur to invention.) The pal is a beer-barrelled alien,
with a club-foot of a head, an enquiring,
extending neck, thousands of years of
wisdom (and a voice to match), no legs,
but feet sticking out below his 4-foot
frame like *Dark Star's* (q.v.) follow-the-
bouncing-ball alien. E.T. is the guy who
missed the bus – *CE3K's* mother ship.
He's afraid, totally alone and three million
light years from home. He's hunted (by
merciless adults, of course), befriended
(by terrific kids, of course) and teaches
them both a thing or two about love,
friendship and all that jazz. Any attempt at
a synopsis makes it too simple to send up.
On-screen, it works – wonderfully. Even
E.T., operated by his maker, Carlo Rambaldi, and a team of ten (occasionally with
small persons in a suit) fast becomes, like
Yoda before and *The Dark Crystal*-ites
afterwards, a real being, not an animated
collation of steel, aluminium, foam-rubber
and the rest. With kid jokes, adult jokes,
in-jokes, there was something for everyone, including as many interpretations as
you care to read into the simplicity of it all.
From John Brosnan's wry line about it
really being *E.T. Come Home* to the insane
(and therefore, American) view that it was

an Easter parable. "I never anticipated," said Spielberg, "religious parallels with the Immaculate Heart, which people find the glowing chest to be. Or, the fact that E.T. goes to sleep/dies and reawakens/ comes back to life ... I'm a nice, Jewish boy from Phoenix, Arizona! My mother, who has a kosher deli restaurant, would not, I think, be giving me my mozah-ball soup ration if I came out and admitted there was any kinda Christ parallel! It was never my intention to draw myself into sainthood. I thought I was making a little film, my most personal film, that only a few of my closest friends would enjoy ..."

| P★★★★ | T★★★★★ | E★★★★★ | A★★★★★ |

Produced by Steven Spielberg and Kathleen Kennedy. Directed by Spielberg. Written by Melissa Mathison. With Henry Thomas, Dee Wallace, Peter Coyote, Robert MacNaughton, Drew Barrymore, K. C. Martel, Sean Frye and Tom Howell (now C. Thomas Howell). (TC)

EVA, LA VENERE SELVAGGIA (1968) see EVE, THE SAVAGE VENUS (1968)

EVEN DWARVES STARTED SMALL (1970) Werner Herzog produced, directed and wrote this film about a tropical island in the future run by dwarves.

With Helmut Doring, Gerd Crickel, Paul Glauer, and Ema Geschwenter.

EVE, THE SAVAGE VENUS (1968) Silly Italian feature about a beautiful savage (Esmerelda Barros) who is brought up by the gorillas. The twist is that the gorillas are being controlled from afar by a mad scientist.

| P★ | T★ | E★ | A |

Directed by Robert Mons. Written by Mario Pupillo. With Brad Harris, Mark Farran, Adriana Alben and Aldo Cecconi.

THE EVIL FORCE (1959) see THE 4-D MAN (1959)

THE EVIL OF FRANKENSTEIN (1963) Third of Hammer's reworkings of the Mary Shelley myth, again starring Peter Cushing as the dedicated, amoral

scientist. Here the monster, revived, falls into the clutches of an evil hypnotist who makes him kill his enemies.

| P★ | T★★ | E★ | A★ |

Directed by Freddie Francis. Written by John Elder. Special Effects by Les Bowie. Make-up by Roy Ashton. With Peter Woodthorpe and Sandor Eles.

EXPEDITION MOON (1950) see ROCKETSHIP X-M (1950)

THE EXTERMINATORS (1965) Atomic-age thriller as criminals build a nuclear rocket in an underground laboratory and plan to destroy New York. Based on Paul Kelly's novel, *Stoppez Coplan*.

| P★ | T★ | E★ | A |

Directed by Riccardo Freda. Written by Claude Marcel Richard. With Richard Wyler, Jany Clair, Gil Delamare and Robert Manuel.

EXTERMINATORS OF THE YEAR 3000 (1982) Yet another Italian version of *Mad Max* (q.v.); a post-Holocaust, water's-precious, hard-case-with-soft-centre-takes-on-baddies film, totally derivative and ultimately as sterile as the landscape through which its predictably spiked cars travel. A nasty, brutish, but alas not short film.

| P★ | T★★ | E★★ | A |

Directed by Jules Harrison. Written by Elisa Briganti, Dardano Sacchetti and Jose Truchado Reyes. Special Effects by Gino De Rossi and Edmondo Natali. With Robert Jannucci, Alicia Moro, Alan Collins and Fred Harris.

THE EYE CREATURES (1965) A made-for-TV cheapie without any finesse and stealing unabashedly the storyline to Paul W. Fairman's "The Cosmic Frame" and *Invasion Of The Saucermen* (1957) (q.v.). Multi-eyed aliens invade, kill, and blame the locals.

| P | T | E | A |

Directed by Larry Buchanan. With John Ashley, Cynthia Hall, Warren Hammack and Chet Davis.

EYES WITHOUT A FACE (1959) see THE HORROR CHAMBER OF DR FAUSTUS (1959)

F

A FABLE (1971) In the US of the future blacks fight whites for supremacy. Based on the play by Leroi Jones, "Slave".

Directed by Al Freeman Jr Written by Leroi Jones. With Al Freeman Jr, Hildy Brooks and James Patterson.

THE FABULOUS WORLD OF JULES VERNE (1958) Loosely based on Jules Verne's novel, *Facing The Flag*, though paying homage to other works of his, this charming film uses numerous cinematic devices (animation, puppets, trick photography, live action and tricks with processing) to tell its story. All of the elements we have grown accustomed to thinking of as Vernian are here – atomic subs, pirate cities inside volcanoes, rocket-firing cannons, etc.

P★	T★★★	E★★	A★★

Directed by Karel Zeman. Written by Zeman and Frantisek Hrubin. With Lubor Tokos, Arnost Navratil, Miroslav Holub and Jana Zatloukalova.

THE FACELESS MONSTER (1965) Mad scientist kills wife and her lover, partly for revenge, partly for his experiments in animating blood. The horror aspects of the film, however, are far better than the thin sf element, with nightmarish hauntings by the dead lovers.

P★	T★★	E★★	A★

Directed by Mario Caiano. Written by Caiano and Fabio de Agostino. With Barbara Steele, Paul Miller, Helga Lune and Laurence Clift.

THE FACE OF ANOTHER (1966) A strange tale of a man whose face is destroyed in an accident and who has a life-like mask made to replace it. But his face has strange properties and causes others, at a distance, to act strangely.

P★★	T★★	E★★	A★★

Directed by Hiroshi Teshigawara. Written by Koko Abe. With Tatsuya Nakadai, Mikijiro Hira, Kyoko Kishida, Maduko Kyo and Eiji Okada.

FACE OF FEAR (1962) *see* FACE OF TERROR (1962)

FACE OF TERROR (1962) An interesting but flawed film about a surgeon working to give beauty to a disfigured and mentally disturbed girl. He succeeds, and she goes out into the world to get a rich husband, but she needs a fluid to keep her looks and reverts to type, becoming a homicidal maniac.

P★	T★★	E★★	A★

Directed by Isidoro Martinez Ferry. Written by Monroe Manning. With Lisa Gaye, Fernando Rey, and Virgilio Teixeira.

FAHRENHEIT 451 (1966) The beautiful visual textures of this film (Nicolas Roeg was the cinematographer) conceal what is a rather poor version of Ray Bradbury's 1954 novel. Where the novel stressed the awakening of Montag, the fireman (in an age where firemen burn books rather than fight fires), to the sterility of his existence – in what might be described as lowest-common-denominator-land – the film merely charts his switched allegiance from one interest group to another, equally sterile (if somewhat more romantic) group. Where the novel asserts Life, the film turns Montag's rebellion into merely another cul-de-sac with its final image of the "Book People" (who are remembering whole works of literature in their heads, ostensibly for a future renaissance) monotonously reciting their fragments in a trance-like manner. This said, Truffaut's love of cinema comes through in certain scenes of utter visual clarity – as in that in which the people come out of their houses to point at the fleeing Montag when ordered to by their TV sets. But I can only summarize my attitude to this film by saying that it should never have been made. Bradbury's tale worked because it was in the literary medium; transferred to another medium the whole tenor of its argument (for film is, to a greater degree than literature, a passive medium) crumbled. That's why Truffaut could not keep Bradbury's black-and-white argument: it argued against *his* medium. What resulted is occasionally beautiful but generally severely flawed.

P★★	T★★★★	E★★	A★★★

Directed by François Truffaut. Written by Truffaut and Jean-Louis Richard. Special Effects by Charles Staffel and Bowie Films. With Julie Christie, Oskar Werner, Cyril Cusack, Anton Diffring and Bee Duffell.

FAIL SAFE (1964) Based on the novel by Eugene Burdick and Harvey Wheeler. Henry Fonda plays the American president who, having accidentally bombed Moscow, has to nuke New York City to prevent World War Three. What could have been a neat parable is blunted by uncharacteristically poor direction.

| P★★ | T★★ | E★★ | A★ |

Directed by Sidney Lumet. Written by Walter Bernstein. Special Effects by Storyboard Inc. With Dan O'Herlihy, Walter Matthau, Frank Overton, Edward Binns, Fritz Weaver, Larry Hagman and Sorrell Booke.

THE FALLS (1980) How simplify this three-hour experience into a paragraph? Peter Greenaway is better known nowadays for his *The Draughtsman's Contract*, but this operates on the same level of intelligent enigma. Ninety-two capsule biographies of witnesses of the Violent Unknown Event. Which was? The Fall itself ...? Armageddon? Lightweight, fascinating and, of course, totally obscure.

| P★★ | T★★★ | E★★ | A★★ |

Directed and written by Peter Greenaway.

THE FANTASTICAL AIRSHIP (1906) Comic short, told as a dream. An inventor envisages he has succeeded in flying his mechanized balloon into space.

Directed by Georges Méliès.

A FANTASTIC COMEDY (1975) A schizophrenic production seemingly at odds with itself as it interweaves a comic story about a robot with an at times horrid story of a boy brought up in the isolation of an orbiting satellite.

| P★ | T★★ | E★★ | A★ |

Directed and written by Ion Popescu-Gopo. With Dem Radulescu and Cornel Coman.

I FANTASTICI TRE SUPERMEN (1967) *see* THE FANTASTIC THREE (1967)

FANTASTIC PLANET (1973) A strange and beautiful animated feature-length version of Stefan Wul's novel *Oms en Série*. The tiny underpeople of the planet Yagam, the Oms, are pets to the gigantic Draags, until an Om, Terr, leads a revolution against the inconsiderate giants. It's a hauntingly imaginative work.

| P★★ | T★★★★ | E★★★ | A★★★ |

Directed by René Laloux. Written by Laloux and Roland Topor.

THE FANTASTIC PUPPET PEOPLE (1958) *see* ATTACK OF THE PUPPET PEOPLE (1958)

THE FANTASTIC THREE (1967) Two comics in Superman suits go in pursuit of a master criminal with a matter transmitter, who keeps making copies of an FBI man helping them out.

| P | T★ | E | A |

Directed by Gianfranco Parolini. Written by Marcello Parolini and G. Parolini. With Luciani Stella, Brad Harris and Nick Jordan.

FANTASTIC VOYAGE (1966) One of the most ingenious ideas to reach the science fiction movies, despite the fact that it would not actually work: a submarine crewed with medics is miniaturized to enter a scientist's bloodstream and remove a blood clot from his brain. There is a time limit, one hour, before the sub returns to full size; and there's a Soviet agent on board. Raquel Welch, Stephen Boyd, Donald Pleasance, Arthur Kennedy, and William Redfield are the crew, battling with white corpuscles, killer enzymes, and running into real trouble when their host develops a cough. The sets inside the body are so pristine and colourful they more resemble a wonderland than an old man's corrupted interior. But that is what a buoyantly exuberant director Richard Fleischer and writer Harry Kleiner seem to be telling us – that the human body *is* a wonderland, just as much a last frontier as Outer Space or the bottom of the ocean – and then they leave us wondering why they sent to explore such a frontier a crew of wooden martinets, stout clean-cut heroes

A scene from Fantastic Voyage

and other such unpoetical types. The 60-minute time limit cuts everything to the chase, makes characterization and interrelationships a flat impossibility and perhaps, all things considered, that proves to be a blessing. But Pleasance is at his morbid best, and when Welch gets attacked by the bloodstream's defence mechanisms, it's almost like a bizarre type of cannibalism, slightly kinky the way all boy-scout adventure movies with pretty female stars are. No lesser personage than Isaac Asimov wrote the novelization, which was serialized in the *Saturday Evening Post*, confirming the popularity of a movie which demands to be enjoyed on its own simple terms or not at all.

P★★★	T★★★	E★★★★	A★

Special Effects by L. B. Abbott, Art Cruikshank, Emil Kosa Jr. Cinematography by Ernest Laszlo. With Edmond O'Brien and Arthur O' Connell. (TR)

THE FBI VERSUS DR MABUSE
(1961) *see* THE RETURN OF DR MABUSE (1961)

FEARLESS FRANK (1967) Comic
turn on the Frankenstein myth, starring Jon Voigt. Killed by a group of gangsters, Frank comes back as a Frankenstein look-alike, possessed of an evil doppelganger.

P★	T★★	E★★	A

Produced, directed and written by Philip Kaufman. With Monique Van Vooren.

FERMATI COPLAN (1965) *see* THE
EXTERMINATORS (1965)

FIEND WITHOUT A FACE (1957)
Based on Amelia Reynolds Long's short story "The Thought-Monster", the unlikely premise of this film is that a scientist's machine, designed to increase and amplify thought-waves, produces instead physical thought-beings – flying brains that, of course, attack people and suck their brains out. Despite the silliness of this, the film still retains quite a powerful charge, particularly at its climax.

P★	T★★	E★★	A★

Directed by Arthur Crabtree. Written by Herbert J. Leder. Special Effects by Puppel Nordhoff and Peter Nielson. Make-up by Jim Hydes. With Marshall Thompson, Terence Kilburn, Kim Parker, Peter Madden and Michael Balfour.

THE FINAL COUNTDOWN (1980)
An ultimately unsatisfying scenario. What if a modern-day aircraft carrier, complete with modern weaponry, were to be sent back in time to the days before Pearl Harbor, with full knowledge of Japanese battle plans? Would they take on the Japanese fleet and defeat them? Apparently not; at least, not in *this* feature. All of our expectations are raised and then dashed as Kirk Douglas takes the USS *Nimitz* through the (impressive) time storm and then back to present-day America, without changing very much at all. This could have been a great film, instead it's a piece of TV fodder.

P★★	T★★★	E★★	A★

Directed by Don Fodder. Written by David Abrose, Gerry Davis, Thomas Hunter and Peter Powell. Special Effects by Maurice Binder. With Martin Sheen and Katharine Ross.

THE FINAL PROGRAMME (1973)
Writer-director Robert Fuest loses some of the ethos, but picks up a lot of the jokes Michael Moorcock missed in this adaptation of the first Jerry Cornelius novel. Cornelius (Jon Finch) was created as a hero-of-the-times in the 1960s, and remains fairly valid today. Sexually and morally ambiguous, his philosophy is *après nous le déluge*, "anything goes", as he

wanders through a doomed world where Trafalgar Square has become a scrap yard, trying to discover the truth behind the enigmatic Miss Brunner, who is planning to create a successor to the human race. It's pure junk style. Broken biscuits and plastic cups line the bottom of an immaculate Rolls-Royce. A mercenary can't get hold of any napalm because "the shops are shut". There is a mansion defended by a device which sends intruders into epileptic fits, and guns which fire needles with a deadly *zzzzip*. A brash, funny comic-strip of a movie.

P★★★   T★★★   E★★★★   A★

Cinematography by Norman Warrick. With Hugh Griffith, Patrick Magee, Jenny Runacre, Sterling Hayden and George Coulouris. (TR)

THE FINAL WAR (1960) After the accidental explosion of an atom bomb over Korea, the USA is forced into nuclear confrontation with the USSR on an escalating basis.

P★★   T★★   E★   A★

Directed by Shigeaki Hidaki. Written by Hisataka Kai. With Tatsuo Umemiya, Yoshiko Mita, Yayoi Furusato and Noribumi Fujishima.

FIN DE SEMANA PARA LOS MUERTOS (1974) *see* THE LIVING DEAD AT THE MANCHESTER MORGUE (1974)

LA FIN DU MONDE (1930) *see* THE END OF THE WORLD (1930)

FIREBIRD 2015 AD (1980) Dull yarn about private roadsters ("burners") in an age where the private car is banned. A crazy Indian with a hand-held shell gun adds mild interest.

P   T★   E   A

Directed by David M. Robertson. Written by Barry Pearson. With Darren McGavin and Doug McClure.

FIREFOX (1982) Craig Thomas (who wrote the novel) never did quite work out the full implications of a thought-controlled weapons system (telepathy, in any other words!) and its potential appli-

cations. In *Firefox* the Russians have developed an aircraft (more like a *Star Wars* fighter) which can fly at 135,000 feet, at Mach 6, and has such a weapons system – only you have to think in Russian. Mitchell Gant (Clint Eastwood) is the ex-Vietnam veteran US pilot chosen to play spy and take the aircraft from deep in the heart of Russia – aided by an underground composed of Jewish Russian dissidents (three of them the plane's inventors). The first half of the film is pure spy-thriller, the second half – the flight from Russia and the dogfight with the second Firefox craft – pure *Star Wars*, including a re-run of the Death-Star-canyon flight. Eastwood (who also produced and directed) is excellent as the fear-ridden but ultimately confident spy/pilot and it's a superior thriller.

P★★★★   T★★★★★   E★★★★★   A★★

Written by Alex Lasker and Wendell Wellman. Special Effects by John Dykstra, Robert Shepherd, Roger Dorney and Apogee, Inc. With Freddie Jones, David Huffman, Warren Clarke and Ronald Lacey.

FIRE MAIDENS OF OUTER SPACE (1955) An accurate description of this film would be to title it *The Lost Women Of Atlantis Fight A Space Monster On Venus* – with the help of some Earth spacemen, of course. Utterly silly apart from its delightful classical score.

P   T★   E★   A

Directed and written by Cy Roth. With Anthony Dexter, Susan Shaw, Paul Carpenter, Harry Fowler and Sydney Tafler.

THE FIRE OF LIFE (1912) A chemist discovers the secret of immortality – a formula for eternal life – but ironically dies with it.

Directed by Schnedler Sorensen. Written by Zenius Rostock. With Valdemar Psitander, Julie Henriksen and Else Frolich.

FIRESTARTER (1984) A chemical compound, Lot 6, is given to a test group of young people – two of whom become telepaths and eventually marry. They have a daughter, Charlie, in whom the powers awoken in them are innate – and more powerful. The drug, developed at the government's research institute, The Shop, was derived from the pituitary gland, and as the girl grows older and approaches puberty, the period when her pituitary gland will be most active, her powers, they believe, will also grow. This is pure sf thus far, and if *Firestarter* seems a little like *Carrie* with sf trimmings, that's not too surprising, because this is another film adaptation of a Stephen King novel. Gone are the pseudo-religious trappings and in their place is a conspiracy thriller, with The Shop and its agents pursuing father and daughter (they've already killed the mother) in order that they might return them to The Shop for "tests". Those moments of peace from pursuit – of normalcy – show that King's concerns have altered over the years from an examination of the manifestations of the abnormal, to the psychology of those afflicted by it – cursed with such gifts (see *The Dead Zone* as a further example of this). Drew Barrymore is convincing as the young girl trying to balance the little bad against the big bad – moralities – and trying to be normal and control her awesome talent. But when, after her potential has been frighteningly tested, the government agency pushes her too far and kills her father, she obeys her father's dying command and burns it all down. In this sense it's opposed to the usual run of horror movies in being intensely moral, violently (literally) opposed to the corruption of institutions, and ultimately for normalcy (the life with the small-town farmer and his wife she chooses at the end). Good performances by David Keith as Andrew McGee (the father), George C. Scott as the murderous assassin Rainbird, and Martin Sheen as the boss of The Shop, add to the quality of this film. A good soundtrack, too, from Tangerine Dream.

P★★★   T★★★★★   E★★★★   A★★★

Directed by Mark L. Lester. Written by Stanley Mann. With Freddie Jones, Heather Locklear, Art Carney, Louise Fletcher and Moses Gunn.

FIRST MAN INTO SPACE (1959)
An astronaut, returning from a routine space flight, has been turned into a blood-drinking, slimy monster.

P★   T★   E★   A

Directed by Robert Day. Written by John C. Cooper and Lance Z. Hargreaves. With Marshall Thompson, Marla Landi, Robert Ayres, Bill Edwards, Bill Nagy and Carl Jaffe.

FIRST MEN IN THE MOON (1919)
Earliest adaptation for the silent screen of Wells's Victorian adventure amongst the Moon-dwelling Selenites.

Directed by J. V. Leigh. With Bruce Gordon, Lionel D'Arragan, Hector Abbas, Cecil Morton York and Heather Thatcher.

FIRST MEN IN THE MOON (1964)
Enjoyable if silly version of Wells's science fantasy about Mr Cavor's journey to the Moon and his encounter with the ant-like Selenites. Wells's tale deserved somewhat better, but this isn't a total dud.

P★★   T★★   E★★   A

Directed by Nathan Juran. Special Effects by Ray Harryhausen. Written by Nigel Kneale and Jan Read. With Edward Judd, Martha Hyer, Lionel Jeffries, Betty McDowall, Hugh McDermott and Peter Finch.

THE FIRST OF JANUARY (1971) *see* ZERO POPULATION GROWTH (1971)

FIRST SPACESHIP ON VENUS (1959) Rather routine space opera with pacifist undertones, based on Stanislaw Lem's first novel, *The Astronauts*. A scientific expedition (with a robot aboard) go to Venus, which they find has been destroyed by atomic war. The moral lesson is, of course, clear.

P★★   T★★   E★★   A★

Directed by Kurt Matzig. Written by J. Barckhausen, J. Fethke, W. Kohlaase, G. Reisch, G. Rucker and A. Stenbock-Fermor. Special Effects by Ernst and Vera Kunstman, Jan Olejniczak and Helmut Grewald. With Yoko Tani and Oldrich Lukes.

FIRST STEPS TO THE MOON (1963) *see* STEPS TO THE MOON (1963)

FIRST WOMAN INTO SPACE (1965) *see* SPACE MONSTER (1965)

FIVE (1951) A disappointing and, in retrospect, rather preachy film about the

last five people on Earth after the Nuclear Catastrophe. Their symbolic characters, their hopes and their despair could have been the ingredients for a superb little film, but this simply falls flat, and only the slightly haunting settings of the film (the house on the cliff, apparently home of director/writer Arch Oboler) really remain in mind long after seeing the film.

P★★	T★★	E★	A★

With Susan Douglas, William Plupps, James Anderson, Charles Lampkin and Earl Lee.

FIVE MILLION YEARS TO EARTH (1967) *see* QUATERMASS AND THE PIT (1967)

THE FLAME BARRIER (1958) One of several films of the time to exploit the common fear that journeys into space would result in some hideous distortion of men. Here a fallen satellite, found in the jungle, is seen to have brought back a living, pyrotechnic, protoplasmic creature.

P★	T★	E★	A

Directed by Paul Landis. Written by Pat Fielder and George Worthing Yates. With Arthur Franz, Kathleen Crowley and Robert Brown.

FLASH GORDON (1980) Earth is under cosmic attack from a distant planet. Flash (Sam J. Jones) and his girlfriend Dale (Melody Anderson) set off in a rocket ship with the frantic Dr Zarkov (Topol) to confront Ming the Merciless of Mongo (Max von Sydow) in an attempt to save civilization as we know it. Yet another in that deluge of space-adventure films which followed in the wake of *Star Wars*, the film ultimately fails horribly, falling into the trap of setting itself up as a spoof and then trying to take its spoofiness seriously – an impressive Queen soundtrack, a lot of rococo sets, and a cinematic gimmick of concentrating on glaring, unreal primary colours all labour to convince us that director Mike Hodges and producer Dino de Laurentiis have produced something artsy and clever. Sometimes they practically succeed – the scene where Flash is forced to compete in a fantasy version of Russian roulette by

Max Von Sydow as the Emperor Ming in Flash Gordon

putting his hand into various holes, one of which contains a creature with a fatal bite, works well, and the Winged Men of Mongo who fly in to save the day are all the fun they are supposed to be – but mostly the film is just campy and cute. It's an attempt to re-create the success of *Barbarella*, but without Vadim's style. Ornella Muti as Princess Aura and Peter Wyngarde as Klytus put in performances which, though sinister and funny to the right degree, seem fuelled out of relief that they never had to play the roles seriously in the 1930s matinee movies. The Winged Men were forbidden lunch during the shooting of the "flight" scenes, to stop them from passing out in their harnesses. Mercifully, there were no sequels.

P	T★★★★	E★★	A

Written by Lorenzo Semple Jnr. Special Effects by Glen Robinson, George Gibbs, Richard Conway, Norman Dorme and Frank Van Der Veer. With Brian Blessed and Timothy Dalton. (TR)

THE FLESH EATERS (1964) Mad scientist on remote island develops a flesh-eating bacteria.

P	T★	E	A

Directed by Jack Curtis. Written by Arnold Drake. Special Effects by Roy Benson. With Matin Kosleck, Rita Morley and Byron Sanders.

FLESH FOR FRANKENSTEIN
(1973) Not content with bodging his one monster, Frankenstein is here seen creating the ultimate super-race of Balkan peasants. Meanwhile, we, the audience, are treated to numerous instances of disembowelling in glorious 3-D. A must for perverts and *Duchess Of Malfi* freaks.

P★★   T★★★·   E★★   A★

Directed and written by Paul Morrissey. Special Effects by Carlo Rambaldi. With Joe Dallesandro, Monique Van Vooren and Udo Kier.

FLESH GORDON (1972) Notorious
for its near-pornographic rendition of the 1936 serial, not enough attention has been paid to the excellent work by directors Michael Benveniste and Howard Ziehm in parodying the style of the original. There's a deliberate 1930s feel to this and the original is faithfully copied in absurd dialogue, costumes, action shots and tableaux. Here a sex-beam from the planet Porno, ruled by his impotence Wang The Pervert strikes Flesh's plane and only he and Dale escape – meeting up with Dr Flexi Jerkoff and, in his penis-shaped rocket, flying off to Porno to save the world from depravity. Amidst scenes of utter depravity, Wang marries Dale while Flesh is kidnapped by the lusty Amora, Wang's daughter. But Dale is held by a group of Amazonian dykes (who do horrifically graphic things to her until freed by Prince Precious and his gay freedom fighters). And so it goes; Wang is defeated (after a King Kong-like scene featuring his pet demon), Dale is saved, the kingdom of Porno returned to Precious. Not for the prudish, the special effects in this are surprisingly professional. Look out, in particular, for Wang's rapist-robots. A delightful hybrid.

P★★   T★★★   E★★★★   A★

Written by Michael Benveniste. Special Effects by Tom Scherman, Ray Mercer, Howard Ziehm, Lynn Rogers and Walter R. Cichy. With Jason Williams, Suzanne Fields, Joseph Hudgins, William Hunt, John Hoyt and Mycle Brandy.

FLICK (1967) *see* DR FRANKENSTEIN ON CAMPUS (1967)

FLIGHT BEYOND THE SUN
(1965) *see* SPACE MONSTER (1965)

THE FLIGHT THAT DISAPPEARED (1961) A nice twist on the scientist's moral dilemma. Here three top scientists are "kidnapped" in mid-air by representatives from the future who persuade them to destroy the notes on their work towards a new super-bomb. Unfortunately, this was only a fiction!

P★★   T★★   E★★   A★

Directed by Reginald LeBorg. Written by Ralph Hart, Judith Hart and Owen Harris. Special Effects by Barney Wolff. With Craig Hill, Paula Raymond, Dayton Lumis and Gregory Morton.

THE FLIGHT THAT VANISHED
(1961) *see* THE FLIGHT THAT DISAPPEARED (1961)

FLIGHT TO FAME (1938) Pedestrian
ray-gun-shoots-down-planes melodrama, where the invention falls into criminal hands.

P★   T★   E   A

Directed by C. C. Coleman Jr. Written by Michael L. Simmons. With Charles Farrell, Jacqueline Wells and Alexander D'Arcy.

FLIGHT TO MARS (1951) Awful film
about a space expedition that crash-lands on Mars. The obligatory 1930s civilization of underground Martians meanwhile plot to conquer the Earth.

P   T★   E   A

Directed by Lesley Selander. Written by Arthur Strawn. With Marguerite Chapman, Cameron Mitchell, Arthur Franz and Virginia Huston.

FLOATING PLATFORM ONE DOES NOT REPLY (1932) *see* F.P.1
DOESN'T ANSWER (1932)

FLOWERS FOR THE MAN IN THE MOON (1975) *Boys' Own* German
style! A little boy wants to grow not merely vegetables but flowers on the Moon. . .

P★   T★   E★   A

Directed by Rolf Losansky. Written by Losansky, Irmgard Speitel and Ulrich Speitel. With Jutta Wachowiak, Stefan Lisewski and Dieter Franke.

THE FLY (1958) Fun as it is, the sf idea behind *The Fly* is ludicrous. A scientist, experimenting with a matter transmitter, exchanges his head and one arm with those of a common housefly. But somehow – never explained in the film – he keeps his own brain and is able to converse and function as a human being still. The fly, complete with miniature human head, can do the same. So popular was this, nonetheless, that two sequels followed, *Return Of The Fly* (1959) (q.v.) and *Curse Of The Fly* (1965) (q.v.).

P★	T★★	E★★★	A★

Directed by Kurt Neumann. Written by James Clavell. Special Effects by L. B. Abbott. Make-up by Ben Nye. With Al Hedison, Patricia Owens, Vincent Price and Herbert Marshall.

THE FLYING DISC (1964) *see* THE FLYING SAUCER (1964)

THE FLYING MACHINE (1901) One of the earliest imaginative uses of special effects techniques, director/writer Ferdinand Zecca used a crude split-screen technique for his tale of a flying motorcycle.

FLYING PHANTOM SHIP (1969) Japanese Vernian adventure with giant robots, crabs, lobsters, a few underwater cities and flying clipper ships. Animated.

Directed by Hiroshi Ikeda. Written by Masaki Tsuji. Animation by Yoichi Otake.

THE FLYING SAUCER (1949) First use of the name "flying saucer" for the UFO phenomenon, this is not an outer space tale, but an invasion from the USSR scare story; though not the last time that the Russians were suspected of sending the saucers!

P★	T★	E★	A

Produced, directed and written by Mikel Conrad. With Mikel Conrad and Pat Garrison.

THE FLYING SAUCER (1964) Mildly comic Italian film, starring Alberto Sordi in several roles. The Martians are slowly abducting Earth people, but the authorities don't want to know and lock up all those who claim to have seen them in an asylum.

P★	T★★	E★★	A★

Directed by Tinto Brassi. Written by Rudolfo Sonego. With Monica Vitti and Eleonora Rossi Drago.

THE FLYING SORCERER (1974) Boy travels back to medieval times and returns with a dragon; a theme resurrected (in slightly different form) in *The Neverending Story* (1984) (q.v.), but here without any value whatsoever. A Children's Film Foundation outing.

P★	T★	E	A

Directed by Harry Booth. Written by Booth and Leo Maguire. Special Effects by John Poyner. With Kim Burfield, Debbie Russ, John Bluthal and Bob Todd.

THE FLYING TORPEDO (1916) An early super-technology-developed-before-its-time story; this time an anti-aircraft, radio-controlled torpedo is developed and then stolen by enemy spies – and then recaptured...

Directed by John O'Brien. With John Emerson, Bessie Love and Spottiswoode Aitken.

FOES (1977) Fourth-rate UFO story without any surprises.

P	T	E	A

Directed and written by John Coats. Special Effects by Coats, Scott Farrar, Christopher George. With McDonald Carey, Jerry Hardin and Jane Wiley.

LA FOLIE DU DOCTEUR TUBE (1915) *see* THE MADNESS OF DR TUBE (1915)

THE FOOD OF THE GODS (1976) Some young Americans, holidaying in the backwoods, discover to their cost that a chemical is making all the woodland creatures grow to a tremendous size. This atrocious adaptation of an H. G. Wells short story is little more than an excuse to show us giant rats devouring people – and even within that sub-genre, there can be few other movies so trite, so dull, so hackneyed and humourless. Pure, nasty exploitativeness wins the day – when one of the young women begins going into labour in a cabin surrounded by the over-sized rodents it becomes difficult to imagine how much lower to induce a cheap frisson Bert I. Gordon, who wrote, produced and directed, could sink. *Food of the Gods* not only has you asking for your money back, it has you threatening to sue the cinema for damages.

P	T	E	A

Special Effects by Bert I. Gordon (!). With Marjoe Gortner, Pamela Franklin, Ida Lupino, Ralph Meeker and John McLiam. (TR)

FORBIDDEN PLANET (1956) The chief claim to fame of director Fred M. Wilcox's movie is that it (very loosely) borrows some of its plot and characters from Shakespeare's *The Tempest*, and, while that most auspicious of literary influences serves to give *Forbidden Planet* a little more heft and durability than its contemporaries, the film derives far more from *Astounding Stories* than it does from the Bard. In true 1950s sci-fi style, everything is given a number – the year is ad 2200; the planet is called Altair 4; the craft which lands on it is relief ship C57D. Commander Adams (Leslie Nielsen) and his crew have been detailed to re-establish contact with a scientific colony which arrived on the planet 25 years ago. They discover that Morbius (Walter Pidgeon) is the only man left of the original team – the rest, he tells them, have been killed long ago by some unknown force, all save for Morbius's wife who died of illness shortly after giving birth to his now full-grown daughter, Altaira (Anne Francis). A genial robot called Robby makes up the third member of the peculiar household – but if the servile robot is Ariel, then where is Caliban? What monster is it that has killed the other scientists? The answer lies in a vast and still-functioning underground laboratory, memento of an advanced alien race called the Krel who inhabited the planet centuries back until they too, like Morbius's colleagues, disappeared. It's one of the best science fiction movies from its decade, with certainly one of the most intelligent ideas ... Freudianism is the

A scene from Forbidden Planet

inspiration here, both in the conception of the monster and the explanation of its motives when Adams falls in love with the untouched, naïve Altaira. The special effects range from the impressive (the movie was shot entirely on sound stages, yet the outdoor scenes have a rich, believable three-dimensionality) to the less-than-effective (when the monster approaches Adams's camp, the way the effects team present huge footprints appearing in the sand leaves us suspecting the planet is inhabited by giant gophers). Robby the robot made a later appearance in the *Lost in Space* television series, starred in *The Invisible Boy*, and was one of the first to whet the moviegoing public's appetite for lovable metal men. It's in the realms of character and dialogue that the movie really falls down. Adams and his men seem to have been transferred directly from the set of some cheap Warner Bros. war movie of the previous decade, the officers are clean-cut bores and the underlings are earthy, blockheaded slobs. The conflict here is between the poetry of idea, mood, and setting and the unimaginative prosaicness of the protagonists. It's a conflict which was forever echoed in the far later *Star Trek* series, whose creator, Gene Rodenberry, must *surely* count this film amongst his major influences – when Altaira, who has never seen any man but her father before now, falls into the arms of the visiting spaceman, Adams and his successor James T. Kirk become completely interchangeable. But, finally and surprisingly, the poetry wins through. Altair 4, with its pink sand, lustrous green sky and twin moons, remains one of the most memorable of science fiction worlds. Morbius's airy domicile, resounding to the music of windchimes, further complements the unearthly mood. The movie's finale is a truly enjoyable edge-of-the-seat experience.

P★★★★   T★★★   E★★★★★   A★★

Produced by Nicholas Nayfack. Written by Cyril Hume. Special Effects by A. Arnold Gillespie, Warren Newcombe, Irving G. Reis and Joshua Meador. With Warren Stevens, Jack Kelly, Richard Anderson and Earl Holliman. (TR)

FORBIDDEN WORLD (1982) Producer Roger Corman's exploitation of the *Alien* (q.v.) theme. Here the nasty mutant (a convincing little nausea-inducer) is eventually killed off when fed one of the ship's scientist's cancer-ridden livers. This dénouement is quite typical of a deeply dark script which maintains tension throughout. Of course, it isn't anything like as good as *Alien*, but it is a thoroughly competent and – in a perverse sense – enjoyable film.

P★★   T★★★   E★★★   A★

Directed by Allan Holzman. Written by Tim Curnen. With Jesse Vint, June Chadwick, Dawn Dunlap, Linden Chiles and Raymond Oliver.

THE FORBIN PROJECT (1967) *see* COLOSSUS, THE FORBIN PROJECT (1967)

THE FORMULA OF THE RAINBOW (1967) *see* CALL ME ROBERT (1967)

THE FORTRESS (1979) A black comedy about a holiday camp where the visitors become participants in real war games. After a few moments of panic they (in true Butlin's style) join in enthusiastically.

P★★   T★★   E★★   A★

Directed by Milos Szinetar. Written by Szinetar and Gyula Hernadi. With Bella Tanai, Sandor Oszter, Istvan Kovacs and Jozsef Madaras.

LE FOU DU LABO 4 (1967) *see* THE MADMAN OF LAB 4 (1967)

THE 4-D MAN (1959) A surprisingly good feature from director Irvin Shortess Yeaworth J., well acted, with convincing special effects throughout (by Barton Sloane). Brothers Scott and Tony Nelson (Robert Lansing and James Congdon) discover a means by which substances can interpenetrate each other, and eventually Scott, his brain impulses amplified by exposure to radiation, is able to walk through walls and so forth. But the Faustian scientific bargain always has its price; each time Scott uses his powers it ages him years. He becomes an energy vampire, killing people (by rapid ageing) simply by touching and draining them of their life force. With a good adult script and fine performances by all involved (including girlfriend Linda, played by Lee Meriwether) this is one of the few sf movies of the 1950s to remain impressive even today.

P★★★   T★★★   E★★★★   A★

Written by Theodore Simonson and Cy Chermak from an idea by co-producer Jack H. Harris. Make-up by Dean Newman. With Robert Strauss, Patty Duke, Edgar Stehli and Jasper Deeter.

400 MILLION MILES FROM THE EARTH (1917) *see* THE SKY SHIP (1917)

FOUR-SIDED TRIANGLE (1953) Two scientists, Robin and Bill (John Van Eyssen and Stephen Murray), love the same female colleague, Lena (Barbara Payton), but only one – Robin – can marry her. Help is at hand, however; the three have developed a matter duplicator and Lena can be duplicated. Unfortunately, the duplicate also loves Robin; but all is solved when Bill, researching into atomic power, blows himself and the duplicate sky-high. This cheap budget reduction of an already silly story by William F. Temple is instantly forgettable.

P★   T★   E★   A

Directed by Terence Fisher. Written by Fisher and Paul Tabori. With James Hayter, Knaston Reeves and Percy Marmount.

64000

F.P.1 ANTWORTET NICHT (1932)
see F.P.1 DOESN'T ANSWER (1932)

F.P.1 DOESN'T ANSWER (1932) In this age where transatlantic flight is an accepted idea (indeed, so much accepted that we're indifferent to it) it is hard to envisage how exciting the idea behind *F.P.1* was back in 1932. F.P.1 is a giant floating platform in mid-Ocean, where planes can land, refuel and the passengers rest before setting off on the next stage of their journey. Even though Curt Siodmak's story was shortly outstripped by science fact, the story still has a certain charge. The giant platform – constructed specially for the film – is an effective piece of futuristic technology, and the plot is strictly thriller stuff, involving saboteurs and brave scientists. The film was also made in three versions, with appropriate cast changes: English, German and French.

P★   T★★   E★★   A★

Produced by Erich Pommer. Directed by Karl Hartl. Written by Walter Reisch and Curt Siodmak. Cinematography by Gunther Rittau and Konstantin Tschet. English Dialogue by Robert Stevenson and Peter MacFarland. With (English): Leslie Fenton, Conrad Veidt, Jill Esmond, George Merritt; (German): Hans Albers, Sybille Schmidt, Paul Hartmann, Peter Lorre; (French): Charles Boyer, Jean Murat, Pierre Brasseur and Daniella Parola.

FRANKENSTEIN (1910) This was the first, brief version of Mary Shelley's mythic novel; the monster played by Charles Ogle (created not by spare-part surgery but from a chemical broth). Its dénouement – love triumphs over evil – is director J. Searle Dawley's own perversion of Shelley's story.

With Augustus Philipps and Mary Fuller.

FRANKENSTEIN (1931) Brian Aldiss (in his history of sf, *Billion Year Spree*) argues that science fiction began with Mary Shelley's story of perverse creation. When James Whale came to film it, however, he took not the original novel but Peggy Webbing's play as his starting point. Nonetheless, his version is taken as being the definitive *Frankenstein*, if only for Boris

Karloff's moody portrait of the monster and Jack Pierce's memorable make-up. Whale may well have borrowed elements from Lang's *Metropolis* (q.v.) in devising the Baron Frankenstein's operating theatre, but the mood of his film was not scientific but gothic – it is much more a horror film than an exposition of the diseased-creator myth. Its visual settings are not as inspired as the later Hammer versions and its effects are often clumsy, but its influence on all that followed is undoubted. It created those clichés that the horror/sf genre was to work to death over the next 50 years.

P★★   T★★★   E★★★   A★★

Written by Garrett Fort, Robert Florey and Francis Edward Faragoh. Special Effects by John P. Fulton. Electrical Effects by Kenneth Strickfaden. With Colin Clive, Mae Clarke, Lionel Belmore and Edward van Sloan.

FRANKENSTEIN AND THE MONSTER FROM HELL (1973) When a young doctor, obsessed with Baron Frankenstein's experiments, is committed to an asylum, not only does he discover that the Baron himself is there (under an assumed name) but that the Baron is effectively in charge of the institution. The doctor joins in with the Baron's experiments yet finds himself horrified by what the Baron is doing – placing the brain of a suicidal genius into the body of a moronic strongman. As ever the experiment goes wrong, but there are a lot of interesting and gory moments.

P★★   T★★★   E★★★   A★

Directed by Terence Fisher. Written by John Elder. With Peter Cushing, Sloane Briant, Madeline Smith, John Stratton and Bernard Lee.

FRANKENSTEIN CONQUERS THE WORLD (1964) Ridiculous addition to the Japanese monster movie cycle as the heart of Frankenstein's monster, saved by the Nazis, becomes a hideous monster child (with buck teeth) who fights with monster Baragon, the giant devil fish, as to who has property-destruction rights for Tokyo.

P   T★   E   A

Directed by Ihoshiro Honda. Written by Kaoru Mabuchi. With Nick Adams, Tadao Takashuma, Kumi Mizuma and Takashi Shimura.

FRANKENSTEIN CREATED WOMAN (1966) Director Terence
Fisher and Hammer Films have the Baron (Peter Cushing) putting the soul of a wrongly executed man into the corpse of a young girl. The "soul" seeks vengeance, but the chance to explore what it would be like to be such a creature of mixed sexuality is missed.

P★	T★★	E★★	A★

Written by John Elder. Special Effects by Les Bowie. With Susan Denberg and Thorley Walters.

FRANKENSTEIN, EL VAMPIRO Y CIA (1961) see FRANKENSTEIN, THE VAMPIRE & CO. (1961)

FRANKENSTEIN ITALIAN STYLE (1976) Like *Transplant* (1970)
(q.v.) this deals with the question of a penis transplant, but mixes this in with the Frankenstein myth, producing a rather funny sex comedy.

P★	T★★	E★★	A★

Directed by Armando Crispino. Written by M. Franciosa and M. L. Montagnana. With Aldo Maccione, Glanrico Tedeschi and Ninetto Davoll.

FRANKENSTEIN LIVES AGAIN
(1935) see BRIDE OF FRANKENSTEIN (1935)

FRANKENSTEIN MEETS THE SPACEMONSTER (1965) Puerto
Rican film about a cyborg (robot body, human brain) who defeats an alien princess and her monster who plan to conquer the Earth. As far away from Mary Shelley as could be possible.

P★	T★	E★	A

Directed by Robert Gaffney. Written by George Garret. With James Karen, Nancy Marshall, Robert Reilly and Marilyn Hanold.

FRANKENSTEIN MEETS THE WOLFMAN (1943) One of several ex-
ploitation movies which capitalized upon the popularity of "creatures" by sticking

two, three or more in the same film. The plot in such cases is rarely coherent and has much in common with the Japanese monster movies of a later generation.

P★	T★★	E★	A

Directed by Roy William Neill. Written by Curt Siodmak. Special Effects by John P. Fulton. Make-up by Jack Pierce. With Lon Chaney Jr, Bela Lugosi, Lionel Atwill and Eddie Parker.

FRANKENSTEIN MUST BE DESTROYED (1969) Perhaps the best of the
Hammer films of the Frankenstein myth, this switches the emphasis from the horror of diseased creation to the psychological condition both of creator and creature. With Peter Cushing as the unswerving man of science, ungoverned by moral law, and Simon Ward as a younger, more moral doctor inspired by the Baron's work, this has a charge that many of the other films do not possess.

P★★★	T★★	E★★★	A★★

Directed by Terence Fisher. Written by Bert Batt. With Veronica Carling and Freddie Jones.

FRANKENSTEIN 1970 (1958)
Rather silly, gimmicky update of the Frankenstein myth, throwing atomic power and cruel Nazis into the formula without great thought.

P★	T★★	E★	A

Directed by Howard W. Koch. Written by Richard Landau and George Worthing Yates. With Boris Karloff, Tom Duggan and Jana Lund.

FRANKENSTEIN ON CAMPUS (1967) see DR FRANKENSTEIN ON CAMPUS (1967)

FRANKENSTEIN'S MONSTER
(1920) Italian working of the Frankenstein myth, based directly on Mary Shelley's novel.

Directed by Eugenio Testa. Written by Giovanni Drovetti. With Luciano Alberti and Umberto Guarracino.

FRANKENSTEIN: THE TRUE STORY (1973) Not quite the "true
story" (ie., the original Mary Shelley tale) but a far truer psychological version than

most that preceded it, and certainly more in keeping with Shelley's original than the 1930s sequence of films. Here the monster is a doppleganger (dark double) of the Baron, and their strange relationship is the focus of the film. Made for TV in two parts, this is a subtler, unsensationalized film with moments of real beauty and genuine horror, and for once the "monster" is not a grotesque.

| P★★★ | T★★★ | E★★★ | A★★★ |

Directed by Jack Smight. Written by Christopher Isherwood and Don Bachardy. Special Effects by Roy Whybrow. With James Mason, Leonard Whiting, David McCallum, Ralph Richardson, Jane Seymour, Nicola Paget and Michael Sarrazin.

FRANKENSTEIN, THE VAMPIRE & CO. (1961) An uncredited Mexican remake of the 1947 Abbot and Costello spoof, with two comic fools encountering Frankenstein's monster.

| P★ | T★ | E★ | A |

Directed by Benito Alazraki. Written by Alfredo Salazar. With Manuel "Loco" Valdes, Martha Elena Cervantes and Nora Vetran.

FRANKENSTEIN UND DIE UNGERHEUER AUS DEM MEER (1966) see GODZILLA VERSUS THE SEA MONSTER (1966)

FRANKENSTEIN VS. THE GIANT DEVIL FISH (1964) see FRANKENSTEIN CONQUERS THE WORLD (1964)

FRANKENSTEIN – ZWEIKAMPF DER GIGANTEN (1966) see WAR OF THE GARGANTUAS (1966)

FRANK'S GREATEST ADVENTURE (1967) see FEARLESS FRANK (1967)

THE FRIEND (1963) Short (20-minute) Polish film by Marek Nowicki and Jerzy Stawicki based on a Stanislaw Lem short story, *Przjaciel*, where atomic war has destroyed life on Earth, but life is continued elsewhere by robots.

With Piotr Kurowski and Josef Pieracki.

FROGS (1971) Rather pointless film, cleverly photographed, where the frogs become super-intelligent and organize other small life-forms to attack mankind on a small, isolated island.

| P★ | T★★ | E★ | A |

Directed by George McCowan. Written by Robert Hutchinson and Robert Blees. With Ray Milland, Sam Elliott and Joan Van Ark.

FROM HELL IT CAME (1957) Man framed and executed on his wife's evidence comes back to life as a walking tree and seeks revenge.

| P★ | T★ | E★★ | A |

Directed by Dan Milner. Written by Richard Bernstein. With Tod Andrews, Tina Carver, Linda Watkins and John McNamara.

FROM THE EARTH TO THE MOON (1958) Joseph Cotten stars in this mundane version of Verne's story of a one-way trip to the Moon.

| P★ | T★★ | E★ | A |

Directed by Byron Haskin. Written by Robert Bless and James Leicester. Special Effects by Lee Zavitz and Albert M. Simpson. With George Sanders, Debra Paget and Don Dubbins.

THE FROZEN DEAD (1966) One might see this as a ghoulish earlier version of *The Odessa File* as an ex-Nazi general plans to have a whole army of his soldiers, kept frozen in suspended animation, thawed out and re-animated, ready to fight for a new Reich.

| P★★ | T★★ | E★★ | A★ |

Produced, directed and written by Herbert J. Leder. With Dana Andrews, Kathleen Breck, Anna Palk and Philip Gilbert.

FUHARANKENSHUTAIN TAI BARAGON (1964) see FRANKENSTEIN CONQUERS THE WORLD (1964)

FUKKATSU NO HI (1980) see VIRUS (1980)

FURANKENSHUTAIN NO KAIJU — SANDA TAI GAIRA (1966) see WAR OF THE GARGANTUAS (1966)

THE FURY (1978) A rather muddled story about children with advanced ESP powers, pursued and manipulated by a mysterious government agency. Kirk Douglas plays the father of a boy kidnapped by these agents and made to believe that his father was brutally murdered by Arab terrorists (this belief fuels his "fury" and makes him, apparently, as dangerous as an atom bomb). A gory ending, followed by a nasty final twist, underline the moral message that you don't tinker with these forces, but otherwise it's all pretty directionless.

P★★	T★★★	E★★	A★

Directed by Brian De Palma. Written by John Farris (from his novel). Special Effects by A. D. Flowers and Rick Baker. With John Cassavetes.

FURY IN THE SKIES (1909) *see* THE AIRSHIP DESTROYER (1909)

FUTUREWORLD (1976) It seems that someone in Hollywood, back at the start of this movie's inauspicious career, stood up at a board meeting and said, "Look, fellas, we've got this successful movie called *Westworld*, see. It takes the theme of berserk robots, and somehow manages to do everything right, so why don't we make a sequel where we do everything *wrong!*" And off they went. They set it back in Delos, several years after the original massacre, but the futuristic adventureland has been changed completely. Gone are the western sets, the fairy-tale castle. Gone too are the humour, suspense, ingenuity, and rational plot. Instead, we have Peter Fonda and Blythe Danner as two journalists who smell a rat in the new set-up. Nothing can possibly go wrong, a recorded voice tells them at the entrance. The recorded voice has the best line of dialogue in the entire script, which is perhaps why Danner and Fonda, who are supposed to be the co-stars after all, wander around looking so bewildered; or perhaps it's because they find themselves in little more than a souped-up amusement arcade. The games they play on are clever enough but, for anyone over twelve years old, there's a law of diminishing returns.

P	T★★	E	A

Directed by Richard T. Heffron. Written by Mayo Simon and George Schenck. With Arthur Hill, Yul Brynner, John Ryan and Stuart Margolin.

FX-18, SUPERSPY (1965) *see* THE EXTERMINATORS (1965)

G

GALAXINA (1980) It is 3008 and the police cruiser 308, piloted by female robot Galaxina, is patrolling the edges of the galaxy. Galaxina (Dorothy R. Stratten) is a robot with feelings, a voluptuous creation who falls in love with Sgt Thor (Stephen Macht) and, on a 27-year journey to Altar 1, teaches herself to speak, changes her body temperature to human normal, removes her anti-human shock defence and gets a set of female sex organs from the catalogue, preparing herself for the man she loves when he comes out of Cryosleep. Before this gets too serious, I should mention that this is an out-and-out spoof of *2001* (q.v), *Star Wars* (q.v.) and *Star Trek* (q.v.) with nods and bows to *Alien* (q.v.), *Welcome To Blood City* (q.v.) and *Buck Rogers* (q.v.) along the way. And for once the end result is reasonably funny, as the crew go in search of the blue star (cue for angelic music). The scene in the Altar bar – a direct parody of the bar scene in *Star Wars* – is quite brilliant.

P★★	T★★★★	E★★★★	A★

Directed and written by William Sachs. Special Effects (Make-up) by Christopher J. Walas (Director) George Berndt/Chuck Colwell (Modelling) J. C. Buechler. With Avery Schreiber and James David Hinton.

THE GALAXY CRIMINALS (1965) *see* WILD WILD PLANET (1965)

GALAXY OF TERROR (1981) *see* MINDWARP: AN INFINITY OF TERROR (1981)

GALVANIC FLUID (1908) Professor Watt, star of *Liquid Electricity* (1907), makes a further discovery. Could be seen as a precursor of the two Flubber movies of the 1960s as the fluid makes things fly.

Produced and directed by J. Stuart Blackton.

GAMERA (1966) First of the adventures of the child-loving giant turtle. Here it is woken by an atomic blast, which thaws it out of the ice, and attacks the Japanese countryside. In sequels it was to be the saviour of that same countryside, much as Godzilla changed nature and thus sides.

P★	T★★	E★	A

Directed by Noriaki Yuasa. Written by Fumi Takahashi and Richard Kraft. With Eiji Funakoshi, Harumi Kiritachi and Brian Donlevy.

GAMERA TAI BARUGON (1966) *see* WAR OF THE MONSTERS (1966)

GAMERA TAI DAIMAJU JAIGA (1970) *see* GAMERA VS. MONSTER X (1970)

GAMERA TAI GYAOS (1967) *see* THE RETURN OF THE GIANT MONSTERS (1967)

GAMERA TAI SHINKAI KAIJU JIGURA (1971) *see* GAMERA VS. ZIGRA (1971)

GAMERA TAI UCHI KAIJO BAIRUSA (1968) *see* DESTROY ALL PLANETS (1968)

GAMERA TAI VIRAS (1968) *see* DESTROY ALL PLANETS (1968)

GAMERA THE INVINCIBLE (1966) *see* GAMERA (1966)

GAMERA VS. BARUGON (1966) *see* WAR OF THE MONSTERS (1966)

GAMERA VS. GUIRON (1969) *see* ATTACK OF THE MONSTERS (1969)

GAMERA VERSUS GYAS (1967) *see* THE RETURN OF THE GIANT MONSTERS (1967)

GAMERA VS. JIGER (1970) *see* GAMERA VS. MONSTER X (1970)

GAMERA VS. MONSTER X (1970) Nasty touch of parasitism creeps into this film, as Jiger, a giant iguana creature, invades Expo '70, lays eggs in Gamera's turtle-like body, and is foiled when two children go into Gamera's bloodstream in a tiny submarine, as in *Fantastic Voyage* (q.v.)

P★	T★★	E★	A

Directed by Noriaki Yuasa. Written by Fumi Takahashi. With Tsutomu Takakuwa, Kelly Varis, Katherine Murphy and Ken Omura.

GAMERA VS. OUTER SPACE MONSTER VIRAS (1968) *see* DESTROY ALL PLANETS (1968)

GAMERA VERSUS THE DEEP SEA MONSTER ZIGRA (1971) *see* GAMERA VS. ZIGRA (1971).

GAMERA VS. VIRAS (1968) *see* DESTROY ALL PLANETS (1968)

GAMERA VS. ZIGRA (1971) Zigra is a giant prehistoric fish from another star. Gamera, the turtle, who loves children, saves the Earth from the Zigrans. Yawn.

P	T★	E★	A

Directed by Noriaki Yuasa. Written by Fumi Takashi. With Ken Utsui and Yusuke Kawazu.

THE GAMMA PEOPLE (1955) A muted anti-Communist satire on Gudavia, where the state's leader is experimenting with gamma ray bombardment, whose unpredictability is producing a few geniuses and numerous morons.

P★★	T★★	E★★	A★

Directed by John Gilling. Written by Gilling and John Gossage. Special Cinematic Effects by Tom Howard. With Paul Douglas, Eva Bartok, Leslie Phillips, Walter Rilla and Martin Miller.

GAMMA SANGO UCHU DAI-SAKUSEN (1968) *see* THE GREEN SLIME (1968)

GAPPA, FRANKENSTEIN FLIEGEND MONSTER (1967) *see* MONSTER FROM A PREHISTORIC PLANET (1967)

GAPPA TRIPHIBIAN MONSTER
(1967) *see* MONSTER FROM A PRE-
HISTORIC PLANET (1967)

THE GARGON TERROR (1958) *see*
TEENAGERS FROM OUTER SPACE
(1958)

GARGOYLES (1972) Silly little mon-
ster movie about gargoyles who live to be
500 years old, inhabit a desert in S. W.
USA, and who aim to conquer the World.

P★	T★★	E★	A

Directed by B. W. L. Norton. Written by Stephen
and Elinor Karpf. Special Effects by Milt Rice and
George Peckham. With Cornel Wilde, Jennifer
Salt, Grayson Hall and Bernie Casey.

GARIBA NO UCHU RYOKO (1965)
see GULLIVER'S TRAVELS BEYOND
THE MOON (1965)

GAS NINGEN DAIICHIGO (1960)
see THE HUMAN VAPOR (1960)

GAS, OR IT BECAME NECES-
SARY TO DESTROY THE
WORLD IN ORDER TO SAVE IT
(1972) *see* GAS-S-S-S! (1972)

GAS-S-S-S! (1972) The youth cult
meets sf in this Roger-Corman-produced
and directed muddle. A poisonous gas
wipes out everyone over 25 (how?), but life
goes on as ever. The Apocalyptic end is
the final silly touch to a thoroughly awful
film.

P	T★★	E★	A

Written by George Armitage. With Robert Corff,
Elaine Giftos, Bud Cort and Talia Coppola.

LE GENDARME ET LES EXTRA-
TERRESTRES (1978) *see* THE
POLICEMAN AND THE EXTRA-
TERRESTRIALS (1978)

GENOCIDE (1968) *see* WAR OF IN-
SECTS (1968)

GHIDORAH, SANDAI KAIJU
CHIKYU SAIDDI NO KESSAN
(1965) *see* GHIDRAH, THE THREE-
HEADED MONSTER (1965)

GHIDRAH, THE THREE-
HEADED MONSTER (1965) Ghidrah
(or Ghidorah) is a three-headed, light-
ning-breathing, flying dragon-like monster who threatens Earth and is defeated
by a group of other Toho studios' monsters (Godzilla, Mothra and Co.). A lot
more fun than most of these Honda monster movies.

P★	T★★	E★★★	A★

Directed by Inoshiro Honda. Written by Shinichi
Sekizawa. Special Effects by Eiji Tsuburaya. With
Yosuke Natsuki, Yuriko Hoshi, Hiroshi Koizumi.

GHOSTBUSTERS (1984) By dealing
with ghosts not as a psychic phenomenon
– and thus in the realm of the intangible –
but as manifestations of a breakthrough
from a different dimension, *Ghostbusters*
allows itself to be considered as science
fiction; a hybrid of 1930s scientifiction and
modern-day *Animal House*-style humour.
The comedy for once heavily outweighs
the horror/sf, and that's a good thing
here. To take any of this too seriously
would be an admission of rampant insanity
or, at least, crankish kookiness. But we're
not really asked to suspend disbelief and
the wise-cracking scepticism of "ghost-
buster" Pete Venkman (Bill Murray) dis-
arms any objections we might have had
towards the cranky plot. Add to this the
fact that the superb special effects (and
there's humour in these, too!) convince us
that such madness *just might* be possible,
and we have a rather unique film. Not, in
its parts, original, but in its totality –
unique. So what's the story? Three investigators of the Paranormal, researching at
the University in New York, are called in
to deal with a psychic occurrence in the
New York Public Library one afternoon
and encounter a floating apparition of an
old woman reading one of the books.
When they go to grab her she turns on
them in the form of a hideous ghoul. This,
the film's most horrific and genuinely
shocking moment, convinces them (and
us?) that something strange is happening
in New York. It's the first sign of a build-
up of psychic energy. Only the University's finance committee remain uncon-
vinced, however, and the three are thrown

Left to right: Bill Murray, Dan Aykroyd and Harold Ramis in Ghostbusters

out of their cosy research job. But on the strength of that first contact they decide to go into business as "Ghostbusters", "Professional Paranormal Investigations and Eliminations" as they bill it. It's seemingly risky, but soon they've more work than they can adequately handle. Venkman has got involved with a female client, Dana Barrett, who discovered that her fridge was being used as a doorway to another dimension – a gateway through which Zuul and, eventually, the ancient god Gozer, are to arrive. She becomes Zuul, taken over by the ancient gatekeeper. The boys, meanwhile, are trapping blobs and ghosts and nasties all over town and storing them, but an over-zealous safety inspector switches off their store and lets the mass of psychic weirdies loose again – to play havoc with New Yorkers. Things are building to a head at the apartment block and Dana (Sigourney Weaver) and a near neighbour, Mr Tully (an accountant, played by Rick Moranis), have got together as gatekeeper and key (a lovely, obviously sexual innuendo) to let Gozer through into the world. But the ghostbusters (including their new black recruit) are there with their special nuclear accelerators to stop Gozer from entering our world. In one of the film's most delightful moments she asks them to choose what form she will enter our world as. They try to blank their minds, but Ray Stantz (Dan Aykroyd) thinks of a childhood form, and so Gozer enters our world – as the Stay-Puft Marshmallow Man, only 200 feet tall.

By a bit of jiggery-pokery (they cross their neutron streams) they roast the Stay-Puft Gozer (hot marshmallow flies everywhere!) and save the day – to general applause from the New Yorkers. Special effects and humour give substance to an otherwise insubstantial tale which seems a refugee from a 1930s *Weird Tales* issue. Anyway, normal standards of criticism don't apply here. Hugely enjoyable!

P★★★   T★★★★★   E★★★★★   A★★

Directed by Ivan Reitman. Written by Dan Aykroyd and Harold Ramis. Special Effects by Richard Edlund. With Harold Ramis.

THE GHOST OF FRANKENSTEIN (1942) This picks up the threads of *Son of Frankenstein* (1939), lifts the monster from the sulphur pit (a miracle enough in itself!) and lets him loose again. A thoroughly dumb exploitation of the Frankenstein myth.

P   T★★   E★   A

Directed by Erle C. Kenton. Written by W. Scott Darling. Make-up by Jack P. Pierce. With Cedric Hardwicke, Ralph Bellamy, Lionel Atwill, Bela Lugosi, Evelyn Ankers, Eddie Parker and Lon Chaney Jr (as the monster).

THE GIANT BEHEMOTH (1958) Willis O'Brien had a hand in this giant-prehistoric-type-monster-threatens-London movie. This behemoth can, however, kill by radiation rays, with a glance.

P★   T★★   E★★   A★

Directed by Eugene Lourie and Douglas Hickok. Written by Lourie. Special Effects by Jack Rabin, Irving Block, Louis DeWitt and Pete Petterson. With Gene Evans and Andre Morell.

THE GIANT CLAW (1957) Years later *Q, The Winged Serpent* (q.v.) was to make good this dreadful tale of an inter-planetary buzzard (the original golden turkey?) which lands and makes its nest in New York. Even the dumb-looking bird's force field couldn't protect it from the derision of most audiences.

P   T   E★   A

Directed by Fred F. Sears. Written by Samuel Newman and Paul Gangelin. With Jeff Morrow, Mara Corday and Morris Ankrum.

THE GIANT GILA MONSTER
(1959) Second-rate even for a B-movie, this isn't even graced with an explanation of where the slimy came from. Acting, sets and special effects are equally dire.

| P | T | E | A |

Directed by Ray Kellogg. Written by Kellogg and Jay Sims. Special Effects by Ralph Hammeras and Wee Risser. With Don Sullivan, Lisa Simone, Shug Fisher and Beverly Thurman.

THE GIANT LEECHES (1959)
Uninspired creature-feature about man-sized leeches from a Florida swamp that attack and kill people.

| P | T★ | E★ | A |

Executive Producer Roger Corman. Directed by Bernard L. Kowalski. Written by Leo Gordon. With Ken Clark and Yvette Vickers.

THE GIANT OF METROPOLIS
(1962) A tale of Atlantis in 10,000 b.c., before it sank. The picture itself sinks early on, leaving the trite gadgetry and mad scientist plot clinging to the wreckage.

| P | T★ | E★ | A |

Directed by Umberto Scarpelli. Written by Sabatino Cuiffino, Oreste Palella, Ambrogio Molteni, Gino Stafford and E. Salvi. With Gordon Mitchell, Bella Carter, Roldano Lupi and Liani Orfei.

THE GIANT SPIDER INVASION
(1975) Radiation-mutated giant spiders attack small town and are defeated by cunning of brave young teenage couple. Seen this one before?

| P | T★ | E | A |

Directed by Bill Rebane. Written by Richard L. Huff and Robert Easton. Special Effects by Richard Albain and Robert Millay. With Barbara Hale, Steve Brodie and Leslie Parrish.

THE GIANT YMIR (1957) see
TWENTY MILLION MILES TO EARTH (1957)

GIBEL SENSATY (1935) see LOSS OF FEELING (1935)

IL GIGANTE DI METROPOLIS
(1962) see THE GIANT OF METROPOLIS (1962)

GIGANTES PLANETARIOS (1963)
see PLANETARY GIANTS (1963)

GIGANTIS, THE FIRE MONSTER
(1955) Godzilla (here called Gigantis) fights monster Angurus on the island where they were awoken by A-bomb blasts, wins, then ravages the countryside, heading towards Tokyo. Formula stuff from the Toho studio.

| P★ | T★ | E★ | A |

Directed by Motoyoshi Odo. Written by Takeo Murata and Sugeaki Hidaka. Special Effects by Eiji Tsuburaya, Akira Watanebe, Hiroshi Mukoyama and Masso Shirota. With Hiroshi Koizumi, Yukio Kasama and Setsuko Wakayama.

THE GILL WOMEN (1966) see
VOYAGE TO THE PLANET OF PREHISTORIC WOMEN (1966)

GILL WOMEN OF VENUS (1966)
see VOYAGE TO THE PLANET OF PREHISTORIC WOMEN (1966)

GIPERBOLOID INGENERA GARINA (1965) see THE HYPERBOLOID OF ENGINEER GARIN (1965)

GIRARA (1967) see THE X FROM OUTER SPACE (1967)

THE GIRL FROM 5000 A.D. (1958)
see TERROR FROM THE YEAR 5000 (1958)

GIRL IN HIS POCKET (1957) Based
on the short story, "The Diminishing Draft", by Waldemar Kaempffert, this is an innocuous comedy on the Shrinking Woman theme involving jealousy and rivalry between two women (one the shrunken pocket-sized girl).

| P★ | T★★ | E★★ | A |

Directed by Pierre Kast. Written by France Roche. With Jean Marais and Agnes Laurent.

GIRL IN THE MOON (1929) see BY ROCKET TO THE MOON (1929)

THE GIRL OF TIN (1970) see THE TIN GIRL (1970)

GIVE US THE MOON (1944) Mild-mannered near-future comedy about a time after the war's end when, conditions being right, it will be possible to choose whether or not to work. From the novel *The Elephant Is White* by Caryl Brahms and S. J. Simon.

P★★	T★	E★★	A★

Directed and written by Val Guest. With Margaret Lockwood, Vic Oliver, Peter Graves, Jean Simmons, Roland Culver and Irene Handl.

THE GLADIATOR (1938) A rather flippant adaptation of a weak novel, Philip Wylie's *The Gladiator*, where a strength-creating serum makes a wimp into a super-strong athlete. Mildly charming.

P★	T★★	E★	A

Directed by Edward Sedgwick. Written by Charlie Melson and Arthur Sheekman. With Joe E. Brown, June Travis and Dickie Moore.

GLADIATORENA (1969) *see* THE GLADIATORS (1969)

THE GLADIATORS (1969) This film has one of those premises which is not subtle enough to work *except* as an sf story: a future world where conflict is resolved by gladiatorial teams rather than full-blooded warfare. Peter Watkins's attempt to convince fails abysmally.

P★	T★★	E★	A★

Directed by Peter Watkins. Written by Watkins and Nicholas Goshing. Special Effects by Stig Lindberg. With Arthur Pentelow, Frederick Danner, Kenneth Lo and Bjorn Franzen.

GLEN AND RANDA (1971) Something of an Adam and Eve story set in post-Holocaust America, with Glen and Randa leaving their natural Edenic home to go in search of the lost city of Metropolis. Director Jim McBride effectively conveys the emptiness of the "wondrous" thing – civilization – that they in their innocence seek.

P★★★	T★★	E★★	A★★

Written by McBride, Lorenzo Mans, Rudolph Wurlitzer. With Steven Curry, Shelley Plimpton, Woodrow Chambliss and Garry Goodrow.

THE GLITTERBALL (1977) A small, shiny, spherical alien is stranded on Earth. Children help reunite it with its alien parents/mother ship. A nice little film from the Children's Film Foundation.

P★★	T★★	E★★	A★

Directed by Harley Cockliss. Written by Howard Thompson. Special Effects by Brian Johnson and Charles Page. With Ben Buckton, Keith Jayne, Ron Pember, Marjorie Yates, Barry Jackson and Andrew Jackson.

GLUMP (1972) *see* PLEASE DON'T EAT MY MOTHER (1972)

GO AND GET IT (1920) A mad scientist puts a dead convict's brain into a gorilla's body. The demented gorilla then goes on a revenge rampage. Not as poor a film as its bare plot synopsis makes it sound.

Directed by Marshall Neilan and Henry R. Symonds. Written by Marion Fairfax. With Pat O'Malley, Wesley Barry, Agnes Ayres, Noah Beery and Bull Montana.

GOD BLESS THE BOMB (1971) *see* WILD IN THE SKY (1971)

GOD SELECTED HIS TRAVELLERS (1964) *see* THE UNKNOWN HOUR (1964)

GODZILLA FIGHTS THE GIANT MOTH (1964) *see* GODZILLA VERSUS MOTHRA (1964)

GODZILLA, KING OF THE MONSTERS (1954) First of more than a dozen features in which Godzilla, a 400-foot prehistoric monster awakened by an A-bomb test blast (or a man in a rubber suit if you prefer to view this as comedy), tramples his way across the Japanese countryside towards Tokyo. Why Tokyo? Well, it's traditional, part of the Kaiju Eiga, the monster movie ethos. And when he's killed at the end, he's never really utterly and irrevocably dead. Just playing possum (in a rubber suit) until the Toho studios can think of another inane plot-line for him (or re-utilize one they've done already). Pure juvenile pap which, unaccountably, was highly popular with American audiences, too, when the film was released there (featuring Raymond Burr as a reporter) in 1956. I cannot, for the life of me, understand why these *are* popular.

P★	T★★	E★	A

Directed by Inoshiro Honda. Written by Honda and Takeo Murata. Special Effects by Eiji Tsuburaya, Akira Watanabe, Hiroshi Mukoyama and Kuichiro Kishida. With Akira Takarada, Akihiko Hirata, Takashi Shimura and Momoko Kochi.

GODZILLA NO GYAKUSHYU
(1955) *see* GIGANTIS, THE FIRE MONSTER (1955)

GODZILLA RADON KINGIDORAH (1956) *see* MONSTER ZERO (1965)

GODZILLA RAIDS AGAIN (1955)
see GIGANTIS, THE FIRE MONSTER (1955)

GODZILLA'S COUNTERATTACK (1955) *see* GIGANTIS, THE FIRE MONSTER (1955)

GODZILLA'S REVENGE (1969)
Most of the Godzilla series are dreadful; this gets a five-star rating for being superdreadful, being a child's daydreams of being on Monster Island with daddy and baby Godzilla.

P	T★	E	A

Directed by Inoshiro Honda. Written by Shinichi Sekizawa. Special Effects by Eiji Tsuburaya. With Kenji Sahara and Tomonori Yazaki.

GODZILLA VERSUS HEDORA
(1971) Godzilla's eleventh bout has him up against a smog monster that feeds on industrial pollution. He wins, but then who cares?

P	T★	E	A

Directed by Yoshimitsu Banno. Written by Banno and Kaoru Mabuchi. Special Effects by Shokei Nakano. With Akira Tamanchi, Toshie Kimura and Hiroyuki Kawase.

GODZILLA VERSUS MEGALON
(1973) The 13th appearance of the 400-foot atomic dinosaur has him fighting a giant cockroach. Imagine being infested with these darlings? Megalon, the cockroach, is also helped by Borodan, a giant black chicken. All of this happens underground and is part of an awful revenge plot by an underground race, the Seatopians. Even if the special effects are better than usual, this is nonetheless utter drivel.

P	T★★	E	A

Directed by Jun Fukuda. Written by Fukuda and Shinichi Sekizawa. With Katsuhiko Sasaki, Hiroyuki Kawase and Yutaka Hayashi.

GODZILLA VERSUS MOTHRA
(1964) The 400-foot tyrannosaurus rex fights the giant moth. Or would do, if Mothra was not dying anyway. Godzilla has to put up with being snared in the silken nets of her caterpillar offspring.

P★	T★	E★	A

Directed by Inoshiro Honda. Written by Shinichi Sekizawa. Special Effects by Eiji Tsuburaya, Sadamasa Arikawa, Mototaka Tomioka and Akira Watanabe. With Akira Takarada, Yuriko Hoshi, Hiroshi Koisumi, Emi Ito and Yumi Ito.

GODZILLA VERSUS THE BIONIC MONSTER (1974) Tiresome addition to the unending Godzilla series (no. 14 to be precise). Alien invaders create a robot replica of Big G for him to fight. A touch of magic and pure sf fails to lift this from the usual monster clichés.

P	T★	E	A

Directed by Jun Fukuda. Written by Fukuda and Hiroyasu Yamamura. Special Effects by Shokei Nakano. With Masaki Daimon, Kazuya Aoyama, Akihiko Hirata and Hiroshi Koizumi.

GODZILLA VERSUS THE GIANT MOTH (1964) *see* GODZILLA VERSUS MOTHRA (1964)

GODZILLA VERSUS THE SEA MONSTER (1966) Ebirah, the evil giant shrimp, pops up out of the waves and gets ready to threaten Tokyo, but Godzilla, that baddie-turned-good, won't let him. Unintelligent pap.

P	T★	E	A

Directed by Jun Fukuda. Written by Shinichi Sekizawa. Special Effects by Eiji Tsuburaya. With Akira Takarada and Toru Watanabe.

GODZILLA VERSUS THE SMOG MONSTER (1971) *see* GODZILLA VERSUS HEDORA (1971)

GODZILLA VERSUS THE THING (1964) *see* GODZILLA VERSUS MOTHRA (1964)

GOG (1954) Gog and Magog are appendages of the super-computer NOVACS, non-humanoid robots which, mysteriously, are slowly destroying the space lab they work at and murdering the scientists there. A slow-paced thriller.

P★★	T★★	E★	A

Directed by Herbert L. Strock. Written by Tom Taggart. Special Effects by Harry Redmond Jr. With Richard Egan, Constance Dowling, Herbert Marshall, John Wengraf and Philip Van Zandt.

GOJIRA (1954) *see* GODZILLA, KING OF THE MONSTERS (1954)

GOJIRA NO GYAKUSHYU (1955) *see* GIGANTIS, THE FIRE MONSTER (1955)

GOJIRA TAI GAIGAN (1972) *see* WAR OF THE MONSTERS (1972)

GOJIRA TAI MEGALON (1973) *see* GODZILLA VERSUS MEGALON (1973)

GOJIRA TAI MEKGOJIRA (1974) *see* GODZILLA VERSUS THE BIONIC MONSTER (1974)

GOKE, BODY SNATCHER FROM HELL (1968) Alien take-over story of an unspectacular kind. An airliner passes through a cloud of alien substance and people in the plane are changed into vampires. Today Japan, tomorrow the World.

P★	T★	E★	A

Directed by Hajime Sato. Written by Susumi Tahaku and Kyuzu Kobayashi. With Hideo Ko, Teru Yoshida and Tomoni Sato.

GOKE THE VAMPIRE (1968) *see* GOKE, BODY SNATCHER FROM HELL (1968)

GOLDEN EARRINGS (1947) Ray Milland stars as a fake mind-reader who suddenly finds himself cursed with the gift of genuine precognition.

P★★	T★★	E★★	A★

Directed by Mitchell Leisen. Written by Abraham Polonsky, Frank Butler and Helen Deutsch. Special Effects by Gordon Jennings. With Marlene Dietrich, Murvyn Wye and Quentin Reynolds.

GOLDFINGER (1964) Easily the best of the early Bond films, with Connery in action against villainous Gert Frobe, who plans to make Fort Knox radioactive. Scriptwriters Richard Maibaum and Paul Dehn hit a peak of inventiveness for the series with an astonishing heavy called Oddjob, an Aston Martin equipped with every lethal device bar a nuclear capability, and, of course, that famous murdered girl painted entirely gold.

P★	T★★★	E★★★★★	A

Directed by Guy Hamilton. From the novel by Ian Fleming. Special Effects by John Stears and Frank George. With Honor Blackman, Harold Sakata, Shirley Eaton and Bernard Lee. (TR)

A GOOD BED (1899) *see* A MIDNIGHT EPISODE (1899)

GORATH (1962) One of Toho studios worst cinematic excursions. A runaway planet is heading for Earth, a space monster has been brought back by a rocketship and the attempts to shift Earth's orbit have caused huge earthquakes and a giant walrus-like monster.

P	T★	E★	A

Directed by Inoshiro Honda. Written by Takeshi Kimura. Special Effects by Eiji Tsuburaya. With Ryo Ikebe, Jun Tazaki and Akiko Hirata.

GORGO (1959) A cheapie British version of Godzilla. A trawler finds an undersea monster tangled in its nets and takes it back to London for display in a circus. What no one realizes is the creature is only a baby, and then its ten-times-larger mother comes looking for it. Frequently screened on late-night TV, it's just the kind of enjoyable trash to tide viewers through until the wee hours.

P	T★★	E★★★★★	A

Directed by Eugene Lourie. Written by John Loring and Daniel Hyatt. Special Effects by Tom Howard. With Bill Travers, William Sylvester, Vincent Winter and Christopher Rhodes. (TR)

GORUNMIYEN ADAM INSTAN-BULDA (1956) see INVISIBLE MAN IN ISTANBUL (1956)

THE GORY CREATURES (1959) see TERROR IS A MAN (1959)

GOSTI IZ GALAKSIJE (1981) see VISITORS FROM THE GALAXY (1981)

GRAVE ROBBERS FROM OUTER SPACE (1956) see PLAN 9 FROM OUTER SPACE (1956)

THE GREAT BET (1915) An early sf comedy about robots in the decadent America of the year 2000.

Directed by Harry Piel. With Mizzi Wirth, Ludwig Hartmann and Harry Piel.

THE GREAT BIG WORLD AND LITTLE CHILDREN (1962) Polish feature with three small stories for children, the last depicting a post-Holocaust world, Vega.

P★	T★★	E★★	A★

Directed by Anna Sokolowska. Written by Sokolowska and Jerzy Broszkiewicz. With Kinja Sienko and Woychiech Purzynski.

THE GREATEST BATTLE ON EARTH (1965) see GHIDRAH, THE THREE-HEADED MONSTER (1965)

THE GREATEST GIFT (1946) see IT'S GREAT TO BE ALIVE (1946)

THE GREATEST POWER (1917) Moralistic tale of a chemist's discoveries, one a cancer cure, the other a super-explosive, "exonite", which he plans to give to every nation so that no one will dare use it. In these more sophisticated days we sense the naivety of such a message.

Directed by Edwin Carewe. Written by Albert Shelby Le Vino. With Ethel Barrymore, William B. Davidson and Harry S. Northrup.

THE GREAT GAMBLER — AN IMAGE OF OUR TIME (1922) see DR MABUSE, THE GAMBLER (1922)

GREAT MONSTER YONGARI (1967) see YONGKARI, MONSTER FROM THE DEEP (1967)

THE GREEN SLIME (1968) Triffids in space, as Earth is first saved from collision with a meteor, then threatened by the green slime creatures who almost take over a space station.Strangely enjoyable, if decidedly minor.

P★	T★★	E★★	A★

Directed by Kinji Fukasaku. Written by Charles Sinclair, William Finger and Tom Rowe. Special Effects by Akira Watanabe. With Robert Horton, Richard Jaeckel and Luciana Paluzzi.

THE GREEN TERROR (1919) A film without gimmicks which, in its premise, is far better science fiction than most films of the time. Based on a story by Edgar Wallace, *The Green Rust*, it is an account of how a German scientist plans to decimate the rest of the world's wheat.

Directed by Will P. Kellino. Written by G. W. Clifford. With Aurele Sydney.

GREMLINS (1984) Spielberg movie with many of the ingredients that we associate with his work: comic family scenes, pathos, horror, juvenile protagonists. Unfortunately, this time the elements do not fit together well. On the one hand the sentimentality gushes over the top and on the other the violence is gratuitous and unnecessarily extreme. A wacky inventor finds a creature, which appears to be a cross between a koala, a flying fox and a nightingale, and gives it to his son. The instructions for its care include not letting it eat after midnight and keeping it away from water, both of which are of course disregarded. The result is a plague of demons, which destroy the town. Some of the characters in the film are on a level with a bad Walt Disney cartoon – the spinster who is cruel to dogs and the girl whose father dresses as Santa Claus and dies climbing down

the chimney. The film does not seem to be able to make up its mind whether it wants to be whimsy, black comedy or horror and the mix is not satisfactory.

P★★★	T★★★★	E★★	A

Directed by Joe Dante. Written by Chris Columbus. With Zach Galligan, Phoebe Cates, Hoyt Axton, Polly Holliday. (GDK)

GRITOS EN LA NOCHE (1961) see THE AWFUL DR ORLOFF (1961)

EIN GROSSE GRAU-BLAUER VOGEL (1970) see A BIG GREY-BLUE BIRD (1970)

DER GROSSE SPIELER – EIN BILD DER ZEIT (1922) see DR MABUSE, THE GAMBLER (1922)

DIE GROSSE WETTE (1915) see THE GREAT BET (1915)

THE GROUNDSTAR CONSPIRACY (1972) After a remarkable and memorable opening, this film settles down to tell an intelligent if familiar story, a hybrid of *Who?* (q.v.) and *Frankenstein* (q.v.), structured like a thriller. A high-security space project is breached and its headquarters blown up; Michael Sarrazin plays the reconstructed victim who might know why and by whom.

P★★	T★★	E★★	A★

Directed by Lamont Johnson. Written by Mathew Howard. Special Effects by Herbert Ewing. With George Peppard, Christine Belford and Cliff Potts.

GUGUSSE ET L'AUTOMATE (1897) see THE CLOWN AND THE AUTOMATON (1897)

GUILALA (1967) see THE X FROM OUTER SPACE (1967)

GUIRARA (1967) see THE X FROM OUTER SPACE (1967)

GULLIVER'S TRAVELS BEYOND THE MOON (1965) Animated feature updating the Gulliver story. Gulliver and a small boy go by spaceship to a planet

beyond the Moon where they encounter both good and bad robots. Sub-Disney.

P★	T★★	E★	A

Directed by Yoshio Kuroda. Written by Shinichi Sekizawa.

GWANGI (1968) see THE VALLEY WHERE TIME STOOD STILL (1968)

THE HALF-WIT (1916) Advanced surgical techniques make it possible for a moron to become normal.

Directed by Wilbert Melville. Written by Arthur Peterman. With L. C. Shumway and Helen Eddy.

HALLOWEEN III: SEASON OF THE WITCH (1983) One of a new generation of cross-bred hybrids of horror and sf. An Irish manufacturer of practical jokes and halloween masks, based in the USA, plans to return America to the 3,000-year old ways of the Druids – with a massive child sacrifice. Chippings from Stonehenge, micro-lasers and a town run by toy replicas of men are the elements in this messy addition to the series.

P★★	T★★★	E★★	A★

Directed and written by Tommy Lee Wallace. Special Make-up by Tom Burman. With Tom Atkins, Stacey Nelkin and Dan O'Herlihy.

HAND OF DEATH (1961) Experiments on a new nerve gas cause a scientist (John Agar) to possess a touch which kills. They also change his looks for the worse, making him a monster.

P★	T★	E★	A

Directed by Gene Nelson. Written by Eugene Ling. Make-up by Bob Mark. With Paula Raymond, Steve Dunne and Ray Gordon.

THE HAND OF PERIL (1916) A criminal thriller involving a government agent who has a device which can see through walls.

Directed and written by Maurice Tourneur. With House Peters, June Elvidge and Ralph Delmore.

HANDS OF A KILLER (1961) see PLANETS AGAINST US (1961)

HANDS OF A STRANGER (1960)

Seemingly an updated reinterpretation of *The Hands Of Orlac* (1925) (q.v.), where the grafting of a new pair of hands on to the severed wrists of a concert pianist slowly turns him into a killer.

P★★	T★	E★★	A★

Directed and written by Newton Arnold. With Paul Lukather, Joan Harvey and Irish McCalla.

THE HANDS OF ORLAC (1925) A

concert pianist, Orlac (Conrad Veidt), loses his hands and has a new pair grafted to his arms – those of a convicted murderer. Orlack, previously a relatively good man, is corrupted by his new hands. From Maurice Renard's novel *Les Mains d'Orlac*. It was re-made as *Mad Love* in 1935.

P★★	T★★	E★★	A★

Directed by Robert Wiene. Written by Louis Nerz. With Fritz Kortner, Carmen Cartellieri, Alexander Sorina and Paul Askonas.

THE HANDS OF ORLAC (1935) see MAD LOVE (1935)

HANGAR 18 (1980) America's late-

1970s conspiracy theories here encompass a cover-up which gets out of hand after a UFO collides with a satellite launched from the space shuttle. The UFO is taken to Hangar 18 in Texas to be investigated, whilst the two astronauts are (unaccountably) blamed for the satellite accident (which resulted in the death of their colleague). Robert Vaughn as the President's aide wants to hush things up (as the President scoffs at UFOs and the election is two weeks off) but fails miserably, eventually bombing the hangar, but not destroying either the UFO or the investigating team – who have meanwhile discovered an alien plan to conquer the Earth. Slow-paced and crammed full of illogical events (why don't the CIA put the astronauts into quarantine for two weeks if they're worried about them?), this is a mixture of *All The President's Men*, a cynical *Close Encounters* (q.v.) and a touch or

two of Erich Von Daniken thrown in for good measure. A film for UFO nuts.

P★★	T★★★	E★★	A★

Directed by James L. Conway. Written by Steven Thornley (from a story by Conway and Tom Chapman). With Gary Collins, James Hampton, Phillip Abbott and Joseph Campanella.

THE HAPPINESS CAGE (1972) see THE MIND SNATCHERS (1972)

HAPPINESS IS A THREE-LEGGED DOG (1967) Australian short

about a totalitarian future society.

Directed and written by Anthony Airey.

HAUNTED PLANET (1965) see PLANET OF THE VAMPIRES (1965)

THE HAUNTING AT CASTLE MONTEGO (1966) see CASTLE OF EVIL (1966)

HAUSER'S MEMORY (1970) Hau-

ser, a dying Nazi scientist, donates some of his brain fluid for an experiment. The recipient of the fluid, a Jewish intellectual, inherits some of Hauser's memories. An intelligent thriller – in search of the dead man's scientific secrets – this is based on Curt Siodmak's novel.

P★★	T★★	E★★	A★

Directed by Boris Sagal. Written by Adrian Spies. With David McCallum, Susan Strasberg, Lilli Palmer and Robert Webber.

HAVE ROCKET WILL TRAVEL

(1959) A gimmick-ridden film starring the Three Stooges. Here they travel to Venus where they encounter giant spiders, a robot, a speaking unicorn and so forth. It's a forced comic exploitation of the genre.

P★	T★	E★★	A

Directed by David Lowell Rich. Written by Raphael Hayes. With Moe Howard, Larry Fine, Joe De Rita, Jerome Cowan and Anna Lisa.

THE HEAD (1959) The inventor of

Serum-2, which keeps severed portions of the human body alive, finds the tables turned upon him and has his own head kept alive. The inevitable laboratory accident ends his misery in this better than usual working of the theme.

P★★   T★★   E★★   A★

Directed and written by Victor Trivas. Special Effects by Theo Nischwitz. With Horst Frank, Michel Simon, Karin Kernke and Paul Dahlke.

A HEAD FOR THE DEVIL (1959) see THE HEAD (1959)

THE HEAD THAT WOULDN'T DIE (1959) see THE BRAIN THAT WOULDN'T DIE (1959)

HEARTBEEPS (1981) An enchanting, if slow-paced, future comedy in which two service robots, Aqua and Val, fall in love, run away, literally make themselves a child, and generally try to cope with a world in which they aren't permitted personal feelings. Add to that mixture Uncle CatSkil, a wise-cracking Jewish robot comedian and a script about as sentimental as *The Wizard of Oz* (1939) (q.v.) – to which this film occasionally seems to nod – then you have something rather unique in the sf cinema.

P★★★   T★★★   E★★★★   A★★

Directed by Allan Arkrush. Written by John Hill. Special Effects by Robert Blalack, Jamie Shourt and Albert Whitlock. With Andy Kaufman, Bernadette Peters, Barry Diamond, Randy Quaid and Kenneth McMillan.

Andy Kaufman and Bernadette Peters as the two robots Aqua and Val In Heartbeeps

HEAVEN ON ONE'S HEAD (1964) see SKY ABOVE HEAVEN (1964)

THE HEAVENS CALL (1959) Good special effects mark this out as superior to the comparable American product, but the tale of travel to the Moon and Mars is slow.

P★   T★★★   E★★   A★★

Directed by Aleksandra Kozyr and Mikhail Karyukov. Written by A. Sazanov and J. Pmieszczykov. With Ivan Pereverzev, Alexander Shworin Taisa Litvienenko and Konstantin Bartashevich.

HEAVEN SHIP (1917) see THE SKY SHIP (1917)

HEAVY METAL (1981) By the nature of the film there was bound to be a mixed response to this: adoration or loathing, with little ground between. There's no doubting that the animation and general standard of the graphics (derived from the French sf comic magazine, *Metal Hurlant*) is exceptional. What's in question is the concept of eight cobbled-together stories linked only by the desire of a glowing green sphere (the Loch Nar) to conquer all Space and Time. If you like comic-books this is fine, and you'll probably find *Heavy Metal* one of the best things in cinema, but if you don't then you might tire easily of this glossy confection. There's a lot of icing and little cake, you see. Its longest sequence is *Taarna*, pure sword-and-sorcery of the John Norman school of gore; though the much-needed dose of (sometimes sick) humour evident elsewhere is strangely lacking here. If you don't like heavy metal *music* the soundtrack too will probably pass you by.

P★   T★★★★★   E★★★   A★★

Directed by Gerald Potterton, Jimmy T. Murakami, Harold Whitaker, Pino Van Lamsweerde, Jack Stokes, Paul Sabella, Julian Szuchopa, Barrie Nelson, John Halas and John Bruno. Written by Dan Goldberg and Len Blum. Animation/Graphics by Angus McKie, Thomas Warkentin, Bernie Wrightson, Richard Corben, Juan Gimenez and Lee Mishkin.

THE HELL CREATURES (1957) see INVASION OF THE SAUCER MEN (1957)

HELP, I'M INVISIBLE (1952) Mediocre German comedy about a nondescript man whose life is changed (so what?) when he accidentally becomes invisible.

| P★ | T★ | E | A |

Directed by E. W. Emo. Written by Herbert Tjadens, Erwin Kreker and Kurt Werner. With Theodor Lingen and Grethe Weiser.

HENRY, THE RAINMAKER (1949) Based on D. D. Beauchamp's story, "The Rainmaker", this is a simple little tale of Henry, who made it start raining ... but can't make it stop.

| P★★ | T★★ | E★★ | A★ |

Directed by Jean Yarbrough. Written by Lane Beauchamp. With Raymond Walburn, Walter Catlett, William Tracy and Mary Stuart.

HERCULES (1983) Ancient myth meets modern-day technology as Hercules (Lou Ferrigno) takes on a series of robot adversaries (in various shapes and sizes) in order to save the Princess (Sybil Danning) and make the galaxy safe for decent iron-pumpers.

| P★ | T★★★ | E★★ | A |

Directed and written by Lewis Coates. With Mirella D'Angelo, Ingrid Anderson and William Berger.

HERCULES AGAINST THE MOON MEN (1965) An sf/sword-and-sorcery mixture as Maciste (Hercules) battles the Moonmen (stone robots) to save the land of Samar and its royalty.

| P★ | T★ | E★ | A |

Directed by Giacomo Gentilomo. Written by Arpad De Riso, Nino Scolaro, Giacomo Gentilomo and Angelo Sangarmano. Special Effects by Ugo Amadoro. With Sergio Ciani, Jany Clair, Anna-Maria Polani and Nando Tamberlani.

HER INVISIBLE HUSBAND (1916) Another comic twist on the invisible man theme, this time with the husband's identity mistaken for a dead man – he watches his own funeral.

Directed by Matt Moore. Written by Samuel Greiner. With Matt Moore and Jane Gail.

DER HERR DER WELT (1934) *see* MASTER OF THE WORLD (1934)

HERRIN DER VELT (1959) *see* MISTRESS OF THE WORLD (1959)

HE WAS CALLED ROBERT (1967) *see* CALL ME ROBERT (1967)

H. G. WELLS' NEW INVISIBLE MAN (1957) *see* THE NEW INVISIBLE MAN (1957)

H. G. WELLS' THE SHAPE OF THINGS TO COME (1979) Somewhere between the title and the opening shots, H. G. Wells was discarded. Earth has been devastated by robot wars and Man's main base is on the Moon. Radioactive-sick humans are dependent on RADIC-Q-2, a miracle drug found only on planet Delta Three. Would-be dictator Omas (Jack Palance) has taken over D3 with robots, against which Nikki (Carol Linley) and her forces fight with spears and shields. A mission of four go to aid her from the Moon, stopping off at Earth halfway there for repairs. This kind of anomaly is indicative of the whole, weak plot-structure. Special effects are poor, using obviously moulded plastic models against stills. Strange anachronistic mixtures of steam boiler rooms and omnipotent computers weaken already weak settings. Six-year-old children who have apparently raised themselves from birth in Earth's woods are inserted for pathos. A village hall production of *Star Trek*.

| P★ | T | E★ | A |

Directed by George McCowan. Written by Martin Lager. Special Effects by Wally Gentleman and Bill Wood. With Barry Morse, Nicholas Campbell, John Ireland and Eddie Benton. (GDK)

THE HIDDEN VALLEY (1957) *see* THE LAND UNKNOWN (1957)

THE HIDEOUS SUN DEMON (1959) A scientist is contaminated by radiation and, when exposed to sunlight, becomes a man-killing lizard creature.

| P★ | T★ | E★ | A |

Directed by Robert Clarke and Thomas Cassarino. Written by E. S. Seeley Jr and Doane Hoag. With Robert Clarke, Patricia Manning, Alan Peterson and Patrick Whyte.

HIGH TREASON (1929) Set 11 years in the future, when television was common and a channel tunnel in existence, the President of the United States kills the leader of a United Europe and then offers himself up for trial – all to prevent a disastrous war. Shabby stuff.

P★	T★	E★	· A

Directed by Maurice Elvey. Written by L'Estrange Fawcett. With Benita Hume, Basil Gill, Humberston Wright, Jameson Thomas, Milton Rosmer, Henry Vibart and Raymond Massey.

LA HIJA DE FRANKENSTEIN (1971) see SANTO VS. FRANKENSTEIN'S DAUGHTER (1971)

HILFE, ICH BIN UNSICHTBAR (1952) see HELP, I'M INVISIBLE (1952)

HIMMELSKIBET (1917) see THE SKY SHIP (1917)

HIS NAME IS ROBERT (1967) see CALL ME ROBERT (1967)

HIS PREHISTORIC PAST (1914) Charlie Chaplin comedy, where Charlie dreams he is back in the prehistoric past as a caveman.

P★	T★	E★★★	A★

Directed and written by Chaplin. With Mack Swain, Gene Marsh and Fritz Schade.

A HITCH IN TIME (1978) Enjoyable juvenile time-travel story from the Children's Film Foundation, with Patrick Troughton as the eccentric scientist who invents the machine (which malfunctions regularly) by which two teenagers visit the past and aid their ancestors.

P★★	T★★	E★★	A★

Directed by Jan Darnley-Smith. Written by T. E. B. Clarke. With Michael McVey, Pheona McLellan and Jeff Rawle.

THE H-MAN (1958) The film that takes the phrase "his knees turned to jelly" literally and has people liquefying all over the place due to the radioactive waste from H-Bomb explosions.

P★	T★	E★	A

Directed by Inoshiro Honda. Written by Takeshi Kimura. Special Effects by Eiji Tsuburaya. With Yumi Shirakawa, Kenji Sahara and Akihiko Hirata.

HOLD TIGHT TO THE SATELLITE (1958) see A DOG, A MOUSE AND A SPUTNIK (1958)

HOLOCAUST 2000 (1977) Kirk Douglas and Simon Ward star in a strange mixture of religious mysticism and ecological nightmare, *The Omen* meets *China Syndrome*, as the building of a nuclear power plant parallels in its details a religious "vision" almost two thousand years old. Simon Ward (Angel Kane) proves to be the Anti-Christ. The film has an ambiguous resolution but otherwise is a successful hybrid.

P★★	T★★	E★★★	A★

Directed by Alberto de Martino. Written by Martino and Sergio Donati. With Agostina Belli, Anthony Quayle and Virginia McKenna.

EL HOMBRE INVISIBLE ATACA (1967) see THE INVISIBLE MAN ATTACKS (1967)

EL HOMBRE QUE LOGRO SER INVISIBLE (1957) see THE NEW INVISIBLE MAN (1957)

EL HOMBRE QUE VINO DE UOMO (1971) see DRACULA VS. FRANKENSTEIN (1971)

EL HOMBRE Y LA BESTIA (1951) see THE MAN AND THE BEAST (1951)

HOMME AU CERVEAU GREFFE (1972) see THE MAN WITH THE BRAIN GRAFT (1972)

LA HORA INCOGNITA (1964) see THE UNKNOWN HOUR (1964)

L'HORRIBLE DR ORLOFF (1961) see THE AWFUL DR ORLOFF (1961)

LA HORRIPLANTE BESTIA HUMANA (1970) see NIGHT OF THE BLOODY APES (1970)

HORROR! (1963) *see* CHILDREN OF THE DAMNED (1963)

THE HORROR CHAMBER OF DR FAUSTUS (1959) Jean Redon wrote the screenplay for and starred in this adaptation of his own novel. A doctor, responsible for the accident which scarred his daughter's face, literally steals the faces of other young women in an attempt to replace her looks. His own face is torn off by dogs at the end in a moment of true poetic justice. A strangely haunting film with distinct surrealist tendencies, it seems now to be much ahead of its time.

| P★★★ | T★★ | E★★★ | A★★★ |

Directed by Georges Franju. With Franju, Claude Santet, Pierre Boileau and Thomas Narcejac.

HORROR CREATURES OF THE PREHISTORIC PLANET (1970) *see* THE HORROR OF THE BLOOD MONSTERS (1970)

HORROR EXPRESS (1972) An ancient alien, trapped in the form of the missing link unearthed by an anthropologist, takes over the minds of various travellers aboard the Trans-Siberian railway as it makes its way back from China to Moscow. What it wants as it drains mind after mind, is the knowledge to build a spacecraft and escape, future invasion by its own kind being its motive.

| P★★ | T★★ | E★★★ | A★ |

Directed by Eugenio Martin. Written by Arnaud d'Usseau and Julian Halvey. With Peter Cushing, Christopher Lee and Telly Savalas.

THE HORROR OF FRANKEN-STEIN (1970) One of the least successful of Hammer studios Frankenstein films, its careless eroticizing of the myth adds little if anything to previous versions.

| P★ | T★★ | E★★ | A★ |

Produced and directed by Jimmy Sangster. Written by Sangster and Jeremy Burnham. Make-up by Tom Smith. With Ralph Bates, Kate O'Mara, Graham James and David Prowse.

THE HORROR OF THE BLOOD MONSTERS (1971) John Carradine plays the ageing Dr Rhining in this pa-thetic film, which stumbles between colour and black-and-white footage (from at least three other films) by way of tinted sequences. An expedition to Tubetan, home planet of the vampire people, involves all the old clichés of tribal warfare, battles with dinosaurs. Ridiculous dialogue in the mouths of bad actors; one for the Golden Turkey brigade!

| P | T | E | A |

Produced and directed by Al Adamson. Written by Sue McNair. With Robert Dix, Vicki Volante, Joey Berison, Jennifer Bishop and Bruce Powers.

HORROR Y SEXO (1970) *see* NIGHT OF THE BLOODY APES (1970)

EL HOTEL ELECTRICO (1905) *see* THE ELECTRIC HOTEL (1905)

HOUSE AT THE END OF THE WORLD (1965) *see* DIE! MONSTER DIE! (1965)

HOUSE OF FRANKENSTEIN (1944) A truly dreadful exploitation by Universal studios of all its monsters, as Boris Karloff takes a travelling show of freaks and monsters about the countryside. Avoid.

| P | T★ | E | A |

Directed by Erle C. Kenton. Written by Edward T. Lowe. Special Effects by John P. Fulton. Make-up by Jack Pierce. With Lon Chaney Jr, John Carradine, Glenn Strange and George Zucco.

HOUSE OF FRIGHT (1960) *see* THE TWO FACES OF DR JEKYLL (1960)

HOW TO STEAL THE WORLD (1968) The Men From U.N.C.L.E. battle against a mad villain who plans to make everyone in the world obedient to him by means of a docility gas.

| P★★ | T★★ | E★★ | A★ |

Directed by Sutton Roley. Written by Norman Hudis. Special Effects by Ted Samuels. With Robert Vaughn, David McCallum, Barry Sullivan, Eleanor Parker, Leo G. Carroll and Dan O'Herlihy.

HU-MAN (1975) Terence Stamp, playing Terence Stamp, travels into the past in a machine that transforms emotional response into energy, only to re-live the death of his wife. In a touching finale he joins his wife in death.

| P★★★ | T★★★ | E★★ | A★★ |

Directed by Jerome Laperrousaz. Written by Laperrousaz, Guillame Laperrousaz, Andre Ruellan and Francis Guilbert. With Jeanne Moreau, Agnes Stevenin and Frederick Van Pallandt.

THE HUMAN DUPLICATORS
(1964) Richard Kiel ("Jaws" in the Bond series) plays an alien, who muscles in on an android-manufacturer's lab with plans to replace leading humans with robots.

| P★★ | T★ | E★★ | A★ |

Directed by Hugo Grimaldi. Written by Arthur C. Pierce. Make-up by John Chambers. With George Nader, Barbara Nichols and George Macready.

THE HUMANOID (1979) Italian
space-opera, complete with mad scientist bent on Universal domination. Richard Kiel (Bond's "Jaws") is the man turned into a humanoid and made to serve the scientist's purpose.

| P★ | T★★ | E★★ | A★ |

Directed by George B. Lewis. Written by Adriano Bolzoni and Aldo Lado. Special Effects by Ermanno Biamonte, Antonio Margheriti and Armando Valcauda. With Corinne Clery, Leonard Mann and Barbara Bach.

THE HUMAN VAPOR (1960) After
experimenting on new gases a scientist finds he can himself change into a vapour and uses this to rob and kill.

| P★ | T★ | E★ | A |

Directed by Inoshiro Hondo. Written by Shinichi Sekizawa. Special Effects by Eiji Tsuburaya. With Tatsuya Mihashi, Kaoni Yachigusa, Yoshio Tsuchiya and Keiko Sata.

THE HYPERBOLOID OF ENGINEER GARIN (1965) Based on Alexei
Tolstoy's novel, this is a fairly routine death-ray story, with the invention falling into the hands of the wrong people.

| P★ | T★★ | E★ | A★ |

Directed by M. Berdicevski. Written by I. Maneric and Alexander Ginzburg. With Yevgeny Evstigneev and Vsevolod Safonov.

I

ICARUS MONTGOLFIER
WRIGHT (1962) Short (20-minute) colour animation of Ray Bradbury's story telling of the urge to fly which results in the first Moonshot by Jedediah Prentiss on 1 April 1971.

| P★★ | T★★★ | E★★★ | A★★ |

Directed by Jules Engel. Written by Ray Bradbury and George Clayton Johnson. Graphics by Joe Mugnaini.

ICEMAN (1984) As the cinematic genre
matures and gets older, the oldest, crudest themes are resurrected, reworked and given a depth of exploration worthy of their mythic basis. *Iceman* is one such – its story, about an ancient human woken from a block of ice in the Antarctic after 40,000 years, is as old as written sf, and yet the film's treatment is thoroughly modern. The iceman, Charlie (played by John Lone), is not the uncontrollable savage of earlier genre offerings, but a sensitive, instinctive and utterly "alien" human being, out of his time. But what will modern Man do with him: will they dissect this "find" or will they attempt to understand him. Lindsay Crouse plays Dr Brady, the biologist, who wants to do the first, Timothy Hutton the anthropologist, Shepherd, who wants the latter and whose comment "Maybe his spirit could teach us more than his flesh" seems the ultimate message of this film. Shepherd wins but has the plug pulled on him by the higher-ups. Nonetheless, he manages to free Charlie from the artificial environment in which they were keeping him and partly accompanies him on the "dream-walk" he had begun 40,000 years earlier, the culmination of which (the coming of a giant bird to take him to heaven – merely a helicopter to our lesser, rational eyes) frees Charlie from torment. A deeply sensitive, highly intelligent and at times moving film.

| P★★★★ | T★★★★ | E★★★★ | A★★★★ |

Directed by Fred Schepisi. Written by Chip Proser and John Drimmer. Make-up by Michael Westmore. With Josef Sommer.

THE ICE PIRATES (1984) In a distant galaxy far far away they've run out of water. Yes, and the stuff is so valuable that star pirates steal the stuff. Throwing together a whole lot of sub-*Star-Wars* clichés, titillating special effects and dog-fight space battles, *Ice Pirates* manages to make *Battlestar Galactica* (q.v.) seem an epic of incomparable subtlety. A film made *by* rather than *for* juveniles.

P	T★★	E★	A

Directed by Stewart Raffill. Written by Raffill and Stanford Sherman. Special Effects by Max W. Anderson, John Short, Praxis Filmworks, Digital Effects and David Stipes. With Robert Urich, Mary Crosby, Michael D. Roberts, Anjelica Huston, Ron Perlman and John Carradine.

ICH LIEVE DICH, ICH TOTE DICH (1971) *see* I LOVE YOU, I KILL YOU (1971)

IDO ZERO DAISAKUSEN (1969) *see* LATITUDE ZERO (1969)

I EAT YOUR SKIN (1964) Simple story of an adventurer who fights scientifically produced zombies on an Atlantic island.

P★	T★	E★	A

Produced, directed and written by Del Tenney. With William Joyce, Heather Hewitt, Betty Hyatt Linton, Dan Stapleton, Walter Coy and Robert Stanton.

IF ALL THE WOMEN IN THE WORLD (1966) *see* KISS THE GIRLS AND MAKE THEM DIE (1966)

I HATE MY BODY (1975) A man's brain is transplanted into a woman's head and, from the start, begins to rebel against the body it has been given. The inevitable death of the confused "hybrid" is the only psychologically convincing moment in the whole film.

P★	T★★	E	A

Directed by Leon Klimovsky. Written by Klimovsky and Solly Wollodarski. With Alexandra Bastedo, Byron Mabe and Gemma Cuervo.

I HAVE A STRANGER'S FACE (1966) *see* THE FACE OF ANOTHER (1966)

IKARIE XB1 (1963) Strangely colourless account of a group of 25th-century space voyagers travelling to a new "green" world, which proves to be Earth. The American version of this film has a different ending.

P★★	T★★	E★	A★

Directed by Jindrich Polak. Written by Polak and Pavel Juracek. With Zdenek Stepanek, Radovan Lakavsy and Dana Medricka.

I KILLED EINSTEIN, GENTLE-MEN (1970) A sterile future sends back time-travellers to assassinate Einstein – to prevent certain developments in physics that led to radioactive fall-out, the source of their problem – but fail. A slow-paced comedy.

P★★	T★	E★	A★

Directed by Oldrich Lipsky. Written by Josef Nesvadba, Milos Macourek and Oldrich Lipsky. With Jiri Sovak and Jana Brejchova.

ILE D'EPOUVANTE (1913) *see* THE ISLAND OF TERROR (1913)

THE ILLUSTRATED MAN (1968) A hitchhiker travelling through the corn-belt during the 1930s comes across a wild-eyed man (Rod Steiger) whose entire body has been tattooed by a witch from the future. At night, each of the pictures comes alive and tells a different story. There were 18 tales in the original classic collection by Ray Bradbury. To say that director Jack Smight and writer Howard B. Kreitsek have adapted three of them – "The Veldt", "The Long Rain", and "The Last Night of the World' – would be a misrepresentation: they've emasculated two and butchered the third. Bradbury's work, heavily reliant on the use of language for its impact, has always been difficult to translate on to the screen (the only director who ever came anywhere near the mark was Franois Truffaut with *Fahrenheit 451* (q.v.)) but this film seems to sleepwalk where others feared to tread. Out of a bad bunch, "The Long Rain" holds the attention at least momentarily, largely because it is impossible to bleed *all* the poetry out of a story of spacemen trapped in a colourless Venusian forest

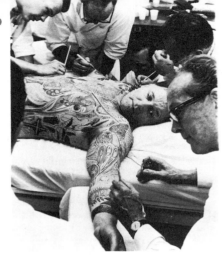

Rod Steiger being tattooed for his part in The Illustrated Man

where the rain never stops. But "The Last Night of the World" achieves an all-time low, leaving you wondering why the producers chose to take that quiet little story and turn it into schlock suspense when they had 15 other ideas to choose from. Rod Steiger is nicely psychopathic as the man himself, but the script demands he play the lead role too in each of the tattooed stories. Poor Steiger, he becomes the first actor in cinema history ever to be hideously miscast by his own epidermis. A disappointment for fans of the book.

P★★	T★★	E★	A

Special Effects by Ralph Webb. With Claire Bloom and Robert Drivas. (TR)

I LOVE YOU, I KILL YOU (1971) A near-future fantasy about power and control. The village people are harmless vegetables, the police keep order under a benevolent totalitarianism, while a group of misfits and rejects exist on the margins of this society. A bleak commentary on the then contemporary German scene?

P★★	T★★	E★	A★★

Produced, directed and written by Uwe Brandner. With Ralf Becker, Hannes Fuchs, Helmut Brasch, Thomas Eckelmann, Nikolaus Dutsch.

I MARRIED A MONSTER FROM OUTER SPACE (1958) A strangely atmospheric piece for all its cheap budget

origins, this has justifiably become a cult film, which has subsequently been interpreted as a female nightmare. What if your husband, so nice before marriage, turned out to be a foul, alien creature? In Gene Fowler Jr's film, this is *almost* what happens. Oh, and just to explain, the alien species are dying out and they are making themselves into duplicates in order to replace human men.

P★★	T★★	E★★★	A★

Written by Louis Vittes. Special Effects by John P. Fulton. With Tom Tryon, Gloria Talbott, Ken Lynch, John Eldredge and Valerie Allen.

IMMEDIATE DISASTER (1954) Yet another alien busybody who wants to stop A-bomb tests. This one's a Venusian. Like Michael Rennie before him, he gets chummy with Patricia Neal and ends up dying. And the A-bomb tests went on . . .

P★	T★	E★★	A

Directed by Burt Balaban. Written by Hans Jacoby. With Helmut Dantine and Derek Bond.

THE IMMORTAL (1969) Based on the novel by James Gunn. A millionaire seeks, by criminal means, to take all the blood from a man who has super-resistant blood and is therefore immune to disease and virtually immortal. Christopher George plays the Immortal, Cartwright, in this clever medical thriller.

P★★★	T★★	E★★★	A★

Directed by Joseph Sargent. Written by Robert Specht. With Jessica Walter, Barry Sullivan, Carol Lynley and Ralph Bellamy.

I, MONSTER (1971) Slight variation on the Jekyll and Hyde story with Dr Marlowe (Christopher Lee) becoming the ugly Mr Blake, an evil creature.

P★	T★★	E★	A

Directed by Stephen Weeks. Written by Milton Subotsky. With Peter Cushing, Mike Raven, Richard Hurndall and George Merritt.

AN IMPOSSIBLE VOYAGE (1904) Georges Méliès fantasy about a space trip to the sun. The spaceship is a train, launched from the top of the Jungfrau.

IM STAHLNETZ DES DR MABUSE (1961) see THE RETURN OF DR MABUSE (1961)

INCONTRI MOLTO RAVVICI-NATI (1979) see VERY CLOSE ENCOUNTERS OF THE FOURTH KIND (1979)

THE INCREDIBLE FLYING MANTIS (1957) see THE DEADLY MANTIS (1957)

THE INCREDIBLE HULK (1977)

David Banner (Bill Bixby) – victim of his own scientific experiments and accused of his own murder – turns into a not-so-jolly green giant of fantastic strength whenever angered. Taken from *Marvel* comics via TV, this tells of the Hulk's origins. For Hulk addicts only.

| P★★ | T★★ | E★★ | A★ |

Directed by Kenneth Johnson and Sigmund Neufeld. Written by Johnson, Thomas E. Szollosi and Richard Matheson. With Susan Sullivan, Jack Colvin, Lou Ferrigno and Susan Batson.

THE INCREDIBLE INVASION (1968)

Notable more for being Boris Karloff's last film than for its overcomplex plot and uninspired visuals. Karloff plays a professor who has invented a radioactive power source. Rather than see it be developed as a weapon, an alien comes to Earth to destroy the invention.

| P★ | T★ | E★ | A |

Directed by Juan Ibañez and Jack Hill. Written by Karl Schanzer and Luis Enrique Vergara. Special Effects by James Tanenbaum. With Enrique Guzman, Christa Linder and Maura Monti.

THE INCREDIBLE MELTING MAN (1977)

With a plot-line straight out of the 1950s – a spaceman returns from Saturn with a mysterious flesh-melting disease that turns him into a monster – this seems to have been made merely to showcase Rick Baker's series of liquefied, decomposing heads.

| P★★ | T★★★ | E★★ | A★ |

Directed and written by William Sachs. Special Effects by Baker and Harry Woolman. With Alex Rebar, Burr DeBenning and Myron Healey.

THE INCREDIBLE SHRINKING MAN (1957)

Despite being badly marred by one of those really dreadful 1950s voice-overs, Richard Matheson's adaptation of his own popular novel stands as a minor classic of its type, depending for its impact not on the shocks and instant thrills of other sf-horror movies, but on a fascination with its own theme which becomes inexorable, obsessive, ultimately chilling. Scott Carey (Grant Williams), everyone's idea of the man in the street, falls victim to a cloud of radioactive gas which gradually makes him shrink. We see him first become an object of almost-academic concern for the medical establishment, and then a figure of fascination and ridicule for the rest of the ordinary joes. But there is more to this movie than the horror of Carey becoming an ineffectual freak, a human being who could die by being stepped on or eaten by the cat. It's the story of one man's descent into primevalism *en route* to oblivion. Carey, in the latter stages of his illness, falls into the cellar of his house and is unable to get out: it's a chilling microcosm of scant light and tangible shadow with matchboxes for houses, orange crates for mountains – the kind of terrain a child would set up to fight his model soldiers in. Carey is the sole infantryman on the side of reason, sapience; on the side of brute hunger and insanity, a black widow spider which becomes all the more dangerous the tinier Carey gets. In the end, he destroys this primal nightmare and transcends, through infinitesimalism, to a new oneness with the universe – a kind of Zen Buddhism with giant insects. It's a shame that the acting, mostly wooden, could not match up to the special effects, and the final 30 seconds of the movie are pure cornball, but there's a darkness and intensity about *The Incredible Shrinking Man* which lingers long after the slavering monsters of most other sci-fi movies are forgotten.

| P★★★ | T★★★★ | E★★★★★ | A★★ |

Directed by Jack Arnold. Special Effects by Clifford Stine, Alexander Golitzin, Robert Clatworthy, Roswell A. Hoffmann and Everett A. Broussard. With Randy Stuart and April Kent. (TR)

THE INCREDIBLE SHRINKING WOMAN (1981) This slight, irritating movie turns Richard Matheson's original idea into a schlock attack on consumerism. Tasty Meadows is consumer-land and housewife Pat Kramer (Lily Tomlin) is reduced by a combination of "products" reacting with her body chemistry. There's no real drama, however, no pathos either, just a kind of ingrained silliness which has Kramer re-appear at the end – only growing bigger by the moment.

P★	T★★	E★	A

Directed by Joel Schumacher. Written by Jane Wagner. Special Effects by Roy Arbogast, Guy Faria and David Kelsey. With Charles Grodin, Ned Beatty, Henry Gibson and Maria Smith.

THE INCREDIBLE TWO-HEADED TRANSPLANT (1970) Unintentionally funny film about the grafting of a maniac's head on to the body of an imbecile (Albert Cole and John Bloom respectively). Bruce Dern is the best thing in this inane movie, playing the mad scientist with a rare devilish glee.

P	T★	E★★	A

Directed by Anthony Lanza. Written by John Lawrence and James Gordon White. Special Effects by Ray Dorn. Make-up by Barry Noble. With Pat Priest, Casey Kasem, Berry Kroeger.

THE INDESTRUCTIBLE MAN (1956) The jolt of electricity which returns a killer to life also gives him incredible strength and seemingly makes him indestructible.

P★	T★	E★	A

Produced and directed by Jack Pollexfen. Written by Sue Bradford and Vy Russell. With Lon Chaney Jr, Marian Carr and Robert Shayne.

INFERNO DEI MORTI-VIVENTI (1981) see ZOMBIE CREEPING FLESH (1981)

INFERNO — MENSCHEN DER ZEIT (1922) see DR MABUSE, THE GAMBLER (1922)

L'INHUMAINE (1923) see THE INHUMAN ONES (1923)

THE INHUMAN ONES (1923) A man-killing female opera star is revived after her death by the special machines of an old admirer.

P★	T★★	E★	A★

Directed by Marcel L'Herbier. Written by Georgette Le Blanc and L'Herbier. With Eve Francis, Georgette Le Blanc and Jacques Catelain.

THE INHUMAN WOMAN (1923) see THE INHUMAN ONES (1923)

IN LIKE FLINT (1967) The sequel to Our Man Flint, with James Coburn in the title role as the 1960s' funniest Bond-spoof hero. The plot concerns the efforts of a group of women to dominate the world. And the script contains one of the most grimly prophetic lines of dialogue ever to emerge from the silver screen: "an actor as President of the United States? Ridiculous!"

P	T★★	E★★★★	A★

Directed by Gordon Douglas. Written by Hal Fimberg. Special Effects by L. B. Abbott, Emil Losa Jr and Art Cruikshank. With Lee J. Cobb, Jean Hall, Andrew Duggan and Anna Lee. (TR)

INSEMINOID (1980) This pedestrian movie reeks of gratuitous violence. Judy Geeson as Sandy is utterly unconvincing – even so she's the best actor here.

P	T	E★	A

Directed by Norman J. Warren. Written by Nich and Gloria Maley. With Robin Clarke, Jennifer Ashley, Stephanie Neacham and Steven Grimes.

INTERPLANETARY REVOLUTION (1924) Comic parody of Aelita (1924) (q.v.) by another Soviet company.

Art directed by E. Komissarenko, Y. Merkulov and N. Khodatayev.

INTERPLANETARY TOURISTS (1960) Inane Mexican comedy about two comedians kidnapped and taken to Venus.

P★	T★	E★	A

Directed by Miguel Zacarias. Written by Zacarias and Roberto Gomez Bolanos. With Marco Antonio Campos, Gaspar Henaine and Gina Romand.

AN INTERPLANETARY WEDDING (1910) An Italian space opera with distinct romantic concerns. An astronomer from Earth falls in love (via his telescope) with a girl from Mars. They exchange messages, then meet on the Moon in a year's time and are married.

Directed and written by Enrico Novelli.

IN THE YEAR 2000 (1912) One of several early films positing what life would be like 100 years hence, this is a spoof on the trends towards women's rights.

Directed by Alice Guy Blanché.

IN THE YEAR 2014 (1914) Another in a series of future glimpses of a world where women's suffrage has gone so far as to reverse the roles of the sexes – in the future of 2014 women control business and hire young men as their secretaries.

Produced by Carl Laemmle. With Max Asher.

IN THE YEAR 2889 (1966) After an Atomic War the survivors in a valley are suddenly threatened by cannibalistic human mutants with telepathic powers.

P★	T★	E★	A

Produced and directed by Larry Buchanan. Written by Harold Hoffman. Special Effects by Jack Bennett. With Paul Petersen, Quinn O'Hara, Charla Doherty and Neil Fletcher.

THE INTRIGUE (1916) An American inventor develops a death-ray weapon which gets sold to a European power.

Directed by Frank Lloyd. Written by Julia Crawford Ivers. With Cecil Van Acker, Lenore Ulrich, Howard Davies and Florence Vidor.

THE INTRUDER (1979) A mysterious man in black comes to the Canadian small town of Holoway, driving a rented car and towing a trailer which contains an enigmatic wooden box. In the box is Howard Turt, a marvel of twentieth-century science, unveiled, to much local interest at a show in the town hall. These Bradburyesque ingredients are used to investigate how the opportunity of being truthful (H. TURT is an anagram of TRUTH) would affect a two-timing, pettily corrupt town like Holoway.

P★★★	T★★	E★★★	A★

Directed by David F. Eustace. Written by Norman Fox. Special Effects by Dennis Pike, Edwin Watkins, Gary Myers and David Eustace. With Trudy Weiss, Tony Fletcher and Pota Oliver.

INVADERS FROM MARS (1953) One of the more interesting films to have emerged from the 1950s, William Cameron Menzies chose to tell this story through the eyes of a young boy who sees the coming of the giant green androids from Mars and witnesses the strange, dehumanizing effect of them upon those about him.

P★★	T★★	E★★★★	A★

Written by Richard Blake. Special Effects by Jack Cosgrove. With Helena Carter, Arthur Franz, Jimmy Hunt, Leif Erickson and Hillary Brooke.

THE INVADERS FROM OUTER SPACE (1967) Spanish juvenile on the invaders from Mars theme, featuring a boy, a girl and a chimpanzee.

P★	T★	E★	A

Directed by Guillermo Ziener. Written by Carlos Serrano and Rafael Henriquez. With Angel Aranda and Jose Maria Prada.

THE INVASION (1964) Italian near-future story of a secret alien invasion.

Directed by Camillio Bazzoni. With Pier Paolo Capponi.

INVASION (1966) A nice little low-budget sf film with a simple but effective storyline. An alien and her prisoner crashland on Earth. An Earth doctor wants to treat the strange girl he accidentally knocked down, and refuses to hand her over to the aliens (more girls) until she's well enough.

P★★	T★★	E★★	A★

Directed by Alan Bridges. Written by Roger Marshall. Special Effects by Ronnie Whitehouse, Jack Kine and Stan Shields. With Edward Judd, Valerie Gearson, Yoko Tani, Lyndon Brook, Tsai Chin.

INVASION OF THE ANIMAL PEOPLE (1960) Aliens land in Lapland and their pet monster escapes from the ship. After terrorizing the local inhabitants (and a few reindeer!) it's recaptured and shipped home. The American version has a tagged-on narration by John Carradine.

P★   T★★   E★   A★

Directed by Virgil Vogel and Jerry Warren. Written by Arthur C. Pierce. With Barbara Wilson, Robert Burton, Stan Gester and Bengt Blomgren.

INVASION OF THE ASTRO MONSTERS (1965) *see* MONSTER ZERO (1965)

INVASION OF THE BEE GIRLS
(1973) The Brandt Institute has, with its swarms of bees, changed ordinary housewives into sex-mad Queen-bee-like creatures who, with their sexual demands, kill off their male lovers from exhaustion. A B-movie (sic) with a soft-core frisson.

P★   T★   E★★   A

Directed by Denis Sanders. Written by Nicholas Meyer. With William Smith, Anitra Ford, Victoria Vetri and "The Bee Girls".

INVASION OF THE BODY-SNATCHERS (1956) It's out of the horror which lurks behind bland, sedate small-town America that this film comes, the same horror which informed *The Circus of Dr Lao* and *Something Wicked This Way Comes*, to name but two equally famous examples. Miles Bennell (Kevin McCarthy) is the local doctor in the unobtrusive Californian town of Santa Mira – it might easily have been Charles G. Finney's "Abalone, Arizona" or Bradbury's "Greentown, Illinois", so uniform is the setting, so typecast and recognizable the characters, and this is where the theme of *Bodysnatchers* lies. Bennell receives a late-night phone call from the town's token nonconformist, a writer called Jack Velichec (King Donovan); the man has found a duplicate of his own body lying dormant in the cellar of his home. Inexplicably, it vanishes before the authorities can be called, but it is not long before other simulacra start appearing ... Bennell's own is discovered growing from a pod inside his greenhouse. The plants come from another planet, producing exact

Left to right: Larry Gates, Kevin McCarthy and King Donovan in Invasion Of The Body Snatchers

copies of all the human beings in the town and then replacing them; Santa Mira is the beachhead for an alien invasion. It's not long before Bennell and his girlfriend Becky Driscoll (Dana Wynter) are the only real humans left. They take to the hills, but Becky, exhausted, falls asleep inside a mine-shaft and is possessed by the aliens. Only Bennell, half-crazy by now, escapes to the big city. Like many of the best science fiction movies, *Bodysnatchers* draws material from other genres but its own. The influence of the classic crime thrillers is strong here – recast Bennell as Alan Ladd and the plot could have become one of small-town graft and corruption with the bare minimum of rewriting; even the cinematography with its plain, unfussy day scenes and shadow-haunted night-time sequences evokes earlier *film noir*. And writer Daniel Mainwaring and director Don Siegel seem to have obtained their lessons in the art of suspense not from the myriad alien invasion cheapies abounding at the time – *Bodysnatchers* was a low-budget production itself – but from the Val Lewton horror classics of a decade before; not one transmutation, not one disposal of a human corpse is shown on screen; the horror occurs just beyond the corners of the audience's vision and is all the more memorable for that. The film, then, has all the hallmarks of a minor classic beyond its obvious strengths, those of ingenuity, tightness of pacing and plot, and the uniformly strong performances.

Only a few lapses into stilted, mock-hysterical dialogue, embarrassedly mouthed, see the film descending briefly towards its B-movie sci-fi origins. Otherwise, it remains one of those small genre landmarks which draws together the best elements of a dozen films gone by, meshes them almost perfectly. What Siegel is also saying – picking up the theme of the original novel by Jack Finney – is that small-town conformity is a kind of living death. The replica humans have all the physical characteristics of their originals, but they are bland, emotionless, virtually mindless on an individual basis. Bennell and Becky Driscoll, upon capture, are urged to relinquish their free will and their individuality; how much better run society could be, the aliens argue, without these human qualities. As a historical footnote, this was the time of McCarthyism in America, of sameness and blind conformity to an alarming degree. And though too much is made of the fact, by editors and producers from that time, science fiction was one of the very few genres where counter-arguments could be expounded safely, because the authorities did not take them seriously. However, it's not the philosophy in *Bodysnatchers* which mesmerizes but the brilliance of a science fiction thriller supremely done.

P★★★   T★★   E★★★★★   A★★★

Produced by Walter Wanger. With Carolyn Jones, Larry Gates and Ralph Dumke. (TR)

INVASION OF THE BODY SNATCHERS (1978) Philip Kaufman's re-make of Don Siegel's 1956 movie, which is far closer in spirit to *The Stepford Wives* (1974) (q.v.) than to the 1950s invasion tale. Unfortunately, this change in emphasis also resulted in the loss of that deeply haunting sense of paranoia the original is justly famous for. In its place is the full armoury of modern-day special effects, used more for its shock value (dogs with human faces) than as illustration for the dehumanization process proceeding apace. The story remains much as was, of course, and Kevin McCarthy is still (in cameo) running

around warning the world, but it's almost as if no one really cares anymore and as if the health inspector (Donald Sutherland) is perverse in even considering opposition against the invasion. All in all, then, this is a slick, enjoyable horror film rather than the intelligent fable it was intended to be.

P★★★   T★★★★   E★★★   A★★

Written by W. D. Richter. Special Effects by Dell Rheaume and Russ Hessey. With Brooke Adams, Leonard Nimoy and Veronica Cartwright.

INVASION OF THE BODY STEALERS (1969) Confusion as to whether these aliens constitute a threat or not mars this rather poor invasion and duplication tale.

P★   T★   E★   A

Directed by Gerry Levy. Written by Mike St Clair and Peter Marcus. With George Sanders, Maurice Evans, Patrick Allen and Neil Connery.

INVASION OF THE FLYING SAUCERS (1956) *see* EARTH VS. THE FLYING SAUCERS (1956)

INVASION OF THE GARGON (1958) *see* TEENAGERS FROM OUTER SPACE (1958)

INVASION OF THE HELL CREATURES (1957) *see* INVASION OF THE SAUCER MEN (1957)

INVASION OF THE LOVE DRONES (1975) Mildly comic soft porn alien invasion tale. But the invasion is merely padding here, most of the footage concentrating on the alien Dr Femme's power source for her ship – sexual energy.

P★   T★   E★★   A

Directed by Jerome Hamlin. Written by Hamlin, Conrad Baunz and Michael Gury. With Eric Edwards, Viveca Ash and Bree Anthony.

INVASION OF THE NEPTUNE MEN (1961) A friendly alien helps fight off an invasion from Neptune.

P★   T★   E★   A

Directed by Koji Ota. Written by Shin Morita. With Shinichi Chiba and Kappei Matsumoto.

INVASION OF THE SAUCER MEN (1957) A low-budget parody of low-budget invasion movies. Little green men from Mars can inject the alcohol from their veins into the bloodstreams of humans who have seen them via their hypodermic fingernails. Despite a brave attempt' this is *too* low budget and inept to succeed. Laughable rather than comic.

P★	T★	E★	A

Directed by Edward L. Cahn. Written by Robert Gurney Jr and Al Martin. Special Effects by Paul Blaisdell and Howard A. Anderson. With Steve Terrell, Gloria Castillo and Frank Gorshin.

INVASION OF THE STAR CREATURES (1962) The star creatures are walking carrots who, through a group of Amazonian women (who can't act), kidnap two American GIs with a vague plan of conquering the Earth. Yes . . . It is *meant* to be a comedy.

P	T	E★	A

Directed by Bruno Ve Sota. Written by Jonathan Haze. Make-up by Joseph Kinder. With Bob Hall, Frankie Ray, Gloria Victor and Dolores Reed.

INVASION OF THE ZOMBIES (1963) Monsters caused through radioactive waste dumped in the sea ravage a popular beach.

P★	T★	E★	A

Directed by Del Tenney. Screenplay and Cinematography by Richard L. Hilliard. With John Scott, Alice Lyon and Allen Laurel.

INVASION UFO (1980) Feature-length story cobbled together from several episodes of the British TV serial "U.F.O"., shown in the early 1970s. Aliens from a solar system a billion miles away (sic) come to Earth to steal organs to replace their own – their race is dying out and sterile. Commander Straker (Ed Bishop) sets up an organization (internationally funded) to stop their nasty shopping trips. I remember the TV series as being better-paced than this rather tedious and repetitive adventure – but then, my memory is probably defective on that point. Gerry and Sylvia Anderson, whose project this is, were best known for their sf-oriented TV puppet serials (like "Stingray", "Thunderbirds" and "Captain Scarlet") before this venture, and the end result here seems stilted and puppet-like, the actors "sculpted" to look somewhat unreal, the action definitely juvenile, for all the quasi-scientific exposition.

P★	T★★★	E★★	A★

Directed by Gerry Anderson, Dave Lane and David Tomblin. Written by Gerry and Sylvia Anderson, David Tomblin and Tony Barwick. Special Effects by Derek Meddings. With George Sewell, Michael Billington, Grant Taylor and Gabrielle Drake.

INVASION USA (1952) Dan O'Herlihy (the alien Grig in *The Last Starfighter*, q.v.) starred in this strange tale of a stranger in a bar who convinces everyone that the USA is at war with Russia and the bombs are falling.

P★★	T★	E★★	A★

Directed by Alfred E. Green. Written by Robert Smith and Franz Spencer. With Gerald Mohr, Peggie Castle, Robert Bice and Phyllis Coates.

AN INVENTION OF DESTRUCTION (1958) *see* THE FABULOUS WORLD OF JULES VERNE (1958)

INVENTIONS OF AN IDIOT (1909) A cruelly comic film about a young inventor's meddlesome creations, including a flying machine that goes at 200 m.p.h. and an automatic hairdressing machine that malfunctions

Produced by Sigmund Lubin.

INVENTOR CRAZYBRAINS AND HIS WONDERFUL AIRSHIP (1906) *see* THE FANTASTICAL AIRSHIP (1906)

THE INVENTORS (1934) A robotic "Frankenstein" is made up out of old car parts – and goes haywire.

Directed by Bud Fisher. Written by William Watson and Sig Herzig. With F. Chase Taylor and Wilbur Budd Hulick.

THE INVENTOR'S GALVANIC FLUID (1907) *see* LIQUID ELECTRICITY (1907)

THE INVINCIBLE INVISIBLE MAN

(1969) One of director Antonio Margheriti's silliest films, this has a young researcher invent an invisibility "filter" so that he can go and rescue his girl from villains who have captured her.

P★	T★	E	A

Written by M. Eller and Luis Marquina. With Dean Jones, Gastone Moschin and Ingeborg Schoener.

INVISIBILITY

(1909) Nice comedy about a hen-pecked man who buys some invisible powder to avoid his wife's scolding.

Directed by Cecil Hepworth and Lewin Fitzhamon. With Lewin Fitzhamon.

INVISIBLE AGENT

(1942) The son of the inventor of the invisibility formula becomes a spy for the Allies in Nazi Germany.

P★★	T★	E★★	A

Directed by Edwin L. Marin. Written by Curt Siodmak. Special Effects by John P. Fulton. With Ilona Massey, Jon Hall and Peter Lorre.

THE INVISIBLE BOY

(1957) Robby the Robot proved so popular in *Forbidden Planet* (q.v.) that the film company decided to feature him again. Taking a story that had no robot in it – "The Invisible Boy" by Edmund Cooper – they dragged bits of Robby back from the future, re-assembled him and had him taken over by a super-computer that wishes to rule the world (don't they all?). But the story is told from the viewpoint of the invisible boy himself (Richard Eyer), a child genius and son of the inventor of the super-computer, who is only invisible briefly. Both "children", Robby and the IB, rebel against parental control, the computer is destroyed and the world saved from a fate worse than ... well, perhaps worse than another Robby film. This is quaint rather than charming, and not greatly intelligent.

P★★	T★★	E★★	A★

Directed by Herman Hoffman. Written by Cyril Hume. Special Effects by Jack Rabin, Irving Block and Louis DeWitt. With Philip Abbott, Diane Brewster and Harold J. Stone.

THE INVISIBLE DR MABUSE

(1961) Norbert Jacques meets H. G. Wells in this cross-pollination of two great cinematic themes – one German, one international. Wolfgang Preiss is impressive as Mabuse, who here discovers how to make himself invisible, but this is not quite as atmospheric as Lang's *The Thousand Eyes of Dr Mabuse*, released the previous year.

P★★	T★★	E★★	A★

Directed by Harald Reinl. Written by Ladislas Fodor. With Lex Barker, Karin Dor, Siegfrid Lowitz and Werner Peters.

THE INVISIBLE FLUID

(1908) Only one of numerous invisibility films of the first decade of sf film, it again played the idea for laughs. Here the invisibility spray gets a delinquent youth into deep trouble.

Directed by Wallace McCutcheon.

THE INVISIBLE HORROR

(1961) *see* THE INVISIBLE DR MABUSE (1961)

INVISIBLE INVADERS

(1959) Formless alien invaders take over corpses which then attack living humans in this thoroughly silly film. Ultra-sonics kill the Moon-aliens.

P	T★	E	A

Directed by Edward L. Cahn. Written by Samuel Newman. With John Agar, Jean Byron, Robert Hutton and John Carradine.

THE INVISIBLE MAN

(1933) To say that Claude Rains starred in this James Whale film of Wells's classic novel is to give more credit to his voice than his body – which is glimpsed very little. A concentration by scriptwriter R. C. Sherriff on the more comic aspects of invisibility rather than on the pathos and horror that this idea involves makes it a light but enjoyable experience. John P. Fulton's special effects are excellent for their time and, of course, provide half the real fun.

P★★★	T★★★	E★★★★	A★

With Gloria Stuart, Henry Travers, William Harrigan, Una O'Connor, Holmes Herbert, Dudley Digges, E. E. Clive and John Carradine.

Claude Rains and Gloria Stuart in The Invisible Man

THE INVISIBLE MAN (1963) *see* THE INVISIBLE TERROR (1963)

THE INVISIBLE MAN ATTACKS
(1967) Argentinian addition to the world-wide invisible man phenomenon – here with a slight homicidal twist.

Produced and directed by Martin Mentasti. Written by Sergio De Cecco. With Martin Karadagian, Gilda Lousek and Tristan.

AN INVISIBLE MAN GOES THROUGH THE CITY (1933) Harry
Piel directed and starred in this comedy about a cab driver who finds a curious gadget on the back seat of his cab. After discovering that it makes him invisible he uses it to his advantage – until a friend steals it and uses it to rob a bank. An inventive wish-fulfilment story.

P★★	T★★	E★★	A★

Written by Hans Rameau. With Fritz Odemar, Ernst Rothemuend and Walter Steinbeck.

INVISIBLE MAN IN ISTANBUL
(1956) Turkish localization of the H. G. Wells story.

Produced and written by Osman Seden. Directed by Lutfu Akad. With Turan Seyfioglu, Nese Yulac and Atif Kaptan.

THE INVISIBLE MAN RETURNS
(1939) A rather tiresome sequel, featuring the invisible man's brother who uses the invisibility serum to clear his name and bring the villain to justice.

P★	T★★	E★	A

Directed by Joe May. Written by Lester Cole and Curt Siodmak. Special Effects by John P. Fulton. With Cedric Hardwicke and Vincent Price.

THE INVISIBLE MAN'S RE-VENGE (1944) Jon Hall plays the criminal who forces a scientist to give him the invisible man's formula so that he can avenge himself on those who framed him.

P★	T★	E★	A

Produced and directed by Ford Beebe. Written by Bertram Millhauser. Special Effects by John P. Fulton. With Lester Matthews, Gale Sondergaard and John Carradine.

THE INVISIBLE POWER (1914)
Two men who can transfer their thoughts and exert their wills, clash over girls.

With William H. West, Paul C. Hurst and Cleo Ridgeley.

THE INVISIBLE RAY (1923) *see* THE CRAZY RAY (1923)

THE INVISIBLE RAY (1935) "There are some things that Man is not meant to know!" Those immortal, oft-repeated words are uttered here in this, Boris Karloff's first outing without horror make-up, as a mad scientist after Radium X, an element that fell to Earth centuries before. Karloff has the touch of death, but his mother eventually stops him.

P★★	T★★	E★★	A★★

Directed by Lambert Hillyer. Written by John Colton. Special Effects by John P. Fulton. With Bela Lugosi, Frances Drake and Frank Lawton.

LES INVISIBLES (1905) *see* AN INVISIBLE THIEF (1905)

THE INVISIBLE TERROR (1963) A
thriller about crooks who obtain a scientist's secret invisibility serum.

P★	T★	E★	A

Directed by Raphael Nussbaum. Written by Nussbaum and Wladimir Smitjof. With Hanaes Hauser, Ellen Schwiers and Herbert Stass.

THE INVISIBLE THIEF (1905)
Comic use of Wells's idea. An invisible thief becomes a practical joker, undressing people and escaping uncaught.

Directed by Gaston Velle and Gabriel Moreau. With Charles Lepire.

THE INVISIBLE WOMAN (1940)
Comic interpretation of the Wells myth rather than the Wells story. Virginia Bruce is the woman made invisible by mad scientist John Barrymore's ray. Foreign spies, of course, try to get their hands on the device.

P★	T★★	E★★	A

Directed by A. Edward Sutherland. Written by Robert Lees, Fred Rinaldo and Gertrude Purcell, from a story by Curt Siodmak and Joe May. Special Effects by John P. Fulton. With John Howard, Charlie Ruggles and Oscar Homolka.

IO E CATARINA (1981) Italian sex comedy, featuring a lascivious and jealous female robot, Catarina, who proves to be programmed for much more than sexual compliancy.

P★★	T★★	E★★	A★

Directed by Alberto Sordi. Written by Sordi and Rodolfo Sonego. With Alberto Sordi, Catherine Spaak, Valeria Valeri and Edwige Fenech.

LA ISLA DE LOS DINOSAURIOS
(1966) *see* THE ISLAND OF THE DINOSAURS (1966)

THE ISLAND AT THE TOP OF THE WORLD (1973) A rather second-rate Disney, featuring the discovery of a lost race of Vikings up in the far north. As ever, the volcano explodes at the end.

P★	T★★	E★	A

Directed by Robert Stevenson. Written by John Whedon. Special Effects by Art Cruikshank and Danny Lee. With Donald Sinden.

THE ISLAND OF DR MOREAU
(1932) *see* ISLAND OF LOST SOULS (1932)

THE ISLAND OF DOCTOR MOREAU (1977) We normally associate eugenics with the Nazis, but racial theor-ies were all the rage in Wells's day; his novel was his humanitarian assault against them. A young shipwrecked sailor, Charles Edward Prendick (Michael York), is washed up on the shore of a lost Pacific island, inhabited by a crazed scientist, Moreau (Burt Lancaster), who is experi-menting with DNA codes by transforming animals into quasi-humans. His failed experimental subjects, the Beast People, lurk in the forests beyond the walled compound. And when York discovers the truth and begins to protest, he finds him-self strapped on to the good doctor's operating table too. It would have taken a Kubrick to evoke the full horrific sweep of the book; director Don Taylor's version has all the ineffectualness of a made-for-TV movie. The only scene which truly frightens is when York, halfway in his transmutation towards an animal, fights against the process by dredging into his human memory. Otherwise, York's fresh-faced innocence is merely irritating – he's so clean and pleasant that the introduction of some feral hair and bad manners seem to make him a little more likeable. Burt Lancaster tries to provide us with a nicely understated Moreau, mad by virtue of his cold, inhuman logic, but he is struggling against the odds of a script which has him cantering around trying to control a mob of semi-humans who look like the Cow-ardly Lion in *The Wizard of Oz*. "He has broken the Law," they chant incessantly – they're trying to bore him to death here, their tediousness bursts over into risibility. It's one of those films which you either do near-perfectly or leave alone – and *Mor-eau*, with its final scene of a beast-man popping again and again over the side of York's escaping boat like something from a Punch and Judy show, was best left untouched.

P★★	T	E	A

Written by John Herman Shaner and Al Ramus. With Nigel Davenport and Barbara Carrera. (TR)

THE ISLAND OF LOST SOULS
(1932) Based loosely on H. G. Wells's *The Island Of Dr Moreau*, and starring Charles Laughton as Moreau (and a young Alan

Ladd as one of the Beast Men!), this is actually less a distortion of Wells's original than most, even though the scientifically curious Moreau is transformed by Waldemar Young and Philip Wylie's script into an evil maniac delighting in the horrific elements of his experiment to change animals into men. Make-up is primitive but the settings marvellously evocative.

P★★★	T★★	E★★★	A★★

Directed by Erle C. Kenton. Special Effects by Gordon Jennings. Make-up by Wally Westmore. With Richard Arlen and Leila Hyams.

ISLAND OF LOST WOMEN (1959)
Another sci-fi version of *The Tempest?* Men are washed ashore an uncharted island where a scientist and his daughters live. He's mad, of course.

P★	T	E★	A

Directed by Frank W. Tuttle. Written by Ray Buffum. With Jeff Richards, Venetia Stevenson, John Smith and Diane Jergens.

ISLAND OF MUTATIONS (1978)
Overdubbed Italian production which manages to create a mixture of Burroughs, Wells and Verne in the story of the survivors of the lost city of Atlantis and genetically altered villagers who become fish men. Tastefully, if rather senselessly, produced by Luciano Martino, it's essentially Moreau's tale again, with voodoo.

P★	T★★	E★★	A★

Directed by Sergio Martino. Written by Cesare Frugoni, Luciano Martino, Sergio Donati and Sergio Martino. With Barbara Bach, Claudio Cassinelli, Richard Johnson and Joseph Cotten.

THE ISLAND OF TERROR (1913)
French version of Wells's *The Island of Dr Moreau*, with a mad scientist on an isolated island experimenting in grafting.

ISLAND OF TERROR (1966) On
Peachey's Isle, off the east coast of Ireland, Dr Phillips has made a breakthrough in cancer research. Or has he? Apparently not: what he's created is a race of quick-breeding, vampiric hot water bottles – silicates, which, until they succumb to Strontium 90, ravage the countryside

eating the bones out of policemen and cattle alike. Peter Cushing and Edward Judd take joint credit in this risible offering. The killer bottles are stopped. But meanwhile in Japan someone is duplicating Phillips's experiments . . .

P★	T	E★★	A

Directed by Terence Fisher. Written by Alan Ramsen and Edward Andrew Mann. Special Effects by John St John Earl. With Carole Gray, Eddie Byrne, Sam Kydd and Niall MacGinnis.

ISLAND OF THE BURNING DAMNED (1967) Globular alien proto-plasmic creatures take over and cause a heatwave on a British island which incinerates the inhabitants. The British weather comes to human aid. Naturally. Based on the novel *Night Of The Big Heat* by John Lymington.

P★	T★	E★	A

Directed by Terence Fisher. Written by Ronald Liles, Pip Baker and Jane Baker. With Christopher Lee, Peter Cushing and Patrick Allen.

ISLAND OF THE DEAD (1966) *see* ISLAND OF THE DOOMED (1966)

THE ISLAND OF THE DINOSAURS (1966) Using extensive footage from *One Million B.C.* (1940) (q.v.), this is a routine explorers-discover-lost-world story, complete with black-and-white dinosaurs and cavemen. Mexican.

P	T★	E	A

Directed by Rafael Lopez Portillo. Written by Alfredo Salazar. With Armando Silvestre, Alma Delia Fuentes and Elsa Cardenas.

ISLAND OF THE DOOMED (1966)
A mad scientist, experimenting on his island, creates a vampiric tree with flexible, limb-like branches that suck blood from people.

P★	T★	E★	A

Directed by Mel Welles. Written by Stephen Schmidt. With Cameron Mitchell, Elisa Montes, Jorge Martin and Kim Fischer.

THE ISLAND OF THE FISH MEN
(1978) *see* ISLAND OF MUTATIONS (1978)

IT CAME FROM BENEATH THE SEA

(1955) As a vehicle for Ray Harryhausen's effects this is a pretty shabby exploitation of the monster from the deeps genre. Here a gigantic octopus attacks San Francisco and eats a few men along the way before it's stopped.

P★	T★★	E★	A

Directed by Robert Gordon. Written by George Worthing Yates and Hal Smith. Special Effects by Harryhausen and Jack Erickson. With Kenneth Tobey, Faith Domergue and Donald Curtis.

IT CAME FROM OUTER SPACE

(1953) An alien "invasion" story with a difference: not an invasion as such but a brief stop to repair the old spacecraft. The invisible aliens, able to duplicate human beings (who are recruited to help in the repairs), aren't really a threat and aren't out to conquer the world, but they do have the most disconcerting habit of staring vacantly when they think no one's watching. Ray Bradbury's short story "The Meteor" was the basis for Harry Essex's screenplay. The 3-D horror effects were all thrown in by director Jack Arnold and special effects man David S. Horsley to give the thing a frisson. Altogether an atmospheric, memorable film with a superb title.

P★★	T★★	E★★★★	A★

Make-up by Bud Wetsmore. With Richard Carlson, Barbara Rush, Charles Drake, Russell Johnson, Kathleen Hughes and Joe Sawyer.

IT CONQUERED THE WORLD

(1956) A thoroughly silly but amusing film where the Venusians are brought to Earth by Lee Van Cleef, who believes they will rule the world better than Man. As it turns out, the Venusians plan to turn us all into zombie slaves using their bat-mites which sting people in the neck. As ever, the Venusian is defeated by fire.

P★	T★	E★★	A

Produced and directed by Roger Corman. Written by Lou Rusoff. Special Effects by (and Monster) Paul Blaisdell. With Peter Graves and Beverly Garland.

IT HAPPENED HERE

(1963) In the alternate world of this film the Nazis won World War Two and occupied England.

P★★	T★★	E★★	A★

Produced, directed and written by Kevin Brownlow and Andrew Mollo. With Pauline Murray, Sebastian Shaw and Floria LeLand.

IT LIVES AGAIN

(1978) Sequel to *It's Alive* (1973) (q.v.). Having learned their lesson from the first birth of a savage mutant baby, the authorities attempt to prevent others. But there are a growing number of people who realize that the mutant babies are also affectionate … A nice, taut thriller with a psychological sting.

P★★	T★★	E★★★	A★

Directed and written by Larry Cohen. Special Effects by Rick Baker. With Frederic Forrest, John Ryan, Kathleen Lloyd and Andrew Duggan.

IT'S ALIVE!

(1968) A man's pet dinosaur needs feeding, so he traps and keeps three men in a cave, planning to feed them to the monster. Based on Richard Matheson's novelette, "Being".

P★	T★★	E★	A

Directed and written by Larry Buchanan. Special Effects by Jack Bennett. With Tommy Kirk, Shirley Bonne and Billy Thurman.

IT'S ALIVE

(1973) As a side-effect of a new drug, a pregnant woman gives birth to the first of a new kind of human, one better adapted to the polluted, cut-throat world of the 1970s. This savage baby mutant, accepted (after a struggle) by the family, is nonetheless hunted down by society, finally meeting its end (in true *Them!* (q.v.) fashion) in the storm drains of LA. A sequel, *It Lives Again* (q.v.), followed in 1978.

P★★	T★★★	E★★★	A★

Directed and written by Larry Cohen. Special Effects by Rick Baker. With John Ryan, Sharon Garrell, Andrew Duggan and Guy Stockwell.

IT'S A WONDERFUL LIFE

(1946) Frank Capra's charming version of the Christmas Carol story isn't, of itself, a science fiction film, but it deserves inclusion for the "What if …?" sequence towards the end of the film, when George Bailey (James Stewart), missing $8,000, and with all his life's ambitions seemingly frustrated, decides to jump off a bridge. His comment, "If only I'd never been born", is taken literally by his guardian angel, who shows him an alternative world in which George Bailey had never existed. The bleak alternative, a loveless, soul-less world, is the purest rendition of a Philip K. Dick-style world yet put on celluloid (*Blade Runner* (q.v.) notwithstanding): good men are tramps, others are dead, his wife is a tired spinster, his mother doesn't know him, and the lovely old town has become mercenary Pottersville. For this brief (15-minute) section the film can be recognized as a genre classic.

P★★★	T★	E★★★★	A★★

Written by Frances Goodrich, Albert Hackett and Frank Capra. With Donna Reed, Lionel Barrymore and Henry Travers.

IT'S GREAT TO BE ALIVE (1933) A

fairly straight re-working of the 1924 film, *The Last Man On Earth* (q.v.). After an epidemic which has killed off all but one man, the world is run by a matriarchy. The hero is re-united with his love (from whom he was fleeing at the beginning, after a tiff), but not before there are one or two arguments about "using" him to re-populate the world. Based on John D. Swain's story.

P★★	T★★	E★★★	A★

Directed by Alfred Werker. Written by Paul Perez and Arthur Kober. With Paul Rowlien, Gloria Stuart and Edna May Oliver.

IT STALKED THE OCEAN FLOOR (1954) *see* MONSTER FROM THE OCEAN FLOOR (1954)

IT! THE TERROR FROM BEYOND SPACE (1958) Poor effects spoil this tale of a Martian monster (a vampire) who stows away on a ship returning to Earth and slowly kills the crew one at a time. There are similarities to the much later *Alien* (q.v.), and the tale was re-made as *Planet of Blood* (q.v.) in 1966.

P★★	T★	E★★	A

Directed by Edward L. Cahn. Written by Jerome Bixby. Special Effects by Paul Blaisdell. Make-up by Lene Britton. With Marshall Thompson, Shawn Smith, Ray Corrigan and Ann Doran.

IT, THE VAMPIRE FROM OUTER SPACE (1958) *see* IT! THE TERROR FROM BEYOND SPACE (1958)

I WAS A TEENAGE CAVEMAN (1958) *see* TEENAGE CAVEMAN (1958)

I WAS A TEENAGE FRANKENSTEIN (1957) Minor key parody of the Frankenstein myth, with a modern-day descendant of the Baron cobbling together a patchwork cadaver which eventually goes on the rampage.

P★★	T★★	E★★	A

Directed by Herbert L. Strock. Written by Kenneth Langtry. Make-up by Philip Scheer. With Whit Bissell, Phyllis Coates, Robert Burton.

I WAS A TEENAGE GORILLA (1960) *see* KONGA (1960)

I WAS A TEENAGE WEREWOLF (1957) A teenage delinquent is regressed by a scientist to a primitive, werewolf stage of development. Gory fun.

P★★	T★★	E★★	A★

Directed by Gene Fowler Jr. Written by Ralph Thornton. With Michael Landon, Yvonne Lime, Whit Bissell and Guy Williams.

IZBAVITELJ (1977) *see* THE RAT SAVIOUR (1977)

JEKYLL AND HYDE TOGETHER AGAIN (1982) Stevenson's tale is given a modern, punk rendering as the staid Jekyll becomes the punk Hyde when his alterego takes over. A high-energy comedy.

P★★	T★★★	E★★★	A★

Directed by Jerry Belson. Written by Belson, Monica Johnson, Harvey Miller and Michael Leeson. With Mark Blankfield, Bess Armstrong, Krista Errickson and Tim Thomerson.

JEKYLL'S INFERNO (1960) *see* THE TWO FACES OF DR JEKYLL (1960)

A JERSEY SKEETER (1900) The "skeeter", a giant mosquito, is perhaps the first case of insect gigantism in sf cinema. Here it abducts a yokel from Jersey, USA.

JESSE JAMES MEETS FRANKEN-STEIN'S DAUGHTER (1966) Cal Bolder stars as the resurrected monster pal of Jesse James, brought back to life by Frankenstein's daughter, alive and well and living in Mexico. It has an undeserved cult following, perhaps for the pure silliness of its title.

P★	T★	E★	A

Directed by William Beaudine. Written by Carl Hittleman. With Narda Onyx, John Lupton, Nestor Paiva, Jim Davis, Estelita and Steven Geray.

JESSIE AND SUPERMAN (1965) *see* WHO KILLED JESSIE? (1965)

JE T'AIME, JE T'AIME (1967) A far more explicit and less enigmatic approach to memory than Alain Resnais's earlier *Last Year In Marienbad* (1961) (q.v.), this uses a time machine as a device to allow the hero to re-live the damaging love affair that resulted in him attempting to commit suicide. An intelligent, haunting film.

P★★★	T★★★	E★★★	A★★★

Directed by Alan Resnais. Written by Resnais and Jacques Sternberg. With Claude Rich, Olga Georges-Picot and Anouk Ferjac.

THE JETTY (1962) Chris Marker's animated photo-novel is, in essence, a story of time-dislocation following a nuclear war and the oscillations between past, present and future of its central character, H. The moment of H's death is the pivot of this enigmatic but visually impressive film. In cinematic terms it's wholly successful, even at the expense of its sf storyline.

P★★	T★★★★	E★★★	A★★★

Directed and written by Marker. Special Effects by C. S. Olaf. Narrated by Jean Negroni. With Helene Chatelain, Jacques Ledoux, Davos Hanich, Andre Heinrich and Pierre Joffroy.

JIKAN NO KYOFU (1960) *see* THE FINAL WAR (1960)

NE JOUEZ PAS AVEC LES MAR-TIANS (1967) *see* DON'T PLAY WITH THE MARTIANS (1967)

JOURNEY BENEATH THE DESERT (1961) Based on Pierre Benoit's *L'Atlantide*, this mixes in modern technology with the discovery of the legendary lost Empire. A poor man's *She* (q.v.).

P★	T★	E	A

Directed by Edgar G. Ulmer and Giuseppe Masini. Written by Ugo Liberatore, Remigio del Grosso, Andre Tabet and Amedeo Nazzari. Special Effects by Giovanni Ventimiglia. With Haya Harareet and Jean-Louis Trintignant.

THE JOURNEY THAT SHOOK THE WORLD (1954) *see* BLAST OFF! (1954)

JOURNEY TO THE BEGINNING OF TIME (1954) Interesting more than entertaining film from Czech puppeteer Karel Zeman, mixing various techniques in telling a story of a group of boys who travel backwards down the river of time into an age of dinosaurs.

P★★	T★★★	E★	A★★

Written by Zeman and J. A. Novotny. With James Lucas, Victor Betral and Peter Hermann.

JOURNEY TO THE CENTRE OF THE EARTH (1909) First screen version of Verne's novel, now lost, but apparently once containing images of ruined cities and dinosaurs.

Directed and written by Segundo de Chomon.

JOURNEY TO THE CENTRE OF THE EARTH (1959) No great variations on Verne's original story; the adventuring party meet their fair share of dinosaurs on the way to the lost city of Atlantis. But here the action seems no more than a vehicle for singer Pat Boone's crooning.

P★	T★★	E★★	A

Directed by Henry Levin. Written by Walter Reisch and C. Brackett. Special Effects by L. B. Abbott, James D. Gordon and Emil Kosa Jr. With James Mason, Arlene Dahl and Diane Baker.

JOURNEY TO THE CENTRE OF TIME (1967) Instantly forgettable time-travel adventure – battling with mutants/aliens in the future and dinosaurs in the past – with poor special effects.

P	T	E	A

Directed by D. L. Hewitt. Written by David Prentiss. Special Effects by Modern Film Effects. With Scott Brady, Gigi Perreau, Anthony Eisley.

JOURNEY TO THE FAR SIDE OF THE SUN (1969) A tenth planet is discovered on the far side of the sun to Earth – a doppleganger planet which proves to be a parallel world. An expedition is sent out and discovers this fact. A touch uninspired.

P★	T★★	E★	A★

Storyline Gerry and Sylvia Anderson. Directed by Robert Parrish. Written by Gerry and Sylvia Anderson and Donald James. Special Effects/Cinematography by Harry Oakes. Special Effects by Derek Meddings. With Ian Hendry, Roy Thinnes, Patrick Wymark and Herbert Lom.

JOURNEY TO THE FOURTH PLANET (1959) see THE ANGRY RED PLANET (1959)

JOURNEY TO THE SEVENTH PLANET (1961) a film about the first manned expedition to Neptune in 2001. They encounter a huge brain which, unknown to them, can replicate whatever exists in their deepest consciousnesses. A good idea poorly developed.

P★	T★	E★	A

Directed by Sidney Pink. Written by Pink and Ib Melchior. Special Effects by Bent Barford Films. With John Agar and Greta Thyssen.

JULES VERNE'S ROCKET TO THE MOON (1954) see BLAST OFF! (1954)

JUNGLE MOON MEN (1954) The "moon men" are actually a tribe of pygmies, but Johnny Weissmuller (not, for once, as Tarzan) here battles against an immortal woman who has lived for thousands of years and knows the secret of eternal life.

P★	T★	E★	A

Directed by Charles S. Gould. Written by Dwight V. Babcock and Jo Pagano. Special Effects by Jack Erickson. With Jean Byron and Helene Stanton.

JUNKET 89 (1970) An eccentric little film from the Children's Film Foundation about an instantaneous transportation device fixed up with chewing gum.

P★	T★★	E★★	A★

Directed by Peter Plummer. Written by David Ash. With Stephen Brassett and John Blundell.

JUST IMAGINE (1930) Big-budget American musical set in 1980. Its financial failure must be one of the major reasons why no further money was invested in this kind of "epic" sf film throughout the next two decades. A story of two non-conformist lovers in an age of conformity seems to prefigure the central theme of Aldous Huxley's *Brave New World* (published two years later), but the thinness of the plot – including the adventures with twin Martians on Mars – and the general appalling standard of writing ensured that this had to be a mammoth flop. The most impressive aspect of the film is the huge model of 1980 New York, which cost a then staggering $250,000 to create. 20th Century-Fox made sure they got their money back by using it as often as they could thereafter! Generally, however, it's a dreadful, unwatchable failure.

P★	T★★	E	A

Directed by David Butler. Written by Butler, Ray Henderson, B. G. DeSylva and Lew Brown. With El Brendel, Frank Albertson, Maureen O'Sullivan, John Garrick and Marjorie White.

K

KADOYNG (1972) Charming little film from the Children's Film Foundation about an alien from a planet of geniuses who comes to Earth to help a group of children.

P★★	T★★	E★★	A★

Directed by Ian Shand. Written by Leo Maguire. With Teresa Codling, Adrian Hall, David Williams, Stephen Bone and Leo Maguire.

KAIJU DAISENSO (1965) *see* MON-STER ZERO (1965)

KAIJU SOSHINGEKI (1968) *see* DESTROY ALL MONSTERS (1968)

KAITEI DAISENSO (1966) *see* TER-ROR BENEATH THE SEA (1966)

KDO CHCE ZABIT JESSII? (1965) *see* WHO KILLED JESSIE? (1965)

THE KEEPERS OF THE EARTH (1958) *see* THE BRAIN EATERS (1958)

KESSEN NANKAI NO DAIKAIJU (1970) *see* YOG – MONSTER FROM SPACE (1970)

KIBERNETICKA BABICKA (1962) *see* CYBERNETIC GRANDMOTHER (1962)

KILLERS ARE CHALLENGED (1965) Italian-French production capital-izing on the sf-spy-thriller craze of the mid-1960s. A super energy source is the glittering prize everyone is fighting over here, though the good agent has a ring which lights up when death threatens. Handy.

P★	T★★	E★	A

Directed by Antonio Margheriti. Written by Ernesto Gastaldi. With Richard Harrison, Wandisa Guida and Susy Anderson.

KILLERS FROM SPACE (1954) Kidnapped scientist becomes servant of aliens from Astron Delta. They plan to conquer Earth but the scientist foils them.

P★	T	E★	A

Produced and directed by W. Lee Wilder. Written by Bill Raynor. With Peter Graves and Barbara Bestar.

THE KILLER SHREWS (1959) Scientist's serum turns shrews into dog-like carnivores who attack anything in sight. Escaping their pens they try to attack the scientist and friends but fail, so eat one another.

P	T	E★	A

Written by Jay Sims. Make-up by Corinne Daniel. With James Best and Ingrid Goude.

KING DINOSAUR (1955) Silly film about an undiscovered planet with primi-tive life. All the best footage is from *One Million B.C.* (1940) (q.v.).

P	T	E	A

Produced and directed by Bert I. Gordon. Written by Tom Gries. Special Effects by Howard A. Anderson Co. With Bill Bryant.

KINGDOM IN THE CLOUDS (1968) Romanian science fantasy about a boy who discovers the secret of immorta-lity, then, after many magical adventures, loses that gift in the fountain of time.

P★★	T★★	E★★	A★

Directed and written by Elisabeta Bostan. (Eng-lish language version written by Janet Waggener.) With Mircea Breazu, Ana Szeles, Ion Tugearu.

KINGDOM OF THE SPIDERS (1977) While still reliant upon our phobic reaction to spiders for its chief effect, this film, like *Phase IV* (q.v.), depicts a radical change in behaviour in one of the smaller species. The cooperation amongst these tarantulas, changed by a chemical in a new crop-dusting formula, is eerily convincing and their conquest of the small Arizona town ultimately quite chilling.

P★★	T★★★	E★★★	A★★

Directed by John Cardos. Written by Richard Robinson and Alan Caillou. Special Effects by Greg Auer. With William Shatner, Tiffany Boll-ing, Woody Strode and Lieuz Dressler.

KING KONG (1933) It's a film centring around *two* great showmen, really. The first is the male lead of the movie, Carl Denham (Robert Armstrong), a Barnum-esque movie mogul who goes to fog-shrouded Skull Island to make a film about the mythical giant ape Kong. But by far the greater showman is director-pro-ducer Merian C. Cooper, who seemed to have in mind solely the production of a spectacular monster movie, only to end up as the creator of cinema's most famous archetypal character. And not even a *hu-man* character at that. Denham sets out

A scene from the original, 1933, version of King Kong

from New York Harbour with Anne Darrow (Fay Wray), a waif he as swept off the shtreets and promised to transform into a movie star. They and the crew reach their destination to fnd an enormous wall ringing the complete interior of Skull Island – it is within this barrier that Kong has been confined for centuries. The savage tribe outside the wall are preparing several of their women to become ritual "brides" of Kong to propitiate what they see as a god. Denham's arrival is discovered. The savage chief (Noble Johnson) demands that Anne Darrow be handed over to be sacrificed. Denham's people refuse and withdraw to their ship, but during the night a native canoe slips alongside and Anne Darrow is kidnapped. Her rescuers – first mate Jack Driscoll (Bruce Cabot), who has fallen in love with her, most prominent amongst them – arrive too late. Kong has already carried the girl off into the jungle. Yet instead of devouring her, he too falls in love with her, protects her from the other giant, prehistoric beasts inhabiting the enclosure until Driscoll finally catches up and rescues her. Enraged, Kong pursues the couple back to the wall, only to fall into a trap which the entrepreneurial Denham has set. Kong is transported to New York but on the first night he is exhibited he breaks out of his cage and rampages through the city, once again in search of Darrow. Capturing her, he clambers to the top of the Empire State Building where he is finally attacked and killed. Looked at coldly, it's a pretty asinine plot, a pure boys' pulp adventure. Worse, you can practically hear, in Cooper's approach to the movie, the cheap tinny cry of the carnival huckster. The ape crushes people like bugs, chews their heads off, molests white virgins. (Some of the scenes of carnage were such strong meat for 1930s audiences that the censor originally cut them.) It's the old story – for other versions of the story look at the success of Tarzan and Sherlock Homes – of an adventure hack turning up a **subconscious**, universal image which crosses all boundaries of age, nationality, and language. And there's a great wealth of those universal images here. The ape becomes an all-purpose victim, a god-figure, a Christ-figure. The "Beauty and the Beast" theme is a strong influence, and one that is referred to in the script. But there is still more going on than that. Certainly far more than the undercurrent of sexuality which was chosen as the main theme of the dismal 1976 remake. Perhaps Kong – and this is an impression reinforced by the eerie, primeval, dream-like quality of his Skull Island habitat – becomes a manifestation of our primal selves all coalesced into one vast figure, a shadow image from our racial memories far more than simply a giant gorilla. It seems pedantic to the point of churlishness to point out that he was simply an 18-inch-tall model clad in dyed rabbits' fur, brilliantly manipulated by Willis O'Brien. It seems futile to remark that, even by the standards of their own time, the values of the film are morally base – the role of the ape as victim is skimmed over in order not to diminish his innate scariness; Denham, crass and money-grubbing, on the other hand, is someone we are asked to empathize with. The movie defies intellectual dissection. How else could a film about a giant monkey join the highest pantheon of Hollywood greats?

P★   T★★★★   E★★★★★   A★★★★

Co-directed by Ernest Schoedsack. Written by James Geelan and Ruth Rose, from a story by Edgar Wallace. With Frank Reicher. (TR)

KING KONG (1976) Despite a promising first 20 minutes, this proves to be a really abysmal remake of the 1933 classic. With Jessica Lange as the blonde "beauty" forced to mouth asinine lines of chic-jokey dialogue at the ape instead of simply screaming, and Jeff Bridges as a hippie ecologist, the "conscience" in a movie so dishonest about its 1970s ideals, it attempts sympathy for the exploited ape and then goes right ahead to depict Third World tribesmen shouting *unga-bunga* and leaping about in true pre-War matinée movie style. All the magic, mystery, and myth of the original are stripped away; Kong becomes merely a horny guy in a hairy coat. And thankfully, despite all the hype, audiences and critics alike shouted *unga-bunga* and leapt for the exits. Absurd schlock.

P	T★★★	E	A

Directed by John Guillermin. Written by Lorenzo Semple, Jnr. With Charles Grodin, John Randolph, Ed Lauter, Julius Harris and John Agar. (TR)

KING KONG ESCAPES (1967) Kong, roped into Toho studios' interminable monster-movie sequence, here battles Gorosaurus, a duplicate of himself called Mechanikong, and a mad scientist (Dr Who, but not to be confused with the British Who) up to no good.

P★	T★	E★	A

Directed by Inoshiro Honda. Written by Kaoru Mabuchi. Special Effects by Eiji Tsuburaya. With Rhodes Reason, Mie Hama and Linda Miller.

KING KONG'S COUNTER-ATTACK (1967) *see* KING KONG ESCAPES (1967)

KING KONG VS. GODZILLA (1962) It's possible to read this symbolically, as a clash of US and Japanese cultures, but it's also possible to see it as just another very silly addition to the Japanese monster movie series.

P	T★	E	A

Directed by Inoshiro Honda and Thomas Montgomery. Written by Shinichi Sekizawa, Paul Mason and Bruce Howard. Special Effects by Eiji Tsuburaya. With Michael Keith and James Yagi.

KING ROBOT (1952) *see* OLD MOTHER RILEY MEETS THE VAMPIRE (1952)

KISSES FOR MY PRESIDENT (1964) Near-future comedy about a time when the USA has a female President.

P★	T★★	E★★	A★

Produced and directed by Curtis Bernhardt. Written by Claude Binyon and Robert G. Kane. With Fred MacMurray, Polly Bergen and Arlene Dahl.

KISS ME QUICK! (1964) *see* DR BREEDLOVE (1964)

KISS THE GIRLS AND MAKE THEM DIE (1966) A Dino De Laurentiis production about a satellite which can emit rays which will sterilize Man. A mad industrialist is responsible, and, in his plan for world conquest, he keeps a number of women in suspended animation.

P★	T★★	E★	A

Directed by Henry Levin and Dino Maiuri. Written by Maiuri and Jack Pulman. Special Effects by Augie Lohman. With Michael Connors, Dorothy Provine, Raf Vallone and Terry Thomas.

KLAUN FERDINAND A RAKETA (1962) *see* CLOWN FERDINAND AND THE ROCKET (1962)

KONCHU DAISENSO (1968) *see* WAR OF INSECTS (1968)

KONEC SRPNA V HOTELU OZON (1965) *see* END OF AUGUST AT THE HOTEL OZONE (1965)

KONGA (1960) A mad scientist, busy raising man-eating plants, manages to turn a charming chimp into killer Konga, a gorilla, which grows to a giant size and ravages London.

P★	T★★	E★★	A★

Directed by John Lemont. Written by Aben Kandel and Herman Cohen. With Michael Gough, Margo Johns and Jess Conrad.

KRAKATIT (1948) Adapted from the novel by Karel Capek, this is a workaday story about a scientist's moral dilemma on inventing the super-explosive Krakatit. A pacifistic statement on the threat posed by atomic weapons after the bombings of Hiroshima and Nagasaki.

P★★	T★★	E★	A★

Produced, directed and written by Otakar Vavra. With Florence Marly and Karel Hoeger.

KRONOS (1957) Surprisingly, this film of a 100-foot cubical robot who comes to Earth in a flying saucer and eats up energy isn't Japanese. There's a side plot about a man taken over by a liquid creature.

P★	T★★	E★	A

Produced and directed by Kurt Newmann. Special Effects by Jack Rabin, Irving Block and Louis DeWitt. Written by Irving Block. With Jeff Morrow, Barbara Lawrence, John Emery and George O'Hanlon.

KRULL (1983) One of the first, pure, fully-fledged examples of science *fantasy* (as opposed to straightforward fantasy) to find its way to the big screen, *Krull* is one of the most disappointing films to result from the boom in sf cinema's technology. A weak script – about Prince Colwyn's quest to free his princess from the clutches of The Beast in his Black Fortress – and a rather indifferent lead performance by Ken Marshall as Colwyn make for a film lacking any dramatic tension whatsoever. The scenery is, of course, marvellously romantic, the effects dazzling, individual moments highly memorable, but the whole is a bit of a mess. The enjoyment here comes from the stunning visuals – the intricate, almost animate insides of the Black Fortress, the Beast itself, the Cyclops (Bernard Bresslaw brilliantly disguised), the shape-changers and the Web. It *is* worth seeing for those alone, but how much better it might have been had they recruited someone with a genuine *feel* for the fantastic (and not just its clichés) to write the story!

P★	T★★★★★	E★★★	A★★

Directed by Peter Yates. Written by Stanford Sherman. Special Effects by: (Visual) Derek Meddings, (Optical) Robin Browne, (Make-up) Nick Maley, (General) John Evans and Mark Meddings. With Freddie Jones, Alun Armstrong and Francesca Annis.

L

THE LADY AND THE MONSTER (1944) Based on Curt Siodmak's novel *Donovan's Brain*, this early mad-scientist-keeps-brain-alive movie (with its twist that the disembodied brain telepathically controls its "keeper") is a fair indication in its indifferent standards of all the brain movies that were to come a decade later.

P★★	T★★	E★★	A

Directed by George Sherman. Written by Dave Lussier and Frederick Kohner. Special Effects by Theodore Lydecker. With Vera Ralston, Richard Arlen and Erich Von Stroheim.

THE LAND THAT TIME FORGOT (1974) Stop-action animation was beyond the budget of this film, so the monsters inhabiting the lost isle of Caprona are glove puppets or wire-operated dummies in this adaptation of the Edgar Rice Burroughs pulp novel. And perhaps that works out for the best – expensive, impressive special effects might have destroyed the enjoyable matinée-movie feel. Survivors of a World War One submarine attack take over a crippled U-boat and drift to an island where prehistoric beasts still roam. The mixed crew – English, Americans, and Germans – are forced into an uneasy truce if they are to survive. The script was written by Michael Moorcock – whose own early novels were tributes to Burroughs – and James Cawthorne.

P★★	T★★★	E★★★★	A

Directed by Kevin Connor. Special Effects by Derek Meddings. With John McEnery, Susan Penhaligon, Keith Barron and Anthony Ainsley. (TR)

THE LAND UNKNOWN (1957) Minor lost world film about a tropical oasis in the Antarctic where dinosaurs and man-eating plants have survived.

P★	T★	E★	A

Directed by Virgil Vogel. Written by Laszlo Gorog. Special Effects by Clifford Stine, Fred Knoth, Orien Ernest, Jack Kevin and Roswell A. Hoffman. With Jack Mahoney, Shawn Smith, William Reynolds and Phil Harvey.

LASERBLAST (1978) Lizard-like giant aliens chase an escaped slave to Earth and kill him, but neglect to collect the laser and controlling neckpiece he was carrying. An American teenager finds and is "changed" by the alien technology, going on the rampage. In the end the lizard men return and kill the boy.

| P★ | T★★★ | E★ | A |

Directed by Michael Rae. Written by Franne Schacht and Frank Ray Perilli. Animation Effects by Dave Allen. Special Effects by Harry Wolman. With Kim Milford, Cheryl Smith, Gianni Russo and Keenan Wynn.

THE LAST CHILD (1971) Made-for-TV film about a near-future USA under a totalitarian regime, which strictly controls population. A couple has an illegal baby.

Directed by John L. Moxey. Written by Peter S. Fischer. With Van Heflin, Michael Cole, Harry Guardino and Edward Asner.

THE LAST DAYS OF MAN ON EARTH (1973) *see* THE FINAL PROGRAMME (1973)

THE LAST HOUR (1930) Slow-paced sf thriller about a prince who steals a death ray and uses it to force down airships and steal their cargoes.

| P | T | E★ | A |

Directed by Walter Forde. Written by H. Fowler Mear. With Stewart Rome, Richard Cooper and Kathleen Vaughan.

THE LAST MAN (1968) Domestic melodrama set in the days after the Holocaust – with only three survivors: a man, his wife, and the other woman.

| P★ | T★★ | E★ | A |

Directed and written by Charles Bitsch. With Jean-Claude Bouillon, Corinne Brill and Sophia Torkelli.

THE LAST MAN ON EARTH (1924) The "What If?" premise here is that women take over the running of the world (filling all male and female roles – badly, as it happens here) when all but one man over 14 have been wiped out in an epidemic.

Directed by Jack G. Blystone. Written by Donald W. Lee, from a story by John D. Swain. With Earle Foxe, Derelys Perdue and Grace Cunard.

THE LAST MAN ON EARTH (1963) A plague, blown across the Earth on the winds, turns humans into nightwalking zombies; all but one man who escapes being a vampire mutant, though in the end he too succumbs. Based on Richard Matheson's *I Am Legend*.

| P★★ | T★ | E★ | A |

Directed by Sidney Salkow and Ubaldo Ragona. Written by Logan Swanson and William P. Leicester. With Vincent Price, Franca Bettoia and Giacomo Rossi-Stuart.

THE LAST STARFIGHTER (1984) In the 1960s a bad producer would stick a few extras in monkey suits and space helmets; in the 1980s there's more than enough money in the kitty to buy the very best in special effects and to hire the top actors from the soaps. What remains the same is the paucity of true creative thought behind the resultant films. *The Last Starfighter* is one of a new generation of sf films – perhaps typifying them – with its use of computer graphics simulation, life-like aliens, marvellous model work and a wide range of sf images. Compared to anything pre-dating *2001* it's a visual treat. Unfortunately one has also to listen to the dialogue, follow the plot-line and attempt to ignore the howling great black holes in the logic of the thing. First let's look at the story. Alex Rogan (Lance Guest) is a teenager stuck in a rut (the Starlite Starbrite Trailer Park). All he's good at is the video game, The Last Starfighter. Yes, you've guessed it ... He beats the record, is recruited as a starfighter, and – after a bout of reluctance – finally goes out into the stars and single-handedly defeats the aliens who want to conquer our galaxy. He even gets to fly his spacecraft home to pick up his girl. Even that aspect of the story where Alex gets an android "double" to take his place while he's gone has its weaknesses – the Zandoran "hit beast" sent to kill him is so inept it's a wonder it doesn't shoot itself. This juvenile power fantasy, complete with its stultifyingly dull "Death Blossom" scene makes about as much sense as any eight-year-old's school essay – especially in scenes where the Frontier of Space is surrounded by huge floating craft which form a kind of web of energy, keeping the aliens out. A simple calculation would convince a low-grade physics student that it just wasn't feasible. But then, feasibility wasn't a criterion.

P	T★★★★	E★★	A

Directed by Nick Castle. Written by Jonathan Betuel. With Dan O'Herlihy, Catherine Mary Stewart, Barbara Bosson, Norman Snow and Robert Preston. Production Design by Ron Cobb. Computer Graphics by John Whitney Jr, Gary Demos (Digital Productions).

THE LAST WAVE (1977) Following his success with *Picnic At Hanging Rock* (1975), Peter Weir decided to push even further his obsession with the intrusion of the inexplicable into our rational, bounded world. Focus of his story is a Sydney lawyer, David Burton (Richard Chamberlain), whose ordered world is shattered by his discovery that he has prescience. His foresight takes the form of a vision of an Apocalyptic "last wave" that will flood Sydney. As with *Picnic*, the irrational element in the tale originates in ancient aboriginal culture, and, though we can never be certain whether the lawyer's vision is objective or subjective (the wave is the last thing we see – through *his* eyes), we are convinced enough by Weir's narrative to accept its strong possibility.

P★★★★	T★★★★	E★★★★	A★★★★

Written by Weir, Tony Morphett and Petru Popescu, from an idea by Weir. With Olivia Hammett, Gulpilil, Frederick Parslow, Vivian Gray and Nandjiwarra Amagula.

THE LAST WOMAN ON EARTH (1960) Roger Corman produced and directed this cheap-budget post-Disaster story, a cliché about two men and one woman – the only survivors – on a tropical island. A weak allegory of pleasure and purpose.

P★	T★	E★★	A

Written by Robert Towne. With Antony Carbone, Betsy Jones-Moreland and Edward Wain.

Giorgio Albertazzi (left) and Sacha Pitoeff (right) in Last Year In Marienbad

LAST YEAR IN MARIENBAD (1961) Alain Robbe-Grillet, the French anti-novelist, wrote the script to this Alain Resnais film about time and memory and uncertainty. Its three characters, X, A and M (Giorgio Albertazzi, Delphine Seyrig and Sacha Pitoeff), enact an enigma which, through repetition of events, of phrases and of images, erodes the certainty of what was remembered. Of course, it isn't science fiction as the pulps would define it, but its games with the malleability of "inner space" (its constant reshaping of what is remembered of an unspecified event) make it a parallel in cinematic terms to the New Wave science fiction of the 1960s. A visual treat, it is one of the few truly original cinematic experiences.

P★★★★	T★★★★★	E★★★	A★★★★★

Cinematography by Sacha Vierny and Philippe Brun. With Pierre Barbaud, François Bertin, Luce Garcia-Ville and Helena Kornel.

LATITUDE ZERO (1969) Vernian bottom-of-the-sea tale with super-subs and exploding underwater volcano. Avoid.

P	T	E	A

Directed by Inoshiro Honda. Written by Ted Sherdeman and Shinichi Sekizawa. Special Effects by Eiji Tsuburaya. With Joseph Cotten, Cesar Romero and Akira Takarada.

LA 2017 (1970) An episode of the TV series "Name Of The Game" which was also released as a feature and notable for being directed by a young Steven Spielberg. A newspaper publisher dreams he is suddenly in a future so polluted that the whole population is living underground.

P★★	T★★	E★★	A★

Written by Philip Wylie. With Gene Barry, Barry Sullivan, Edmond O'Brien and Severn Darden.

LAUGHING AT DANGER (1924) Rather standardized film about the inventor of a death ray, crooks who steal it, and the threat to the US Navy the ray presents.

P	T★	E	A

Directed by James W. Horne. Written by Frank Howard Clark. With Richard Talmadge, Joe Girard, Joe Harrington and Eva Novak.

THE LEECH WOMAN (1960) Dull working of a tired old theme. To regain her youthful beauty a woman uses an African tribal serum which requires a male pineal gland. But its effects are only temporary and so she has to keep killing.

P	T★	E	A

Directed by Edward Dein. Written by David Duncan. With Colleen Gray, Phillip Terry and Grant Williams.

LEGALLY DEAD (1923) A scientist uses an adrenalin-based drug to bring a wrongly hanged man back to life.

Directed by William Parke. Written by Harvey Gates. With Milton Sills and Clair Adams.

LIBERXINA 90 (1971) Spanish film about an anarchist group who have control of a drug, Liberxina 90, which can wipe a man's mind clean.

Directed by Carlos Duran. Written by Joaquin Jorda and Carlos Duran. With Serena Vergano, William Pirie and Edward Meeks.

LIFE IN THE NEXT CENTURY (1909) Usual gimmick-filled vision of life 100 years hence, with automation supposedly causing ennui.

Directed by Gerard Bourgeois.

LIFE WITHOUT SOUL (1915) A feature-length (70-minute) version of Mary Shelley's *Frankenstein*. It keeps fairly closely to her novel without accentuating

the grotesque elements of the monster that later films were to capitalize upon.

Directed by Joseph W. Smiley. Written by Jesse J. Goldburg. With Percy Darrell Standing, William A. Cohill, Jack Hopkins and Lucy Cotton.

THE LIFT (1983) An interesting idea given a flawed interpretation. The lift is a machine with an organic mind of its own which begins to take vengeance on those unwitting enough to travel in it. The liftman and a young woman reporter investigate and, eventually, take on the lift. If anything the atmosphere is not claustrophobic enough.

P★★	T★★★	E★★	A★★

Directed and written by Dick Maas. Special Effects by Leo Cahn and Rene Stouthamer. With Huub Strapel, Willeke Van Ammelrooz, Piet Romer and Josine Van Dalsum.

LIGHTNING BOLT (1965) Rather silly sub-Bond thriller with a beer magnate who wants to control the world from his underwater city.

P	T★	E★	A

Directed by Antonio Margheriti. Written by Alfonso Balcazar and José Antonio De La Loma. With Anthony Eisley and Wandisa Leigh.

THE LIGHT THAT KILLS (1913) A good invention, the "A"-ray, can heal, but too great an exposure to it can kill.

LIGHT YEARS AWAY (1981) Similar in many respects to Ray Bradbury's "Icarus Montgolfier Wright", this is the story of a modern-day Icarus, an old man who dreams of flight, and the young man who becomes his admirer and helper.

P★★	T★★★	E★★	A★★

Directed and written by Alain Tanner. With Trevor Howard, Mick Ford and Odile Schmitt.

THE LION'S BREATH (1916) A nice variant on the brain transplant theme. Here a scientist switches the characters of a lion and a meek, retiring man, making the latter a bold go-getter.

Directed by Horace Davey. Written by Al E. Christie. With Neal Burns, Billie Rhodes and Jean Hathaway.

LIQUID ELECTRICITY (1907) A chemist synthesizes a new fluid which stores electricity. Spraying this on himself he realizes that it accelerates his movements. Further experiments allow producer/director J. Stuart Blackton to indulge in some speeded-up photography.

LIQUID SKY (1982) Perhaps the point of *Liquid Sky* is that the modern New Wave New Yorker is an alien – in the Bowie mould? – and that his/her obsession with sex and drugs and rock 'n' roll is about as divorced from reality as the tiny UFO that lands on the roof of Margaret's Manhattan penthouse in this film. The aliens – who take Margaret over – are heroin addicts, but they can make do on a chemical reproduced in the brain at the moment of orgasm. Margaret works her way sexually through all her male friends and acquaintances – vengefully de-materializing them at the moment of orgasm – until the moment comes when she herself is threatened and seeks aid from the aliens. It's a humorously perverse film, bleakly funny rather than comic, but with a great deal of style. Of course.

P★★	T★★★★	E★★★	A★★

Directed by Slava Tsukerman. Written by Tsukerman, Anna Carlisle and Nina V. Kerova. Cinematography by Yuri Neyman. With Anna Carlisle, Paul E. Sheppard and Susan Doukas.

THE LITTLE SHOP OF HORRORS (1960) Remarkable little sf comedy made, so it's said, in two days. Roger Corman, more noted for his sf rip-offs, produced and directed this rough-edged gem about a florist's assistant who develops and raises a talking ("feed me!"), man-eating plant. Its pacing, acting and script (courtesy of Charles Griffith) transcend the minuscule budget effects.

P★★★	T★	E★★★★	A★

With Jonathan Haze and Jackie Joseph.

THE LIVING DEAD AT THE MANCHESTER MORGUE (1974) An Italian film shot in the Lake District and, in true George Romero tradition, dealing with zombies created when a new chemical spray (used on crops) resurrects the dead. A nicely dark ironic twist at the end makes this enjoyable if bloodthirsty.

P★★	T★★	E★★	A★

Directed by Jorge Grau. Written by Sandro Continenza and Marcello Coscia. Special Effects by Giannetto De Rossi and Luciano Bird. With Ray Lovelock and Christine Galbo.

LLEGARON LOS MARCIANOS (1964) *see* THE MARTIANS ARRIVED (1964)

LOCK YOUR DOORS (1943) *see* THE APE MAN (1943)

LOGAN'S RUN (1976) Authors William F. Nolan and George Clayton Johnson disowned this adaptation of their novel, which is easy to understand. But how it became the paradigm, within the clannish sf world, of all that is bad in science fiction movies, is somewhat harder to follow. There are many hundred far worse movies contained in, for instance, this book. In a futuristic city sealed beneath an impenetrable dome and run by a computer, Logan (Michael York) is a Sandman, a policeman trained to hunt and kill those who would destroy the dome's delicate ecological balance by refusing to die at the mandatory age of 30. When his own time is made, artificially, to run out, he and rebel Jenny Agutter decide to make their own run for the exit. It's a quest story, some of it through the gaudy, plastic city, the rest through an outside world which, unfortunately, looks even more plastic – presumably it was the numbing effect of the latter which stunned Peter Ustinov into the hammiest performance of his life as the Old Man the runaway couple encounter amongst the ruins of Washington D.C., who travels back to prove to the dome-dwellers there is life after 30. The ending, with the city erupting and the inhabitants swarming for freedom *Metropolis*-style, is coy and truly dreadful. And there are loose-ends and idiocies all the way through. But *Logan's Run* does not pretend to have anything important to say, does not portend to be anything more than what it is – a fast,

Michael York and Jenny Agutter in a scene from Logan's run

colourful adventure movie, and as such it succeeds fairly well. Some of the special effects are spectacular – the scene of the "Carousel" ritual, when the 30-year-olds levitate and disappear in a puff of smoke, is especially good. But sf fans abhorred this movie. A couple of years later they were holding *Star Wars* up as their answer to *Citizen Kane*, which shows what a peculiar mob they are.

P★★	T★★★★	E★★★	A

Directed by Michael Anderson. Written by David Zelag Goodman. Special Effects by L. B. Abbott and Glen Robinson. With Richard Jordan, Roscoe Lee Browne. Farrah Fawcett-Majors and Michael Anderson Jnr. (TR)

LOLA (1916) *see* WITHOUT A SOUL (1916)

LOOKER (1981) Flawed thriller about near-future high-tech society where 3-D computer-generated human images are used in advertising (with the same kind of effect as subliminals, partly hypnotizing people). Further investigations turn up something even more sinister – that the original human models are being killed off . . . Either this was made to defy comprehension or it was cut badly before release. And, as ever in Michael Crichton's films, there's a sense of corporate conspiracy.

P★★	T★★★	E★★	A★

Directed and written by Michael Crichton. Special Effects by Joe Day. With Albert Finney, James Coburn, Susan Dey and Leigh Taylor-Young.

LOOKING FORWARD (1910) Scientific variant on the Rip Van Winkle tale, with a man, put to sleep for 100 years by a potion, waking to a future world run by women.

LORD OF THE FLIES (1963) William Golding's novel tells of a group of schoolboys stranded on a coral island after their plane has crashed. It is made clear that the Bomb has fallen, civilization is threatened, and, through the slow deterioration of ingrained patterns of behaviour and restraint in the boys, we see – in microcosm – what would happen to society at large. There's more to the novel than that, of course – a level of experience beyond the social, glimpsed by the saintly Simon – but Peter Brook's film (he directed and wrote) keeps to the tangible. Something is therefore lost in translation from one medium to the other – the powerful savagery of the book and its sense of the sea and the darkness beneath the trees. The definitive film of this book is yet to be made.

P★★★	T★★	E★★★	A★★

With James Aubrey, Tom Chapin, Hugh Edwards, Roger Elwin and Tom Gaman.

LOSS OF FEELING (1935) Intelligent adaptation of Karel Capek's famous novel, *Rossum's Universal Robots*, about a fully-automated future where machines have become what men were – slaves to the economic process.

P★★★	T★★	E★★	A★★

Directed by Aleksander Andrievski. Written by G. Grebner. With S. Vecheslov and V. Gardin.

LOSS OF SENSATION (1935) *see* LOSS OF FEELING (1935)

LOST ANGEL (1943) A pleasant child prodigy story, about a six-year old foundling who, raised by a child psychologist, has the intellect and verbal abilities of a college professor.

P★★	T★	E★★	A★

Directed by Roy Rowland. Written by Isobel Lennart. With Margaret O'Brien, James Craig, Marsha Hunt and Keenan Wynn.

LOST ATLANTIS (1921) Simple story of two married men who, on their travels, discover the legendary Atlantis and fall beneath the sway of its powerful queen.

Directed and written by Jacques Feyder. With Stacia Napierkovska, Jean Angelo, Marie-Louise Iribe and Georges Melchoir.

LOST ATLANTIS (1923) The beautiful Brigitte Helm starred as Antinea, the Queen of Atlantis, whose lovers are preserved for ever in mummified form. Based on Pierre Benoit's novel, *The Queen Of Atlantis*.

P★	T★	E★	A★

Directed by Georg Wilhelm Pabst. Written by Ladislaus Vajda and Hermann Oberlaender. With (German): Gustav Diessl, Heinz Klingenberg and Tela Tschai; (French): Pierre Blanchard and Odette Florelle; (English): John Stuart and Gibb McLaughlin.

LOST CONTINENT (1951) A lost atomic rocket is traced to a mountainous island in the South Seas. There, uranium deposits are discovered, the radioactivity from which has preserved a primeval world of dinosaurs.

P★	T★	E★	A

Directed by Samuel Newfield. Written by Richard H. Landau. Special Effects by Augie Lohman. With Cesar Romero and Hillary Brooke.

THE LOST CONTINENT (1968) Based on Dennis Wheatley's novel *Uncharted Seas*, this tells of an area of the sea inhabited by giant crabs and jellyfish and a colony of Spanish conquistadores, trapped in time. Thoroughly nondescript.

P★	T★	E	A

Produced and directed by Michael Carreras. Written by Michael Nash. Special Effects by Robert A. Mattey and Cliff Richardson. With Eric Porter, Hildegard Kneff, Suzanna Leigh and Nigel Stock.

THE LOST FACE (1965) A nicely worked comedy about a doctor who can change his face and imitate people.

P★★	T★★	E★★	A★★

Directed by Pavel Hobl. Written by Hobl and Josef Nesvadba. With Vlastimil Brodsky, Jana Brejehova and Fred Delmare.

LOST HORIZON (1936) By a strict definition, this adaptation of James Hilton's well-known novel is not science fiction at all; but on its own terms, this is excellent light entertainment with some good moments of pure hokum. Nowadays (apart from science itself) the most common source of new words in English has been science fiction, and here we are presented with a memorable new word – Shangri-La, that magical land of love and eternal youth that lies, always, just beyond the next mountain range, where the sun shines when you need it to and every man can be good and kind if he chooses. The film begins with an exciting escape from an armed Chinese rabble, and there is a spectacular flight through the Himalayas; the frigid, alien mountainscape lingers in the memory. The paradise itself is perhaps less memorable. Even for 1937, the love-affair (not acted with any particular passion) is somewhat conventionalized, and the long ethical debates are, indeed, very long. However, Ronald Colman is excellent, and though the film is dated and inconsistent, it provides many pleasurable moments and the lovely word *Shangri-La*.

P★★★	T★★★	E★★★★	A★★★

Produced and directed by Frank Capra. Written by Robert Ruskin. Special Effects by E. Roy Davidson and Ganahl Carson. With Jane Wyatt and Sam Jaffe. (RS)

LOST HORIZON (1972) Dire musical re-make of Frank Capra's 1936 classic where stray travellers are taken to the lost city of Shangri-La, high in a Himalayan valley. The near immortality of those in the valley – the High Lama (Charles Boyer) is over 200 years old – fades quickly when they are taken from the valley, a seemingly young girl ageing to her true 100 years and dying. Peter Finch and Liv Ullman are only two of the talented cast who waste themselves on this tediously long production (150 minutes!).

P★★	T★★	E★	A★

Directed by Charles Jarrott. Written by Larry Kramer. Special Effects by Butler-Glouner. With Sally Kellerman, George Kennedy, Michael York, Olivia Hussey, Bobby Van, James Shigeta, John Gielgud and Kent Smith.

LOST IN SPACE (1983) *see* SPACE RAIDERS (1983)

THE LOST MISSILE (1958) Utterly ridiculous tale of an alien missile which orbits Earth at a very low altitude and incinerates all below its flight path.

P	T★	E	A

Directed by Lester W. Berke. Written by John McPartland and Jerome Bixby. With Robert Loggia, Ellen Parker and Larry Kerr.

THE LOST VALLEY (1968) *see* THE VALLEY WHERE TIME STOOD STILL (1968)

THE LOST WORLD (1925) Lost world stories were a staple of the pulp magazines in the 1920s and this adventure, based on Conan Doyle's novel, was the model for many later cinematic ventures into this sub-genre. Willis O'Brien (later the creator of King Kong) and Marcel Delgado made the model dinosaurs – one of which, a brontosaurus, is captured by the expedition members and taken back to London, where it escapes and wreaks havoc (perhaps anticipating the Japanese monster-ravages-Tokyo obsession of the 1960s).

P★	T★★	E★★	A★

Directed by Harry O. Hoyt. Written by Marion Fairfax. With Wallace Beery, Lewis Stone, Bessie Love, Lloyd Hughes and Arthur Hoyt.

THE LOST WORLD (1960) A tame, even banal, re-working of the 1925 version of Conan Doyle's novel. Claude Rains starred, hampered rather than helped by Irwin Allen and Charles Bennett's script, and the dreadful special effects of L. B. Abbott, Emil Kosa Jr and James B. Gordon. It adds nothing and loses much, and after a while you begin to wish it *were* a silent movie like the original. The plateau is filled this time not with model monsters but with photographically enlarged lizards. Rather silly.

P★	T★★	E	A

Produced and directed by Irwin Allen. With Michael Rennie, Jill St John, David Hedison and Fernando Lamas.

LOVE AND SCIENCE (1912) An early glimpse of video-phones, as an inventor produces a machine that lets you see who you're phoning.

THE LOVE DOCTOR (1917) A case of medical neatness as a doctor transplants the brain of a girl who loves him into the body of the woman he loves.

Directed by Paul Scardon. Written by Louis Garfinkle. With Earle Williams, Corinne Griffith.

THE LOVE MICROBE (1907) A lovely idea – of finding and separating the microbe which causes love in people – extrapolated in true sf fashion. The doctor develops a love serum, which he tries on the unsuspecting with glorious success.

Directed by Wallace McCutcheon.

LOVERS BEYOND THE TOMB (1965) *see* THE FACELESS MONSTER (1965)

LUANA, DAUGHTER OF THE VIRGIN FOREST (1968) Mundane throw-back to the days of serums, man-eating plants and distant, isolated parts.

Directed by Bob Raymond. Written by Louis Road. With Mei Chin and Evi Marandi.

LAS LUCHADORAS CONTRA EL MEDICO AESINO (1965) *see* DOCTOR OF DOOM (1965)

LUCHI SMERTI (1925) *see* THE DEATH RAY (1925)

M

MA AND PA KETTLE BACK ON THE FARM (1951) A film important for its influence on the impressionable young Steven Spielberg, it was based on Betty MacDonald's characters. Pa Kettle's overalls become radioactive and provide power for the kitchen appliances.

P★	T★★	E★★	A

Directed by Edward Sedgwick. Written by Jack Henley. With Marjorie Main, Percy Kilbride, Richard Long and Meg Randall.

MACISTE CONTRO GLI UOMINI DELLA LUNA (1965) *see* HERCULES AGAINST THE MOON MEN (1965)

MADAME SIN (1971) Bette Davis and Robert Wagner starred in this rather slight thriller-with-gimmicks tale of a Chinese scientific mastermind (a woman) who develops sonic guns, mind-controlling drugs and other devices for evil uses.

P★	T★	E★	A

Directed by David Greene. Written by Greene and Barry Oringer. With Denholm Elliott, Gordon Jackson, Roy Kinnear and Pik-Sen Lim.

MAD DOCTOR OF BLOOD ISLAND (1969) Rare Philippines excursion into the mad scientist genre – this time creating a chlorophyll monster (yes, you read that right!). Fortunately rare.

P	T★	E	A

Directed by Eddie Romero and Gerardo de Leon. Written by Reuben Conway. With John Ashley, Angelique Pettyjohn and Eddie Garcia.

THE MAD DOCTOR OF MARKET STREET (1941) Strictly horror-oriented mad scientist movie, as Lionel Atwill tries to raise the dead and experiments with suspended animation.

P★	T★	E★★	A

Directed by Joseph H. Lewis. Written by Al Martin. With Una Merkel, Nat Pendleton, Claire Dodd, Anne Nagel and Hardie Albright.

MAD LOVE (1935) An intelligent, atmospheric re-making of *The Hands Of Orlac* (1925) (q.v.) starring Peter Lorre and Colin Clive. Clive plays the pianist who, after a train crash, is given the hands of a murderer to replace his own lost ones. Lorre plays the surgeon who impersonates worse injuries (decapitation and mutilation, warranting a new head and arms). Lorre's presence adds to the film's essential darkness, as does the underlying theme of sexual jealousy and insane desire.

P★★★	T★★★	E★★★★	A★★★

Directed by Karl Freund. Written by P. J. Wolfson and John L. Balderston. With Frances Drake, Henry Kolker, Isabel Jewell and Keye Luke.

THE MADMAN OF LAB 4 (1967) A chemist invents a formula for a gas which makes people love one another, and is pursued for his secret by the underworld. A rather low-key comedy.

P★	T★	E★★	A★

Directed by Jacques Besnard. Written by Jean Halain. With Jean Lefebvre, Maria Latour, Bernard Blier and Pierre Brasseur.

MAD MAX (1979) There's an oddness about the social set-up of *Mad Max* that makes you wonder just when this is set, and where. It's obvious that director/writer George Miller was aiming at the American car-chase market with this first Max movie in which Max (Mel Gibson) loses his wife and child and goes after the amoral, leather-clad bikers for revenge. As cop-turned-killer, an MCP Interceptor who is pushed just *too* far and freaks, Max is not quite the mythic figure he becomes in the sequel, but elements of the film – Anarchie Road, The Halls Of Justice, the Toecutter – point towards the comic-book post-Apocalyptic vision of *Mad Max II* (q.v.). This is an amateurish production with touches of melodrama (and the death of Max's family is signalled long before it occurs; the only drama is when).

P★★	T★★	E★★★★	A★

Written by James McCausland and George Miller. With Joanne Samuel, Roger Ward, Steve Bisley, Tim Burns and Hugh Keays-Byrne.

MAD MAX II (1981) "A time of chaos, ruined dreams, this wasted land …" As the talk-over at the beginning of *Mad Max II* introduces the idea of a post-War, post-Economic Collapse world and the central plot-mechanism of a fuel-less society where wealth is oil, we move from the adventure-based Americanized world of *Mad Max* to a land of myth – a future parallel of the old West, with barbarian savages (led by the Lord Humungus – Kjell Nilsson) battling to get control of a refinery run by more civilized (white-clothed) types; pure Fort Apache stuff, with bikes for horses and some nasty gimmicks thrown in. And amidst all, moves Max (Mel Gibson), an emotionally

A scene from Mad Max II.

emptied, practical man – a survivor and, ultimately, a hero in the classic ancient mould (the final shot really does impress this upon your every sense), the "Road Warrior". The plot, of course, isn't anything special; any imaginative kid in his early teens could have thrown it together. What is important is the overall mythic feel of this movie. In two years George Miller learned a lot about film-making, and the sequel is in a different league to the original, almost hallucinatory in some scenes. Much time, of course, is given up to the final grand chase as the battle-truck, loaded (so we believe) with oil, makes a break through the Humungus's camp on its way North (to where Civilization still exists in some form). It's a bloody, cruel, but ultimately moralistic movie – is Max just as bad as those he seems to despise? – which hits just the right tone.

P★★	T★★★★	E★★★★★	A★★

Directed by George Miller. Written by Terry Hayes, George Miller and Brian Hannant. Special Effects by Jeffrey Clifford, Monte Fieuth, David Hardy and Steve Courtley. With Bruce Spence, Mike Preston, Max Phipps and Vernon Wells.

MADMEN OF MANDORAS (1963)
On the island of Mandoras a group of Nazi fanatics have kept Hitler's brain alive, meanwhile developing Nerve Gas G which will destroy the world. An almost comically bad film

P	T★	E★★	A

Directed by David Bradley. Written by Richard Miles and Steve Bennett. With Walter Stocker, Audrey Caire, Carlos Rivas and Nestor Paiva.

MADMEN'S TRIAL (1962) A scientist develops the means of paralysing wills within a range of several miles.
Directed and written by Grigori Roshal. With Irina Skobtseva and Vasili Livanov.

THE MADNESS OF DR TUBE
(1915) Early special effects fantasia about a doctor who can split light with prisms.
Directed by Abel Gance. Cinematography by L. H. Burel.

MADRID IN THE YEAR 2000
(1925) Almost documentary vision of Madrid's future as a city – in fact, as a port (Madrid is more than 200 km inland) thanks to a huge canal system.

P★	T★★	E★	A

Directed and written by Manuel Noriega. With Roberto Iglesias, Roberto Rey, Javier Rivera, Amelia Sanz Crusado and Juan Nada.

THE MAGIC GLASS (1914) An early
science fantasy about a fluid which makes the scientist's reading glass have x-ray properties.
Directed by Hay Plumb. With Eric Desmond.

MAGIC SPECTACLES (1961) Slight
film about X-ray glasses which allow a man to see women in the nude.

P	T★	E★	A

Produced, written and narrated by Arch Hall. Directed by A. H. Mehling. With Tommy Holden, Margo Mehling, June Pari and Kay Kramer.

MAGIC TOWN (1970) Enjoyable story
of a small US town so typical that it provides poll results which accurately reflect how the rest of the US will vote in an election.

P★★	T★★	E★★★	A★

Produced and written by Robert Riskin. Directed by William A. Wellman. With James Stewart, Jane Wyman, Wallace Ford, Ann Doran and Kent Smith.

THE MAGNETIC MONSTER
(1953) A man-made isotope gets out of control, eating up energy and doubling its size every 12 hours, giving off radiation and magnetizing metal. But like all mon-

sters (animate and inanimate) in 1950s
horror movies, a huge electric shock from
a handy cyclotron kills the beastie.

P★	T★★	E★★	A

Directed by Curt Siodmak. Written by Siodmak
and Ivan Tors. Special Effects by Jack Glass. With
Richard Carlson, King Donovan, Harry Ellerbe.

THE MAID AND THE MARTIAN
(1964) Neo-Disney comedy starring
Tommy Kirk as the Martian who comes to
Earth to plan an invasion and instead falls
in love with Annette Funicello.

P★★	T★★	E★★★	A★

Directed by Don Weiss. Written by Louis M.
Heyward. Special Effects by Roger George. With
Elsa Lanchester, Buster Keaton, Harvey Lem-
beck, Jesse White, Dorothy Lamour and Frankie
Avalon.

MAIDSTONE (1971) Norman Mailer's
flawed movie-about-a-movie; supposedly
a documentary about a future USA after
the assassination of all political leaders.
The "documentary" traces the events
during the presidential elections.

P★	T★	E★	A

Directed and written by Norman Mailer. With
Mailer, Rip Torn, Beverly Bentley and Joy Bang.

LES MAITRES DU TEMPS (1982)
see THE MASTERS OF TIME (1982)

MALEVIL (1981) A post-Holocaust
scenario, taken from Robert Merle's
lengthy novel of the same name. It's curiously unconvincing, despite some lyrical
cinematography and a sense (though not
the factual reality) of the desolation following the event. A French pastoral community tries to rebuild, is twice threatened
and eventually succumbs to outside forces.
Unfortunately this is one of the slowest,
dullest sf movies of the last decade.

P★	T★★★	E	A★

Directed by Christian de Chalonge. Written by de
Chalonge and Pierre Dumayet. With Michel Ser-
rault, Jacques Dutronc, Robert Dhery, Hanns
Zischler and Jean-Louis Trintignant.

MAN AND HIS MATE (1940) see
ONE MILLION B.C. (1940)

THE MAN AND THE BEAST
(1951) Argentinian version of the Jekyll
and Hyde myth which, whilst it blunts
Stevenson's split-personality theme, is
memorable for its stark cinematography by
Antonio Merayo and Alberto Muñoz.

P★★	T★★	E★★	A★★

Directed by Mario Soffici. Written by Ulises Petit
de Murat, Soffici and Carlos Marin. Make-up by
Alberto Neron and Angel Salerno. With Mario
Soffici, Ana Maria Campoy and Olga Zubarry.

MAN BEAST (1955) Himalayan ex-
pedition to seek the Yeti achieves its
objective, is attacked, and discovers that
the Yeti are of primitive human stock and
want to breed with human women to raise
their average intelligence. I think one of
them wrote this.

P	T★	E★	A

Produced and directed by Jerry Warren. Written
by Arthur Cassidy. With Rock Madison, Virginia
Maynor and George Skuff.

A MAN CALLED DAGGER (1967)
Run-of-the-mill mad scientist spy thriller
involving a gadget-laden wheelchair (a
crippled Bond?).

P★	T★★	E★★	A

Directed by Richard Rush. Written by James
Peatman and Robert S. Weekley. With Terry
Moore, Jan Murray, Sue Ann Langdon and Paul
Mantee.

MANDRAGORE (1952) see
ALRAUNE (1952)

MANDRAKE (1918) see ALRAUNE
(1918)

MAN EATER OF HYDRA (1966) see
ISLAND OF THE DOOMED (1966)

THE MAN FROM BEYOND (1921)
An early, slightly ludicrous variation on
the thawed-out human theme. Harry
Houdini starred as the man frozen in the
Arctic ice for 100 years, who finds his
reincarnated fiancée.

Directed by Burton King. Written by Coolidge
Streeter, from Houdini's story. With Jane Connelly, Arthur Maude and Albert Tavernier.

THE MAN FROM 1997 (1957) An episode of the TV series "King's Row" shown as a feature. A man from 1997 appears in 1957 with a book which tells of his own age.

With James Garner, Gloria Talbott, Jacques Sernas and Charles Ruggles.

THE MAN FROM PLANET X (1950) Before all 1950s aliens became hostile to Earth, director Edgar G. Ulmer presented us with an alien who only wants to get help for his dying, ice-gripped planet and who receives only cold antagonism from those he meets on Earth. The production values are awful but something in its atmosphere remains impressive.

| P★★ | T★ | E★★ | A★ |

Written by Aubrey Wisberg and Jack Pollexfen. Special Effects by Andy Anderson and Howard Weeks. With Robert Clarke, Margaret Field, Raymond Bond and William Schallert.

MAN FROM THE FIRST CENTURY (1961) *see* MAN IN OUTER SPACE (1961)

THE MAN IN HALF MOON STREET (1943) A scientist has discovered a means of keeping perpetually unageing, but every ten years he has to replace a gland. When he is prevented from changing that gland he ages 60 years in minutes and dies. Re-made in 1959 as *The Man Who Could Cheat Death* (q.v.).

| P★★ | T★ | E★ | A★ |

Directed by Ralph M. Murphy. Written by Charles Kenyon. Make-up by Wally Westmore. With Nils Asther, Helen Walker, Reinhold Schunzel and Paul Cavanagh.

MAN IN OUTER SPACE (1961) Czech satire on the dangers of over-automation. A man from 1961 is accidentally fired into space in a rocket ship and encounters aliens, who take him 500 years into the future, to a machine-ruled Earth, before returning him to his own age.

| P★★ | T★★ | E★★ | A★ |

Directed by Oldrich Lipsky. Written by Lipsky and Zdenek Blaha. Special Effects by Zdenek Liska. With Milos Kopecky.

MAN IN THE MIDDLE (1959) *see* 48 HOURS TO LIVE (1959)

MAN IN THE MIRROR (1936) Slightly fantastic tale of a man whose more spontaneous, less social self steps out from the mirror to replace him every now and then. Based on William Garrett's novel.

| P★★ | T★ | E★★ | A★ |

Directed by Maurice Elvey. Written by Hugh Mills and Edward Everett Horton. With Edward Everett Horton, Genevieve Tobin, Ursula Jeans.

MAN IN THE MOON (1960) A British farce about a man (Kenneth More) whose exceptional health gets him chosen as the first British astronaut. The moonshot, however, fails and he's dumped in the wilds of Australia.

| P★★ | T★ | E★★ | A★ |

Directed by Basil Dearden. Written by Michael Relph and Bryan Forbes. With Shirley Anne Field, Michael Hordern and Norman Bird.

THE MAN IN THE RUE NOIR (1959) *see* THE MAN WHO COULD CHEAT DEATH (1959)

THE MAN IN THE WHITE SUIT (1951) An excellent comedy from the British Ealing Studios, starring Alec Guinness as the scientist who makes a fabric that does not wear out or get dirty. But such an invention doesn't suit the economy of the time; it would reduce the need for new clothes and cripple the fabric industry. The inventor is put upon by those with vested interests (entrepreneurs and workers alike). The end has a nice double twist, with the fabric of the white suit rotting away, but the inventor struck by an idea as to how he might improve it. Based on a play by Roger MacDougall.

| P★★★ | T★★ | E★★★★ | A★★ |

Directed by Alexander Mackendrick. Written by Roger MacDougall, John Dighton and Mackendrick. With Joan Greenwood, Cecil Parker, Michael Gough and Ernest Thesiger.

MAN MADE MONSTER (1941) A mad scientist takes a performer from a sideshow and turns him into an electrically powered freak whose touch electro-cutes. When the freak (Lon Chaney Jr) is arrested for murder they find they cannot electrocute him – only give him more power. Based on the story "The Electric Man" by H. J. Essex, Sid Schwartz and Len Golos.

P★★	T★	E★★	A★

Directed by George Waggner. Written by Joseph West. Special Effects by John P. Fulton. With Lionel Atwell, Anne Nagel and Frank Albertson.

EIN MANN GEHT DURCH DIE WAND (1959) see THE MAN WHO WALKED THROUGH THE WALL (1959)

DER MANN MIT DEM OBJECTIV (1963) see THE MAN WITH THE GADGET (1963)

THE MANSTER (1959) Mad chemist develops a serum which makes its taker grow a second, monstrous head. Then his own head becomes monstrous. Finally he splits into two beings, his normal self and the monster. This murderous beastie is polished off inside an erupting volcano.

P★	T★	E★	A

Directed by George P. Breakston and Kenneth G. Crane. Written by Walter J. Sheldon. With Peter Dyneley, Jane Hylton and Satoshi Nakamura.

THE MAN THEY COULD NOT HANG (1939) Boris Karloff plays the evil (rather mad) scientist who, sentenced to death for an experimental murder, survives the execution through his own invention (a mechanical heart), then seeks vengeance on those who tried him.

P★★	T★★	E★★	A★

Directed by Nick Grinde. Written by Karl Brown.

THE MAN THEY COULDN'T ARREST (1931) A scientist invents a machine which can overhear conversations anywhere.

Directed by T. Hays Hunter. Written by Hunter, Angus MacPhail and Arthur Wimperis. With Hugh Wakefield and Gordon Barker.

MANUTARA (1966) see THE VULTURE (1966)

THE MAN WHO CHANGED HIS MIND (1936) see THE MAN WHO LIVED AGAIN (1936)

THE MAN WHO COULD CHEAT DEATH (1959) A re-make of Barré Lyndon's play The Man In Half Moon Street (filmed in 1945 with Boris Karloff) is another mad-doctor-obtains-immortality-by-replacing-a-growth-gland tale. This Hammer version is pleasingly gothic. Dr Bonêt (Anton Diffring) is a sculptor obsessed with beautiful women. Deprived of his gland he ages 60 years in a minute and dies at the end.

P★★	T★★	E★★	A★

Directed by Terence Fisher. Written by Jimmy Sangster. Cinematography by Jack Asher. With Hazel Court, Christopher Lee and Arnold Marle.

THE MAN WHO COULD WORK MIRACLES (1936) Given wish-fulfilment powers by the Gods, clothing-store clerk George McWhirter Fotheringay (Roland Young) tinkers with his powers and then, not thinking of the consequences, orders the Earth's rotation to stop. The Gods set things right, but only after lots of fun and games in director Lothar Mendes's lightweight adaptation of H. G. Wells's story.

P★★	T★★	E★★★	A★

Written by H. G. Wells. Special Effects by E. Cohen, Ned Mann and Laurence Butler. With Ralph Richardson, Joan Gardner, Ernest Thesiger, Sophie Stewart and George Zucco.

THE MAN WHO FELL TO EARTH (1976) The original "man who fell", from whom Tevis got the title and theme of his novel, was the mythical Icarus, who flew too close to the sun and was destroyed. Another, no less pervasive, source of heat is portrayed as the melting, destroying force in Nicolas Roeg's screen adaptation. It is human sexuality, the co-mingling of eroticism and violence, passion and possession. David Bowie plays a lone visitor from another world who takes on human appearance and the name

David Bowie as Jerome Newton in The Man Who Fell To Earth

Thomas Jerome Newton. Innocent, pallid, visually almost sexless, he is here to fetch back water to his home world, where his family are dying (might already be dead) of drought. For this most common of the world's commodities, he makes the mistake most uninitiated innocents make of offering too much in return – in terms not only of new technology but of power and prestige for those few people he collects around him. A megalithic corporation is formed, and Newton becomes engulfed and isolated at the centre of it; another mythical figure, Howard Hughes this time. He is impressive on paper but in reality powerless and lacklustre in the face of the needs and desires of even a burnt-out university professor (Rip Torn) and a none-too-bright chambermaid (Candy Clark), his two closest human cohorts. The only occasion in the film where he finds real sway over anyone is when he scares Candy Clark witless by revealing himself in his true form, and then her terror is short-lived, quickly replaced by a probing and, yes, sexual, curiosity. At this point, Roeg and writer Paul Mayersberg start trying to build in, unsuccessfully, political undertones – on the night when a rocket ship, its construction funded by Newton's accumulated wealth, stands ready to take him home, Newton is kidnapped by government agents, confined, tortured, crippled … and, finally, totally embittered by the realization that he will never get home, reunited with Candy Clark to indulge in a bout of violent sex-play – complete with toy gun – a million miles away from the tenderness of touch

and the Olympian eroticism we saw him sharing with his wife in earlier flashbacks. Alcoholism, despair, and a brief career as a rock star are the final brief stages in the alien's descent. By the end, Newton has become simply human. All of the standard Roeg trademarks are here. A sweaty sex scene intercut with flashes of display of oriental ritual fighting; a wall of television sets, each screen giving a different but curiously interconnected view of our seething, madhouse world. But Roeg's real brilliance lies in his depiction of Earth as a world of hazy deserts, luminous lakes, jigsaw-puzzle skyscrapers: Earth as a visitor would see it, as an alien planet. Perhaps his ultimate message is that we are all "men who fall to earth", ultimately crushed by forces well beyond our control. After all, Candy Clark and Rip Torn both become seedy, bedraggled too as age sets in – their distanced concern for Newton's well-being, his born out of scientific curiosity, hers out of simple affection, provide the only redeeming view of the human race in this brilliant, eerie gem of a movie.

P★★   T★★★★★   E★★★★   A★★★★

Produced by Michael Deeley and Barry Spikings. With Buck Henry and Bernie Casey. (TR)

THE MAN WHO LIVED AGAIN
(1936) Flawed story of mind transference, starring Boris Karloff as an experimenting doctor using his electrical apparatus to obtain perpetual youth and the hand of a fair maiden. As in all such films, he fails.

P★   T★   E★   A

Directed by Robert Stevenson. Written by L. du Garde Peach, Sidney Gilliat and John L. Balderston. With Anna Lee, John Loder, Frank Cellier.

THE MAN WHO LIVED TWICE
(1936) Anticipating *A Clockwork Orange* (q.v.), this tells of a criminal who, through an operation, has his criminal instincts removed; at the same time his face is changed and he becomes a servant to mankind, a famous doctor.

P★   T★   E★   A★

Directed by Harry Lachman. Written by Tom Van Dycke, Fred Niblo Jr and Arthur Strawn. With Frank Bellamy and Marian Marsh.

THE MAN WHO STOLE THE SUN

(1980) Japanese black comedy about a teacher who builds his own A-bomb at home. When he threatens the government with his device, it isn't to end all war, nor to seek world domination, but to get his own way as far as TV shows and concerts are concerned. A rather silly idea which could have made excellent comic material is wasted in this tedious production.

| P★★ | T★★ | E★ | A★ |

Directed by Kazuhiko Hasegawa. Written by Hasegawa and Leonard Schrader. With Kenji Sawada, Bunta Sugawara and Kimiko Ikegami.

THE MAN WHO TURNED TO STONE

(1956) Some scientists from the eighteenth century have kept themselves alive into the twentieth by using a formula derived from the energy of young women (whom they murder). But when the men fail to get their regular treatment they turn to stone and die.

| P★ | T★ | E★★ | A★ |

Directed by Leslie Kardos. Written by Raymond T. Marcus. With Victor Jory, Ann Doran, Charlotte Austin and William Hudson.

THE MAN WHO WALKED THROUGH THE WALL (1959)

Story of a drab clerk who discovers he has the power to walk through solid objects. A comic exploration of drabness.

| P★ | T★ | E★ | A |

Directed by Ladislao Vajda. Written by Istvan Bekelfi and Hans Jacoby. With Heinz Ruhmann, Nicole Courcel and Anita von Ow.

THE MAN WHO WANTED TO LIVE FOREVER

(1970) Burl Ives stars as a billionaire cripple who is trapping and keeping young men, planning to use them as a future source for organ transplants to restore him to health.

| P★ | T★ | E★ | A |

Directed by John Trent. Written by Henry Denker. With Stuart Whitman, Sandy Dennis, Tom Harvey and Robert Goodier.

THE MAN WITHOUT A BODY

(1957) The head of Nostradamus is resurrected and used to help a businessman plan his business strategy. The head is then grafted on to a body and begins to rebel against the petty tasks assigned it.

| P★★ | T★ | E★★ | A★ |

Directed by W. Lee Wilder and Charles Saunders. Written by William Grote. Make-up by Jim Hydes. With Robert Hutton, George Coulouris, Julia Arnall, Nadja Regin and Sheldon Lawrence.

THE MAN WITH THE BRAIN GRAFT

(1972) A brain-damaged young man has the brain of a doctor transplanted into his skull, but complications set in when it transpires that the doctor's daughter was the young man's lover.

| P★★ | T★★ | E★★ | A★★ |

Directed and written by Jacques Doniol-Valcroze. With Mathieu Carriere.

THE MAN WITH THE GADGET

(1963) East German film about a man from the future sent back to 1960, who brings a mind-reaching machine with him.

| P★ | T★ | E★ | A★ |

Directed by Frank Vogel. Written by Paul Wiens. With Rolf Ludwig and Christine Laszar.

MAN WITH THE YELLOW EYES

(1961) see PLANETS AGAINST US (1961)

THE MAN WITH TWO HEADS

(1971) Slight variant on the Jekyll and Hyde legend, with Jekyll's scientific experiments to separate his good side from his evil resulting in the unleashing of his dark doppleganger, Dr Blood.

| P★ | T★ | E★ | A★ |

Directed and written by Andy Milligan. With Denis DeMarne, Julia Stratton and Gay Feld.

THE MAN WITH TWO HEADS

(1972) see THE THING WITH TWO HEADS (1972)

THE MAN WITH X-RAY EYES

(1963) see X – THE MAN WITH X-RAY EYES (1963)

THE MARK OF THE CLAW (1957)

see THE GIANT CLAW (1957)

MAROONED (1969) Minor piece of pseudo-documentary about cooperation between American and Russian astronauts when an American manned craft is stranded on the Moon. Its not particularly impressive special effects swamp a wholly unimpressive script (by Mayo Simon from Martin Caidin's novel).

P★	T★★	E★	A

Directed by John Sturges. Special Effects by Lawrence W. Butler, Donald C. Glouner and Robbie Robinson. With Gregory Peck, Gene Hackman, Richard Genna and David Janssen.

A MARRIAGE IN THE MOON (1910) see AN INTERPLANETARY WEDDING (1910)

MARS AT EASTER (1967) see DON'T PLAY WITH THE MARTIANS (1967)

MARS CALLING (1923) see RADIO MANIA (1923)

MARS EN CAREME (1967) see DON'T PLAY WITH THE MARTIANS (1967)

MARS NEEDS WOMEN (1966) Disney studios' young star Tommy Kirk features in this enjoyable if trite tale of Martian men who come to Earth to seek breeding stock. Larry Buchanan produced, directed and wrote – in thorough conformity to B-movie standards.

P★	T★	E★★	A★

Make-up by Annabelle Weeinck. With Yvonne Craig, Byron Lord and Roger Ready.

A MARTIAN IN PARIS (1960) A Martian (Darry Cowl) lands on Earth in his flying saucer, his mission to find out about the disease called love so that an antidote can be developed. In a comic twist he falls foul of the disease.

P★★	T★	E★★	A

Directed by Jean-Daniel Daninos. Written by Daninos and Jacques Vilfrid. With Nicole Mirel, Henri Vilbert, Gisele Grandre and Roland Segur.

THE MARTIANS (1964) see THE FLYING SAUCER (1964)

THE MARTIANS (1979) Feature released from the TV series "The Martian Chronicles"; actually the third and final part, including three of Ray Bradbury's original Martian tales, "The Silent Towns", "The Long Years" and "The Million Year Picnic" (where the Earth family discard their Earth identity and become the new Martians, staring down at their image in a Martian canal). In places this is highly tedious and it, naturally, loses much of the sheer poetry of the originals (what film *could* capture that?), but the visual splendour of the envisaged Mars is occasionally glimpsed.

P★★	T★★★	E★★	A★★

Directed by Michael Anderson. Written by Richard Matheson. Special Effects by John Stears. With Rock Hudson, Gayle Hunnicut, Bernie Casey, Christopher Connelly, Nicholas Hammond, Roddy McDowall, Maria Schell, Fritz Weaver, Barry Morse and Nyree Dawn Porter.

THE MARTIANS ARRIVED (1964) Four Martians come to Earth to plan an invasion but are seduced by our lifestyle in this charming little comedy.

P★★	T★	E★★★	A★

Directed by Guiseppe Moccia and Franco Castellano. Written by Moccia, Castellano and Leonardo Martin. With Paolo Panelli. Alfredo Landa, Carlo Croccolo and Raimondo Vianello.

MARTIANS HAVE TWELVE HANDS (1964) see THE MARTIANS ARRIVED (1964)

I MARZIANI HANNO DODICI MANI (1964) see THE MARTIANS ARRIVED (1964)

MASTER MINDS (1945) Mad scientist turns ape into man and has to find a human brain for his creature, incurring a switch of personalities.

P★	T★	E★	A

Directed by Jean Yarbrough. Written by Charles R. Marion and Bert Lawrence. Make-up by Jack Pierce. With Leo Gorcey, Huntz Hall, Glenn Strange, Minerva Urecal and William Benedict.

MASTER OF TERROR (1959) see THE 4-D MAN (1959)

MASTER OF THE WORLD (1933)
see AN INVISIBLE MAN GOES THROUGH THE CITY see (1933)

THE MASTER OF THE WORLD
(1934) A mad scientist movie which might, these days, be seen as an allegory of over-industrialization, with automaton-like workers operating real automatons. Of course, the scientist here wants his robot army to conquer the world for him.

| P★ | T★★ | E★ | A★ |

Directed by Harry Piel. Written by George Muehlen-Schulte. With Walter Janssen, Sybille Schmitz and Walter Franck.

MASTER OF THE WORLD (1961)
A Vernian adventure with a nice Victorian feel. Set in the middle of the nineteenth century, Robur (Vincent Price) builds an enormous flying machine (out of compressed paper and powered by electricity) with which he bullies the world into giving up war. He fails, but it's fun and games all the way to the end. Based on Verne's novels, *The Clipper Of The Clouds* and *Master Of The World*.

| P★★ | T★★★ | E★★★ | A★ |

Directed by William Whitney. Written by Richard Matheson. Special Effects by Ray Mercer, Tim Barr, Wah Chang and Gene Warren. With Charles Bronson and Henry Hull.

MASTER OF THE WORLD (1983)
Italian imitation (?) of the more successful and much more professional, *Quest For Fire* (q.v.). Again we're back in the past of Man, 200,000 years in this instance, witnessing the rather disjointed happenings in the life of Bog, a rather too good-looking (Swedish) type who encounters some real primitives. Less coherent than *Quest For Fire*, yet treading the same ground (that is, there's no speech, only grunts, and meaning is conveyed by mime), there are several fights with a rather docile bear, a few inter-tribal battles and the odd gruesome beheading with a flint knife. Ignore this, see the original.

| P★ | T★★ | E★ | A★ |

Directed and written by Alberto Cavallone. With Sven Kruger, Sasha D'Arc and Viviana M. Rispoli.

THE MASTERS OF TIME (1982)
Animated adaptation of Stefan Wul's novel, *L'Orphelin de Perdide*. Stylish if slow-paced spaceship rescue story.

| P★★ | T★★★★ | E★★ | A★★ |

Directed by Rene Laloux. Written by Laloux, Jean Giraud, Jean-Patrick Machette. Special Effects by Sandor Reisenbuchler.

MATANGO, FUNGUS OF TERROR (1963) see ATTACK OF THE MUSHROOM PEOPLE (1963)

UN MATRIMONIO INTERPLANETARIO (1910) see AN INTERPLANETARY WEDDING (1910)

THE MAZE (1953)
A strange, haunting tale of a Scots laird hidden at the heart of a maze, who turns out to be part-man, part-frog and more than 200 years old.

| P★ | T★ | E★★ | A★ |

Directed by William Cameron Menzies. Written by Dan Ullman. With Richard Carison, Veronica Hurst, Michael Pate and Hilary Brooke.

THE MECHANICAL MAN (1915)
Short film about a mechanical life-sized doll controlled by buttons on its back. But when it breaks down a normal man impersonates it.

Directed by Allen Curtis. Written by Clarence Badger. With Max Asher and Phroso.

MECHANICAL MARY ANNE (1910)
A robot servant goes haywire.

Directed by Lewin Fitzhamon.

THE MECHANICAL STATUE AND THE INGENIOUS SERVANT (1907)
A servant takes the place of a runaway mechanical statue of a gladiator. A brief, semi-comic film.

Produced and directed by J. Stuart Blackton.

MEET THE GHOSTS (1948) see ABBOTT AND COSTELLO MEET FRANKENSTEIN (1948)

MEIN IST DIE WELT (1933) see AN INVISIBLE MAN GOES THROUGH THE CITY (1933)

Director David Gladwell and actress Julie Christie shooting a scene from Memoirs Of A Survivor

MEMOIRS OF A SURVIVOR (1981)
Talent and sheer intelligence saved Julie Christie from becoming a redundant Swinging Sixties girl and led her to roles such as the lead in this careful adaptation of the Doris Lessing novel. Society has collapsed, Britain is engaged in the kind of limited nuclear war which leaves us suspecting Armageddon might be more honest and less painful. Tribes of homeless nomads roam the streets, stealing where they can. Julie Christie has billeted on her a teenaged girl (Leonie Mellinger) who, at the dawn of her awakening sexuality, becomes bored and listless quickly in her new environment. This might have been the cue for a surge of melodrama, but the movie is subtle enough to present us with a world where not only houses and bodies but emotions are burnt-out. The girl, wanting to find a home, can only keep walking away from the one she has been given. The woman, wanting to show maternal concern and affection, can only gaze out of the window after her. The eerie, understated direction is by David Gladwell, with urban ruin scenes which chill us without straining our credulity, and a genuinely frightening episode when a group of almost-neanderthal children emerge *en masse*, from the underground station where they have been living, like a gigantic primal shadow from our racial memories. It is a film about different *kinds* of survival, ranging all the way from the mindless, cannibalistic existence of the children, through the attempts of Christo-

pher Guard to rebuild society within a commune, to, ultimately, Christie's escapes into fantasies of an earlier, more sedate world. It's also a film which tells us that the Christopher Guard line will always fail, our egos will ensure we make the same mistakes over and over again until, finally, only the fantasies are left.

P★★★   T★★★   E★★★   A★★★★

Directed by David Gladwell. Written by Gladwell and Kerry Grabbe. Special Effects by Effects Associates. With Debbie Hutchings, Nigel Hawthorne and Pat Keen. (TR)

MEN MUST FIGHT (1933) Set in
1940 and depicting the bombing of New York as part of World War Two, the Empire State Building being destroyed.

P★   T★   E★   A

Directed by Edgar Selwyn. Written by C. Gardner Sullivan. With Diana Wynyard and Lewis Stone.

THE MESA OF LOST WOMEN
(1952) Rather potty mad scientist movie. Dr Spider is making big spiders and aggressive women on his lost mesa.

P★   T★   E★   A

Directed by Herbert Tevos and Ron Ormond. Written by Tevos. With Jackie Coogan, Allan Nixon, Richard Travis and Mary Hill.

MESHTE NASTRESHU (1963) see A
DREAM COME TRUE (1963)

A MESSAGE FROM MARS (1913)
Feature-length adaptation of the stage play by Richard Ganthony. Re-made in 1921, this is a fairly straightforward morality play about a Martian sent to Earth to reform a young rascal. Meanwhile the Martian leader observes his progress.

Directed and written by J. Wallett Waller. With Charles Hawtrey and E. Holman Clark.

A MESSAGE FROM MARS (1921) A
moral story about a selfish man who is approached by a messenger from Mars and is shown the suffering in the world.

Produced and directed by Maxwell Karger. Written by Arthur Zellner and Arthur Maude. With Bert Lytell, Raye Dean, Gordon Ash and Maude Milton.

METALSTORM: THE DESTRUCTION OF JARED-SYN (1983)

Charlie Band is the man who would be Corman. Via a fistful of genre actioners. Flavour-of-the-month stuff. His *Gremlins* (or *Goonies?*) is *Ghoulies*. This is Mad Max vs. Darth Vader. Supported by his semi-machine brother, Nomad and Cyclopean warriors, evil Mike (*Max I*) Preston is sucking people's life-forces with death crystals. Nasty! Another galactic Western, sure. But full of Band's enthusiasm for movies; two-word colliding titles; *Star Wars/Trek* chapter-headings, as if it were a series (you *can* fool some people); and 3-D, which Band and cinematographer Mac Ahlberg handle better than most.

P★   T★★   E★★   A★★

Directed by Charles Band. Written by Alan J. Adler. With Jeffrey Byron, Tim Thomerson, Kelly Preston, Richard Moll and David Smith. (TC)

METEOR (1979)

Ronald Neame deserves thanks for directing one of the films which finally, mercifully, put the disaster movie into the unmarked grave it so deserved. This one is about a giant meteor knocked towards Earth by a wayward comet – and if the odds against that seem tremendous, then it's another kind of mathematics which seems to have attracted the all-star cast. They appear to be in it for the money. The scenes of devastation – as chips off the larger block crash prematurely into our world – are truly lousy, and only Sean Connery, as the scientist trying to avert the big cataclysm, makes any effort to inject some life. It's like watching a doctor go on and on after the patient's died.

P   T   E★   A

Written by Stanley Mann and Edmund H. North. Special Effects by William Cruse, Margo Anderson, Robert Staples and Glen Robinson. With Natalie Wood, Karl Malden, Brian Keith, Martin Landau, Trevor Howard and Henry Fonda. (TR)

METEOR MONSTER (1957) see

TEENAGE MONSTER (1957)

METROPOLIS (1926)

To say that the plot of *Metropolis* is both naïve and rather ridiculous is to state the obvious, but this doesn't detract from its undeniable visual power. As a piece of pure cinema it remains an extraordinary achievement and one which is still appreciated by audiences of today, as is witnessed by the success of Giorgio Moroder's reconstructed 1984 version with a disco soundtrack (it's difficult to imagine such an approach working with the ossified *Things To Come* (q.v.)). The screenplay was written jointly by the film's director, Fritz Lang, and his then wife, Thea von Harbou, who was also the author of the novel it was based on. The action in *Metropolis* is set in a vast gothic city of the future neatly divided into a ruling elite and a mass of downtrodden workers. Freder (Gustav Froehlich), the hedonistic son of the city's ruler, John Frederson (Alfred Abel), doesn't even know about the workers until he encounters the beautiful Maria (Brigitte Helm) and a group of ragged children from "down below". He follows her back to the lower levels and finds himself in a nightmarish world where men work unceasingly to tend vast machines and have become mere cogs within the city's mechanical bowels. He finds Maria in a church where she is preaching to the workers on the subject of good worker-employer relationships. The gist of her message seems to be that the two parties should at least meet and discuss the situation occasionally. Hardly revolutionary but it alarms John Frederson who is also spying on the meeting ... Frederson then instructs an evil scientist/magician called Rotwang (Rudolf Klein-Rogge) to build a robot duplicate of Maria who will lead the workers into a violent revolt. The plan works; the workers go beserk and smash up the machines, causing a serious flood. But the real Maria, who's been imprisoned in Rotwang's house, escapes and succeeds in saving the workers' children from the flood waters. All ends happily for everyone but Rotwang and his lovely robot (Rotwang has a fatal fall, the robot is incinerated); Freder gets Maria and the workers get a sort of promise from Frederson that he'll be nicer to them in the future. The main absurdity in the plot, of course, is why Frederson would want to

Rudolf Klein-Rogge as Rotwang, the evil scientist, with his robot Maria in Metropolis

engineer a revolt that would destroy the city. *Metropolis* took over nine months to shoot and put the German studio UFA heavily into debt. It did well in its initial European release but not well enough to recover its costs. It was re-edited for its American release in 1927 and lost several reels. When Paramount later bought out the bankrupt UFA studio it decreed that the American version of the film only should be circulated and had the negative of the three-hour original destroyed; the later American version was shortened even further. Moroder located copies of the longer American print and though his version is only 83 minutes long it contains restored scenes that have been missing from prints since the 1920s. The film wasn't a popular success in America but it had a great impact on American film-makers, who were impressed by its huge sets, its imaginative design and its use of visual effects. Lang's directing style also impressed the Americans; his ability to manipulate huge crowds of extras so that they formed giant, fluid sculptures was particularly admired – and imitated (Cecil B. DeMille adopted many of Lang's crowd techniques). Its influence, in terms of design, persists to this day as, for example, *Blade Runner* (q.v.) testifys.

P★★	T★★★★	E★★	A★★★

Directed by Fritz Lang. Written by Lang and Thea von Harbou. Cinematography by Karl Freund and Gunther Rittau. Designed by Otto Hunte, Erich Kettelhut, and Karl Vollbrecht. With Alfred Abel and Gustav Froehlich. (JB)

MEZHOLANETNAYA REVO-LUTSIYA (1924) *see* INTERPLANETARY REVOLUTION (1924)

A MIDNIGHT EPISODE (1899) Outsize bugs plague the residents of a guesthouse. A man sets fire to the insects.

Made by Georges Méliès.

MIDNIGHT MENACE (1937) The reality was far more dreadful, of course, but this pre-War vision of a fleet of radio-controlled planes bombing London was as much menace as they could imagine.

P★	T★	E★	A

Directed by Sinclair Hill. Written by G. H. Moresby-White. With Charles Farrell, Fritz Kortner, Margaret Vyner and Danny Green.

MIDSTREAM (1929) Once again the theme is rejuvenation, but here the ageing industrialist given the perpetual youth treatment reverts to norm during a performance of *Faust*.

P★	T★	E★	A

Directed by James Flood. Written by Frances Guihan. With Ricardo Cortez, Claire Windsor, Montagu Love and Larry Kent.

THE MIGHTY GORGA (1970) Rather uninspired lost plateau story, set in Africa, featuring a prehistoric region complete with monsters and giant gorilla (Gorga).

P★	T★	E★	A

Directed by David Hewitt. Written by Jean Hewitt and David Prentiss. With Anthony Eisley, Scott Brady, Megan Timothy and Kent Taylor.

MIGHTY JOE YOUNG (1949) Joe is a 15-foot gorilla, Kong in miniature, brought back to America as a night club act. Revolted by their table manners he wrecks the place. A reworking of the Beauty and the Beast theme from *King Kong* (q.v.).

P★	T★★	E★	A

Directed by Ernest B. Schoedsack. Written by Ruth Rose. Special Effects by Harold Stine, Bert Willis, Willis H. O'Brien and Ray Harryhausen. With Terry Moore, Ben Johnson, Robert Armstrong and Frank McHugh.

MILCZACA GWIZADA (1959) *see*
FIRST SPACESHIP ON VENUS (1959)

**THE MILLION EYES OF SU-
MURU** (1967) Su-Muru is the Amazonian head of a group of villainous women
intent on world domination and using
their ray-guns which turn their enemies to
stone. Characters taken from the stories of
Sax Rohmer.

P★	T★★	E★	A★

Directed by Lindsay Shonteff. Written by Kevin
Kavanagh. With Frankie Avalon, George Wader,
Shirley Eaton, Wilfrid Hyde-White and Klaus
Kinski.

MILL OF THE STONE WOMEN
(1960) Set in 1912 in a Dutch windmill,
this concerns the bloody exploits of a
scientist who can continually resuscitate
his dead daughter by using the blood of
young women lured to the mill. But his
process turns the women to stone and he
keeps them like showpiece statues.

P★★	T★★	E★★	A★

Directed by Giorgio Ferroni. Written by Remigio
Del Grosso, Ugo Liberatore, Giorgio Stegani and
Ferroni. With Pierre Brice, Scilla Gabel, Dany
Carrel and Wolfgang Preiss.

THE MIND BENDERS (1963) An
interesting study of the effects of brain-
washing via sensory deprivation, with Dirk
Bogarde starring as the slightly unhinged
lab assistant trying to prove the danger of
these experiments.

P★★	T★★	E★★	A★

Directed by Basil Dearden. Written by James
Kennaway. With Mary Ure, John Clements,
Michael Bryant and Wendy Craig.

THE MIND-DETECTING RAY
(1918) A villain steals the mind-reading
machine, but all of his wrongdoings are
revealed by the machine at the end.

Directed by Alfred Desy. Written by Istvan Lajar.
With Robert Faith and Gustav Turan.

THE MIND OF MR SOAMES
(1969) A thoughtful study of the effect on
a 30-year-old man of being brought out of
long coma (since birth) into the modern

world. Based on Charles Eric Maine's
novel, it doesn't quite work on the level of
a fable about innocence.

P★★	T★★	E★★	A★

Directed by Alan Cooke. Written by John Hale
and Edward Simpson. With Terence Stamp,
Robert Vaughn and Nigel Davenport.

THE MIND SNATCHERS (1972)
Similar in theme to Phil José Farmers's
award-winning story, "Riders Of The
Purple Wage", this stars a young Christopher Walken as the incorrigible prisoner
subject to US Army experiments on
stimulating pleasure centres in the brain.
Based on Dennis Reardon's play *The Happiness Cage.*

P★★	T★★	E★★	A★

Directed by Bernard Girard. Written by Ron
Whyte. With Joss Ackland and Ralph Meeker.

**MINDWARP: AN INFINITY OF
TERROR** (1981) An old sf idea given an
uninspired treatment. A spaceship landing
on an alien planet confronts a mysterious
force which pits creations from the crew-
members' ids against them. A gory piece
of fairly mindless borderline horror from
Roger Corman's New World studios.

P★	T★★★	E★★	A★

Directed by B. D. Clark. Written by Clark and
Marc Siegler. With Edward Albert, Erin Moran,
Ray Walston, Zalman King and Robert Englund.

MIRACLE FROM MARS (1952) *see*
RED PLANET MARS (1952)

**THE MIRROR DEATH RAY OF
DR MABUSE** (1964) *see* SECRET OF
DR MABUSE (1964)

**THE MISADVENTURES OF
MERLIN JONES** (1963) A college student (Tommy Kirk) invents an electric
brain machine which can read people's
thoughts. In a rather limpid comedy he
has a few games with the machine. Disney
at low ebb.

P★	T★★	E★	A

Directed by Robert Stevenson. Written by Tom
and Helen August. With Annette Funicello, Leon
Ames and Stuart Erwin.

THE MISER'S REVERSION (1914)

Fun with evolution theory as rejuvenation treatment fails and the subject of the experiment devolves back to "missing link" state.

With Sidney Brace and Harry Benham.

MISSILE TO THE MOON (1958)

Dreadful story of an expedition to the Moon which has gangster stowaways aboard. They encounter a tribe of lost women and battle rock creatures before returning to Earth.

| P | T★ | E | A |

Directed by Richard Cunha. Written by H. E. Barrie and Vincent Fotre. Special Effects by Ira Anderson and Harold Banks. With Richard Travis, Cathy Downs and K. T. Stevens.

MISSING HUSBANDS (1921) *see* LOST ATLANTIS (1921)

THE MISSING LINK (1926) One of

the favourite themes of the 1920s, this is a lighthearted, romantic search for the link which results in eventual success.

| P★ | T★ | E★ | A |

Directed by Charles F. Reisner. Written by Darryl Francis Zanuck. With Syd Chaplin, Ruth Hiatt, Tom McGuve and Cranford Kent.

MISSIONE PLANETA ERRANTE

(1965) *see* WAR BETWEEN THE PLANETS (1965)

MISSION GALACTICA: THE CYLON ATTACK (1979) This, the

second film in the *Battlestar Galactica* sequence, shares much with the dreadful Disney film, *The Black Hole* (q.v.), in being scientifically inept – ignoring so many of the laws of physics that one could readily believe that this was taking place in an alternate universe where different laws appertain. With a second instalment of The Battle Of Midway (mother ships as aircraft carriers, fighters as planes, with kamikaze tactics from the Cylons/Japanese) and atrociously shallow characterization, this is only really enjoyable for its first-rate special effects. But what are clouds doing in space? And how can a

starship flame in the void? Ah well, the *Galactica* lives to fight another day and the re-discovered *Battlestar Pegasus*, with its loony strategist, Kane (Lloyd Bridges), sails off again into the deeps of space, having helped the convoy fight off another Cylon threat. A juvenile, tacked together from the TV series of *Galactica*, this is perhaps purer space opera than *Star Wars*.

| P | T★★★★ | E★★ | A |

Directed by Vince Edwards and Christian I. Nyby II. Written by Glen A. Larson, Jim Carlson and Terrence McDonnell. With Lorne Greene, Richard Hatch and Dirk Benedict.

MISSION MARS (1968) An American

expedition to Mars encounters dead Russian astronauts and alien presences ("polarities"), embodied in glowing metallic spheres. A low-key film.

| P★ | T★★ | E★ | A★ |

Directed by Nick Webster. Written by Mike St Clair. Special Effects by Haberstroh Studios. With Darren McGavin and Nick Adams.

MISSION   STARDUST   (1968)

Another film from the Perry Rhodan series is an uninspired adventure on the Moon where an alien spacecraft is encountered.

| P★ | T★ | E★ | A |

Directed by Primo Zeglio. Written by Karl H. Vogelman and Federico d'Urrutia. With Lang Jeffries, Essy Persson and Luis Davila.

MISSION WANDERING PLANET

(1965) *see* WAR BETWEEN THE PLANETS (1965)

MR JARR'S MAGNETIC FRIEND

(1915) Mildly comic treatment of an sf idea – that a man could be magnetized by a dynamo.

Directed by Harry Davenport. Written by Roy L. McCardell. With Harry Davenport.

MR JOSEPH YOUNG OF AFRICA

(1949) *see* MIGHTY JOE YOUNG (1949)

MR KRANE (1957) Feature first tele-

cast as an episode of Matinee Theater on NBC TV, starring Cedric Hardwicke as the leader of an alien race who, five years ahead, in 1962, gives Earth an ultimatum about nuclear weapons.

With John Hoyt and Peter Hansen.

IL MISTERO DE TREI CONTI-NENTI (1959) *see* MISTRESS OF THE WORLD (1959)

IL MISTERO DI ATLANTIDE (1962) *see* THE GIANT OF METROP-OLIS (1962)

MR SERVADAC'S ARK (1970) *see* ON THE COMET (1970)

MISTER, YOU ARE A WIDOW (1971) *see* SIR, YOU ARE A WIDOW (1971)

MISTRESSES OF DR JEKYLL (1964) *see* DR ORLOFF'S MONSTER (1964)

THE MISTRESS OF ATLANTIS (1932) *see* LOST ATLANTIS (1932)

MISTRESS OF THE WORLD (1959) A lengthy film, made in two parts, it features a spy trying to locate and steal a formula for controlling gravitational and magnetic fields.

P★★	T★★	E★	A★

Directed by William Dieterle. Written by Jo Esinger and M. G. Petersson. With Martha Hyer, Carlos Thompson, Micheline Presle and Wolfgang Preiss.

MODERN PROBLEMS (1981) After suffering an accident with nuclear waste, a loser develops telekinetic powers and sets about avenging himself on his heartless companions – heartlessly, as it turns out.

P★★	T★★	E★★	A★

Directed by Ken Shapiro. Written by Shapiro, Tom Sherohman and Arthur Sellers. With Chevy Chase, Patti d'Arbanville and Mary Kay Place.

MOLCHANIYE   DOKTORA IVENS (1973) *see* THE SILENCE OF DR EVANS (1973)

THE MOLDEN METEOR (1958) *see* THE BLOB (1958)

THE MOLE PEOPLE (1956) Archeologists, investigating the ancient Sumerians, find some instances alive and well and living underground, together with their slaves, the Mole People. A bit like *The Time Machine* (q.v.) without the Eloi and set in the past. The albino Sumerians die in sunlight and the un-mole-like Mole People do their killing for them. Avoid.

P	T★	E★	A

Directed by Virgil Vogel. Written by Laszlo Gorog. Special Effects by Clifford Stine. With John Agar, Cynthia Patrick, Hugh Beaumont, Nestor Paiva, Alan Napier and Eddie Parker.

LA MOMIA CONTRA EL ROBOT HUMANO (1957) *see* THE ROBOT VERSUS THE AZTEC MUMMY (1957)

LE MONDE TREMBLERA (1939) *see* THE WORLD WILL SHAKE (1939)

THE MONITORS (1968) Based on Keith Laumer's novel, this is a rather limp satire on an alien invasion of a love-and-peace kind: the monitoring protects humans from themselves and others.

P★	T★★	E★	A★

Directed by Jack Shea. Written by Myron J. Gold. Cinematography by Vilmos Zsigmond. With Guy Stockwell, Susan Oliver and Avery Schreiber.

THE MONKEY MAN (1908) Comic vision of a monkey's brain transplanted into a human skull, with predictable results.

THE MONKEY'S UNCLE (1965) The sequel to *The Misadventures Of Merlin Jones* (1963) (q.v.) with Tommy Kirk again as the College genius, Jones, who develops sleep-teaching methods and a drug which increases strength. As ever in a Disney film, this is used for a trite purpose – to help the College football team out.

P★	T★★	E★★	A★

Directed by Robert Stevenson. Written by Tom and Helen August. Special Effects by Robert A. Mattey and Eustace Lycett. With Annette Funicello, Leon Ames and Frank Faylen.

THE MONOLITH MONSTERS (1957) An interesting, rather than entertaining, invasion-from-outer-space story, this time by an inanimate crystalline form which turns humans to stone. The giant crystals threaten a small town.

P★★	T★★	E★	A

Directed by John Sherwood. Written by Norman Jolley and R. M. Fresco (Jack Arnold co-authored the original story). Special Effects by Clifford Stine. Make-up by Bud Westmore. With Grant Williams, Lola Albright, Les Tremayne, Trevor Bardette and William Schallert.

MONSTER A GO-GO (1965) A trendy, second-rate movie about an astronaut who returns from a space expedition as a 10-foot-tall monster.

P★	T	E★	A

Produced and directed by Herschell Gordon Lewis and Bill Rebane. With Phil Morton and June Travis.

MONSTER FROM A PREHIS-TORIC PLANET (1967) A film that parodies the rest of the Japanese monster movie cycle. The baby monster, Gappa, taken not from a prehistoric planet but an isolated island, is pursued to Tokyo by its irate parents who cause havoc until baby G is returned.

P★	T★	E★	A

Directed by Haruyasa Noguchi. Written by Iwao Yamazak and Ryuzo Nakamishi. Special Effects by Akira Watanabe. With Tamio Kawaji, Yoko Yamamoto, Tatsuya Fuji and Koji Wada.

THE MONSTER FROM GALAXY 27 (1958) see THE CREATURE FROM GALAXY 27 (1958)

MONSTER FROM MARS (1953) see ROBOT MONSTER (1953)

THE MONSTER FROM THE GREEN HELL (1958) An experimental rocket with its cargo of wasps crashes in Africa. The wasps, exposed to radiation, have mutated into giant, flightless monsters. A team goes in to retrieve the rocket and encounters the giant wasps, but the obligatory volcano ends the threat.

P★	T★	E★	A

Directed by Kenneth Crane. Written by Louis Vittes and Endre Bohen. With Jim Davis, Robert E. Griffin and Barbara Turner.

MONSTER FROM THE MOON (1953) see ROBOT MONSTER (1953)

MONSTER FROM THE OCEAN FLOOR (1954) Roger Corman produced this awful tale about a giant amoeba which is killed by ramming a miniature sub into its eye.

P	T★	E	A

Directed by Wyott Ordung. Written by William Danch. With Anne Kimbell and Stuart Wade.

MONSTER IN THE NIGHT (1958) see MONSTER ON CAMPUS (1958)

MONSTER MAKER (1954) see MONSTER FROM THE OCEAN FLOOR (1954)

MONSTER OF MONSTERS GHIDORAH (1965) see GHIDRAH, THE THREE-HEADED MONSTER (1965)

THE MONSTER OF PIEDRAS BLANCAS (1958) Horror offering about a creature from the depths (vaguely humanoid – to allow the obligatory man-in-a-rubber-suit) who is fed by the local light-house keeper and has the unpleasant habit of ripping heads from bodies.

P★	T★	E★	A

Directed by Irvin Beswick. Written by Haile Chace. With Les Tremayne, Forrest Lewis, John Harmon and Jeanne Carmen.

MONSTER OF TERROR (1965) see DIE! MONSTER DIE! (1965)

MONSTER ON THE CAMPUS (1958) Ludicrous tale of a scientist whose devolutionary serum gets into his pipe and turns him into an ape-man with murderous instincts.

P	T★	E★	A

Directed by Jack Arnold. Written by David Duncan. Make-up by Bud Westmore. Special Effects by Clifford Stine. With Arthur Franz, Joanna Moore, Judson Pratt and Troy Donahue.

MONSTERS FROM THE UNKNOWN PLANET (1975) In a re-run of/sequel to *Godzilla Versus The Bionic Monster* (1974) (q.v.), Godzilla has once more to fight his robot double, Mekago-jira, as well as another huge dinosaur creature, Titanosaurus.

P★	T★★	E★★	A★

Directed by Inoshiro Honda. Written by Yukiko Takayama. Special Effects by Teruyoshi Nakano. With Katsuhiko Sasaki, Tomoko Ai, Akihiko Hirata and Tadao Nakamura.

MONSTERS INVADE EXPO '70
(1970) see GAMERA VS. MONSTER X (1970)

MONSTERS OF THE NIGHT
(1965) see THE NAVY VS. THE NIGHT MONSTERS (1965)

THE MONSTER THAT CHALLENGED THE WORLD (1957) Giant caterpillars attack US naval bases and are defeated in this slightly better than usual creature feature.

P★	T★	E★★	A★

Directed by Arnold Laven. Written by Pat Fielder. With Tim Holt, Audrey Dalton, Hans Conreid and Barbara Darrow.

MONSTER ZERO (1965) In what is perhaps the silliest plot in all the ridiculous Japanese monster movie sequence, aliens borrow Godzilla and Rodan to ostensibly fight off Ghidrah, but instead plan to use them to conquer Earth.

P	T★	E★	A

Directed by Inoshiro Honda. Written by Shinichi Sekizawa. Special Effects by Eiji Tsuburaya. With Nick Adams, Akira Takarada and Kumi Mizumo.

MONSTROSITY (1963) Uninspired brain movie, with walking zombies as results of a scientist's transplant experiments. Just for fun he also transplants a cat's brain into a young woman's skull.

P★	T★	E★	A

Directed by Joseph Mascelli. Written by Vi Russell, Sue Dwiggens and D. Dillman Jr. With Frank Gerstle, Erika Peters and Judy Bamber.

MOONCHILD (1972) A deformed, man-made man is forced to repeat his life every 25 years – reincarnated – a fate he has suffered for 225 years as the film begins. Similar, in some ways, to P. D. Ouspensky's *Strange Life Of Ivan Osokin*, but given a horror bias.

P★★	T★	E★★	A★

Directed and written by Alan Gadney. With Victor Buons, John Carradine, William Challee and Janet Landgard.

MOON PILOT (1961) Dreadful Disney about a girl from space who comes to warn the (US, naturally) authorities that "proton rays" are endangering their astronauts. A sickly love interest and weak comedy make this even more of a mess.

P★	T★★	E★	A

Directed by James Neilson. Written by Maurice Trombragel. Special Effects by Eustace Lycett. With Tom Tryon, Brian Keith, Edmond O'Brien, Dany Saval and Tommy Kirk.

MOONRAKER (1979) How to spot when a series has run completely out of steam? – Well, an impressive series villain is introduced, and hogs much of the camera space, and the script begins cashing in on all the current movie trends, regardless of plausibility. "Jaws" (Richard Kiel) is back again, presumably to add a little bite to a movie where Roger Moore's pallid, weary-looking Bond fails to capture the attention. And *Star Wars* (q.v.) is the theme, as 007 plods into space to combat a mad scientist (Michel Lonsdale) who wants to kill off the human race and replace it with his own genetically perfect acolytes. The Bond movies, a send-up in the first place, had long been incestuously sending themselves up by now. And director Lewis Gilbert's only idea for an inventive killing is to show us a victim being pursued in slow motion by a couple of dobermans. 007 has gone to the dogs. Producer Albert R. Broccoli ought to have scrapped him and introduced a new series about "Jaws".

P	T★★★★	E★	A

Written by Christopher Wood, from the title of a completely different novel by Ian Fleming. Special Effects by Derek Meddings, Paul Wilson, Robin Browne and John Richardson. With Lois Chiles, Connie Clery and Blanche Ravalec. (TR)

MOONSHOT (1967) *see* COUNT-DOWN (1967)

MOON ZERO TWO (1969) Fairly uninspired Western in space, set in 2021, when a space shuttle pilot is blackmailed into trying to capture a sapphire-rich asteroid. Almost but not quite comedy.

P★	T★	E★	A★

Produced and written by Michael Carreras. Directed by Roy Ward Baker. Special Effects by Kit West, Nick Allder and Les Bowie. With James Olson, Catherine von Schell, Warren Mitchell, Adrienne Corri, Bernard Bresslaw and Sam Kydd.

MORE FUN WITH LIQUID ELECTRICITY (1908) *see* GALVANIC FLUID (1908)

MORONS FROM OUTER SPACE (1985) From an opening shot of a massive starship thundering overhead – towing a 1950s caravan on a long length of chain – through to the final *Close Encounters* ending, with its appropriate twist, this is a film strong on visual comedy. Indeed, it's one of a rare few films – sf or otherwise – capable of making a whole audience laugh time and again. Individual touches – the decor of the spacecraft (1960s kitsch this time); the morons' spacecraft crashing on to the M1 motorway at Junction 7 (a brilliant visual scene, both exciting and funny); the dead and rotting alien coming to rescue Bernard (Mel Smith) and then dumping him when it discovers he's not female; the mental asylum parody of *One Flew Over The Cuckoo's Nest* (complete with giant Indian) – guarantee that this is a good evening's enjoyment, but unfortunately the central idea, of four aliens coming to Earth by accident and proving to be highly unintelligent life-forms, is squandered. Their emergence by the end of the film as super-stars with a huge travelling stageshow is somehow not merely unconvincing but stale, too. As is the pure 1960s (and purely British) depiction of bumbling yet sinister British and American authorities trying to cope with the "invasion". A bit more imaginative input might easily have transformed this funny-in-places film into a comedy classic; it

unfolds too predictably, and the character development of Griff Rhys Jones from bumbling TV tea "boy" into shark-like manager of three of the aliens is again unbelievable. As for the aliens, they aren't quite dumb enough – only Jimmy Nail remains amusing throughout the film. As for the other plot-oriented jokes – that they're from the planet Blob, and their spacecraft is merely hired (a repossession man emerges from the massive mother ship at the end!) – they need a stronger storyline to give them their punch. As it is, this is a film I found both very funny and very tiresome, and, after its opening 20 minutes, highly unoriginal.

P★★	T★★★★	E★★★★	A★★

Directed by Mike Hodges. Written by Mel Smith and Griff Rhys Jones. Special Effects by Dennis McTaggart. With Smith, Jones, Paul Brown and Joanne Pierce.

MORTAL ORBIT (1968) *see* MISSION STARDUST (1968)

MOSCOW – CASSIOPEIA (1974) A starship heads off to Cassiopeia with its small adult crew and complement of young teenage scientists. An accident happens and, towards the end of the journey, the youngsters have to take over. A sequel, *Teenagers In Space* (q.v.), was made in 1975. A stylish high-tech Soviet film.

P★★	T★★★	E★★	A★★

Directed by Richard Viktorov. Written by Avenir Zak and Isai Kuznetsov. With Innokenty Smoktunovsky, Volodya Basob and Ira Popova.

THE MOST DANGEROUS MAN ALIVE (1958) The poor production values of this film hide what is quite a powerful little film about a prisoner escaping, being exposed to a cobalt bomb explosion and slowly turning to steel. It is comic-book myth, admittedly, but nonetheless effective for all that, with Ron Randell, as the prisoner, turning to dust at the climax.

P★★	T★	E★★★	A★

Directed by Allan Dwan. Written by James Leicester and Phillip Rock. With Debra Paget, Elaine Stewart, Anthony Caruso, Gregg Palmer and Morris Ankrum.

THE MOST DANGEROUS MAN IN THE WORLD (1969) *see* THE CHAIRMAN (1969)

MOSURA (1961) *see* MOTHRA (1961)

MOSURA TAI GOJIRA (1964) *see* GODZILLA VERSUS MOTHRA (1964)

MOTHRA (1961) First appearance of the giant moth from Toho studios' relentless production line of monster movies. Features two 6-inch twin Japanese girls. For once the menacing monster isn't a man in a rubber suit. Elseways it's the same plot as ever, with Mothra the result of H-bomb tests.

P★	T★★	E★	A★

Directed by Inoshiro Honda. Written by Shinichi Sekizawa. Special Effects by Eiji Tsuburaya and Hiroshi Mukonyama. With Frankie Sakai, Hiroshi Koizumi, Ken Uehara, Kyoko Kagawa, Emi Ito and Yumi Ho.

THE MOTOR CAR OF THE FUTURE (1910) German film about a new super-speed car which can fly, leap over trains and go underwater.

THE MOTORIST (1906) Frank Paul's short fantasy about a couple whose car takes off after exceeding the speed limit and, after driving round Saturn's rings, returns home.

Directed by Walter R. Booth.

THE MOTOR VALET (1906) Very short film about a robot servant which goes haywire, smashes the furniture and finally – in good sf tradition – blows up.

Directed by Arthur Cooper.

LE MOULIN DES SUPPLICES (1960) *see* MILL OF THE STONE WOMEN (1960)

THE MOUSE ON THE MOON (1963) This director can usually be relied upon for zany action scenes at least. Unfortunately, this damp squib has overdone acting and characterization and a slow script, and its jokes are never quite funny enough. Though the idea of a rocket going to the Moon on a fuel of home-made wine is a good one, the film lacks conviction; it is not really a worthy successor to its 1959 prequel.

P★★	T★★	E★★	A★

Directed by Richard Lester. Written by Michael Pertwee. With Margaret Rutherford, Bernard Cribbins, Terry Thomas, Ron Moody, David Kossoff and John LeMesurier. (RS)

THE MOUSE THAT ROARED (1959) This is an amusing exercise with a quite original central idea. At least, the film is amusing if you have no objection to long and endlessly re-cycled jokes about nuclear holocausts. The Ruritanian Grand Duchy of Fenwick declares war on the United States; their cunning plan is to suffer a bloodless defeat and then "accept" Marshall Aid. Peter Sellers (among other roles here) leads a party of men-at-arms through New York, and accidentally captures a nuclear scientist and – provoking much fumbling slapstick – his hair-trigger doomsday weapon. Washington surrenders – to the surprise of just about everyone. The scenes in Europe after victory is announced, and the duchy is courted by the great powers, are really very funny indeed – although some may be put off by the racial stereotyping.

P★★★	T★★	E★★★	A★★

Directed by Jack Arnold. Written by Roger MacDougall and Stanley Mann. With Jean Seberg, David Kossoff, William Hartnell and Leo McKern. (RS)

IL MULINO DELLE DONNE DI PIETRA (1960) *see* MILL OF THE STONE WOMAN (1960)

MURDER AT DAWN (1932) Weird happenings at an old house prove fatal as a madman activates his death-ray.

Directed by Richard Thorpe. With Jack Mulhall, Josephine Dunn and Mischa Auer.

MURDER BY PHONE (1981) *see* BELLS (1981)

MURDER BY TELEVISION (1935) Bela Lugosi stars in this simple thriller about a device which can kill at a distance

– a phone call makes a TV camera act as a death-ray.

P★	T★	E★	A★

Directed by Clifford Sanforth. Written by Joseph O'Donnall. With June Collyer.

MURDERER'S ROW (1966) The Matt Helm spoofs of the Bond series strive for new depths in this trite tale of a terrifying helio-beam, lost to baddies and threatening to destroy Washington D.C. Dean Martin as Helm is suitably dreadful.

P	T★★	E★	A

Directed by Henry Levin. Written by Herbert Baker. Special Effects by Danny Lee. With Ann Margret, Karl Malden and James Gregory.

THE MURDERS IN THE RUE MORGUE (1914) Dr Mirakle's experiments in cross-breeding apes and humans are only partially successful, and his trained ape becomes a savage killer.

Produced and written by Sol. A. Rosenberg.

THE MURDERS IN THE RUE MORGUE (1932) Lengthy re-make of the 1914 film, with an accent on the properties of ape blood. Bela Lugosi starred in this atmospheric tale of a mad doctor's experiments in cross-breeding of species.

P★★	T★★	E★★	A★

Directed by Robert Florey. Written by Tom Reed and Dale van Every. Make-up by Jack Pierce. Special Effects by John P. Fulton. With Sidney Fox, Leon Waycroff and Bert Roach.

MUTANT (1982) see FORBIDDEN WORLD (1982)

MUTANT (1983) A small town, a large company experimenting in chemicals with huge vats of waste substances, two boys out on a vacation in redneck country, USA – these elements blend together in a professional but rather clichéd story of an epidemic which changes normal people into blue-skinned mutants with zinc in their blood and a voracious apetite for more, fresh blood. In the nick of time the state troopers appear.

P★★	T★★	E★★★	A★

Directed by John Cardos. Written by Peter Z. Orton, Michael Jones and John C. Kuize. With Wings Hauser, Bo Hopkins and Cary Guffey.

THE MUTATIONS (1973) A mad scientist (Donald Pleasance) attempts to create a life-form midway between plant and human and is, in part, successful.

P★	T★★	E★	A★

Directed by Jack Cardiff. Written by Garson Raye. Special Effects by Ken Middleham and Mike Hope. Make-up by Charles Parker. With Tom Baker, Michael Dunn and Julie Ege.

MUTINY IN OUTER SPACE (1964) When an expedition to caves on the Moon brings back a fungus to the space station, the heat revives it and makes it grow. Before it can kill everyone and get back to Earth they kill it – by freezing the station.

P★	T★★	E★	A

Directed by Hugo Grimaldi. Written by Arthur C. Pierce. With William Leslie, Dolores Faith, Pamela Curran and Richard Garland.

MUZZ PRRNIHO STOLETI (1961) see MAN IN OUTER SPACE (1961)

MY FRIEND, DR JEKYLL (1963) Italian adaptation of the Jekyll/Hyde story, about a professor who develops a method of switching minds. He first chooses a handsome new body, but ends up in the body of a chimpanzee, trapped.

P★	T★	E★	A★

Directed by Marino Girolani. Written by Girolani, Scarnicci and Tarabusi. With Ugo Toguazzi, Raimondo Vianello, Abbe Lane and Carlo Croccolo.

THE MYSTERIANS (1957) Aliens, who have ruined their own planet through nuclear war, come to Earth with their giant robot bird, Mogella, in search of women for a breeding programme. The aliens choose to land in Japan (because Toho studios made this, essentially) but are thwarted by the Japanese. For its time a reasonable slice of space opera.

P★	T★★	E★★	A

Directed by Inoshiro Honda. Written by Takeshi Kimura. Special Effects by Eiji Tsuburaya. With Kenji Sahara and Yumi Shirakawa.

THE MYSTERIOUS CONTRA-GRAV (1915) Inventor and thieves thriller surrounding the invention of a device – the contragrav – which allows planes to float and use little fuel; its "negative electricity" power-source is a rather confused explanation.

Directed by Henry McRae. With Frank Stites.

MYSTERIOUS DR R (1941) see MAN MADE MONSTER (1941)

THE MYSTERIOUS INVADER (1958) see THE ASTOUNDING SHE MONSTER (1958)

MYSTERIOUS ISLAND (1929) An early sound production based very loosely on Jules Verne's novel and starring the melodramatic Lionel Barrymore. Barrymore (as Count Dakkar, the Nemo figure) goes investigating the ocean bed, looking for lost races (he finds them!) and meanwhile a friend steals his island kingdom. The obligatory battle with a giant octopus survives.

P★	T★★	E★★	A★

Directed by Lucien Hubbard, Maurice Tourneur and Benjamin Christiansen. With Pauline Starke, Karl Dane and Warner Oland.

MYSTERIOUS ISLAND (1941) Soviet juvenile faithful to Verne's original novel. Nemo aids castaways on the island, using the *Nautilus*, his atomic submarine.

Directed by E. Penzline and B. M. Chelintzev. Written by Chelintzev and M. P. Karukov. With M. V. Commisarov and A. S. Krasnopolski.

THE MYSTERIOUS ISLAND (1961) Jules Verne's story is tampered with here in this tale of a group of prisoners who escape by balloon from a Confederate prison, fight giant monster creatures and are rescued by Captain Nemo (who created these mutated beasts).

P★	T★★	E★	A

Directed by Cy Endfield. Written by John Prebble, Daniel Ullman and Crane Wilbur. Special Effects by Ray Harryhausen. With Michael Craig, Herbert Lom and Joan Greenwood.

MYSTERIOUS SATELLITE (1956) For once in Japanese cinema Tokyo isn't threatened by monsters, but is contacted by benign aliens who want to stop the nuclear arms race and, as a bonus, save Earth from a rogue planet on collision course with it. The aliens are rather nice – Cyclopean starfish from Paira. Based on the novel *Uchujin Tokyo ni Arawaru* by Gentaro Nakajima.

P★	T★★	E★	A★

Directed by Koji Shima. Written by Hideo Ogumi. With Toyoni Karita and Keizo Kawasaki.

THE MYSTERY OF THREE CONTINENTS (1959) see MISTRESS OF THE WORLD (1959)

N

DIE NACKTE UND DER SATAN (1959) see THE HEAD (1959)

THE NAKED VAMPIRE (1969) French borderline sf-horror film, where a young man discovers that both he and a young girl he believed to be a vampire are mutants, first in a new breed of Man.

P★★	T★★	E★★	A★

Directed by Jean Rollin. Written by Rollin and S. H. Moati. With Olivier Martin, Maurice Lemaitre, Caroline Cartier and Ly Letong.

NAKUSEI DAISENSO (1977) see WAR OF THE PLANETS (1977)

NANKAI NO DAIKAIJU (1970) see YOG – MONSTER FROM SPACE (1970)

NANKAI NO DAI KETTO (1966) see GODZILLA VERSUS THE SEA MONSTER (1966)

LA NAVE DE LOS MONSTRUOS (1959) see THE SHIP OF THE MONSTERS (1959)

THE NAVY VS. THE NIGHT MONSTERS (1965) Based on Murray Leinster's novel, *Monster From Earth's End*, it has perambulating trees from a hot

part of the South Pole taken to a US naval base where they begin to kill people. A rather second-rate *Thing* (q.v.) but with a growing cult following.

P★	T★★	E★	A

Directed and written by Michael Hoey. Special Effects by Edwin Tillman. With Mamie Van Doren, Anthony Eisley and Pamela Mason.

THE NEANDERTHAL MAN (1952) Mad scientist develops serum and becomes ape man. A film as trite as that plot synopsis suggests.

P	T★	E	A

Directed by E. A. DuPont. Written by Aubrey Wisberg and Jack Pollexfen. Special Effects by Jack Rabin and David Commons. With Robert Shayne, Richard Crane and Doris Merric.

NECROPHAGUS (1971) Nasty little story of a scientist who becomes a mixture of animal, vegetable and mineral. His brother buries the hairy thing and feeds it fresh corpses every day.

P★	T★	E★	A★

Directed and written by Miguel Madrid. Special Effects by Antonio Molina. With Bill Curran, Francisco Braun, Beatrice Lacy and Victor Israel.

NEMO (1984) *see* DREAM ONE (1984)

NEVER SAY NEVER AGAIN (1983) I never was convinced by Roger Moore as Bond; here the impersonation is cast aside and Sean Connery, older but no less suave and sophisticated, is back, preventing SPECTRE from blowing up large parts of the world with captured cruise missiles and saving them the blackmail monies (25 per cent of their total oil incomes). It's a humorous film without ever stooping to the low levels of spoof the Moore films dredge regularly, though the plot elements and the settings are predictable enough. One delight, however, is the World Domination game Bond plays against SPECTRE's Max Largo (Klaus Maria Brandauer – one of Europe's finest actors); a marvel of computer graphics. A sub-theme of old-style aggression versus new-style bureaucracy is nicely summarized in Q's comment to the old-style Bond: "Now you're on this I hope we're

Sean Connery and Klaus Maria Brandauer in a scene from Never Say Never Again

going to have some gratuitous sex and violence." And, of course, we do. Note also the lovely cameo by Rowan Atkinson as the inanely English Embassy official.

P★★★	T★★★★★	E★★★★★	A★★

Directed by Irvin Kershner. Written by Lorenzo Semple Jr. Special Effects by Ian Wingrove. Optical Effects by Apogee Inc, Los Angeles. Special Visual Effects by David Dryer. Cinematography by Douglas Slocombe. With Max Von Sydow, Barbara Carrera and Kim Baringer.

THE NEW ADVENTURES OF THE BIONIC BOY (1978) *see* DYNAMITE JOHNSON (1978)

THE NEW BARBARIANS (1983) Italian cowboys and Indians working of the post-Holocaust American dream. Could be sub-titled "a Fistful of Mad Max" as Scorpion (Timothy Brent) and his black Tonto (Fred Williamson) battle the nasty "Templars" who want to purify the world of people. The deranged morality and logical inconsistencies of the plot are almost (but not quite) laughable. Baddies leap on to cars to make good targets and leap four feet in the air when shot ...

P★	T★	E★	A

Directed by Claude King. Written by Tito Carpi and Enzo Girotamii. With Anna Kanakis, George Eastman and Thomas Moore.

THE NEW INVISIBLE MAN (1957) Man invents invisibility serum and administers it to his brother in prison. His brother escapes, but the serum drives him mad and, after a hunt, he is killed by the police.

P★	T★	E★	A

Directed by Alfredo Crevena. Written by Alfredo Salazar. With Arturo de Cordova, Ana Luisa Peluffo, Augusto Benedico and Paul Meraz.

NEW TRIP TO THE MOON (1909)
A fantasy about a trip to the Moon which allowed director/writer/special effects expert Segundo de Chomon to practise his trick effects.

THE NEXT VOICE YOU HEAR
(1950) Based on a story by George Sumner Albee. A small town in America has a strange voice contact them on the radio – the voice of God.

P★★	T★	E★★	A★

Directed by William Wellman. With James Whitmore, Nancy Davis and Gary Gray.

THE NIGHT CRAWLERS (1965) see
THE NAVY VS. THE NIGHT MONSTERS (1965)

THE NIGHT CREATURES (1963)
see THE LAST MAN ON EARTH (1963)

NIGHT KEY (1937) Gimmick-filled
film about the inventor of a special, advanced burglar alarm and the devices he develops.

P★	T★★	E★	A

Directed by Lloyd Corrigan. Written by Tristram Tupper and John C. Moffit. Special Effects by John P. Fulton. With Boris Karloff.

NIGHTMARE CASTLE (1965) see
THE FACELESS MONSTER (1965)

NIGHTMARE CITY (1980) Poor reworking of the radiation mutants theme – this time the cause is a leak at a nuclear plant. The dying red blood cells of the resultant monster-men need replenishing, hence they become vampires.

P★	T★★	E★	A

Directed by Umberto Lenzi. Written by Piero Regnoli and Toni Corti. With Hugo Stiglitz, Laura Trotter, Francisco Rabal and Mel Ferrer.

NIGHT OF ANUBIS (1968) see
NIGHT OF THE LIVING DEAD (1968)

NIGHT OF THE BIG HEAT (1967)
see ISLAND OF THE BURNING DAMNED (1967)

NIGHT OF THE BLOOD BEAST
(1958) see THE CREATURE FROM GALAXY 27 (1958)

NIGHT OF THE BLOODY APES
(1970) Rather silly twist on the Frankenstein idea. A doctor transplants a gorilla's heart into his dying son's chest, only to have the boy turn into a murderous ape.

P★	T★	E	A

Directed by Rene Cardona. Written by Cardona and Rene Cardona Jr. With Armando Silvestre, Norma Lazareno and José Elias Moreno.

NIGHT OF THE DOOMED (1965)
see THE FACELESS MONSTER (1965)

NIGHT OF THE FLESH EATERS
(1968) see NIGHT OF THE LIVING DEAD (1968)

NIGHT OF THE LEPUS (1972) Experiments in trying to control fast-breeding rabbits produce a serum which instead of killing off the pests turns the bunnies into huge voracious carnivores. Perhaps one of the silliest monster-mutation movies about.

P	T★	E★	A

Directed by William F. Claxton. Written by Don Holliday and Gene R. Kearney (from the novel by Russell Braddon, *The Year Of The Angry Rabbit*). With Stuart Whitman, Janet Leigh, Rory Calhoun, DeForest Kelley, Paul Fix and Melanie Fullerton.

NIGHT OF THE LIVING DEAD
(1968) A cult movie with a tenuous sf pretext: space radiation revives the recently dead and turns them into crazed killers. It can be seen as one of the films that founded the spate of modern "zombie" movies and, despite its low-budget origins, remains excellent entertainment for strong stomachs.

P★★	T★★	E★★★	A★

Directed by George Romero. Written by John A. Russo. Special Effects by Regis Survinski and Tony Pantanello. With Duane Jones, Judith O'Dea, Russell Streiner and Karl Hardman.

NIGHT OF THE SILICATES (1966)
see THE ISLAND OF TERROR (1966)

NIGHT SLAVES (1970) Soft-edged
alien invasion story. The aliens have only come to Earth to mend their spacecraft, and take over the local small town's inhabitants to help in the task. When they leave they take one of the humans who has fallen in love with a female alien. Based on the novel by Jerry Sohl.

| P★ | T★★ | E★ | A★ |

Directed by Ted Post. Written by Everett Chambers and Robert Specht. With James Fransiscus, Lee Grant and Scott Marlowe.

NIGHT THE SILICATES CAME
(1966) *see* THE ISLAND OF TERROR (1966)

THE NIGHT THE WORLD
EXPLODED (1957) Scientists discover a highly explosive element, E-112, which is causing earthquakes. An extraordinarily dull offering.

| P★ | T★ | E | A |

Directed by Fred F. Sears. Written by Luci Ward and Jack Natteford. With Kathryn Grant, William Leslie, Tristram Coffin and Raymond Greenleaf.

1984 (1955) Washed clean of its frightening political significance, Michael Anderson's adaptation of Orwell's bleak dystopia reduces the novel's complexity to a simple story of a defiant love affair in the face of extreme conformity. There were two endings to this, the one most often shown having the two lovers defiantly die together, the other being more faithful to the book – where Winston Smith recants and betrays Julia, as she does him. Unlike the later version the settings are not so much evocative of a despairing, hopeless system but of 1950s technological sterility, and the only real bonus is Michael Redgrave's excellent portrayal of O'Brien (not to be confused with Edmund O'Brien, who played Smith) which, like the later

Edmund O'Brien as Winston Smith in 1984

portrayal by Burton, really brought out the terrifying reality of totalitarianism. Too brief, though, are such moments in this highly disappointing film.

| P★★ | T★★ | E★★ | A★★ |

Written by William P. Templeton and Ralph Bettinson. Special Effects by B. Langley, G. Blackwell and N. Warwick. With Jan Sterling, David Kossoff and Mervyn Johns.

1984 (1984) Veracity and fidelity are the cornerstones of the movie; a large final caption informs us that all the scenes were shot not only in the parts of London George Orwell's book describes, but in the exact months of the precise year. The makers realized, with a display of good sense rare in the cinematic world, that they could contribute little worthwhile in terms of plot and substance – all they've added are a couple of brief flashbacks to the central character's childhood; otherwise, Orwell's classic novel has been transferred scene for scene, and often line for line, directly on to celluloid. Does this work any better than the more standard approach of reworking a novel's plot around its central theme? The answer is yes, but only halfway. The film is partly strangled and partly saved by its own mythology. So strongly has the book become embedded in our culture that every schoolchild above O-level age is by now familiar with the story of Winston Smith, his love for fellow Party-member Julia, and their personal rebellion against the nightmarish future dictatorship of which Big Brother is the figurehead. Writer and director Michael Radford has had the savvy to recognize that the story is a fable, describing a state of mind – with us always – rather than a specific time and place. The world they present us with is Orwell's England of the 1940s gone horribly wrong. The bomb sites are permanent, rationing has become a weapon more than a necessity, the quaint old-fashionedness of cubicle-style offices and mouldering railway stations takes on a grim, sordid quality – this is the bleak and joyless best Smith can ever hope to expect. His personal dwelling – a dilapidated brick slum dominated by a giant television screen – and his constant dreadful state of health complete the picture of a society humans should never be required to exist in. There's no disbelief on the part of the audience, therefore, when he plunges into an illegal relationship with the girl ... yet because the story is a fable, and because fables rely so heavily on their dénouements, Michael Radford seems impatient to get to the crunch. The first half of the movie, up until Smith's capture, is marginally slow and disjointed, holding us on an intellectual level but failing to touch our emotions. John Hurt as Smith and Suzanna Hamilton as Julia perform as strongly as they can, but their dialogue is often weak, monosyllabic; all the best lines belong to the second half of the movie, to O'Brien, the interrogator. Here, in the torture chambers of the Ministry of Love, *1984* truly comes to life; the viewer is engulfed with rather than simply fascinated by its horror. Burton's last performance, as O'Brien (he died shortly afterwards and the film is dedicated to his memory), is his finest before the camera. He was quoted as deliberately toning down that famous voice of his and, subdued, it becomes an instrument of terror in itself, the calm voice of unreason as O'Brien holds up four fingers and asks Winston·Smith to see five. On a technical level, the film is a small masterpiece of location shooting, paying a degree of attention to its camerawork and lighting which the vastly expensive blockbusters of

the year might have done well to emulate. As an unhappy sidenote, the original soundtrack was replaced, by the film's distributors, with a totally inappropriate backing by the pop group The Eurythmics. *1984* took the major British screen award for "Best Movie" of its year, though it may well be that – so wrapped up is the production in its own small mythos of controversies, deaths, and dates – its true value might not be assessed for some while to come. What *is* certain is that it is a brave and honest attempt at Orwell's novel, one which you walk away from shaken, even depressed, but never cheated.

P★★★★   T★★★★   E★★   A★★★★

Produced by Simon Perry. Special Effects by Ian Scoones. Cinematography by Roger Deakins. With Cyril Cusack, Gregor Fisher, James Walker, Peter Frye, Rupert Baderman, Phyllis Logan, Pam Gems and Bob Flag. (TR)

1990: BRONX WARRIORS (1982) In the future, New York's Bronx district has been made a no-go area by the authorities and the gangs have taken over. Trash, leader of the riders (Hells Angels), encounters a girl runaway (the richest girl in America, heir to the Manhattan Corporation) and becomes her defender against all-comers (gangs and Hammer, the homicidal cop who's sent in to get her back). An attractive juvenile film with aggression all the way. Better, however, than Carpenter's *Escape From New York* (q.v.); it echoes some of the predilections of 1960s American sf (particularly Delany).

P★★   T★★★   E★★★   A★

Directed by Enzo G. Castellari. Written by Castellari, Dardano Sacchetti and Elisa Livia Briganti. With Christopher Connelly, Vic Morrow, Fred Williamson and Mark Gregory.

1990: BRONX WARRIORS 2 (1983) A more original film than its predecessor, yet still somewhat derivative, this has Trash, star of Bronx 1, orphaned by the G.C. Corporation, whose men (under the evil Wangler) are clearing the Bronx ready for a new super-development scheme. Genocide is the central issue of this film;

the Corporation's morals make gang-land ethics seem almost Christian, and the film is interesting for winning our sympathies for the punks – almost an inverse *Death Wish* if you like. Most of the film's second half is taken up with a huge (and somewhat repetitious) battle for the Bronx. The unquestioned ethic of violence may dismay many, but that aside, this is as good an entertainment as any war film. It could be read as a modern-day re-enactment of what happened in Eastern Europe in the late 1930s – an indictment of Fascist approaches to life, final solutions and abstract projects – but it's perhaps best viewed as punk myth.

P★★	T★★★	E★★★	A★

Directed by Enzo G. Castellari. Written by Castellari and Tito Carpi. With Henry Silva, Valeria D'Obiri, Timothy Brent and Mark Gregory.

NIPPON CHIUBOTSU (1973) *see* THE SUBMERSION OF JAPAN (1973)

NIYA-ISKUSSTVENNYI CHELO-VEK (1981) *see* PER ASPERA AD ASTRA (1981)

NO BLADE OF GRASS (1970) Film of John Christopher's novel *The Death Of Grass* in which a blight sweeps the world, killing off all grass, including corn and rice, leaving famine in its wake. The hero, John Custance (played by Cornel Wilde), makes his way north and encounters roving gangs of bikers and other riff-raff trying to survive in a dying world. As one of the first movies of a disaster novel it works within the limitations of its time, though subsequent films glutted with violence and better special effects have tended to make *No Blade Of Grass* look a little tame in comparison. Some of the moorland shots are quite haunting but a low budget seems to have kept crowd scenes to a mere handful of extras.

P★★★★	T★★	E★★★	A★★

Directed by Cornel Wilde. Written by Sean Forestal. Special Effects by Terry Witherington. With Nigel Davenport, Jean Wallace, John Hamill, Anthony May and Lynne Frederick.

NO SURVIVORS, PLEASE (1963) Aliens from Orion want to take over Earth,

so plan to impersonate world leaders and start a nuclear war.

P★	T★	E★	A★

Directed by Hans Albin and Peter Berneis. Written by Berneis. With Maria Perschy, Robert Cunningham and Uwe Friedrichsen.

NOTHING BUT THE NIGHT

(1972) Straight horror treatment of an sf idea. Children are injected with the life essence of dead people and take on the memories of the dead. Based on the novel, *Children Of The Night*, by John Blackburn.

P★★	T★★	E★★	A★

Directed by Peter Sasdy. Written by Brian Hayles. Special Effects by Les Bowie. With Christopher Lee, Peter Cushing, Diana Dors, Georgia Brown and Keith Barron.)

NOT OF THIS EARTH (1956) Produced and directed by Roger Corman, this dwells on the horror aspects of a standard sf tale: a blood-drinking alien comes to Earth to collect blood to take back to his dying planet. He is telepathic and has psi powers (he can drain people simply by removing his dark glasses) but succumbs in the end to a simple noise. A colourful, haunting nightmare of a film.

P★★	T★	E★★	A★

Written by Charles Griffith and Mark Hanna. Special Effects by Paul Blaisdell. With Paul Birch, Beverly Garland and Morgan Jones.

A NOVICE AT X-RAYS (1897) Brief comedy skit in which a man's skeleton separates from his flesh and leaves him in a pile on the floor.

Directed, written by and starring Georges Méliès.

NO VIOLENCE BETWEEN US (1973) *see* WHERE IS BETA? (1973)

NOW WE'LL TELL ONE (1933) A Charley Chase comedy about a belt that can transmit the personality of a person to someone wearing the receiving belt.

P★	T★	E★★	A★

Directed by James Chase. With Muriel Evans, Lillian Elliot and Frank Darien.

NOW YOU SEE HIM, NOW YOU DON'T (1971)
Sequel to *The Computer Wore Tennis Shoes* (1969). This time the super-computer boy (Kurt Russell) accidentally makes an invisibility spray-on serum and is pursued by criminals. A better comedy than the original.

P★★	T★★	E★★★	A★

Directed by Robert Butler. Written by Joseph L. McEveety. Special Effects by Eustace Lycett and Danny Lee. With Cesar Romero and Joe Flynn.

N.P. (–THE SECRET) (1968)
An Italian socio-political vision of life at the end of the twentieth century. An industrialist is prevented from imposing his scheme of full automation.

P★★	T★	E★	A★

Directed and written by Silvano Zaccaria. With Francesco Rabal, Ingrid Thulin and Irene Papas.

THE NUDE BOMB (1980)
Rather weak spin-off from the 1960s TV series, "Get Smart" (a James Bond spoof starring Don Adams). A scientist has, in this new film version, developed a bomb that will destroy the fabric of clothes and leave him free to conquer a naked world. Tiresome rather than comic.

P★	T★★	E★	A★

Directed by Clive Donner. Written by Arne Sultan, Bill Dana and Leonard B. Stern. Special Effects by Whitey Krumm and Richard Lea. With Sylvia Kristel and Vittorio Gassman.

NUDE IN HIS POCKET (1957) see GIRL IN HIS POCKET (1957)

I NUOVI BARBARI (1983) see THE NEW BARBARIANS (1983)

THE NUTTY PROFESSOR (1963)
Professor Kelp (Jerry Lewis) develops a potion which turns him into nauseously handsome but malicious Buddy Love in this asinine version of the Jekyll/Hyde legend.

P★	T★	E★	A★

Directed by Jerry Lewis. Written by Lewis and Bill Richmond. Special Effects by Paul K. Lerpae. With Stella Stevens and Del Moore.

002 OPERAZIONE LUNA (1967) see TWO COSMONAUTS AGAINST THEIR WILL (1967)

OCTOPUSSY (1983)
The formula for a Bond film rarely changes, and this is no exception – unless, perhaps, that it's probably the best of the Roger Moore Bond films. Action all the way, exotic locations, Q's ingenious contraptions, the suggestion in Bond of deep resources of knowledge, and the sense of omnicompetence in the great man himself. Here Bond struggles against a conspiracy to start World War Three, involving a mad Russian general (played rather over the top by the usually brilliant Steven Berkoff), an island of female smugglers (Octopussy herself in charge of them – and, ultimately, in love with Bond) and one Kamal Khan, an ex-Afghan prince with a line in nasty servants. The plot is fairly thin and melodramatic, with the plan hinging on a circus troupe setting off an A-bomb in a US base in West Germany – thus precipitating European demands for the removal of US forces – but that's scarcely noticeable as the pyrotechnics of a Bond adventure keep all disbelief firmly suspended. There's far less spoof humour here, but the sense of total escapism remains.

P★★	T★★★★★	E★★★★	A★★

Directed by John Glen. Written by George MacDonald Fraser, Richard Maibaum and Michael G. Wilson. Special Effects by John Richardson. With Maud Adams, Louis Jordan and Kristina Waybon.

ODIO MI CUERPO (1975) see I HATE MY BODY (1975)

OFF TO BEDLAM (1901)
Georges Méliès fantasy about four blacks who, after a shock, turn white and later become one giant black.

Directed by Georges Méliès.

OFF TO BLOOMINGDALE ASYLUM (1901) see OFF TO BEDLAM (1901)

OLD MOTHER RILEY MEETS THE VAMPIRE (1952) The popular comic character here struggles against Bela Lugosi, a master criminal with powerful weapons and a large robot, who believes he's a vampire.

P★	T★	E★	A

Directed by John Gilling. Written by Val Valentine. With Arthur Lucan, Richard Wattis and Dora Bryan.

O LUCKY MAN (1973) Lindsay Anderson's picaresque morality play contains moments of sf horror and apocalypse – a glimpse of a man's head grafted to a sheep, an atomic explosion from which our hero, Mick Travis (Malcolm McDowell), emerges unscathed in his golden suit.

P★★★	T★★★	E★★★	A★★★

Written by David Sherwin. With Ralph Richardson, Rachel Roberts, Arther Lowe and Helen Mirren.

THE OMEGA MAN (1971) A plague of vampires was the theme of Richard Matheson's classic sf novel *I Am Legend* – it seems a couple of them escaped to make this dreadful movie so loosely based on the original book that the word "adaptation" seems a mockery. Gone are the bloodsuckers from the original idea: instead, a plague brought on by germ warfare has transformed all but Robert Neville (Charlton Heston) into crazed albinos whose injured eyes cannot stand the sunlight. Cowled like medieval monks, they are led by Mathias (Anthony Zerbe) in a holy war against anything reminiscent of the technology which brought them to this pass, and that includes Neville himself, who is on the verge of developing a cure. He finds two things during the course of the movie: the daytime hideaway of the plague-bearers; and another group of humans immune like himself. It's a shame that director Boris Sogal and writers John William and Joyce M. Corrington could not find some impetus to put behind this basically decent premise for a science fiction flick. The mood is all wrong – instead of American gothic, we're presented with all the technocratic flashiness

of chitinous-looking motor bikes and bristling submachine guns. The action sequences are obvious – chitinous-looking motor bikes racing up stairways – and the gaps between them sedentary, aswamp with turgid dialogue and, when a black female character appears, embarrassing racial sidewiping. And Heston, so perfect in a similarly superhuman role in *Planet of the Apes* (1968), dies a million deaths before his screen death at the movie's feeble dénouement – he's a hipster Christ-figure besieged within a swinging bachelor penthouse, so cardboard that when the mutants finally get him you expect him to slap down flat, completely two-dimensional. He could justly claim he was keeping in line with the whole feeling of the movie.

P★★	T★	E	A

With Rosalind Cash and Paul Koslo. (TR)

OMICRON (1963) A bodiless being from another world – an omicron – takes over the body of an Italian factory worker and plans to invade Earth. But he's persuaded to invade Venus instead.

P★	T★	E★	A

Directed and written by Ugo Gregoretti. With Renato Salvatori and Rosemarie Dexter.

ONE HOUR TO DOOMSDAY
(1970) *see* CITY BENEATH THE SEA (1970)

ONE HUNDRED YEARS AFTER (1911) A male scientist puts himself into suspended animation and wakes in the year 2011 when women are emancipated and where men have become second-class citizens (even in physical stature).

Pathé.

100 YEARS FROM NOW (1952) *see* CAPTIVE WOMEN (1952)

ONE MILLION B.C. (1940) Set, as the title says, back in the distant caveman past, this is a nice caveman vs. dinosaurs (they were extinct, but who cares) romp with a love interest between Victor Mature

and Carole Landis thrown in. D. W. Griffiths's creation of the prehistoric animal sequences is a disputed point.

P★	T★★	E★★	A

Directed by Hal Roach and Hal Roach Jr. Written by Mickell Novak, George Baker and Joseph Frickert. Special Effects by Roy Seawright. With Lon Chaney Jr, John Hubbard, Nigel de Bruher, Robert Kent, Ed Coxen and Creighton Hale.

ONE MILLION YEARS B.C. (1966)

Based on the 1940 film, *One Million B.C.*, this is another anachronistic caveman versus dinosaurs romp with the much publicized presence of Raquel Welch as the world's first pin-up.

P★	T★★	E★	A★

Produced and written by Michael Carreras. Directed by Don Chaffey. Special Effects by Ray Harryhausen and George Blackwell. Make-up by Wally Schneiderman. With John Richardson and Robert Brown.

ONE THOUSAND MILES AN HOUR (1916)

Very short film about a super-fuel which makes an old flivver travel at incredible speed.

Produced by Louis William Chaudet. Written by Bess Meredyth. With Eddie Lyons, Lee Moran, Harry Nolan and Edith Roberts.

ONE WAY STREET (1925)

A fairly routine melodrama about an aristocratic lady kept young by means of operations and monkey-gland treatment. Under psychological stress she begins to age rapidly.

P★	T★	E★	A

Directed by John Francis Dillon. Written by Arthur Stratte and Mary Alice Scully. With Ben Lyon, Anna Q. Nilsson and Marjorie Daw.

ON HER MAJESTY'S SECRET SERVICE (1969)

The publicity surrounding George Lazenby's taking over the role of 007 was enormous. The publicity surrounding his being dropped was even greater – all of which has gone to obscure the fact that this is one of the strongest of the Bond series, with far more of a story than its precursors, and an attempt by writer Richard Maibaum to invest Bond with a little more character than we'd previously seen him display.

The evil Blofeld (Telly Savalas) has set up a supposed allergy clinic in the Alps, where he is in fact developing a deadly mutant virus. The clinic is such an odd combination of old and modern that its strangeness – and thus its menace – seems believable, and Lazenby, who was hammered by the critics, at least looks the part, and his throwaway lines are nicely delivered. Like the clinic, this Bond too seems trapped between times and moods, he's a pure old-fashioned gentleman at times – as every playboy, deep down, would like to imagine himself. He even marries the heroine (Diana Rigg), though only for five minutes.

P★★★	T★★★★	E★★★★	A

Directed by Peter Hunt. From the novel by Ian Fleming. Special Effects by John Stears. With Ilse Steppat, Gabrieli Ferzetti and Bernard Lee.

THE ONLY WAY OUT IS DEAD

(1970) *see* THE MAN WHO WANTED TO LIVE FOREVER (1970)

ON THE BEACH (1959) Movies which open to massive publicity are nothing new, and Stanley Kramer's adaptation of the Nevil Shute novel was a major blockbuster in its time, opening simultaneously in 18 cities worldwide and heralded by full-page adverts in the national newspapers. Not that Kramer admitted he was simply after big box-office returns, for *On The Beach* stands as the most polemical of the director-producer's Message movies. After a nuclear war has devastated the rest of the world, neutral Australia stands faced with doom as clouds of radioactive fallout begin to close in; rather than suffer a slow, agonizing death, the populace is issued with suicide tablets. Anthony Hopkins does some extra agonizing, over whether to give the pill to his wife and child; Fred Astaire is a racing driver who wants to go out in one cataclysmic final burn-up; Ava Gardner is the spinster who finds love all too late with the commander of a visiting American submarine, Gregory Peck. There are genuinely touching moments in the film. Peck's submarine finally leaves for home to find only the dead, echoey shell of San Francisco; Astaire, unable to die in the race, locks himself in his garage and chokes on his racing car's exhaust. And it's impossible not to shudder at the final scenes of Aussies lining up to receive, like some final sacrament, their suicide pills. But the movie has not dated well, largely thanks to Kramer's gift for simplistic pulpit-thumping, and the story is so inert at times it seems hard to believe that what is being discussed is the end of the world. Peck's stone-faced dignity seems to be a virus-form which has spread across the whole Antipodes; only Astaire stands out in a too rare example of how well he can handle drama of this kind. It's a massively inadequate piece of propaganda by today's standards, but though there is no real telling how much it affected public opinion (the USA and USSR signed a treaty banning nuclear tests four years later) it was hugely embraced by 1959 audiences, and remains a minor landmark.

| P★★★ | T★★ | E★★★ | A★ |

Written by John Paxton. With Donna Anderson. (TR)

ON THE BRINK (1961) *see* THE DAMNED (1961)

ON THE COMET (1970) Based on Verne's novel *Hector Servadac*, this tells of a man's adventures when a part of the Earth (including prehistoric beasts) breaks off and becomes a comet.

| P★ | T★ | E★ | A |

Directed and written by Karel Zeman. With Emil Horvath and Magda Vasarykova.

OPERACIONE GOLDMAN (1965) *see* LIGHTNING BOLT (1965)

OPERATION GANEYMEDE (1977) Most of this German film takes place in the Mexican desert, where the crew members of a "lost" expedition to Ganeymede proceed to eat one another.

| P★★ | T★★ | E★★ | A★ |

Produced, directed and written by Rainer Erler. With Horst Frank, Dieter Laser, Uwe Friedrichsen, Juergen Prochnow and Claus Theo Gaestner.

OPERATION GOLDMAN (1965) *see* LIGHTNING BOLT (1965)

OPERATION KID BROTHER (1967) Sean's brother, Neil Connery, starred in this Bond look-alike, complete with sf gimmicry (underground atomic-run cities and a radiation device 'that deactivates weapons). An exploitative run-of-the-mill master criminal/spy tale.

| P★ | T★★ | E★ | A★ |

Directed by Alberto De Martino. Written by Paul Levi, Frank Walker and Canzio. Special Effects by Gagliano. With Daniela Bianchi.

OPERAZIONE PARADISO (1966) *see* KISS THE GIRLS AND MAKE THEM DIE (1966)

ORBITA MORTAL (1968) *see* MISSION STARDUST (1968)

ORLAC, THE HELL OF FRANKENSTEIN (1960) Mexican Frankenstein movie – Orlac is the creature here, brought back to life with a metal head and super-human strength. The monster is used by a criminal to seek vengeance on his enemies.

| P★ | T★ | E★ | A★ |

Directed by Rafael Baledon. Written by Alfredo Ruanova and Carlos E. Taboada. With Joaquim Cordero, Armando Calva and Rosa de Castilla.

ORLAC HANDE (1925) *see* THE HANDS OF ORLAC (1925)

ORLOFF AND THE INVISIBLE MAN (1970) Sequel to *The Awful Dr Orloff* (1961) (q.v.). Here the mad Orloff has made a man invisible, which is slowly driving the man insane.

| P★ | T★ | E★ | A★ |

Directed by Pierre Chevalier. Written by Juan Fortuny and P. Chevalier. With Howard Vernon, Isabel del Ruo and Francisco Valladares.

ORU KAIJU DAISHINGEKI (1969) *see* GODZILLA'S REVENGE (1969)

OS SOIS DA ILHA DE PASCOA (1971) *see* THE SUNS OF EASTER ISLAND (1971)

OTEL 'U POGIBSCHCHEGO
ALPINISTA (1979) *see* THE DEAD
MOUNTAINEER HOTEL (1979)

OTROKI VO VSELENNOI (1975) *see*
TEENAGERS IN SPACE (1975)

OUR MAN FLINT (1965) Flint
(played by James Coburn) is one step
beyond James Bond, armed with a cigar-
ette lighter that can kill in innumerable
ways. A successful parody of the super-spy
ethos, with Flint battling not one but three
mad scientists for control of the world.
Based on a story by Hal Finberg. A sequel,
In Like Flint (q.v.), was made in 1967.

Sean Connery as Marshall O'Niel in Outland

P★★	T★★	E★★	A★

Directed by Daniel Mann. Written by Hal Finberg
and Benn Starr. Special Effects by L. B. Abbott,
Howard Lydecker and Emil Kosa Jr. With Lee J.
Cobb, Gila Golan and Edward Mulhare .

OUTER SPACE JITTERS (1957) A
Three Stooges comedy about a visit to the
planet Zunev, with its strange electrically
powered women. To add to the fun a
prehistoric man is brought to life on the
journey.

P★	T★	E★★	A

Produced and directed by Jules White. Written by
Jack White. With Moe Howard, Larry Fine, Joe
Besser, Gene Roth Emil Sitka and Dan Blocker.

OUTLAND (1981) Harlan Ellison, the
sf writer, doesn't like *Outland*. In print
he's said that it's "derivative shuck" and
that it has a "rip-off comic-book plot".
But in his nit-picking he neglects to say
that 99.9 per cent of all sf films get some
science wrong somewhere, and that *Outland*, to its credit, has a gripping, involving
plot which is about an individual acting
against a system – a moral, ethical being
trying to come to terms with a totally
corrupt ethos. It isn't, as director/writer
Peter Hyams has stated, "High Noon in
Space", though that gives an idea of the
film's conclusion, yet it does share something of that frontier feeling that good
Westerns possess. It is set on the Con-
Amalgamated mining base on Io, the third
moon of Jupiter, somewhere in the next
century, and Marshall O'Niel (Sean Con-

nery) is the newly appointed Security chief
for the base. An increase in the numbers of
suicides leaves him suspicious and his
investigations reveal drug abuse – illegal
drugs are being given to men to increase
their output and keep the base at the top of
Con-AM's production league. The
powers-that-be want it that way, and O'Niel
is bucking the system in exposing it. The
indifference of the miners to his fate (and,
indeed, of his police force) leaves him
almost alone (only a female scientist, Dr
Lazarus, played by Frances Sternhagen,
assists him). None of this is brilliantly
innovative, and the overall effect is of a
workable sf story made into a tolerably good
and enjoyable film. What's more, its psychology is good (Ellison finds it dumb, more
a reflection on his reading of people than of
this film) and it's the first sf film to show what
a mining colony would probably be like.

P★★	T★★★	E★★★	A★

Special Effects by Roy Field, John Stears, Bob
Harman. Cinematography by Stephen Goldblatt.
With Peter Boyle, James B. Sikking, Kika Mark-
ham, Steven Berkoff and Chris Williams.

OUTLAW PLANET (1965) *see*
PLANET OF THE VAMPIRES (1965)

OUT OF THE DARKNESS (1958)
see TEENAGE CAVEMAN (1958)

AN OVER-INCUBATED BABY
(1901) An incubator developed for human
babies goes wrong and turns a tiny baby
into a wrinkled old man.

Directed and written by Walter Booth.

PACT WITH THE DEVIL (1968)
Tired old theme done tiresomely. Mexican version of the Jekyll/Hyde myth with a scientist kept young by a potion taken from living women. Presented as a deal with the devil.

P★	T★	E	A

Directed by Jaime Salvador. Written by Ramon Obon Jr and Adolfo Torres Portillo. With John Carradine and Miguel Angel Alvarez.

PAJAMA PARTY (1964) see THE MAID AND THE MARTIAN (1964)

PANE VY JSTE VDOVA (1971) see SIR, YOU ARE A WIDOW (1971)

PANIC IN THE YEAR ZERO (1962)
Ray Milland directed and starred in this post-Holocaust scenario about an American family from Los Angeles who adopt survivalist tactics to cope with a suddenly amoral world. If it weren't for the fact that it's dubious *anyone* would survive a nuclear war, I'd say that this was brutally realistic.

P★★	T★★	E★★	A★

Written by Jay Simms. Special Effects by Pat Dinga and Larry Butler. With Jean Hagen, Frankie Avalon, Mary Mitchell, Joan Freeman, Richard Garland and Richard Bakalyan.

PANICO EN EL TRANSIBERIANO (1972) see HORROR EXPRESS (1972)

PARASITE (1982) Post-Apocalypse-mad-scientist-*Alien*-movie, complete with giant leeches ripping their way out of various parts of human anatomies. A 3-D guts and gore unoriginal with obligatory post-Apocalypse gangs.

P★	T★★	E★★	A

Directed by Charles Band. Written by Alan J. Adler, Michael Shoob, Frank Levering. Special Effects by Doug White. With Robert Glandini, Demi Moore, Luca Glandini and Cherie Currie.

THE PARASITE MURDERS (1974)
see SHIVERS (1974)

PARIS QUI DORT (1923) see THE CRAZY RAY (1923)

PARTS: THE CLONUS HORROR
(1979) A film much in the *Coma* mould, but with a degree more intelligence. Clones of important people are being created by the George Walker Organization, bred to maturity and then killed and frozen ready for their organs to be used for their originals. One clone escapes from Clonus and traces his original. The plot is exposed, then, it seems, with the powers-that-be killing off all those who found out and the clone recovered, covered up again. But a last twist sees the media finding things out. This realistic, utterly honest exploration of a future possibility is excellent cinema. The ethics of breeding clones and of organlegging are brought to the fore, and there's a lovely sub-theme on the corruptness of American government.

P★★★★	T★★	E★★★★	A★

Directed by Robert S. Fiveson. Written by Ron Smith and Bob Sullivan, from a story by Sullivan. With Timothy Donnelly, Dick Sargent, Peter Graves, Keenan Wynn and David Hooks.

PAS DE VIOLENCE ENTRE NOUS (1973) see WHERE IS BETA? (1973)

PASI SPRE LUNA (1963) see STEPS TO THE MOON (1963)

THE PASSIONATE PEOPLE EATER (1960) see THE LITTLE SHOP OF HORRORS (1960)

PASSION OF DR MABUSE (1922)
see DR MABUSE, THE GAMBLER (1922)

PAWNS OF MARS (1915) Mars is the god of war, rather than the planet, in this story of a fictional arms race between two fictional East European countries (one with a new super-explosive, the other with a super-ray which can explode bombs).

Directed and written by Theodore Marston. With Dorothy Kelly and James Morrison.

THE PEACE GAME (1969) see THE GLADIATORS (1969)

THE PEOPLE (1971) An understated and genuinely moving film, intelligently presented and based on Zenna Henderson's lyrical novel on The People, a group of aliens who, hundreds of years before, had come to Earth, fleeing from their dying world. These outcasts from Eden – the witches and wizards of our demonology – are simply trying to exist in harmony, but, learning that Man will not let them be, the survivors and descendants are settled in a Mid-Western town called Bendo, cut off from all contact with Man. They seem, to the young teacher (Kim Darby) who comes to run the schoolhouse, like stern Christian fundamentalists, without music or any form of joy. It is she who catalyses a change in them that makes them willing to share what they know with Man. Without calling on modern special effects know-how, this film manages to convey alienness in an effective and touching manner.

P★★★★   T★★   E★★★★   A★★

Directed by John Korty. Written by James M. Miller. With William Shatner, Diane Varsi and Dan O'Herlihy.

THE PEOPLE THAT TIME FORGOT (1977) Michael Moorcock had no hand in the scripting of this sequel to *The Land That Time Forgot* (1974), and it shows. The plot concerns the return of a team headed by Doug McClure to the prehistoric island of Caprona – where dinosaurs and ape-men roam – in search of a lost explorer. It's little more than a tired reworking of the original, and as such even the puppet monsters have lost their early sparkle. Doug McClure struggles to keep the whole thing going with the bouncy, cheerful style of performing we have come to expect from him.

P★   T★★   E★★   A

Directed by Kevin Connor. Written by Patrick Tilley, from the novel by Edgar Rice Burroughs. Special Effects by Ian Wingrove. With Patrick Wayne, Sarah Douglas and Dana Gillespie. (TR)

PER ASPERA AD ASTRA (1981) The survivor of an alien spacecraft, Niya, is brought back to Earth and learns of our ways. Eventually the people of her distant planet come to get her, and Earth sends a mission to help them (the people of the polluted planet Dessa) solve their problems. Made in two parts, this Russian production repays in charm what it lacks in special effects sophistication.

P★★   T★★   E★★★   A★★

Directed by Richard Viktorov. Written by Viktorov and Kir Bulychev. With Elena Metelinka, Nadezhda Sementsova and Vadim Ledogorov.

PERCY PUMPERNICKLE, SOUBRETTE (1914) One of several films of the period which, in predicting the future, see it as a time when the sex roles will be reversed – thus the 1950 depicted here is run as a matriarchal society. Percy is the put-upon, slightly effeminate male.

Directed by Albert Hale. Written by Edwin Ray Coffin. With John E. Brennan.

THE PERFECT WOMAN (1949) A delightful comedy involving a scientist who builds a robot (a simulacrum of his niece) and tests it out on a young man. But, unknown to the young man (Nigel Patrick) and the scientist (Stanley Holloway), the niece (Patricia Roc) takes the place of the robot. The humour of the mistaken identity theme outweighs the sf element, of course, though there are nice scenes of the robot girl blowing up at the end, and sf fans – who like their subject-matter treated with reverence – generally didn't appreciate the comedy.

P★★   T★★   E★★★   A★

Directed by Bernard Knowles. Written by George Black and Bernard Knowles. With Miles Malleson, Irene Handl and Anita Sharp-Bolster.

THE PERILS OF PARIS (1924) Pearl White stars in a fairly routine adventure, where her scientist father develops a power ray and has it stolen by criminals. White sets out to regain the device and avenge her father's death.

Directed by Edward José. Written by Gerard Bourgeois. With Robert Lee and Henry Baudin.

PERRY RHODAN – SOS IN WELTALL (1967) From disastrously bad novels a suitably bad film. This, and its sequal, *Mission Stardust* (1968) (q.v.), are, fortunately, the only cinematic offerings from the seemingly endless Perry Rhodan series of pulp sf space opera.

P	T★	E	A

Directed by Primo Zeglio. Written by K. H. Scheer and K. H. Vogelmann. Special Effects by Antonio Margheriti. With Lang Jeffries, Essy Persson and Joachim Hansen.

THE PETRIFIED MAN (1956) *see* THE MAN WHO TURNED TO STONE (1956)

PHANTASM (1979)
The Frankenstein myth given a modern-day gore treatment, as the "Tall Man" plans to conquer the world with the legion of cadavers he has animated. Mildly humorous.

P★	T★★	E★	A

Produced, directed and written by Don Coscarelli. Special Effects by Paul Pepperman. Cinematography by Coscarelli. With Michael Baldwin, Bill Thornbury and Reggie Bannister.

PHANTOM FROM SPACE (1952)
Rather dull little tale of an invisible humanoid alien who can't actually remain invisible because he needs to wear a helmet containing a special atmospheric mixture.

P	T★	E	A

Produced and directed by W. Lee Wilder. Written by Bill Raynor and Myles Wilder. Special Effects by Alex Welden and Howard Anderson. With Ted Cooper, Noreen Nash and James Seay.

THE PHANTOM FROM 10,000 LEAGUES (1955)
Derived rather obviously from that other creature from 20,000 fathoms, this beast is a mixture of turtle and alligator, made by Man and busy defending uranium treasure.

P★	T★	E★	A

Directed by Dan Milner. Written by Lou Rusoff. With Kent Taylor and Cathy Downs.

THE PHANTOM PLANET (1961)
The phantom planet is, in fact, an asteroid, whose inhabitants shrink a visiting spaceship's crew down to their own size and recruit them in the fight against a monster.

P★	T★	E★	A

Directed by William Marshall. Written by William Telaak, Fred De Gorter and F. Gebhardt. With Dean Fredericks, Coleen Gray and Dolores Faith.

PHASE IV (1973)
Ken Middleton's superb footage of ants opens this intelligent exploration of the evolution of a species; in particular one memorable shot of an ant looking up into space from the mouth of the ant hole. Number theory, alien intrusion and astronomical event all seem to lie behind this story of an ant colony which becomes sentient and begins to organize ways and means of conquering all other living life forms. Some of this involves standard monster-movie scare-them-out-of-their-pants tactics, but mainly it's a thoughtfully developed movie which, with the scene when the ants, one after another, give up their lives to get a poisonous substance back to the Queen in the heart of the nest, actually captures our sympathy for the ants. We see them as beautiful, flexible, highly intelligent aliens. Perhaps the only *true* aliens in all sf cinema. The attempts at communication between the ants and the young research scientist, Jim Lesco (Michael Murphy), are well handled, as are the cruder confrontations between Doctor Hubbs (Nigel Davenport) and the ants – his solution is to attack the little buggers; but he finds they're smarter and more vicious than him. There are amazing scenes in this, such as when the black ants lay out all the newly mutated yellow ants (killed by Davenport) in rows in a mourning chamber, and the ant towers (looking like something from an ancient star-watching cult) again evoke a sense of the alien. Towards the end of the film Hubbs is eaten alive by the ants and Lesco gives up all thought of communicating. He goes outside in a hardsuit, a cloud of poisonous blue chemicals sprayed about him, determined to go down into the nest and kill the Queen. Instead (in a wash of semi-mystical photography) he is *changed* and made "part of their world", together with the young girl who sought refuge in the scientists' dome (Lynn Frederick). We are left in no uncertain terms, however, that it will not be Man but the ants who will very soon be running the Earth. The strength of the

Lynn Frederick in a scene from Phase IV

movie lies in the fact that we can, at the end of this experience, share something of the ethos of the ants.

P★★★   T★★★★★   E★★★   A★★★★

Directed by Saul Bass. Written by Mayo Simon. Special Effects by John Richardson. Cinematography by Dick Bush.

THE PHILADELPHIA EXPERIMENT (1984) The publicity people for this film claimed that its story was based on the sober truth. The film is *supposed* to be inspired by a World War Two attempt to make a US warship in Philadelphia harbour "radar invisible". This alleged experiment has been a legend within the science fiction community for many years, though usually in versions that temporarily displace the vessel in space (matter transmission) rather than the time-travel which is the fulcrum of the plot here. But it is only a story – though one piquant detail is that "the crew all went stark, staring *mad* . . ." – and it is unlikely that anybody today *really* believes that anything exciting happened. It seems that the creators of this film have the same problem. They alternate uneasily between orthodox sf, special-effects sf, car-chase thriller, and even boy-meets-girl! This film's answer to the problem of what happened in Philadelphia harbour involves time-travel. Two of the sailors (well played by Bobby Di Cicco and Michael Paré) are whirled from 1944 into 1984. This one unoriginal idea is the basis of the entire plot, and though there is some amusement in the clean-cut sailors'

earnest enquiries about the result of "the war" and their dubious feelings about 1984 America, the film has by now lost touch with believability. In spite of some good action scenes and a generous measure of special-effects lightning and thunder, not even the time vortex that follows the two sailors around – threatening to destroy the entire world needless to say – can really retain much dramatic tension in the film.

P★★   T★★★   E★★   A★

Directed by Stewart Raffill. Written by William Gray and Michael Janover. Visual Effects by Max Anderson. With Nancy Allen, Eric Christmas and Kene Holliday. (RS)

PICNIC ON THE GRASS (1966)
French vision of a Utopian future where all problems have been solved.

P★★   T★★   E★★   A★★

Directed and written by Jean Renoir. With Paul Meurisse, Catherine Rouvel and Fernand Sardon.

THE PIER (1962) *see* THE JETTY (1962)

THE PIRATES OF 1920 (1911) Piracy future style – from the air. Here the pirates' airship attacks an ocean liner and steals its cargo before sinking it.

Directed by A. E. Colby and Dave Aylott.

THE PIT (1963) *see* THE MIND BENDERS (1963)

PLAGUE (1978) Research into DNA leads to the development of a strain, N-3, which creates rapid crop growth. It might solve world food-shortage problems, but it has a deadly side-effect – when it enters the human bloodstream it triggers a reaction which leads to all the nerves firing at once. Spread like a plague virus, it almost gets out of hand. The film follows the usual step-by-step escalation – it escapes first from the lab, then is carried farther afield, until, in time, an antidote is found. But two of the scientists working on the antidote are held culpable at the end, and the strain one of them developed, N-4, has been isolated by the authorities while

the two of them are indefinitely quaran-
tined. A good medical sf thriller without
over-sensationalizing matters.

P★★★   T★★   E★★   A★★

Directed by Ed Hunt. Written by Hunt and Barry
Pearson. With Daniel Pilon, Kate Reid, Celine
Lomez and Michael J. Reynolds.

PLANETA BURG (1962) *see* PLANET
OF STORMS (1962)

PLANETARY GIANTS (1963) Mexican juvenile about a journey to an alien
planet to prevent Earth from being destroyed. The young crew and professor
take along a boxer and his manager.

P★   T★   E   A

Directed by Alfredo B. Crevenna. Written by
Alfredo Ruanova. With Guillermo Murray, Lorena Velazquez, José Galvez and Adriana Roel.

I PLANETI CONTRO DI NOI
(1961) *see* PLANETS AGAINST US
(1961)

PLANET OF BLOOD (1965) *see*
PLANET OF THE VAMPIRES (1965)

PLANET OF BLOOD (1966) *see*
QUEEN OF BLOOD (1966)

**THE PLANET OF EXTIN-
GUISHED MEN** (1960) *see* BATTLE
OF THE WORLDS (1960)

PLANET OF HORRORS (1981) *see*
MINDWARP: AN INFINITY OF TER-
ROR (1981)

PLANET OF STORMS (1962) Tech-
nically well-made Russian film about a
space journey to Venus. The human crew
are assisted by an unpredictable robot
helper and eventually encounter lizard
men and native Venusians. Excerpts from
this film were used (without credit) in
Voyage To The Prehistoric Planet (1965)
(q.v.) and *Voyage To The Planet Of Prehistoric Women* (1968) (q.v.).

P★★   T★★   E★   A★

Directed by Pavel Klushantsev. Written by Alexander Kazantsev and Klushantsev. With Gennadi
Vernov, Yuri Sarantsev and Vladimir Temelianov.

PLANET OF TERROR (1965) *see*
PLANET OF THE VAMPIRES (1965)

PLANET OF THE APES (1968) Despite all of its commercial auspices, this
adventure-movie adaptation of Pierre
Boulle's novel *Monkey Planet* stands, at
times, as a very pleasant little piece of
satire. Taylor (Charlton Heston) is an
astronaut who finds himself stranded on a
world where simians are the dominant
species and human beings little more than
dumb animals, to be hunted, caged, and
experimented on by the chimps. The film
turns into partly an anti-vivisection lecture
on the level of "how would *you* like it?",
but mercifully that debate is framed within
the context of a larger theme; what's being
sent up is not merely our attitude towards
lesser species but our arrogance as a
whole. The apes' world is a strange mock-
ery of our own, advanced in such techniques as surgery and armaments, but
pre-Galilean – there's a deftly clever reason for all this – in its social structure and
philosophy. And the creatures themselves
are given character by being imbued with
that most simultaneously endearing and
worrying of human qualities, an unintentional comicality born out of their own
self-centredness, the fragility of their
egos. These apes have been flicking
through *Pickwick Papers* – we look in the
mirror of Michael Wilson and Rod Serling's script and see a little bit of ourselves
loping back towards us, furrily. Taylor, in
counterpoint, believes he stands as the
sole representative of his race and behaves
accordingly, violent and aggressive, but
impressive too, convinced of his own
superiority right up until the end. Some of
his dialogue is pure spaghetti Western – a
mood which visually filters into the movie
at points – and in his occasional de-
pressions he becomes self-critical without
reaching any conclusions, but otherwise
he's a self-appointed superman, battling
with shadow images he does not realize
are his own. None of which is to say that
director Franklin Schaffner has given us
some concealed work of art here, for
Planet of the Apes is a fun movie and the
satire is of a zippy, collegiate kind, used

Charlton Heston and Kim Hunter in a scene from
Planet Of The Apes

more as a mortar to the action than an end in itself. There's some excellent humour, like the young hippie-chimp who doesn't trust the older generation. And the final shot contains one of the classic images of the sf movie genre.

P★★★★	T★★★★★	E★★★★★	A★★

Special Effects by L. B. Abbott, Art Cruikshank and Emil Kosa Jr. Make-up by John Chambers. With Kim Hunter, Roddy McDowall, Maurice Evans, James Whitmore, James Daly and Linda Harrison. (TR)

PLANET OF THE APES RE-VISITED (1969) *see* BENEATH THE PLANET OF THE APES (1969)

PLANET OF THE DEAD (1959) *see* FIRST SPACESHIP ON VENUS (1959)

PLANET OF THE MEN (1969) *see* BENEATH THE PLANET OF THE APES (1969)

PLANET OF THE VAMPIRES (1965) Italian/Spanish collaboration, directed by Mario Bava. Astronauts find themselves drawn down on to the surface of an alien planet, where disembodied aliens take over their bodies, prepared to go to Earth and conquer it. Based on Renato Pestriniero's short story, "One Night Of 21 Hours".

P★	T★★	E★	A★

Written by Castillo Cosulich, Antonio Roman, Alberto Bevilacqua, Mario Bava and Rafael J. Salvia (English language version by Ib Melchior and Louis M. Heyward). With Barry Sullivan, Norma Bengell, Angel Aranda and Evi Morandi.

PLANETS AGAINST US (1961) Runaway humanoid robots (identical to humans) with deadly touches are hunted and killed by the Earth authorities in this interesting Italian movie.

P★	T★★	E★	A★

Directed by Romano Ferraro. Written by Ferraro and Piero Pierotti. With Michel Lemoine, Maria pia Lozi, Jany Clair and Marco Guglierno.

PLAN 9 FROM OUTER SPACE (1956) A predictable, amateurish production – aliens try to conquer Earth by reviving the dead and using them as zombies – which has received undue attention (if not huge cult status) for its sheer awfulness. But this is a dull, incoherent film which is funnier as a lecture subject than in its own right. The two minutes of film that director Edward D. Wood bought up that have Bela Lugosi in them (as a cloaked vampire) are edited in with footage of a healer (hired for the occasion and nothing like Lugosi) who holds a cloak in front of his face at all times. Memorable for its ineptness alone.

P	T	E★	A

Produced, directed, written and edited by Edward D. Wood. With Bela Lugosi, Vampira, Lyle Talbot, Tor Johnson and Gregory Walcott.

PLEASE DON'T EAT MY MOTHER! (1972) Man in his forties feeds various authority figures (mother, policeman, etc.) to his pet carnivorous plant. A comedy (of sorts) in bad taste.

P★	T★	E★	A

Produced and directed by Carl Monson. With Rene Bond, Buck Kartahan, Flora Wisel and Alicia Friedland.

PLUCKED (1967) Light-hearted spoof on mutation tales with a radioactive accident at a chicken-food factory.

P★	T★★	E★★	A★

Directed by Giulio Questi. Written by Questi and Franco Arcalli. With Gina Lollabrigida, Eva Aulin, Jean-Louis Trintignant and Jean Sabieski.

THE POLICEMAN AND THE EXTRATERRESTRIALS (1978)
Weak French sf comedy about a comic policeman (Louis de Funes) who encounters a flying saucer.

P★	T★★	E★	A

Directed by Jean Girault. Written by Jacques Vilfrid. With Michel Galabru, Maurice Risch, Jean-Pierre Rambal and Maria Mauban.

POPDOWN (1968) Psychedelic, swinging London attracts a pair of aliens, who observe 1960s youth culture.

P★	T★★	E★★	A★

Directed and written by Fred Marshall. With Diane Keen, Jane Bates and Carol Rachell.

PORT SINISTER (1952) A sunken Caribbean pirate city is raised from the ocean bed by an earthquake.

P★	T★	E★	A

Produced and written by Jack Pollexfen and Aubrey Wisberg. Directed by Harold Daniels. Special Effects by Jack Rabin and Rocky Cline. With James Warren, Lynne Roberts, Paul Cavanaugh and William Schallert.

THE POSSIBILITIES OF WAR IN THE AIR (1909) see THE AIRSHIP DESTROYER (1909)

THE POWER (1967) An interesting but severely flawed film from the George Pal (producer)/Byron Haskin (director) stable. In a research institute a doctor tries to track down who amongst his colleagues is the super-mutant with incredible psychic/telekinetic powers. Based on Frank M. Robinson's novel, this was one of the first serious attempts to capture the dangers of such ESP powers on the screen. Since *The Power* there have been several better attempts (*The Fury, Scanners, The Dead Zone*) but none quite as frightening in its implications (the super-mutant can erase the identity of people by degrees).

P★★★	T★★	E★★★	A★★

Written by John Gay. Special Effects by J. MacMillan Johnson, Merrill Pye and Wah Chang. With George Hamilton, Suzanne Pleshette, Michael Rennie and Nehemiah Persoff.

THE PREHISTORIC MAN (1917) A scientist develops a ray which makes an ape as clever as a human. It gains political power, but its lusting after human women has it changed back to original simian state.

Directed by Alfred Desy. Written by Zoltan Somlyo and Erno Gyori. With Viktor Kurd and Myra Corthy.

PREHISTORIC PLANET (1965) see VOYAGE TO THE PREHISTORIC PLANET (1965)

PREHISTORIC VALLEY (1961)
Rather lacklustre adaptation of Jules Verne's novel, *Hector Servadac*, with a chunk of Earth swept off by a comet – a chunk containing prehistoric monsters and cavemen.

P★	T★	E	A

Directed and written by Edward Bernds. Special Effects by Dick Albain. Make-up by Ben Lane. With Cesare Danova and Sean McLory.

PREHISTORIC WOMEN (1950)
Fairly uninspired story about the year 20,000 B.C. with Stone Age women capturing men, discovering fire and fighting winged dragons.

P★	T★	E★	A

Directed by Greg Tallas. Written by S. X. Abarbanel and Greg Tallas. With Laurette Luez, Allan Nixon, Tony Devlin and Mara Lynn.

PREHISTORIC WORLD (1958) see TEENAGE CAVEMAN (1958)

THE PRESIDENT'S ANALYST (1967) The comic sinister touches throughout this film are typical of its schizophrenic time, and the revelation that the Telephone Company and their robots *really* run things could have come straight from the pages of a Philip K. Dick novel. James Coburn plays the title role with panache and humour.

P★★	T★★	E★★	A★

Directed and written by Theodore J. Flicker. Special Effects by Westheimer Co. With Godfrey Cambridge, Severn Darden, Pat Harrington, Joan Delaney and Barry McGuire.

THE PREVIEW MURDER MYSTERY (1936) A haunting thriller about images of murder picked up by a television; images received despite absence of lighting.

P★★	T★	E★★	A★

Directed by Robert Florey. Written by Brian Marlow and Robert Yost. With Reginald Denny, Frances Drake, Ian Keith and George Barbier.

THE PRIMITIVE MAN (1913) see BRUTE FORCE (1913)

PRISONERS OF THE LOST UNIVERSE (1983) A professor builds a machine which taps into a parallel universe. Earthquakes in the Los Angeles district tip him, and then two others, into the rays of the machine and over into the alternate world. Split seconds in our world prove to be days in theirs, so the Prof. has been there a year when our hero, Dan (Richard Hatch), and heroine, Carrie (Kay Lenz), arrive. The Prof. becomes sorcerer to the Warlord, Kleel (John Saxon), while the two others find themselves abused and misused by said Kleel. After a series of adventures involving pygmies with glowing red eyes, green men (goodies), a man mountain (goody), water-creatures (baddies), fire men (baddies), a sneak-thief (semi-goody), and various ghouls belonging to the Warlord, the Warlord is killed, his fortress blown up, and our intrepid twosome escape (leaving the Prof. in the alternate world – serves him right for tinkering ... there are some things ...). All in all a mindless, enjoyable romp, part *Conan*, part *Raiders*, part 1950s schlock costume drama.

P★	T★★	E★★★	A★

Directed by Terry Marcel. Written by Marcel and Harry Robertson. Special Effects by Roy Hanson.

PRIVILEGE (1967) If the idea of Paul Jones as a rock and roll Messiah impresses you, then make sure you see *Privilege*. The rest of us, though, quickly come to the sad realization that everything about this film (except perhaps for Johnny Speight's original idea) is now dated: dialogue, music, human attitudes and – worst of all – the "Swinging London" ambience that extends to turning Jean Shrimpton into an actress. There is something interesting struggling to emerge here, but what the film really makes you realize is that 1967 was a long, long time ago.

P★★	T★★	E★	A★

Directed by Peter Watkins. Written by Norman Bogner. With Mark London and Max Bacon. (RS)

PROFESSOR HOSKIN'S PATENT HUSTLER (1913) Short comedy about a machine which makes things speed up.

Directed by Dave Aylott.

PROFESSOR PUDDENHEAD'S PATENTS: THE ELECTRIC ENLARGER (1909) Fun and games with a wand which makes everything it touches grow huge. The Professor's assistant misbehaves with the invention.

Directed and written by Walter R. Booth.

PROFESSOR PUDDENHEAD'S PATENTS: THE AEROCAB AND VACUUM PROVIDER (1909) Charming gimmick-ridden film from director Walter Booth (who also wrote). The flying car (complete with flapping wings) and suction vacuum provide an excuse for special effects fun.

THE PROFESSOR'S ANTI-GRAVITATIONAL FLUID (1908) Gimmicky film about a fluid (or powder) which makes things float in the air.

Directed by Lewin Fitzhamon. With Bertie Potter.

PROFESSOR WEISE'S BRAIN SERUM INJECTOR (1909) The meddlesome Professor develops a serum that increases brain size and intelligence.

Produced by Sigmund Lubin.

THE PROJECTED MAN (1966) The inventor of a matter-transmitter is disfigured in an accident with machine and becomes a killer with an electric shock touch. But eventually he is remorseful and destroys both his machine and himself.

P★	T★	E★★	A★

Directed by Ian Curteis. Written by John C. Cooper and Peter Bryan. Special Effects by Flo Nordhoff, Robert Hedges and Mike Hope. With Bryant Halliday and Mary Peach.

PROJECT MOONBASE (1953) Con-
structed from the opening episodes of an unsold TV series, this is about an orbital space station and an ill-fated expedition to the Moon. Co-written by Robert A. Heinlein and Jack Seaman, it has little of the zest of Heinlein's written work of the period.

| P★ | T★ | E★ | A★ |

Directed by Richard Talmadge. Special Effects by Jacques Fresco. With Donna Martell, Ross Ford, Hayden Rourke and James Craven.

PROJECT X (1967) Future thriller about
a secret agent in 2118 who knows how the Sino-Asians plan to destroy the West. Under interrogation his subconscious splits off and becomes a ferocious monster creature. In the end it seems that the spy is in himself the means for destroying the West, his body filled with delayed-action germ viruses. Based on L. P. Davies's novels, *The Artificial Man* and *Psychogeist*.

| P★★ | T★★ | E★★ | A★ |

Produced and directed by William Castle. Written by Edmund Morris. Special Effects by Paul K. Lerpae. With Christopher George and Greta Baldwin.

PROPHECY (1979) A strong ecology
theme runs throughout this poor movie. An industrial plant is causing animals in the woods to mutate and grow to giant proportions – the modern variant on radiation mutation – and a government man is sent in to investigate.

| P★ | T★★ | E★ | A★ |

Directed by John Frankenheimer. Written by David Seltzer. Special Effects by Robert Dawson. With Talia Shire, Robert Foxworth, Armand Assante, Richard Dysart and Victoria Racino.

THE PROTECTORS: BOOK 1
(1981) Marilyn Chambers (star of *Rabid* (q.v.) and numerous hard-core movies) plays lead in this soft-core, low-budget, battle-for-control-of-the-Earth, high-tech, neo-spy-thriller. No *Book 2* has so far appeared.

| P★ | T★★ | E★★ | A |

Produced and directed by Myrl A. Schreibman. Written by Helen Sanford. With Stephen Johnson, Mary Woronov, Milt Kogan and Dan Jesse.

PROTOTYPE (1983) A surprisingly in-
telligent film about the development of the first humanoid robot who, with his creator, flees from military intervention. Christopher Plummer plays the Nobel Prize winning creator and David Morse prototype 2VR. 2VR, or Dr Michael Smith as he becomes, grows fascinated with the Frankenstein myth, identifying with the creature's fate, but recognizing that he is *less* than the creature – "I'm not anything. I'm what anyone wants me to be." Michael is a result of the ghost in the machine – of the uncertainty principle. In a poignant final scene, knowing they cannot run any longer, the robot agrees to destroy himself so that Plummer can build a new model and, in doing so, have greater controls over how that model is *used*. 2VR/Michael is the ultimate realist, dealing only in certainties. This excellent script is by Richard Levinson and William Link.

| P★★★★ | T★★ | E★★★ | A★★ |

Directed by David Greene. With Frances Sternhagen, James Sutorius, Stephen Elliot, Doran Clark, Alley Mills and Arthur Hill.

P.T.BARNUM'S ROCKET TO
THE MOON (1954) *see* BLAST OFF! (1954)

THE PULVERIZER (1909) A scientist
invents a pulverizer (and antidote) and has it stolen by pranksters.

THE PUMAMAN (1980) Italianate
comic-book hero, part alien god, part Aztec, part Italian, who – as Pumaman – fights Cobras (Donald Pleasance) who wants to control the world via his ancient Aztec mask of power. Not as bad as it sounds, even though the special effects are distinctly second rate.

| P★★ | T★ | E★★ | A |

Directed by Alberto De Martino. Written by Massimo De Rita and Luigi Angelo. With Walter George Alton and Miguelangelo Fuentes.

PUNISHMENT PARK (1970) In the near future the Vietnam War has escalated and political control back in the USA has tightened to a repressive degree. Dissenters against the war can choose between a three-year jail sentence and a long weekend at Punishment Park, where, in effect, they live out a microcosm of the war. The nasty twist in the tale is that even the survivors of the park are killed.

P★★   T★★   E★★   A★

Directed and written by Peter Watkins. With Paul Alelyanes and Carmen Argenziano.

Q PLANES (1937) *see* CLOUDS OVER EUROPE (1937)

Q, THE WINGED SERPENT (1982) Ritual killings (in which the bodies are completely skinned) bring back the ancient Aztec god, Quetzalcoatl, a giant flying lizard. It builds its nest at the top of New York's Chrysler building and begins to terrorize the city. A small-time hood, Jimmy Quinn (Michael Moriarty), knows where it is and so strikes a bargain with the Mayor's office. The beast is killed (in scenes reminiscent of *King Kong*) but in a derelict building a new egg is hatching. It's a clever, highly entertaining and at times horrific film with David Carradine and Richard Roundtree as the cops out to solve the mystery.

P★★   T★★★   E★★★   A★

Produced, directed and written by Larry Cohen. Special Effects by David Allen, Randy Cook, Peter Kuran; Lost Arts Inc. With Lee Louis, Candy Clark and Fred J. Scollay.

QUANDO GLI UOMINI AMAR-ANO LA CLARA . . . E CON DONNE FECERO DIN-DON (1971) *see* WHEN WOMEN PLAYED DING DONG (1971)

QUANDO LE DONNE AVE-VANDO LA CODA (1970) *see* WHEN WOMEN HAD TAILS (1970)

QUATERMASS AND THE PIT (1967) Most of the usual flaws of science fiction B-movies are here, yet this, the third in the series, remains an enjoyable example of what can be done in a low-budget movie with a halfway decent idea. The intrepid Professor Q. is called in to investigate when excavation works reveal an alien capsule buried beneath the heart of London. Strange things begin happening to anyone who comes near the site – the script manages to tie in the idea of Martians visiting our world in prehistoric times with a variety of supernatural legends ranging from poltergeists to diabolism. There's a tense finale as the Martians re-emerge to destroy a good deal of London – the Wyndham-obsessed British seemed to revel in the idea of the Apocalypse back then – and the film is shot in that inky, claustrophobic version of *noir* which was the trademark of British suspense movies of that era.

P★★★★   T★★★   E★★★★   A★

Directed by Roy Ward Baker. Written by Nigel Kneale. Special Effects by Bowie Films. With Andrew Keir and James Donald.

THE QUATERMASS EXPERI-MENT (1955) First of Hammer Films' adaptations of Nigel Kneale's television series, it's a fairly standard rocketship-brings-back-something-nasty-from-space story, as the sole survivor of a spaceship crash becomes a giant fungus and terrorizes London, ultimately succumbing to a massive electric shock. Brian Donlevy played the capable man of science, Quatermass, in both of the first two films, giving what was an otherwise undistinguished storyline a touch of authority.

P★★   T★★★   E★★★   A★

Directed by Val Guest. Written by Richard Landau and Guest. Special Effects by Leslie Bowie. With Margia Dean, Jack Warner, Richard Wordsworth and David King Wood, Thora Hird, Gordon Jackson, Harold Lang and Lionel Jeffries.

QUATERMASS II (1957) Sequel to the popular and successful *The Quatermass Experiment* (q.v.), this second cinematic episode had Professor Quatermass battling against alien invaders who are con-

Left to right: John Longden, Brian Donlevy and Sidney James in Quatermass II

trolling the minds of humans and attempting to change Earth's environment to suit their physical needs. It's a tauter, darker film than either of the other two Quatermass movies and has a sub-text which became more widely popular in the late 1960s and 1970s – that of governmental conspiracy to hush things up. It seems the aliens (recognizable by a V-shaped scar on their human hosts) have taken over whole strata of government. Things work out well in the end, but there's a genuine sense of threat that remains with you after the film has ended: always a good sign.

P★★★   T★★★   E★★★★   A★★

Directed by Val Guest. Written by Nigel Kneale and Val Guest. With Brian Donlevy, Vera Day, Bryan Forbes, John Longden, Sidney James, Michael Ripper and Charles Lloyd Pack.

QUEEN OF ATLANTIS (1947) *see* SIREN OF ATLANTIS (1947)

QUEEN OF BLOOD (1966) An Earth expedition to Mars discovers a crashed alien spacecraft and takes its female survivor aboard, but she proves to be a vampire and kills several of them before she is cut and bleeds to death. But she has left a nest of eggs which are taken back to Earth.

P★★   T★   E★   A★

Executive Producer Roger Corman. Directed and written by Curtis Harrington. Make-up by William Condos. With John Saxon and Basil Rathbone.

QUEEN OF OUTER SPACE (1958) An off-course spacecraft lands on Venus

and finds it ruled by a tribe of Amazons who want to destroy Earth. Zsa Zsa Gabor plays a rebellious Venusian woman in this ham-fisted farce of a movie.

P   T★   E   A

Directed by Edward Bernds. Written by Charles Beaumont. Special Effects by Milt Rice. With Eric Fleming, Laurie Mitchell and Paul Birch.

QUEST FOR FIRE (1982) An everyday story of apish folk with a couple of ideas from William Golding's "The Inheritors", set 80,000 years ago when a tribe of our ancestors lose their fire and send out three of their warriors to find some more. Different periods of human evolution have become mixed up in this Jean-Jacques Annaud film – there are sub-humans even more hirsute than our heroes, and, incredibly, another tribe several thousand years more advanced, already at the pots-and-mud-huts stage. A girl from this tribe falls in with the three apes and teaches them more interesting things than how to rub two sticks together. The dialogue, all grunts, was devised by Anthony Burgess; the gestures and sign language by Desmond Morris. The clowning humour of the three heroes is the strongest point in a film which is little more than an intriguing curiosity.

P★   T★★★★   E★★★   A★

Written by Gerard Brach, from a novel by J. H. Rosny. Special Effects by Martin Malivoire, Colin On and Christopher Tucker. With Rae Dawn Chong, Everett McGill and Ron Perlman.

QUEST FOR LOVE (1971) Romantic use of the parallel worlds idea (rarely used in sf cinema), with a man accidentally cast into a world where Kennedy wasn't assassinated and the Vietnam War wasn't fought. There he meets and falls in love with a girl who then dies. The shock of her death returns him to his own world, where he searches for and finds her equivalent and saves her life. Based on John Wyndham's short story, "Random Quest".

P★★   T★★   E★★★   A★

Directed by Ralph Thomas. Written by Bert Batt. With Joan Collins, Tom Bell, Denholm Elliott, Juliet Harmer and Simon Ward.

QUINTET (1979) Robert Altman directed and co-wrote (with Frank Barhydt and Patricia Resnick) this elegant little gem of an sf movie. In the future the Earth has suffered another Ice Age and, in one of the last cities, Mankind is dying out. Essex (Paul Newman) enters the city with his mate, Vivia (Brigitte Fossey), looking for his brother. In its opulent decay the city and its inhabitants resemble a Renaissance Italian city state set at the wrong end of time. Within the city people are obsessed with pentagons and with a game, Quintet. But the game has been extended into real life and made to contain all that remains of Man's cultural wealth and vitality, though ironically the game itself is about death – the death of those participating. Essex discovers his brother is dead, then has his wife, Evi, killed in the game (accidentally). Her death – while pregnant, in a world where pregnancy is almost a miracle – seems to emphasize the film's message of "No Hope" – "Hope is an obsolete word" says one of the players. But Essex confronts the "Adjudicator" after winning the game (i.e. *surviving*), then goes north. In spite of all, he still has hope, following the path of a goose which he saw flying north. Beautifully photographed in Montreal, Canada, by Jean Boffety, and with a memorable and evocative musical score by Tom Pierson, this isn't the easiest of films to follow, but rewards attention. One of the few sf films to reflect the current literary state of the written genre.

| P★★ | T★★★ | E★★★ | A★★★★ |

Script Supervision by Monique Champagne. Special Effects by Tom Fisher and John Thomas. With Vittorio Gassman, Fernando Rey, Bibi Andersson and Nina Van Pallandt.

RABBITS (1972) *see* NIGHT OF THE LEPUS (1972)

RABID (1976) Experiments in skin-grafting at the Keloid Clinic save the life of a girl, Rose (Marilyn Chambers), almost killed in a motorcycle accident, but the graft of neutral tissues have a strange side-effect. Like Typhoid Mary she becomes the carrier of a hideous strain of super-rabies which spreads throughout Montreal, Canada. The film sees Rose as a victim rather than as a gleeful murderer – and the film ends with her as the final victim of the vicious circle of death, carried off by white-suited men and dumped unceremoniously in a rubbish van. Between times we see the effects of the rabid strain, red-eyed frothing maniacs – horror film fodder one and all. David Cronenberg wrote and directed, and his dark (some might say perverse) trademarks are evident throughout the film, along with certain clumsinesses – scenes inserted purely for their shock value rather than as integral to the unwinding story. It's far from Cronenberg at his best, but even second-rate Cronenberg is morbidly fascinating.

| P★★ | T★★★ | E★★★ | A★ |

Make-up by Joe Blasco. With Frank Moore, Joe Silver and Howard Ryshpan.

RADIO MANIA (1923) In a dream, a man imagines a two-way radio connection with Mars (the Martians are large-brained humanoids), by means of which he is given various alchemical secrets. But it *is* only a dream...

Directed by R. William Neill. Written by Lewis Allen Brown. With Grant Mitchell, Margaret Irving and Gertrude Hillman.

RADON THE FLYING MONSTER (1956) *see* RODAN (1956)

LA RAGAZZA DE LATTA (1970) *see* THE TIN GIRL (1970)

RAGEWAR (1984) Paul Bradford (Jeffrey Byron) has undergone an "experiment" and can communicate direct with his computer, Cal. A dracula-like figure, Mestema (Richard Moll) draws him – through his computer-sensitive glasses – into a world of magic where he has to face seven challenges and save his fiancée, Gwen (Leslie Wing). Predictable, juvenile stuff, without any real challenge and only superficial adventure. The seven sections (individually written and individually directed by seven different people) are unsatisfyingly derivative. Showy special effects do not make a film, and the opening scene – gratuitously sexual – is somehow at odds with the juvenile emotions and plot-lines.

P	T★★★	E★	A

Directed by Rosemary Turko, John Buechler, Charles Band, David Allen, Steve Ford, Peter Manoogian and Ted Nicoldon. Overall scenario by Allen Actor. Special Effects by John Buechler. Visual Effects by David Allen.

RAIDERS OF THE LOST ARK
(1981) Spielberg and Lucas brilliantly evoked the all-action-adventure spirit of the 1920s pulp magazines for boys in this story of Indiana Jones's pursuit of the Lost Ark of the Covenant. The Ark, when it's found and dusted off (with a few words of Hebrew muttered over it for good measure), proves to be a transmitter of awesome power – angels turning into demons which can melt your face! A lovely quasi-sf touch in a film from another genre.

P★★	T★★★	E★★★★★	A★

Written by Lawrence Kasdan. With Harrison Ford and Karen Allen.

THE RAJAH'S TIARA (1914) Using
an X-ray machine to see through walls is a help for a gang of jewel thieves.

Directed by H. D. Martinek. Written by L. C. MacBean. With James Carew and Ivy Montford.

RAMPER DER TIERMENSCH
(1927) see THE STRANGE CASE OF CAPTAIN RAMPER (1927)

RAT (1960) see WAR (1960)

RATATAPLAN (1979) A social failure
builds a robot duplicate which proves a social success. But when the robot blows a fuse (at a critical moment) its creator steps in and we have a happy ending. A mild-mannered comedy which amuses rather than delights, despite its excessive energy.

P★★	T★★	E★★	A★

Directed and written by Maurizio Nichetti. With Nichetti, Angela Finocchiaro and Edy Angelillo.

THE RAT SAVIOUR (1977) An invasion from within our eco-system as shape-changing rats kill and duplicate their human victims. Based on a story by Alexandre Greene, this has an investigative writer combating the rats with a new chemical. A good, enjoyable film from this Jugoslavian team.

P★★	T★★	E★★★	A★★

Directed by Krsto Papic. Written by Papic and Ivo Brexan. With Ivica Vidovic, Mirjana Majurec, Relja Basic and Fabijan Sovagovic.

THE RAVAGERS (1979) Unsavoury
post-Holocaust tale of a man seeking revenge for his wife's rape and murder by a motorcycle gang. Should have starred Bronson!

P★	T★★	E★	A

Directed by Richard Compton. Written by Donald Sanford. With Richard Harris, Art Carney, Alana Hamilton, Ernest Borgnine and Ann Turkel.

RAW MEAT (1972) see DEATHLINE
(1972)

EL RAYO DESINTEGRADOR
(1965) see THE DISINTEGRATING RAY (1965)

LE RAYON INVISIBLE (1923) see
THE CRAZY RAY (1923)

LES RAYONS MORTELS DU DOCTEUR MABUSE (1964) see
SECRET OF DR MABUSE (1964)

LES RAYONS ROENTGEN (1897)
see A NOVICE AT X-RAYS (1897)

THE READER OF MINDS (1914) A
mind-reading machine is used to steal military secrets.

Written by Philip Longerman.

THE REDEEMER (1977) see THE
RAT SAVIOUR (1977)

RED LIGHTS (1923) Typical 1920s
gimmick film. An inventor perfects a device which can transmit his voice anywhere, by means of a red light. Based on

the play "The Rear Car" by Edward E. Rose.

Directed by Clarence G. Badger. Written by Carey Wilson. With Marie Prevost, Raymond Griffith, John Walker and Alice Lake.

RED PLANET MARS (1952) One of the maddest Born-again-Christian, anti-Communist conspiracy films from the early 1950s, with God ruling an efficient, Christian Mars and knowledge of this toppling the USSR. Meanwhile an ex-Nazi, who invented the "communicator", is trying to cripple capitalism. Based on the play "Red Planet" by John L. Balderston and John Hoare.

| P | T | E | A |

Produced and co-written by Anthony Weiller. Directed by Harry Horner. With Peter Graves, Andrea King, Marvin Miller and Morris Ankrum.

RED PLANET MARS (1968) *see* MISSION MARS (1968)

REGULAR AS CLOCKWORK (1967) *see* DON'T PLAY WITH THE MARTIANS (1967)

THE RELUCTANT ASTRONAUT (1966) Rather poor comedy about an astronaut who suffers badly from vertigo.

| P★ | T★ | E★ | A |

Produced and directed by Edward J. Montague. Written by Jim Fritzell and Everet Greenbaum. With Don Knotts, Arthur O'Connell and Leslie Nielsen.

REPO MAN (1984) If Philip K. Dick had been – in some alternate, drug-induced world – a film director, he might have gone under the name of Alex Cox and directed (and written) *Repo Man*. Emilio Estevez plays Otto, the punk who becomes a repossession man (stealing back cars) and goes after a bounty of $20,000 offered for the capture and return of a '64 Chevy Malibu. In the car are a lobotomized nuclear scientist with a boot full of dead (yet curiously active) aliens. In the totally nihilistic landscapes of "Edge City" relationships are tenuous at best and life a compromise with entropy. This is a brilliant, hilarious, *weird* film.

Emilio Estevez (left) and Harry Dean Stanton (right) in Repo Man

| P★★★★ | T★★★ | E★★★★★ | A★★★★ |

With Harry Dean Stanton, Tracey Walter, Olivia Barash, Sy Richardson and Susan Barnes.

REPTILICUS (1962) The tail of a prehistoric nasty is brought up by an oil-drilling crew. In the laboratory it regenerates itself into the full-bodied reptile, which spits poison, flies and generally does nasty things to humans. In the end it's knocked unconscious and dies.

| P★ | T★ | E★ | A |

Produced, directed and written by Sidney Pink. Co-written by Ib Melchior. With Carl Ottosen, Ann Smyrner, Mimi Heinrich and Asbjorn Andersen.

THE RESURRECTION OF ZACHARY WHEELER (1971) One of the earliest organ-legging films. A US senator is brought back to life and given necessary organ transplants (by means of "somas" – specially bred zombie-like humans). But this sf idea serves the normal political thriller ends, and was better handled in the later *Parts: The Clonus Horror* (1979) (q.v.).

| P★★ | T★★ | E★★ | A★ |

Directed by Robert Wynn. Written by Jay Sims and Tom Rolf. With Leslie Nielsen, Bradford Dillman, James Daly and Angie Dickinson.

THE RETURN (1980) A surprisingly good UFO tale, owing much to both Spielberg's *Close Encounters* (q.v.) (mountain and light motifs) and splatter movies (a mad prospector, unageing, and busy mutilating cattle and people with his light-dagger), but ultimately original in its thinking. Two children experience an UFO encounter as four-year-olds, in Little Creek, New Mexico. Twenty-five years later they meet again at the same place. He's Deputy Marshall, she's a scientist investigating strange fuzzy areas on photographs from space. These aliens prove benevolent, the prospector a mistake of theirs, and the pre-destined couple are returned safe after being taken to the far side of the galaxy and back in a few hours. Raymond Burr plays a nice cameo as the girl's father, Dr Kramer, with his personally funded scientific institute.

| P★★★ | T★★★ | E★★★ | A★★ |

Directed by Greydon Clark. Written by Ken Wheat, Jim Wheat and Curtis Burch. Special Effects by Dana Rheaume. With Jean-Michael Vincent, Cybill Shepherd and Martin Landau.

RETURN FROM WITCH MOUNTAIN (1978) The sequel to *Escape To Witch Mountain* (1974) (q.v.) from Walt Disney's studios. Our two super-powered alien children get separated (one of them is kidnapped by a pair of stock villains), then are reunited thanks to a bunch of cute Disney scallywags (brats by any other name). Dire.

| P | T★★ | E★ | A |

Directed by John Hough. Written by Malcolm Marmorstein. Special Effects by Eustace Lycette, Art Cruikshank and Danny Lee. With Kim Richards, Ike Eisenmann, Bette Davis, Christopher Lee and Anthony James.

THE RETURN OF DR MABUSE (1961) Without Lang at the directorial helm, this sequel to *The Thousand Eyes Of Dr Mabuse* (1960) (q.v.) is less effective than it ought to have been. Mabuse's criminal plan here is to subjugate a whole city to his will, and he tries out his powers at a local prison, producing an army of hypnotized zombies.

| P★★ | T★★ | E★★ | A★ |

Directed by Harald Reinl. Written by Ladislas Foder and Marc Behm. With Curt Frobe, Lex Barker, Daliah Lavi and Wolfgang Preiss.

THE RETURN OF DR X (1939) Not a sequel to *Dr X* (1932) but based on

William J. Makin's short story "The Doctor's Secret". Humphrey Bogart played the electrocuted criminal returned to life who needs transfusions of a rare blood group to keep alive. A curious but entertaining mixture of then modern science and the Frankenstein myth.

| P★★ | T★ | E★★★ | A★ |

Directed by Vincent Sherman. Written by Lee Katz. Make-up by Perc Westmore. With Rosemary Lane, Dennis Morgan and Wayne Morris.

THE RETURN OF FRANKENSTEIN (1935) see BRIDE OF FRANKENSTEIN (1935)

THE RETURN OF MAURICE DONNELLY (1915) One of the earliest films on the theme of a wrongly executed man being brought back to life by electricity and then finding the real killers.

Directed by William Humphrey. Written by William Addison Lathrop. With Leo Delany, Leah Baird and Anders Randolph.

THE RETURN OF MR H (1963) see MADMEN OF MANDORAS (1963)

RETURN OF THE APE MAN (1944) Bela Lugosi puts John Carradine's brain into the skull of a prehistoric ape man discovered frozen in the ice – and it's all in the cause of science! The resultant ape man goes on the rampage (of course) in this rather weak exploitation of the success of *The Ape Man* (1943) – to which this was *not* a sequel.

| P★ | T★ | E★ | A |

Directed by Philip Rosen. Written by Robert Charles. With George Zucco and Frank Moran.

RETURN OF THE FLY (1959) It's the turn of the son of the man who became a fly in *The Fly* (q.v.) to become a fly! Once again experiments with matter transmission cause him to end up with a fly's head, arm and leg. Despite meddling villains, it's just as silly as the original . . .

| P | T★★ | E★★ | A |

Directed and written by Bernard Glasser. Make-up by Hal Lierley. With Vincent Price, Brett Halsey, David Frankham and John Sutton.

THE RETURN OF THE GIANT MONSTERS (1967) Child-loving giant turtle Gamera fights fox-like giant Gaos.

P★	T★	E★	A

Directed by Noriaki Yuasa. Written by Fumi Takahashi. Special Effects by Kazufumi Fujii. With Kojiro Hongo and Kichijiro Ueda.

RETURN OF THE JEDI (1983)

Chapter Six of George Lucas's proposed nine-part *Star Wars* series, this is the third of the films to have been made and features the same cast as in *The Empire Strikes Back* (1980) (q.v.), with its story continuing straight on from where that film left off. The existence in *Return* ... of the cuddly teddy-bear-like Ewoks (on sale at your local shop *now*!) has led to many critics nicknaming this "Return of the Teddi", but it would be wrong to judge the whole by this unfortunately twee part. George Lucas, who shares screenwriting credits with Lawrence Kasdan, has set down the parameters of each tale in advance – and here he tends towards slight repetition with the Death Star sequence from *Star Wars* (1977) (q.v.) being re-vamped, and a further battle between Luke Skywalker (Mark Hamill) and his father, Darth Vader, bringing matters to a climax. This aside, the all-action carry-you-along style of Lucas's film-making is preserved by director Richard Marquand, though some of the acting (particularly of Harrison Ford) reveals a slightly jaded quality not necessarily to do with having – yet again! – to act in the thinnest of plots, but with – once more! – being upstaged by a barrage of special effects (many repetitious) and a group of increasingly Muppet-like extra-terrestrials. Once again the plot is derivative and (worse here than elsewhere) full of logical holes you could fly a Death Star through. So what? It's still the third biggest box-office grosser of all time, and it *is* – quite definitely *is* – a marvellous entertainment, maintaining a sense of wonder in the viewer. But I've the feeling that this conclusion of the middle trilogy should have been far better, far richer and far more original. Lucas has gone on record as saying that the whole *Star Wars* thing was more fairy-tale than science fiction

proper, and that is nowhere more evident than in *Return* ... and especially in those sequences in the tree city of the Ewoks and the forests of Endor. But what of the story? Well, bearing Lucas's comment in mind, and remembering that much of the traditional form of fairy story has to do with quest, rescue, riddle and eventual confrontation with evil, this fits the format well. It begins with rescue – the rescue of the carbon-frozen Han Solo (Harrison Ford) from the criminal Emperor, Jabba the Hutt, on the planet Tatooine. Between them (Luke, Chewbacca, Leia and the two robots) they eventually succeed. Then begins the quest. Luke goes to Dagobah again (where Yoda and the spirit of Obi-Wan are) and learns that he must – yes! confront the evil of Darth Vader. He's also told (in a stroke which I find more unacceptable coincidence than fulfilment of a mythic level to the story) that Princess Leia (Carrie Fisher) is his sister. Well, meanwhile the evil forces are gathering, a new Death Star is being built, and the Emperor himself (a thoroughly convincing performance by Ian McDiarmid) has taken charge of events. The rebels (Leia and Lando Calrissian amongst them) are planning to sabotage the Emperor's carefully laid plans. The setting is Endor's green Moon, where the foursome (Han, Luke, Leia and Chewy) are captured by the Ewoks, but then persuade them to join their struggle. Luke then sets out to confront his father and does so – walking into Vader's trap. He fights his father before the Emperor's gaze and defeats him, but then the Emperor turns on Luke and focuses all his vast, evil power on him. Released from the Emperor's control, Vader, almost with his last gasp, helps Luke defeat and kill the Emperor. You can't keep an old Jedi Knight down, can you? So there it is, confrontation. But what about the riddle? Riddles demand intelligence, and the one thing all three *Star Wars* films so far have demonstrated beyond doubt is that they lack any real degree of intelligence. However, it was never Lucas's intention to create something "realistic". He was concerned with story-telling; likewise, he isn't primarily concerned with exploring an idea so much as animating a feeling. With this in mind we can see that the *Star Wars* series is much more a form of fantasy than of science fiction, despite the incredible sf trappings. There's no real scientific extrapolation evident anywhere, no sf riddles to be solved and no use of the sf hardware except as analogues for the fantastic powers of wizards and warlocks (of whom the Emperor, Darth Vader, Obi-Wan and Luke are all examples). All of the essential elements of the three films are fantastic, the colour alone derived from space opera of the 1930s and 1940s. Lucas was clever enough to realize that, given these two, the third ingredient, an intelligent idea at the heart of things, was irrelevant and might stand in the way of his swashbuckling tale. For that reason the question of "realism" was by-passed from the opening scene of *Star Wars*. So we're left with the fairy-tale, pure and simple: quest, rescue and the confrontation with evil. And that's the secret – the *real* secret – of the success of the *Star Wars* films: they pose no riddles, no questions; demand no *intellectual* engagement on our part. They demand only that we let our deep-rooted attachment to (if not love of) things fantastic take charge of us and meet the films halfway. And, for all their failings as science fiction, we must admit to their excellence as fairy stories.

P★★   T★★★★★   E★★★★★   A★★★

Special Effects by Dennis Muren, Ken Ralston, Richard Edlund, Phil Tippett and Stuart Freeborn. With Billy Dee Williams, Anthony Daniels, Peter Mayhew, Sebastian Shaw, David Prowse, Bob Anderson, Frank Oz, Alec Guinness, James Earl Jones and Jeremy Bulloch.

REVENGE OF THE COLOSSAL MAN (1958) *see* WAR OF THE COLOSSAL BEAST (1958)

THE REVENGE OF THE CREATURE (1955) First sequel to *Creature From The Black Lagoon* (q.v.), it has little of the dark, haunting quality of the original, though the stark contrasts of the ancient creature (from a race prior to Man) against modern, sanitized life (Florida and its

modern architecture) is effective. This is essentially a monster-seeks-bride scenario, with the monster (bride-less) returning to the deeps at the film's conclusion, freed from captivity.

P★★   T★★★   E★★★   A★★

Produced and storyline by William Alland. Directed by Jack Arnold. Written by Martin Berkeley. Make-up by Bud Westmore. With John Agar, Nori Nelson and John Bromfield.

THE REVENGE OF FRANKENSTEIN (1958) Sequel to *The Curse Of Frankenstein* (1957) (q.v.), with Michael Gwynn as the monster. The Baron, continuing his experiments in a prison hospital, is still after creating the perfect being (physically and mentally) but again manages only to create deformed cannibals. Eventually he is killed and his own brain transferred into an assembled body.

P★★   T★★★   E★★★   A★★

Directed by Terence Fisher. Written by Jimmy Sangster. Make-up by Phil Leakey. With Peter Cushing, Francis Matthews and Eunice Grayson.

REVERSING DARWIN'S THEORY (1908) *see* THE DOCTOR'S EXPERIMENT (1908)

LA REVOLTE DES VIVANTS (1939) *see* THE WORLD WILL SHAKE (1939)

REVOLT OF THE ROBOTS (1924) *see* AELITA (1924)

RIDERS TO THE STARS (1953) At the time it must have seemed an accurate scientific vision of the space-travelling age to come, but in retrospect it's just a dull, lecturing, scientifically inadequate piece of poor movie-making. The storyline? Well, in trying to create a friction-proof coating for spacecraft, they try to capture some small meteors outside the Earth's atmosphere.

P★   T★★   E   A

Directed by Richard Carlson. Written by Curt Siodmak. Special Effects by Harry Redmond Jr and Jack R. Glass. With William Lundigan, Herbert Marshall, Richard Carlson, Dawn Addams and King Donovan.

THE RISE AND RISE OF MICHAEL RIMMER (1970) Sinister

satire starring Peter Cook as Michael Rimmer, the man from nowhere who works his way inexorably to the top of British society. His ruthless rise to the top results in some lovely comic touches – an old couple attempting to answer stacks of referendum papers; proof that most people are unqualified and unable to make important decisions – but also in moments of bleak revelation – the murder of the Prime Minister and the final accession of Rimmer to totalitarian leader.

| P★★★★ | T★★★ | E★★★★ | A★★★ |

Directed by Kevin Billington. Written by Peter Cook, John Cleese, Graham Chapman and Kevin Billington. With Denholm Elliott, Ronald Fraser, Vanessa Howard, Arthur Lowe, Harold Pinter, John Cleese and Dennis Price.

THE ROAD TO HONG KONG

(1961) Bob Hope takes a drug which gives him a photographic memory, and within minutes has memorized a secret formula for rocket fuel. Along with Bing Crosby he's then sent to the Planet Plutonium. The last and least of the 'Road' films.

| P★ | T★★ | E★★ | A★ |

Directed by Norman Panama. Written by Panama and Melvin Frank. Special Effects by Wally Veevers and Ted Samuels. With Joan Collins, Robert Morley, Dorothy Lamour, Peter Sellers, David Niven, Frank Sinatra and Dean Martin.

THE ROAD WARRIOR (1981) see MAD MAX II (1981)

ROBINSON CRUSOE ON MARS

(1964) Byron Haskin's attempt to translate Defoe's novel into sf by having his spaceship wreck occur on Mars is held in considerable affection by the sf community. Its early sequences – shot in Death Valley – are, indeed, highly atmospheric and evoke the desert world of Mars, but its adventure elements, as the Crusoe figure (Paul Mantee) encounters humanoid aliens, are trite B-movie stuff.

| P★ | T★★ | E★ | A |

Written by Ib J. Melchior and John C. Higgins. With Vic Lundin and Adam West.

ROBOT MONSTER (1953) The ro-

men from the Moon kill everyone on Earth bar a family of six with their calcinator ray. The ro-men come (dressed in gorilla suits with space helmets perched on top) to finish off the survivors, but then the little boy wakes up and we find it's all a dream. This film now has a large cult following for its pure awfulness.

| P | T | E★★ | A |

Produced and directed by Phil Tucker. Written by Wyatt Ordung. Special Effects by Jack Rabin and David Commons. With George Nader, Claudia Barrett, Selena Royle and Gregory Moffet.

THE ROBOT VERSUS THE AZTEC MUMMY (1957) Truly third-

rate Mexican movie which steals bits from Frankenstein movies in its story of mad scientist out to gain the sacred jewels defended by the Aztec mummy.

| P★ | T★ | E★ | A |

Directed by Rafael Portillo. Written by Alfred Salazar. With Ramon Gray and Rosita Arenas.

ROCKET ATTACK USA (1960)

Second-rate thriller with Russia launching a nuclear strike on New York City at the film's end, starting World War Three.

| P★ | T★ | E★ | A |

Produced and directed by Barry Mahon. With John McKay, Monica Davis and Daniel Kern.

A ROCKET FROM FENWICK

(1963) see THE MOUSE ON THE MOON (1963)

THE ROCKET MAN (1953) Lenny

Bruce and Jack Henley wrote this satire on modern society and its untruthfulness. A boy's toy spacegun forces people to be honest. But the "toy" proves to be an alien gadget, given to him by a benign invisible spaceman.

| P★★ | T★★ | E★★ | A★ |

Directed by Oscar Rudolph. With Charles Coburn, George Winslow, Spring Byington, Anne Francis and John Agar.

ROCKETSHIP X-M (1950) Producer,

director and writer Kurt Neumann

exploited his knowledge that George Pal was making *Destination Moon* (q.v.) to rush out this far cheaper and, in terms of enjoyment, better version of the same basic tale. Apart from the unlikelihood of a Moon expedition missing its course and landing on Mars (where it finds a post-Atomic civilization) this is good pulp sf.

P★	T★	E★★	A★

Special Effects by Jack Rabin and I. A. Block. With Lloyd Bridges, Osa Massen, John Emery, Noah Beery Jr and Hugh O'Brien.

ROCKET TO THE MOON (1953) *see* CATWOMEN OF THE MOON (1953)

ROCKET TO THE MOON (1954) *see* BLAST OFF! (1954)

THE ROCKY HORROR PICTURE SHOW (1975) Perhaps the definitive *homage* to the "science fiction double feature", a musical comedy which, both as theatre and as film, has attained a justifiable cult status. Richard O'Brien, obviously a devotee of 1950s sf, created this show, and the film has Jim Sharman join him on the screenplay credits as well as direct. From the opening song, "Science Fiction/Double Feature", to its reprise at the end, this is thoroughly, utterly entertaining. Its working of the obvious genre clichés into a coherent plot is ingenious. I suppose it might be reduced thus: Brad and Janet, two straight American teenagers, are un-straightened (some would say perverted) when their car breaks down and they – by unfortunate chance – knock at the door of Frank-N-Furter, whose scheme is to create the perfect male sex object. Jokes about sex, transvestites and, of course, sf are backed up by an enjoyable (if not entirely original) rock and roll soundtrack. And look out for Meatloaf as "Eddie".

P★★★	T★★★	E★★★★★	A★

Special Effects by Wally Veevers. With Tim Curry, Susan Sarandon, Barry Bostwick, Richard O'Brien and Patricia Quinn.

RODAN (1956) Rodan hatches from a giant egg and proves to be a huge ptero-dactyl which can fly at supersonic speed.

The military, of course, defends Japan against the monster.

P★	T★	E★	A

Directed by Inoshiro Honda. Written by Takeshi Kimura and Takeo Murata. Special Effects by Eiji Tsuburaya. With Kenji Sahara, Yumi Shirakawa, Akihiko Hirata and Akio Kabori.

ROLLERBABIES (1976) Rather awful variation on the idea of future population control, with sex as an entertainment form, procreation illegal unless licensed and a roller-derby orgy to cap it all.

P★	T★★	E★★	A

Produced and directed by Carter Stevens. Written by Wesson Smith. With Robert Random, Suzanne McBain, Terri Hall and Yolanda Savalas.

ROLLERBALL (1975) It's actually quite rare for an sf film to create a credible future environment within which the story is told, and *Rollerball*'s plot – the story of rollerball champion, Jonathan E. – is integral to the nature of that future society. Rollerball itself is a violent, brutish game, where faces are punched in with spiked gloves and contestants crushed and run-over by motorbikes. But rollerball is also a channel for violence in a peaceful, harmonized society that has no other channels. It serves a purpose in a world run by the big Corporations, and the champion, Jonathan, has grown too big for the game. And so the game is changed, some of the restraining rules (penalties, time limits) are removed. It becomes overtly a battle between the players of contesting towns. The Executives want Jonathan out, their argument being that no player is bigger than the game, but Jonathan refuses to go, and at the end of the film he rejects the Corporation's new notion that this *is* organized warfare by refusing to kill his last remaining opponent and scoring the winning goal instead. The set pieces of this film – the three rollerball games with their steadily escalating violence; the confrontations between Jonathan and the Executive Mr Bartholomew; the attempt by Jonathan to discover information about the past of his world; the revealed facts about Jonathan's wife having been taken by an Executive; the multivision "special"

James Caan as Jonathan E. in Rollerball

on the rollerball career of Jonathan E. – are extremely well choreographed and the film has a compulsive edge to it that few sf films ever achieve. It's a film that involves us deeply with Jonathan E.'s challenge to the system; he represents individuality against the system and takes on a mythic stature which, perhaps, only sporting heroes ever achieve these days. James Caan, as Jonathan, the half-articulate, natural man, is a perfect choice for the role, and it's fitting that we carry away his image from the film as a symbol of the triumph of individual man over corporate man.

P★★★   T★★★   E★★★★   A★★

Directed by Norman Jewison. Written by William Harrison. Special Effects by Sass Bedig, John Richardson and Joe Fitt. With John Houseman, Maud Adams, Ralph Richardson, John Beck and Moses Gunn.

ROME 2033: THE FIGHTER CENTURIONS (1982)
A highly polished Italian production which owes something to both *Rollerball* (q.v.) and *Blade Runner* (q.v.) (the latter are its textural landscapes). In 2033 media ratings are only achieved through violence. World Video Services plan to resurrect the gladiatorial contest and choose killbike champion Drake (Jared Martin) as the centrepin for this production. They frame him for a murder and, along with 19 other condemned prisoners, obtain his release to fight for his life (to the death against the others). A sub-plot about Sam (space animate module) the controlling computer links up with the main plot at the end

rather messily. The film, while entertaining enough, seems to revel in those values (sensationalism and violence) that its plot condemns.

P★★   T★★★   E★★   A

Directed by Lucio Fulci. Written by Elisa Briganti, Cesare Frugoni, Dardano Sacchetti and Lucio Fulci. Special Effects by Corridori. With Fred Williamson and Howard Ross.

THE RUBBER MAN (1909)
An automated man made of rubber goes haywire and fights off the police. Finally it is trapped and fused by being doused in water.

Made by Sigmund Lubin.

THE RUNWAY (1962) *see* THE JETTY (1962)

S

SANNIKOV'S LAND (1973)
A Russian variant on the lost world theme. An explorer in nineteenth-century Alaska finds a warm area, heated by a volcano. A lost tribe lives there (of course), but in the end (as ever) the volcano explodes and . . .

P★   T★   E★   A★

Directed by A. Mkrtician and L. Popov. Written by M. Zaharov and V. Fedoseev. With Ugadilav Dvorgezki, Georghi Vizin and Yuri Nasarov.

SANTA CLAUS CONQUERS THE MARTIANS (1964)
Santa is kidnapped by the Martians who want to brighten up their own children's lives. The acting is abysmal at best.

P   T   E★   A

Directed by Nicholas Webster. Written by Glenville Mareth. With John Call.

THE SATAN BUG (1965)
Based on the novel by Ian Stuart (i.e. Alistair McLean) this is a thriller about the theft and limited use of a highly deadly virus developed by a special government research station in California.

P★★   T★   E★★   A★

Produced and directed by John Sturges. Written by James Clavell and Edward Anhalt. Special Effects by Paul Pollard. With George Maharis, Richard Basehart, Anne Francis, Dana Andrews and Edward Asner.

SATAN'S SATELLITES (1958) A
trimmed-down version of the 1952 serial, *Zombies Of The Stratosphere*, which – perhaps – reflects American xenophobia at that time. Aliens invade Earth covertly, build a bomb (with the help of a traitorous scientist) and plan to blast Earth out of its orbit. Leonard Nimoy plays Lane Bradford's henchman/assistant in this costume drama.

P★	T★	E★★	A

Directed by Fred C. Bannon. Written by Ronald Davidson. Special Effects by Howard and Theodore Lydeckers. With Judd Holdren, Aline Towne, Wilson Wood, John Crawford and Craig Kelly.

SATELLITE IN THE SKY (1956)
Experimental bomb test goes wrong and fails to launch from the spacecraft it is attached to. The inventor of the bomb sacrifices himself to save the spaceship's crew. Wally Veevers provided what were then most adequate special effects.

P★	T★★	E★	A

Directed by Paul Dickson. Written by John Mather, J. T. McIntosh and Edith Dell. With Kieron Moore, Lois Maxwell, Donald Wolfit, Bryan Forbes and Jimmy Hanley.

SATELLITE OF BLOOD (1959) *see*
FIRST MAN INTO SPACE (1959)

SATURN 3 (1980) Saturn 3 Experimental Station is working on a hydroponics food project to feed the over-populated hungry Earth. It isn't doing too well as far as results are concerned, and so the Earth authorities send in a trained human who will put together and get operational one of the new demi-god series robots. Adam (Kirk Douglas) and Alex (Farrah Fawcett) are the team who run the Station and have the unstable Captain Vince and his robot, Hector, descend on them in this bleak vision of the teeming future. Hector has a huge brain which the Captain (Harvey Keitel) links directly with. But just as the Captain is warped (he's a killer and a psychological failure), so those qualities

Farrah Fawcett as Alex with the robot Hector in Saturn 3

pass on to his (literal) brainchild. He wants Alex (who is Adam's lover as well as helper) and so the robot also wants her. He has superiority complexes, and so too does the robot. Almost predictably, the robot kills its creator, yet spares the other two, using them – or planning to, for whilst the robot does not understand the concept of "sacrifice", Adam does, and gives his own life to save his beloved Alex and kill Hector (who by now is running things far too smoothly and sinisterly). With extremely good visuals (my only complaint was about the scenes where the rocketship passes through Saturn's rings) and robust acting from all concerned, this suggests a credible future, with an emphasis placed upon the new breed of man, typified by the Captain, who is replacing Major Adam in the solar system, humanistic values being lost in the face of growing technological expertise and the alienation resulted from overcrowding and lack of privacy. All in all, then, an intelligent, mature sf movie.

P★★★	T★★★	E★★★	A★

Produced and directed by Stanley Donen. Written by Martin Amis, from a story by John Barry. Special Effects by Roy Field, Wally Veevers, Colin Chilvers, Roy Spencer, Peter Parks and Jeff Luff.

SCANNERS (1981) This marked a
change of pace for the Canadian filmmaker David Cronenberg after his pre-

vious three feature films *Shivers* (q.v.), *Rabid* (q.v.) and *The Brood* (q.v.). The usual Cronenberg ingredients – bizarre psychosexuality and grotesque manifestations of the flesh – are absent. Instead, the emphasis in *Scanners* is more on action and pyrotechnics, though there are a few typical Cronenbergisms such as the exploding-head sequence near the start of the movie and the final duel between the protagonist, Vale (Stephen Lack), and Revok (Michael Ironside) during which they use their mental powers to inflict gross physical mutilations on each other. As far as plot goes *Scanners* bears a passing resemblance to George Pal's 1968 film *The Power*. Both films begin with a super-mind revealing itself during an ESP demonstration; a middle section where the renegade super-mind destroys his enemies one by one, and both end with a telekinetic duel. *Scanners*, with its visceral and visual impact, is superior to the bland Pal film in most ways but in terms of plot construction it is definitely inferior. For financial reasons Cronenberg had to start shooting *Scanners* before he'd even finished the screenplay and there are several gaps in the storyline as well as lapses in logic. For example, the scanners are supposedly unable to block the unwanted thoughts of other people from their minds, unless they take a special drug, yet throughout the movie they are constantly being caught unawares by people sneaking up on them. The biggest flaw is the casting of the aptly named Stephen Lack. Lack's lack of any evident acting ability is hard for Cronenberg to conceal.

P★★	T★★★★	E★★★	A★★

Directed and written by David Cronenberg. Make-up by Dick Smith. With Jennifer O'Neil, Michael Ironside, and Patrick McGoohan. (JB)

SCARED TO DEATH (1980) Kermit Eller (not the frog, but in a rubber suit nonetheless) plays the rampaging, murderous alien in this horror-sf crossover. We feel a touch of pity for the alien – who is only, after all, attempting to protect its young and feed them the odd human.

P★	T★★	E★★	A★

Directed and written by William Malone. Special Effects by Malone and Robert Short. With John Stinson, Toni Janotta and Diana Davidson.

THE SCARLET JUNGLE (1963) *see* SCOTLAND YARD HUNTS DR MABUSE (1963)

DIE SCHARLACHROTE DSCHUNKE (1963) *see* SCOTLAND YARD HUNTS DR MABUSE (1963)

SCHLOCK (1973) Written and directed by John (*Animal House*) Landis, this is a reasonably successful sf spoof about the schlockthropus, an ape-like missing link, and its exploits.

P★★	T★★	E★★★	A★

With John Landis, Saul Kahn, Joseph Piantodosi, Richard Gillis, Eliza Garrett and John Chambers.

DER SCHWEIGENDE STERN (1959) *see* FIRST SPACESHIP ON VENUS (1959)

SCOTLAND YARD HUNTS DR MABUSE (1963) The boys in blue are after the spirit of Mabuse, actually, because West Germany's favourite villain has here taken over the body of a famous psychiatrist, who has invented a hypnotizing machine.

P★	T★★	E★★	A★

Directed by Paul May. Written by Ladislas Fodor. With Peter va Eyck, Sabine Bethman, Walter Rilla, Dieter Borsche, Werner Peters, Klaus Kinski and Hans Nielsen.

SCREAM AND SCREAM AGAIN (1969) Entertaining mixture of the Frankenstein and Vampire myths in a tale of super-beings assembled from human spare-parts who plan to conquer the world.

P★★	T★★	E★★★	A★

Directed by Gordon Hessler. Written by Christopher Wicking. With Vincent Price, Christopher Lee, Peter Cushing and Alfred Marks.

THE SCREAMING HEAD (1959) *see* THE HEAD (1959)

SCREAMS IN THE NIGHT (1961) *see* THE AWFUL DR ORLOFF (1961)

SECONDS (1966) The Faust myth has been reinterpreted countless times on screen within the context of modern American society – it seems to have been tailor-made to bridge the gap between those two conflicting United States mythologies of the "honest homesteader" and the "American dream" – but few times so successfully as in this John Frankenheimer effort. A middle-aged, middle-class bank manager (John Randolph) becomes so unhappy with his life, so deeply imbedded in a rut he cannot see the edges any more, that he approaches a covert organization specializing in rebuilding people into young, virile men. Randolph is restructured as Rock Hudson. He is given a new identity, as an artist, moved to Malibu, and left on his own – so he thinks – to take his second chance at life. There are other problems, but the main one is, he simply has no idea what to do. Unlike a lot of movies which aim for a mainstream feel and ethos based upon a pure sf idea, this one works. Writer Lewis John Carlino takes us a nice depth into the character of the banker, an experience which proves more frightening than all of the operating theatres and scalpels of the earlier scenes. The man, as his wife puts it in the movie's grimmest scene when Randolph goes back to visit her, has died years before in the physical sense; he simply has no comprehension of what life is about, and, bereft of even the inarticulate violence of a James Dean, all he can display in the face of his predicament is the stasis of an injured turtle waiting for its death. It's society's wearing away of human potential which is the real horror here. Frankenheimer's manic over-use of camera angles, and an ending which dissolves into rubbishy fable, are the only serious flaws in this intelligent and engrossing science fiction movie.

P★★★	T★★	E★★★★	A★★★

Adapted from the novel by David Ely. With Salome Jens, Jeff Corey and Murray Hamilton. (TR)

THE SECRET KINGDOM (1928) One of the better "gimmick" stories of its time, this has a machine which can read people's minds. By this means a husband learns of his wife's infidelity and is made unhappy. In the end he destroys the machine. Based on the novel *Hidden Fires* by Bertram Askey.

P★★	T★	E★★	A★

Produced and directed by Sinclair Hill. Written by Alicia Ramsey. With Matheson Lang, Stella Arbenia and Eric Branby Williams.

EL SECRETO DEL DR ORLOFF (1964) *see* DR ORLOFF'S MONSTER (1964)

THE SECRET OF DR CHALMERS (1970) Italian/Spanish standard about a man who suffers a brain transplant and undergoes a confusion between bodily and mental responses. A kind of Frankenstein/Jekyll and Hyde melding.

P★	T★	E★	A

Directed by Juan Logar. Written by Logar and Giorgio Marcelli. With Eduardo Fajardo, Silvia Dionisio, Frank Wolff and Muria Torray.

SECRET OF DR MABUSE (1964) Norbert Jacques's Mabuse is here given a rather tired treatment by writer Ladislas Fodor and director Hugo Fregonese in this Italian/West German/French production. The evil genius's plans to destroy the world are again (yawn) foiled. Perhaps for good, as to date no further sequels have been produced.

P★	T★	E★	A★

With Peter Van Eyck, Werner Peters, Leo Genn, Walter Rilla and Wolfgang Preiss.

THE SECRET OF DR ORLOFF (1964) *see* DR ORLOFF'S MONSTER (1964)

THE SECRET OF N.I.M.H. (1982) In an electrically lit headquarters under the rose bush, the rats prepare for their move to Thorn Valley where they might live without stealing power off the local farmer. They are outlaws from NIMH (the National Institute for Mental Health) where, as experimental lab animals, they were injected with a serum that gave them intelligence, and from where they escaped. This much is background; the real story is that of Mrs Brisby and her attempts to move her house so that her son Tim, suffering from pneumonia, will not be killed when the farmer ploughs his field after the frosts. It should be explained that Mrs Brisby is a mouse. Don Bluth's cartoon fable is an excellent juvenile entertainment, even if it blunts some of Robert C. O'Brien's original theme of "intelligence demands morality" (in his novel *Mrs Frisby And The Rats of NIMH*). The film, more than the novel, is a sequence of adventures done in what is best termed High-Disney, and if it's lightweight in retrospect, it's also brilliant to watch.

P★★★   T★★★★★   E★★★★★   A★★★

Directed by Don Bluth. Written by John Pomeroy, Don Bluth, Gary Goldman and Will Finn. Special Effects Animation by Dorse A. Lanpher. Voices: Hermione Baddeley, John Carradine, Dom DeLuise, Elizabeth Hartman, Derek Jacobi, Arthur Malet and Paul Shenar.

SECRET OF THE TELEGIAN
(1960) A break for Japan's Toho studios from their monster movie format produced a clever, understated little story about a Japanese soldier who develops a teleportation device by which he gains a murderous revenge on those he believes betrayed him.

P★★   T★★   E★★   A★

Directed by Jun Fukuda. Written by Shinichi Sekizawa. Special Effects by Eiji Tsuburaya. With Koji Tsuruta and Akihiko Hirata.

THE SECRET ROOM (1915) Director Tom Moore creates an effective mad scientist story in which a normal man and an idiot are made to exchange minds. Moore also starred.

With Ethel Clifton and Robert Ellis.

SECRETS OF F.P.1 (1932) see F.P.1 DOESN'T ANSWER (1932)

SEDDOCK, L'ERECE DI SATANA (1960) see ATOM AGE VAMPIRE (1960)

SEDMI KONTINENT (1966) see THE SEVENTH CONTINENT (1966)

THE SEED OF MAN (1969) The collapse of civilization and its after-effects

are painted bleakly (if unrealistically) in Marco Ferreri's film. One of the surviving men drugs and rapes one of the few surviving women (his wife) after she refuses to bring a child into the new world. Unfortunately, the film falls far short of the intelligent examination of this predicament it could have been.

P★   T★   E★★   A

Written by Ferreri and Sergio Bazzini. With Marco Margine, Anne Wiazemsky, Annie Girardot, Rada Rassimov and Maria Teresa Piaggio.

IL SEGRETO DEL DR CHALMERS (1970) see THE SECRET OF DR CHALMERS (1970)

IL SEME DELL'UOMO (1969) see THE SEED OF MAN (1969)

SENGOKU JIETAI (1981) see TIME SLIP: THE DAY OF THE APOCALYPSE (1981)

SERGEANT DEADHEAD THE ASTRONAUT (1965) A none-too-funny comedy in which meek army sergeant Frankie Avalon (the pop singer) gets fired into space and returns an extrovert.

P★   T★   E★   A

Directed by Norman Taurog. Written by Louis M. Heyward. Special Effects by Roger George. With Deborah Walley, Cesar Romero, Fred Clark, Gale Gordon and Buster Keaton.

SERVICE WITH A SMILE (1934) Slight comedy about a futuristic gas station run by machine-like gadgets.

P★   T★   E★   A

Directed by Roy Mack. Written by Eddie Moran and A. Dorian Otvos. With Leon Errol, Maxine Doyle, Herbert Evans and Marie Wells.

SE TUTTE LE DONNE DEL MONDO (1966) see KISS THE GIRLS AND MAKE THEM DIE (1966)

SEVEN CITIES TO ATLANTIS (1978) see WARLORDS OF ATLANTIS (1978)

SEVEN DAYS IN MAY (1964) John Frankenheimer's intensely tough and taut

political thriller, set in the near future, and based along the lines of "this is the way something awful might happen", in this case a military take-over of the United States. Burt Lancaster is the martinet general who commands such popular support no one dare challenge him. Kirk Douglas is the aide who lays his career on the line, when he uncovers the plot, by reporting his suspicions to the White House. The suspense is expertly constructed, without any trace of flashiness. The plotting is intelligent. It's the kind of movie you arrive at the end of with a slow release of breath.

| P★★★★★ | T★★★ | E★★★★★ | A★★★ |

Written by Rod Serling, from the novel by Fletcher Knebel. With Frederic March, Ava Gardner, Martin Balsam, Edmond O'Brien, George Macready and John Houseman. (TR)

SEVEN DAYS TO NOON (1950) The
shade of Oppenheimer sits over this film, which describes how a guilt-ridden scientist builds his own A-bomb, plants it in London and attempts to blackmail the government into abandoning their nuclear development programme. A rare too-sane-scientist story it's a tense, moral thriller.

| P★★ | T★★ | E★★ | A★ |

Produced and directed by John and Roy Boulting. Written by Frank Harvey and Roy Boulting, from a story by Paul Dehn and James Bernard. With Barry Jones, Olive Sloane and Andre Morell.

THE SEVENTH CONTINENT
(1966) Part-Yugoslav, part-Czech film (with animated sections) about a magic island where children's fantasies come true (and drawings come to life). Freed from adult supervision, director Dusan Vukotic pictures a world of harmony and imaginative wealth.

| P★ | T★★ | E★ | A★ |

Written by Vukotic and Andro Lusicic. With Iris Vrus, Tomislav Pasaric, Adbulaie Seck, Hermina Pipinic and Demeter Bitenc.

SEX CHARGE (1973) see 2069: A SEX
ODYSSEY (1973)

SEX KITTENS GO TO COLLEGE
(1960) Albert Zugsmith produced, dir-

ected and wrote this little comedy involving "Thinko", an electronic brain which can pick horse-race winners (amongst other things).

| P★ | T★ | E★★ | A |

Written by Robert Hill. Special Effects by Angie Lohman. With Mamie Van Doren, Tuesday Weld, Mijanou Bardot, Mickey Shaughnessy, Louis Nye, Pamela Mason, Martin Milner, Jackie Coogan, John Carradine, Vampira, Norman Grabowski, Charles Chaplin Jr, Harold Lloyd Jr and Conway Twitty.

SHADOW ON THE LAND (1968) A
near-future political thriller where the United States is controlled by a neo-Fascist organization. Not so far from the truth if you believe Philip K. Dick's accounts of the times.

| P★★ | T★★ | E★★ | A★ |

Directed by Richard C. Sarafian. Written by Nedrick Young. With Jackie Cooper, John Forsythe, Carol Lynley and Gene Hackman.

THE SHADOW VERSUS THE
THOUSAND EYES OF DR
MABUSE (1960) see THE THOUSAND EYES OF DR MABUSE (1960)

SHAME (1967) Ingmar Bergman dir-
ected and wrote this story of a near-future war in a mythical land.

With Liv Ullman, Max Von Sydow, Gunnar Bjornstrand, Sigge Furst and Birgitta Vallberg.

SHE DEMONS (1958) Ex-Nazi war
criminal takes the beauty from young girls to restore beauty to his scarred wife. The young girls become monstrous animals. An inept allegory.

| P★ | T★★ | E★ | A |

Directed by Richard E. Cunha. Written by Cunha and H. E. Barrie. Special Effects by David Koehler. With Irish McCalla, Tod Griffin, Victor Sen Yung, Charlie Opuni and Gene Roth.

THE SHERIFF AND THE SATEL-
LITE KID (1979) Affectionate comedy involving Cary Guffey (the little boy in Close Encounters (q.v.)) as an extra-terrestrial H-725 stranded on Earth. An evil army captain is after his "photonic ray", but Sheriff Hole of Coweta County (Bud

Spencer) ultimately saves him. Joe Bugner plays town no-good Brennan and joins Spencer in some excellent and funny fight scenes. The sf element is played strictly as a gimmick. A sequel, *Why Did You Pick On Me?* (q.v.), appeared from the same Italian film company.

P★	T★★	E★★★	A

Directed by Michele Lupo. Written by Marcello Fondato and Francesco Scardamaglia. With Raimund Harmstorf, Carlo Reali and Gigi Bonos.

THE SHIP OF THE MONSTERS
(1959) Comic-book characterization is well suited to a comic-book script about an interplanetary craft come to Earth to collect samples of the local life-forms (and containing samples from other worlds).

P	T★	E	A

Directed by Rogelio A. Gonzales. Written by Fredo Varela Jr. Special Effects by Juan Munoz Ravelo. With Lalo Gonzalez, Ana Bertha Lepe, Lorena Velazquez and Consuelo Frank.

SHIRLEY THOMPSON VERSUS THE ALIENS (1972) Director/producer/writer Jim Sharman was responsible for *The Rocky Horror Picture Show* (q.v.), and this is just as bizarre, rooted deeply in B-movie clichés and made for a reputed Aus. $17,000. Back in 1956 Shirley Thompson (Jane Harders) saw aliens in the Tunnel of Love. Years later she is trying to convince her friends that they have taken over the Duke of Edinburgh and plan to conquer the world. As an insane send-up of the Is-it-madness-or-is-it-true? genre it's a classic with excellent fantasy sequences – particularly at the film's opening.

P★★★	T★★	E★★★★	A★★

Co-written by Helmut Bakaitis. With John Ivkovitch, Tim Elliot and Ron Haddrick.

SHIVERS (1974) A university professor, experimenting in replacing human organs with specially developed parasites which can do the jobs of those organs, decides instead that mankind is over-cerebral and needs to re-establish contact with his guts. The parasite he develops, therefore, is a large, slug-like creature which takes over its host and is, in its effects, a mixture of aphrodisiac and venereal disease. This premise allows director David Cronenberg to indulge in a gory, sex-oriented story set in a luxury apartment block on Starliner Island, just outside Montreal. The block's doctor, Roger St Luke (Paul Hampton), stages a one-man fight against the parasite's take-over, but is ultimately defeated (in an orgiastic scene in the block's swimming pool). The scene where the parasites breed inside a host and then break out is graphically depicted, prefiguring the famous scene in *Alien* (q.v.), but ultimately the viewer comes to realize that realism is not Cronenberg's aim, and that this is a fable upon modern promiscuity and sexual deviancy – THEM! have become US! in effect. We are the monster slowly taking over ourselves. In some respects it's a cluttered, unprofessional movie – the modern Cronenberg would have done it all far better – but it remains an important variation on the take-over theme.

P★★	T★★	E★★★	A★

Written by David Cronenberg. Special Effects Make-up and Creatures by Joe Blasco. With Joe Silver, Lynn Lowry, Alan Migicovsky, Susan Petrie, Ronald Mlodzik and Barbara Steele.

SHOCK! (1955) *see* THE QUATERMASS EXPERIMENT (1955)

SHOCK TREATMENT (1973) A return to the themes and concerns of the 1920s in this French/Italian production. To create a rejuvenation serum a group of young boys are incarcerated in a French sanitorium and their blood and bodies used.

P★	T★★	E★	A★

Directed and written by Alain Jessua. With Alain Delon, Annie Girardot and Robert Hirsch.

SHOCK WAVES (1970) More zombies coming back from the dead to savage a group of unsuspecting folk – this time a Nazi battalion.

P★	T★★	E★	A★

Directed by Ken Wiederhorn. Written by Wiederhorn and John Harrison. With Peter Cushing, John Carradine, Brooke Adams and Fred Buch.

THE SHOES OF THE FISHER-MAN (1968)

THE SHOES OF THE FISHER-MAN (1968) One of the more unlikely sf-ish visions (if only because of the reputed state of Vatican politics) has a future Pope releasing all of the Catholic Church's wealth to aid severe famine in communist China.

P★★	T★★	E★★★	A★★

Directed by Michael Anderson. Written by John Patrick and James Kennaway. With Anthony Quinn, Oskar Werner, Vittorio De Sica, John Gielgud, Rosemary Dexter, Laurence Olivier, David Janssen, Leo McKern and Frank Finlay.

SHONEN TANTEIDAN – KABU-TOMUSHI NO YOKI & TETTO NO KAIJIN (1957)

SHONEN TANTEIDAN – KABU-TOMUSHI NO YOKI & TETTO NO KAIJIN (1957) *see* 20 FACES (1957)

SHORT WALK TO DAYLIGHT (1972)

SHORT WALK TO DAYLIGHT (1972) Made-for-TV feature about an earthquake which flattens New York. Eight survivors are trapped in a subway tunnel.

P★	T★	E★★	A★

Directed by Barry Shear. Written by Philip H. Reisman Jr and Gerald DiPego. With James Brolin, Don Mitchell and James McEachin.

THE SHOUT (1978)

THE SHOUT (1978) Charles Crossley (Alan Bates) is either a madman – relating his strange tale to a partly reluctant listener in a score-box during a game of cricket between the villagers and the mental home inmates – or a man possessed of strange super-normal powers. His soul, he claims, is shattered into four. He spent, he claims, 18 years amongst the aborigines in the deep outback of Australia. He can, he claims, kill with "the shout" which he learned from a powerful magician. In another's hands this Robert Graves story might have remained an exercise in sensationalism, but Jerzy Skolimowski transforms Graves's rich tale into a visual and intellectual treat which, paradoxically, denies the sufficiency of intellect alone. The Shout is beyond what our science can comprehend. When experimental musician Anthony (John Hurt) and his wife Rachel (Susannah York) have their home invaded by Crossley – an intrusion which their essential English politeness cannot properly handle – their small world is expanded by Crossley's "magic". But this isn't supposed to be a fantasy. What Crossley talks of is also enacted. He does control Rachel by means of a personal trinket. He *can* shout and kill a man (and a few sheep besides!). He is, therefore, what he claims to be. Or so it *seems*, because Skolimowski keeps returning us to that score-box and the fact that Crossley is an inmate and what he is telling is a story. Until the very end, during the thunderstorm, when Crossley shouts for the last time. I make no excuses for claiming this as a science fiction film, as it stretches the bounds of the possible in ways that fantasy – utterly divorced from reality – doesn't. It is also one of the finest crafted films of the 1970s – in any genre.

P★★★★★	T★★★★	E★★★★★	A★★★★★

Directed and written by Skolimowski. Co-written by Michael Austin. Cinematography by Mike Molloy. Theme and Incidental Music by Anthony Banks and Michael Rutherford (Electronics by Rupert Hine). With Tim Curry.

SIAMO QUATTRO MARZIANI (1964)

SIAMO QUATTRO MARZIANI (1964) *see* THE MARTIANS ARRIVED (1964)

SIDEREAL CRUISES (1941)

SIDEREAL CRUISES (1941) A nice little story illustrative of the factor of Einsteinian relativity involved in space travel. A girl, gone two weeks, finds that the Earth and her lover have aged 25 years by comparison.

P★★	T★	E★★	A★

Directed by André Svoboda. Written by P. Guerlais and Pierre Bost. With Madeleine Sologne, Jean Marchat, Julien Carette and Robert Arnoux.

SIGNALS – A SPACE ADVENTURE (1970)

SIGNALS – A SPACE ADVENTURE (1970) An East German/Polish space opera of a competent but uninspired nature revolving about a lost spacecraft. Apparently based on Carlos Rasch's novel *Asteroidenjaeger*.

P★	T★★	E★	A★

Directed by Gottfried Kolditz. Electronic Special Effects by Karl-Ernst Sasse. With Piotr Pawlowski, Gojko Mitic and Alfred Muller.

THE SILENCERS (1965)

THE SILENCERS (1965) Like *The Ambushers* (q.v.), this is a Matt Helm

(Dean Martin) film; essentially a spy thriller with gadgets *à la Bond*. Atom bombs and laser beam weapons provide the limp threat in this spy spoof.

P★	T★★	E★	A

Directed by Phil Karlson. Written by Oscar Saul. With Stella Stevens, Daliah Lavi, Victor Buono, Arthur O'Connell, Robert Webber, Nancy Kovack and Cyd Charisse.

THE SILENCE OF DR EVANS
(1973) Russian film with a curiously pessimistic vision of humanity – as a being almost beyond saving. Three aliens from the planet Oraina, a balanced society, visit Earth and are disheartened by what they discover.

P★★	T★★	E★	A★

Directed and written by Budimir Metalnikov. With Sergei Bondarchuk, Zhanna Bolotova, I. Kuznetsov and Leonid Obolenski.

SILENT EVIDENCE
(1922) Wireless was a novelty in the 1920s and here an inventor's wireless-vision reveals to him his wife's flirtations. Slight but fun.

Directed by C. C. Calvert. Written by Alicia Ramsey. With David Hawthorne, Marjorie Hume, Frank Dane, H. R. Hignett and Cecil due Gue.

THE SILENT PLANET
(1959) *see* FIRST SPACESHIP ON VENUS (1959)

SILENT RUNNING
(1971) Without flora Earth's atmosphere would die; yet in this film that is the premise upon which all else rests. Because Earth is built over and sterile, huge spacecraft have been set up as greenhouses in space – museums of horticulture which no one could ever see. Useless artifacts if ever there were such. Of course, these plants are supposed to be used to eventually regenerate the Earth (which has suffered a nuclear war), but it seems a ludicrously expensive way of doing things. The company running the show order the keeper of one of these craft to destroy his floral charges. His refusal to do so and his flight from the company spacecraft take up most of the film, which ends with a single robot watering the Earth's last patch of green (paradoxically no longer belonging to the Earth!). Doug-

A scene from Silent Running

las Trumbull, fresh from his success as special effects genius on *2001* (and using clips not used in that film), directed and co-wrote what some see as a charming film about humane qualities, but which is – when viewed with a clear eye – a rather dull, senseless film. The "charm" of the three robots, Louie, Huey and Dewey, keeper Bruce Dern's sole companions (he's crazy at the start, it seems), is a plus factor, but the senselessness of this film and its stultifyingly slow pace more than cancel them out.

P★	T★★★★	E★★	A★

Written by Trumbull, Deric Washburn, Mike Cimino and Steve Bochco. Special Effects by Trumbull, John Dykstra, Richard Yuricich and Richard O. Helmer. With Cliff Potts.

THE SILICATES
(1966) *see* THE ISLAND OF TERROR (1966)

SILVER DUST
(1953) Russian film about an American scientist's development of a lethal radioactive dust which is tested on US soldiers and prisoners. Condemned as anti-US propaganda, it has an element of truth reminiscent of Thomas Disch's later *Camp Concentration*.

P★★	T★	E★★	A★

Directed by Abram Room. Written by August Jakobson and A. Filimonov. With M. Bolduman, Valentina Utchakova and Vladimir Larionov.

SIMON
(1980) Simon (Alan Arkin) is a professor of psychology who undergoes various experiments in sensory deprivation

and regression, but his "altered state" is a belief that he is an extra-terrestrial come to Earth with a mission – to awaken minkind to its wrong-headedness (primarily about over-mechanization, it seems). Part comedy, part preachment, it's neither one nor the other. A severely flawed comic exposition of an idea taken at face value in *Altered States* (q.v.), released the same year.

P★★	T★★★	E★★	A★★

Directed and written by Marshall Brickman. With Madeline Kahn and Austin Pendleton.

THE SINISTER HANDS OF DR ORLAK (1925) see THE HANDS OF ORLAC (1925)

SINNERS IN SILK (1924) The cult of eternal youth was popular in the 1920s, and this is an intelligent examination of the psychology of that desire. A rich man takes rejuvenation treatment that makes him young enough to pursue an attractive "flapper"; but rivalry between rejuvenated father and naturally young son gives the film an added twist. Unlike other treatments of this theme it avoids the horror cliché of the suddenly ageing man.

P★★	T★	E★★	A★★

Directed by Hobart Henley. Written by Carey Wilson, from a story by Benjamin Glazer. With Adolphe Menjou, Eleanor Boardman, Conrad Nagel, Jean Hersholt and Edward Connelly.

SINS OF THE FLESHAPOIDS (1964) In a world one million years in the future, the fleshapoids – pleasure robots – exist to serve mankind (an atrophied, hedonistic bunch), until they begin to want sexual freedom and progeny of their own. Deliberately comic strip, this brief (44-minute) film is a pleasant departure from the usual earnest B-feature.

P★★	T★★	E★★★	A★

Directed and written by Mike Kuchar. With Bob Cowan, Donna Kerners and George Kuchar.

SIREN OF ATLANTIS (1947) Join the Foreign Legion and ... stumble upon ancient Atlantis in the middle of the Sahara. Based on Pierre Benoit's *L'Atlantide*, it is far inferior to the earlier version,

Lost Atlantis (1932) (q.v.), though notable for Maria Montez's portrayal of the ruthless but sensuous Queen Antinea.

P★★	T★★	E★★	A★

Directed by Arthur Ripley, Douglas Sirk, John Brahm and Greg G. Tallas. Written by Roland Leigh and Robert Lax. Special Effects by Rocky Cline. With Jean-Pierre Aumont, Dennis O'Keefe, Henry Daniell and John Shelton.

SIR, YOU ARE A WIDOW (1971) A delightful Czech exercise in utter craziness (with dark touches) as spare-parts abound, a precognitive man has his brain transplanted into a female android, and a king avoids assassination.

P★★★	T★★	E★★★	A★★

Directed by Vaclav Vorlicek. Written by Baclave Vorlicek and Milos Makourek. With Olga Schoberova, Iva Janzurova, Jiri Sovak and Jiri Hrzan.

SIX HOURS TO LIVE (1932) A good idea wasted. An assassinated diplomat is restored to life by a scientist's ray, allowing him to prevent a disastrous trade agreement for his country, catch his murderer and destroy the ray before his second death. Based on the story "Auf Wiedersehen" by Gordon Morris and Morton Barteaux.

P★★	T★	E★	A

Directed by William Dieterle. Written by Bradley King. With Warner Baxter, Irene Ware, George Marion, John Boles and Edwin Maxwell.

SIX INCHES TALL (1958) see ATTACK OF THE PUPPET PEOPLE (1958)

THE SIX MILLION DOLLAR MAN (1973) Pilot film for the TV series, this was an adaptation of Martin Caidin's novel, *Cyborg*, about the reconstruction of a badly mutilated test pilot which gives him exceptional physical gifts.

P★★	T★★	E★★	A

Produced and directed by Richard Irving. Written by Henri Simoun. With Lee Majors, Barbara Anderson, Martin Balsam and Darren McGavin.

SKELETON ON HORSEBACK (1937) Based on Karel Capek's play, *Bila Nemoc*, this fable of a leprous disease that

decimates the Earth can be read as a fable on Nazism or simply as an anti-war film.

P★★★	T★★	E★★	A★★

Directed by Hugo Haas. With Hugo Haas, Bedrich Karen, Karla Olicova and Zdenek Stepanek.

SKULLDUGGERY (1970) Vercors's intelligent missing-link novel, *You Shall Know Them*, about the ape-like men, Tropis, was treated with little reverence by director Gordon Douglas and Vercors requested that his name be taken from the credits.

P★	T★★	E★★	A

Written by Nelson Gidding. Make-up by Bud Westmore. With Burt Reynolds, Susan Clark, Roger C. Carmel, Paul Hubschmid, Chips Rafferty, Pat Suzuki and Wilfrid Hyde-White.

SKY ABOVE HEAVEN (1964) Rather tiresome anti-nuclear adventure focusing on an aircraft carrier which is periodically threatened by an unidentified satellite.

P★	T★★	E	A

Directed by Yves Ciampi. Written by Alain Saton, Yves Ciampi, Jean Chapot, Maurice Auberge and Jean Raymond. With Andre Smagghe, Marcel Bozzufi, Jacques Monod and Yves Brainwille.

THE SKY CALLS 1959 *see* THE HEAVENS CALL 1959

THE SKY SHIP (1917) This Danish intergalactic romance is the first instance of space opera to reach the cinema screen (a genre in which *Star Wars* (q.v.) sits comfortably). A group of Earthmen travel to Mars in a craft resembling a high-speed train with propellers. On Mars they encounter a peace-loving race, complete with flowing white robes and well-mown gardens. The love interest involves a beautiful Martian girl brought back to Earth.

Directed by Forest Holger-Madsen. Written by Ole Olsen and Sophus Michaelis. With Zanny Petersen and Gunnar Tolnaes.

THE SKY SPLITTER (1922) A scientist invents a new rocket-ship which exceeds the speed of light. He travels back in time to his own childhood and relives the events of the past 50 years.

Directed by Ashley Miller and J. A. Norling. Written by Norling.

SLAPSTICK (1984) An inept and rather clumsy adaptation of Kurt Vonnegut Jr's 1976 novel, which suffers badly from Jerry Lee Lewis's own highly unsubtle form of inanity. Most of the original's hilarious inventiveness is squandered through director Steven Paul's too literal use of slapstick comedy, while the second half of Vonnegut's novel is jettisoned entirely – replaced by a blatant copy of the finale to *Close Encounters* … (q.v.). Six-inch Chinamen, cars and planes run by chickenshit (literally!), benevolent-but-meddlesome superior aliens, and highly intelligent twins (dumb when separated) remain in a violently disordered (in all senses) movie. A shame, because it could have been superb. As it is, whilst they lack the special effects budget of *Slapstick*, most B-movies of the 1950s manage more plot coherence. Marty Feldman's presence as the butler suggests this has been held back from release for some time.

P★	T★★	E★	A

Written by Steven Paul. Special Effects by Private Stock Effects Inc. With Madeline Kahn, John Abbot, Jim Backus and Samuel Fuller.

SLAUGHTERHOUSE FIVE (1971) Director George Roy Hill stuck very closely to Vonnegut's original, where ex-GI and perpetual innocent, Billy Pilgrim (Michael Sacks), comes unstuck in time after experiencing the Dresden firebombing while a prisoner at 5, Slaughterhouse Street. His oscillations in time between past and present (where he is a rather mundane optometrist) are further exacerbated by his capture by superior aliens from the planet Tralfamadore. They keep him as their entertainment in a bubble-like zoo where, with the sex-film starlet Montana Wildhack (Valerie Perrine), he eats, drinks, sleeps and makes love – all things the Tralfamadorians have left behind in their evolution. This almost surreal switching in time, acceptable in the book, is rather distracting in the film and undermines rather than reinforces the original's dark message of bewilderment in the face of uncontrollable forces whilst keeping Vonnegut's deep-rooted humanity and bleak humour.

| P★★★ | T★★★ | E★★★ | A★★ |

Written by Stephen Geller. With Ron Leibman, Eugene Roche and Sharon Gans.

SLEEPER (1973) Woody Allen, who directed, and co-wrote with Marshall Brickman, goes into hospital with an ingrowing toenail, develops complications, and is cryogenically frozen, to awake several hundred years later in a society where Central Park West meets 1984. The health fads of Allen's time have been reversed; cigarettes and red meat are considered healthy. Unfortunately, the trendy New Yorkers of his time sphere are still there, living in white plastic homes amongst the verdant pastures now, reading each other their awful poetry and indulging in habits which make cocaine seem tame. There's also a brutal police service, and a Big-Brother-style dictator who has fallen victim to a terrorist ambush – all that remains of him is his nose. Allen, unfrozen illegally by dissidents, first finds himself on the run from the police, then joins the revolutionary guerillas in an attempt to overthrow the dictator. Diane Keaton is the girl who, unwillingly, finds herself on the run with him. The humour constantly hits the mark – there is one classic scene where Keaton and the revolutionaries try to snap Allen out of a brainwashed stupor by regressing him to his Jewish childhood – but the script borrows heavily for its laughs, from Chaplin's *Modern Times* particularly, and the movie is for once so dependent on its story it loses some of the free-ranging zaniness of Allen's earlier efforts. But the funny scenes are side-splitting, often acid in their satire, and you're prepared to forgive anything of a movie which has as its closing line Allen explaining to Keaton what the important things in life are.

| P★★★ | T★★★ | E★★★★ | A★★ |

Special Effects by Ralph Rosenblum, A. D. Flowers and Gerald Endler. With John Beck. (TR)

SLEEP NO MORE (1955) *see* INVASION OF THE BODY SNATCHERS (1955)

THE SLIME PEOPLE (1963) Prehistoric humanoid slimers are awakened by nuclear testing and take over Los Angeles. They actually like the fog and build a dome over the city to keep it in, before they're eventually defeated. The silliness of the idea did not daunt director Robert Hutton.

| P | T★ | E★ | A |

Written by Vance Skarstedt. Special Effects by Charles Duncan. With Robert Hutton, Les Tremayne, Robert Burton and Judee Morton.

THE SNOW CREATURE (1954) Abominable snowman is captured and brought to Los Angeles where it escapes, rampages and is killed in the sewers. The yeti isn't the only one who should have stayed at home.

| P | T | E★ | A |

Directed by W. Lee Wilder. Written by Myles Wilder. Special Effects by Lee Zavitz. With Paul Langton, Leslie Denison and Teru Shimada.

SNOW DEVILS (1965) Variation on the abominable snowman tale as these yetis prove to be blue-skinned humanoids from the planet Aytia (which, as in most Antonio Margheriti films, is a wandering planet). Their plan to take over the Earth is thwarted.

| P★ | T★ | E★ | A |

Written by Charles Sinclair, William Finger, I, Reiner and Moretti. Special Effects by Victor Sontolda. With Giacomo Rossi-Stuart, Ombretta Colli, Renato Baldini and Archie Savage.

SOLARIS (1971) Andrei Tarkovsky is undoubtedly one of the finest film directors now working in the cinema, and his choice of science fiction for two of his films (this and *Stalker* (1979) (q.v)) graces the genre. Never content to use his source material direct, he alters it subtly, emphasizing the contrast between the ordinary (mundane, perhaps) life most humans have to live and the extraordinary and rich inner life made manifest through the sci-

Yuri Jarvet and Natalya Bondarchuk in a scene from Solaris

ence-fictional metaphor he chooses as his starting point (the planet in *Solaris*, the Zone in *Stalker*). Indeed, in the case of *Solaris* one might almost glimpse – in the planet which can make solid forms of the images in men's minds; of people, memories, things – a metaphor for Tarkovsky's own creative processes. Unlike Lem's original, Tarkovsky frames his vision of Solaris with visions of Earth and of its central character, Kris Kelvin's life (from child to old man – in the fashion of his later, non-sf film, *Mirrors*). This emphasis (on a human psyche) shifts much of the novel's emphasis on Solaris, but is justified, for Solaris is an entity which whilst it can mimic and mirror our forms, yet remains alien, incomprehensible, and Kelvin provides us with a mirror, within which we might glimpse aspects of the incomprehensible (just as Stalker does in *Stalker*). Realism jostles against the fantastic in this film (as, again, in all of Tarkovsky's work); the space satellite orbiting Solaris is functional, even cluttered, and yet its field of study is fantastic. What *is* Solaris? A kind of God? Can we communicate with such alienness? Or is it simply a kind of intelligent, mind-reading mechanism, simply mimicking? Kelvin is sent, as psychologist, to discover what is going wrong on the satellite: why only two of its 80-plus crew members are still there. But to understand the whys, he must first attempt to understand Solaris. And, in a very literal, very substantial manner, he is haunted by the planet – which makes a copy of his wife, which he falls in love

with. But she is a phantom who has substance only near to and through Solaris. To be with her Kelvin must stay on the satellite, or on Solaris itself. There are paradoxes, of course: how can you study something which, when you reach out your mind to comprehend it, merely echoes what is in the mind that struggles to comprehend it? The alien is, Tarkovsky (and Lem) is saying, untouchable, ungraspable. It is inviolate. You cannot even infer what it is by what isn't there, for it fills the gaps by mirroring, mimicking. As in *Stalker*, you can only crawl about the edges of the alien, approach it tangentially, and find yourself no wiser. Visually, *Solaris* is superb. Few films have matched its invocation of the alien through images of the familiar. But ultimately its richness lies in its depiction of Kelvin and of Solaris (via Kelvin), and – in the style of *Mirrors*, though perhaps less effective – its conjuring of a man's deepest psyche, his deepest fears and desires.

P★★★★   T★★★★   E★★★★   A★★★★

Directed by Andrei Tarkovsky. Written by Tarkovsky and Friedrich Gorenstein. With Donatas Banionis, Nikolai Grinko, Yuri Jarvet, Vladislav Dvorzetsky and Anatoly Solitsyn.

LES SOLEILS DE L'ISLE DE PAQUES (1971) *see* THE SUNS OF EASTER ISLAND (1971)

SOME GIRLS DO (1969) Sapper's

Bulldog Drummond takes on a madman with an infrasonic ray and an army of girl robots in this spy-thriller with sf gimmicks

P★★   T★★   E★★   A

Directed by Ralph Thomas. Written by David Osborn and Liz Charles-Williams. Special Effects by Kit West. With Richard Johnson, Daliah Lavi, Belsa Loucar, James Villiers, Sydney Rome, Ronnie Stevens and Robert Morley.

SOMETHING WICKED THIS WAY COMES (1983) Based on Ray

Bradbury's book of the same title, this is a film which manages to make the poetic transfer from novel to screen so often lost. The "Bradbury" atmosphere of the American small town, during the early part of the century, with its whimsical characters and dream-like days, is captured completely. Nothing much happens in the town until the autumn carnival arrives with its malevolent proprietor, Mr Dark (one of the October people), whose nefarious activities attract the attention of two small boys. Mr Dark and his troupe feed on misery and his only fear appears to be the secrets of the lightning-conductor pedlar. The special effects are not startling, but they are adequate for the film's needs. There are slow, sentimental patches and a scene with tarantulas that could have been grafted from a Spielberg movie, but the essence of childhood fears and boyish heroism, which is what Bradbury does best, is dealt with admirably.

| P★★★★ | T★★★ | E★★★★ | A★★★★ |

Directed by Jack Clayton, Written by Ray Bradbury. With Jason Robards and Jonathon Price. (GDK)

SOMEWHERE IN TIME (1980)

Sometimes slow, and at all times reeking in pastiche, Richard Matheson's adaptation of his novel *Bid Time Return* still manages to be an engaging movie for all but the last 30 seconds. A young, successful playwright (Christopher Reeve) becomes obsessed with the portrait of a turn-of-the-century actress (Jane Seymour) and wills himself back in time to consummate an affair with her. Christopher Plummer is the manager who becomes suspicious – and if he never does anything much with those suspicions, more than anyone does much in the entire 103 minutes, then that's a passable fault, because what we have here are Matheson and director Jeannot Schwarc playing about with time-travel ideas and with atmosphere – and it becomes contagious. Matheson's recent obsession with life after death provides the one massive boo-boo in the movie: When Reeve is reunited with his love in the hereafter, we're presented with a spectacle of arc lights and dry ice which would have Busby Berkeley stumbling for the exit.

| P★★ | T★★ | E★★★★ | A★ |

With Teresa Wright, Bill Erwin and George Voskovec. (TR)

SON OF BLOB (1971) *see* BEWARE! THE BLOB (1971)

SON OF FLUBBER (1962) Sequel to *The Absent-Minded Professor* (q.v.), Fred MacMurray once again plays the professor, this time inventing a ray-gun which produces "dry-rain", a substance which causes the growth of giant vegetables. Flubber (the extremely buoyant material) is added to here by flubber-gas. It's all good clean Disney fun.

| P★★ | T★★ | E★★★ | A |

Directed by Robert Stevenson. Written by B. Walsh and Ron Miller. Special Effects by Peter Ellenshaw, Eustace Lycett, Robert A. Mattey, Jack Boyd and Jim Fetheroff. With Nancy Olson, Keenan Wynn, Tommy Kirk and Elliot Reid.

SON OF FRANKENSTEIN (1939)

The last of Universal's three 1930s Frankenstein movies, this is the farthest from Shelley's original conception. Bela Lugosi plays the evil shepherd Ygor (hanged but a survivor of that) who leads Wolf von Frankenstein, son of the baron, to the monster, who is then revived. Wolf is as altruistic as his father, but Ygor uses the monster to avenge himself on those who convicted him. It was also Boris Karloff's last performance as the monster, and whilst we see the monster toppled into molten sulphur, he was resurrected by Universal a few more times.

| P★★ | T★★ | E★★ | A★ |

Produced and directed by Rowland Lee. Written by Willis Cooper. Make-up by Jack Pierce. With Basil Rathbone and Lionel Atwill.

SON OF GODZILLA (1967) Toho studios were obviously out to win the very young over to their rubber-suited monster series (this was Godzilla Number 8!) by having a baby Godzilla hatch out and then be threatened by all manner of other giant nasties. Tokyo isn't threatened in this film, and father and son monster go into a snow-enforced hibernation at the end.

| P★ | T★★ | E★ | A |

Directed by Jim Fukuda. Written by Shinichi Sekizawa and Kazue Shiba. Special Effects by Sadamasa Arikawa and Eiji Tsuburaya. With Tadao Takashima and Akira Kubo.

THE SON OF KONG (1933) Quickly made sequel to *King Kong* (q.v.). Denham returns to Skull Island and finds a baby Kong (a white-haired cutie only 12 feet tall). After various battles with prehistoric animals Skull Island is destroyed by a volcanic eruption and baby Kong saves Denham before he too dies. It hasn't any of the original's epic, mythical feel but is played almost as comedy, hence it's rather a disappointment.

P★★	T★★	E★★	A

Directed by Eernest B. Schoedsack. Written by Ruth Rose. Special Effects by Willis O'Brien. Models built by Marcel Delgado. With Robert Armstrong, Helen Mack and Frank Reicher.

THE SORCERORS (1967) Boris Karloff starred in this story of an elderly inventor who creates a machine which allows him and his wife to control others and receive their sensations. When the young man burns alive the feedback kills the controlling "parasites".

P★★	T★	E★★	A★

Directed by Michael Reeves. Written by Reeves and Tom Baker. With Catherine Lacey, Elizabeth Ercy, Ian Ogilvy, Victor Henry and Ivor Dean.

S.O.S INVASION (1969) Spanish alien-takeover story about females who are making robots out of corpses.

P★	T★	E★	A

Directed by Silvio F. Balbuena. Written by J. L. Navarro Basso. With Jack Taylor and Mara Cruz.

S.O.S. TIDAL WAVE (1939) One oft-forgotten fact is that TV is a post-War phenomenon (there were only 5,000 sets in the whole of the USA in 1945). The near-future disaster movie showed the effects on society of TV being a common phenomenon and borrows the scene where New York is destroyed by a tidal wave from *Deluge* (1933) for a fake TV story. As one of the earliest media-corruption stories, however, it's worth nothing.

P★★	T★★	E★★	A

Directed by John H. Auer. Written by Maxwell Shane and Gordon Kahn, from a story by James Webb. With Ralph Byrd, Kay Sutton, George Barbier, Marc Lawrence and Frank Jenks.

Chuck Connors (left) and Charlton Heston (right) in a scene from Soylent Green.

SOYLENT GREEN (1973) Based loosely on Harry Harrison's novel *Make Room, Make Room*, an overpopulation story enhanced by a crime detection element. Charlton Heston plays the detective on the trail of a murderer in a world where food and water are distributed from trucks to an overcrowded city populace. Soylent green is the staple diet of the inhabitants of a city simmering with violent mobs – a foodstuff which is later found to be derived from sinister sources. There are some poignant moments between Heston and Edward G. Robinson, playing his last role before his death in 1973. Robinson is Heston's friend, confidant and researcher who discovers "the truth" and decides he does not want to live in a world where governments are forced into ugly corners to keep the living alive. The death scene has enough pathos to carry it through some very sentimental revelations of what the old world was like before everyone started breeding in earnest. Much of the impact and seriousness of the novel is destroyed by a desire to sensationalize the screen version, and Heston's overacted portrayal of a man suffering in anguish at the end does not help to alleviate this unnecessary rewriting of an excellent work. The corruption and manipulation of police is inevitable, but only because there is nothing futuristic or fictional about such a state. The film has the right atmosphere, however, and, if not exactly gripping, is interesting and entertaining as one follows the trials and tribulations of a detective attempting to retain his integrity in a world seething with hungry people, several of whom are intent on blocking the course of justice. A romantic element provides an interesting sub-plot without too much sentimentality interfering with the grim business of attempting to stay alive and sane.

P★★★	T★★	E★★★	A★★

Directed by Richard Fleischer. Written by Stanley R. Greenberg. Special Effects by Braverman Productions. With Leigh Taylor-Young, Chuck Connors, Joseph Cotten, Brock Peters and Paula Kelly. (GDK)

SPACE AMOEBA (1970) see YOG-MONSTER FROM SPACE (1970)

THE SPACE CHILDREN (1957) An evocative film which, despite its sf trappings, is essentially a juvenile view of adulthood – as rather a quarrelsome, spiteful phenomenon. In the caves near a beach the children find a glowing brain which acts to prevent adult violence.

P★★	T★★	E★★	A★

Directed by Jack Arnold. Written by Bernard C. Schoenfeld. Special Effects by John P. Fulton. Make-up by Wally Westmore. Cinematography by Ernest Laszlo. With Adam Williams, Peggy Webber, Michael Ray and Johnny Crawford.

SPACE DEVILS (1965) see SNOW DEVILS (1965)

SPACE CRUISER YAMATO (1977) Full-length Japanese cartoon feature set in 2199 with aliens from Gorgo (148,000 light-years away) devastating the Earth. Only Battle Cruiser *Yamato* (a mixture of World War Two battleship, submarine and flying boat) can save Earth. A ludicrous plot, silly graphics and hideous juvenile characters make this unendurable.

P	T★	E	A

Directed by Ginei Tanasesen. Japanese version written by Eiishi Nishizaki and Keisuke Fujikawa. English language version written by Bernard Tabakin.

SPACE FIREBIRD 2772 (1980) Japan churns out genre animation like there was no tomorrow to watch it in. TV series mainly. Characters are usually Western;

influences catholic, Huxley to Disney; animation is often *el cheapo*, more effort being lavished on the technology (on-screen) and the pointed anti-war moral. This one's beastie, a.k.a. *Phoenix 2772*, ruins our spacecraft, yet could save the nearly fuel-less world with its blood. Godoh (no waiting) is sent to snare it, helped by a girl robot, which like all Japanese robots changes shape and functions (never *that* one). Far too long, the film – not best/worst example – could lose Godoh's pets, one based on the bagpipes, and his brother. He's named Rock Schlock. Honest, the Japanese.

P★	T★★	E★	A★

Directed and written by Taku Sugiyama. (TC)

SPACEFLIGHT IC-1 (1965) Set 50 years in the future (2015) a spacecraft sets out to colonize new worlds, but finds trouble in the form of an authoritarian captain who provokes a mutiny. A rather dull tale.

P★	T★	E★	A

Directed by Bernard Knowles. Written by Harry Spalding. With Bill Williams, Norma West, John Cairney, Linda Marlowe and Jeremy Longhurst.

SPACE GREYHOUND (1961) see INVASION OF THE NEPTUNE MEN (1961)

SPACEHUNTER: ADVENTURES IN THE FORBIDDEN ZONE (1983) It's only recently that the cinema has been able – through great advances in special effects – to convey the full colour of science fiction. *Spacehunter* is one of the better fruits of the new technological expertise, a not unintelligent adventure which, by using so many familiar elements from sf, is thoroughly entertaining without making you howl at the scriptwriters' ineptness and lack of scientific knowledge. A tourist spaceship blows up, but three women escape in a sealed rescue pod and land on a habitable planet, Terra 11. There they are captured by the followers of the Overdog, once the joint leader of a colonization mission but now – following a great plague – the part-machine dictator of the planet's Forbidden Zone. Wolff (Peter Strauss) is a good-for-little space tramp who, up to his neck in debt, is tempted by the 3000 Megacredit reward for rescuing the three Earth women. Almost at once he encounters a huge metallic land-galleon (on rails) which is attacked by the Overdog's men. They take the Earth women and Wolff goes in pursuit, accompanied by a dirty female waif, Niki (Molly Ringwald) and, later on, by a space chief of police, Washington (Ernie Hudson). After various adventures on this highly colourful planet (with Amazonian fish-women and glutinous, maggot-like dwarves) they penetrate the Forbidden Zone and release the women from under the nasty eyes of Overdog (Michael Ironside). It's a 1950s plot in many respects, but with mature touches – the relationship between Wolff and Niki in particular – yet the sets, the costumes and the special effects transform mundane elements into something quite memorable. It could so easily have been done as spoof and have failed; as it is it's one of the first of a new breed of "little" sf films, not epics but the real thing nonetheless.

| P★★ | T★★★★★ | E★★★★★ | A★★ |

Directed by Lamont Johnson. Written by Stewart Harding and Jean Lafleur. Special Effects by Gene Warren Jr, Peter Kleinow, Gary Bentley, George Erschbamer, Darrell Pritchitt, Michael Clifford, Keith Richins, Paul Smith, Robert Burns, Steve Luport and Bob Tiller. Special Visual Effects by Fantasy 11 Films.

THE SPACEMAN AND KING ARTHUR (1979) A better-than-average Disney space comedy, based (very loosely) on Mark Twain's novel, *A Connecticut Yankee In King Arthur's Court*. Twain has his misplaced-in-time narrator hit on the head with a shovel, Disney do it as in *Buck Rogers* (q.v), by rocket. And Disney's hero (Dennis Dugan) has a robot companion, Hermes, to help him out. A fun film. Leave your brain at home.

| P★★ | T★★★ | E★★★ | A★ |

Directed by Russ Mayberry. Written by Don Tait. Special Effects by Cliff Culley, Ron Ballanger and Michael Collins. With Jim Dale, Ron Moody, Kenneth More and John Le Mesurier.

SPACE MASTER X-7 (1958) A space satellite returns to Earth contaminated with a space fungus which, when mixed with blood, becomes "Blood Rust". Two security agents investigate this pestilence (which devours people) and one discovers an antidote. Unlike the later *Andromeda Strain* (q.v.) it fails to maintain dramatic tension.

| P★ | T★ | E★★ | A |

Directed by Edward Bernds. Written by George Worthing Yates and Daniel Mainwaring. With Bill Williams, Lyn Thomas and Robert Ellis.

SPACE MONSTER (1965) An expedition to another planet (including the first female astronaut) lands on the ocean floor and battles sea monsters, then a tiny alien spaceship.

| P★ | T★ | E★ | A |

Directed and written by Leonard Katzman. With Russ Bender, Francine York and James B. Brown.

SPACE RAIDERS (1983) I come to bury Corman, not to praise him. Really! This is Cormania at its penny/script-pinching worst. It rips off everything in the galaxies from Lucas to Peter Hyams, from *Alien* (q.v.) to … well, much footage, models and all the score (not *again?*) stem from *Battle Beyond The Stars* (q.v.). That was a good 'un. This is t'other side of the coin. Counterfeit, too. James Horner's score, now used in three or more Corman quickies, can't gee up Ben Casey's … er, Col. Hawkins's space battles against The Company (read: Corman's against Hollywood). He steals spacecraft, tackles a robot destroyer *and* a stowaway kid! The kid should have been dropped on Proscian 3 earlier. With the print. Alternate title: *Lost In Space*.

| P | T | E | A |

Produced by Roger Corman. Directed and written by Howard R. Cohen. With Vince Edwards, David Mendenhall, Patsy Pease, Thom Christopher, Luca Bercovici, Drew Snyder and Dick Miller. (TC)

SPACESHIP (1981) The Starship Vertigo (an *Airplane*-style rip-off and comic

exaggeration of sf themes) picks up an alien that grows into a face-eating monster. The film isn't as funny as it ought to be, even while borrowing heavily from *This Island Earth* (q.v), *War Of The Worlds* (q.v.), *Alien* (q.v.) and *Star Trek* (q.v.).

| P★ | T★★ | E★★★ | A★ |

Directed and written by Bruce Kimmel. With Cindy Williams and Leslie Nielsen.

THE SPACE SHIP (1935) Early Soviet paean to space travel, with enthusiastic scientists and dreary bureaucrats. They get to the Moon despite official hindrance.

| P★ | T★ | E★ | A |

Directed by Vasili Zhuravlev. Written by A. Filimonov. With Sergey Komarov, Nicolai Feokistov and Vassili Gaponenko.

SPACE SHIP SAPPY (1957) A fortunately brief outing for the Three Stooges as they fly to a planet of vampire girls.

| P★ | T★ | E★ | A |

Produced and directed by Jules White. Written by Jack White. With Moe Howard and Larry Fine.

SPACE STATION X (1964) *see* MUTINY IN OUTER SPACE (1964)

SPACEWAYS (1953) Romance and marital infidelity in space in this rather nonsensical murder mystery revolving around a new rocket/satellite system.

| P★ | T★★ | E★ | A |

Directed by Terence Fisher. Written by Paul Tabori and Richard Landau. With Howard Duff, Eva Bartok and Alan Wheatley.

SPAZIALE K.1 (1964) *see* THE HUMAN DUPLICATORS (1964)

SPERMULA (1976) Attack of the virgin vampire women! This B-format movie is based on the idea that the women are vampiric upon sperm, not blood.

| P★ | T★★ | E★★ | A★ |

Produced, directed and written by Charles Matton. With Dayle Haddon, Udo Kier and Georges Geret.

SPIDER-MAN (1977) A feature designed as the pilot for the teleseries, this is based on Stan Lee's *Marvel* Comic's super-hero, schoolboy Peter Parker, who, in need, becomes spider man, a super-hero in the usual mould. A rather pointless film, lacking any real humour or interest.

| P★ | T★★★ | E★ | A |

Directed by E. W. Swackhamer. Written by Alvin Boretz. Special Effects by Don Courtney. With Nicholas Hammond, Lisa Eilbacher, Michael Pataki, Thayer David and David White.

SPIDER-MAN STRIKES BACK (1978) Another teleseries feature, this time a sequel to *Spider-Man* (1977) (q.v.). As any comic-book follower knows, the normally harmless Peter Parker is but a very pale imitation of the caped crusader. Juvenile pap.

| P★ | T★★★ | E★ | A |

Directed by Ron Satlof. Written by Robert Janes. Special Effects by Don Courtney. With Nicholas Hammond, Robert F. Simon and Michael Pataki.

THE SPIDER WOMAN STRIKES BACK (1945) Gale Sondergaard plays the spider woman (not to be confused with the comic-book super-hero) who murders young women to feed her poisonous blossoms.

| P★ | T★ | E★★ | A |

Directed by Arthur Lubin. Written by Eric Taylor. With Brenda Joyce, Kirby Grant, Rondo Hatton and Milburn Stone.

LE SPIE VENGO DEL SEMI-FREDDO (1966) *see* DR GOLDFOOT AND THE GIRL BOMBS (1966)

DIE SPINNEN (1920) *see* THE BRILLIANT SHIP (1920)

THE SPIRIT OF 1976 (1934) Brief futuristic glimpse of a society where work has been abolished and people play all day.

Directed by Leigh Jason. Written by Ernest Pagano and Leigh Jason. With Walter King and Betty Grable.

THE SPLIT (1959) *see* THE MANSTER (1959)

SPUTNIK (1958) *see* A DOG, A MOUSE AND A SPUTNIK (1958)

THE SPY (1928) Fritz Lang's film of the master-criminal, Haghi (Rudolph Klein-Rogge), prefigures many of the elements used in Ian Fleming's James Bond spy-thrillers years later – worldwide criminal webs using beautiful female spies, British agents that they fall for (Tremaine, played by Willy Fritsch), all-action adventure (with then-not-so-obligatory car chase) and gimmicks (a button-hole camera here). Lang's criminal world, however, is far more chilling than Fleming's, and his arch-criminal is frighteningly inhuman.

P★★★   T★★   E★★★   A★★★

Written by Lang and Thea Von Harbou. With Gerda Maurus, Lien Deyers, Lupu Pick, Fritz Rasp, Craighall Sherry and Julius Falkenstein.

SPY IN YOUR EYE (1965) Mundane spy-thriller with the interesting idea of an American spy having his eye replaced (in an operation, but unknown to him) by a Russian spy camera.

P★★   T★★   E★★   A

Directed by Vittorio Sala. Written by Romano Ferrara, Adriano Baracco, Adrano Bolzoni and L. Marcuzzo. With Brett Halsey, Pier Angeli, Dana Andrews, Gaston Moschin and Taina Beryl.

THE SPY WHO LOVED ME (1977) Practically a re-run of *You Only Live Twice* (1967) (q.v.), only this time it's nuclear submarines and not spaceships that are being kidnapped by the baddies. As ever, the aim is to blow up the world – the villains having constructed their now Nemo-like underwater haven away from it all. Roger Moore as Bond stops them – of course – but has a lot of fun with "Jaws" (Richard Kiel) along the way. More tech-nologically oriented than previous Roger Moore versions of the Bond "myth", this had a delightful supertanker swallowing the subs and the usual huge cave-like set.

P★   T★★★   E★★★   A★

Directed by Lewis Gilbert. Written by Christo-pher Wood and Richard Maibaum. With Barbara Bach, Caroline Munro, Curt Jurgens, Walter Gotell, Geoffrey Keen and Bernard Lee.

THE SPY WITH MY FACE (1965) Feature-length adaptation of Clyde Ware's Man From U.N.C.L.E. episode "The Double Affair" in which Napoleon Solo (Robert Vaughn) battles a robot duplicate of himself, while Ilya Kuryakin (David McCallum) fights an army of miniature robots.

P★★   T★★★   E★★★   A★

Directed by John Newland. Written by Clyde Ware and Joseph Cavelli. With Senta Berger, Leo G. Carroll, Michael Evans and Sharon Farrell.

SQUIRM (1976) Scraping the barrel these film-makers have come up with the idea of ... flesh-eating worms! Usual pap, but scarcely threatening.

P   T★   E   A

Directed and written by Jeff Lieberman. Special Effects by Bill Milling, Don Farnsworth and Lee Howard. With John Scardino, Patricia Pearcy, Peter MacLean and Fran Higgins.

SROUBEK'S ADVENTURE (1960) Czech animated short about a little boy robot, Sroubek, whose super strength lands him in prison.

Directed by Frantisek Vystrcil. Written by N. Argilli and G. Parca. Graphics by Josef Pelc.

SSSSSSS (1973) A particularly mad scientist, obsessed with pollution and snakes, decides to change mankind into snake-like creatures. His experiments produce a snake-man and, to hide him from inquisitive eyes, the scientist is forced to kill. In the finale the snake-man fights a mongoose.

P★   T★★   E★   A★

Directed by Bernard Kowalski. Written by Hal Dresner. Make-up by John Chambers. With Strother Martin and Dirk Benedict.

STALKER (1979) What is The Zone? Is it merely an acausal pocket left after the visit of an alien spacecraft to Earth? Or is it, in the scheme of Andrei Tarkovsky's movie, the heartland of the imagination itself? And is the grey, monochrome area that exists around the Zone representative of physical reality, or simply of modern-day Soviet Russia? The only problem with *Stalker* as far as a critic is concerned is that

Tarkovsky has created a work of art that admits to all of these explanations and many more. His film does not merely transform its original source (the novel, *Roadside Picnic*, by Arkady and Boris Strugatsky) but transcends its terms of reference. *Stalker* is, ultimately, *pure* cinema – a wonderful succession of multiple expressive images which accumulate in the viewer's mind and attain deep significance. *Stalker*, like Tarkovsky's non-sf film, *Mirrors*, reflects not merely the director's concern with the quality of our spiritual existence, but the viewer's own deepest response to our increasingly sterile and mechanized world: the bleak world which we lingeringly see in the long opening of *Stalker*. But what has this to do with science fiction? The finest sf has always used the metaphoric value of a science-fictional idea to express something much more than the thing to hand. Thus the Zone becomes the spiritual heartland, the imagination, life itself in the midst of non-life, the colourful inner self denied in "real" life. The Strugatskys, of course, understood this. Their book reflects a similar concern to Tarkovsky's own – but to Tarkovsky's advantage is the medium. Film allows far subtler suggestion than print and here, with no special effects whatsoever, Tarkovsky implies that the Zone is something wholly alien and almost incomprehensible. This is the science-fictional level: the journey by the guide, Stalker (the shaven-headed Alexander Kaidanovsky), into the Zone, with the Scientist (Nikolai Grinko) and the Writer (Anatoli Solonitsin) to find the elusive "Wishing Room" at its heart. The acausality of the Zone and the nature of the mysterious central artifact (which can grant whoever penetrates it their heart's desire) mean that they must approach it indirectly, almost *intuitively*. What would, in another's hands, have been a rather dull section of the film, in Tarkovsky's proves one of the most genuinely tense sequences in cinema; a tension created not through over-the-top *Raiders Of The Lost Ark*-style Hollywood special effects but by tapping some level of ourselves which is universal and unchanging. It is a sequence which, in

Alexander Kaidanovsky as the guide, Stalker, in Stalker

its final stages, is almost unbearable – the journey down the tunnel which leads to the Wishing Room is not matched in cinema, even by Hitchcock, for its creation of an intense, almost nightmarish sense of anticipation. It is, in a very real sense, both the entrance to Hell and to Heaven. *Abandon hope all ye who enter here* is a literal necessity for admittance to the Zone and the Wishing Room at its heart. Going into the Zone is a gamble which can lead to sudden death unless those venturing there place their utter trust in the Zone and do not try to manipulate it. Thus the Scientist and the Writer have reached a point of spiritual vacuity – an absence of hope – and can survive in the Zone. As for the Stalker, he is the eternal Divine Fool, perhaps Intuition itself, unbridled by Intellect: acting upon what feels right and what seems right rather than by what he *thinks* to be right. And when he returns, to his grey, "real" world outside the Zone, it is to a daughter who, unlike himself and his wife, is somehow connected to the Zone. In a final, brilliant sequence, we sense that she is the only colourful thing beyond the Zone's borders. *Stalker* is not merely an exceptional science fiction film, it is a great work of art, and perhaps the most memorable experience in sf cinema.

P★★★★★   T★★★★★   E★★★★★   A★★★★★

Written by Arkady and Boris Strugatsky. With Alisa Freindlikh, Natasha Abramova, F. Yurma, E. Kostin and R. Rendi.

STAR CHILD (1983) see SPACE RAIDERS (1983)

STARCRASH (1979)

With an opening straight out of *Star Wars* (q.v.) and highly polished special effects, *Starcrash* doesn't really claim to be anything more than straightforward, fairly mindless adventure. The plot contains innumerable scientific idiocies (spacecraft that can turn like speedboats!) and the acting is cardboard, yet the whole thing has a certain charm. Stella Star (Caroline Munro) is the semi-clad heroine of this intergalactic saga, helped by Akton (Marjoe Gortner), rescuing the Emperor's son, Simon (David Hasselhoff), and fighting for the Emperor (Christopher Plummer) against the evil Count Zarth Arn (Joe Spinell). It gets more ludicrous as time passes. The Emperor can stop time; even so he's about to lose to the Count when ... yes, Stella and Akton fly a floating city through the 4th dimension (Starcrash) and destroy the Count. A juvenile for the undiscerning juvenile.

P	T★★	E★★	A

Directed by Lewis Coates. Written by Lewis Coates and Nat Washsberger. Special Effects by Studio Quattro, Armando Valcauda, Matteo Verzini and Germano Natali.

THE STAR CREATURES (1962) see INVASION OF THE STAR CREATURES (1962)

STARFLIGHT ONE (1982)

Soap in near space; Lee Majors plays Cody, pilot of a new super-jet which by accident goes into orbit. Stale, lifeless plot has space shuttle Columbia come to the rescue.

P★	T★★	E	A

Directed by Jerry Jameson. Written by Robert Malcolm Young. Special Effects by John Dykstra. With Hal Linden and Lauren Hutton.

THE STAR INSPECTOR (1980)

Greedy Western space pirates fall foul of the upright Space Kommissariat in this strange Russian space opera which blends Western film techniques (and images) with Soviet orthodoxy.

P★★	T★★	E★★	A★

Directed by Mark Kovalyov and Vladimir Polin. Written by Kovalyov and Vladislaw Smirnov. With Vladimir Ivashov, Yuri Gusev, Timofei Spivak and Valentina Titova.

STARMAN (1985)

It starts off well with shots of the Voyager II probe hurtling through space while accompanied by the Rolling Stones' "I Can't Get No Satisfaction", a scene that misleadingly suggests that *Starman* might be a return by director John Carpenter to the off-beat wit and intelligence of his first film *Dark Star* (q.v.). But, alas, *Starman* is anything *but* witty or intelligent. Though lavishly mounted (and at a cost of $20,000,000 that's not surprising), and with an intriguing opening which has a disembodied alien growing a body for itself by using the genetic code from a dead man's hair, *Starman* quickly degenerates into a mawkish, illogical, and unoriginal pastiche of *E.T.* (q.v.) and *Close Encounters* (q.v.). Jeff Bridges's performance as the alien in human form is frankly embarrassing with its jerky movements, silly walk and Dalek-like speech patterns (yet he received an Academy Award nomination!), though Karen Allen, in the thankless role of the girl who befriends the alien wearing her dead husband's body, falls in love with him and ends up having his baby, almost overcomes the puerile script with her acting ability alone. But even Ms Allen's talents can't disguise the fact that *Starman* is nothing but an episode of TV's *Mork and Mindy* writ large.

P★★	T★★★★★	E★★★	A★

Directed by John Carpenter. Written by Bruce A. Evans and Raynold Gideon. Special Effects by Bruce Nicholson and Industrial Light & Magic. With Charles Martin Smith. (JB)

STAR ROCK (1980) see THE APPLE (1980)

THE STAR ROVER (1920)

Albert Shelley Le Vino adapted Jack London's novel about a soul reincarnated.

Directed by Edward Sloman. With Courtenay Foote, Thelma Percy and Jack Carlysle.

STARSHIP INVASIONS (1977)

A pedestrian UFO story which is curiously

dated. Both script and special effects are reminiscent of something from the late 1950s, with a race from a dying planet seeking to invade and colonize Earth, an intergalactic league and some of the worst modern space effects committed to screen. Good aliens battle bad aliens to save the Earth (plagued with a spate of suicides caused by an alien ship transmitting bad vibes!). Good triumphs, of course, and everything is, literally, hugs and kisses at the end, UFOlogist Robert Vaughn's wife being returned from the dead after slitting her wrists. In fact, it's so mediocre and modest a film that its glaring failings are almost charming – the plucky robot that saves the league's base; the notion that humankind uses only 1 per cent of its mental capacity, etc. – yet ultimately bore.

The crew of the Enterprise in Star Trek with William Shatner as Captain Kirk (left) and Leonard Nimoy as Spock (right) in the foreground

P★	T★	E★	A

Directed by Ed Hunt. Written by Hunt. Special Effects by Warren Keilor. With Christopher Lee, Daniel Pilon, Tiiu Leek, Kate Parr, Sherri Ross, Helen Shaver and Henry Ramer.

STAR TREK – THE MOTION PICTURE (1979)

Producer Gene Roddenberry seemed to have a clear choice here – he could either create a full-length version of his internationally famous sf television series which could be enjoyed by a wide and varied audience, or he could bring to the screen a film specifically aimed at "Trekkies". For the most part, unfortunately, he opted for the latter ... and the gulf between those who enjoyed and were affectionately amused by the series, and those to whom *Star Trek* has become a cult, an obsession, with some of the trappings of a bizarre minor religion, has never been more apparent than in this most motionless of motion pictures. "*Star Trek – The Television Series*" began in the early 1960s as a low-budget production with a future as certain as the *Lusitania*'s and a cast made up almost entirely of unknown actors. Viewers were introduced to the world of the Federation, an intergalactic alliance of planets run from Earth, of which the starship USS *Enterprise* was the pride of the peacekeeping fleet. A different world was visited each week – Captain James T. Kirk (William Shatner), Lieutenant Spock (Leonard Nimoy made up with pointy ears to resemble an alien "Vulcan"), Dr McCoy (DeForest Kelley) and the rest of the crew did battle with either some unspecified alien menace or with the Federation's arch-enemies, the Klingons. For all its faults – an infuriating undertone of pious Republican morality, for instance – the series caught on; only the most cynical of television viewers could completely resist "Star Trek"'s ready-mixed brand of imagination, action, and humour. Extra money was poured into the production, Roddenberry began hiring world-class science fiction authors – Robert Bloch, Robert Silverberg, A. E. Van Vogt and Harlan Ellison amongst them – to contribute scripts. The "Trekkie" cult was born, fed by a new industry of "Star Trek" T-shirts, toys, novelizations, the hideous "photobooks". Years after the series' demise, massive "Star Trek" fan conventions persist in most Western countries. After what must have seemed to those fans an unbearable delay, director Robert Wise and writers Harold Livingstone and Alan Dean Foster gave them precisely what they had been waiting for. We begin the movie with the information that a gigantic force of unknown nature has destroyed an entire Klingon fleet and is moving through space towards Earth. The *Enterprise* is sent to intercept it ... and, like the film, the famous starship seems to take for ever getting off the ground. (In dock, Robert Wise photographs it from every loving angle conceivable, pandering to such a degree of obsessional fascination that he practically turns set-design into a new form of pornography.) Worse is to come. Word goes around the ship that Kirk is about to board – it's made very clear to the audience that this is a *high point* of the movie, breaths are held, the tension mounts to fever pitch. He arrives. Relief! Picking up Mr Spock, later, from his home world takes about half an hour and seems to take for ever. The fans in the audience are whimpering with anticipation and flailing each other with their photobooks by now. A good part of the movie trudges along these lines. Those in the audience who simply *liked* the series gaze on bemused. The story, when we get to it through all the dreary ritual, is quite a decent science fiction concept, with origins in part in Arthur C. Clarke's *Rendezvous with Rama* – the unknown force proves to be one of our own "Voyager" space probes; departing our solar system, it has been intercepted by an advanced alien race who have "repaired" it, modifying it so vastly that it now possesses enormous power, sentience, and an insane mistranslation of its original mission. The tension actually does mount as the *Enterprise* gets closer to its Nemesis, only to be undermined when Wise slops over into a lengthy metaphysical sequence, all space warps, confused dimensions, and life-after-death, when the cast venture into the area of void affected by the probe. It's all horribly portentous, like the worst of the television episodes. So reverential is this film towards its subject matter that the humour needed to balance it out is lost completely. The good moments Kirk and Co. have are lost amongst the morass. The special effects, by Douglas Trumbull and John Dykstra, are superb but ultimately wasted; all the visual wizardry in the world can't make *Star Trek – The Motion Picture* anything more than an epic of self-importance. News reports preceded the film by months – some of the cast, underpaid in the original television series, were holding out for massive fees which they eventually managed to obtain. But many of the principals were already middle-aged when the series first began – their somewhat time-worn appearance in the same roles over a decade later moved one critic to term the movie "Wigs in Space". Presumably, "Star Trek"'s die-hard fans wouldn't settle for anything less than the original cast. The only new blood is introduced in the forms of Stephen Collins and Persis Khambatta, neither of whom are given enough material to make their tours of duty memorable. There was the inevitable novelization, by Alan Dean Foster, and two inevitable sequels. But the movie's doom lies in that inevitability – that a commercial phenomenon should have grown out of an enjoyable, inventive, but undeniably *slight* television series. Expanded to wide screen size and movie length, the makers have nothing to fill in the gaps with save the original series' own ludicrous mythology. Special mention ought to be made of Leonard Nimoy, whose retention of dignity throughout the film would win medals in a war. This is not a good vehicle for him. Nor is it, by any yardstick save that of undiscriminating devotee, any more than a disappointing and rather silly major motion picture.

P★★   T★★★★   E★   A

With DeForest Kelley, James Doohan, George Takei, Majel Barrett, Walter Koenig, Nichelle Nichols, Mark Lenard and Billy Van Zandt. (TR)

STAR TREK II: THE WRATH OF KHAN (1982)

After the disaster of the first *Star Trek* movie, the only direction for the series to go was up. The appeal was more general and less directed at devout "Star Trek" fandom in this sequel, which was a welcome approach – but claims that *Wrath of Kahn* stays closer to the ethos of the television series are true only in terms of superficialities. Khan was the 21st-century warlord the crew of the *Enterprise* inadvertently re-animated in the "Space Seed" episode of the television series; the story ended with Kirk marooning the ferocious character on a deserted planet. In this – perhaps a cinema first, a full-length sequelization of a TV programme – Khan (Ricardo Montalban) has escaped his Ben

Gunn existence and is seeking to wreak revenge on Kirk. Infinitely faster paced and funnier than the original, the film contains some nice wry moments of self-parody – "there's no such thing as a no-win situation", Kirk proclaims with an impish grin. But the climactic battle scenes seem on a scale too vast for *Star Trek*, they seem more an effort to cash in on the series' heir to the title of "junk phenomenon", *Star Wars*, and the whole movie appears ill-fitting and often down-right tatty around the edges. Part of *Star Trek's* success on television lay in the fact that, for just 50 minutes, viewers were willing to accept the inconsistencies, the portentousness, the boy scout morality and the sometimes weak acting in favour of the series' few but very obvious strengths. It came in capsule form. *Wrath of Khan* comes as a horse pill – a little hard to swallow.

P★★   T★★★   E★★★   A

Directed by Nicholas Meyer. Written by Jack Sowards and Harve Bennett. Special Effects by Jim Veillux and Ken Ralston, Industrial Light & Magic. With William Shatner, Leonard Nimoy, DeForest Kelley, Ricardo Montalban, Bibi Besch, Paul Winfield, George Takei, Walter Koenig and Nichelle Nichols. (TR)

STAR TREK III: THE SEARCH FOR SPOCK (1984)

"Star Trek" was first of all a television series – and, writ large, it still shows. This may give the film some strengths. There are familiar characters (or at least familiar caricatures), a strong and predictable plot, and momentum and interest from what has gone before. But the atmosphere is irredeemably pre-pubescent, and too much here is trite and pompous – the score, much of the script, and most of what passes for acting, to begin with. Still, the good special effects get across the notion that space is *big*; there are some genuinely touching moments; Admiral Kirk's larger-than-life role is convincing in its own terms (although not in any others); and the Klingons and their guttural language are, as usual, excellent. The plot, carrying over from earlier episodes, is complicated. Mr Spock's soul is apparently in the possession of Dr McCoy; his body is on "the

Genesis planet", where Admiral Kirk's son will soon be landing; lastly, a Klingon warlord with an entertainingly carnivorous hell-hound also wishes to investigate "the Genesis effect". In a good sequence Admiral Kirk and his crew hijack the soon-to-be-scrapped *Enterprise* and head off. The film has been lacklustre until now, but when the action shifts to the spectacularly disintegrating new world it becomes genuinely exciting. Blood is shed as the world falls apart. Needless to say, Spock *is* resurrected – he is probably needed to star in sequels, after all – by means of some usual Hollywood pseudo-religious hocus-pocus; the heavenly choirs and the Grecian staging are unconvincing, though. Overall, this film certainly can be enjoyed (even if you are over twelve), but only if you suspend your disbelief and your critical faculties.

P★★★   T★★★★   E★★★   A★★

Directed by Leonard Nimoy. Written by Harve Bennett. Special Effects by Industrial Light & Magic. With William Shatner, Leonard Nimoy, Mark Lenard, Robin Curtis, Walter Koenig, DeForest Kelley and Nichelle Nichols. (RS)

STAR WARS (1977)

Unoriginal as its parts may be, this is the definitive space opera – in celluloid terms the original, from which all else has been subsequently cloned. From its opening sequence of a giant starship roaring through the skies above a planet (a sequence copied in countless movies since) in pursuit of the smaller rebel vessel, to its final triumphal march, it is non-stop big screen adventure. This is not to say that it's completely thoughtless, simply that Lucas is not concerned so much with realism as with riveting story-telling; any attempt to analyse this too deeply could result (and indeed does) in a deep-rooted dissatisfaction with the over-simplistic and hack-neyed storyline. Ignoring analysis for the moment, what *Star Wars* and no film before – even *2001* – had, was a sense of wonder. Luke Skywalker (Mark Hamill) is the teenage orphan, staying on his aunt and uncle's farm (what do they grow? all we see is sand!) but itching to get away to college when his life is changed dramatically by events. By amazing coincidence a 'droid (R2D2) containing the plans to the Empire's "Death Star" comes into his possession and leads him to Obi-Wan Kenobi (Alec Guinness) who is a Jedi Knight and knew his father. The Jedi were once guardians of the Republic, before it fell to the Emperor and "the dark times came". This much is pure *Flash Gordon* with a touch of *Lord Of The Rings* (Obi-Wan is a Gandalf-like figure if ever there was one in sf; representing the light side of the force against Darth Vader – Sauron? – and the dark side). *The force*? Ah yes, that's the "energy field created by all living things; it surrounds us and penetrates us and binds the galaxy together," Obi-Wan explains to Luke. Zen Buddhism meets

Mark Hamill, Carrie Fisher, Peter Mayhew (as Chewbacca) and Harrison Ford in Star Wars

Gibbon's *Rise And Fall Of The Roman Empire* (which was almost a set text for 1940s sf writers, particularly those in John Campbell's *Astounding* camp!). Anyway, Luke's aunt and uncle are killed by Empire stormtroopers and he vows not merely to seek vengeance, but to aid the rebel forces against the Empire. The visit to the space-port and the scene in the bar there is one of the film's highlights, for the first time committing one of science fiction's finest images to celluloid: that of numerous alien races meeting and mixing in one (disreputable, naturally) place. It's also a good illustration of Lucas's techniques, for he allows us no glimpse of aliens in the streets of the port (except the Jawas who we've already encountered – and they're only dwarves, really!) until after this scene – thus getting maximum effect from it. Again, I stress, it isn't realism he's after but the means of creating the greatest impact in terms of storytelling. With the character of Han Solo (Harrison Ford) firmly established, the group – with the alien Chewbacca (Peter Mayhew) and C-3PO (Anthony Daniels) – set off for Alderaan and the Rebel Alliance, only to find the planet gone (blasted by the Death Star) and to find themselves drawn into the Death Star by force fields. The rest of the film is in two parts: the finding of the Princess Leia (Carrie Fisher) and the escape from the Death Star; and the attempts by the rebel

fighters to fire a photon torpedo into one of the outlets of the Death Star to set off a chain reaction. Both sequences are tense, fast-paced adventures – straight from the pages of the 1940s pulps – and again bear little logical examination. (Why, for instance, didn't the Imperial Stormtroopers work out where Solo, Chewbacca, Luke and the Princess had gone and fire in on them through the hole in the wall when they were in the garbage chute? And what was all that junk doing in the garbage hole anyway – spaceship parts?!) It's very lightweight stuff with cardboard characterization, and yet somehow – perhaps because the effects are so excellent, and also because the acting of all concerned hits just the right tone, balanced between utter seriousness and wry humour, never spoof – it works. Works beautifully. It becomes, in the end, pure escapism. The film cost, apparently, only $11 million to make and has subsequently (without spin-off merchandising) earned over $400 million (only *E.T.* has done better). Its success was vital to the genre because it allowed funds to be invested into sf as never before. Some of those funds were, of course, squandered, but the continual success of the *Star Wars* sequence (three films to date and one – *The Clone Wars* – apparently in production) has meant that the big film companies are now committed to science fiction as major features as they never were before. It should also be noted that Lucas's original scheme was for *nine Star Wars* films. The first, known as *Star Wars*, is actually *Episode Four: A New Hope*. This sense of vast schemes was also something new to the genre – something only Fritz Lang, with *Das Spinnen*, and the very long original version of *Metropolis* (q.v.) (12 reels) had previously come near to planning. My own feeling for *Star Wars* is, as this piece suggests, a mixture of love and hate. Certain scenes still have the power to move me no matter how often I see them, whereas the dialogue becomes tiresome very quickly. My own solution is to watch and try not to listen.

P★   T★★★★★   E★★★★★   A★★

Produced by Gary Kurtz. Directed and written by George Lucas. Special Effects by John Dykstra, John Stears, Richard Edlund and Grant McClune. Cinematography by Gilbert Taylor. With Peter Cushing, David Prowse and Kenny Baker.

THE STEEL MONSTER (1958) *see* THE MOST DANGEROUS MAN ALIVE (1958)

THE STEPFORD WIVES (1975) A

family move from New York to the suburban town of Stepford. Katherine Ross is the wife – she's strong-willed, a feminist, an amateur photographer aspiring to professional success, and she is horrified to find that the remainder of the married women in this commuters' Utopia seem to have arrived directly out of a TV soap commercial. They are beautiful, vacuous, smile as brightly and whitely as though their lives depend on it, all the while exalting the virtues of household products and the joy of being unpaid drudges. And as Ross digs deeper into the mystery – the answer to which you guess less than halfway through – she begins to realize that the men are behind it all. American gothic is nothing entirely new, but here – right down to an old dark house revealed by lightning flashes – director Bryan Forbes is allowed to be stylish and tongue-in-cheek in a way he never quite succeeded in his English films. Even his wife, Nanette Newman, joins in the fun – she plays a simulacrum of herself in all her twee-est roles. It's a movie which needs

almost total suspension of disbelief. And the twist at the end is so standard and such obvious science fiction fare that it simply would not have worked in half a dozen other movies. But this adaptation of the bestselling Ira Levin novel – pure entertainment with the "message" thrown in as a sideline – is more about the dehumanizing horror of the suburban housewife role than it is about technological terror. When Katherine Ross asks the chief male-pig; "Why are you doing this?" and he replies: "Because we can," you feel it's not simply an explanation of why he's swapped his wife for a machine, it is a life philosophy.

P★   T★★★   E★★★★★   A★

Written by William Goldman. With Paula Prentiss, Patrick O'Neal and Peter Masterson. (TR)

STEPS TO THE MOON (1963)

Romanian comic fantasy about an astronaut's dreams of the history of spaceflight as he waits to be launched to the Moon.

P★   T★   E★   A

Directed and written by Ion Popesco-Gopo. Special Effects by Alexandru Popescu. With Radu Beligan, Grigori Vasiliu-Birlic and Emil Botta.

STEREO (1969) David Cronenberg's

obsession with telepathy and the intrusion of privacy that it entails is here, even in his first film, where an experiment is being carried out to increase people's telepathic abilities in various ways. A disturbing quasi-documentary film.

P★★   T★★   E★★   A★

Produced, directed, written, cinematography and edited by David Cronenberg. With Ronald Mlodzik, Iain Ewing, Jack Messinger, Clara Mayer, Paul Mulholland and Arlene Mlodzik.

STING OF DEATH (1966) Uncon-

sciously funny B-movie about a mad scientist who is experimenting on giant jellyfish and who finally turns himself into a half-man, half-jellyfish monster with poisonous tentacles – a killer! Punctuated by the odd song from teen hero Neil Sedaka.

P★   T★   E★★★   A

Directed by William Grefe. Written by Richard S. Flink. Make-up and Special Effects by Harry Kerwin. With Joe Morrison and Valerie Hawkins.

STORM PLANET (1962) see PLANET OF STORMS (1962)

STORY OF A MADMAN (1915) see THE MADNESS OF DR TUBE (1915)

THE STORY WITHOUT A NAME (1924) Another death-ray story, this one capable of being transmitted by the radio (!). The sane scientist (sane because he does not wish to conquer the world with his invention) is kidnapped, but the US Navy comes to his aid, frees him, and, unfortunately for them perhaps, the ray is destroyed.

Produced and directed by Irwin Willat. Written by Victor Irwin. With Agnes Ayres, Antonio Moreno, Tyrone Power Sr, Louis Wolheim and Dagmar Godowsky.

THE STRANGE CASE OF CAPTAIN RAMPER (1927) An Arctic explorer, trapped in the wilds, devolves back to ape-man with a hairy coat and a dormant brain. He is taken back to civilization and displayed in a circus as an ape-man. A scientist restores him to his old, human self, but Ramper (Paul Wegener), sick of civilization, returns to the Arctic.

P★★	T★★	E★★	A★

Directed by Max Reichmann. Written by Kurt J. Braun and Paul Wegener. With Mary Johnson, Max Schreck and Camilo Kossath.

THE STRANGE CASE OF THE MAN AND THE BEAST (1951) see THE MAN AND THE BEAST (1951)

STRANGE HOLIDAY (1942) see THE DAY AFTER TOMORROW (1942)

STRANGE INVADERS (1983) A B-movie is not defined by the amount of money spent on the production nor by the excellence or otherwise of the special effects, but by the attitudes of writer, director and actors and by the amount of imaginative input – creative input, perhaps – they instil into their picture. *Strange Invaders* is a modern phenomenon, a highly polished, large-budget B-movie. Indifferent acting, an illogical, at times silly script, and a failure by the director, Michael Laughlin, to make any kind of

coherent whole out of this mish-mash of B-movie clichés. Centreville, Illinois, is the town the aliens have invaded and taken over, but this bunch of extraterrestrial uglies (they have smaller heads than us with pulsing scalps) have made a deal with the government that they can have a 25-year tenure before they return the inhabitants (melted down into blue balloons which glow) to their normal state and go home. Meanwhile they emanate menace and take hotel rooms in the New York Hilton – ostensibly to get hold of a little girl who is the first human-alien, result of the mating of Charles Bigelow (an entomologist, but that really plays no part in this bug-eyed-monster movie, unless it's too subtle a joke for me to follow) with his (unknown to him) alien wife, Margaret. They have, of course, green blood, which pumps out of them when shot. They can also blow the backs off estate wagons with their eyes – electric thunderbolts – if they choose to. This is a kind of *Close Encounters* written by an amnesiac – William Condon and Michael Laughlin couldn't remember if this was to be an alien-terror movie or a "they're really nice and they'll decide our fate" (as in *The Day The Earth Stood Still* (q.v.), a brief clip of which is glimpsed on a TV screen) movie. In the end it's neither and, once again, only the UFO nuts will enjoy this.

P★	T★★★★	E★	A

Special Visual Effects by Private Stock Effects Ltd. Mechanical Special Effects by Martin Malivoire. (Special crews on Alien Effects and Special Effects were used, too numerous to list here.) With Nancy Allen and Diana Scarwid.

THE STRANGER FROM VENUS (1954) see IMMEDIATE DISASTER (1954)

THE STRANGE WORLD OF PLANET X (1957) Based on the BBC TV serial of the same name (itself based on the novel by René Ray), this is a "man should not tinker with nature" movie, where experiments rip a hole in the ionosphere, with side-effects ranging from giant insects to maniacal humans.

P★	T	E★	A

Directed by Gilbert Gunn. Written by Paul Ryder and Joe Ambor. With Forrest Tucker, Gaby Andre, Martin Benson and Wyndham Goldie.

STRIKING TONIGHT (1951) A mad psychiatrist combines two brains in his quest to create the perfect mind.

P★	T★	E	A

Directed by Mario Bonnard. Written by Nicola Manzari and Alberto Vecchietti. With Marisa Merlini, Clelia Mantania and Laura Gore.

STRYKER (1983) Yet another *Mad-Max*-inspired road movie, with the opening premise that, after the Holocaust, water is short (see also *Exterminators Of The Year 3000*). Uninspired and not greatly exciting either.

P★	T★★	E★	A

Directed by Cirio H. Santiago. Written by Howard R. Cohen. With Steve Sandor, Andria Savio, William Ostrander and Julie Gray.

THE SUBMERSION OF JAPAN (1973) For once an intelligent sf movie from Japan, ostensibly about the slipping of Japan into the sea as a trench beneath its islands begins to open up. A sub-text about Japan's relationship to the rest of the world is less interesting in the face of spectacular special effects.

P★★	T★★★	E★★	A★★

Produced and directed by Shiro Moritani. Written by Shinobu Hashimoto. Special Effects by Tereyoshi Nakano. With Keiji Kobayashi and Testsuro Tanba.

SUMURA (1967) *see* THE MILLION EYES OF SU-MURU (1967)

THE SUNS OF EASTER ISLAND (1971) *Close Encounters* was anticipated in this story of six strangers drawn to Easter Island by mysterious brands on their palms. There they encounter aliens who decide that Earth isn't yet ready for a full encounter with aliens. Obviously they changed their minds by 1977!

P★★	T★★	E★★	A★

Produced, directed and written by Pierre Kast. With Norma Bengell, Françoise Brion, Jacques Charrier and Alexander Stewart.

SUPERBEAST (1972) Cheap production filmed in the Philippines with a mad doctor story; here he experiments on the minds of criminals and is, himself, turned into a monster.

P	T★	E★	A

Directed and written by George Schenk. Make-up by John Chambers and Fred C. Blan. With Antoinette Bower and Craig Littler.

SUPERGIRL (1971) Second-rate West German film unrelated to the D.C. Comics character. This supergirl is simply an alien, threatening the Earth with invasion.

P★	T★★	E★	A

Produced and directed by Rudolf Thome. Written by Thome and Max Zihlmann. With Iris Berben, Marquand Bohn and Karina Ehret-Brander.

SUPERGIRL (1984) A film designed to involve teenage American girls in the Superman craze sweeping America in the late 1970s and early 1980s. Based on the old D.C. Comics again, and fairly true to its comic-strip origins, but strangely lacking in humour, and even Peter Cook playing it all reasonably straight-faced. Supergirl, Zara (Helen Slater), is a native of Argo City, somewhere in "Inner Space" (a kind of negative state to our own) – she's also Superman's cousin, and gets a chance to go to her cousin's adopted home (he's meanwhile gone on a peace mission several hundred trillion light years away!) when the Omega Hedrin, power-source for Argo City, somehow gets away and flees to Earth (why? – a point never answered). There it's discovered by a witch called Selena (Faye Dunaway), who battles with Supergirl over a hunk, Ethan, and then over the land rights to Earth. Supergirl (or Linda Lee, friend of Lucy Lane, Superman's girlfriend's sister ...) becomes, for a time, an ordinary school-girl, then is hurled into the Phantom Zone (where Zaltar (Peter O'Toole), creator of Argo City, has already gone before her) and escapes (with Zaltar playing Obi-Wan to her Luke Skywalker) to allow her to defeat the darkly evil Selena (who has merged the Omega Hedrin with a Burundi wand of evil origins and summoned

up the Beast himself). Confused? The Omega Hedrin, for a start, is a little black-and-white glowing crystal ball. Argo will die unless it's returned. It's all a rather fantastic, melodramatic scheme to link together a whole series of spectacular special effects: a small black hole ripping up earth, trees and the odd brick wall (it must have been *very* small to have been so weak); the "quantum vortex" (a red and blue hurricane leading from the Phantom Zone to Selena's house), and Argo City itself. Indeed, the first ten minutes – in Argo –. are the best in the film. Pure science fiction. The rest? Schoolgirl adventure, if enjoyable enough as that.

| P★★ | T★★★★ | E★★★ | A★ |

Directed by Jeannot Szwarc. Written by David Odell. Special Visual Effects by Derek Meddings. Optical Visual Effects by Roy Field. With Hart Bochner, Mia Farrow, Marc McLure, Maureen Teefy and Simon Ward.

SUPER - HOOPER - DYNE - LIZ-ZIES (1925) Perhaps the movie with the least comprehensible title. An inventor (Billy Bevan) devises a means of using hot air from speeches to run motorcars.

Directed by Del Lord. Written by Jefferson Moffitt and Frank Capra. With Andy Clyde, Lillian Knight and J. J. Richardson.

THE SUPER INFRAMAN (1975) The bionic Kung Fu man meets witch woman from the underworld! Control of the world is at stake in this Hong Kong production. Rather silly comic-book stuff for stunted juveniles.

| P | T★ | E★ | A |

Directed by Hua Shan. With Li Hsiu-Hsien, Terry Liu, Wang Hsieh and Lu Sheng.

SUPER INVISIBLE MAN (1969) *see* THE INVINCIBLE INVISIBLE MAN (1969)

SUPERMAN (1960) Indian tale about a drug which gives a man invisibility and super-human powers. Not based on the D.C. Comics super-hero.

Directed by Anant Thakur. With Nirupa Roy, Neeta, Jairaj and Tiwari.

SUPERMAN AND THE MOLE MEN (1951) A feature-length movie eventually used to launch the TV series, "The Adventures Of Superman". Here our super-hero (George Reeves) encounters a race of furry mole men who possess a radiation ray. Their kingdom under the Earth was drilled into by an oil company and they're hopping mad. But our caped crusader is a good liberal and stops the local inhabitants and the mole men from fighting, helping the furries to return home.

| P★★ | T★ | E★★ | A★ |

Directed by Lee Sholem. Written by Richard Fielding. Special Effects by Ray Mercer. With Phyllis Coates, Jeff Corey and Walter Reed.

SUPERMAN FLIES AGAIN (1954) Three adventures of the comic-book hero taken from the TV series "The Adventures Of Superman" and tagged together as a cinema feature. George Reeves plays the caped crusader, fighting a jewellery caper, saving a private detective and eventually battling deadly kryptonite.

| P★★ | T★ | E★★ | A |

Directed by Thomas Carr and George Blair. Written by David Chantler. With Noel Neill, Jack Larson, John Hamilton and Robert Shayne.

SUPERMAN: THE MOVIE (1978) There were several previous attempts at getting D.C. Comics' most famous character on to the screen, but the real hero in director Richard Donner's mega-budget version is author Mario Puzo's script. The elements of religious legend which the original creators, Jerry Siegel and Joe Schuster, most conceivably drew on without even realizing it – Moses in the bulrushes, the Christ story – are pulled into the open here. As is that other great myth, that of old-fashioned Americanness. *Superman: The Movie* is so American it makes Mom's apple pie look like a Commie confection packed post-haste from the Kremlin – and the result, which could have been nauseating, is pure enchantment. Kansas cornfields roll into the distance like seas of molten gold; the city of Metropolis has that grainy, bustly look we

Christopher Reeves as Superman in Superman: The Movie

associate with the most romantic in the works of Runyon and Saroyan; there are decent, honest mid-Western parent figures; gruff editors with hearts of gold; wide-eyed, freckle-faced office juniors ... and God, how we long for a world as simple and romantic as that. It's the dream of simplicity, after all, which provides Superman's universal appeal just as much as the old fantasy of unlimited power. The movie traces the Man of Steel's life from infancy and escape on Krypton, through adolescence in the mid-West, to adulthood and his first real adventure in the big bad city, taking in a platonic affair with Lois Lane on the way. Margot Kidder's version of the ruthless girl reporter, who we first encounter typing up stories of massacres and bloodbaths with the heartless glee of a child dissecting hamsters, is several long steps up from the irritating, hapless comic-book original. She's definitely not the kind of girl you would take home to Kansas to show Mom and Pop – she's too much fun for one thing – yet Kidder manages to invest her, too, with a soft centre of naïve, dewy innocence. Christopher Reeve, in his first major role, looks, talks and moves just right for both Superman and alter-ego Clark Kent; in one lovely scene when, in the Kent guise, he seems ready to reveal his true identity to Lois, then changes his mind, he seems to grow in stature, swell within his baggy suit, and then deflates again. It's an illusion rarely used, and then generally on stage by experienced actors, but Reeve makes it work perfectly. Yet the movie does have its debit side. The film covers such an elongated time scale and is so thin on actual plot that the final effect becomes a slightly patchy one. And the villains, played by Valerie Perrine, Ned Beatty, and Gene Hackman as criminal genius Lex Luthor, are so camp and bumbling they bear far closer relation to the criminal clowns in the old "Batman" television series; though you're prepared to forgive them almost anything when Perrine sighs wistfully to your hero: "Why can't I ever get it on with the good guys?" All in all, though, it's a thinking-child's *Star Wars* (q.v.), appealing to us with a great swamp of nostalgia, and a magical quality which owes much to our own rose-tinted memories of comic-reading days. The action sequences include a scene – Lois Lane in a doomed helicopter – which must count as one of the best crafted suspense episodes in modern cinema. The special effects are not only convincing but used as the original intended – Superman enters Luthor's underground hideaway by spinning around until he drills himself through the soil. Marlon Brando, who was paid a million dollars for his five-minute appearance as Superman's father, plays the role with such overblown presence he is worth every cent – though, calculatedly, the publicity that gigantic payment fuelled proved to be a massive box-office draw in itself. It's a film which stands head and shoulders above the rest as an example of how to do a fun-fantasy movie, a gorgeous film.

P★★   T★★★★★   E★★★★★   A★

Produced by Pierre Spengler. Co-written by David Newman, Leslie Newman, Tom Mankiewicz, Robert Benton and Norman Enfield. Special Effects by Colin Chilvers, Roy Field, Derek Meddings, Brian Smithies, Denis Rich, Zoran Perisic, John Richardson, Bob MacDonald, Derek Botell and Bob Harman (!!). With Glenn Ford, Phyllis Thaxter, Terence Stamp, Susannah York, Jeff East, Trevor Howard, Jackie Cooper, Larry Hagman, Maria Schell and Aaron Smolinski (as the young Superman). (TR)

SUPERMAN II (1980) In this sequel to *Superman: The Movie*, the Kryptonian arch villains – General Zod (Terence Stamp), Non (Jack O'Halloran), and Ursa (Sarah Douglas) – whom we saw banished in the opening sequences of the original movie, descend on Earth to conquer it and, especially, to humiliate the President of the USA. It's thoroughly disappointing, a pure power-fantasy leavened only by a sub-plot in which Superman loses his powers and, having become human, finally consummates his affair with Lois Lane. Christopher Reeve and Margot Kidder are excellent again – in the space of two movies they have polished their routine until it seems like verbal choreography – and the rest of the cast perform their roles competently enough, although almost all they're required to do is snarl and throw skyscrapers about or yelp and duck them. The special effects, though well done, are so immediately obvious they lose their impact – we *know* the instant that, say, General Zod spots a Greyhound bus he's going to pick it up and hurl it, and when he does just that we lean back with a blasé 1980s monchalance. And as for the humour – there's more of it than there was in the original, but little of it is integral to the plot, or seems to make any sense in terms of what is happening on the screen. (In the final battle scene, for instance, an elderly couple suffer a comic mishap while walking out of a fried-chicken take-away; but why, with four super-beings battling above their heads, are they buying a chicken dinner anyway? Are they blind and deaf? And if so, what is the movie doing making fun of such people?) You're left with the impression that the writers had a pile of unused jokes lying around and decided to jam them, higgledy-piggledy, into the screenplay. The movie has the aura of something slapped together carelessly to cash in on the success of the original.

P★   T★★★★   E★★   A

Directed by Richard Lester. Written by David Newman, Leslie Newman, Mario Puzo and Tom Mankiewicz. Special Effects by Roy Field, Colin Chilvers and Zoran Perisic. With Gene Hackman and E. G. Marshall. (TR)

SUPERMAN III (1983) A change of direction for the *Superman* format and a surprisingly successful one, relying heavily on comedy for its entertainment value, and successful because the comedy relies on Richard Pryor. He plays a no-gooder off the street who accidentally discovers he's a computer genius, gets sacked from his job for putting that genius to embezzlement, and is promptly picked up by ruthless billionaire Ross Webster (Robert Vaughn), who wants him to run a supercomputer which can, in turn, run the world. Inevitably, the machine starts getting ideas of its own. Pryor really is at his best – his strength lies in his impression of someone who wants to be a super-cool, streetwise black dude but can never find the courage and conviction to make it work. And the opening sequence, with Pamela Stephenson causing mayhem by walking through Metropolis in a skimpy dress, is a bravura performance of extended slapstick reminiscent of the silent classics. Inventive set pieces abound – a snow-clad mountainside proves to be an artificial ski-slope on the roof of Webster's company skyscraper; and his female partner's transformation into a half-human, half-robotic monster is so close to the ethos of the comic-book stories it might have been lifted directly from the three-colour printed page. Superman (Christopher Reeve), meanwhile, his brain affected by a new kind of Kryptonite, is transformed from a goody two-shoes into an unpleasant lout – before the audience's delighted gaze he gets drunk in bars, picks up loose women, and his uniform becomes shabby and discoloured; it's only spoilt by a resolution scene in which he splits in two, and his good and evil sides physically battle with each other.

P★★   T★★★★   E★★★★★   A

Directed by Richard Lester. Written by David Newman and Leslie Newman. Special Effects by Roy Field, Colin Chilvers, Martin Gutteridge and Brian Warner. With Annette O'Toole and Annie Ross. (TR)

SUPERMAN AND THE STRANGE PEOPLE (1951) *see* SUPERMAN AND THE MOLE MEN (1951)

SUPERMAN'S PERIL (1954)   *see*
SUPERMAN FLIES AGAIN (1954)

SUPERSONIC SAUCER (1956)
Low-key juvenile about a group of children who save a flying saucer from Venus.

P★	T★	E★	A

Directed by S. G. Ferguson. Written by Dallas Bower. With Marcia Monolescue and Fella Edmonds.

SUPERZAN AND THE SPACE BOY (1972) Rather silly juvenile from Mexico about a space boy who naïvely comes to Earth to pass on scientific information and contacts a scientist who wants to rule the Earth. Superzan, a good superman figure, battles Sartillo, a baddie, to decide the fate of the boy and of Earth.

P★	T★★	E★	A★

Directed and written by Rafael Lanuza. With Superzan, Giovanni Lanuza and Claudio Lazuna.

SURVIVAL (1962) *see* PANIC IN THE YEAR ZERO (1962)

THE SURVIVOR (1980) New twist on an old story. After an aircraft crashes, the pilot walks away from the carnage unharmed. It seems that he has been brought back from the dead to avenge those killed. A well-wrought, if slightly over-enigmatic thriller with a powerful ending as the pilot is found, charred and dead, in the ruins days after the crash investigation has ended.

P★★	T★★★	E★★★	A★★

Directed by David Hemmings. Based on a novel by James Herbert. With Robert Powell, Jenny Agutter and Angela Punch-McGregor.

SWAMP THING (1982) Old-fashioned monster movie where a relatively sane scientist, working on developing a plant-animal hybrid (vegetables with animal cells) is drenched in his own solution and becomes the "swamp thing" of the title.

P★	T★★	E★★	A★

Directed and written by Wes Craven. Special Effects by William Munns. With Louis Jordan, Dick Durock, Adrienne Barbeau and Ray Wise.

THE SWARM (1978) A cloud of African killer bees threatens to destroy America. By unanimous consensus, the worst large-budget movie ever made – and as such it has become a minor cult classic by virtue of the fun of seeing an all-star cast struggle with a script which seems to have been typed by an imaginative three-year-old. Unintentional "bee" puns abound in the dialogue. The penultimate scene, in which the swarm pours in through the doors of military headquarters, looks as though the cast have become trapped in a popcorn vending machine. So bad it's un*bee*lievable.

P	T★	E★★★★★	A

Produced and directed by Irwin Allen. Written by Stirling Silliphant, from the novel by Arthur Hertzog. Special Effects by L. B. Abbott, Howard Jensen and Van Der Veer Photo Effects. The cast includes Michael Caine, Katherine Ross, Richard Widmark, Richard Chamberlain, Olivia de Havilland, Fred MacMurray, José Ferrer, Slim Pickens and Henry Fonda. (TR)

SWORDKILL (1984) A samurai warrior, Yoshimitsu, is killed in 1552, falling into freezing water. His body is preserved in the ice until, in the present day, it is discovered, taken to America, thawed out and resuscitated. From there on it's a predictable storyline, with the samurai forced to kill – thieves, streetpunks and men from the institute – yet establishing a friendship with the girl reporter covering his "case". An enjoyable rather than fascinating film, held together by the dignity of Hiroshi Fujioka as the moral samurai.

P★★	T★★	E★★	A★

Directed by Larry Carroll. Written by Tim Curnen. With John Calvin, Janet Julian, Charles Lampkin and Frank Schuller.

TAINSTVENNI OSTROV (1941) *see* MYSTERIOUS ISLAND (1941)

TAIYO O NUSUNDA OTOKO (1980) *see* THE MAN WHO STOLE THE SUN (1980)

TAMIN NO KAO (1966) *see* THE FACE OF ANOTHER (1966)

TARANTULA (1955) Atmospheric Jack Arnold film, where experiments into creating artificial strains of food causes acromegaly in people and gigantism in animals. Amidst the mounting tension this wee spider grows to a 100-foot monster, devouring people and cars alike (can it tell the difference?) until the US Airforce blows it apart with fire bombs. Based on an episode of the Science Fiction Theatre TV series, "No Food For Thought" by Robert M. Fresco.

| P★★ | T★★ | E★★★ | A★ |

Written by Fresco and Martin Berkeley. Special Effects by Clifford Stine. Make-up by Bud Westmore. With John Agar, Mara Corday, Leo G. Carroll, Nestor Paiva and Eddie Parker.

TARGET EARTH (1954) Giant robots from Venus attack a small town and destroy most of the inhabitants with head-mounted death rays. A local scientist takes them on.

| P★ | T★ | E★★ | A |

Directed by Sherman A. Rose. Written by William Raynor. Special Effects by Dave Koehler. With Richard Denning and Virginia Grey.

DIE TAUSEND AUGEN DES DR MABUSE (1960) *see* THE THOUSAND EYES OF DR MABUSE (1960)

TEACHER WAS A SEXPOT (1960) *see* SEX KITTENS GO TO COLLEGE (1960)

TEENAGE CAVEMAN (1958) What seems like a prehistoric world is given a lovely twist when the curious caveman (Robert Vaughn) discovers that this is not a primitive time but the results of a Holocaust. Awful special effects and a whole castful of awful actors (Vaughn included) somehow don't manage to blunt the impact.

| P★★ | T | E★★★ | A |

Produced and directed by Roger Campbell. Written by R. Wright Campbell. With Leslie Bradley, Darrah Marshall, Jonathan Haze, Robert Shayne, Frank de Kova and Beech Dickerson.

TEENAGE FRANKENSTEIN (1957) *see* I WAS A TEENAGE FRANKENSTEIN (1957)

TEENAGE MONSTER (1957) A meteor sends down rays which turn a harmless mother's boy into a hairy rampaging monster and mum looks after her boy by hiding him in the cellar.

| P★ | T★ | E★ | A★ |

Produced and directed by Jacques Marquette. Written by Ray Buffum. Make-up by Jack Pierce. With Anne Gwynne, Gloria Castillo and Stuart Wade.

TEENAGERS FROM OUTER SPACE (1958) Teenage aliens land on Earth with their pet giant lobster (seen only in shadow form), a "gargon". But their leader falls in love with an Earth teenager (female, Dawn Anderson) and the invasion is thwarted. The love-sick alien dramatically aborts his mission.

| P | T | E★ | A |

Produced, directed and written by Tom Graeff. With David Love, Harvey B. Dunn, Bryan Grant, Tom Lockyear, King Moody and Helen Sage.

TEENAGERS IN SPACE (1975) Russian film, second section of *Moscow – Cassiopeia* (1974) (q.v.), dealing with the events on Planet Alpha – where robots maintain an Utopia of vegetable-like people. Nothing much happens before they go home to Earth.

| P★★ | T★★ | E★ | A★ |

Robert Vaughn and Darrah Marshall in Teenage Caveman

Directed by Richard Viktorov. Written by Avenir Zac and Isai Kuznetsov. With Misha Yershov, Sasha Grigorieve and Voldoya Savin.

TEENAGE ZOMBIES (1957) In-
stantly forgettable film about a nerve gas changing harmless teenagers into mindless slaves of an evil man.

| P | T★ | E | A |

Produced and directed by Jerry Warren. Written by Jacques Lecotier. With Don Sullivan, Katherine Victor, Steve Conte and Paul Repper.

THE TELEGIAN (1960) see SECRET OF THE TELEGIAN (1960)

TEMPS DE MOURIR (1969) see TWICE UPON A TIME (1969)

THE TENTH VICTIM (1965) A
weak, curiously humourless adaptation of Robert Sheckley's short story "The Seventh Victim", in which Ursula Andress, on her tenth challenge in the "Big Hunt" (a legitimized future murder game), falls in love with and eventually marries Marcello Mastroianni, rather than killing him.

| P★★ | T★★ | E★ | A★ |

Directed by Elio Petri. Written by Petri, Ennio Flaiano, Tonino Guerra and Giorgio Salvione. With Elsa Martinelli and Massimo Serato.

THE TERMINAL MAN (1973) Based
on Michael Crichton's novel, this is a superior high-tech thriller about a murderer implanted with a tiny computer supposedly to control his murderous desires, but in fact proving to accentuate his desire for such violent pleasure. The inadequacy of the machines as controlling devices is writ large here.

| P★★★ | T★★★ | E★★★ | A★★ |

Produced, directed and written by Michael Hodges. With George Seal and Joan Hackett.

THE TERMINATOR (1984) A slick,
powerful and fast-paced amalgam of a lot of other people's sf ideas from novels, stories, television and films, which is not surprising seeing that the writer and director of The Terminator, James Cameron,

is a former sf fan and an admirer of the films of Ridley Scott and George Miller. Apart from elements of Alien (q.v.) and especially Mad Max 2 one can also detect in The Terminator's magpie structure echoes of the two Harlan Ellison Outer Limits episodes (Soldier and Demon With A Glass Hand), Philip K. Dick's short story "Second Variety" and the Beserker series of novels and stories by Fred Saberhagen. According to Cameron, The Terminator came about because "I'd never really seen a good robot in a movie ever. Not a really great one the way they used to be portrayed on the covers of Analog ..." What John W. Campbell Jnr would have thought of The Terminator is anyone's guess. In it Arnold Schwarzenegger is cunningly cast as a killer robot sent by its computer masters in the future back to present-day Los Angeles to kill a girl who will eventually give birth to a freedom fighter who will threaten the rule of the computers. One of the freedom fighters also travels back in time to protect her and the stage is set for a violent game of pursuit during which unfortunate bystanders, mainly policemen, get mown down by the score. As the hunt continues the robot's outer layer of flesh is progressively destroyed until finally he's a glittering, mechanized skeleton. And even when reduced to bits and pieces he keeps coming ... Despite one or two car chases too many it's an exciting and well-made piece of sf entertainment. True, it's basically an exploitation movie, but an intelligent and witty one. And it features good performances from Linda Hamilton as the prey and Michael Biehn as her protector. Schwarzenegger is Schwarzenegger.

| P★★★ | T★★★★ | E★★★ | A★ |

Written by James Cameron and Gale Anne Hurd. Make-up Effects by Stan Winston. With Paul Winfield. (JB)

TERROR (1924) see THE PERILS OF PARIS (1924)

TERROR BENEATH THE SEA
(1966) Nemo meets the mad scientist in this tale of the insane scientist ruler of an underwater city who is experimenting on

turning men into water-breathing monsters under his control.

P★   T★★   E★★   A★

Directed by Hajime Sato. Special Effects by Nobuo Yajima. With Shinichi Chiba, Peggy Neal, Franz Gruber and Gunther Braun.

TERROR EN EL ESPACIO (1965)
see PLANET OF THE VAMPIRES (1965)

TERRORE NELLO SPAZIO (1965)
see PLANET OF THE VAMPIRES (1965)

TERROR FROM THE SUN (1959)
see THE HIDEOUS SUN DEMON (1959)

TERROR FROM THE YEAR 5000
(1958) A machine is developed which can retrieve objects from the future. In one of its "sweeps" it brings back a hideously disfigured woman (badly irradiated and highly radioactive) who, it seems, is seeking men to take back with her to revivify the human race.

P★   T★   E★   A

Produced, directed and written by Robert Gurney Jr. With Ward Costello and Joyce Holden.

TERROR IN SPACE (1965) see
PLANET OF THE VAMPIRES (1965)

TERROR IN THE MIDNIGHT SUN (1960) see INVASION OF THE ANIMAL PEOPLE (1960)

TERROR IS A MAN (1959) Mad
scientist movie drawing heavily on Moreau's tale. On isolated Blood Island a scientist tries to surgically transform a leopard into a man. The resultant killer beast gets loose.

P★   T★   E★   A

Directed by Gerry De Leon. Written by Harry Paul Harber. With Francis Lederer, Greta Thyssen and Richard Derr.

THE TERRORNAUTS (1966) Based
on Murray Leinster's The Wailing Asteroid, this slight piece of sf is cluttered and rather dull, despite a script from sf writer John Brunner – too many elements clamour to be fitted into its 75-minute length. A group of unlikely enough people are

taken by alien spacecraft to the alien fortress on the asteroid (the alien race being now dead, but its computers work on) which gives them the knowledge to fight off a fleet of nasty alien spacecraft.

P★★   T★★   E★   A★

Directed by Montgomery Tully. Special Effects by Bowie Films. With Simon Oates, Zena Marshall, Charles Hawtrey and Patricia Hayes.

TERROR OF MECHAGODZILLA
(1975) see MONSTERS FROM THE UNKNOWN PLANET (1975)

THE TERROR OF THE AIR (1914)
British pre-War film about a ray which can activate explosive at a distance. A spy steals the apparatus and blows up a ship.

Directed by Frank Wilson. With Tom Powers, Stewart Rome, Violet Hopson and Harry Royston.

TERROR OF THE DEEP (1966) see
DESTINATION INNER SPACE (1966)

TERROR ON BLOOD ISLAND
(1968) see BRIDES OF BLOOD (1968)

TERROR OUT OF THE SKY (1978)
Slightly more intelligent killer bee movie than usual, lacking the inanity of The Swarm (q.v.) but, unfortunately, not creating any true sense of menace from the potentiality of total agricultural collapse should the bees spread.

P★★   T★★   E★★   A★

Directed by Lee H. Katzin. Written by Guerdon Trueblood and Doris Silverton. Special Effects by Allen L. Hall. With Efrem Zimbalist Jr, Dan Haggerty, Tovah Feldshuh and Lonny Chapman.

THE TERROR STRIKES (1958) see
WAR OF THE COLOSSAL BEAST (1958)

TESTAMENT (1983) This made-for-
TV film was given a wider distribution; not another The Day After (q.v.) – with its romanticized, soap-opera undertones – but an honest examination of what a normal family in the Californian town of Hamlin do after the Bomb. The bleakness, futility and heartbreaking reality of the film make it depressing but ultimately

necessary viewing. Radiation sickness, rationing, the burial of the dead – these are taken as documentary fact not sensationalized spectacle. A subtle, in some ways brilliant, film.

| P★★★ | T★★★ | E★★★ | A★★★★ |

Directed by Lynne Littman. Written by John Sacret Young. With Jane Alexander, William Devane, Ross Harris, Roxana Zal and Lukas Haas.

DAS TESTAMENT DES DR MABUSE (1933) see THE TESTAMENT OF DR MABUSE (1933)

LE TESTAMENT DU DR MABUSE (1933) see THE TESTAMENT OF DR MABUSE (1933)

THE TESTAMENT OF DR MABUSE (1933) Direct sequel to *Dr Mabuse, The Gambler* (1922) (q.v.). Rudolf Klein-Rogge again plays the master-criminal, controlling his underworld empire from an insane asylum. He dies here, but, in true Mabuse tradition, takes over the personality of the asylum's director and so achieves a form of immortality. Banned by the Nazis (perhaps because Lang claimed the dialogue of his criminals was taken direct from their doctrines) it was Lang's parting shot within the German cinema, until 1958.

| P★★ | T★★ | E★★ | A★★ |

Directed by Fritz Lang. Written by Thea Von Harbou. With Otto Wernicke, Oscar Beregi, Gustav Diessl and Theodor Loos.

THE TESTAMENT OF DR MABUSE (1962) Re-make of Fritz Lang's 1933 film, with Wolfgang Preiss as Mabuse and Walter Rilla as the director of the insane asylum taken over by the will of Mabuse.

| P★★ | T★★ | E★★ | A★ |

Directed by Werner Klinger. Written by Ladislas Fodor and Robert Adolf Stemmle. With Gert Froebe, Senta Berger and Helmut Schmid.

THE TEST OF PILOT PIRIX (1978) A crew of robots and humans (and who can really tell who is who?) go to Saturn, to place the crew under stress and test who is better – man or machine. Based on Stanislaw Lem's ingenious and amusing tales (in particular, "Inquiry"), it falls far short of the original.

| P★★★ | T★★ | E★★ | A★ |

Directed by Marek Piestrak. Written by Piestrak and Vladimir Valutski. With Sergiusz Desnitsky, Boleslaw Abart and Vladimir Ivashov.

TEST PILOTA PIRXA (1978) see THE TEST OF PILOT PIRIX (1978)

TEST PILOT PIRX (1978) see THE TEST OF PILOT PIRIX (1978)

THEM! (1953) This is, perhaps, *the* monster movie. The classic of the subgenre. The only giant-mutation film with any real coherence and dramatic tension. All else is imitation, this – from the opening sequence introducing the giant ants to the final showdown in the storm drains beneath Los Angeles (itself a stroke of genius) – is the real thing. It's the ultimate scare story: what powers might we let loose if we carry on testing atomic bombs? what are the side effects? *THEM!* gives us an answer which, in its way, is as allegorically effective as Mary Shelley's *Frankenstein*, another diseased-creation myth. But this is creation by inadvertence. The gi*ANTS* are caused by Man's meddling not his maliciousness or scientific curiosity. Thirty years on and the images of the film (and its effects) are still enough to convince and frighten, and its developing sense, first of mystery, and then of threat, result in a thoroughly absorbing piece of cinema. The human actors in this drama are for once dwarfed by events (even Professor Medford, played by Edmund Gwenn) – by the utter hostility of "Them!", perhaps of Nature itself.

| P★★★★ | T★★★ | E★★★★★ | A★★★ |

Directed by Gordon Douglas. Written by Russell Hughes and Ted Sherdemann, from an original story by George Worthing Yates. Special Effects by Ralph Ayers. With James Whitmore, James Arness, Joan Weldon and Leonard Nimoy.

THEM (1970) A lyrical French film about an old man who invents a machine which allows an artist to tap his deep

unconscious and create art directly from his dreams. Based on the novel *Ils* by Andre Hardellet.

| P★★ | T★★ | E★★ | A★★ |

Directed by Jean-Daniel Simon. Written by Simon and Jean-Paul Petrolacci. With Michel Duchaussoy and Charles Vanel.

THESE ARE THE DAMNED (1961)
see THE DAMNED (1961)

THEY CALL ME ROBERT (1967)
see CALL ME ROBERT (1967)

THEY CAME FROM ANOTHER WORLD (1955) *see* INVASION OF THE BODY SNATCHERS (1955)

THEY CAME FROM BEYOND SPACE (1967)
What seems like a nasty alien invasion proves – after several misunderstandings – to be a friendly first contact. The aliens have crashed on the Moon and want help with their repairs, but their first attempts at recruitment (taking over people and spreading plague) are rather heavy-handed. A confused and rather dull film.

| P★ | T★ | E★ | A★ |

Produced by Max J. Rosenberg and Milton Subotsky. Directed by Freddie Francis. Written by Subotsky. Special Effects by Bowie Films. With Robert Hutton and Jennifer Jayne.

THEY CAME FROM WITHIN (1974) *see* SHIVERS (1974)

THEY SAVED HITLER'S BRAIN (1963) *see* MADMEN OF MANDORAS (1963)

THIN AIR (1969) *see* INVASION OF THE BODY STEALERS (1969)

THE THING (1982)
When Howard Hawks made the first version of *The Thing* in 1951 he changed essential elements of John W. Campbell's original storyline ("Who Goes There?") beyond recognition whilst maintaining the sense of threat and deep paranoia. In re-making *The Thing* John Carpenter was more faithful to Campbell's version – able to show us

Kurt Russell as McCready in The Thing

graphically (and gruesomely) what the "Thing" would be like and act like. The resultant film is one of the most imaginative pieces of sf put on celluloid, for the "Thing" is a shape changer, able to assimilate and copy exactly (down to cellular level) any life form. It can be destroyed by fire, but the problem is in finding out what and where the "Thing" is. From the opening scene of the giant alien spacecraft coming to Earth more than one hundred thousand years ago, to the final scene where McCready (Kurt Russell) faces Childs (Keith David) as the Antarctic base flames nearby and says "Why don't we sit here and see what happens?" the film is a tour-de-force of slow-building tension, easily the equal of the original movie. The special effects are superb, particularly in one scene where the head of a human victim detaches itself (melting away from the body), drops to the floor, throws out a tendril-like tongue, then re-emerges a moment later as a giant spider-like creature. One of the real humans comments for us when he says "You've got to be fucking kidding." It's all borderline horror, of course, but its evocation of alien menace is more genuine than the usual run of Satan's-brood films.

| P★★★ | T★★★★★ | E★★★★ | A★★ |

Written by Bill Lancaster. Special Effects by Roy Arbogast. Special Visual Effects by Albert Whitlock. Cinematography by Dean Cundey. With Wilford Brimley, T. K. Carter, David Clennon, Richard Dysart and Charles Hallahan.

THE THING (FROM ANOTHER WORLD) (1951)

When John Carpenter made a new version of *The Thing* in 1982, he was careful to avoid those areas of emphasis that the original had chosen. Howard Hawks's production (Christian Nyby was, by all accounts, only director in name) created several visual images which have stood the test of time – the moment when the investigating team form a circle about the spacecraft, frozen beneath the ice, is one of them. The monster, however, was less memorable – an 8-foot "intellectual carrot". It was as hostile and inimical to human life as the "Thing" in John W. Campbell's "Who Goes There?", but somewhere along the line it had lost its ability to change its shape and mimic any form. The human interactions save the film from being just another monster movie; scriptwriter Charles Lederer provides some excellent dialogue, and the mounting sense of paranoia is almost tangible. As in the original story and the later film version, the "Thing" is unthawed, takes over almost all of the Antarctic camp and is eventually destroyed – by electrocution in this instance. Five years later *Invasion Of The Body Snatchers* (q.v.) was to take the theme of alien mimicry avoided by this film and make the movie Hawks *should* have made and Carpenter *did* make some 31 years later.

| P★★★ | T★★ | E★★★ | A★★ |

Special Effects by Donald Stewart. With Margaret Sheridan, Kenneth Toby, Robert Cornthwaite, Douglas Spencer and Dewey Martin.

THINGS TO COME (1936)

This film stands like a great monument on the sf cinema landscape: huge and impressive but basically a cold and lifeless structure – a memorial to H. G. Wells's obsolete ideas about how the world *should* be. Its producer, Alexander Korda, was a great admirer of Wells and it's to his credit that he asked the author to adapt his book *The Shape Of Things To Come* for the screen, but surely Korda's showman instincts should have warned him from the start that the result would be short on drama and strong on polemics. For Wells, by this time, had long since ceased to present his ideas within the context of well-written, and entertaining, stories and novels, but had become a pamphleteer who was delivering his messages to the masses straight and unadorned by fiction. Most of Wells's answers to the problems of the world in the 1930s resided in a touching faith in science and technology, and this is the message he promoted in his screenplay for Korda, a screenplay that was to undergo many transformations before it was in a filmable state. It begins in a city square captioned "Everytown" in "1940". War is obviously imminent and in the home of the film's central character, and Wells's mouthpiece, John Cabal (Raymond Massey) comes the first of the many author's messages: "If we don't end war, war will end us." But war does start, as it did in reality, and in the film's most successful piece of prophecy, Everytown is blitzed into ruins. Wells's World War Two continues on until the mid-1960s. By that time Everytown is in a feudal state and ruled over by a warlord called the Chief (Ralph Richardson giving the liveliest performance in the picture). Then John Cabal arrives in a mysterious aeroplane and tells the Chief that he is part of a society of scientists who call themselves the Airmen and who intend to reform the world. The Airmen are Wells's *deus ex machina* – his cavalry who arrive from nowhere and save the day. The Chief and his kind are overthrown and Everytown is rebuilt. By 2036 it is a vast white and gleaming underground complex with all the appeal of a modern shopping centre. In charge of it is John Cabal's grandson Oswald (Massey again) but he's got problems with a reactionary artist, Theotocopulous (Cedric Hardwicke) who heads a band of 21st-century Luddites. They want to wreck a planned Moonshot involving a manned projectile being fired from a huge cannon. But despite the Luddite uprising the gun is fired and Wells, through Cabal, delivers his final message which ends with: "All the universe or nothingness. Which shall it be ...?" At times *Things To Come* exhibits a certain visual grandeur but compared to the earlier *Metropolis* (q.v.) (which

Wells didn't like) it's a static, ponderous film. Wells's dialogue is stilted and most of the characters aren't even two-dimensional but are symbols set up by Wells to either be knocked down or lauded. The film is a classic case of the message overwhelming the medium.

P★	T★★★	E★	A★★

Produced by Alexander Korda. Directed by William Cameron Menzies. Written by H. G. Wells and Lajos Biro. Special Effects by Ned Mann. Designed by Vincent Korda. With Sophie Stewart and Margaretta Scott. (JB)

THE THING WITH TWO HEADS

(1972) Ray Milland plays the racist doctor who, riddled with cancer, plans to have his head grafted on to a donor body. Unfortunately (for him) it's mistakenly grafted on to the body of a falsely charged black convict (Rosey Grier). A lovely tongue-in-cheek vision of racism in America.

P★★	T★★	E★★★	A★

Directed by Lee Frost. Written by Frost, Wes Bishop and James Gordon White. Special Effects by Dan Striepeke, Gail Brown, Tom Burman, Charles Schram, James White and Pete Peterson. With Don Marshall, Roger Perry, Kathy Baumann, Chelsea Brown and Lee Frost.

THE THIRD FROM THE SUN

(1973) Bulgarian time-travel story about extraterrestrials who meddle with human evolution.

P★★	T★	E★	A

Directed by Gueorgui Stoyanov. Written by Pavel Vejinov. With Dobrinka Stankova, Ivan Mikolaichuk, Iziak Fintzi and Naoum Chopov.

THE THIRTY-FOOT BRIDE OF CANDY ROCK

(1958) Inane mishmash of sf ideas as an inventor wreaks havoc in a small town by turning a girl into a giant, inventing a time-displacement machine and giving a friend the ability to fly. Lou Costello, without Abbott, died shortly after making this ...

P	T★	E★	A

Directed by Sidney Miller. Written by Rowland Barber and Arthur Ross. Special Effects by Jack Rabin, Irving Block and Louis DeWitt. With Dorothy Provine and Gale Gordon.

THIS ISLAND EARTH

(1954) Cal Meacham, a young physicist, receives strange electronic parts through the post – parts ordered from a catalogue which contains remarkably advanced developments – and a blueprint for building what seems like a highly sophisticated television screen. When he builds and activates the screen he comes into contact with a man with white hair and high forehead (Jeff Morrow) who invites him to join a secret project. Meacham (Rex Reason) and a female colleague, Dr Ruth Adams (Faith Domergue), are slightly suspicious and eventually discover that these high-browed, white-haired men are aliens, whose homeworld, Metaluna, is engaged in an interplanetary war. They are taken to Metaluna, a daunting landscape in the final throes of destruction, and escape just as the planet is being destroyed – with the help of Exeter, the alien who recruited them. They fly back to Earth in one of the Metalunan spacecraft, but with a stowaway aboard – one of the grotesque, huge aliens the Metalunans had bred as slaves. Exeter is attacked and fatally wounded by the slave mutant, but manages to get Meacham and Adams home before crashing the ship (plus mutant) into the sea. The plot of *This Island Earth*, borrowed from Raymond Jones's novel, is sparse, the acting not particularly impressive, but the whole film *is* impressive for making concrete familiar images from the written genre: Metaluna and its attackers are vividly and colourfully created, as is the slave mutant (Eddie Parker), a marvellous B.E.M. (Bug-Eyed Monster). The combination of simplicity (in plot) and richness (in visuals) makes for a genuine piece of speculative cinema, something rare in the 1950s.

P★★	T★★★★	E★★★★	A★★

Directed by Joseph Newman. Written by Franklin Coen and Edward G. O'Callaghan. Special Effects by Clifford Stine and Stanley Horsley. Make-up by Bud Westmore. Cinematography by Clifford Stine. With Lance Fuller and Russell Johnson.

THE THOUSAND EYES OF DR MABUSE

(1960) Fritz Lang's final film was a return to territory he had first explored in 1922 with *Dr Mabuse, The Gambler* (q.v.), and returned to in 1933 with *The Testament Of Dr Mabuse* (q.v.). In this claustrophobic feature the will of Mabuse lives on in Professor Jordan who runs a worldwide criminal web from the depths of the Hotel Luxor. The multiplicity of visual devices within the hotel (constantly suggestive of evil watchers) is counterpointed by the activities of the blind visionary, Dr Cornelius. But the core of the film concerns police investigations into the mysterious Hotel Luxor and all is presented as a fast-paced thriller. However, it's important to note that Lang's starting point was an article he read about Nazi plans for post-War hotels which would be designed on the lines of Hotel Luxor, allowing full 1984-like observation of all the guests.

| P★★ | T★★★ | E★★★ | A★★ |

Directed by Fritz Lang. Written by Lang and Heinz Oscar Wuttig. With Dawn Addams, Peter Van Eyck, Gert Frobe and Wolfgang Preiss.

THE THREE FANTASTIC SUPERMEN (1967) *see* THE FANTASTIC THREE (1967)

THE THREE STOOGES IN ORBIT (1962) Martians are out to steal a special tank-helicopter-submarine invention, but the Stooges stop them.

| P★ | T★ | E★ | A |

Directed by Edward Bernds. Written by Elwood Ullman. With Moe Howard, Larry Fine, Joe De Rita, Carol Christensen and Emil Sitka.

3000 AD (1952) *see* CAPTIVE WOMEN (1952)

THROUGH SOLID WALLS (1916) An inventor traps a pair of jewel thieves and proves the value of his machine which can see through solid walls.

Directed by Walter Morton. Written by E. J. Clauson. With Jay Belasco and Marc Fenton.

THUNDERBALL (1965) Villain Adolfo Celi has stolen some nuclear warheads. Bond (Sean Connery) is sent to the Caribbean to get them back. Standard 007

fare, with the sharks – Celi keeps a pool full of them – as the real heroes. The movie depends almost entirely on underwater spectacle for its thrills, and the showdown scene is so vast it loses everything when screened on television. It's the only Bond movie Broccoli and Saltzman ever made without a complete stranglehold on the adaptation rights, so Connery produced a medium-budget remake in 1983, *Never Say Never Again.*

| P | T★★★ | E★★★★ | A |

Directed by Terence Young. Written by Richard Maibaum and John Hopkins. Special Effects by John Stears. With Claudine Auger, Luciana Paluzzi, Bernard Lee and Lois Maxwell. (TR)

THUNDERBIRDS ARE GO (1966) The first manned flight to Mars is attacked by the red planet's denizens, creatures which look like whorls of hardened lava until they uncoil to reveal themselves as gigantic rock snakes. Returning to Earth, the crew find they cannot land their crippled ship, and only the intrepid men of International Rescue, a covert organization of do-gooders headed by a reclusive billionaire, can save them. If it sounds childish it's because the movie is for children – the characters are puppets, the film is a spin-off from the famous TV series by Gerry Anderson. All the familiar crew of Scott, Virgil, Brains, Parker and Lady Penelope are here. Anderson probably reached a high peak of imaginative puppeteering around this period, and has never managed to regain it.

| P★★ | T★★★★ | E★★★ | A |

Directed by David Lane. Written by Sylvia and Gerry Anderson. Special Effects by Derek Meddings and Shaun Whittacker-Cook. (TR)

THUNDERBIRDS 6 (1968) Feature derived from the TV series *Thunderbirds*, about a group of rich altruists, International Rescue, who, with their advanced rocket technology, get people out of trouble.

| P★ | T★★ | E★ | A★ |

Directed by David Lane. Written by Gerry and Sylvia Anderson. Special Effects by Derek Meddings.

Robert Duvall as THX and Maggie McOmie as his wife, LUH, in THX 1138

THX 1138 (1970) With hindsight this bleak variation on *1984* might at first seem to have little in common with the relentlessly juvenile and up-beat later movies of George Lucas, such as *Star Wars* (q.v.) and *Return Of The Jedi* (q.v.), yet on closer examination the seeds of his subsequent works can be detected in this early "experimental" work. After a prologue consisting of scenes from the old *Buck Rogers* movie serial Lucas skilfully leads the viewer into an unsettling dystopia where the human race lives in a subterranean, totalitarian society run by computers and bland technocrats. Everyone is fed a constant supply of sedative drugs and any sign of individuality is forbidden, along with sexual intercourse. The protagonist, THX (Robert Duvall), unexpectedly has his consciousness raised when his wife, LUH (Maggie McOmie), deliberately alters his drug intake. Very quickly he discovers sex, love and where babies come from. With LUH pregnant they are both arrested and separated. LUH is "terminated" but THX is thrown into an all-white prison which doesn't seem to have any boundaries. In this eerie setting he meets a black man who claims he isn't real but a hologram that decided to get out of the "entertainment circuits". The two of them escape and at this point the film changes its mood from one of grim "reality" to one of exhilarating fantasy as THX proceeds to outrun, outdrive (Lucas, a fast-car fanatic, most reveals his true colours in these

sequences) and outwit his pursuers. One of the several *Star Wars* seeds in *THX 1138* is the obvious fun Lucas has with robots. For all the apparent efficiency of the tall, chrome-faced robot policemen, dressed like LA cops, they're far from perfect and their foibles provide the film's main source of humour, culminating in the final scenes when they plead to the escaping THX to come back because they've exceeded their pursuit budget.

P★★　　T★★★　　E★★★　　A★★

Directed by George Lucas. Written by Lucas and Walter Murch. With Robert Duvall, Donald Pleasance, Maggie McOmie and Don Pedro Colley. (JB)

THX 2238 – 4EB (1967) George Lucas's first production was a 20-minute short which, re-vamped and slightly retitled (*THX 1138* (1970) (q.v.)), became his first feature. Francis Ford Coppola saw this short, made for Lucas's college degree, and agreed that Lucas could make it as the first feature for Coppola's new film company.

TICKLED PINK (1961) *see* MAGIC SPECTACLES (1961)

TIGER MAN (1944) *see* THE LADY AND THE MONSTER (1944)

TIME AFTER TIME (1979) A clever adaptation of H. G. Wells's *The Time Machine* by writers Karl Alexander and Steve Hayes was picked up by director/screenwriter Nicholas Meyer here. In this film Wells (Malcolm McDowell) has actually built the time machine and, on the eve of demonstrating it to his friends, discovers that one of their number – a doctor, John Stevenson – is Jack the Ripper. Stevenson (David Warner) uses Wells's machine to escape into the future – into San Francisco, 1979. The machine has, however, an in-built homing device and returns to Wells in 1893. Wells, fearful but determined, pursues Stevenson into the future. This part of the film is perhaps the most interesting, especially in the eccentric encounter with bank-teller Amy Robbins (Mary Steenburgen) who finds him quaint. Through Amy he traces Stevenson and tries to persuade him to return. This confrontation is crucial to the "message" of the film, as Stevenson says to Wells "I belong here completely and utterly. I'm home ... The world has caught up with me and surpassed me ... The future isn't what you thought, it's what I am." In this condemnation of Modern Man and rejection of Victorian values (the ethic of the gentleman) lies the ambiguity of the film, for we sense Stevenson is right, but pray that Wells triumphs. This level of the film, separate from the sf story, the thriller and the love story – all of which exist within the film's framework – is where we engage with Wells's Utopianism and reject it. The world Wells glimpses on the TV screen is not merely fantastic (compared to his own age) but far more violent. He realizes that Man has become more efficient – at killing. Stevenson returns to the bank to change more money, and realizes that Amy is in connivance with Wells. From this point on her life is endangered and, when Wells takes her into the future to prove to her that he isn't a nutcase, they discover that she will soon be a victim – Stevenson's fifth in San Francisco. For a time this becomes a straightforward thriller – with the twist of Wells not being believed when he tells the truth to the police. Eventually, however, he pursues Stevenson back to the machine, saves the girl and removes a special key from the side of the machine as Stevenson is about to use it, sending him into infinity. All comes well in the end, even to the extent of Wells taking Amy Robbins back into the past and marrying her. Of course, if you know the work of H. G. Wells at all, this is all nonsense, even as fanciful hypothesis, because no one, having glimpsed the truth of the future, would have written *The Shape Of Things To Come*.

P★★★   T★★★   E★★★★   A★★★

Special Effects by Larry Fuentes and Jim Blount. With Charles Cioffi and Kent Williams.

TIME BANDITS (1981) An 11-year-old boy has boring, materialistic parents who virtually ignore him. One evening,

while in bed, his wardrobe shatters and a knight on horseback thunders out of the debris. This is the beginning of a series of adventures through time for the young hero and a set of dwarves – God's little helpers – who have stolen a map of the Creation which shows where the time holes are located. Special effects are good, and the humour is Pythonesque, flagging in few places, the action remaining pacy. The brilliant sense of the absurd is typified by John Cleese's portrayal of Robin Hood, and squeamish viewers should prepare for scenes of dwarves eating live rats. The tangle of classical myth and history in no way detracts from the visual impact of the film. A macabre ending in modern times adds a final superb touch.

P★★★   T★★★★   E★★★★★   A★★★

Directed by Terry Gilliam. Written by Gilliam and Michael Palin. Special Effects by John Bunker. With John Cleese, Michael Palin, Ralph Richardson, Sean Connery, Ian Holm and Kenny Baker. (GDK)

TIME FLIES (1944) The "time ball" by which comedian Tommy Handley gets back to Tudor England is about the only sf element in this third-rate comedy.

P★   T   E★   A

Directed by Walter Forde. Written by Howard Irving Young, J. O. C. Orton and Ted Kavanagh. With Evelyn Dall and George Moon.

THE TIME MACHINE (1960) This begins as an intelligent examination of time travel and ends as a schlock romance between George (Rod Taylor) from the year 1900 and Weena (Yvette Mimieux) from the year 802701. George Pal directed and produced, which explains something of the ham-fisted handling of Wells's original. There's no journeying into the past, nor into the very-far future, only to the time of the Eloy and Morlocks. Pal, and writer David Duncan, added material appertaining to World Wars One, Two and Three (the last in 1966!), yet spoiled the veracity this seemed to give the story by having people from 800,000 years in the future remember the events of the 326-year-long Third World War. The Morlocs themselves are surprisingly clumsy and stupid (they're stunted and green with glowing eyes and mops of whitish hair) and their introduction sees the film plummet to the depths of unintelligent adventure pulp. Some of the time-travel effects were good and the machine itself is a marvellous piece of Victoriana, but generally it's an enervated performance by all concerned.

P★	T★★	E★★	A

Special Effects by Gene Warren and Wah Chang. Make-up by William Tuttle. With Alan Young, Whit Bissell, Sebastian Cabot and Doris Lloyd.

TIMERIDER: THE ADVENTURE OF LYLE SWANN (1983) Slow-paced, rather uninspired, time-travel story. A motorcycle champion is accidentally transferred back into 1877 and gets into trouble with some bad men who want to steal his motorcycle. But the limp storyline is all an excuse for Swann to make love to his great-great grandmother and so start the Swann dynasty. Heinlein come back, all's forgiven!

P★★	T★★	E★	A★

Directed by William Dear. Written by Dear and Michael Nesmith. With Belinda Bauer, Peter Coyote, L. Q. Jones and Ed Lauter.

TIMESLIP (1956) Based on Charles Eric Maine's novel, *The Isotope Man* (he also wrote the screenplay here), this is the story of a man, clinically dead, who, because of an atomic accident is $7\frac{1}{2}$ seconds ahead in time. Maine reduces his own complex plot into a spy thriller with horror elements.

P★★	T★	E★★	A★

Directed by Ken Hughes. With Gene Nelson, Faith Domergue and Joseph Tomelty.

TIME SLIP: THE DAY OF THE APOCALYPSE (1981) The physical mechanics of the "time warp" which throws a group of modern Japanese soldiers back into the Samurai past isn't ever explained, but it really doesn't matter as the film unfolds in all its gory glory. It's all very simple really; the Colonel in charge (a modern-day Samurai) reasons that if they

can conquer Japan they'll change history and thus effect a second time warp, getting them back home. What happens, however, is that they encounter the ferocious lunacy of Samurai armies which eventually win a costly but certain victory over them. In a delightfully ironic final scene the Samurai leader shoots the Colonel (armed with a sword) with a machine pistol. A gripping film, though not for the squeamish.

P★★★	T★★	E★★★★	A★★

Directed by Kosei Saito. Written by Toshio Kaneda and Ryo Hanmura. With Sonny Chiba, Isao Natsuki, Miyuki Ono and Jana Okada.

THE TIME TO DIE (1969) *see* TWICE UPON A TIME (1969)

TIME TRAP (1964) *see* THE TIME TRAVELLERS (1964)

THE TIME TRAVELLERS (1964) Scientists from 1964 are trapped in 2064, in a world that has suffered a nuclear war, with the last few normal humans living underground and the surface of Earth inhabited by mutants. They escape back into the past eventually, but have discovered that they cannot change a thing, and that their time-travel experiments are part of a set cycle of events.

P★★	T★★	E★★	A★

Directed and written by Ib Melchior. Special Effects by David Hewitt. With Preston Foster, Philip Carey, Merry Anders and John Hoyt.

TIME WALKER (1982) Updated version of *The Mummy* with science fiction element. Previously overlooked mummy from Tutankhamen's tomb is found and then ravages a University campus. Five crystals are stolen and the eventual possessors hunted by the mummy (the "noble traveller") and repossessed. Scrolls resembling wiring diagrams, green killer fungus and a mummy whose natural habitat is power-houses; all point to the word *alien*. A stale though repeatable plot is spoiled by a murdered caretaker who is immediately forgotten and a nefarious alien killer who is suddenly a benign and sympathetic character.

P★★	T	E★★	A

Directed by Tom Kennedy. Written by Karen Levitt and Tom Friedman. With Ben Murphy, Nina Axelrod and Ken Brophy. (GDK)

TIMEWARP (1981) Colonel Weston wants the wife of Mark DeVore, an astronaut, so sends him off on a two-year mission into deep space and sabotages his ship (via a computer message) when it is three days out from Earth. But the ship and Devore (Chip Johnson) pass through a time warp and appear back on Earth a year later, to the day. By various means they return to Jupiter and through the warp again, reversing all that happened. Adam West plays Weston with suitable stuffiness.

P★★	T★★	E★★★	A★

Produced and written by Anne Spielberg. Directed by Robert Emenegger and Allan Sandler. With Gretchen Corbett, Peter Kastner and Steven Mond.

TINERETE FARA BATRINETE (1968) see KINGDOM IN THE CLOUDS (1968)

THE TIN GIRL (1970) What seems to begin as a love story set in the future becomes a story of independent thinking in the face of growing conformity. The girl who fascinates a bored executive proves to be a robot, and he destroys her.

P★★	T★	E★	A★

Directed by Marcello Aliprandi. Written by Fernando Imbert and Aliprandi. With Sydne Rome, Roberto Antonelli and Elena Persiani.

THE TINGLER (1959) Interesting idea given a horror treatment. A man (Vincent Price) discovers that fear isn't an instinct but an insect-like creature which develops on the spines of fearful people but is killed when they scream. He uses this knowledge to kill his mute wife, terrifying her by various means.

P★★	T★★	E★★	A★

Produced and directed by William Castle. Written by Robb White. With Judith Evelyn, Darryl Hickman and Patricia Cutts.

THE TIN MAN (1935) Short film about two women who encounter a mad scientist whose robot had been programmed to kill all women, but the robot disobeys and attacks its creator.

P★	T★	E★	A★

Directed by James Parrott. With Thelma Todd, Patsy Kelly and Mathew Betz.

TOBOR THE GREAT (1954) Tobor, the palindromic robot, is one of the rare breed of good robots in sf cinema. With his gifts of telepathy and empathy he saves his creator, the professor, and the professor's grandson. Visually Tobor is unwieldy to say the least.

P★	T★	E★★	A★

Directed by Lee Sholem. Written by Phillip MacDonald and R. Goldstone. Special Effects by Howard and Theodore Lydecker. With Charles Drake, Karin Booth and Billy Chapin.

TOMEI NINGEN TO HAI OTOKO (1957) see THE TRANSPARENT MAN VS. THE FLY (1957)

THE TOMORROW MAN (1981) Bleak future thriller which demands that its viewers piece the jigsaw of events together for themselves. A Fascist organization, the Movement, under a Dr Fontayne, win an election and begin to take over all levels of society. One man, Tom Weston, will neither conspire against them nor allow them to dominate him, but when the anti-Movement conspiracy blow up Fontayne with a portable nuclear device (thus triggering World War Three, it seems), then Weston is incarcerated and questioned – for ten years. We know little of the results – i.e. the War – until the very last frame when we gaze out at the sterile world "outside" Weston's prison, and the charade is rather tiresome both for Weston and us. Shades of Zamyathin's *We* are evident throughout this, as are *1984* and the bleaker, anti-Nazi works of Philip K. Dick.

P★★★	T★★	E★★	A★

Directed by Tibor Takacs. Written by Stephen Zoller and Peter Chapman. With Stephen Markle, Don Francks, Stan Wilson and Gail Dahms.

TOMORROW YOU DIE! (1963) *see*
THE CRAWLING HAND (1963)

TOOMORROW (1970) A soul-less,
silly film about a group of aliens, Alphoids,
who kidnap a pop group (art students all –
including Olivia Newton-John!) to revita-
lize their own stagnant music.

P.	T★	E★	A

Directed and written by Val Guest. Special Cinematic Effects by Ray Caple and Cliff Culley.
Special Effects by John Stears. With Benny Thomas, Vic Cooper and Karl Chambers.

**TORTICOLA AGAINST FRANK-
ENSTEIN** (1952) Rather confused
French use of elements from the Frankenstein myth. The mad scientist patches
together a number of corpses and names
the result Torticola (Frankenstein-like –
though he never fights Frankenstein as the
title suggests). The scientist's mad experiments (man into cat, cat into man) are
thwarted by his own monster when he
oversteps the mark and plans to transfer a
girl's blood into the monster. Beauty and
the beast . . .

P★	T★	E★	A

Directed by Paul Paviot. Written by Louis Sapin
and Albert Vidalie. With Vera Norman, Roger
Blin and Michel Piccoli.

TORTURE SHIP (1939) Aboard a
mysterious vessel a scientist conducts experiments in curing men's criminal tendencies through gland injections. Based
on Jack London's "A Thousand Deaths".

P★	T★	E★	A★

Directed by Victor Halperin. Written by George
Sayre. With Irving Pichel, Lyle Talbot, Jacqueline
Wells and Anthony Averill.

**EIN TOTER SUCHT SENIER
MORDER** (1962) *see* THE BRAIN
(1962)

**TO THE CENTRE OF THE
EARTH** (1950) *see* UNKNOWN
WORLD (1950)

TOTO IN THE MOON (1957) Popular Latin comic in this space farce; he

proves to be the only person on Earth
(mistakenly) to be capable of space travel.
Meanwhile, the moon men are invading
Earth, duplicating people (including
Toto).

P	T★	E★	A

Directed by Stefano Steno. Written by Steno,
Alessandro Continenza and Sandra Milo. With
Toto, Sylva Koscina and Ugo Tognazzi.

THE TOY BOX (1971) Sexploitation
movie which prefigures *Liquid Sky* (1982)
(q.v.). An extraterrestrial subjects people
to a wide variety of sexual perversions so
that his race can eat the stimulated brains
of their victims.

P★	T★	E★	A

Directed and written by Ron Garcia. With Evan
Steele, Ann Myers and Deborah Osborne.

TRAITEMENT DE CHOC (1973) *see*
SHOCK TREATMENT (1973)

**THE TRANS-ATLANTIC TUN-
NEL** (1935) An English version of the
German film *Der Tunnel* (1933) (q.v.)
about the building of a transatlantic tunnel
– memorable not so much for its standard
Vernian-adventure plot but for its then-
impressive modelling.

P★	T★★	E★	A

Directed by Maurice Elvey. Written by Clemence
Dane and L. du Garde Peach. With Richard Dix,
Leslie Banks, Madge Evans and Helen Vinson.

**THE TRANSPARENT MAN VER-
SUS THE FLY** (1957) Japanese exploitation movie. A scientist develops a trans-
parency formula and helps the Tokyo
police track down a killer who is only
inches tall.

P★	T★	E★	A

Directed by Mitsuo Murayama. Written by
Hajime Takaiwa. With Ryuji Shinagawa, Yoshiro
Kitabara and Joji Tsunumi.

TRANSPLANT (1970) First of several
Italian movies obsessed with this subject:
an old man married to a beautiful young
girl feigns interest in a hyper-sexual young
man in order to get a penis transplant.

P★	T★★	E★★	A★

Directed by Stefano Vanzina. Written by Nino Longobardi and Giulio Scarnicci. With Carlo Guiffré, Fernando Bilbao and Renato Rascel.

TRANSPLANTE A LA ITALIANA (1970) *see* TRANSPLANT (1970)

TRASPLANTE DE UN CEREBRO (1970) *see* THE SECRET OF DR CHALMERS (1970)

I TRE FANTASTICI SUPERMEN (1967) *see* THE FANTASTIC THREE (1967)

TRIP TO A STAR (1906) *see* A VOYAGE AROUND A STAR (1906)

A TRIP TO MARS (1910) A professor of chemistry discovers a gravity-reversing formula; two powders which when combined – on his head – take him to Mars, where he encounters giant Martians.

A TRIP TO THE MOON (1902) Perhaps George Méliès's first true sf film (and not merely a gimmick piece), this is a lengthy 845-foot (20-plus minutes) and was based on Jules Verne's *From The Earth To The Moon* and H. G. Wells's *The First Men In The Moon*. A shell-like spacecraft is fired at the Moon, hits it bang in the eye, and its crew encounter lobster-clawed aliens, who, when struck, explode violently. Voilà! – a means of getting home! Back in Paris all involved are celebrated by the Mayor. Whilst a comic fantasy, the whole film is quite remarkable for its time.

P★★	T★★	E★	A★

Produced and directed by, and starring George Méliès. With the Ballerinas of the Théâtre du Châtelet and acrobats of the Folies Bergère.

THE TRITON (1917) Unlike the Creature (from 20,000 fathoms) this Hungarian sea monster had a thin skin when it came to human emotions and suffered both love for and betrayal by a human woman. A sensitive little comedy.

Produced and directed by Alfred Deesy. Written by Karloly Huszar. With Huszar, Annie Goth and Viktor Kurd.

TROG (1970) Unimpressive story about a caveman found in England. A device reads his mind and gets back pictures of encounters with dinosaurs (sequences taken from *The Animal World*, a 1955 O'Brien/Harryhausen effort). Eventually, when all attempts to civilize him fail, the army get him.

P★	T★	E	A

Directed by Freddie Frances. Written by Alben Kandel. With Joan Crawford, Michael Gough, Joe Cornelius, David Griffin and Kim Braden.

THE TROLLENBERG TERROR (1958) Based on the British TV serial, written by Peter Key, this tells of a radioactive cloud which mysteriously descends on a mountain village. The cloud contains cyclopean aliens possessed of telepathy who have the nasty habit of decapitating their Earth victims. In the end the good old RAF fire-bomb the aliens to death.

P★★	T★	E★★	A

Directed by Quentin Lawrence. Written by Jimmy Sangster. Special Effects by Les Bowie. With Forest Tucker, Janet Munro, Laurence Payne, Jennifer Jayne and Warren Mitchell.

TRON (1982) Walt Disney studios aren't noted for their originality these days, but *Tron*, whilst very much a child of its age (computer games and escapism into different dimensions), is an original. On one level it's a swindler-pinches-ideas-and-takes-over-company computer thriller, on another a subtle, understated threat to humanity (as the computer's Master Control, MCP, decides it can run Earth better than the humans can and prepares to take over the Pentagon's and the Kremlin's computer systems). But the best part of *Tron* is the adventure *within* the computer as computer-whizz-kid Kevin Flynn (Jeff Bridges) is taken out of the Users world (our reality) and into the world of the Programs (inside the computer system) by means of a computer/laser reconstruction system. There he meets Tron (Bruce Boxleitner) who is struggling to communicate with the Users world and get his Program, *Tron*, into the system and in control of MCP. MCP, meanwhile, is out to kill both of them and they fight their way through various video games – as participants – before they confront MCP (a whirling, giant, red face – satanic and a symbol of totalitarianism) and its front-man, Sark (David Warner). Flynn jumps into the power beam, distracts MCP, and allows Tron to throw his frisby-like pro-gram into the heart of MCP, killing it and making the world of Program healthy and "free" again. The film works rather well on all its chosen levels, but is most impres-sive as a visual treat – just sit back and enjoy the light-show.

P★★★	T★★★★★	E★★★★★	A★★★

Directed by Steven Lisberger. Written by Lis-berger, from a story by Lisberger and Bonnie MacBird. Conceptual Artists of the Electronic World: Syd Mead, Jean Giraud and Peter Lloyd. Visual Effects Concepts by Steven Lisberger. Technical Effects by John Scheele. Computer Effects by Richard Taylor. Cinematography by Bruce Logan. With Cindy Morgan, Barnard Hughes, Dan Shoa and Peter Jurasik.

THE TROUBLESOME DOUBLE
(1971) Children's Film Foundation sequel to *Egghead's Robot* (1971) (q.v.), featuring this time a twin robot girl for the boy inventor's sister.

P★	T★★	E★★	A★

Directed by Milo Lewis. Written by Leif Saxon. With Keith Chegwin and Julie Collins.

THE TROUBLE WITH 28 (1972)
Children's Film Foundation sequel to *Junket 89* (1970) (q.v.), with an eccentric science teacher demonstrating various sprays to his pupils – strength potions, truth elixirs, rejuvenation sprays, etc. A six-part quasi-scientific comedy.

P★★	T★	E★★	A★

Directed by Peter K. Smith. Written by David Ash. With Richard Wilson, Stephen Brassett, Peter Newby and Linda Robson.

A TRYTON (1917) see THE TRITON (1917)

THE TUNNEL (1933) Based on the
novel by Bernhard Kellerman about the building of a tunnel under the Atlantic, this was filmed in English (see *The Trans-*

atlantic Tunnel) (1935), French and Ger-man versions, with different casts. Its monomania – the building of the tunnel overrides all other considerations – makes it an interesting piece even today, though the predictable sabotage attempts are standard thriller fodder.

P★★	T★★	E★★	A★

Directed by Kurt Bernhardt. Written by Bern-hardt and Reinhart Steinbicker (and Alexandre Arnoux for French version). With (Germany): Paul Hartmann, Olly Von Flint, Attila Horbiger and Elga Brink; (France): Jean Gabin, Madeleine Renaud and Gustaf Grundgens.

THE TUNNEL (1935) see THE TRANS-ATLANTIC TUNNEL (1935)

TUNNELLING THE ENGLISH CHANNEL (1907) An ever-popular
subject, Georges Méliès presents this as the dream of two leaders, King Edward VII and President Fallières. But in Méliès's vision of things a train crash and the pressure of the sea above destroy the tunnel.

With George Méliès and Fernande Albany.

IL TUNNEL SOTTO IL MONDO
(1968) see THE TUNNEL UNDER THE WORLD (1968)

LE TUNNEL SOUS LA MANCHE
(1907) see TUNNELLING THE ENG-LISH CHANNEL (1907)

THE TUNNEL UNDER THE WORLD (1968) Rather lame adaptation
of Fred Pohl's excellent short story, con-cerned with the manipulation by a giant corporation of a town – a town which proves to be the testing ground for con-sumer products.

P★★	T★	E★	A★

Directed by Luigi Cozzi. Written by Alfredo Castelli and Tito Monezo. Special Effects by Roberto Scarpa, Studio Marosi and Sergio Zam-boni. With Alberto Morso, Bruno Salviero, Anna Mantovani and Lello Maraniello.

TURISTAS INTERPLANETAR-IOS (1960) see INTERPLANETARY
TOURISTS (1960)

TURKEY SHOOT (1982) Set in the future, *Turkey Shoot* uses the age-old plot of the man-hunt with little or nothing else to raise it from the dust. Interns of a concentration camp for civil convicts are let loose in twos and threes and pursued by fat politicians and overseers, who hunt them down with a variety of weapons. One of the prey manages to turn the tables on his trackers and a successful prison revolt is engineered. Nude shower scenes presumably titillate viewers who normally watch soap operas. Poor effects.

P	T★	E★	A

Directed by Brian Trenchard Smith. With Steve Railsback and Olivia Hussey. (GDK)

THE TWELVE-HANDED MEN OF MARS (1964) *see* THE MARTIANS ARRIVED (1964)

12 TO THE MOON (1960) An internationally mounted expedition to the Moon encounters beings who threaten to freeze Earth unless we give up war.

P★	T★★	E★	A★

Directed by David Bradley. Written by DeWitt Boden. Special Effects by Howard A. Anderson and E. Nicholson. With Ken Clark, Anthony Dexter, Tom Conway and Francis X. Bushman.

A TWENTIETH CENTURY SUR-GEON (1897) Delightful comic short about a surgeon's tinkering with nature, as a tramp finds first his legs and then the rest of his body replaced.

Directed, written by and starring George Méliès.

20 FACES (1957) Japanese futuristic thriller about a villain who can change faces and who, in an attempt to steal atomic power, uses an armoury of devices (including robot beetles and man-made monsters).

P★	T★	E★	A★

Directed by Hideo Sekigawa. Written by Tadashi Ogawa. With Eiji Okada, Juan Usami, Takashi Kanda, Masako Nakamura and Mitsue Komiya.

TWENTY MILLION MILES TO EARTH (1957) An Earth expedition to Venus crashes into the sea off Italy, losing its specimen of Venusian life. The egg of the creature hatches and a giant, lizard-like creature, Ymir, results, growing furiously until the military get him in the Colosseum in Rome.

P★	T★★	E★★	A

Directed by Nathan Juran. Written by Bob Williams and Christopher Knopf, from a story by Charlotte Knight and Ray Harryhausen. Special Effects by Ray Harryhausen. With William Hopper, Joan Taylor and Frank Puglia.

THE 27TH DAY (1956) A silly idea which would work better as a story than a film. Aliens give five people weapons capable of destroying all human life, then let them choose whether or not to use them. The capsule-weapons have a life-cycle of 27 days before they become inert, and the aliens hope Mankind will (via these five) kill themselves and allow the aliens to take over. Its main point of interest is its deep anti-Soviet theme; the Soviets declare war and the capsules are used, the meek inheriting the Earth.

P★	T★★	E★★	A★

Directed by William Asher. Written by John Mantley. With Gene Barry, Valerie French, George Voskovec and Arnold Moss.

TWENTY THOUSAND LEAGUES UNDER THE SEA (1905) First cinematic version of Verne's novel about Nemo and the Nautilus.

A scene from 20,000 Leagues Under The Sea *(1905 version)*

TWENTY THOUSAND LEAGUES UNDER THE SEA (1907) *see* UNDER THE SEAS (1907)

20,000 LEAGUES UNDER THE SEA (1916) A lengthy (almost two-hour) version of the Nemo legend, describing his origins as an Indian prince, his underwater empire, the existence of his daughter on an isolated island, and depicting various of his adventures in the *Nautilus*. Based partly on Verne's novel, *L'Ile Mystérieuse*.

Directed and written by Eugene Gaudio. With Allen Holubar, Matt Moore and Jane Gail.

20,000 LEAGUES UNDER THE SEA (1954) This colourful, all-action version of Jules Verne's novel is Disney at its best; director Richard Fleischer's almost juvenile approach to his source material perfectly suited. Set in the late nineteenth century it chronicles some of the adventures of the atomic-powered submarine, the *Nautilus*, whose mysterious captain, Nemo (James Mason), is also Emperor of the Ocean's floor. Battles with a giant squid and a finale which has Nemo's island hideout blown sky-high are highlights, and one can only really complain about the casting of Kirk Douglas as the shipwrecked harpoonist.

P★★   T★★★   E★★★★   A★★

Written by Earl Fenton. Special Effects by John Hench, Josh Meador and Ub Iwerks. With Paul Lukas, Peter Lorre and Robert J. Wilke.

TWICE UPON A TIME (1969) A chilling thriller about a man who discovers a video film from the future showing his own murder. A great idea given a less than adequate presentation.

P★★★   T★★   E★★   A★

Directed by Andre Farwagi. Written by Farwagi and Alain Morineau. With Anna Karina, Bruno Cemer, Jean Rochefort and Catherine Rich.

TWILIGHT PEOPLE (1971) Roger Corman was executive director on this Moreau-influenced movie about a mad scientist on an isolated South Pacific island trying to create the super-man by experiments in vivisection.

P★   T★   E★   A★

Directed by Eddie Romero. Written by Jerome Small and Eddie Romero. Special Optical Effects by Richard Abelardo. With John Ashley, Pat Woodell, Jan Merlin and Pam Grier.

TWILIGHT ZONE — THE MOVIE (1983) No escaping it ... There remains a dreadful pall over this attempt at an anthology of stories. It started out as "a lark", said Spielberg. Instead, it created its own horrorshow during shooting on 23 July 1982, when Vic Morrow and two Vietnamese child extras were killed (two of the trio being decapitated) by a crashing helicopter. This horrendous accident cannot be forgotten, particularly as the episode in question, the movie's only new story (from Landis) forms the first act and the least effective or coherent. Spielberg, last to shoot, when the pall was still tangibly thick, understandably lacks much gusto; although *Kick The Can* (by George Clayton Johnson, 1962) suits the wunderkind's ethos of touching the child within us. With everything to play for, the winners are the outsiders: a pre-*Gremlins* (q.v.) Dante creates vivid live-action cartoon from *It's A Good Life* (Jerome Bixby, 1961) around a bright boy, Jeremy Licht, who should have been lighting up more films than he has since. Best of all, the last-minute invitee, *Mad Max*'s Dad ... George Miller takes Richard Matheson's *Nightmare at 20,000 Ft.* to the heights of (hilarious) paranoia, far beyond that played by a dullard William Shatner in 1963. This is due to an inspired John Lithgow occupying Shatner's old airline seat. Even before glimpsing a gremlin on the wing, Lithgow's fear-of-flying visage is unforgettable – and obviously won him his fear-of-space-walking astronaut in *2010* (q.v.). Not quite Rod Serling's 1959–64 "dimension as vast as space and timeless as infinity". More a reminder that anthologies work best on the box, in the wee small hours, which explains why Walter Hill (Bartel, Scorsese, *et al*) scrapped his similar notion and Spielberg is producing 44 *Amazing Stories* for TV.

P★★   T★★   E★★   A★★

Produced by Steven Spielberg and John Landis. Directed by Landis and Spielberg, Joe Dante and George Miller. Written by Landis, Richard Matheson, George Clayton Johnson and Josh Rogan. Effects: *Prologue*: Special Effects by Mike Wood. *Segment 1*: Special Effects by Paul Stewart. Make-up by Craig Reardon. *Segment 3*: Special Make-up by Rob Bottin and Craig Reardon. *Segment 4*: Special Make-up Michael McCracken. Visual Effects by Peter Kuran, Jim Danforth and David Allan. With Vic Morrow, Scatman Crothers, Kathleen Quinlan, Kevin McCarthy, Abbe Lane, Dan Aykroyd and Albert Brooks. (TC)

TWO COSMONAUTS AGAINST THEIR WILL (1967) When the Russians lose contact with the two cosmonauts they sent to the Moon, they decide to send up two more to welcome home. Only the first two aren't lost . . .

P★   T★   E★   A★

Directed by Lucio Fulci. Written by Vittorio Metz, Jose Luis Dibildos and Amedeo Sollazo. With Franco Franchi and Ciccio Ingrassia.

THE TWO FACES OF DR JEKYLL (1960) A fairly straightforward version of the Stevenson story with a good script by Wolf Mankovitz. Hammer studios and director Terence Fisher seemed at the height of their powers when this was made.

P★★★   T★★★   E★★★   A★★

Make-up by Roy Ashton. With Paul Massie, Dawn Addams, Christopher Lee, David Kossof and Oliver Reed.

THE TWO MAFIOSI FROM THE FBI (1966) *see* DR GOLDFOOT AND THE GIRL BOMBS (1966)

THE TWONKY (1952) The Twonky is a meddlesome creature from the future which invades a present-day man's TV set and attempts to protect and perfect its new master. But its master hates the Twonky and destroys it. Based on Lewis Padgett's short story (alias Henry Kuttner).

P★★★   T★★   E★★   A★

Produced, directed and written by Arch Oboler. With Hans Conried, Bill Lynn and Gloria Blondell.

2 × 5: MISSION HYDRA (1966) A spaceship from Hydra lands in Italy and

kidnaps some humans, but aliens and humans unite in the face of a greater threat.

P★   T★   E★   A

Directed by Pietro Francisci. Written by Francisci, Ermanno Curti and Aldo Calamara. With Leonor Curtis, Antony Freeman and Kirk Morris.

2001: A SPACE ODYSSEY (1968) My own feeling is that the true science fiction film *began* with this joint Stanley Kubrick, Arthur C. Clarke venture. Everything previous – even the worthy stuff – was Sci-Fi. This was the first real hybrid of cinematic technique and literary science fiction. Intelligent, accurate, brilliantly visual and – perhaps its saving grace – ultimately mystical. The special effects prefigured everything that has been done in the last 15 years – and in most cases haven't really been bettered – while the storyline remains quite unique in its breadth and scope; for this is no less a story than the evolution of Mankind, *Homo sapiens*, from Ape to Starchild. *2001* is, of necessity, five separate but inter-linked films. The first film deals with the "Dawn Of Man", some 4 million years ago. Amongst the tribes of apes appears a mysterious huge black obelisk which seems to awaken the consciousness of one of the apes such that he begins to use the bones of animals as weapons to kill meat (thus increasing the protein diet of his tribe) and fight off their rivals for the water-hole. In a memorable scene he casts a bone high into the air and at its zenith we cut to the second sequence, set some 30 years or so in our future, in 1999. The bone is transposed into a space shuttle seen heading towards a giant orbital spacecraft which is circling the Earth like a vast carousel. Strauss's "Thus Spake Zarathustra" is replaced by the "Blue Danube" as we waltz silently through space. Bald, symbolic story-telling has been replaced by a sophisticated exhibition of gimmickry as we become tourists on a future shuttle flight to the Moon. Dr Heywood R. Floyd (William Sylvester), a member of the National Council of Aeronautics, is going to Clavius Base to investigate a strange occurrence there. There's a

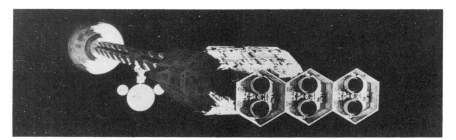

The Discovery *in a scene from* 2001: A Space Odyssey

semi-documentary feel to this section of the film (perhaps the weakest part of this epic) which ends with a second confrontation with one of the black obelisks as it sends out a pulsed signal towards Jupiter. The third film deals with the journey of the Jupiter Mission ship *Discovery 1* some 18 months later. Three of its crew are in hibernation while Commander Dave Bowman (Keir Dullea) and his assistant, Frank Poole (Gary Lockwood) run the ship. Or oversee it, to be more precise, because charge of the ship is firmly in the hands of HAL 9000, one of a new generation of super-computers with massive brain capacity and an almost-human personality. HAL is both the hero and villain of this third segment, his professed infallibility and his ultimate nervous breakdown providing the drama here as the ship nears Jupiter and the great enigma. Dave Bowman succeeds, after being shut outside the ship, in getting back in and switching off HAL (another notable sequence in which HAL regresses as if to childhood, singing "Daisy" as it runs down). But with HAL gone the ship is crippled and merely drifts towards Jupiter. Film four is often called "the light show" because of its lengthy sequence of unexplained visuals. In the novelization Clarke took care to explain what was happening here, but it's probably best to ignore that and take the experience on its own terms. As the planets coincide (a moment that parallels the film's opening shot) Dave Bowman is shot through some kind of warp in space – a doorway, perhaps – and travels what seem galactic distances to an uncharted, unexplained

destination. We see alien worlds, the sense of their strangeness achieved by strange colorations for natural phenomena: mauve skies, neon-green seas. Then, with Dave, we are inside a suite of rooms, as if in some eighteenth-century hotel. The pod sits incongruously beside baroque furniture; eighteenth-century paintings adorn the walls. In the next room sits an older version of Bowman, eating a meal like a guest at a spa. It is the film's most surreal section. Then we see Bowman as an extremely aged man – in his nineties it seems – at the moment of death confronting the obelisk again and . . . becoming the starchild. The film then closes with the foetal starchild gazing down in wonder at the Earth. This fifth, final section seems to bring us full circle, to another new awakening for Man – a new stage of evolution, once more sparked off by the enigmatic obelisk. If it were only about the technology *2001* would be a rather dull, showy film. Its significance lies in the way it takes all of these disparate parts and moulds them into a highly potent statement about Mankind and its development. Its perspectives are huge and force us not to look at the smallness of single lives but at the development of a species. This can, of course, be a flaw. Clarke, as a writer, was always weak in his characterization, and that weakness transfers itself to this film. But it's a forgivable weakness in view of what we're being given here. What so many sf films talk about – usually in stilted dialogue about sizes and ages of things – *2001* enacts.

P★★★★   T★★★★★   E★★★★   A★★★

Produced and directed by Stanley Kubrick. Production Design by Tony Masters, Harry Lange and Ernest Archer. Special Effects by Stanley Kubrick, Wally Veevers, Douglas Trumbull, Con Pederson, Tom Howard. With Douglas Rain (voice of HAL 9000), Dan Richter, Leonard Rossiter, Margaret Tyzack and Robert Beatty.

2010 (1984) If there were flaws with *2001* they were that the film was too episodic and the characters too thinly drawn, too cardboard. The spectacle and the grand story of Mankind's evolution – with its schizophrenic connection between knowledge and aggression – were enough, however, to make the film quite outstanding. Sixteen years later in real time (nine in fiction) comes the direct sequel to Kubrick's epic, this time produced, directed and written by Peter Hyams. And this time from an already existent novel by Arthur C. Clarke (*2001* was developed by Clarke and Kubrick from Clarke's 1953 short story, "The Sentinel"). The difference is immediately apparent. Characterization is strong, the storyline tense, effective and, all important, homogenous. The spectacle becomes secondary as we are engrossed in the voyage of the Russian spacecraft, the *Leonov*, to rendezvous with the abandoned *Discovery* near Jupiter and what it discovers in doing so. This is not to say that the special effects are poor by comparison with *2001*, if anything they're several degrees better – the inside of *Leonov* and its manoeuvres are thoroughly convincing – but the accent is no longer on spectacle. The new emphasis is upon the marvellous, mystical event that ultimately turns Jupiter into a second sun, burning in the Earth's night sky. In *2001* Dr Heywood Floyd, played there by William Sylvester, was a rather anonymous-seeming bureaucrat in charge of the Jupiter Mission. In *2010* Roy Scheider takes on a more dynamic role as Heywood; this time as a man who, made the scapegoat for the first Mission's apparent failure, gets back in on the act when he learns that the Russians have built a craft which will rendezvous with the *Discovery* long before the Americans can get a ship out to Jupiter. Learning that the *Discovery* is on a decaying orbit and will soon fall into one of Jupiter's satellites, and that the Russians need help to reactivate *Discovery*'s

systems (and particularly HAL 9000), Heywood persuades his government to let him and two other experts, Walter Curnow (John Lithgow) and Dr Chandra (Bob Balaban) join the Russian crew. Two days out from their destination Floyd is woken up from hibernation by the Russian crew (headed by Tanya Kirbuk, played superbly by Helen Mirren) to try to help explain a strange phenomenon occurring on the moon Europa. A probe makes a close approach towards what seems like a source of life and is greeted by what seems like a warning shot – an effect rather like a brilliantly white shooting star hurtles out and past the *Leonov*. Unable to investigate this further, the *Leonov* goes on to "brake" by entering the periphery of Jupiter's atmosphere – a dangerous, brilliantly realized manoeuvre that (along with *The Right Stuff*) is one of the highlights of realism in the cinema of space fiction. Their speed successfully slowed, they rendezvous with *Discovery* and reactivate both the ship and HAL. In space all seems to be going well, but back on Earth things have degenerated badly and a US naval blockade on the Honduras has led to an open confrontation between America and Russia, with a Russian warship sunk and an American satellite shot down. World War Three seems imminent and orders are given for the crew members to go to their own respective ships and break off all contact. It's a scene more effective even than the novel in demonstrating how ludicrous the East/West division is – a re-enactment of the ape tribes of *2001*'s opening sequence, squabbling over the waterhole. It also underlines what is *2010*'s principal message: "Cooperate Or Else". From an initial atmosphere of paranoic mistrust, the Russian and American crew members had grown to like and respect one another: their joint quest for knowledge had eroded the underlying aggression of their nationalities. This moment of crystallization underlines the absurdity of nationalism and, in a moment poignant with symbolism, the bridge between the craft floats free. It is at this low point that Clarke plays his mystical ace, having Dave Bowman (changed dramatically by his contact with

Keir Dullea as Dave Bowman in 2010

the unspecified aliens) return to the *Discovery* to contact Floyd and tell him that they must leave Jupiter within two days. Floyd returns to the Russian ship, persuades them to ignore nationalistic rivalries and – using a nice touch of scientific logistics – gets them to link up with *Discovery* again to get out of orbit and head back to Earth. In a scene in which HAL is "redeemed" (the seemingly malicious behaviour of *2001* is explained as National Security Council meddling with his essential truthfulness) they escape, just as Jupiter is eaten up by the enigmatic black obelisks (with their 1,4,9 ratio) and turned into a sun. It's a marvellous ending, even if the aliens' message – ALL THESE WORLDS ARE YOURS – EXCEPT EUROPA – is merely a variation on Cooperate Or Else. And there's one last twist reserved for a beautifully visual last scene (a scene which returns us, in one sense, to the opening sequence of *2001*), where we see rudimentary life developing on Europa. Are we, it suggests, the result of an alien experiment? Were we begun by these mysterious benefactors in the same way that life was seeded on Europa, where no life existed previously? It's hard to judge, yet, whether *2010* is the classic of sf cinema. What is undoubted is that it is the most scientific sf film yet made and, in respect of visuals and accuracy, it is unmatched. It's genuinely dramatic without resorting to space opera (à la *Star Wars*) (q.v.) or melodrama (à la *Dune*) (q.v.) and its character studies are mature and sophisticated. Mention should be made of Elya Baskin's warming performance as "Max", the Russian who is

"lost" when investigating the giant 2-kilometre-long obelisk. But credit overall goes to Hyams for transforming a first-rate novel into an even better film.

P★★★★   T★★★★★   E★★★★★   A★★★★

Visual Effects by Richard Edlund. Visual Futurist Syd Mead. Special Effects by Entertainment Effects Group, Los Angeles. Key Effects by Man Bob Spurlock. Cinematography by Peter Hyams. With Keir Dullea, Dougls Rain (the voice of Hal), Madolyn Smith, Dana Elcar, Taliesin Jaffe, James McEachin, Mary Jo Deschanel, Savely Kramarov, Oleg Rudnik, Natasha Schneider, Vladimir Skomarovsky, Victor Steinbach and Jan Triska.

2019: AFTER THE FALL OF NEW YORK (1983) Italian production by Luciano Martino (a modern-day Antonio Margheriti) set 20 years after the Holocaust. Eurac (Europe/Africa/Asia) have bombed the PanAmerican confederacy out of existence – or nearly so – the remnants plan to fly to Alpha Centauri and set up life there with the help of the last fertile woman. But at present she's in Manhattan, a Eurac-controlled area. The PanAm president sends in Mad-Max-like Parsifal (Michael Sopkiw) and friends to get her out. A confusing, episodic and often rambling adventure demonstrates its essential ignorance by mixing gratuitous violence with pseudo-philosophy and High School polemic. Ape-men, dwarves, spiky cars, mutants and lots of rats provide the local colour.

P★   T★★★   E★★   A

Directed by Martin Dolman. Written by Julian Berry, Martin Dolman and Gabriel Rossini. With Valentine Monnier and Anna Kanakis.

2069: A SEX ODYSSEY (1973) Sexploitation movie of the shoddiest kind, as women from Venus come to mate with Earthmen to keep their species alive.

P   T★   E★   A

Directed by Hans Sternbeck. Written by Willy Pribil. With Nina Frederic.

2889 (1966) *see* IN THE YEAR 2889 (1966)

THE TWO WORLDS OF JENNY LOGAN (1979) A year after she gave up being TV's Bionic Woman, Lindsay Wagner made this moderately intelligent if slow-paced time-travel story. Schizophrenia or genuine travel into a past age? The paintings behind the attic wall reveal that it all *was* real. A nice cameo by *Dallas*'s Linda Gray as Aunt Betty/Elizabeth. Similarities to *Somewhere In Time* (q.v.) do strike you, but this is filmed from David Williams's novel *Second Sight*.

P★★	T★	E★★	A★

Directed and written by Frank de Fellita. Make-up by Stan Winston. With Marc Singer.

UCHU DAIKAIJU GUILALA (1967) *see* THE X FROM OUTER SPACE (1967)

UCHU DAI SENSO (1959) *see* BATTLE IN OUTER SPACE (1959)

UCHUI DAIKAYU DOGORA (1964) *see* DAGORA THE SPACE MONSTER (1964)

UCHUJIN TOKYO NI ARAWARU (1956) *see* MYSTERIOUS SATELLITE (1956)

UCHU KAISOKU-SEN (1961) *see* INVASION OF THE NEPTUNE MEN (1961)

UFO (1979) *see* THE SPACEMAN AND KING ARTHUR (1979)

THE ULTIMATE WARRIOR (1975) The Baron (Max Von Sydow) runs a peaceful commune in the midst of post-Collapse New York, a.d. 2012. Behind barricaded walls he is rebuilding a small patch of civilization, but the attempt is failing. He calls upon mercenary Carson (Yul Brynner) to help him fight off Carrott and his gang of mean street-punks who want to take over the commune. Carson, attracted by the offer of cigars, accepts and for a time prevents Carrott from destroying the commune. But he is only buying time, and when the Baron asks him to take his pregnant daughter out, he does so – fighting off the gang in New York's subway system. Compared to what followed in the way of devastated-New-York films, this is tame, but Brynner is utterly convincing as the intelligent killer, the perfect fighting machine.

P★★★	T★★	E★★	A★★

Directed and written by Robert Clouse. With Joanna Miles and Richard Kelton.

L'ULTIMO UOMO DELLA TERRA (1963) *see* THE LAST MAN ON EARTH (1963)

THE UNDERWATER CITY (1961) A project to build an underwater city goes disastrously wrong when the Ocean floor collapses beneath it. So it goes. A thoroughly poor film.

P★	T★	E★	A

Directed by Frank McDonald. Written by Owen Harris. Special Effects by Howard C. Lydecker and Howard A. Anderson. With William Lundigan, Julie Adams, Roy Roberts and Paul Dubov.

L'UMANOIDE (1979) *see* THE HUMANOID (1979)

UNDER THE SEAS (1907) George Méliès adapts Verne's 20,000 Leagues to 200,000 for a visually exciting journey to the seabed.

With the Corps de Ballet du Chatelet.

UNDERWATER WARSHIP (1963) *see* ATRAGON (1963)

THE UNEARTHLY (1957) Mad scientist (John Carradine) seeks immorality by glandular operation technique, but creates only immortal monsters, who, in the film's climax, gang up on him.

P★	T★	E★	A

Directed by Brooke L. Peters. Written by Geoffrey Dennis and Jane Mann. With Allison Hayes, Myron Healey, Sally Todd and Marilyn Buferd.

UNEARTHLY STRANGER (1963)
A scientist working on a space-time project discovers that his wife is an alien,
spearheading an invasion force. Her
inability to kill him leads to her own death,
but it's implied that more aliens are
amongst us – taking over.

P★★★	T★★	E★★★	A★★

Directed by John Krish. Written by Rex Carlton.
With John Neville, Gabriella Lucidi, Philip Stone,
Patrick Newell, Jean Marsh and Warren Mitchell.

**DIE UNHEIMLICHEN HANDE
DES DR ORLAK** (1925) *see* THE
HANDS OF ORLAC (1925)

UNHOLY LOVE (1928) *see* ALRAUNE
(1928)

**UNIDENTIFIED FLYING ODD-
BALL** (1979) *see* THE SPACEMAN
AND KING ARTHUR (1979)

UNINHABITED PLANET (1962)
Eleven-minute Polish animation of a
Stanislaw Lem tale, depicting the adventures of a robot on an "Uninhabited"
planet.

Directed and designed by Krzysztof Debowski.
Written by Stanislaw Lem.

THE UNKNOWN HOUR (1964)
Spanish film of an atomic accident which
devastates one of their cities.

Directed and written by Mariano Ozores. With
Emma Penella and José Luis Ozores.

UNKNOWN ISLAND (1948) Uninspired variation on the Lost World theme:
an island with dinosaurs and giant sloth.

P★	T★	E★	A

Directed by Jack Bernhard. Written by R. T.
Shannon and Jack Harvey. With Virginia Grey,
Barton MacLane and Phillip Reed.

UNKNOWN PEOPLE (1951) *see*
SUPERMAN AND THE MOLE
PEOPLE (1951)

THE UNKNOWN PURPLE (1923)
Framed scientist makes himself invisible
on his release from prison. Pursues ex-
wife and lover and gets revenge.

P★★	T★★	E★	A★

Directed by Roland West. Written by West and
Paul Schofield. With Henry B. Walthall, Johnny
Arthur, Dorothy Phillips and Alice Lake.

THE UNKNOWN TERROR (1957)
Set in the "legendary cave of death" on a
Caribbean island, this is about experimen-
tation with hallucinogenic fungi, which
turns the native population into walking
fungoid creatures. The island blows up
before it can spread. Phew! Special effects
are particularly dire.

P	T	E★	A

Directed by Charles Marquis Warren. Written by
Kenneth Higgins. With John Howard, Mala
Powers, Paul Richards and May Wynn.

UNKNOWN WORLD (1950) A scientific talk-over fails to conceal a hideous
lack of geophysical facts in this ludicrous
but enjoyable story of a scientific expedition to find a refuge from nuclear war,
deep in the Earth (1,640 miles to be
precise!). Its anti-nuclear arguments are
cogent but its plot is inane.

P★	T★★	E★★	A

Directed by Terrell O. Morse. Written by Millard
Kaufman. Special Effects by J. R. Rabin & I. A.
Block. Mechanical Effects by Willis Cook. With
Bruce Kellogg, Marilyn Nash and Victor Killian.

UNNATURAL (1952) *see* ALRAUNE
(1952)

DER UNSICHTBARE (1963) *see*
THE INVISIBLE TERROR (1963)

**EIN UNSICHTBARER GEHT
DURCH DIE STADT** (1933) *see* AN
INVISIBLE MAN GOES THROUGH
THE CITY (1933)

UNTAMED WOMEN (1952) One to
miss. World War Two pilot lands on
uncharted island complete with beautiful
savage women, man-eating plants, prehistoric monsters and an exploding volcano.
A dreadful use of clichés.

P	T	E	A

Directed by W. Merle Connell. Written by George
W. Sayre. Special Effects by P. Sprunck and
Alfred Schmid. With Mikel Conrad, Doris Mer-
rick, Richard Monahan and Mark Lowell.

UOMINI H (1958) *see* THE H-MAN (1958)

L'UOMO CHE VISSE DUE VOLTE (1970) *see* THE SECRET OF DR CHALMERS (1970)

L'URLO (1965) *see* THE SCREAM (1965)

THE VALLEY OF GWANGI (1968) *see* THE VALLEY WHERE TIME STOOD STILL (1968)

VALLEY OF THE DRAGONS (1961) *see* PREHISTORIC VALLEY (1961)

THE VALLEY OF THE ZOMBIES (1946) Mad scientist returns from the grave and, to prolong his life, steals blood. He's killed at the end, of course, and the only surprise is that the scientist is the only "zombie" about.

P★	T★	E★	A

Directed by Philip Ford. Written by Dorrell McGowan and Stuart McGowan. Special Effects by Howard and Theodore Lydecker. With Robert Livingston, Adrian Booth, Ian Keith, Thomas Jackson and Charles Trowbridge.

THE VALLEY WHERE TIME STOOD STILL (1968) A none too inspired twist on the lost world formula, allowing special effects man Ray Harryhausen to animate an old Willis O'Brien idea about a circus in Mexico which enters a forbidden valley full of dinosaurs and takes a few exhibits.

P★	T★★	E★	A

Directed by James O'Connolly. Written by William E. East and Julian More. With James Franciscus, Gila Golen and Richard Carlson.

THE VAMPIRE BAT (1932) The culprit isn't a vampire but a mad doctor whose "creation" needs a constant supply of fresh blood.

P★	T★	E★	A

Directed by Frank Strayer. Written by Edward T. Lowe. With Lionel Atwill, Melvyn Douglas, Fay Wray and Dwight Frye.

THE VAMPIRE BEAST CRAVES BLOOD (1967) A detective attempting to solve a string of mysterious murders discovers that a mad scientist's daughter is, in fact, a giant blood-drinking moth, for whom Daddy is constructing a mate.

P★	T★★	E★★	A★

Directed by Vernon Sewell. Written by Peter Bryan. Special Effects by Roger Dicken. Make-up by Rosemarie Peattie. With Peter Cushing, Robert Flemyng and Wanda Ventham.

VAMPIRE MEN OF THE LOST PLANET (1970) *see* HORROR OF THE BLOOD MONSTERS (1970)

VANITY'S PRICE (1924) A morality play on the rejuvenation theme. An ageing actress is made younger by a Viennese surgeon, but then finds her operation estranges her from her lover and ex-husband. The stress of this ironically ages her and a happy ending is achieved.

P★★	T★	E★★	A

Directed by Roy William Neill. Written by Paul Bern. With Anna Q. Nilsson, Stuart Holmes, Wyndham Standing and Arthur Rankin.

VARAN THE UNBELIEVABLE (1958) Varan, a giant flying prehistoric reptile, is brought back to life when a salt lake is desalinized. The army attempts to contain the monster. Rather dull fare from Toho studios.

P★	T★	E★	A

Directed by Inoshiro Honda. Written by Shinichi Sekizawa and Sid Harris. With Myron Healy, Tsuruko Kobayashi and Kozo Nomura.

THE VENETIAN AFFAIR (1966) Fairly standard spy-thriller with a rather nasty drug involved, which turns people into human zombie-like robots.

P★	T★	E★	A★

Directed by Jerry Thorpe. Written by E. Jack Newman. Special Effects by Carroll L. Shepphird. With Robert Vaughn, Elke Sommer and Boris Karloff.

VENGEANCE (1952) *see* ALRAUNE (1952)

VENGEANCE (1962) *see* THE BRAIN (1962)

VENTO DI MORTE (1963) *see* THE LAST MAN ON EARTH (1963)

THE VENUSIAN (1954) *see* IMMEDIATE DISASTER (1954)

VERLDENS UNDERGANG (1916) *see* THE END OF THE WORLD (1916)

VERY CLOSE ENCOUNTERS OF THE FOURTH KIND (1979) Inevitable sexploitation of the Spielberg epic, with little to recommend itself. Soft porn with the scantiest sf clothing.

P	T★	E★	A

Directed by Mario Garriazo. Written by Garriazo and Augusto Finnocchi. With Maria Baxa, Monica Zanchi and Marina Duania.

DOS VIAJEROS DEL ESPACIO (1960) *see* INTERPLANETARY TOURISTS (1960)

VIDEODROME (1982) If there is a side darker than Hitchcock's it's Cronenberg's. At last, he slips it loose and gloriously comes of age. (So, it flopped, of course.) More a warning than any attack on the tube, it's a mite late. *Dallas* warps more minds than Max Renn's kinky Civic TV (more boob than tube). How long, then, before O'Blivion's Mission for tele-addicts becomes reality? TV has gone to pot; a cypher here for social/personal responsibility. Brilliantly assisted by Rick Baker and Jimmy Woods as Max, Cronenberg's Eighth, written before his Third, is his most ambiguous, energetic, complex and dangerous. He doubts if he'd choose to see it, himself. Ironically, the only way we can is on cassette! (Do it.)

P★★★	T★★★★	E★★★★	A★★★★

Directed and written by David Cronenberg. With James Woods, Sonja Smits, Deborah Harry, Peter Dvorsky, Les Carlson, Jack Creley, Lynne Gorman and Julie Khaner. (TC)

VILLAGE OF THE DAMNED (1960) A cut above most of the Wyndham adaptations to appear on the big screen, this is Wolf Rilla's version of *The Midwich Cuckoos*, and if it's a largely successful attempt at that chilling little tale, it's because Rilla, who co-wrote the script with Sterling Silliphant and George Barclay, had the sense to employ that most Wyndhamesque of British virtues, modesty. The sleepy little English village of Midwich becomes even sleepier one day, for no apparent reason; when the inhabitants awake from their 24-hour blackout, all of the women are pregnant. It sounds like the beginning of a bar-room joke, but the mass impregnations have an alien origin, and when the new children start to be born they prove to be blond-haired, golden-eyed beings, with telepathy amongst the least of their bizarre mental powers. We are told, never shown, that the same has occurred in villages all over the world, and an identical pattern repeats itself in each, the adults find themselves slaves to the children; the theme is that classic science fiction mainstay, not of alien invasion, but of the horror of great power being invested in something as amoral as a child. (Jerome Bixby's "It's a Good Life" and Stephen King's *Carrie* are two of the successful examinations of that allegorical theme.) It's this turning of tables that is the unsettling element. *Village of the Damned* might easily have become risible with its spectacle of adults cowering before a group of deadpan kiddies half their size, but Rilla's sense of restraint prevails. He turns the children's natural cuteness in on itself to give us a chilling vision of the bland, remote little monsters. Nobody bothers to explain exactly where the children came from, or what they precisely plan to do, and you end up so riveted you don't precisely care.

P★★★	T★★★	E★★★★★	A★★

Special Effects by Tom Howard. With George Sanders, Martin Stephens, Barbara Shelley, Michael Gwynne, Laurence Naismith, Richard Vernon and John Phillips. (TR)

VILLAGE OF THE GIANTS (1965) Based very loosely on Wells's *The Food Of*

The Gods, Bert I. Gordon delivers something slightly more than his usual pap here in this story of teenagers grown huge who terrorize a small town.

P★	T★	E★★	A

Written by Alan Caillon. Special Effects by Bert and Flora Gordon. With Tommy Kirk, Charla Doherty, Johnny Crawford and Timmy Rooney.

THE VIRGIN PRESIDENT (1967)

Rather poor and slightly incredible notion of a future America, governed by an ineffectual president, invaded and conquered by Ecuador.

P★	T	E★	A

Produced and directed by Graeme Ferguson. Written by Ferguson and Severn Darden. With Severn Darden, Peter Boyle and Conrad Yama.

VIRUS (1980) Overcomplex end-of-the-world story. MM-88, a "DNA" reconstitutor, can mimic any form of virus and make that virus more toxic and faster-breeding. It has no known antidote, and becomes active when exposed to air above −10°C. Suffice to say it gets loose and everyone but 800-plus people in Antarctica are killed. *On The Beach* (q.v.) style scenes with subs lead into another thriller element involving a self-controlled computer weapons system, earthquakes epicentred on Washington (where the weapons trigger is) and a second Disaster, almost avoided. The world blows up but – as we know from the opening scene – the Japanese hero survives, in a dead world. Simplified, it might have been all right, but as it is it's tedious.

P★★	T★★★	E★★	A★

Directed by Kuiji Fukasaku. Written by Koji Takada, Gregory Knapp and Fukasaku (based on the novel, *Fukkatsu No Hi* by Sakyo Komatsu). With Chuck Connors, Glenn Ford, Olivia Hussey, George Kennedy, Masao Kusakari, Edward J. Olmos, Henry Silva, Bo Svenson and Robert Vaughn.

VISITORS FROM THE GALAXY

(1981) A young boy begins to turn his favourite fictional aliens into living entities. Trouble, naturally, results until time itself is reversed and the damage healed. Yugoslavian juvenile.

P★	T★★	E★	A★

Directed by Dusan Vukotic. Written by Vukotic and Milos Macourek. With Zarko Potocnjak, Lucie Zulova and Ljubisa Samardzic.

A VISITOR FROM VENUS (1954)

see IMMEDIATE DISASTER (1954)

VISIT TO A SMALL PLANET

(1959) Based on Gore Vidal's satirical play, this is killed stone dead by Jerry Lewis's inane portrayal of an alien humanoid visiting Earth and falling in love (with Joan Blackman) before returning home.

P★★	T★★	E★	A

Directed by Norman Taurog. Written by Edmund Beloin and Henry Garson. Special Effects by John P. Fulton. Make-up by Wally Westmore. With Earl Holliman, Gale Gordon and Fred Clark.

THE VOLCANO MONSTER (1955)

see GIGANTIS, THE FIRE MONSTER (1955)

VOODOO BLOOD BATH (1964) *see* I EAT YOUR SKIN (1964)

VOODOO WOMAN (1956) Awful, silly mad scientist film. The insane doctor here is trying to create obedient female killers under his telepathic command, but fails, producing only shambling monsters.

P	T	E	A

Directed by Edward L. Cahn. Written by Russell Bender and V. I. Voss. With Marla English, Tom Conway, Touch Connors and Lance Fuller.

A VOYAGE AROUND A STAR

(1906) Like most early shorts, this is essentially fantasy: an astronomer sails away to another star in a huge soap bubble, then is thrown back to Earth and killed by an angry god.

Directed by Gaston Velle.

LE VOYAGE A TRAVERS L'IMPOSSIBLE (1904) *see* AN IMPOSSIBLE VOYAGE (1904)

VOYAGE AUTOUR D'UNE ETOILE (1906) *see* VOYAGE AROUND A STAR (1906)

VOYAGE BEYOND THE SUN
(1965) *see* SPACE MONSTER (1965)

LE VOYAGE DANS LA LUNE
(1902) *see* A TRIP TO THE MOON (1902)

VOYAGE INTO SPACE (1965)
Cheap-budget Japanese monster movie, a feature-length version of a popular TV series. A young boy and his giant robot battle the evil emperor from space who is out to control the universe.

P★	T	E	A

Produced and directed by Savatore Billitteri. With Mitsunobu Kaneko and Akiro Tito.

VOYAGE TO THE BOTTOM OF THE SEA (1961) The film which spawned the TV series. A super-sub comes to the surface (after fighting giant squids, etc) and finds the Van Allen Belt on fire and the polar icecaps about to melt. Against opposition they manage to put out the fire and save Earth.

P★	T★★	E★★	A★

Produced and directed by Irwin Allen. Written by Allen and Charles Bennett. Special Effects by L. B. Abbott. With Walter Pidgeon, Joan Fontaine, Peter Lorre, Barbara Eden and Frankie Avalon.

VOYAGE TO THE END OF THE UNIVERSE (1963) *see* IKARIE XB1 (1963)

THE VOYAGE TO THE MOON
(1902) *see* A TRIP TO THE MOON (1902)

VOYAGE TO THE OUTER PLANETS (1973) An sf documentary, notable for having John Dykstra (*Star Wars*) as its special effects cinematographer. A simple description of a future exploration of the outer planets of the solar system.

Directed and written by Colin Cantwell.

VOYAGE TO THE PLANET OF PREHISTORIC WOMEN (1966)
Producer Roger Corman bought up footage from *Planet Of Storms* (1962) (q.v.) and built a vague narrative structure around it; a cheap means of constructing a reason-able B-movie. An expedition of Earth men land on the prehistoric planet, kill the women's god and are driven from the planet. Encounters with robots, lizard-men and prehistoric monsters make this an interesting experience.

P★	T★★	E★★	A★

Directed and narrated by Peter Bogdanovich. Written by Henry Ney. Make-up by Mary Jo Wier. With Mamie van Doren and Mary Mark.

VOYAGE TO THE PREHISTORIC PLANET (1965) Roger Corman's exploitation of footage from the Russian film, *Planet Of Storms* (1962) (q.v.). An Earth spaceship crash-lands on an alien planet and encounters aliens, dinosaurs, lizard-men and a robot, as in the later *Voyage To The Planet Of Prehistoric Women* (1966) (q.v.).

P★	T★	E★	A

Directed and written by John Sebastian. With Basil Rathbone and Faith Domergue.

THE VULTURE (1966) Following the success of the awful *Fly* films, this production used the same idea – experiments with a matter transmitter – to blend a man and a vulture (200 years old, to boot!) which then terrorizes the local (Cornish) inhabitants.

P★	T★	E★	A

Produced, directed and written by Lawrence Huntingdon. Make-up by Geoffrey Rodway. With Robert Hutton, Akim Tamiroff, Broderick Crawford and Diane Clare.

VYNALEZ ZHAKY (1958) *see* THE FABULOUS WORLD OF JULES VERNE (1958)

THE WALKING DEAD (1936) Boris Karloff plays the man framed for a murder, executed, then brought back to life by a doctor. Recovered, he pursues the real murderers and frightens them to death before returning to the peace of his own grave. A good working of this theme.

P★★	T★★	E★★	A★

Directed by Michael Curtiz. Written by Ewart Adamson and Joseph Fields. With Edmund Gwenn and Margurite Churchill.

WANGMAGWI (1967) Korean version of the Japanese monster movie with a monster 500 times the size of a man sent by aliens to conquer the world. To begin with he treads on Seoul and crushes it. Thoroughly poor.

P	T	E	A

Directed by Hynkjin Kwon. Written by Hayong Byun. Special Effects by Soonjai Byun. With Kungwon Nam, Haekyung Kim and Unjin Hahn.

WAR (1960) Yugoslavian anti-nuclear war film, revolving about the dropping of the bomb upon a city and the reactions of a newly wedded couple to the catastrophe.

P★★	T★★	E★	A★

Directed by Veljko Buljic. Written by Blazenka Jencik, from a story by Cesat Zavattini. With Eva Krizevska, Anton Vrdoljak and Ita Rina.

WAR BETWEEN THE PLANETS (1965) Director/producer Antonio Margheriti was responsible for several of this kind of spaghetti-sci-fi tale. Here the woodenly overdubbed cast of never-to-make-its destroy a rogue asteroid (the insides of which resemble a giant pasta dish) with an anti-matter bomb, thereby saving Earth from total ruin. The funniest scenes, however, are those where the space crew dangle from visible threads, supposedly in space.

P	T	E★	A

Written by Ivan Reiner. With Giacomo Rossi-Stuart (Jack Stuart), Ombretta Colli (Amber Collins), Halina Zalewska and Freddy Unger.

THE WAR GAME (1965) What is *The War Game* to us now? It has the cachet of being banned by its original commissioners, the BBC. As a film, its grainy and in every sense monochrome British "realism" is heavily dated, and to a contemporary eye (used, like it or not, to big budgets and slickness and "production values") it has many technical awkward-

nesses. Nevertheless, it has *impact*: this pseudo-documentary view of what nuclear war would mean in 1963 can still send thrills of horror through the viewer. Refused television screening, it has still had more than 20 years of life as an effective revelation of the horrors of war. This does not necessarily say anything about the quality of this film *as a film*, but it does say something about the lack (until very recently) of competitive attempts on this theme, as well as the perennial horror of nuclear war. *The War Game* is still worth seeing.

P★★★	T★★	E★★★	A★★

Produced, directed and written by Peter Watkins. Make-up by Lilian Munro. Narrated by Michael Aspel and Dick Graham. (RS)

Matthew Broderick, Ally Sheedy and John Wood in Wargames

WARGAMES (1983) The kind of movie that just *had* to be made that year: Matthew Broderick plays an adolescent home-computer genius who accidentally taps into the machine controlling America's nuclear defence and, thinking that he has discovered a new video game, goes and starts the countdown to Armageddon. From that point on, he and his girlfriend struggle to convince the authorities that everyone's due for a Big Bang – and it would be far easier to sympathize with these teenage heroes in their flight, their plight, their burgeoning romance, if they weren't two of the most vapid brats ever to hit the silver screen. James Dean was a dumb rebel, these two are just *dumb*. Even John Wood, as a scientist who's so disillusioned he does not care if the world goes down the tubes, fails to pull our attention one iota. The action is tight, but only just, and runs the constant risk of verging over into sloppiness. And there's barely one shred of real darkness, real chill, in the entire 113 minutes save for one early sequence when the humans are kicked out of missile command and the computer originally brought in. The people have already left, what we see are their chairs being carried out; a neat, slick piece of symbolism. As what it portends to be, a moral for our times, a dreadful warning, the movie fails horribly. The control centre and the computer itself have a varicoloured prettiness, like a soufflé of flashing lights, which does little to warn us of their function, and the film is shot in a range of colours which remind us more of Disney than of Doomsday. Put the kids into a Volkswagen and it could easily have been re-titled "Herbie Destroys the Universe".

P★★   T★   E★★   A

Directed by John Badham. Written by Lawrence Lasker and Walter F. Parkes. With Matthew Broderick, Barry Corbin and Dabney Coleman. (TR)

WAR GODS OF THE DEEP (1965)
A muddled period piece about an underwater kingdom off the coast of Cornwall in 1903. Lyonesse, the city, is ruled by Vincent Price who kidnaps a girl believing her to be his dead wife reincarnate. Suggested by Edgar Allen Poe's "The City In The Sea", it's ultimately a jaded adventure.

P★   T★★   E★   A

Directed by Jacques Tourneur. Written by Charles Bennett and Louis M. Heyward. Special Effects by Frank George and Les Bowie. With David Tomlinson, Tab Hunter, Susan Hart, John Le Mesurier and Henry Oscar.

WARLORDS OF ATLANTIS (1978)
A follow-up to the Land/People That Time Forgot series. Set in the same period, the movie deals with the crew of a ship, headed by Doug McLure, who are dragged by a giant octopus into a world beneath the sea, the legendary sunken Atlantis. It's populated by all variety of monsters, and by an alien race with nasty

mental powers, who enslave the crews of sunken vessels. The action is the silly kind of fun you would expect, the sets and costumes have the same feel as early episodes of Doctor Who. Basically, it's an enjoyable kids' film.

P★   T★★★   E★★★   A

Directed by Kevin Connor. Written by Brian Hayles. Special Effects by John Richardson, George Gibbs and Roger Dicken. With Peter Gilmore, Shane Rimmer, Lea Brodie and Michael Gothard. (TR)

WARNING FROM SPACE (1956) see
MYSTERIOUS SATELLITE (1956)

THE WAR O' DREAMS (1915)
Scientist invents a world-shattering explosive, Trixite, which can be detonated from a distance by ether waves, but a dream shows the inventor the consequences of his invention – a devastated world – and when he wakes he destroys his formula. An unheeded parable.

Directed by E. A. Martin. Written by W. E. Wing. With Edwin Wallock and Lillian Hayward.

WAR OF INSECTS (1968) Japanese
film about a girl's revenge on mankind. A victim of Auschwitz, she discovers she can control swarms of insects and uses this to crash a plane containing an A-bomb.

P★   T★   E★   A

Directed by Kazui Nihonmatsu. Written by Susumu Takahisa. With Yusuke Kawazu, Emi Shindo, Keisuke Sonoi and Cathy Horan.

WAR OF THE COLOSSAL BEAST
(1958) Bert I. Gordon strikes again! He produced, directed and originated the storyline for this tale of a 60-foot man discovered in Mexico. The Colossal Beast (actually the same Colossal Man as in The Amazing Colossal Man (1957) (q.v.)) goes to Los Angeles, goes on the rampage, and then kills himself on high-voltage cables when his sister tells him he's a baddie. This black-and-white film suddenly becomes colourful for this climactic scene.

P★   T★   E★   A★

Written by George Worthing Yates. Special Effects by Bert and Flora Gordon. With Roger Pace, Sally Fraser, Dean Parkin and Russ Bender.

WAR OF THE GARGANTUAS

(1966) Dreadful Japanese monster movie from the Toho studios. A giant green monster (Gaila) battles a more friendly brown one (Sanda). Tokyo is destroyed and a volcano erupts, killing both monsters.

P	T★	E	A

Directed by Inoshiro Honda. Written by Honda and Kaoru Mabuchi. Special Effects by Eiji Tsuburaya. With Russ Tamblyn and Kumi Mizuno.

WAR OF THE MONSTERS (1966)

Giant, child-loving turtle Gamera battles a dinosaur-like creature called Barugon.

P★	T★	E★	A

Directed by Shigeo Tanaka. Written by Fumi Takahashi. Special Effects by Takahashi. With Kojior Hongo, Kyoko Enami and Akira Natsuki.

WAR OF THE MONSTERS (1972)

Aliens from a dying, ultra-polluted planet make their monsters (Ghidorah and Gaigan) attack Earth. Godzilla fights for us.

P★	T★	E★	A

Directed by Jun Fukuda. Written by Shinichi Sekizawa. Special Effects by Shokei Nakano. With Hiroshi Ichikawa and Yuriko Hishimi.

WAR OF THE PLANETS (1954) see THIS ISLAND EARTH (1954)

WAR OF THE PLANETS (1965)

Fairly routine offering from Antonio Margheriti and his Italian cast. Bodiless light creatures from Mars attack Earth, taking over human bodies.

P★	T★★	E★	A★

Written by Ivan Reiner and Renato Moretti. With Tony Russell, Lisa Gastoni and Carlo Guistini.

WAR OF THE PLANETS (1977)

Japan's Toho studios rushed this film out to exploit the success of *Star Wars* (q.v.). A rather tired and tiresome story about a space battle that decides the fate of the Galaxy, and featuring another variation on the Spacecruiser Yamato.

P★	T★★	E★	A★

Directed by Jun Fukuda. Written by Ryuzo Nakanishi. Special Effects by Shokei Nakano. With Kensaku Morita, Yuke Asano and Ryo Ikebe.

WAR OF THE SATELLITES (1957)

To exploit public interest in the first Russian sputnik, Roger Corman rushed this film out in months. Aliens attempt to prevent the UN from exploring space by kidnapping a top scientist and, at the same time, placing an invisible barrier about the Earth.

P★	T★	E★★	A

Produced and directed by Roger Corman. Written by Lawrence Louis Goldman. Special Effects by Jack Rabin, Irving Block and Louis DeWitt. With Dick Miller and Susan Cabot.

WAR OF THE WORLDS (1952)

Writing about making *War Of The Worlds* in the sf magazine *Astounding* in 1953, producer George Pal stated: "I'll wager that if I could climb into the Time Machine which Wells wrote about in another story and flash back fifty-six years for a conference with the gentleman, he'd have approved the changes." Ignoring the fact that Wells only died in 1946, Wells would have sued for defamation of the character of his novel. Orson Welles's radio version (which apparently petrified American audiences) set the trend for modernizing H. G. Wells, and Pal went the whole hog, making what was a story of genuine alien intrusion into a simple Atom Bombs and Tanks power struggle with a love interest and religious undertones thrown in for good measure. The special effects were good for 1952 (they cost $1,400,000 of a total $2,000,000 budget), and the alien fighting craft – looking like standard lamps attached to huge boomerangs – are quaintly effective, though by no means as threatening as the original illustrations. In spite of the budget, Pal used the B-movie trick of inter-cutting stock documentary film for some scenes. Most damaging, however, is that the modernization makes the Martian strategy – understandable in the terms of the 1890s – seem ludicrous in the 1950s. If they have observed Earth, why haven't *they* got Atomic weapons? Why don't they simply bomb the major cities from flying craft? There's also a noticeable absence of any Russians – the only World War Two allies of the USA getting any mention are of the non-communist variety. Finally the distortion of Wells's apocalypse into a mild cinematic frisson is completed in what must be one of the most orderly evacuations of a major city ever – that of LA shortly before the "mental giants", the Martians, show just how grossly inefficient they really are by destroying systematically thousands of empty buildings.

P★	T★★	E★★	A

Directed by Byron Haskin. Written by Barré Lyndon. Special Effects by Gordon Jennings, Wallace Kelley, Paul Lerpae, Ivyl Burks, Jan Domela and Irmin Roberts. Narration by Sir Cedric Hardwicke. Excellent planetary artwork by Hal Pereira and Albert Nozaki. Technical Adviser Chesley Bonestell. With Gene Barry, Ann Robinson, Les Tremayne, Robert Cornthwaite and Lewis Martin.

THE WAR OF THE WORLDS – NEXT CENTURY (1981)

Set in 1999 with a Wellsian invasion of Earth by the Martians, but made in the shadow of the Russian invasion of Poland, this Polish film differs from Wells in that the public of 1999 seem not to care.

P★★	T★★	E★★	A★

Directed and written by Piotr Szulkin. With Roman Wilhelmi and Krystyna Janda.

WARPSPEED (1980)

The first manned mission to Saturn has an accident six months into its 5½-year journey and cannot complete its mission. If it turns about and returns to Earth it might *just* get there – but all surplus weight has to be jettisoned, including, eventually, six of its seven crew members. The story is re-discovered by a psychic "sensitive", Janet Trask (Camille Mitchell) who boards the *Marie Céleste*-like craft, the *Atlas*, and re-lives the "game". The story idea is similar to Tom Godwin's 1954 *Astounding* story, "The Cold Equations", but with its own special twists and turns. A superior new-generation B-movie.

P★★★	T★★★	E★★	A★

Directed by Allan Sandler. Written by Peter Dawson. Special Effects by John Bertram, Carol Johnsen and R. J. Anderson. With Adam West, David Chandler, Joanne Nail and Barry Gordon.

THE WARRIORS (1979)

Writer-director Walter Hill's third film, and the beginning of his love affair with re-interpreting Greek legend. It's Xenophon's *Anabasis* this time, and the hoplites have become gang kids in New York. The action takes place in one night, as a potential gangland messiah is assassinated and the Warriors have to fight their way right back across the city, unjustly accused of the crime, hunted by every other kid gang in the metropolis. Visually, the film is a spectacular *tour de force* of darkness and iridescent colours, as mesmerizing and fantastical as though the reels had been processed in neon. But the dusk-till-dawn deadline gives Hill little time to develop the characters, the kids end up seeming rather bland and nice, and we would have been better able to identify with their plight if, paradoxically, they were a little rougher around the edges.

P★	T★★★★	E★★★	A★★

From the novel by Sol Yurick. With Michael Beck, Dorsey Wright, Deborah Van Valkenburgh and David Patrick Kelly.(TR)

WARS OF THE PRIMAL TRIBES (1913)

see BRUTE FORCE (1913)

THE WASP WOMAN (1959)

Roger Corman produced and directed this rather slight story about a woman whose wasp enzyme beauty treatment goes drastically wrong. She seeks rejuvenation but gets more than she bargained for, turning into a wasp after dark. A trite twist on the Jekyll-Hyde formula.

P★	T★	E★	A

Written by Kinta Zertuche; adapted by Leo Gordon. With Susan Cabot, Fred Eisley, Barboura Morris, Michael Mark and Frank Wolff.

THE WATCHER IN THE WOODS (1980)

Made completely in England, with an all-British crew, *The Watcher In The Woods* is essentially a supernatural thriller with a small science fiction element. An American family takes over an Old English house owned by an ageing woman (Bette Davis). The elder girl begins to be haunted by events that happened 30 years before. There are some good "buses" (false scares) and the visual effect of the woods is well realized. Some of the intricacies of the plot seem superfluous to the final revelation, but the pace is fast enough to gloss over these.

P★★   T★★★   E★★★   A★★★

Directed by John Hough. With Carroll Baker and David McCallum. (GDK)

WATER CYBORGS (1966) see TERROR BENEATH THE SEA (1966)

WAY...WAY OUT (1966) I'll admit my bias: I've never liked Jerry Lewis. But here he's particularly awful as a weather-man on the moon trying, with Connie Stevens, to beat the Russians at having a baby.

P★   T★★   E★   A

Directed by Gordon Douglas. Written by William Bowers and Laslo Vadnay. Special Effects by L. B. Abbott, Emil Kosa Jr and Howard Lydecker. With Robert Morley, Dennis Weaver, Howard Morris, Anita Ekberg and Brian Keith.

WEAPONS OF DESTRUCTION (1958) see THE FABULOUS WORLD OF JULES VERNE (1958)

WELCOME TO BLOOD CITY (1977) Director Peter Sasdy could have done much more with this material, but allows this potentially interesting film to fall between the sf and Western stools. Project Killmaster has been set up to find an exceptional man – "a man who can lead and kill yet think and act for himself whilst working for the state". To this end men and women are "kidnapped", placed under computer-surveillance (being programmed to do certain things) and dumped in a Wild-West-style environment where Hobbesian thought (life as brutish, violent and short without social restraints) prevails – Blood City. Lewis (Keir Dullea) looks good exceptional-man material, but he escapes the programme, discovers what Killmaster is about, and flees back into the "dream-reality" of the programme, preferring it to the more hideous reality of the present. Somewhere along the way the film becomes incoherent and even rather uninteresting.

P★   T★   E★★   A

Written by Stephen Schneck and Michael Winder. With Jack Palance, Samantha Eggar, Barry Morse and Hollis McLaren.

DIE WELT IST MEIN (1933) see AN INVISIBLE MAN GOES THROUGH THE CITY (1933)

WESTWORLD (1973) It seems inapt to plug this Michael Crichton effort (he wrote and directed) as a major motion picture; it's a nice little movie, with a nice little idea, and none the worse for all that. The scene is Delos, an adult Disneyland set in the near future where visitors can stay to act their fantasies – there is an ancient Roman setting, a medieval castle, and a recreation of the Wild West of someone else's movie. Richard Benjamin and James Brolin opt for the Colt .45s and black hats. The first half of the film is an agile comedy as Benjamin and Brolin shoot down the local android gunfighter – Yul Brynner, playing a robot of his character in *The Magnificent Seven* – become outlaws, and bed the robotic whores – it's the technological dream taken to its logical conclusion, middle-class Americans can not only drive, cook, and brush their teeth with machines, they can sleep with them too. Then the robots start turning against their human brutalizers – and that very smooth transition from humour to horror

Yul Brynner and Norman Bartold in a scene from Westworld

is significant. Crichton understands the thin divide between "funny" and "frightening", and however much we may guffaw at the two men's antics in the first half of the film, their astonishment at their own audacity, a chill remains at the idea that two perfectly ordinary guys want to shoot down what seems like a man, or have sex with what they know only appears to be a woman. At midnight, when the day's mayhem is done, the main street of Westworld lies in corpse-strewn wreckage, to be rebuilt before the morning. And in the complex's repair shop, a constant stream of androids with faces blown off, limbs torn away, remind us just what the average citizen is capable of given the right stimulus. If the movie had been a pure action-pulp effort – it contains one of the few wholly successful extended chase sequences in modern cinema – then it might have been less memorable, but that intertwining of a thin, piercing thread of real horror amongst the thrills and spills gives it a special edge.

P★★★★	T★★★★	E★★★★★	A★★

Special Effects by Charles Schulthies. With Norman Bartold, Victoria Shaw and Alan Oppenheimer. (TR)

WHAT'S SO BAD ABOUT FEELING GOOD?

(1968) Lightweight comedy about a toucan infected with a happiness virus which it spreads throughout New York, causing a plague of happiness (which proves economically disastrous).

P★★	T★★	E★★	A★

Produced and directed by George Seaton. Written by Seaton and Robert Pirosh. With George Peppard, Mary Tyler Moore and Dom De Luise.

WHAT WOULD YOU SAY TO SOME SPINACH?

(1976) Czech comedy about a faulty rejuvenation machine which can either reduce the patient by error, or, if the patient has eaten spinach, function at a heightened rate of efficiency. Eastern Europe's answer to Popeye?

P★★	T★★	E★★★	A★★

Directed and written by Vaclav Vorlicek. With Vladimir Mensik, Jiri Sovak and Josef Somr.

WHEN DINOSAURS RULED THE EARTH

(1969) An everyday tale of cavefolk and dinosaurs (forget that the co-existence of the two is an utter anachronism!) with the Moon being ripped from the Earth and creating vast natural disasters. Dreadful!

P	T★★	E★	A

Directed and written by Val Guest. Special Effects by Jim Danforth, David Allen, Allan Bryce, Roger Dicken and Brian Johnstock. With Victoria Vetri, Robin Hawdon and Patrick Allen,

WHEN THE DEVIL COMMANDS

(1941) *see* THE DEVIL COMMANDS (1941)

WHEN THE MAN IN THE MOON SEEKS A WIFE

(1908) Very Earth-like Man-In-The-Moon, fed up with celibacy, decides he would like a London girl for a mate and comes to Earth in a gas balloon to find one. He succeeds and takes her back to the Moon in this charming comedy.

Directed by Percy Stow. Written by Langford Reed.

WHEN WOMEN HAD TAILS

(1970) An Italian film about the everyday occurrences in the lives of simple prehistoric folk. The women, as the title suggests, have tails. The sequel to this was the gloriously titled *When Women Played Ding Dong* (q.v.).

P★	T★	E★	A★

Directed by Pasquale Festa Campanile. Written by Luia Westmuller, Ottavio Jemma, Marcello Costa and Campanile. Special Effects by Walfrido Traversari. With Giuliano Gemma.

WHEN WOMEN PLAYED DING DONG

(1971) A much better film than *When Women Had Tails* (1970) (q.v.), to which this is a sequel; loosely based on Aristophanes's *Lysistrata*, this is a satire on modern arms races, setting a parallel situation in prehistoric times.

P★★	T★★	E★★	A★

Directed by Bruno Corbucci. Written by Fabio Pitorru, Massumo Felisatti and Corbucci. Special Effects by Eugenio Ascani. With Antonio Sabato, Aldo Guiffre, Vittorio Caprioli and Nadia Cassini.

The rocket in a scene from When Worlds Collide

WHEN WORLDS COLLIDE (1951)

Producer George Pal spent approximately $936,000 to make this adaptation of the novel by Edwin Balmer and Philip Wylie, and hired astronomical artist Chesley Bonestell as technical adviser and draughtsman on the project. Nonetheless, rather than being spectacular, the end result is rather workaday (the exceptions being Bonestell's depictions of the alien planets). The story is a simple one: Bellus, a small star, and its single planet, Zyra, enter the solar system from deep space; it becomes clear that they will collide with Earth; to save a few of Mankind's billions a spaceship is built to transfer them to Zyra when the Earth is – inevitably – destroyed. The attempt to convey this epic resulted in a rather stilted, sensationalized 1930s film with 1950s effects. Director Rudolph Maté and writer Sydney Boehm seemingly worked hard on trying to bring out the human aspects of the disaster, but even this seems like an afterthought or a sop to those who might justifiably claim that it's all set up for the grand destruction of the world at the end.

P★★	T★★★	E★★	A★

With Richard Derr, Barbara Rush, John Hoyt, Mary Murphy, Laura Elliott and Larry Keating.

WHERE DO WE GO FROM HERE?

(1945) Perhaps the only musical time-travel fantasy. The Aladdin-lamp method of getting about in time is no more fantastic, really, than Dr Who's police box, the *Tardis*, but Fred MacMurray's travels in time are specifically American (George Washington's army, Columbus's ship, etc).

P★★	T★★	E★★★	A★

Directed by Gregory Ratoff. Written by Morrie Ryskind. Special Effects by Fred Sersen. With Joan Leslie, June Haver, Gene Sheldon, Anthony Quinn, Carlos Ramirez and Alan Mowbray.

WHERE IS BETA? (1973) Joint Brazilian-French project about the divisions in society (between the tainted and the untainted) after the Holocaust.

P★	T★	E★	A

Directed by Nelson Pereira Dos Santos. Written by Dos Santos and Gerard Levy Clerc. With Frederic De Pasquale and Regina Rosembourg.

THE WHIP HAND (1951) A political thriller with an sf twist; in a small American town a group of ex-Nazi communists (!) are using US citizens as experimental guinea-pigs to perfect a germ which will wipe out the population of the United States. It was apparently adapted from one of director William Cameron Menzies's previously unreleased films and is a haunting little piece, better than its low-budget origins might have made us suspect.

P★★	T★	E★★★	A★

Written by Roy Hamilton. With Carla Balenda, Elliott Reid, Edgar Barrier and Raymond Burr.

THE WHITE DISEASE (1937) *see* SKELETON ON HORSEBACK (1937)

WHITE PONGO (1945) A late exploitation of *King Kong*'s popularity, but without Kong's style or pathos. Here an expedition discovers a large (though not huge) white ape, which they consider to be the missing link. In a fairly dull adventure story it kills the villain and carries off the girl. What's new?

P★	T★	E★	A★

Directed by Sam Newfield. Written by Raymond L. Schrock. With Richard Fraser.

WHO? (1974) One of the sf-suspense movies' most ingenious ideas, but in a milk-and-water version, in this adaptation of the Algis Budrys novel. Martino (Joseph

Bova) is a top scientist who was injured in a laboratory explosion near the Warsaw Pact border and "rescued" by the Russians before anyone else could get to him. When he is handed back, CIA man Shawn Rogers (Elliot Gould) is expecting at best a simple exchange, at worst a man who has been brainwashed. But the Soviets have not used plastic surgery on the man – instead, they've turned him into a creature half-human, half-android, with an alloy face and an artificial arm, a man in an impenetrable iron mask. He is completely unidentifiable, and as Rogers delves deeper into the mystery of whether the man in his custody is Martino or a double-agent, he realizes that the Soviets have presented him with an insoluble problem on the scale of a horrible practical joke. It's excellent grounding for psychological suspense, and a neat little allegory about the way the covert war between the great powers takes individual human beings and dehumanizes them. But the film aims for an aura of subtlety and quiet suspense it never achieves – it doesn't help that directors Jack Gold and John Gould throw in the odd chase scene or exploding car to remind us, by way of stock images, that this is supposed to be an exciting thriller. And the inconclusive ending, so strong a feature of the book, is merely unsatisfying here. Elliot Gould is barely convincing as Rogers – he tries to present us with an agent rumpled and nonchalant on the outside, with a tough inner core, but Gould has had too much exposure in comic roles to convince us he's at all tough.

P★★★★   T★★   E★★   A★

Written by John Gould. With Trevor Howard, James Noble, John Lehne and Ed Grover. (TR)

WHO GOES THERE? (1956) Poorly made 8 mm film of John Campbell's famous story, which has been filmed twice as *The Thing* (q.v.). This keeps strictly to Campbell's original.

Directed by Tony Brezezinski. Cinematography by John Mate.

WHO KILLED JESSIE? (1965) Delightful Czech comedy about a dream-

actuator, a "somnigraph", which begins to produce comic-strip heroes and villains. Jessie, the heroine of the inventor's husband, is pursued by the comic villains.

P★★   T★★   E★★★   A★★

Directed and written by Milos Macourek and Vaclav Vorlicek. Cinematography by Jan Nemecek. With Jiri Sovak and Dana Medricka.

WHOOPS APOCALYPSE (1981) A long feature put together from episodes of the British TV series. World events have moved on and the focus has shifted from the Shah of Iran, but this hard-hitting satire of Cold War mentality, incompetent government and human frailty remains as brilliantly effective as ever. Barry Morse plays the simpleton President Johnny Cyclops (clearly modelled on Reagan) whose advisers slowly edge him towards Nuclear War (mainly through absurd CIA schemes). The complex plot revolves about a Quark Bomb, stolen (with CIA knowledge) by L'Acrobat (alias, The Devil – played by John Cleese). Inexorably, things escalate – though everything is played way over the top, with hilarious results – until the last scene where Cyclops has to sign the retaliation order. Only then are we allowed to glimpse the reality of the situation – the pathos behind the dark comedy of events.

P★★★★   T★★★   E★★★★★   A★★

Written by Andrew Marshall and David Renwick. With John Barron, Richard Griffiths, Alexei Sayler, Ed Bishop, Peter Jones, Richard Davies, Geoffrey Palmer, Rik Mayall, Bruce Montague and David Kelly.

WHY DID YOU PICK ON ME? (1979) Sequel to *The Sheriff & The Satellite Kid* (1979) (q.v.), presumably shot at the same time, and with the same cast. More fights, gimmickry and this time a few baddy aliens trying to get hold of H-725 (Cary Guffey) before they're foiled by the Sheriff (Bud Spencer).

P★   T★★   E★★★   A

Directed by Michele Lupo.

WILD IN THE STREETS (1968) A wildly inventive comedy set in a near-future America where the voting age has been reduced to 14, everyone over 35 is incarcerated and forced to take LSD and a rock singer has just become President. It's *Logan's Run* hippy-style! with the 10-year-olds planning a revolution as the film comes to its hectic conclusion.

| P★★ | T★ | E★★★ | A★ |

Directed by Barry Shear. Written by Robert Thom. With Shelley Winters, Christopher Jones, Diane Varsi, Richard Pryor and Dick Clark.

WILD, WILD PLANET (1965) One of Antonio Margheriti's better offerings, this is set early in the twenty-first century where villainous criminals are kidnapping world leaders, using their four-armed robots and artificial women, shrinking people down to miniature size from their base in space.

| P★ | T★★ | E★★ | A★ |

Written by Ivan Reiner and Renato Moretti. With Tony Russell, Lisa Gastoni and Massimo Serato.

WILD WOMEN OF WONGO (1958) Second-rate movie about two islands of primitive people, one lot beautiful, one lot ugly. When a band of ape-men attack the two tribes merge. A terrible use of the lost world theme.

| P | T | E★ | A |

Directed by James L. Wolcott. Written by Cedric Rutherford. With Jean Hawkshaw, Jonny Walsh, Mary Ann Webb and Cande Gerrard.

THE WILD WORLD OF BAT-WOMAN (1966) A rather silly adaptation of comic-book fodder. The costumed super-heroine fights against a mad doctor who has an atom bomb made from a hearing aid.

| P | T★ | E★ | A |

Produced, directed and written by Jerry Warren. With Katherine Victor and George Andre.

WILLARD (1971) A borderline sf-horror film playing heavily on most people's phobia for rats. An adolescent, cut off from contact with young people his own

age, makes friends with a couple of super-intelligent rats and controls their rat-pack through them. But when he finds a girl they refuse to be abandoned and turn on him. Based on the novel *Ratman's Notebooks* by Stephen Gilbert. A sequel, *Ben* (q.v.), was made in 1972.

| P★★ | T★★ | E★★ | A★ |

Directed by Daniel Mann. Written by Gilbert A. Ralston. Special Effects by Bud David. With Bruce Davison and Ernest Borgnine.

WIND OF DEATH (1963) *see* THE LAST MAN ON EARTH (1963)

WINGS OF DOOM (1938) *see* FLIGHT TO FAME (1938)

THE WISHING MACHINE (1967) Czech film which stresses the virtues of realism. Two boys develop a machine that grants wishes. They want to go to the Moon, but are not aware of the hazards involved.

| P★★ | T★★ | E★★ | A★ |

Directed and written by Josef Pinkava. With Milan Zeman and Vit Weingaertner.

WITHOUT A SOUL (1916) An experimental scientist's daughter is killed in a car crash and her father brings her back to life using his electrical machine. But in the moments of death, Death has come to steal her soul, and when she is revived she is soul-less, heartless and rejects her faithful fiancé. But the soul-lessness itself causes a wasting disease of the heart and she dies a second time. Her father, frightened by the change in her from loving daughter to cruel and selfish stranger, refuses to revive her a second time and destroys his machinery. Based on the play *Lola* by Owen Davis, but with definite affinities to Shelley's *Frankenstein*.

Produced, directed and written by James Young. With Clara Kimball Young, Edward M. Kimball, Alec B. Francis, Irene Tams and Mary Moore.

WITHOUT WARNING (1924) *see* THE STORY WITHOUT A NAME (1924)

WITHOUT WARNING (1980) Blood and gore feature starring a none-too-friendly alien who can fire blood-sucking parasites at its victims. Set, as most of these films now are, in the backwoods country of America, it owes less to sf than to the sickest kind of splatter movie.

P★	T★★	E★	A

Produced and directed by Greydon Clark. Written by Lyn Freedman, Daniel Grodnick, Ben Nett and Steven Mathis. With Jack Palance, Martin Landau and Tarah Nutter.

THE WIZARD (1927) The misleading title aside, this is based on Gaston Leroux's novel, *Balaoo*, and concerns itself with the obligatory mad scientist trying to graft human heads on to apes; to use the result to avenge himself on his enemies. Re-made in 1942 as *Dr Renault's Secret*.

Directed by Richard Rosson. Written by Harry O. Hoyt and Andrew Bennison. With Edmund Lowe, Leila Hyams and Gustav von Seyffertitz.

THE WIZARD OF MARS (1964) Burroughsian science fantasy as an expedition to Mars encounters an ancient civilization.

P★	T	E★	A

Produced, directed and written by David L. Hewitt. Technical Adviser Forrest J. Ackerman. With John Carradine, Roger Gentry and Vic McGee.

WIZARDS (1977) A curious fantasy with a science fiction rationale. This is the far future and a million or so years after the Nuclear Holocaust. Dwarves and goblins exist – from mutated human stock – and battle for the allegorical Goodlands. Excellent animation with some memorable images, but lousy sf. One of the new hybrids, more comic-oriented than anything.

P★★	T★★★★★	E★★★	A★★★

Produced, directed and written by Ralph Bakshi.

WOJNA SWIATOW – NASTEPNE STULECIE (1981) *see* THE WAR OF THE WORLDS – NEXT CENTURY (1981)

THE WOMAN EATER (1957) A madman in search of the fluid which will revive the dead feeds a number of women to a tree.

P★	T★	E★	A★

Directed by Charles Saunders. Written by Brandon Fleming. With George Coulouris.

THE WOMAN IN THE MOON (1929) *see* BY ROCKET TO THE MOON (1929)

WOMEN OF THE PREHISTORIC PLANET (1965) Pedestrian story about a strange planet with prehistoric life forms, which turns out to be Earth. Adam and Eve become, in the scheme of this, two alien astronauts who decided to stay on.

P★	T	E★	A

Directed and written by Arthur C. Pierce. Special Effects by Howard A. Anderson. With Wendell Corey, Keith Larsen, John Agar and Irene Tsu.

THE WONDERFUL ELECTRO-MAGNET (1909) The device sends out magnetic rays which attracts not merely metallic objects but humans, too. A local church minister utilizes the device to reverse the trend of non-attendance at his church.

Made by Thomas Edison.

THE WONDERFUL RAYS (1913) An invention which taps into electrical vibrations in the air is used to re-enact crimes.

WONDER WOMAN (1973) Made for TV feature about a woman raised on an isolated island who becomes a super-heroine (in the comic-book mould), with expertise in martial arts combat.

P★	T★★	E★	A★

Directed by Vincent McEveety. Written by John D. F. Black. Special Effects by George Peckham. With Cathy Lee Crosby and Kaz Garas.

WON IN THE CLOUDS (1914) One of several slightly futuristic films predicting the advent of war from the air – here airships attack a village in Africa.

Produced and written by Otis Turner.

WORK IS A FOUR-LETTERED WORD (1967) A futuristic anti-automation comedy, based on Henry Living's play *Eh?.*

| P★★ | T★ | E★★ | A★ |

Directed by Peter Hall. Written by Jeremy Brooks. Special Effects by Michael Stainer-Hutchins. With David Warner, Cilla Black, Elizabeth Spriggs, Julie May and Alan Howard.

THE WORLD, THE FLESH AND THE DEVIL (1958) A sophisticated film from a rather stereotyped situation. After World War Three has ended, a black worker (Harry Belafonte) digs his way to the surface and finds himself alone. He travels to New York City and there meets a white woman (Inger Stevens). All would be well but for the arrival of a white racist (Mel Ferrer) who pursues Belafonte through the deserted streets of the ruined metropolis with a gun. It's a nice way to allegorize the racial question but ignores all the (even then) known facts about post-Holocaust scenarios. Suffice to say that both men make their peace and, at the film's end, head off into the sunset with their shared woman; a point where many modern film-makers might have begun.

| P★★ | T★★ | E★★★ | A★★ |

Directed by Ranald MacDougall (who also wrote the screenplay, based lossely on M. P. Shiel's "The Purple Cloud"). Special Effects by Lee LeBlanc.

WORLD WAR III (1980) A lengthy (almost 3 hours) made-for-TV feature tracing the steps by which America and Russia come to fight the third, nuclear (and final) war. The setting is the near future, America has set up a grain embargo against the Soviet Union (needing the grain itself) and, owing to diminishing supplies from the Middle East, has opened up its own Alaskan oil fields (which supply 30 per cent of its oil requirements). A KGB-inspired plan to blackmail America into stopping its embargo has a crack Soviet platoon break

into Alaska and, under cover of foul weather, try to take an important (but strangely unguarded) oil pumping station. If they blow it up (and the 30 miles of pipeline attached) it would cut off Alaskan oil supplies and could cripple the American economy. But, in view of Russian food riots, they gamble on the Americans backing down. Things escalate gradually and an attempt to defend the station (against overwhelming odds) eventually fails. The anti-war Russian Premier is killed and the KGB General takes over. Rock Hudson, as President McKenna (a man of peace), is forced, degree by degree, into countering every Russian move. The inevitable occurs. For all its action-adventure and thriller-style tension, this is, surprisingly, a strong anti-war film, and Hudson is excellent as an intelligent, compassionate man forced slowly into decisions he does not wish to make. Despite several plot glitches (why don't the American soldiers blow up this end of the pipeline and save the other 30 miles?) and a few TV-oriented moments of pure soap, there's a general seriousness to this well-suited to its subject matter. And for a film this long its pace rarely slows.

| P★★★ | T★★★ | E★★★★ | A★★ |

Directed by David Greene. Written by Robert L. Joseph. With David Soul, Brian Keith, Cathy Lee Crosby, Jeroen Krabbé, Robert Prosky, Katherine Helmond and James Hampton.

WORLD WAR III BREAKS OUT (1960) *see* THE FINAL WAR (1960)

THE WORLD WILL SHAKE (1939) The existence of a machine which can predict the moment of death for anyone results in social disorder and a rash of killings and suicides. Schrodinger's cat lives! Based on a story by Charles Robert Dumas and R. F. Didelot.

| P★★ | T★ | E★★ | A★ |

Directed by Richard Pottier. Written by Henri-Georges Clouzot and J. Villard. With Madeleine Solonge and Erich Von Stroheim.

THE WORLD WITHOUT A MASK (1934) A comedy thriller revolving about a machine which can see through walls.

P★	T★	E★	A

Directed by Harry Piel. Written by Hans Rameau. With Harry Piel, Kurt Vespermann, Annie Markart and Olga Tschechowa.

WORLD WITHOUT END (1955) A

classic case of a good idea squandered. A spacecraft orbiting Mars passes through a time warp and returns to Earth 100 years in the future (ad 2058). The crew discovers that Earth has been decimated by a nuclear war, with the sterile remnants of Mankind surviving underground and a race of hideous mutants (and giant insects) living on the planet's ruined surface. This promising scenario is let down by a stilted, awful script and threadbare, unconvincing special effects.

P★★	T★	E★★	A★

Directed and written by Edward Bernds. Special Effects by Milton Rice. With Hugh Marlowe, Nancy Gates, Rod Taylor, Lisa Montell and Nelson Leigh.

WORLD WITHOUT WOMEN (1960) see THE LAST WOMAN ON EARTH (1960)

THE X FROM OUTER SPACE

(1967) Seventh Japanese Mars expedition encounters UFOs, discovers a new "living" element, Gulalium, which absorbs energy, and brings it back to Earth. The Gulalium crystal hatches into the rubberoid monster Gulala who proceeds to destroy half of Japan, threaten Tokyo and devour energy plants. A rather tiresome formulaic offering with indifferent special effects.

P★	T★	E★	A

Directed (and co-written) by Kazui Nihonmatzu. Written by Eibi Motomochi and Morujoshi Ishida. Special Effects by Hiroshi Ikeda. With Eiji Okada, Toshiya Wazaki and Peggy Neal.

THE X-RAY FIEND (1897) see X-RAYS (1897)

X-RAYS (1897) Two years after Roentgen's discovery, director George A. Smith made this brief confection showing a courting couple embracing – as skeletons.

THE X-RAYS (1897) see A NOVICE AT X-RAYS (1897)

X – THE MAN WITH THE X-RAY EYES (1963) Ray Milland plays Dr

Xavier, a scientist who crosses into the forbidden zone of research by imbuing himself with X-ray vision. The humorous aspects of the idea are dealt with first, with Milland cheating at cards and peeking through women's clothes. But as the weird new vision becomes stronger, an effect implied by discolouring the doctor's eyes until they become, in the ghastly final scenes, orbs of perfect black, he finds himself a freak trapped in a nightmare world of jostling skeletons and worse. There was a tendency to build religious overtones into the endings of sf movies around this period, and here is no exception – the message seems to be that tampering with nature is a sin – or, more simply, post-Hiroshima curiosity kills the cat – but the thriller moves along at a fair lick, and the final frame is a true horror.

P★★	T★★	E★★★★	A★

Produced and directed by Roger Corman. Written by Robert Dillon and Ray Russell. Special Effects by Butler-Grove Inc. With Don Rickles, John Hoyt and Diana Van Der Vlis. (TR)

X – THE UNKNOWN (1956) Much in

the *Quatermass* mould, this is about an ancient radiation monster discovered on the Scottish moors during an army training exercise. A suspense-filled, evocative film (shot in black and white) it nonetheless is weakened by having a blob as its monster.

P★★	T★★	E★★★	A★★

Directed by Leslie Norman. Written by Jimmy Sangster. Special Effects by Jack Curtis and Bowie Margutti Ltd. With Dean Jagger, Leo McKern, Edward Chapman, Anthony Newley, Jameson Clark and William Lucas.

XTRO (1982) A man, Sam, is abducted by aliens in a blaze of brilliant light, witnessed by his son. For three years his wife believes that he ran out on her and that her son is psychologically compensating with his tale. Then the husband returns, but not, at first, as himself. We see an alien creature "rape" a woman in a cottage, then see her wake to her quickly swelling body. She gives birth not to a child, but to a full-sized replica of Sam. Sam, feigning loss of memory, then goes back to his wife, who has meanwhile found a new boyfriend. Balanced between alien invasion tale and domestic drama this *might* have been quite superb, but sloppy editing (in the sense of which material director Harry Bromley Davenport should have discarded, the animated toy scenes amongst them) blunts its credibility and slows its pace. At moments it's quite excellent, despite its cheap-budget effects (using *Alien*-like pulsing eggs which burst open and smother people's faces), and evokes perfectly what it might be like to be an alien, indifferent to the quality of human life and assertive of the necessity of one's own.

P★★★	T★★★	E★★★★	A★

Written by Iain Cassie and Robert Smith. Special Effects by Tom Harris and (Creature Effects) Francis Coates. With Philip Sayer, Bernice Stegers, Danny Brainin and Maryam D'Abo.

Y

YEAR 2889 (1966) *see* IN THE YEAR 2889 (1966)

YEUX SANS VISAGE (1959) *see* THE HORROR CHAMBER OF DR FAUSTUS (1959)

YEVO ZOVUT ROBERT (1967) *see* CALL ME ROBERT (1967)

YOG — MONSTER FROM SPACE (1970) A spacecraft travelling through the asteroid belt picks up an alien force which, when returned to Earth, gets into various creatures – crabs, an octopus, a turtle – making them huge rampagers. This Toho production gives monster-value for money, if nothing else.

P★	T★	E	A

Directed by Inoshiro Honda. Written by Ei Ogawa. Special Effects by Sadamasa Sunokura, Sadamasa Arikawa, Yoichi Manoda and Yasuyuki Inoue. With Akira Kubo, Atsuko Takahashi, Yoshio Tsuchiya, Kenji Sahara and Noritake Saito.

YONGKARI, MONSTER FROM THE DEEP (1967) An earthquake in China, caused by a nuclear explosion, releases the gasoline-guzzling monster, Yongkari, but the beastie is eventually killed by an ammonia-based spray. A South Korean production.

P★	T★	E★	A

Directed by Kiduck Kim. Written by Yungsung Suh. With Yungil Oh and Chungim Nam.

YOR, THE HUNTER FROM THE FUTURE (1983) Antonio Margheriti strikes again! The Italian film-director here gives us a far future time when Man has reverted to ... prehistoric state (as in *Teenage Caveman*, 1958 (q.v.)). Rocket-ships and flint implements rub (metaphoric) shoulders in this abysmal outing.

P★	T★	E★	A

Written by Margheriti and Robert Bailey. With Reb Brown, Corinne Clery and John Steiner.

YOU ARE A WIDOW, SIR (1971) *see* SIR, YOU ARE A WIDOW (1971)

THE YOUNG DIANA (1922) A twist upon Oscar Wilde's *A Picture Of Dorian Gray*, but based on Marie Corelli's novel. A woman stays perpetually youthful in appearance after a doctor's experiment, yet her heart ages and, still looking strikingly young, she dies of a heart attack.

Directed by Albert Capellani and Robert G. Vignola. Written by Luther Reed. With Marion Davies, Maclyn Arbuckle and Forrest Stanley.

P = Plot   T = Technical Skill

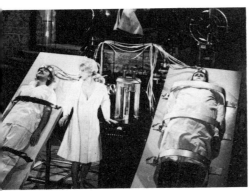

Left to right: Gene Wilder, Teri Garr and Peter Boyle in a scene from Young Frankenstein

YOUNG FRANKENSTEIN (1974)

Good taste never has been a true artistic criterion, rather a bogus value imposed on art by the middle-classes. Enter one Jewish vaudeville comedian from a poor suburb of New York, who understands this instinctively, without even having to rationalize it, and, while what he produces may not be exactly art, Mel Brooks comes closest in this gorgeous-looking tribute to the early *Frankenstein* flicks. It's filmed in the kind of black-and-white which makes colour movies look pallid, and permission was obtained to use the set from the 1931 *Frankenstein* (q.v.). The plot concerns the grandson of the mad scientist, who's trying to live down the infamy of his ancestor, until he receives grandpa's entire inheritance, spooky castle, secret formulae and all, and gets wrapped up in the entire monster-making obsession once again. He also inherits the old bat of a housekeeper who used to be Frankenstein's lover, a beautiful assistant, and Marty Feldman as Igor – it's pronounced "I-gore". Feldman's over-the-top goggling is perfect for this style of humour; Cloris Leachman turns in the kind of venomously nasty performance she would also take over the top in *High Anxiety* (1977); Madeleine Khan is at her enervating best as the frigid fiancée. Only Gene Wilder, who co-wrote the script as well as starring as the grandson, slightly disappoints; he cranks out that bug-eyed, red-faced hysteria attack he introduced in *The Producers* as though

he were doing a party piece. Kenneth Mars has some of the funniest moments, as a police chief who looks like the Kaiser, lumbered with an outrageous Teutonic accent and an artificial arm which has a life of its own (it walked all the way from *Dr Strangelove*). Very highly recommended.

| P★★★ | T★★★ | E★★★★★ | A★★ |

Special Effects by Hal Millar and Henry Miller Jr. With Peter Boyle (as the Monster), Gene Hackman and Richard Haydn. (TR)

THE YOUNG MONK (1978) Post-

Apocalyptic comedy set in a desert-like Earth.

| P★★ | T★★ | E★★ | A★ |

Produced, directed and written by Herbert Achternbusch. With Achternbusch, Karolina Herbig, Brank Samarovski and Heinz Braun.

YOU ONLY LIVE ONCE (1968) *see*
MISSION STARDUST (1968)

YOU ONLY LIVE TWICE (1967)

Bond (Sean Connery) fakes his own death in order to pursue Blofeld (Donald Pleasance in excellent camp form) to the Japanese island from which the arch-villain is kidnapping American and Soviet hardware in order to start a third world war. Scenes like those in which satellites and subs are literally devoured by Blofeld's craft served to put the Bond films in the forefront of spectacular sf effects until Kubrick's *2001* set the definitive tone in 1968. The action is a little stodgy at times, and Connery looks self-conscious and silly in Japanese peasant get-up, but director Lewis Gilbert makes amends at the climax by giving us the spectacular intrusion by several hundred Ninja into Blofeld's secret hideout, contained in an extinct volcano and one of the largest interior sets ever made for a motion picture.

| P★ | T★★★★ | E★★★★ | A |

Written by Roald Dahl, from the novel by Ian Fleming. Special Effects by John Stears. With Teshuro Tamba and Akiko Wakabuyashi. (TR)

YOUTH WITHOUT AGE (1968) *see*
KINGDOM IN THE CLOUDS (1968)

ZAAT (1972) A researcher in marine biology succeeds in transforming himself into an underwater creature, Zaat, and begins to wage war against land dwellers using mutant fish.

P★	T★★	E★	A

Produced and directed by Dan Barton. Written by Ron Kivett and Lee Larew. With Dave Dickerson, Sanna Ringhaver and Paul Galloway.

ZABIL JSEM EINSTEINA, PANOVE (1970) *see* I KILLED EINSTEIN, GENTLEMEN (1970)

ZANDORI'S SECRET (1914) French film starring Renée Sylvaine about a serum developed which can cure insanity.

ZARDOZ (1973) John Boorman's *tour-de-force* exploration of sf themes and images should, perhaps, be sub-titled "A Fable of Vitality and Death". From simple sf elements he creates a rich intellectual fabric while maintaining a lucid and coherent plotline. This is as far from *Star Wars* (q.v.) as sf film could be and yet retain dramatic tension. Unlike *Star Wars* and that ilk of space opera it works on more than a visual/melodramatic level and rewards each new viewing with further discoveries about Boorman's purpose. Zed is the savage from the Outlands who, his curiosity awoken by a book (The Wi*ZARD* of *OZ*), climbs into the giant floating Godhead, kills the creator of the God (Arthur Frayn, played by Niall Buggy) and re-enters 'Civilization'. Civilization, in the post-Atomic world of 2293, takes the form of small, isolated valley-communities, Vortexes, protected by force-shields. In these Vortexes live the Eternals, custodians of Mankind's culture and, in their immortality, a stage beyond *Homo sapiens*. The Eternals view Zed as an animal and are both fascinated and repelled by his brutal passions; what they do not realize is that Zed (Sean Connery) is also third-generation mutant, genetically stable, with an enlarged brain and perfect eidetic recall – thus *superior* to the Eternals. More central to the plot, however, is the sense of Zed bringing back to the Vortex sexuality, violence, fear and death, things lost to the Eternals. Long before Zed's arrival the cracks in the wall of Eternality had begun to show, with Eternals becoming either apathetics or renegades. Through Zed – and the response of the hostile, sexless Consuela (Charlotte Rampling) and the studious May (Sara Kestelman) – Boorman demonstrates how fragile a crystal is pure knowledge and how easily broken it is by a creature of potency. Indeed, intelligent as the schema from this film is, it could not have been successfully conveyed on celluloid without the aggressive, convincing acting of Connery and the (equally difficult) portrayal of human sterility by the cast of Eternals. Were Boorman to end the film with Zed destroying the culture of the Eternals, however, his purpose would not have been served. His intention is to show us – through his future allegory – that "Knowledge is not enough", and to emphasize this there is a reversal towards the end of the film when the defenders of civilization (like Consuela) become its destroyers and Zed (no longer simply an allegorical figure of Death, nor the last letter of a defunct alphabet) becomes a potent Re-storer, replacing the decapitated heads of the statues. Zed brings death, certainly – destroying the Eternals' Tabernacle – but he also brings re-birth, fulfilling his Corn-God role. More important, he brings back mortality and all its accompanying human qualities. While the Vortex perishes, the now-mortal Eternals throwing themselves on the guns of the Liberators from the Outlands, Zed and Consuela escape, make love in a cave and have a child. Human order – *natural* order – is restored. On another level, *Zardoz* is about creation itself. Arthur Frayn, who returns to life late in the film, is a creator with a sense of humour, and this is, in many senses, *his* comedy; a dumb-show with levels of illusion. His words, early in the film, echo throughout this visual tale: "And you, poor creature, who conjured you out of the clay? Is God in show business, too?"

Sean Connery as Zed in Zardoz

P★★★   T★★★★   E★★★★   A★★★★

Produced and written also by John Boorman. Special Effects by Gerry Johnston. Cinematography by Geoffrey Unsworth. With Sally Anne Newton, John Alderton and Bosco Hogan.

ZAVINIL TO EINSTEIN (1961) *see* MAN IN OUTER SPACE (1961)

ZERO POPULATION GROWTH (1971) I simply cannot accept the central premise of this film that the inhabitants of an overpopulated future (unspecified) would agree to World Government laws banning childbirth for 30 years on pain of death. Any examination of the emotional consequences would dismiss the idea out of mind. This film, however, takes up this ideative challenge (a variation on *1984*, with an ecological twist) as a couple, Russ and Carol McNeil (Oliver Reed and Geraldine Chaplin), have an illegal baby and, threatened by their neighbours, first share it with them and then escape from the confines of their civilization (to an island). It's shot full of emotional rather than logical holes – doll-like androids as child substitutes are just one emotionally unacceptable element, whilst a logical enough *idea* – and part of its general limpness stems from this weakness. The futuristic settings are nicely constructed and the sense of uniformity (in dress particularly) suggests a sterile social set-up, but this film goes to prove that having an idea is

insufficient; having an idea that is *feasible* is necessary.

P★★   T★★★★   E★★   A★

Directed by Michael Campus. Written by Max Ehrlich and Frank De Felitta. Special Effects by Derek Meddings. With Don Gordon, Diane Cilento, David Markham and Bill Nagy.

ZETA ONE (1969) Semi-pornographic comic-strip stuff as secret agents battle the alien Angvians (super-women) in more than one sense.

P★   T★★   E★★   A★

Directed by Michael Cort. Written by Cort and Christopher Neame. With Robin Hawdon, Yutte Stensgaard, James Robertson Justice, Charles Hawtrey, Lionel Murton and Dawn Addams.

ZEX, THE ELECTRONIC FIEND (1957) *see* THE ELECTRONIC MONSTER (1957)

ZOMBIE CREEPING FLESH (1981) A Third World research station develops a gas which turns people into flesh-eating ghouls – a solution to the problem of over-population. Really just an excuse for more blood and gore.

P★   T★★   E★   A

Directed by Vincent Dawn. Written by Claudio Fragrasso and J. M. Cunillis. Special Effects by Giuseppe Ferranti. With Margit Evelyn Newton, Frank Garfield, Selan Karay and Robert O'Neil.

ZOMBIES (1964) *see* I EAT YOUR SKIN (1964)

ZONTAR: THE THING FROM VENUS (1966) Uncredited remake of Roger Corman's *It Conquered The World* (1956) (q.v.) where the Venusians control humans' minds after stinging them with their bat-mites.

P★   T   E★   A

Produced and directed by Larry Buchanan. Written by Buchanan and H. Taylor. With John Agar, Susan Bjurman and Anthony Houston.

ZTRACENA TVAR (1965) *see* THE LOST FACE (1965)

ZVYOZDNYI INSPECTOR (1980) *see* THE STAR INSPECTOR (1980)

The Sf Serials 1913–1956

A regular feature of the cinema for more than 40 years was the long-running serial, usually in 10 to 15 "chapters" of approximately 20 minutes duration. The principal demand of the serial form seems to have been that each action-packed, gimmick-filled "chapter" end at a moment of crisis, the resolution of which kicked off the next episode. Serials were, therefore, usually repetitious, if sometimes inventive – a cinematic equivalent, perhaps, to the prose of A. E. Van Vogt! – and, like the more formally accomplished features, were more likely to use an sf element as a central gimmick (a death ray, a special machine) in a thriller plot about master criminals than attempt to tell an sf story. Only from 1936 onward did a sci-fi orientation creep into the serials, and even then it was derived not from the pulp magazines but from the comic-strips. In the list of serials that follows, the figure in parenthesis gives the number of chapters in the sequence.

1914	*The Exploits Of Elaine* (14)	1940	*Flash Gordon Conquers The Universe* (12)
1915	*The Black Box* (15)		*The Mysterious Dr Satan* (15)
	Lady Baffles & Detective Duck (11)	1941	*The Adventures of Captain Marvel* (12)
	The New Exploits Of Elaine (10)		
	The Romance Of Elaine (12)		*Dick Tracy Versus Crime Inc.* (15)
1918	*The Master Mystery* (15)		*Captain Midnight* (15)
1919	*The Carter Case* (15)	1943	*Batman* (15)
1920	*The Branded Four* (15)	1944	*Captain America* (15)
	The Flaming Disk (18)		*The Great Alaskan Mystery* (13)
	The Invisible Ray (15)	1945	*Manhunt Of Mystery Island* (15)
	The Screaming Shadow (15)		*The Monster And The Ape* (15)
1921	*The Sky Ranger* (15)		*The Purple Monster Strikes* (15)
1922	*The Radio King* (10)	1946	*The Crimson Ghost* (12)
1925	*The Power God* (15)	1947	*Brick Bradford* (15)
1926	*Officer 444* (10)		*Jack Armstrong* (15)
	The Scarlet Streak (10)	1948	*Bruce Gentry – Daredevil Of The Skies* (15)
1930	*Voice From The Sky* (10)		*Superman* (15)
1934	*The Vanishing Shadow* (12)		
1935	*The Lost City* (12)	1949	*Batman And Robin* (15)
	The Phantom Empire (12)		*King Of The Rocket Men* (12)
1936	*Flash Gordon* (13)	1950	*Atom Man Versus Superman* (15)
	Undersea Kingdom (12)	1951	*Flying Disc Man From Mars* (12)
1937	*Dick Tracy* (15)		*Mysterious Island* (15)
	S.O.S. Coastguard (12)	1952	*Radar Men From The Moon* (12)
1938	*Fighting Devil Dogs* (12)		*Zombies Of The Stratosphere* (12)
	Flash Gordon's Trip To Mars (15)	1953	*The Lost Planet* (15)
1939	*Blake Of Scotland Yard* (15)	1954	*Rocky Jones, Space Ranger* (14)
	Buck Rogers (12)	1956	*Supergiant* (9)
	Dick Tracy's G-Men (15)		
	The Phantom Creeps (12)		

Creators of Sf on Screen: A–Z

Where appropriate, additional contributions are indicated after film titles as follows:
A=ACTING SE=SPECIAL EFFECTS
C=CINEMATOGRAPHY
D=DIRECTION SP=SCREENPLAY
P=PRODUCTION

ABBOTT, Lyle B. American special effects expert, active mainly in the 1960s, often with Art Cruikshank and Emil Kosa Jr. Little of his work is memorable and some – as on *Journey To The Centre Of The Earth* (1959) – is best forgotten. He did, however, share an Oscar for special visual effects on *Logan's Run* (1976) and was given a "special achievement" Oscar for his work on *Superman – The Movie* (1978).

The Fly (1958); *The Lost World* (1960); *Voyage To The Bottom Of The Sea* (1961); *Our Man Flint* (1965); *Batman* (1966); *Fantastic Voyage* (1966); *Way ... Way Out* (1966); *In Like Flint* (1967); *Planet Of The Apes* (1968); *Beneath The Planet Of The Apes* (1969); *The Challenge* (1970); *City Beneath The Sea* (1970); *The Amazing Captain Nemo* (1977); *The Swarm* (1978).

AGAR, John American actor, born 1921, whose career never evolved beyond B-features, mainly in sf and Westerns.

The Rocket Man (1953); *The Revenge Of The Creature* (1955); *Tarantula* (1955); *The Mole People* (1956); *Attack Of The Puppet People* (1958); *The Brain From Planet Arous* (1958); *Invisible Invaders* (1959); *Hand Of Death* (1961); *Journey To The Seventh Planet* (1961); *Women Of The Prehistoric Planet* (1965); *Zontar: The Thing From Venus* (1966); *King Kong* (1976).

ALLAND, William American producer of several memorable B-movies, he was also writer on two of his productions.

The Creature From The Black Lagoon (1953); *It Came From Outer Space* (1953);

This Island Earth (1954); *The Revenge Of The Creature* (1955) (and SP); *The Mole People* (1956); *The Deadly Mantis* (1957) (and SP); *The Space Children* (1957).

ALLEN, Irwin American producer, born in 1915, better known for his disaster movies (like *Towering Inferno* and *The Poseidon Adventure*) than for his lukewarm sf films. He occasionally directed.

The Lost World (1960) (and D/SP); *Voyage To The Bottom Of The Sea* (1961) (and D); *The Silencers* (1965); *City Beneath The Sea* (1970) (and D); *The Swarm* (1978) (and D).

ANDERSON, Gerry and Sylvia British husband and wife team whose puppet productions for British television pioneered sf programmes for children and included *Stingray*, *Thunderbirds*, *Captain Scarlet* and *Terrahawks*. They were involved at all stages of film-making; producing, directing, making costumes and scriptwriting.

Thunderbirds Are Go (1966) (P/SP); *Thunderbirds 6* (1968) (P/SP); *Journey To The Far Side Of The Sun* (1969) (P); *Alien Attack* (1979) (P); *Invasion UFO* (1980) (P/D/SP).

ANDERSON, Howard A. American special effects man.

The Day After Tomorrow (1942); *Phantom From Space* (1952); *Invasion Of The Saucer Men* (1957); *12 To The Moon* (1960); *The Underwater City* (1961); *Women Of The Prehistoric Planet* (1965).

ARNOLD, Jack American director, born in 1916. Arnold was one of very few directors working on low-budget B-movie science fiction who had a feel for the genre and his work is generally highly atmospheric. He occasionally worked under producer William Alland.

The Creature From The Black Lagoon (1953); *It Came From Outer Space* (1953);

The Revenge Of The Creature (1955); *Tarantula* (1955); *The Incredible Shrinking Man* (1957); *The Space Children* (1957); *Monster On The Campus* (1958); *The Mouse That Roared* (1959).

ATWILL, Lionel English actor, born in 1885. A horror actor, his involvement in sf films is, like that of Boris Karloff, more a question of definition than design. He died in 1946.

Doctor X (1932); *The Vampire Bat* (1932); *Son Of Frankenstein* (1939); *The Mad Doctor Of Market Street* (1942); *The Ghost of Frankenstein* (1941); *Frankenstein Meets The Wolfman* (1943).

BAKER, Kenny At only 3 ft 8 in, Baker is better known to fans of the "Star Wars" sequence when encased in the shell of Artoo Detoo (R2 D2), the cute robot trusted by Princess Leia to carry the message to Obi Wan.

Star Wars (1977); *The Empire Strikes Back* (1980); *Return Of The Jedi* (1983).

BAKER, Rick American special effects and make-up artist, born in 1950. He specializes in facial distortions, apes and aliens, and is perhaps the finest make-up artist working in the genre. He won an Oscar for his work on the non-sf film *An American Werewolf in London* (1982) and was also responsible for the excellent work on *Greystoke* and (under the supervision of John Landis) on Michael Jackson's *Thriller* video. He has occasionally worked alongside the special effects expert Carlo Rambaldi.

It's Alive (1973); *Live And Let Die* (1973); *Schlock* (1973); *King Kong* (1976); *The Incredible Melting Man* (1977); *Star Wars* (1977); *The Fury* (1978); *It Lives Again* (1978); *The Incredible Shrinking Woman* (1981); *Videodrome* (1982).

BALDERSTON, John L. American scriptwriter.

Bride Of Frankenstein (1935); *Mad Love* (1935); *The Man Who Lived Again* (1936); *Red Planet Mars* (1952).

BAVA, Mario Italian film director born in 1914. He began as a cameraman and worked under the names John Foam and John M. Old. Occasionally involved in special effects and scriptwriting, his strength nevertheless was as an imaginative B-movie director.

Caltiki, The Immortal Monster (1959); *Planet Of The Vampires* (1965); *Dr Goldfoot And The Girl Bombs* (1966); *Danger: Diabolik* (1967).

BENDER, Russ American actor who never graduated from the B-movie format. He also tried his hand at writing, with a screenplay to *Voodoo Woman* (1956), in which he also acted.

It Conquered The World (1956); *The Amazing Colossal Man* (1957); *Invasion Of The Saucer Men* (1957); *War Of The Colossal Beast* (1958); *Panic In The Year Zero* (1962); *The Navy Vs. The Night Monsters* (1965); *Space Monster* (1965).

BERNDS, Edward American director working mainly on low-budget B-movies.

World Without End (1955) (and SP); *Queen Of Outer Space* (1958); *Space Master X-7* (1958); *Prehistoric Valley* (1961) (and SP); *The Three Stooges In Orbit* (1962).

BISSELL, Whit American actor who played supporting roles in a number of 1950s B-movies, many of them within the sf genre.

Lost Continent (1951); *The Creature From The Black Lagoon* (1953); *The Atomic Kid* (1954); *Target Earth* (1954); *I Was A Teenage Frankenstein* (1957); *I Was A Teenage Werewolf* (1957); *Monster On The Campus* (1958); *The Time Machine* (1960).

BLACKTON, J. Stuart English producer and director of early trick movies, born in 1875. He helped form Vitagraph in the USA in the early years of this century and died in 1946.

Liquid Electricity (1907); *The Mechanical Statue And The Ingenious Servant* (1907); *Galvanic Fluid* (1908).

BLAISDELL, Paul American special effects expert who worked on several of Roger Corman's productions. He sometimes even played the monster!

The Beast With A Million Eyes (1955); *The Day The World Ended* (1956); *It Conquered The World* (1956); *Not Of This Earth* (1956); *Voodoo Woman* (1956); *Invasion Of The Saucer Men* (1957); *It! The Terror From Beyond Space* (1958).

BLALACK, Robbie One of the new generation of special effects experts who are making a radical change in American cinema and extending what is possible to express in the sf cinema. He shared a special effects Oscar for his work on *Star Wars* (1977).

Altered States (1980); *Heartbeeps* (1981); *Cat People* (1982).

BLOCK, Irving American special effects man, most of whose work was done in collaboration with Louis DeWitt and Jack Rabin. Little of their combined work stands up to modern-day standards of comparison.

Unknown World (1950) (and P); *The Invisible Boy* (1957); *Kronos* (1957) (and SP); *War Of The Satellites* (1957); *The Giant Behemoth* (1958); *The Thirty Foot Bride Of Candy Rock* (1958); *The Atomic Submarine* (1959).

BONESTELL, Chesley American expert in astronomical art, whose advice was sought on several of the bigger sf film projects in the early 1950s. The "feel" of the 1955 film, *The Conquest Of Space*, came from a coffee table book by Bonestell and Willy Ley. Born in 1888, he produced the excellent astronomical art for *Destination Moon* (1950) and was technical adviser on *When Worlds Collide* (1951).

BOOTH, Walter British producer/director, whose work pioneered the tricks of sf cinema in the first decade of this century.

An Over-Incubated Baby (1901); *The Motorist* (1906); *The Airship Destroyer* (1909); *Professor Puddenhead's Patents: The Electric Enlarger* (1909); *Professor Puddenhead's Patents; The Aerocab and Vacuum Provider* (1909); *The Electric Vitaliser* (1910) (and SP); *Aerial Anarchists* (1911); *The Automatic Motorist* (1911).

BOWIE, Les English special effects expert who formed his own company, Bowie Films, in the mid-1960s to produce special effects. He shared an Oscar for his work on *Superman: The Movie* (1978).

Blast Off! (1954); *X – The Unknown* (1956); *The Trollenberg Terror* (1958); *The Day The Earth Caught Fire* (1961); *The Evil Of Frankenstein* (1963); *War Gods Of The Deep* (1965); *Frankenstein Created Woman* (1966); *The Terrornauts* (1966); *Quatermass & The Pit* (1967); *They Came From Beyond Space* (1967); *Moon Zero Two* (1969); *Nothing But The Truth* (1972).

BROCCOLI, Albert "Cubby" and SALTZMAN, Harry American-born (1909) Broccoli and Canadian-born (1916) Saltzman teamed up specifically for *Dr No* (1962) and produced a further seven Bond films together, until in the mid-1970s. Broccoli went on to produce *Moonraker* (1979) alone.

Goldfinger (1964); *Thunderball* (1965); *You Only Live Twice* (1967); *On Her Majesty's Secret Service* (1969); *Diamonds Are Forever* (1971); *Live And Let Die* (1973); *The Man With The Golden Gun* (1974).

BUCHANAN, Larry Distinctive American director/producer of B-movies with a horror emphasis.

The Eye Creatures (1965); *Curse Of The Swamp Creature* (1966); *In The Year 2889* (1966); *Zontar: The Thing From Venus* (1966) (and SP); *It's Alive* (1968) (and SP).

CAHN, Edward L. American B-movie director, whose works added little that was new to the genre.

Robot Wrecks (1941); *The Creature With The Atom Brain* (1955); *Voodoo Woman* (1956); *Invasion Of The Saucer Men* (1957); *It! The Terror From Beyond Space* (1958); *Invisible Invaders* (1959).

CARLSON, Richard American actor, born 1914. He directed one sf film, *Riders To The Stars*, but was otherwise undistinguished in his roles. He died in 1977.

The Creature From The Black Lagoon (1953); *It Came From Outer Space* (1953); *The Magnetic Monster* (1953); *Riders To The Stars* (1953); *The Valley Where Time Stood Still* (1968).

CARPENTER, John American director, born 1948, extended his film-school thesis, *Dark Star*, from a 16 mm short to a 35 mm feature and became, at a stroke, one of the best-loved sf directors of all time. His knowledge of and use of the written form of sf gives an added dimension to his work – particularly in his debut.

Dark Star (1974) (and SP); *Escape From New York* (1981); *The Thing* (1982); *Starman* (1985).

CARRADINE, John American actor, born 1906. Real name Richmond Reed Carradine, one of his first screen appearances was in *The Invisible Man* (1933), where he was credited as Peter Richmond. In the 50 years he's been in cinema he is better noted for the quantity rather than the quality of his acting, much of which is tongue-in-cheek.

The Bride Of Frankenstein (1935); *House Of Frankenstein* (1944); *The Invisible Man's Revenge* (1944); *Return Of The Ape Man* (1944); *The Black Sleep* (1956); *The Unearthly* (1957); *Invisible Invaders* (1959); *Invasion Of The Animal People* (1960) (Voice only); *Sex Kittens Go To College* (1960); *The Wizard Of Mars* (1964); *The Astro Zombies* (1968); *Pact With The Devil* (1968); *Shock Waves* (1970); *The Horror Of The Blood Monsters* (1971); *Everything You Ever Wanted To Know About Sex* (1972); *Moonchild* (1972); *The Secret Of NIMH* (1982) (Voice only); *The Ice Pirates* (1984).

CHAMBERS, John American make-up expert whose work on *Planet Of The Apes* (1968) was innovatory and won him a "special award" Oscar for make-up. His work has certainly influenced Rick Baker amongst others.

The Human Duplicators (1964); *Beneath The Planet Of The Apes* (1971); *Escape From The Planet Of The Apes* (1971); *Superbeast* (1972); *Schlock* (1973); *SSSSSSSS* (1973).

CHANEY, Lon, Jr American actor, born 1906, he is best known for his horror-oriented roles, and for his marvellous performance in the non-sf film, *Of Mice And Men* (1939), where he played the simpleton big man, Lennie. He died in 1973.

One Million B.C. (1940); *Man Made Monster* (1941); *The Ghost Of Frankenstein* (1942); *Frankenstein Meets The Wolfman* (1943); *House Of Frankenstein* (1944); *Abbott and Costello Meet Frankenstein* (1948); *The Black Sleep* (1956); *The Indestructible Man* (1956); *The Cyclops* (1957); *The Alligator People* (1959).

CHILVERS, Colin Special effects expert given a "special achievement" Oscar for visual effects work on *Superman – The Movie* (1978).

Superman II (1980); *Saturn 3* (1980); *Superman III* (1983).

CHRISTIE, Julie British actress, born in Assam, India, in 1941. Her appearances in sf cinema have been few but memorable.

Fahrenheit 451 (1966); *Don't Look Now* (1973); *Demon Seed* (1976); *Memoirs Of A Survivor* (1981).

COHEN, Larry American director, born 1938, whose work in TV (as scriptwriter mainly) led to his graduation to the big screen. His work is usually horror or tinged with horror.

It's Alive (1973) (P/SP); *It Lives Again* (1978) (and SP); *Q, The Winged Serpent* (1982) (P/SP).

CONNERY, Sean Born in Edinburgh, Scotland, in 1930, Connery graduated to the big time with his first portrayal of James Bond in *Dr No* (1962), but is also to be found in several other interesting sf films.

Goldfinger (1964); *Thunderball* (1965); *You Only Live Twice* (1967); *On Her Majesty's Secret Service* (1969); *Diamonds Are Forever* (1971); *Zardoz* (1973); *Meteor* (1975); *Outland* (1981); *Time Bandits* (1981); *Never Say Never Again* (1983).

CORMAN, Roger American producer/director born in 1926, Corman is the most prolific maker of sf movies, even though he has yet to produce one major or influential sf film. A master of the quick exploitation of trends, he began his career as messenger boy at the offices of 20th Century Fox and, besides his sf films has produced a number of movies based on Edgar Allen Poe stories. Excluding Lucas and Spielberg, he remains one of the most successful movie-makers in cinema.

The Beast With A Million Eyes (1955); *Attack Of The Crab Monsters* (1956) (and D); *The Day The World Ended* (1956) (and D); *It Conquered The World* (1956) (and D); *Not Of This Earth* (1956) (and D); *War Of The Satellites* (1957) (and D); *The Creature From Galaxy 27* (1958); *Beast From Haunted Cave* (1959); *The Giant Leeches* (1959); *The Wasp Woman* (1959) (and D); *The Last Woman On Earth* (1960) (and D); *Little Shop Of Horrors* (1960) (and D); *Creature From The Haunted Sea* (1961) (and D); *Battle Beyond The Sun* (1963); *X – The Man With X-Ray Eyes* (1963) (and D); *Voyage To The Prehistoric Planet* (1965); *Queen Of Blood* (1966); *Voyage To The Planet Of Prehistoric Women* (1966); *Twilight People* (1971); *Death Race 2000* (1975); *Deathsport* (1978); *Battle Beyond The Stars* (1980); *Forbidden World* (1982); *Space Raiders* (1983).

CRICHTON, Michael American director who has written the screenplays for all three sf movies he's so far made. His own novels, *Terminal Man* and *The Andromeda Strain*, were also filmed, though without his direct involvement in the projects.

Westworld (1973); *Coma* (1978); *Looker* (1981).

CRONENBERG, David Canadian director, born in 1943, whose work in the cinema has been single-minded and distinctive. He now appears to be moving towards a no-less-horrific, but less morbid set of subject matters, but his early fascination with monsters which reflected a disease in humankind (he has been called "the king of venereal horror") was often marred by his attempt to do everything – produce, direct, write, film, edit. With better backing and a decade's experience, his more recent films mark him out as one of the directors likely to make the sf classics of the future.

Stereo (1969) (P/D/SP/C); *Crimes Of The Future* (1970) (P/D/SP/C); *Shivers* (1974) (D/SP); *Rabid* (1976) (D/SP); *The Brood* (1979) (D/SP); *Scanners* (1981) (D/SP); *Videodrome* (1982) (D/SP); *The Dead Zone* (1983) (D).

CRUIKSHANK, Art American special effects expert, whose work has sometimes been in collaboration with L. B. Abbott and Emil Kosa Jr, with much of it for the Disney studios. He won a Special Visual Effects Oscar for *Fantastic Voyage* (1966).

In Like Flint (1967); *Planet Of The Apes* (1968); *Beneath The Planet Of The Apes* (1969); *City Beneath The Sea* (1970); *Earth II* (1971); *The Island At The Top Of The World* (1973); *Escape To Witch Mountain* (1974); *Return From Witch Mountain* (1978); *The Cat From Outer Space* (1978); *The Black Hole* (1979).

CUSHING, Peter English actor, born 1913, famous for his horror roles for Hammer studios. His most famous sf role is as the Empire's general, Grand Moff Tarkin, in *Star Wars* (1977).

The Abominable Snowman Of The Himalayas (1957); *The Curse Of Frankenstein* (1957); *The Revenge Of Frankenstein* (1958); *The Evil Of Frankenstein* (1963); *Dr Who And The Daleks* (1965); *Daleks: Invasion Earth 2150 AD* (1966); *Island Of Terror* (1966); *Caves Of Steel* (1967); *Island Of The Burning Damned* (1967); *The Vampire Beast Craves Blood* (1967); *Frankenstein Must Be Destroyed* (1969); *Scream and Scream Again* (1969); *Shock Waves* (1970);

I, Monster (1971); *Dr Phibes Rides Again* (1972); *Horror Express* (1972); *Nothing But The Truth* (1972); *Frankenstein And The Monster From Hell* (1973); *At The Earth's Core* (1976).

DANIELS, Anthony Well-spoken actor who, in his shell of golden metal, plays C-3PO in the three Star Wars films.

Star Wars (1977); *The Empire Strikes Back* (1980); *Return Of The Jedi* (1983).

DEHN, Paul British scriptwriter, born 1912, who won an Oscar (together with James Bernard) for his screenplay for *Seven Days To Noon* (1950). He died in 1976.

Goldfinger (1964); *Beneath The Planet of The Apes* (1969); *Escape From The Planet Of The Apes* (1971); *Conquest Of The Planet Of The Apes* (1972).

DE LAURENTIIS, Dino Italian producer, born 1919, whose interest in and support of the sf cinema has not always been matched by the "taste" of the end product.

Kiss The Girls And Make Them Die (1966); *Barbarella* (1967); *Danger: Diabolik* (1967); *King Kong* (1976); *Flash Gordon* (1980); *Dune* (1984) (Exec P).

DeWITT, Louis American special effects man, working often with Jack Rabin and Irving Block.

The Black Sleep (1956); *The Invisible Boy* (1957); *Kronos* (1957); *War Of The Satellite* (1957); *The Giant Behemoth* (1958); *The Monster From The Green Hell* (1958); *The Thirty Foot Bride Of Candy Rock* (1958); *The Atomic Submarine* (1959).

DOMERGUE, Faith American actress, perhaps best known to sf film fans for her role in *This Island Earth* (1954).

It Came From Beneath The Sea (1955); *Timeslip* (1956); *Voyage To The Prehistoric Planet* (1965).

DONLEVY, Brian Irish actor, born 1901. His portrayal of the scientist, Quatermass, in the first two of the three

Quatermass films, earned him justifiable critical acclaim, though he did little else of mention in the sf cinema.

The Quatermass Experiment (1955); *Quatermass II* (1957); *The Curse Of The Fly* (1965); *Gamera* (1966).

DOUGLAS, Kirk American actor, born Issur Danielovitch Demsky in 1916. He seems to grow younger by the year and, in a film like *Saturn 3* (1980), it's difficult to believe that he is a 64-year-old man – perhaps there's an sf film in that! He seems, in recent years, to have moved into the sf cinema quite naturally.

20,000 Leagues Under The Sea (1954); *Seven Days In May* (1964); *Holocaust 2000* (1977); *The Fury* (1978); *The Final Countdown* (1980).

DULLEA, Keir American actor, born 1936, whose portrayal of astronaut Dave Bowman in *2001: A Space Odyssey* (1968) and its sequel *2010* (1984) will undoubtedly be the role for which he will be remembered.

Welcome To Blood City (1977); *Brainwaves* (1982).

DUNCAN, David American sf writer, born 1913, whose scriptwriting is, perhaps, the least significant part of his work.

The Black Scorpion (1957); *Monster On The Campus* (1958); *The Leech Woman* (1960); *The Time Machine* (1960).

DYKSTRA, John American special effects expert whose work on *Star Wars* (1977) earned him a shared Oscar for special effects. He utilized what he learned on that film in his own production of *Battlestar Galactica* (1977), which George Lucas threatened to sue him over. Like Douglas Trumbull he has led the recent revolution in special effects.

The Andromeda Strain (1971); *Silent Running* (1971); *Voyage To The Outer Planets* (1973); *Star Trek – The Motion Picture* (1979); *Starflight One* (1982); *Firefox* (1982).

EDLUND, Richard American special effects expert who, as part of George Lucas's team from Industrial Light And Magic, won Oscars for *Star Wars* (1977) and *The Empire Strikes Back* (1980).

Return Of The Jedi (1983); *Ghostbusters* (1984); *2010* (1984).

ELLIOT, Denholm English actor, born 1922.

The Rise And Rise Of Michael Rimmer (1970); *Madame Sin* (1971); *The Boys From Brazil* (1978); *Raiders Of The Lost Ark* (1980).

FIELD, Roy Special effects expert who won a "special achievement" Oscar for his special effects work on *Superman – The Movie* (1978).

Saturn 3 (1980); *Superman II* (1980); *Outland* (1981); *Superman III* (1983); *Supergirl* (1984).

FISHER, Carrie American actress, born 1956, and daughter of Debbie Reynolds and Eddie Fisher. Despite how it seems, she has appeared in films other than the Star Wars sequence (where she plays the heroic Princess Leia), as, for example, *Wise Blood* (1979).

Star Wars (1977); *The Empire Strikes Back* (1980); *Return Of The Jedi* (1983).

FISHER, Terence English director, born 1904, whose work for Hammer studios – mainly on horror – re-enlivened their reputation. His first film for them was the memorable *The Curse Of Frankenstein* (1957), though Fisher had been a director since the late 1940s after having been a film editor. He died in 1980.

Spaceways (1953); *Four-Sided Triangle* (1953) (and SP); *The Revenge Of Frankenstein* (1958); *The Man Who Could Cheat Death* (1959); *The Earth Dies Screaming* (1964); *Frankenstein Created Woman* (1966); *Island Of Terror* (1966); *Island Of The Burning Damned* (1967); *Frankenstein Must Be Destroyed* (1969); *Frankenstein and The Monster From Hell* (1973).

FORD, Harrison American actor, born 1942, who has starred in five of the seven biggest grossing films of all time (and the 46th, if you want to be pedantic). Either as Han Solo in the Star Wars films, or as the hero of the two (so far) Indiana Jones films, he has recaptured the spirit of the 1930s serial on a grand scale, and as the "blade runner", Rick Deckard, in Ridley Scott's *Blade Runner* (1982) he has become identified with the sf cinema. It may surprise some to discover that he has also appeared in at least a dozen non-sf films.

Star Wars (1977); *The Empire Strikes Back* (1980); *Raiders Of The Lost Ark* (1981); *Return Of The Jedi* (1983).

FRANCO, Jesus Spanish director/ scriptwriter, sometimes working in the medical-horror genre.

The Awful Doctor Orloff (1961) (D/SP); *Attack Of The Robots* (1962) (D); *Dr Orloff's Monster* (1964) (D/SP); *The Diabolical Dr Z* (1965) (D/SP); *Dr Mabuse* (1971) (D/SP).

FUKUDA, Jim Japanese director who worked for the Honda studios and took over the Kaiju Eiga (the monster movie cycle begun with *Godzilla*), from director Inoshiro Honda.

Secret of The Telegian (1960); *Godzilla Vs. The Sea Monster* (1966); *Son Of Godzilla* (1967); *War Of The Monsters* (1972); *Godzilla Versus Megalon* (1973) (and SP); *Godzilla Vs. The Bionic Monster* (1974) (and SP); *War Of The Planets* (1977).

FULTON, John P. American special effects expert, born 1902, whose work on *Frankenstein* (1931) (alongside Kenneth Strickfaden) was, at the time, innovative and exciting – he also worked on James Whale's *The Invisible Man* (1933). He died in 1966 after a prolific career both within the sf cinema and outside.

Bride Of Frankenstein (1935); *The Invisible Ray* (1935); *Night Key* (1937); *The Invisible Man Returns* (1939); *The Invisible Woman* (1940); *Man Made Monster* (1941); *Invisible Agent* (1942); *Frankenstein Meets The Wolfman* (1943); *House Of Frankenstein* (1944);

The Invisible Man's Revenge (1944); *The Naked Jungle* (1953); *The Conquest Of Space* (1955); *The Space Children* (1957); *The Colossus Of New York* (1958); *I Married A Monster From Outer Space* (1958); *Visit To A Small Planet* (1959); *Bamboo Saucer* (1967, released posthumously).

GORDON, Bert I. American director, born 1922, whose sense of science fiction as spectacle was not, alas, matched by his film-making ability. He often did almost everything himself (with some support from wife, Flora) and, subsequently, has produced some of the worst sf films in existence.

King Dinosaur (1955) (P/D); *The Amazing Colossal Man* (1957) (D/SP); *The Cyclops* (1957) (P/D/SP/SE); *Attack Of The Puppet People* (1958) (P/D/SP/SE); *Earth Vs. The Giant Spider* (1958) (P/D/SE); *War Of The Colossal Beast* (1958) (P/D/SE); *Village Of The Giants* (1965) (P/D/SE); *The Food Of The Gods* (1976) (P/D/SP/SE); *Empire Of The Ants* (1977) (P/D/SE).

GUEST, Val English director, born 1911, who began by writing comedies (for Will Hay amongst others) and spent some time as a gossip columnist in the USA, but who produced what were then considered classics of the British sf cinema. Certainly his Quatermass films still bear watching.

Give Us The Moon (1944); *The Quatermass Experiment* (1955) (and SP); *The Abominable Snowman Of The Himalayas* (1957); *Quatermass II* (1957) (and SP); *The Day The Earth Caught Fire* (1961); *Bees In Paradise* (1964) (and SP); *When Dinosaurs Ruled The Earth* (1969) (and SP); *Toomorrow* (1970) (and SP).

GUFFEY, Cary American actor, born 1973, whose appearance as the little boy kidnapped by the aliens in *Close Encounters Of The Third Kind* (1977) endeared him to millions. A bit older and a bit bigger, he's done three films since, playing upon cuteness rather than acting ability.

The Sheriff And The Satellite Kid (1979); *Why Did You Pick On Me?* (1979); *Mutant* (1983).

GUINNESS, Alex Distinguished English actor, born 1914, whose appearance as Obi Wan Kenobi in the Star Wars sequence of films added a necessary ingredient of authority to the proceedings ("Use the force Luke!"). His only previous encounter with a science-fictional idea in a film was in the brilliant 1951 satirical comedy, *The Man In The White Suit*, where he played the naïve inventor.

Star Wars (1977); *The Empire Strikes Back* (1980); *Return Of The Jedi* (1983).

HAGMAN, Larry American actor, born 1931, whose directorial debut was *Beware! The Blob!* (1971), a film only a degree or so more dreadful than its prequel, *The Blob*. Hagman, best known as TV's JR in *Dallas*, has made only two other acting appearances in sf films.

Fail Safe (1964); *Superman: The Movie* (1978).

HAMILL, Mark American actor, born 1952, who made his TV debut on the *Bill Cosby Show* and then found himself cast as Luke Skywalker in George Lucas's Star Wars films. He has only made a couple of very minor films outside of *Star Wars*.

Star Wars (1977); *The Empire Strikes Back* (1980); *Return Of The Jedi* (1983).

HARDWICKE, Cedric English actor, born 1893, his dignified appearance and gentlemanly voice grace a number of sf films, and his voice perfroms the narrative to *War Of The Worlds* (1952). He died in 1964.

Things To Come (1936); *The Invisible Man Returns* (1939); *The Invisible Agent* (1942); *The Ghost Of Frankenstein* (1942); *A Connecticut Yankee At King Arthur's Court* (1948); *Mr Krane* (1957)

HARRYHAUSEN, Harry American special effects expert, born 1920. His work has been in the tradition of Willis O'Brien, whose work Harryhausen admired and tried emulate. Nowadays the stop-go animation techniques look rather too artificial for our tastes, but at the time they were spectacular. He is also to be remembered for his work on the Sinbad and Jason And The Argonauts films.

Mighty Joe Young (1949); *The Beast From 20,000 Fathoms* (1953); *It Came From Beneath The Sea* (1955); *Earth Vs. The Flying Saucers* (1956); *Twenty Million Miles To Earth* (1957); *The Mysterious Island* (1961); *First Men In The Moon* (1964); *One Million Years B.C.* (1966); *The Valley Where Time Stood Still* (1968).

HASKIN, Byron American director, born 1899, who, under producer George Pal, made some of the biggest budget sf movies of the 1950s, if not necessarily the "classic" films they were claimed to be at the time. He began his career as a newspaper cartoonist and for most of his early cinematic career was a cameraman.

War Of The Worlds (1952); *The Conquest Of Space* (1955); *From The Earth To The Moon* (1958); *Robinson Crusoe On Mars* (1964); *The Power* (1967).

HELM, Brigitte German actress, born 1908, who played the beautiful working-class heroine, Maria, in Fritz Lang's *Metropolis* (1926), doubling-up her role as the robot-Maria (a cast was taken of Helm's body for this). It was, surprisingly, her screen debut.

At The Edge Of The World (1927); *Alraune* (1928); *Alraune* (1930); *Lost Atlantis* (1932); *Gold* (1934).

HESTON, Charlton American actor, born in 1923, who has added a slight epic quality to the few sf films he has been in. He is better known, perhaps, for his full-blown epics like *Ben Hur* and *El Cid*.

Planet Of The Apes (1968); *Beneath The Planet Of The Apes* (1969); *The Omega Man* (1971); *Soylent Green* (1973); *Earthquake* (1974).

HONDA, Inoshiro Japanese director who might be said to have created the monster movie cycle, the Kaiju Eiga, with its monsters like Godzilla, Mothra, Rodan and so forth – actors in rubber suits trampling down reduced scale models of

Tokyo. Mindless repetitions, these were, surprisingly, also highly popular in America. For his effects he usually used Eiji Tsuburaya, with Shinichi Sekizawa as his screenwriter. His work for Toho studios ended with *Yog – Monster From Space* (1970), which was without Tsuburaya, who died that year.

Godzilla, King Of The Monsters (1954) (and SP); *Rodan* (1965); *The Mysterians* (1957); *The H-Man* (1958); *Varan The Unbelievable* (1958); *Battle In Outer Space* (1959); *The Human Vapor* (1960); *Mothra* (1961); *Gorath* (1962); *King Kong Vs. Godzilla* (1962); *Atragon* (1963); *Attack Of The Mushroom People* (1963); *Dragora, The Space Monster* (1964); *Frankenstein Conquers The World* (1964); *Godzilla Vs. Mothra* (1964); *Ghidorah, The Three-Headed Monster* (1965); *Monster Zero* (1965); *War Of The Gargantuas* (1966) (and SP); *Destroy All Monsters* (1968) (and SP); *Godzilla's Revenge* (1969); *Latitude Zero* (1969).

HUDSON, Rock American actor, born Roy Scherer in 1925, he graduated from being a truck driver to one of Hollywood's most popular actors. His excursions into sf have been intelligent, sensitive roles.

Seconds (1966); *Embryo* (1976); *The Martians* (1979); *World War III* (1980).

HUNTER, Kim American actress, born Janet Cole in 1922, she is best known as the chimpanzee intellectual, Dr Zira, in the *Planet Of The Apes* series. She hasn't, it seems, chosen to work in the genre without her ape make-up.

Planet Of The Apes (1968); *Beneath The Planet Of The Apes* (1969); *Escape From The Planet Of The Apes* (1971).

HYAMS, Peter American director, born 1943, who writes the screenplays for his own films. His three major sf outings have shown a progression from competence towards excellence. He is, at this moment, perhaps the only successful director of space realism.

Capricorn One (1978); *Outland* (1981); *2010* (1984).

JENNINGS, Gordon American special effects expert at Paramount studios until his death in 1953. He won Oscars for both *When Worlds Collide* (1951) and *War Of The Worlds* (1952).

The Island Of Lost Souls (1932); *Dr Cyclops* (1939); *Golden Earrings* (1947).

JOHNSON, Brian Special effects expert whose work on *Alien* (1979) and *The Empire Strikes Back* (1980) won him special visual effects Oscars.

The Glitterball (1977); *Alien Attack* (1979).

JONES, Freddie Talented English actor who seems only recently to have moved over almost exclusively into sf cinema.

Frankenstein Must Be Destroyed (1969); *Firefox* (1982); *Krull* (1983); *Dune* (1984); *Firestarter* (1984).

KARLOFF, Boris English actor, born William Henry Pratt (1887), his portrayal of Frankenstein's monster in the 1931 film, *Frankenstein*, made his name. Most of his contributions to sf cinema were in the horror vein, with several variants upon the mad scientist theme. He died in 1969.

Bride Of Frankenstein (1935); *The Invisible Ray* (1935); *The Man Who Lived Again* (1936); *The Walking Dead* (1936); *Night Key* (1937); *The Man They Could Not Hang* (1939); *Son Of Frankenstein* (1939); *Black Friday* (1940); *The Boogie Man Will Get You* (1942); *House Of Frankenstein* (1944); *Abbott and Costello Meet Dr Jekyll and Mr Hyde* (1953); *Frankenstein 1970* (1958); *Die! Monster Die!* (1965); *The Venetian Affair* (1966); *The Sorcerors* (1967); *The Incredible Invasion* (1968).

KASDAN, Lawrence American screenwriter, chosen by George Lucas to work with him on the storylines of three of his biggest moneyspinners. Kasdan, an unknown prior to Lucas's decision, has subsequently directed his own films, including *Body Heat*.

The Empire Strikes Back (1980); *Raiders Of The Lost Ark* (1981); *Return Of The Jedi* (1983).

KELLEY, DeForest American actor, born 1920, forever typecast now as Dr McCoy ("Bones") in the *Star Trek* TV and feature film series.

Night Of The Lepus (1972); *Star Trek – The Motion Picture* (1979); *Star Trek II: The Wrath Of Khan* (1982); *Star Trek III – The Search For Spock* (1984).

KENTON, Earl C. American director, born 1896, whose sf films were a very small part indeed of an incredible output of B-movies between 1919 and 1951.

The Island Of Lost Souls (1932); *The Ghost Of Frankenstein* (1942); *House Of Frankenstein* (1944).

KERSHNER, Irvin American director, born 1923, who has been making films since the late 1950s, most of them low-budget crime-oriented movies.

The Empire Strikes Back (1980); *Never Say Never Again* (1983).

KIDDER, Margot American actress, born 1948, who has many facets to her talented nature, including directing documentaries. She is best known, however, for her portrayal of Superman's admirer/lover, Lois Lane.

Superman: The Movie (1978); *Superman II* (1980); *Superman III* (1983).

KIEL, Richard American actor whose chief merit is his size. He's better known, perhaps, as "Jaws" in the Bond films.

The Phantom Planet (1961); *The Human Duplicators* (1964); *The Spy Who Loved Me* (1977); *Moonraker* (1979).

KINSKI, Klaus Polish actor, born Nikolas Nakszynski Zoppot in 1926, his prolific career has not prevented him from putting in some very fine performances, amongst them his portrayal of Dr Mabuse, in *Scotland Yard Hunts Dr Mabuse* (1963).

Blast Off! (1954); *Coplan Saves His Skin*

(1967); *The Million Eyes Of Su-Muru* (1967); *Android* (1982).

KIRK, Tommy American actor who, as a child, appeared in a number of Walt Disney juveniles with an sf bias.

The Absent-Minded Professor (1961); *Moon Pilot* (1961); *Son Of Flubber* (1962); *The Misadventures Of Merlin Jones* (1963); *The Monkey's Uncle* (1965); *Village Of The Giants* (1965); *Mars Needs Women* (1966); *It's Alive!* (1968).

KLEINE-ROGGE, Rudolph German actor whose portrayal of the mad-scientist Rotwang in *Metropolis* (1926) (parodied by Klaus Kinski in the 1982 film, *Android*) is only one of several memorable roles he undertook, mainly with Fritz Lang.

The Cabinet Of Dr Caligari (1919); *Dr Mabuse, The Gambler* (1922); *The Spy* (1928); *The Testament Of Dr Mabuse* (1933).

KNEALE, Nigel English scriptwriter, whose *Quatermass* TV series was adapted for the big screen.

The Abominable Snowman Of The Himalayas (1957); *Quatermass II* (1957); *First Men In The Moon* (1964); *Quatermass And The Pit* (1967).

KOSA, Emil Jr American special effects expert who usually worked with L. B. Abbot and Art Cruikshank.

Journey To The Centre Of The Earth (1959); *The Lost World* (1960); *Our Man Flint* (1965); *Fantastic Voyage* (1966); *Way ... Way Out* (1966); *In Like Flint* (1967); *Planet Of The Apes* (1968).

KUBRICK, Stanley American director/producer, born 1928, responsible for three of the most remarkable sf films made, one of which, *2001: A Space Odyssey* (1968), won him a Best Visual Effects Oscar, and is probably the first of a new generation of space fiction films. He produced, directed, co-scripted and organized special effects on *2001!*

Dr Strangelove, Or How I Learned To Stop Worrying And Love The Bomb (1963) (p/d/sp); *A Clockwork Orange* (1971) (p/d/sp).

KURTZ, Gary Associate of George Lucas and producer of the first two Star Wars films.

Star Wars (1977); *The Empire Strikes Back* (1980); *The Dark Crystal* (1982).

LAEMMLE, Carl Jr. German producer, born 1867. He emigrated to the USA in 1884 and set up as a distributor in 1907. He died in 1939.

Dr Jekyll and Mr Hyde (1913); *In The Year 2014* (1914); *Frankenstein* (1931); *The Invisible Man* (1933).

LANG, Fritz Born in Vienna, Austria, in 1890, Fritz Lang might well be considered to have formed several of the sub-themes of the sf cinema by himself: space flight as realism; dystopias; the technological spy-thriller. He worked with his wife (they married in 1924) Thea Von Harbou on many of his major films and often took a hand in writing the screenplay. He left Germany in 1933 and worked in America until the 1960s while his wife stayed. His film *Metropolis* (1926) must be considered the first major feature in the history of sf cinema. He died in 1976.

The Cabinet of Dr Caligari (1919) (sp only); *The Brilliant Ship* (1920) (and sp); *Dr Mabuse, The Gambler* (1922) (and sp); *The Spy* (1928) (and sp); *By Rocket To The Moon* (1929); *(and* sp); *The Testament Of Dr Mabuse* (1933); *The Thousand Eyes Of Dr Mabuse* (1960) (and sp).

LARSON, Glen A. American scriptwriter whose production company brought out the *Battlestar Galactica* TV series and films.

Battlestar Galactica (1977); *Buck Rogers In The 25th Century* (1979); *Mission Galactica: The Cylon Attack* (1979); *Conquest Of The Earth* (1980).

LEE, Christopher English actor, born 1922, whose work has been in the horror/sf crossover of cinema, much of it of competent B-movie standard.

The Curse Of Frankenstein (1957); *The Man Who Could Cheat Death* (1959); *The Two Faces Of Dr Jekyll* (1960); *Island Of The Burning Damned* (1967); *Scream And Scream Again* (1969); *I. Monster* (1971); *Deathline* (1972); *Horror Express* (1972); *Nothing But The Night* (1972); *The Man With The Golden Gun* (1974); *The End Of The World* (1977); *Starship Invasions* (1977).

LESTER, Richard American director, born 1932, famous for his two Beatles films, *Help* and *Hard Day's Night*, and usually interested in injecting a comic element into films.

The Bedsitting Room (1969); *Superman II* (1980); *Superman III* (1983).

LEWIS, Jerry American comic actor, born 1926. You either love Lewis or you loathe him. He's not to my taste, but his "zaniness" does appeal to some.

Visit To A Small Planet (1959); *The Nutty Professor* (1963) (and d); *Way ... Way Out* (1966); *Slapstick* (1984).

LOHMAN, Augie American special effects expert.

Lost Continent (1951); *The Bowery Boys Meet The Monsters* (1954); *Sex Kittens Go To College* (1960); *Kiss The Girls And Make Them Die* (1966); *Barbarella* (1967).

LORRE, Peter Hungarian actor, born Laszlo Lowenstein in 1904. His first screen part was in Fritz Lang's *M* in 1931 and his sf film appearances have usually been in horror/sf crossovers. He died in 1964.

F.P.1 Doesn't Answer (1932); *Mad Love* (1935); *The Boogie Man Will Get You* (1942); *Invisible Agent* (1942); *Voyage To The Bottom Of The Sea* (1961).

LOURIE, Eugene Russian director, born 1905, who worked primarily as an art director and graduated to full director.

The Beast From 20,000 Fathoms (1953); *The Colossus Of New York* (1958); *The Giant Behemoth* (1958) (and sp); *Gorgo* (1959).

LUCAS, George American director/ producer, born 1944, whose sf short film, *THX 2238 – 4EB* (1967) won an award at the National Student Film Festival and won Lucas the attention of film producer Francis Ford Coppola. With five of his films amongst the ten biggest grossing films of all time, he must (alongside Spielberg, with whom he worked on the Indiana Jones movies) be considered the most successful movie-maker in the world. Much of his profit has been channelled back into his own production company, Lucasfilms, and his special effects team, Industrial Light And Magic, as well as into large grants for film schools. But even without this process, *Star Wars* alone re-vivified sf cinema merely by existing and proving to the big movie houses that not only was sf film good business but the biggest business.

THX 1138 (1970) (d/sp); *Star Wars* (1977) (d/sp); *The Empire Strikes Back* (1980) (p); *Raiders Of The Lost Ark* (1981) (p/d/sp); *Return Of The Jedi* (1983) (p/ sp).

LUGOSI, Bela Born Béla Blaskó in Hungary (1888), Lugosi was a horror film regular and, like Karloff, is included only because so much of the horror output of the 1930s and 1940s had a science-fictional rationale. He died in 1956.

The Invisible Ray (1935); *Murder By Television* (1935); *Son Of Frankenstein* (1939); *Black Friday* (1940); *The Corpse Vanishes* (1942); *The Ghost Of Frankenstein* (1942); *The Ape Man* (1943); *Frankenstein Meets The Wolfman* (1943); *Return Of The Ape Man* (1944); *Abbott and Costello Meet Frankenstein* (1948); *Bela Lugosi Meets A Brooklyn Gorilla* (1952); *Old Mother Riley Meets The Vampire* (1952); *Bride Of The Monster* (1955); *The Black Sleep* (1956); *Plan 9 From Outer Space* (1956).

LYDECKER, Howard and Theodore American brothers who worked on special effects projects together. Theodore worked on *The Lady And The Monster* (1944) without his brother, and Howard's solo services were used on *The Underwater City* (1961), *Our Man Flint* (1965) and *Way ... Way Out* (1966).

The Valley Of The Zombies (1946); *The Atomic Kid* (1954); *Tobor The Great* (1954); *Satan's Satellite* (1958).

LYNCH, David American producer/director/writer, born 1946, whose early experimental works, short films like *The Alphabet* and *The Grandmother*, were preparations for his bizarre but excellent film *Eraserhead* (1979) (where he also provided all the special effects) but hardly prepare *us* for the epic sf saga *Dune* (1984), which he apparently worked at for three years.

McCALLUM, David Scottish actor, born 1933, who became famous as Ilya Kuryakin, the hero (alongside Robert Vaughn's Napoleon Solo) of TV's *The Man From U.N.C.L.E.* series. Two of his sf films, *The Spy With My Face* (1965) and *How To Steal The World* (1968), are feature-length adaptations of the series.

Around The World Under The Sea (1966); *Hauser's Memory* (1970); *Frankenstein: The True Story* (1973); *The Watcher In The Woods* (1980).

McCARTHY, Kevin American actor, born 1914, and brother of well-known novelist Mary McCarthy. He is most famous as the hero of *Invasion Of The Body Snatchers* (1956) and made a cameo return in the re-make in 1978.

Twilight Zone – The Movie (1983).

McDOWALL, Roddy English actor, born 1928, who was evacuated to America during the blitz in 1940. A versatile performer, his career was somewhat typecast by his role as the chimpanzee, Cornelius, in *Planet Of The Apes* (1968) and its sequels.

It! (1966); *Escape From The Planet Of The Apes* (1971); *Conquest Of The Planet Of The Apes* (1972); *Battle For The Planet Of The Apes* (1973); *Embryo* (1976); *The Cat From Outer Space* (1978).

McDOWELL, Malcolm English actor, born 1943, whose roles as Alex, the leader of the Droogs (a futuristic gang), in *A Clockwork Orange* (1971) and as H. G.

Wells in *Time After Time* (1979) demonstrate his versatility.

O Lucky Man (1973); *Cat People* (1982); *Blue Thunder* (1983).

MacMURRAY, Fred American actor, born 1908, who starred as the professor who invents the anti-gravity substance flubber in *The Absent-Minded Professor* (1961) and its sequel.

Where Do We Go From Here? (1945); *Son Of Flubber* (1962); *Kisses For My President* (1964); *The Swarm* (1978).

MARGHERITI, Antonio English-born director Anthony Dawson used this Italian pseudonym for his output of sf films in the 1960s. Never an innovator, there are certain obsessions, nonetheless, in his work – such as roving planets.

Assignment Outer Space (1960); *Battle Of The Worlds* (1960); *Killers Are Challenged* (1965); *Lightning Bolt* (1965); *War Between The Planets* (1965); *War Of The Planets* (1965); *Wild, Wild Planet* (1965); *Perry Rhodan – SOS In Weltall* (1967) (SE only); *The Invincible Invisible Man* (1969); *The Humanoid* (1979) (SE only).

MAYHEW, Peter American actor recognizable only by his grunts and roars beneath the make-up for Chewbacca in the Star Wars sequence of films.

Star Wars (1977); *The Empire Strikes Back* (1980); *Return Of The Jedi* (1983).

MEDDINGS, Derek English special effects expert who won a "special achievement" Oscar for his special visual effects work on *Superman: The Movie* (1978). He worked mainly in the British cinema until the 1970s, often with Gerry and Sylvia Anderson.

Thunderbirds Are Go (1966); *Thunderbirds 6* (1968); *Journey To The Far Side Of The Sun* (1969); *Zero Population Growth* (1971); *The Land That Time Forgot* (1974); *Moonraker* (1979); *Invasion UFO* (1980); *Krull* (1983); *Supergirl* (1984).

MELCHIOR, Ib American director/ screenwriter whose work (even on the fondly-remembered *Robinson Crusoe On Mars* (1964) which he co-wrote) leaves much to be desired.

The Angry Red Planet (1959); *Journey To The Seventh Planet* (1961) (and SP); *Repticilus* (1962) (and SP); *The Time Travellers* (1964) (and SP); *Planet Of The Vampires* (1965) (SP only).

MELIES, Georges French director, born 1861, who many feel was the father of the science fiction film. What he was, in fact, was a man who ran stage magic shows and discovered a new medium for presenting his illusions. If he used Verne and Wells as sources for his later, slightly longer pieces, this does not essentially make him a science fiction film-maker (neglecting, for the moment, that the term "science fiction" was not coined until 1926). His films are, in essence, brief fantasies; what *is* interesting about his work is the way in which it prefigures the way the special effects for sf movies were to be achieved for the following 60 years in a slightly more sophisticated form. He died in 1938, penniless and without any sense of his own achievements.

The Clown And The Automaton (1897); *A Novice At X-Rays* (1897); *A Twentieth Century Surgeon* (1897); *A Midnight Episode* (1899); *Off To Bedlam* (1901); *A Trip To The Moon* (1902); *An Impossible Voyage* (1904); *The Fantastical Airship* (1906); *Tunnelling The English Channel* (1907); *Under The Seas* (1907); *Conquest Of The Pole* (1912).

MENZIES, William Cameron American director, born 1896, who began as an art director and graduated to full director. Besides his interesting (if flawed) sf work, he might also be remembered for directing *Gone With The Wind* (1939). He died in 1957.

Chandu, The Magician (1932); *Things To Come* (1936); *The Whip Hand* (1951); *Invaders From Mars* (1953); *The Maze* (1953).

MILLAND, Ray Welsh actor, born 1905, who starred in several sf B-movies.

Panic In The Year Zero (1962); *X – The Man With X-Ray Eyes* (1963); *Frogs* (1971); *The Thing With Two Heads* (1972); *Escape To Witch Mountain* (1974); *Battlestar Galactica* (1977); *Starflight One* (1982).

MILLER, George Australian director who is currently working on the third of his Mad Max movies. His "quarter" of the *Twilight Zone – The Movie* (1983) experiment, "Nightmare At 20,000 Ft" is by far the most interesting.

Mad Max (1979) (D/SP); *Mad Max II* (1981) (and SP).

MIMIEUX, Yvette American actress, born 1939, who played the insipid woman from the future, Weena, in *The Time Machine* (1960).

Fahrenheit 451 (1966); *The Black Hole* (1978).

MOORE, Roger English actor, born 1928, who took over the James Bond role from Sean Connery, and now shares it with him. He began as a tea-boy in a cartoon studio before progressing to RADA.

The Man With The Golden Gun (1974); *The Spy Who Loved Me* (1977); *Moonraker* (1979); *Octopussy* (1983).

MORROW, Jeff American actor who starred in *This Island Earth* (1954).

The Creature Walks Among Us (1956); *The Giant Claw* (1957); *Kronos* (1957).

MORSE, Barry English actor rarely allowed to express his talent, though outstandingly funny as President Johnny Cyclops in *Whoops! Apocalypse* (1981).

Welcome To Blood City (1977); *Alien Attack* (1979); *H. G. Wells' The Shape Of Things To Come* (1979); *The Bells* (1981).

NIMOY, Leonard American actor, born in 1931, who will, no matter what else he now does, be typecast and remembered as Lieutenant Spock in the *Star Trek* TV episodes and films. But Nimoy was in a long-running science fiction serial back in the 1950s, too – in *Zombies Of The Stratosphere*, which ran from 1952 and was made into a feature, *Satan's Satellites*, in 1958. He has also graduated away from being simply an actor, not merely on the small screen, but as director of *Star Trek III: The Search For Spock* (1984).

Them! (1953); *The Brain Eaters* (1958); *Invasion Of The Body Snatchers* (1978); *Star Trek: The Motion Picture* (1979); *Star Trek II: The Wrath Of Khan* (1982).

O'BANNON, Dan American scriptwriter whose work on *Dark Star* (1974) with John Carpenter probably won him the job on *Alien* (1979). He also played a small acting part in the former film.

Blue Thunder (1983).

OBOLER, Arch American producer/director whose "bubble-vision" experiment and tinkering with 3-D were not very successful.

The Day After Tomorrow (1942) (D/SP); *Five* (1951) (D/SP); *The Twonky* (1952) (P/D/SP); *The Bubble* (1966) (P/D/SP).

O'BRIEN, Edmond American actor, born 1915, chosen to play the part of Winston Smith in the 1955 version of Orwell's *1984*.

Moon Pilot (1961); *Seven Days In May* (1964); *Fantastic Voyage* (1966); *LA 2017* (1970).

O'BRIEN, Willis American special effects expert, born 1886, whose work on *The Lost World* (1925) and *King Kong* (1925) pioneered animation techniques. His first attempts at creating something in this vein was in 1915, with a short piece called *The Dinosaur And The Missing Link*, and his fascination with the prehistoric lasted the rest of his life. Certainly the whole Japanese monster movie cycle (which, ironically, did not use O'Brien's techniques, but took the short cut of having actors in rubber suits) stems from O'Brien's work, and Ray Harryhausen admits to having been first inspired by O'Brien's work. I doubt whether O'Brien was ever conscious of the huge anachronism he was perpetuating in juxtaposing men and dinosaurs, but if he did he

certainly didn't care about it. He died in 1962, but his techniques are undergoing a brief resurgence.

The Son Of Kong (1933); *Mighty Joe Young* (1949); *The Black Scorpion* (1957); *The Giant Behemoth* (1957).

O'HERLIHY, Dan Irish actor, born 1919, who has long been known to both the small and large screen in America. He has played a wide range of heroes and villains, but his most interesting part yet was, perhaps, as the lizard-like alien, Grig, in *The Last Starfighter* (1984).

Fail Safe (1964); *How To Steal The World* (1968); *The People* (1971); *Halloween III: Season Of The Witch* (1983).

PAIVA, Nestor American actor whose appearances were limited to low-budget and often uinspired films, with the exception of *The Creature From The Black Lagoon* (1953).

The Revenge Of The Creature (1955); *Tarantula* (1955); *The Mole People* (1956); *Jesse James Meets Frankenstein's Daughter* (1966); *Madmen Of Mandoras* (1966).

PAL, George Hungarian producer, born in 1908, whose work in the 1950s typifies all that was wrong with sf cinema during that period. One might say of Pal that his heart was in the right place but his head was in another galaxy. His films bear little intelligent examination, though they were colourful enough in their time. He died in 1980, still trying to find the funds for sf-oriented projects.

Destination Moon (1950); *When Worlds Collide* (1951); *War Of The Worlds* (1952); *The Conquest Of Space* (1955); *Atlantis, The Lost Continent* (1960) (and D); *The Time Machine* (1960) (and D); *The Power* (1967); *Doc Savage: Man Of Bronze* (1975) (and SP).

PARKER, Eddie American actor who you're not likely to recognize from the films he was in – he invariably played the monster and was in a rubber suit of some description!

The Ghost Of Frankenstein (1942); *Franken-stein Meets The Wolfman* (1943); *Abbott and Costello Meet Dr Jekyll and Mr Hyde* (1953); *This Island Earth* (1954); *Bride Of The Monster* (1955); *Tarantula* (1955); *The Mole People* (1956); *Monster On The Campus* (1958).

PECK, Gregory American actor, born 1916, best known in his sf roles as Dr Mengele, the ex-Nazi geneticist in *The Boys From Brazil* (1978), and as the submarine commander in *On The Beach* (1959).

The Chairman (1969); *Marooned* (1969).

PEPPARD, George American actor, born 1928.

What's So Bad About Feeling Good? (1968); *The Groundstar Conspiracy* (1972); *Damnation Alley* (1977); *Battle Beyond The Stars* (1980).

PIEL, Harry German director and comic actor, born 1892, whose three sf ventures were gimmicky comedies in which he starred.

The Great Bet (1915); *The Master Of The World* (1934); *The World Without A Mask* (1934).

PIERCE, Arthur C. Prolific American screenwriter whose specialty was science fiction. He also directed one of his own scripts, *Women Of The Prehistoric Planet* (1965).

Frankenstein (1931); *The Cosmic Man* (1958); *Beyond The Time Barrier* (1960); *Invasion Of The Animal People* (1960); *Mutiny In Outer Space* (1964); *Destination Inner Space* (1966); *The Destructors* (1966); *Dimension 5* (1966).

PIERCE, Jack American make-up artist, born 1889, whose work for Universal in the 1930s and 1940s helped give them an edge over their competitors. Some of his creations have passed into popular modern mythology. He died in 1968.

Frankenstein (1931); *Bride Of Frankenstein* (1935); *Son Of Frankenstein* (1939); *The Ghost Of Frankenstein* (1942); *Captive Wild*

Women (1943); *Frankenstein Meets The Wolfman* (1943); *House Of Frankenstein* (1944); *Master Minds* (1945); *Teenage Monster* (1957).

PLEASANCE, Donald English actor, born 1919, whose portrayal of villains has added to the enjoyment of many films.

1984 (1955); *Fantastic Voyage* (1966); *You Only Live Twice* (1967); *THX 1138* (1970); *Deathline* (1972); *The Mutations* (1973); *Escape To Witch Mountain* (1974); *Pumaman* (1980); *Escape From New York* (1981).

POLLEXFEN, Jack American producer, who often worked with Aubrey Wisberg.

The Man From Planet X (1950) (and SP); *Captive Women* (1952) (and SP); *The Neanderthal Man* (1952) (and SP); *Port Sinister* (1952) (and SP); *The Indestructible Man* (1956) (and D).

PREISS, Wolfgang German actor best known for his several portrayals of Mabuse.

Mistress of The World (1959); *Mill Of The Stone Women* (1960); *The Thousand Eyes Of Dr Mabuse* (1960); *The Invisible Dr Mabuse* (1961); *The Return Of Dr Mabuse* (1961); *The Testament Of Dr Mabuse* (1962); *Secret Of Dr Mabuse* (1964).

PRICE, Vincent American master of the horror genre, born in 1911, he has played the title role in many sf-horror films and was involved in Roger Corman's series of Edgar Allen Poe-inspired films.

The Fly (1958); *The Return Of The Fly* (1959); *The Tingler* (1959); *The Last Man On Earth* (1963); *Dr Goldfoot and The Bikini Machine* (1965); *War Gods Of The Deep* (1965); *Dr Goldfoot and The Girl Bombs* (1966); *Scream And Scream Again* (1969).

PROWSE, David English actor whose size made him a candidate to play Darth Vader in the Star Wars sequence, though he shared the role with Bob Anderson and Sebastian Shaw in *Return Of The Jedi* (1983).

The Horror Of Frankenstein (1970); *Star Wars* (1977); *The Empire Strikes Back* (1980).

RABIN, Jack American special effects expert who, for most of his projects, worked in collaboration with Irving Block and Louis DeWitt. Sadly, little of his work is memorable and some (*Robot Monster*) just laughable.

Unknown World (1950) (and P); *The Neanderthal Man* (1952); *Port Sinister* (1952); *Cat Women Of The Moon* (1953); *Robot Monster* (1953); *The Black Sleep* (1956); *The Invisible Boy* (1957); *Kronos* (1957); *War Of The Satellites* (1957); *The Giant Behemoth* (1958); *The Monster From Green Hell* (1958); *The Thirty Foot Bride Of Candy Rock* (1958); *The Atomic Submarine* (1959); *Death Race 2000* (1975); *Deathsport* (1978).

RAINS, Claude English actor, born 1889, most fondly remembered for his depiction of H. G. Wells's *The Invisible Man* in James Whale's 1933 production. The irony is that he was barely seen in that movie. He died in 1967.

The Day After Tomorrow (1942); *Battle Of The Worlds* (1960); *The Lost World* (1960).

RAMBALDI, Carlo Italian-born special effects expert who won Oscars for his special effects work on *Alien* (1979) and *E.T.* (1982), the latter having become the most popular alien ever to have appeared on the big screen.

Flesh For Frankenstein (1973); *Close Encounters Of The Third Kind* (1977); *Dune* (1984).

RATHBONE, Basil South African actor, born 1892 and bred as an Englishman. In films since 1923, he did little of real interest in the sf genre. He died in 1967.

Son Of Frankenstein (1939); *The Black Sleep* (1956); *Voyage To The Prehistoric Planet* (1965); *Queen Of Blood* (1966).

REEVE, Christopher Intelligent American actor, born 1952, who has managed to avoid being typecast as Clark

Kent, alias Superman, yet brought what seem to be perfect qualities to the role.

Superman: The Movie (1978); *Somewhere In Time* (1980); *Superman II* (1980); *Superman III* (1983).

RENNIE, Michael English actor, born 1909, best known as Klaatu in *The Day The Earth Stood Still* (1951). He died in 1971.

The Lost World (1960); *Cyborg 1087* (1966); *The Power* (1967); *Dracula Vs. Frankenstein* (1971).

RICE, Milt American special effects expert.

World Without End (1955); *Queen Of Outer Space* (1958); *Gargoyles* (1972); *Damnation Alley* (1977).

RICHARDSON, John One of the new generation of special effects experts.

Rollerball (1975); *Superman: The Movie* (1978); *Warlords Of Atlantis* (1978); *Moonraker* (1979); *Octopussy* (1983).

RICHARDSON, Ralph Respected English actor, born in 1902, whose portrayal of the "Boss" in the future, ruined city of Everytown in *Things To Come* (1936) enlivened an otherwise dull film. Forty-five years later he was boss of another kind in *Time Bandits* (1981), where he played the Divine Being. He died in 1983.

The Man Who Could Work Miracles (1936); *Clouds Over Europe* (1937); *Frankenstein: The True Story* (1973); *O Lucky Man* (1973); *Rollerball* (1975).

ROBINSON, Glen American special effects expert who shared an Oscar for special visual effects on *Logan's Run* (1976).

Earthquake (1974); *Meteor* (1979); *Flash Gordon* (1980).

ROEG, Nicolas English director, born 1928, who began as a cinematographer and was cameraman on David Lean's

Lawrence Of Arabia (1962). His own work has shared some of that same visual beauty, and he was cinematographer also on François Truffaut's *Fahrenheit 451* (1966).

Don't Look Now (1973); *The Man Who Fell To Earth* (1976) (and SP).

ROSSI-STUART, Giacomo English actor, born Jack Stuart, who starred in several of Antonio Margheriti's 1960s space movies.

The Day The Sky Exploded (1958); *Caltiki, The Immortal Monster* (1959); *The Last Man On Earth* (1963); *Snow Devils* (1965); *War Between The Planets* (1965).

RUSOFF, Lou American scriptwriter.

The Phantom From 10,000 Leagues (1955); *The Day The World Ended* (1956); *It Conquered The World* (1956).

RUSSELL, Kurt American actor, born 1951. He might well be nicknamed "The man who escaped Disney and found John Carpenter", because from juvenile roles he went on to become known as Snake Plisken in Carpenter's boisterous *Escape From New York* (1981).

The Computer Wore Tennis Shoes (1969); *Now You See Him, Now You Don't* (1971); *The Thing* (1982).

SAHARA, Kenji Popular Japanese actor who has appeared in a number of the monster movies (Godzilla and company!).

Rodan (1956); *The Mysterians* (1957); *The H-Man* (1958); *War Of The Gargantuas* (1966); *Son Of Godzilla* (1967); *Godzilla's Revenge* (1969); *Yog – Monster From Space* (1970).

SAMUELS, Ted English special effects expert.

The Road To Hong Kong (1961); *Daleks – Invasion Earth 2150 AD* (1966); *How To Steal The World* (1968).

SANGSTER, Jimmy British scriptwriter who worked mainly for director

Terence Fisher on his Hammer Horror offerings.

X – The Unknown (1957); *The Curse Of Frankenstein* (1957); *The Trollenberg Terror* (1958); *The Man Who Could Cheat Death* (1959); *The Horror Of Frankenstein* (1970) (and P/D).

SAXON, John American actor, born Carmen Orrico in 1935. He was a regular B-movie star, and has recently taken to playing villains.

Blood Beast From Outer Space (1965); *Queen Of Blood* (1966); *The Bees* (1978); *Battle Beyond The Stars* (1980); *Prisoners Of The Lost Universe* (1983).

SAYLES, John American scriptwriter, born 1950, now turned director in *The Brother From Another Planet* (1984).

Alligator (1980); *Battle Beyond The Stars* (1980).

SCHALLERT, William American actor whose career never seemed to rise above the second rate.

Port Sinister (1952); *Tobor The Great* (1954); *The Monolith Makers* (1957); *Colossus, The Forbin Project* (1967); *The Computer Wore Tennis Shoes* (1969); *Hangar 18* (1980).

SCHOEDSACK, Ernest B. American director, born 1893, most famous for his Kong films.

King Kong (1933); *The Son Of Kong* (1933); *Dr Cyclops* (1939); *Mighty Joe Young* (1949).

SCOTT, Ridley English director, born in South Shields in 1939, he began in commercials and as a TV director on *Z Cars*. With the impressive feature *The Duellists* (1977) under his belt, he moved into the sf cinema with two of its finest films. He co-scripted *Alien* (1979) with Dan O'Bannon.

Blade Runner (1982).

SEKIZAWA, Shinichi Japanese scriptwriter whose work was mainly with director Inoshiro Honda, for the Toho studios. Repetitive plot-lines and the demands of the monster movie sequence he was working on mean that his work never evolved beyond the trite.

Varan The Unbelievable (1958); *Battle In Outer Space* (1959); *The Human Vapor* (1960); *Mothra* (1961); *King Kong Vs. Godzilla* (1962); *Dagora, The Space Monster* (1964); *Godzilla Vs. Mothra* (1964); *Ghidrah, The Three-Headed Monster* (1965); *Gulliver's Travels Beyond The Moon* (1965); *Monster Zero* (1965); *Godzilla Vs. The Sea Monster* (1966); *Son Of Godzilla* (1967); *Godzilla's Revenge* (1969); *Latitude Zero* (1969); *War Of The Monsters* (1972); *Godzilla Vs. Megalon* (1973).

SELLERS, Peter English actor, born 1925, whose finest moments (as far as sf cinema is concerned) are in *Dr Strangelove* (1963), where he played three parts. He was also quite brilliant as the Gardener in *Being There* (1979). He died in 1980.

The Mouse That Roared (1959); *The Road To Hong Kong* (1961); *Casino Royale* (1967).

SEMPLE, Lorenzo Jr American screenwriter.

King Kong (1976); *Flash Gordon* (1980); *Never Say Never Again* (1983).

SHATNER, William Canadian actor, born in Quebec in 1931, he is best known to sf fans as Captain Kirk in *Star Trek* (Admiral in the later films).

The People (1971); *Kingdom Of The Spiders* (1977); *Star Trek: The Motion Picture* (1979); *Star Trek II: The Wrath Of Khan* (1982); *Star Trek III: The Search For Spock* (1984).

SHOURT, James American special effects expert.

The Andromeda Strain (1971); *Altered States* (1980); *Heartbeeps* (1981).

SILLA, Felix American midget actor best known for his role as "Twiki" in the *Buck Rogers* TV series, a part he repeated

in the adaptation. He also took the part of the "shell baby" in *Demon Seed* (1976).

Buck Rogers In The 25th Century (1979).

SIMMS, Jay American scriptwriter whose work on *Creation Of The Humanoids* (1962) shows a remarkable understanding of the written genre.

The Killer Shrews (1959); *Panic In The Year Zero* (1962).

SIODMAK, Curt German scriptwriter and novelist, born 1902, who emigrated to America in 1937. Several of his own novels have been filmed, but little of his work demonstrates any true feel for science fiction, being essentially gimmick stories with thriller plot-lines.

F.P.1 Doesn't Answer (1932); *The Invisible Man Returns* (1939); *Black Friday* (1940); *The Invisible Woman* (1940); *Invisible Agent* (1942); *Frankenstein Meets The Wolfman* (1943); *The Magnetic Monster* (1953); *Riders To The Stars* (1953); *The Creature With The Atom Brain* (1955); *Earth Vs. The Flying Saucers* (1956).

SMIGHT, Jack American director, born 1926. His work in the sf field constitutes a very small part of a large output.

The Illustrated Man (1968); *Frankenstein: The True Story* (1973); *Damnation Alley* (1977).

SPIELBERG, Steven The "Wunderkind" of American cinema, he was born in Ohio in 1947 and entered television filmmaking at a surprisingly young age, with features like *LA 2017* (1970) and *Duel* (1971). Like his friend and (on the Indiana Jones movies) co-director, George Lucas, his extraordinary success at the box office has given the whole sf film field a new lease of life and encouraged film companies to take the genre seriously after decades of neglect. Rumour has it that, when Henry Thomas grows up, we'll get a sequel to his biggest-grossing movie, *E.T. The Extra-Terrestrial* (1982), and that a screenplay written for the sequel will shortly see the light of day as a novel.

Close Encounters Of The Third Kind (1977)
(D/SP); *Close Encounters – Special Edition*
(1980); *Raiders Of The Lost Ark* (1981) (P/
D/SP); *Twilight Zone – The Movie* (1983)
(P/D); *Gremlins* (1984) (P).

STAMP, Terence English actor, born
1940, and memorable for his role as Mr
Soames, the man "born late to life".

The Mind Of Mr Soames (1969); *Hu-Man*
(1975); *Superman: The Movie* (1978);
Superman II (1980).

STANTON, Harry Dean American
actor.

Alien (1979); *Deathwatch* (1979); *Escape
From New York* (1981); *Repo Man* (1984).

STEARS, John Special effects expert
whose work on *Thunderball* (1965) won
him a Special Visual Effects Oscar. He
won another Oscar in 1977 for *Star Wars*.

You Only Live Twice (1967); *On Her Majesty's Secret Service* (1969); *Toomorrow*
(1970); *The Martians* (1979).

STEVENSON, Robert English director, born 1905, who is perhaps most
famous for *Mary Poppins* (1964). He
worked for Disney studios from 1956
onwards and, over the next two decades,
directed a whole series of enjoyable films
oriented towards a juvenile audience.

The Man Who Lived Again (1936); *The
Absent-Minded Professor* (1961); *Son Of
Flubber* (1962); *The Misadventures Of Merlin Jones* (1963); *The Monkey's Uncle*
(1965); *The Island At The Top Of The World*
(1973).

STINE, Clifford American special effects expert who often worked alongside
Bud Westmore for Universal studios.

This Island Earth (1954); *Tarantula* (1955);
The Creature Walks Among Us (1956); *The
Mole People* (1956); *The Deadly Mantis*
(1957); *The Incredible Shrinking Man*
(1957); *The Land Unknown* (1957); *The
Monolith Monsters* (1957); *Monster On The
Campus* (1958).

STROCK, Herbert L. American director of rather poor B-movies.

Gog (1954); *I Was A Teenage Frankenstein*
(1957); *The Crawling Hand* (1963) (and
SP).

SUBOTSKY, Milton English producer
and scriptwriter, prominent in the 1960s.
He often co-produced with Max J. Rosenberg.

Dr Who And The Daleks (1965) (SP); *Daleks
– Invasion Earth 2150 AD* (1966) (P/SP);
The Terrornauts (1966) (P); *They Came
From Beyond Space* (1967) (P/SP); *The
Mind Of Mr Soames* (1969) (P); *Scream And
Scream Again* (1969) (P); *I. Monster* (1971)
(SP); *At The Earth's Core* (1976) (SP).

TARKOVSKY, Andrei Russian director, born in Zavroshe in 1932. He has
made few films, and his material has
brought him into conflict with the authorities, though it must be said that they have
found little overt to criticize in his work. It
is significant that of his six major films,
two are science-fictional, even though they
reflect the same concerns as films like
Andrei Rublev (1965) and *Mirrors* (1974).
An art director rather than a commercial
director, he is probably the only cinematic
genius working in the sf field.

Solaris (1971) (D/SP); *Stalker* (1979) (D).

THOMPSON, J. Lee British director,
born 1914, who was prolific until the end
of the 1960s. He is probably best remembered for his non-sf film, *The Guns Of
Navarone* (1961).

The Chairman (1969); *Conquest Of The
Planet Of The Apes* (1972); *Battle For The
Planet Of The Apes* (1973).

TRUMBULL, Douglas American
special effects expert and director, born
1942, who has done more than anyone
else in his field to usher in the new age of
special effects wizardry. His participation
in *2001; A Space Odyssey* (1968) can be
identified as the turning point in the
history of sf film, giving the genre a range

it had previously lacked. Trumbull's recent work has been part of his attempt to change the very nature of the cinematic experience, and he has been steadily developing a "Showscan" system which would surround us. Whether this, like 3-D, would simply prove a gimmick, remains to be seen, though Trumbull does – it must be said – have the ability to carry out his dreams. His move into directing, begun with *Silent Running* (1971), has proved less successful.

The Andromeda Strain (1971); *Close Encounters Of The Third Kind* (1977); *Star Trek – The Motion Picture* (1979); *Blade Runner* (1982); *Brainstorm* (1983) (P/D/SE).

TSUBURAYA, Eiji Resident special effects expert at Japan's Toho studios, he worked closely with director Inoshiro Honda on the monster movie cycle, fitting actors into garish rubber suits of the various super-monsters and building scale models of the Japanese countryside for the beasts to trample upon. His death in 1970 ended a chapter in Toho's history.

Godzilla, King Of The Monsters (1954); *The Invisible Man* (1954); *Gigantis, The Fire Monster* (1955); *Rodan* (1956); *The Mysterians* (1957); *The H-Man* (1958); *Varan The Unbelievable* (1958); *Battle In Outer Space* (1959); *The Human Vapor* (1960); *Secret Of The Telegian* (1960); *Mothra* (1961); *Gorath* (1962); *King Kong Vs. Godzilla* (1962); *Atragon* (1963); *Attack Of The Mushroom People* (1963) (and D); *Dagora, The Space Monster* (1964); *Godzilla Vs. Mothra* (1964); *Ghidrah, The Three-Headed Monster* (1965); *Monster Zero* (1965); *Godzilla Vs. The Sea Monster* (1966); *War Of The Gargantuas* (1966); *King Kong Escapes* (1967); *Son Of Godzilla* (1967); *Destroy All Monsters* (1968); *Godzilla's Revenge* (1969); *Latitude Zero* (1969).

ULMER, Edgar G. Austrian director, born in Vienna in 1904. He produced some interesting rather than "good" sf B-movies, the best of them, perhaps, *Beyond The Time Barrier* (1960). He had moved to America in 1930 and died in 1972

The Man From Planet X (1950); *The Amazing Transparent Man* (1959); *Journey Beneath The Desert* (1961).

VAUGHN, Robert American actor, born 1932, who is best known, perhaps, for his portrayal of super-spy Napoleon Solo, in the sf/spy-thriller TV series, *The Man From U.N.C.L.E.* An intelligent but limited actor, he has joined in the current sf boom with enthusiasm.

Teenage Caveman (1958); *The Spy With My Face* (1965); *The Venetian Affair* (1966); *The Mind Of Mr Soames* (1969); *Starship Invasions* (1977); *Battle Beyond The Stars* (1980); *Hangar 18* (1980); *Virus* (1980); *Superman III* (1983).

VEEVERS, Wally Special effects expert currently enjoying a renaissance of his work.

Satellite In The Sky (1956); *The Road To Hong Kong* (1961); *Day Of The Triffids* (1963); *Dr Strangelove* (1963); *2001: A Space Odyssey* (1968); *Diamonds Are Forever* (1971); *The Rocky Horror Picture Show* (1975); *Saturn 3* (1980).

VON HARBOU, Thea Novelist and scriptwriter, born in Bavaria, Germany (1888) and married (1924) to Fritz Lang. She parted from Lang after writing *The Testament Of Dr Mabuse* (1933), her sympathies with the Nazis separating the two. She died in 1954.

Dr Mabuse, The Gambler (1922); *Metropolis* (1926); *The Spy* (1928); *By Rocket To The Moon* (1929).

VON SYDOW, Max Swedish actor, born 1929, who brings authority to the parts he has played in the sf cinema.

Shame (1967); *The Ultimate Warrior* (1975); *Deathwatch* (1979); *Flash Gordon* (1980); *Dreamscape* (1983); *Never Say Never Again* (1983); *Dune* (1984).

WARD, Simon English actor, born 1941, whose portrayal of the satanic son in *Holocaust 2000* (1977) reveals another side to his talents.

Frankenstein Must Be Destroyed (1969); *Duet For Love* (1971); *Supergirl* (1984).

WATANABE, Akira Japanese special effects expert, working for the Toho studios, sometimes in collaboration with Eiji Tsuburaya.

Godzilla, King Of The Monsters (1954); *Gigantis, The Fire Monster* (1955); *Godzilla Versus Mothra* (1964); *Monster From A Prehistoric Planet* (1967); *The Green Slime* (1968).

WATKINS, Peter English director, born 1935, whose BBC TV documentary, *The War Game* (1965), was banned by his bosses, then, when released as an independent feature, won the Oscar that year for best documentary. He began by working in commercials and, since 1969, has been working mainly in Scandinavia.

Privilege (1967); *The Gladiators* (1969); *Punishment Park* (1970).

WEAVER, Sigourney American actress, born 1949 (as Susan Weaver) and who made her screen debut in *Annie Hall* (1977). As Ripley, the capable female crewmember in *Alien* (1979), she excelled, and her comic portrayal of Dana in *Ghostbusters* (1984) suggests that the sf cinema will see much more of her.

WEIR, Peter Acclaimed Australian director, born 1944, whose first feature, *The Cars That Ate Paris* (1974), which Weir directed and wrote, probably started the whole series of road movies with spiky cars. His subject matter might be considered "mystical", but his skill at film-making is undeniable.

The Last Wave (1977) (and SP).

WESTMORE, Bud American make-up artist, born 1918, most active in the 1950s for Universal studios. His work on the creature in *The Creature From The Black Lagoon* is memorable and probably accounted for the success of the film. He died in 1973.

Abbott and Costello Meet Frankenstein (1948); *Abbott and Costello Meet The Invisible Man* (1951); *Abbott and Costello Meet Dr Jekyll & Mr Hyde* (1953); *It Came From Outer Space* (1953); *The Creature From The Black Lagoon* (1953); *This Island Earth* (1954); *The Revenge Of The Creature* (1955); *Tarantula* (1955); *The Creature Walks Among Us* (1956); *The Mole People* (1956); *The Deadly Mantis* (1957); *The Incredible Shrinking Man* (1957); *The Monolith Monsters* (1957); *Monster On The Campus* (1958); *Skullduggery* (1970).

WESTMORE, Wally Make-up expert.

Dr Jekyll and Mr Hyde (1931); *The Island Of Lost Souls* (1932); *The Man In Half Moon Street* (1943); *The Space Children* (1957); *The Colossus Of New York* (1958); *Visit To A Small Planet* (1959).

WHALE, James English director, born 1889, whose work includes two of the seminal works of the science fiction cinema, *Frankenstein* (1931) and *The Invisible Man* (1933). He died in 1957.

WHITLOCK, Albert American special effects expert.

Colossus, The Forbin Project (1967); *Diamonds Are Forever* (1971); *Short Walk To Daylight* (1972); *The Day Of The Dolphin* (1973); *Earthquake* (1974); *Heartbeeps* (1981); *Cat People* (1982); *The Thing* (1982).

WINGROVE, Ian English special effects expert.

At The Earth's Core (1976); *The People That Time Forgot* (1977); *Never Say Never Again* (1983).

WISBERG, Aubrey American producer, who worked with Jack Pollexfen.

The Man From Planet X (1950); *Captive Women* (1952); *Port Sinister* (1952).

WISE, Robert American director, born 1914, whose classic work, *The Day The Earth Stood Still* (1951), looks a very rickety old production in the face of modern sf films, but still has a strong (if naïve) charm.

The Andromeda Strain (1971) (and P); *Star Trek: The Motion Picture* (1979).

WOOD, Edward D. Jr American producer/director, born 1922, whose reputation has grown considerably owing to Michael Medved's *Golden Turkey* books, which have established him as the worst director of all time. It's doubtful whether there are any worse films than *Plan 9 From Outer Space* (1956) which Wood wrote, produced and directed, but too much fuss has been made over one man's ineptitutde. He died in 1978.

Bride of the Monster (1955) (P/D/SP).

WRAY, Fay Canadian actress, born in Alberta in 1907, she was immortalized as Ann, the woman King Kong falls in love with and carries up the Empire State Building. Her career went downhill all the way from there.

Doctor X (1932); *The Vampire Bat* (1932).

WYNN, Keenan American actor, born 1916. His participation in sf cinema has usually been as a supporting actor in unremarkable films.

Lost Angel (1943); *The Absent-Minded Professor* (1961); *Son Of Flubber* (1962); *Dr Strangelove* (1963); *Around The World Under The Sea* (1966); *Laserblast* (1978); *The Dark* (1979); *Parts: The Clonus Horror* (1979).

YARBROUGH, Jean American director, born 1900, prolific between 1936 and 1949, though never escaping the B-format treadmill.

Masterminds (1945); *The Creeper* (1948); *Henry, The Rainmaker* (1949).

YATES, George Worthing American scriptwriter, prolific in the late 1950s. He was responsible for the original storyline of *Them!* (1953).

It Came From Beneath The Sea (1955); *Earth Vs. The Flying Saucers* (1956); *Attack Of The Puppet People* (1958); *Earth Vs. The Giant Spider* (1958); *The Flame Barrier* (1958); *Frankenstein 1970* (1958); *Space Master X-7* (1958); *War Of The Colossal Beast* (1958).

YORK, Michael English actor, born 1942, who has never really matched his performance in *Cabaret*, particularly in his few sf roles.

Lost Horizon (1972); *Logan's Run* (1976); *The Island Of Dr Moreau* (1977).

YOUNG, Sean Young American actress whose performances as Rachel in *Blade Runner* (1982) and as Chani in *Dune* (1984) have already established her as one of the leading actresses in the sf cinema.

YUASA, Noriaki Japanese director for the Daiei studios.

Gamera (1966); *Destroy All Planets* (1968); *Attack Of The Monsters* (1969); *Gamera Vs. Monster X* (1970); *Gamera Vs. Zigra* (1971).

YURICICH, Richard American special effects expert who shared an Oscar for best visual effects on *Logan's Run* (1976).

Silent Running (1971); *Blade Runner* (1982).

ZAVITZ, Lee American special effects expert who won an Oscar for his work on *Destination Moon* (1950).

The Snow Creature (1954); *From The Earth To The Moon* (1958).

The Literary Sources: Books into Film

ALBEE, George Sumner. His short story "The Next Voice You Hear" was filmed in 1950.

ASIMOV, Isaac. He wrote the novelization for *Fantastic Voyage* (1966) and had his own novel, "The Caves Of Steel" (1954), filmed in 1967.

ATHERTON, Gertrude. Her novel *Black Oxen* was filmed in 1923.

BALMER, Edwin. His novel *When Worlds Collide* (1933) (written with Philip Wylie) was filmed in 1951.

BARRY, John. His short story "Saturn 3" was filmed in 1980.

BATES, Harry. His 1940 story "Farewell The Master" was filmed in 1951 as *The Day The Earth Stood Still.*

BEAUCHAMP, D. D. He wrote the screenplay of his short story "The Rainmaker" for the film *Henry, The Rainmaker* (1949).

BELYAYEV, Alexander. His novel *The Amphibian Man* (1928) was filmed in 1961.

BENOIT, Pierre. His novel *L'Atlantide* was filmed twice, as *Siren Of Atlantis* (1947) and as *Journey Beneath The Desert* (1961).

BIXBY, Jerome. He contributed the story-line for the 1958 film *It! The Terror From Beyond Space* while his own short story "It's A Good Life" was filmed as one of the four parts of *Twilight Zone – The Movie* (1983).

BLACKBURN, John. His novel *Children Of The Night* (1966) was filmed as *Nothing But The Night* (1972).

BOULLE, Pierre. His novel *La Planète Des Singes* ("Planet Of The Apes" or "Monkey Planet") (1963) was the basis for the five films in the "Apes" sequence: *Planet Of The Apes* (1968); *Beneath The Planet Of The Apes* (1969); *Escape From The Planet Of The Apes* (1971); *Conquest Of The Planet Of The Apes* (1972); *Battle For The Planet Of The Apes* (1973).

BRADBURY, Ray. His short story, "The Fog Horn", became the basis of his own screenplay for *The Beast From 20,000 Fathoms* (1953), and he also wrote scripts for his own "Icarus Montgolfier Wright" short story in 1962 and for the novel *Something Wicked This Way Comes* (1962) in 1983. His novel *Fahrenheit 451* (1953) was filmed in 1966, and his collection of linked stories "The Illustrated Man" (1951) was filmed in 1968.

BRADDON, Russell. His novel *The Year Of The Angry Rabbit* became *Night Of The Lepus* (1972).

BRAHMS, Caryl and SIMON, S. J. Their novel *The Elephant Is White* was filmed as *Give Us The Moon* (1944).

BROWN, Fredric. His short story "Arena" (1944) was filmed in 1969.

BUDRYS, Algis. His novel *Who?* (1958) was filmed in 1974.

BURGESS, Anthony. His novel *A Clockwork Orange* (1962) was filmed in 1971.

BURROUGHS, E. R. His works have probably influenced many films indirectly, but direct book-to-film transformations have been made of only three works. *Pellucidar* (1923) became *At The Earth's Core* (1976), while the two connected novellas "The Land That Time Forgot" (1918) and "The People That Time Forgot" (1918) were filmed in 1975 and 1977 respectively.

CAIDIN, Martin. His novel *Marooned* (1964) was filmed in 1969, and his novel *Cyborg* (1972) became *The Six Million Dollar Man* (1973).

CAMPBELL, John W. His short story "Who Goes There?" (1938) has been thrice filmed, as *The Thing (From Another World)* (1951), *Who Goes There?* (1956) and *The Thing* (1982).

CAPEK, Karel. His play *Bila Nemoc* was filmed as *Skeleton On Horseback* (1937) and his novel *Krakatit* (1925) has been twice filmed, as *Krakatit* (1948) and as *Black Sun* (1979).

CHAYEFSKY, Paddy. His novel *Altered States* (1978) was filmed in 1980.

CHRISTOPHER, John. His novel *The Death Of Grass* (1956) was filmed as *No Blade Of Grass* (1970).

CLARKE, Arthur C. His 1948 short story "The Sentinel" was filmed as *2001: A Space Odyssey* (1968), with Clarke sharing scriptwriting duties with Stanley Kubrick. His novel sequel *2010: Odyssey Two* (1982) was filmed as *2010* (1984).

COMPTON, D. G. His novel *The Continuous Katherine Mortenhoe* (1975) was filmed as *Deathwatch* (1979).

COOK, Robin. His novel *Coma* (1976) was filmed in 1978.

COOPER, Edmund. His short story "The Invisible Boy" was filmed in 1957.

CORELLI, Marie. Her novel *The Young Diana* was filmed in 1922.

CRICHTON, Michael. His novel *The Andromeda Strain* (1969) was filmed in 1971, and his novel *The Terminal Man* (1972) was filmed in 1973. He also wrote the screenplay for and directed a 1978 film version of Robin Cook's novel *Coma* (1976) and an original script for *Westworld* (1973).

DAVIES, L. P. Two of his novels, *The Artificial Man* (1965) and *Psychogeist* (1966), were combined to make the film *Project X* (1967).

DEIGHTON, Len. His novel *Billion Dollar Brain* (1966) was filmed in 1967.

DICK, Philip K. His novel *Do Androids Dream Of Electric Sheep?* (1968) was given the title of an Alan Nourse book and filmed as *Blade Runner* (1982).

DOYLE, Arthur Conan. His novel *The Lost World* (1912) was filmed twice, in 1925 and 1960.

DUMAS, Charles Robert and **DIDELOT, R. F.** Their story "Le Monde Tremblera" was filmed as *The World Will Shake* (1939).

DU MAURIER, Daphne. Her short story "The Birds" (1952) was filmed in 1963, and another short, "Don't Look Now" (1971), in 1973.

ELLISON, Harlan. His Nebula Award-winning story, "A Boy And His Dog" (1969), was filmed in 1975.

ELY, David. His novel *Seconds* (1963) was filmed in 1966.

EWERS, Hans Heinz. His novel *Alraune* was filmed four times, in 1918, 1928, 1930 and 1952.

FAIRMAN, Paul W. His story "The Cosmic Frame" (1953) was filmed twice, as *Invasion Of The Saucer Men* (1957) and as *The Eye Creatures* (1965).

FARRIS, John. His novel *The Fury* was filmed in 1978.

FINNEY, Jack. His novel *The Body Snatchers* (1955) was twice filmed as *Invasion Of The Bodysnatchers*, in 1956 and 1975.

FLAMMARION, Camille. His novel *La Fin Du Monde* (1894) was filmed as *The End Of The World* (1930).

FLEMING, Ian. Most of Fleming's work has now been filmed, including several short stories. The resultant films are *Dr No* (1962); *Goldfinger* (1964); *Thunderball* (1965); *You Only Live Twice* (1967); *Casino Royale* (1967); *On Her Majesty's Secret Service* (1969); *Diamonds Are Forever* (1971); *The Man With The Golden Gun* (1974); *The Spy Who Loved Me* (1977); *Moonraker* (1979); *Octopussy* (1983); *Never Say Never Again* (1983).

GEORGE, Peter. His novel *Two Hours To Dream* (1958) was filmed as *Dr Strangelove; Or, How I Learned To Stop Worrying And Love The Bomb* (1963).

GILBERT, Stephen. His novel *Ratman's Notebooks* (1968) was filmed as *Willard* (1971).

GLAZER, Benjamin. His story "Sinners In Silk" was filmed in 1924.

GOLDING, William. His novel *Lord Of The Flies* (1954) was filmed in 1963.

GUNN, James. His novel *The Immortals* (1962) was filmed in 1969.

HARDELLET, Andre. His novel *Ils* was filmed as *Them* (1970).

HARRISON, Harry. His novel *Make Room! Make Room!* (1966) was filmed as *Soylent Green* (1973).

HARRISON, William. His short story "Rollerball" was filmed in 1975.

HEARD, H. F. His novel *A Taste For Honey* (1941) was filmed as *The Deadly Bees* (1966).

HEINLEIN, Robert A. His novel *Rocketship Galileo* (1947) was filmed as *Destination Moon* (1950). The novel *The Puppet Masters* (1951) was adapted and filmed as *The Brain Eaters* (1958). He also co-scripted *Project Moonbase* (1953).

HENDERSON, Zenna. Her two fix-up novels, *Pilgrimage: The Book Of The People* (1961) and *The People: No Different Flesh* (1966), were the basis for the 1971 film, *The People*.

HERBERT, Frank. His novel *Dune* (1965), which won the Hugo and Nebula awards in its year of publication, was filmed in 1984.

HERTZOG, Arthur. His novel *The Swarm* (1974) was filmed in 1978.

HILTON, James. His novel *Lost Horizon* (1933) was filmed in 1936 and 1972.

JACQUES, Norbert. His character, Dr Mabuse, became, like Fleming's Bond, the central focus of a number of German films: *Dr Mabuse, The Gambler* (1922); *The Testament Of Dr Mabuse* (1933); *The Thousand Eyes Of Dr Mabuse* (1960); *The Invisible Dr Mabuse* (1961); *The Return Of Dr Mabuse* (1961); *The Testament Of Dr Mabuse* (1962); *Scotland Yard Hunts Dr Mabuse* (1963); *Secret Of Dr Mabuse* (1964).

JOHNSON, George Clayton. Co-author, with William F. Nolan, of *Logan's Run* (1967), which was filmed in 1976, and writer of the short story "Kick The Can" which was filmed as one of the four parts of *Twilight Zone – The Movie* (1983).

JONES, D. F. His novel *Colossus* (1966) was filmed as *Colossus, The Forbin Project* (1967).

JONES, Raymond F. His novel *This Island Earth* (1952) was filmed in 1954.

KAEMPFFERT, Waldemar. His short story "The Diminishing Draft" was filmed as *Girl In His Pocket* (1957).

KELLERMANN, Bernhard. His novel *Der Tunnel* (1913) was filmed as *The Tunnel* (1933) and as *The Transatlantic Tunnel* (1935).

KELLY, Paul. His novel *Coplan Paie le Cercueil* was filmed as *Coplan Saves His Skin* (1967), and his *Stoppez Coplan* as *The Exterminators* (1965).

KEYES, Daniel. His novel version of *Flowers For Algernon* was filmed as *Charly* (1968).

KING, Stephen. Whilst most of King's novels have now been filmed, two qualify as sf: *The Dead Zone* (1979), filmed in 1983, and *Firestarter* (1980), filmed in 1984.

KLIMA, Ivan. His short story "Cybernetic Grandmother" was filmed in 1962.

KNEALE, Nigel. Mainly known as a scriptwriter, his play *The Creature* became *The Abominable Snowman Of The Himalayas* (1957).

KNEBEL, Fletcher. His novel *Seven Days In May* was filmed in 1964.

KOMATSU, Sakyo. Two of his novels have been filmed, *Nippon Chimbotsu* (1973) as *The Submersion Of Japan* (1973), and *Fukkatsu No Hi* (1980) as *Virus* (1980).

KOONTZ, Dean R. His novel *Demon Seed* (1973) was filmed in 1976.

KUHNE, David. Two of his novels have been filmed, *The Awful Dr Orloff* in 1961, and *Dr Mabuse* in 1971.

LABRYS, Michel. His novel *Les Sextuplets de Locqmaria* was filmed as *Don't Play With The Martians* (1967).

LANGELAAN, George. His story "The Fly" (1957) was filmed in 1958 and formed the basis for the two sequels, *Return Of The Fly* (1959) and *Curse Of The Fly* (1965).

LAUMER, Keith. His novel *The Monitors* (1966) was filmed in 1968.

LAWRENCE, Henry L. His novel *The Children Of Light* (1960) was filmed in 1961 as *The Damned*.

LEINSTER, Murray. Two of his novels have been filmed: *Monster From Earth's End* (1959) as *The Navy Vs. The Night Monsters* (1965), and *The Wailing Asteroid* (1961) as *The Terrornauts* (1966).

LEM, Stanislaw. His early novel *The Astronauts* (1951) was filmed as *First Spaceship On Venus* (1959); the short story "Uninhabited Planet" filmed in

1962; and "Prazjaciel", as *The Friend* in 1963. "Inquiry", a short story in the Pirix sequence, was filmed as *The Test Of Pilot Pirix* (1975), and *Solaris* (1971) was a film of the 1961 novel.

LEROUX, Gaston. His novel *Balaoo* was filmed twice, as *The Wizard* (1927) and as *Dr Renault's Secret* (1942).

LESSING, Doris. Her novel *Memoirs Of A Survivor* (1974) was filmed in 1981.

LEVIN, Ira. Two of his sf-oriented novels have been filmed: *The Stepford Wives* (1972) in 1975 and *The Boys From Brazil* (1976) in 1978.

LONDON, Jack. His first sf story "A Thousand Deaths" (1899) was filmed as *Torture Ship* (1939), and his novel *The Star Rover* (1915) was filmed in 1920.

LONG, Amelia Reynolds. Her short story "The Thought Monster" was filmed as *Fiend Without A Face* (1957).

LOVECRAFT, H. P. His story "The Color Out Of Space" (1927) was filmed as *Die! Monster Die!* (1965).

LUCAS, George. His storyline for *Star Wars* (1977) was extended into a novel.

LYMINGTON, John. His novel *Night Of The Big Heat* (1959) was filmed as *Island Of The Burning Damned* (1967).

McLEAN, Alistair. His novel *The Satan Bug* was filmed in 1965.

MAINE, Charles Eric. Four of his novels have been filmed: *Spaceways* (1953), which was also a radio play, was filmed in 1953; *Escapement* (1956) was filmed as *The Electronic Monster* (1957); *The Isotope Man* (1956) was filmed as *Timeslip* (1956); and *The Mind Of Mr Soames* (1961) was filmed in 1969.

MAKIN, William J. His short story "The Doctor's Secret" was filmed as *The Return Of Dr X* (1939).

MALZBERG, Barry. He wrote the book of the film *Phase IV* (1973).

MATHESON, Richard. His debut novel *I Am Legend* (1954) has been twice filmed, as *The Last Man On Earth* (1963) and as *The Omega Man* (1971). Another early novel, *The Shrinking Man*, was adapted by Matheson himself for the screen as *The*

Incredible Shrinking Man. A novelette, *Being*, was filmed as *It's Alive* (1968), and the short story "Duel" was again adapated for the screen by Matheson, in 1971. His 1975 novel *Bid Time Return* became *Somewhere In Time* (1980), and the earlier short story "Nightmare At 20,000 Ft" was adapted by Matheson for a section of *Twilight Zone – The Movie* (1983). Matheson has also written screenplays for *Master Of The World* (1961) and *The Incredible Hulk* (1977).

MAY, Julian. Her early novel *Dune Roller* (1951) was filmed as *The Cremators* (1972).

MERLE, Robert. Two of his novels have been filmed: *The Day Of The Dolphin* (1967) in 1973, and *Malevil* (1972) in 1981.

MERRITT, Abraham. His story "Burn, Witch, Burn!" (1932) was filmed as *The Devil Doll* (1936).

MOORCOCK, Michael. His Jerry Cornelius novel *The Final Programme* (1968) was filmed in 1973. Moorcock also did the screenplay for *The Land That Time Forgot* (1975).

MORRIS, Gordon and BARTEAUX, Morton. Their short story "Auf Wiedersehen" was filmed as *Six Hours To Live* (1932).

NOLAN, William F. and JOHNSON, George Clayton. Their novel *Logan's Run* (1967) was filmed in 1976.

O'BRIEN, Robert C. His novel *Mrs Frisby And The Rats of N.I.M.H.* (1971) was filmed as *The Secret Of N.I.M.H.* (1982).

ORWELL, George. His novel *Animal Farm* (1945) was filmed in 1954, and the novel *1984* (1949) has been twice filmed, in 1955 and 1984.

PADGETT, Lewis. Pseudonym of Henry Kuttner, whose story "The Twonky" (1942) was filmed in 1952.

PESTRINIERO, Renato. His story "One Night Of 21 Hours" was filmed as *Planet Of The Vampires* (1965).

POE, Edgar Allen. His poem "The City In The Sea" (1845) inspired the film *War Gods Of The Deep* (1965), while his short story "Murders In The Rue Morgue" was filmed twice, in 1914 and 1932.

POHL, Frederik. His 1955 short story "The Tunnel Under The World" was filmed in 1968.

RASPE, Rudolph Erich. His novel *The Adventures Of Baron Munchhausen* was twice filmed, in 1927 and 1943.

RENARD, Maurice. His novel *Les Mains D'Orlac* (1920) was filmed twice, as *The Hands Of Orlac* (1925) and *Mad Love* (1935).

RICHARD, Jay. His novel *The Chairman* was filmed in 1969.

ROBBE-GRILLET, Alain. His literary treatment of *Last Year In Marienbad* appeared in 1961, when the film was made.

ROBINSON, Frank M. His novel *The Power* (1956) was filmed in 1967.

ROSNY, J. H. Sr. His novel *Le Felin Géant* (1918, a.k.a. "Quest Of The Dawn Man") was heavily re-written as the basis for *Quest For Fire* (1982).

SANDOZ, Maurice. His novel *The Maze* was filmed in 1953.

SCHEFF, Werner. His novel *The Arc* was filmed in 1919.

SEARLES, Hank. His novel *The Pilgrim Project* (1964) was filmed as *Countdown* (1967).

SHECKLEY, Robert. His short story "The Seventh Victim" (1953) was filmed as *The Tenth Victim* (1965), which Sheckley then novelized!

SHELLEY, Mary. Her 1818 novel, *Frankenstein: Or, The Modern Prometheus* has been made into numerous films, few anywhere near to the original. The following are amongst them: *Frankenstein* (1910); *Life Without Soul* (1915); *Frankenstein's Monster* (1920); *Frankenstein* (1931); *Bride Of Frankenstein* (1935); *Son Of Frankenstein* (1939); *The Ghost Of Frankenstein* (1942); *Frankenstein Meets The Wolfman* (1943); *The Curse Of Frankenstein* (1957); *Frankenstein 1970* (1958); *The Revenge Of Frankenstein* (1958); *Frankenstein Conquers The World* (1964); *Frankenstein Created Woman* (1966); *Frankenstein Must Be Destroyed* (1969); *Frankenstein And The Monster From Hell* (1973); *Frankenstein: The True Story* (1973); *Young Frankenstein* (1974).

SHIEL, M. P. His novel *The Purple Cloud* (1901) became *The World, The Flesh And The Devil* (1958).

SHUTE, Nevil. His novel *On The Beach* (1957) was filmed in 1959.

SIODMAK, Curt. His novel *F.P.1 Does Not Reply* (1930) was filmed as *F.P.1 Doesn't Answer* (1932). *Donovan's Brain*, his 1943 novel, was filmed three times, as *The Lady And The Monster* (1944), *Donovan's Brain* (1953) and *The Brain* (1962). His novel *Hauser's Memory* (1968) was filmed in 1970.

SLOANE, William. His novel *The Edge Of Running Water* (1939) was filmed as *The Devil Commands* (1941).

SOHL, Jerry. His novel *The Night Slaves* (1970) was filmed that same year.

STEVENSON, Robert Louis. His short novel *The Strange Case Of Dr Jekyll And Mr Hyde* (1886) has spawned numerous film versions; by the same title in 1912, 1913, 1920 (twice), 1931, 1941; as *The Man And The Beast* (1951); as *Dr Jekyll And Sister Hyde* (1971); as *I, Monster* (1971); and as *The Man With Two Heads* (1971).

STRUGATSKY, Arkadi and Boris. They were scriptwriters for both film adaptations of their work. "The Dead Mountaineer Hotel", a short story, became a film in 1979, and their novel *Roadside Picnic* (1972) became *Stalker* (1979).

SWAIN, John D. Two of his stories have been filmed: "The Last Man On Earth" in 1924, and "It's Great To Be Alive" in 1933.

TAYLOR, Samuel. His short story "A Situation Of Gravity" was filmed as *The Absent-Minded Professor* (1961).

TEMPLE, William F. His novel *The Four-Sided Triangle* (1949, itself an expansion of a 1939 story) was filmed in 1953.

TEVIS, Walter S. His novel *The Man Who Fell To Earth* (1963) was filmed in 1976.

THOMAS, Craig. His novel *Firefox* (1977) was filmed in 1982.

TOLSTOY, Alexei. Two of his novels were filmed: *Aelita* (1922) in 1924, and *The Hyperboloid Of Engineer Garin* (1926) in 1965.

TWAIN, Mark. His novel *A Connecticut Yankee In King Arthur's Court* was filmed under that title in 1948, as *The Connecticut Yankee At King Arthur's Court* in 1920, as *A Connecticut Yankee* in 1931, and (heavily adapted) as *The Spaceman And King Arthur* in 1979.

VERCORS. His novel *You Shall Know Them* (1952) was filmed as *Skullduggery* (1970).

VERNE, Jules. Seven of Verne's 64 novels have been filmed for the sf cinema: *Journey To The Centre of The Earth* (1864) was filmed in 1909 and 1959. *From The Earth To The Moon* (1870) was filmed in 1902 as *A Trip To The Moon*. *Twenty Thousand Leagues Under The Sea* (1873) is the most filmed, with the following versions: *Under The Seas* (1907); *20,000 Leagues Under The Sea* (1954); *Captain Nemo And The Underwater City* (1969); and, *The Amazing Captain Nemo* (1977). The 1916 film, *20,000 Leagues Under The Sea*, combined the 1873 novel with its 1875 sequel, *The Mysterious Island*, of which a separate film was made in 1941. *The Clipper Of The Clouds* (1886) and its sequel *Master Of The World* (1914) were combined as the film *Master Of The World* (1961). His novel *Hector Servadac* was filmed as *On The Comet* (1970) and as *Blast Off!* (1954). A further Verne offering is the 1958 film *The Fabulous World Of Jules Verne*, a montage of Verne plots and images.

VICAS, Victor and Franck, Alain. Their novel *Homme Au Cerveau Greffe* became the film *The Man With The Brain Graft* (1972).

VON HARBOU, Thea. Her two novels *Metropolis* (1926) and *By Rocket To The Moon* (1928) were filmed in 1926 and 1929. She wrote the screenplays for both (with Fritz Lang).

VONNEGUT, Kurt Jr. Two of his novels have been filmed: *Slaughterhouse Five; Or, The Children's Crusade* (1969) as *Slaughterhouse Five* (1971) and *Slapstick; Or, Lonesome No More* (1976) as *Slapstick* (1984).

WALLACE, Edgar. His novel *The Green Rust* (1919) was filmed that year as *The Green Terror*.

WELLS, H. G. Much of Wells's sf work has been filmed. The novel *The Time Machine* (1895) was filmed in 1960 and was adapted for the thriller *Time After Time* (1979). *The Island Of Dr Moreau* (1896) was filmed as *The Island Of Terror* (1913), *The Island Of Lost Souls* (1932) and *The Island Of Dr Moreau* (1977). The novel *The Invisible Man* (1897) has seen many versions, chiefly *The Invisible Man* (1933), *The Invisible Man Returns* (1939) and *The Invisible Man's Revenge* (1944). The 1898 short story, "The Man Who Could Work Miracles" was filmed in 1936, and the novel *The War Of The Worlds* (1898) was filmed in 1952. The novel *The First Men In The Moon* (1901) was filmed as *A Trip To The Moon* (1902) and as *First Men In The Moon* in 1919 and 1964. The novel *The Food Of The Gods And How It Came To Earth* (1904) has been filmed as *Village Of The Giants* (1965) and *The Food Of The Gods* (1976). Finally, Wells's polemical novel *The Shape Of Things To Come* (1933) was filmed as *Things To Come* (1936), for which Wells wrote the screenplay, as he did for *The Man Who Could Work Miracles* (1936).

WILLIAMS, David. His novel *Second Sight* was filmed as *The Two Worlds Of Jenny Logan* (1979).

WRIGHT, Sydney Fowler. His novel *Deluge* (1928) was filmed in 1933.

WUL, Stefan. Two of his novels have been filmed: *Oms En Serie* (1957) as *Fantastic Planet* (1973) and *L'Orphelin De Perdide* (1958) as *The Masters Of Time* (1982).

WYLIE, Philip. His solo novel *Gladiator* (1930) was filmed in 1938, and his collaborated novel with Edwin Balmer, *When Worlds Collide* (1933), was filmed in 1951.

WYNDHAM, John. His novel *The Day Of The Triffids* was filmed in 1963. His 1957 novel, *The Midwich Cuckoos*, has been filmed twice, as *Village Of The Damned* (1960) and as *Children Of The Damned* (1963). A short story, "Random Quest", became the film *Quest For Love* (1971).

YURICK, Sol. His novel *The Warriors* was filmed in 1979.

ZELAZNY, Roger. His novel *Damnation Alley* (1969) was filmed in 1977.

Special Effects in Science Fiction Cinema
John Brosnan

As far as today's cinema audiences are concerned "science fiction" and "special effects" are synonymous. In recent years the commercial cinema has been dominated by the big "science fiction" blockbusters and, while sf purists may argue, justifiably, that the sf label is a misnomer, to the general public the term "science fiction" conjures up images of exploding planets, space-ships manoeuvring like World War Two fighters and aliens that are miracles of engineering. The problem is that the field of special effects has made such a technical leap forward during this period that the skills of the effects men far outstrip those of the scriptwriters. It's a case of 1980s technology being used to embroider scripts that have less substance and imagination, with some exceptions, than a 1930s sf pulp magazine.

In the past it was almost a reverse situation: despite their ingenuity and undoubted skills the old Hollywood effects men were usually unable to match the ambitious visions of the writers. Take the 1953 *War of the Worlds*, for example; its effects are certainly spectacular and exciting, but far from convincing. The effects technicians of that era not only lacked the equipment that's available today but also the money. The effects budget on *War of the Worlds* was minuscule compared to that of *Star Wars*. But then the overall budget for *War of the Worlds* was quite small, even in terms of 1950s production costs. Sf films in those days were never allotted "A picture" budgets by the studios; it wasn't until the 1960s that this changed, first with the expensive *Fantastic Voyage* in 1966 and then the even more expensive *2001: A Space Odyssey* in 1968.

There had been relatively big-budget sf movies in the past, such as *Metropolis* (1926), *Just Imagine* (1930) and *Things to Come* (1936), but as none of them were financially successful film companies were deterred from experimenting again with such productions for several decades (it was the fact that both *Fantastic Voyage* and *2001* were box office successes that paved the way for the sf film boom of the 1970s and 1980s).

Of the three films above *Things to Come* is generally regarded as being the nearest to genuine sf film, with its attempt to realistically portray the future as it might be (the future city in *Metropolis* is of an allegorical nature rather than the result of scientific or social extrapolation while the world of 1980 in *Just Imagine* is a satirical reflection of the 1920s).

Things to Come is also regarded as the first major British sf film but its producer, Alexander Korda – himself a Hungarian – imported most of the crew from Hollywood, including the director, William Cameron Menzies, a former set designer, and Ned Mann, who was in charge of all the effects.

Brigitte Helm (top) in a scene from Metropolis

A Hollywood colleague of Menzies, Mann had produced the effects for such films as *Thief of Baghdad* (1924), *Madam Satan* (1930) and the apocalyptic *Deluge* (1934). He brought several of the top Hollywood effects experts with him to the UK, each of whom specialized in a particular effects skill. Harry Zech, for example, was an expert on rear projection; Jack Thomas specialized in optical effects; Ross Jacklin was a model builder; Paul Morell a travelling matte expert; Eddie Cohen an effects cameraman and Lawrence Butler handled full-scale mechanical effects.

The late Wally Veevers, a British effects man who won an Oscar for his work on *2001*, was hired by Mann as an apprentice. "The Board of Trade would only allow work permits for the twelve Americans if they agreed to train some of us in effects work while they were in the country," said Weevers (in an interview in 1972). "I happened to be one of the four British students that Mann chose. It was a marvellous opportunity. We were taken to London Films' Isleworth studio where Mann had set up a machine shop, a plastering shop, an effects camera set-up, an optical printing set-up and an art department. We had to go through all these various departments, spending two weeks in each one, then we could take up any craft we wanted. I took on camerawork and hanging miniatures. I was very lucky with the decision as I got to work with Ross Jacklin, the miniature specialist. We did all the hanging miniatures in *Things to Come* and I learnt a lot from him."

Another Oscar-winning British effects man, Tom Howard, worked with Mann's team during that period. "I trained with Jack Thomas as an optical effects expert that Mann had brought from RKO. To be honest, even though photography had always been my hobby, I looked upon Thomas as rather a miracle man because he was using projection equipment and optical printers that appeared to be the most complicated types of machinery imaginable to me."

But, despite all the Hollywood know-how and equipment, one has to admit that the effects in *Things to Come* vary greatly in quality. Butler's mechanical effects, such as in the bombing raid on "Everytown's" main square, are fine and some of the optical set-ups involving hanging miniatures and the Shuftan process to create the illusion of huge sets are impressive, but much of the model work is unconvincing, particularly in the montage sequences showing futuristic

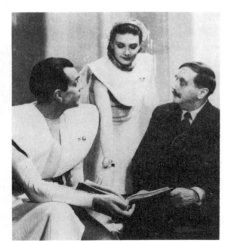

tank battles and in the climactic scenes where a supposedly vast crowd storming the giant space gun obviously consists of hundreds of little model people being pulled jerkily along tracks.

Still, the film did serve as a valuable training ground for British technicians and it's significant that two of them, 30 years later, were Effects Supervisors on Kubrick's *2001*.

There were very few "science fiction" films between *Things to Come* and the sf movie boom that began in 1950, apart from oddities like the

Left to right: Raymond Massey, Margaretta Scott and H. G. Wells on location in Shape Of Things To Come

1939 *Dr Cyclops* which had a mad scientist miniaturizing a group of people. The effects were cleverly contrived and occasionally convincing, the illusion of miniaturization being achieved, with varying success, by a combination of giant props and rear projection, the latter under the supervision of Farciot Edouart, Hollywood's leading exponent of this optical technique in the 1930s and 1940s when it was known as "process photography".

With the arrival of the sf movie boom, which began with *Destination Moon* in 1950, the Hollywood effects men were kept busy trying to create believable visions of "unreality" when, in the past, their job had been to create believable illusions of reality; e.g., that Jon Hall and Dorothy Lamour sitting beside a tepid studio tank were really beside a lagoon on a tropical island. The tools and techniques available to them for the creation of flying saucers and monsters from outer space hadn't really changed since the early 1930s. About the only new development was that rear projection, which had tended to be over-used by the studios in the 1930s and 1940s, was being superseded by improved techniques in travelling mattes, in particular the blue screen process. "Automatic" travelling mattes are cheaper to produce than rear projection and have the added advantage that if an actor makes a mistake with his lines a retake can be done immediately whereas with rear projection the background footage must be halted on the projector and rewound.

It was also considered that the blue screen process provided a more realistic combination of image components in colour movies than rear projection could produce (filming in colour in the 1950s still demanded a lot more light than black-and-white photography – though this changed with the development of faster film stocks – but the rear projection screen couldn't satisfy this demand, with the result that the background scenery was dimmer than the foreground component. Later front projection overcame this handicap), but blue screen has its own disadvantages, the main one being the fringe line around the actors, models or whatever that are filmed in front of it.

The early 1950s sf films, being cheap, tended to be in black-and-white, with the exception of the films made by George Pal. They were just as cheap as the others but the colour, as Pal had wisely realized, made them seem more lavish productions.

Pal, a Hungarian, had enjoyed some success in Europe before World War Two as a model animator, utilizing stop-motion photography to make commercials and entertainment shorts which he called "Puppetoons". On his arrival in America in 1939 he was hired by Paramount to make a series of American "Puppetoons" which they hoped would compete with Disney's cartoons. They proved popular but were increasingly expensive to produce and at the end of the 1940s he began producing live-action feature films. His second was science fiction – *Destination Moon* – the movie that really got the sf boom underway

He then made *When Worlds Collide* in 1951 and *War of the Worlds* in 1953, both of which contained plenty of apocalyptic effects scenes supervised by Paramount's then effects chief Gordon Jennings. As an indication of how important the effects had become, in *War of the Worlds* filming the effects took six months whereas only 40 days were spent filming the actors.

Pal's fourth sf film ended his run of good luck with the genre. *The Conquest of Space* (1955), a would-be serious story about the first manned flight to Mars, was a box office disaster. Apart from an absurd script it was also handicapped by poor effects even though they were supervised by one of the doyens of Hollywood effects men, John P. Fulton. Seen today, one glaring difference in technique between the effects in sf films of that period and contemporary ones is the manner in which spaceship models were built and photographed. While the effects men of the 1940s and 1950s were adept at building and shooting convincing miniature buildings (most of the time), miniature vehicles, such as ships and trains and aircraft tended to be less successfully re-created (with notable exceptions). Spaceships presented even more of a problem and those in *The Conquest of Space*, with their smooth, featureless surfaces lit by bland, sourceless lighting, resemble plastic toys compared to the spaceships of *Star Wars* and *2001: A Space Odyssey* with their starkly lit, busy surfaces.

Another specialist in stop-motion photography became involved with sf movies in the early 1950s but, unlike Pal, he adapted model animation to the genre. He was Ray Harryhausen, protégé of Willis H. O'Brien of *King Kong* fame. His first success was *The Beast from 20,000 Fathoms* (1953), in which he animated a model of a dinosaur and set it loose in New York City. In his second picture, *It Came from Beneath the Sea* (1955), the animated monster was a giant octopus and the city under threat was San Francisco. Animated flying saucers featured in his third movie, *Earth Versus the Flying Saucers* (1956), and in his fourth, and final sf movie for some years, *Twenty Million Miles to Earth* (1957), the monster was a dinosaur-like alien from Venus who won't stop growing.

Harryhausen's sf movies were made on much smaller budgets than Pal's but Harryhausen's unique effects lifted them above similar poverty-row productions. But getting around the restrictions imposed by the budgets often taxed his ingenuity and energy to the limits. For example, in *Earth Versus the Flying Saucers* he couldn't shoot the destruction of the model buildings representing various landmarks in Washington DC at high speed (high speed shooting uses up, obviously, a lot of expensive film stock). "Instead," he said, "the collapse of the buildings had to be animated frame-by-frame. That meant each brick was suspended with wires and had to change position with every frame of film. It was something I'd never do again."

Harryhausen's animated models, even in the low-budget films mentioned above, are always interesting to watch, but, despite the unique visual charm of stop-motion photography, *realism*, one has to admit, is not their strong point. The problem lies in the fact that the model being "animated" is, in reality, frozen in a static position during each frame of exposure and this results in a strobing effect, or jerkiness, when the film is projected.

Recently, however, technicians at the George Lucas effects facility, Industrial Light and Magic, have overcome this problem with a technique they call "go-motion". Utilizing a similar computer system that operates their motion control cameras they move the models by means of attached rods (which are later matted out of the shot) as each frame is exposed. This slight blurring of the model on each frame imparts a smoothness to the animation and eliminates the strobing effect.

As the 1950s progressed the budgets for sf films grew even smaller. One of the last sf movies to enjoy a reasonable effects and production design budget was *Forbidden Planet* in 1956 but this happened almost by accident. The MGM executives regarded it, at first, as a "B picture", assigning a journeyman director to it and casting it with young and relatively unknown contract players, with the exception of Walter Pidgeon. The studio executives were not pleased when the art and special effects departments got carried away with what they were doing and almost doubled the film's official budget.

There are some very impressive effects in *Forbidden Planet*, in particular the early space scenes showing the flying-saucer-like spaceship entering the Altair system and landing on the planet, and the later sequences within the underground complex full of giant, alien machinery. There are some crude effects as well, such as the arrival of the robot jeep – which is obviously just a

spurt of dust being projected along a painted cyclorama – but overall the picture's effects, supervised by MGM's department chief A. Arnold Gillespie, represent a peak in those of the 1950s sf cinema.

Forbidden Planet was by no means a box office failure but it wasn't a spectacular financial success either. If it had been no doubt more big-budget sf movies would have been made in the 1950s but instead the genre became dominated by the cheap exploitation film-makers, such as Roger Corman and Bert I. Gordon; directors who never used two shoe-strings if they could make do with just one. The latter half of the decade saw the making of such sf classics as *Attack of the Crab Monsters*, *The Amazing Colossal Man* and *Attack of the Fifty Foot Man* (all 1957 – a vintage year), in which the main source of entertainment was the risibility of their special effects.

It was not until 10 years after *Forbidden Planet* that another big budget sf movie came to be made – *Fantastic Voyage*. Its story about a journey through a human body in a miniature (*very* miniature) submarine utilized many spectacular effects and some very impressive stylized sets representing the various organs but the special effects still *looked* like special effects. The budget may have been huge for that time, $6,500,000, but the techniques used by the effects unit – made up of Hollywood veterans like L. B. Abbott, Art Cruikshank and Emil Kosa – hadn't changed much since the 1950s.

It was Stanley Kubrick who changed the face of special effects in science fiction movies. When he came to make *2001* he decided to film the effects in such a way that "every special effects shot in it would be completely convincing". To achieve this Kubrick eschewed many of the effects processes that had been in vogue for years, such as the blue screen system, and went back to basics. Kubrick and his team of experts, which included Tom Howard, Wally Veevers and Douglas Trumbull, utilized the trick photography techniques established by the silent film cameramen who were obliged, as there were no optical printers in use in those days, to combine the various image components in the camera (i.e., one element of the scene was shot and then the same piece of film was wound back and then another element was added to it).

For example, to obtain the scenes where either the spaceship *Discovery* or the space station are moving through space with members of their crews visible in the windows it was necessary to film the models at least twice. First, say, the model of the *Discovery* was photographed moving slowly along a track with its window areas blacked out. Then the same movement would be repeated, after the film had been wound back, but this time the exterior of the model was covered with black velvet apart from the window areas which were covered with glossy white cards. On to these cards would be projected the scenes of the interior action.

"The models had to move absolutely smoothly," Veevers later said. "When you come to consider that the space station was nine feet across and we were only moving it three-eighths of an inch a *minute* while shooting it rotating you can appreciate why it had to be so smooth. The same applied to the model of the *Discovery* which was 54 feet long and moved along a track 150 feet in length. It took four-and-a-half hours to reach the end of the track and each time we shot it it had to travel at *exactly* the same speed."

To combine the footage of the various models with a background of star fields Kubrick again refused to use any automatic travelling matte system ("I feel that it is impossible to get original-looking quality with travelling mattes," he said), and insisted that *hand-drawn* mattes be used. This meant that, for example, for a scene of the *Discovery* moving through space the outline of the spaceship had to be rotascoped frame by frame on to animation cells which were used to produce mattes to blank out the corresponding areas on the star-background footage.

Kubrick's methods certainly achieved impressive results but they were both time-consuming and very expensive (*2001* took nearly two-and-a-half years to make and $6,500,000 was spent on the effects alone). Years later when George Lucas wanted a similar look in his space opera *Star Wars* he was obliged to resort to quicker, less expensive methods.

The quality of the effects in *2001* altered the expectations of audiences in this area for good. For instance, the space scenes in the James Bond blockbuster *You Only Live Twice*, released shortly before *2001*, suddenly looked very feeble indeed in spite of their high cost. From now on any film-maker who set a movie in space would have to compete with Kubrick's high standards of visual verisimilitude.

Not surprisingly, seeing as they lacked his budget and luxurious shooting schedule, none of the subsequent makers of space films came close to his achievements during the following decade. But the one who came closest was Douglas Trumbull, an effects supervisor on *2001*, who, in his own production of *Silent Running*, recreated some of the visual majesty of *2001* with similar shots of huge spaceships gliding through space.

Then, in 1976, George Lucas started work on *Star Wars* and very quickly set off a revolution in special effects which is still going on. Wanting the realistic look of *2001* in his space scenes but lacking either the time or a comparable budget Lucas set up an experimental special effects facility, staffed it with young and enthusiastic technicians, such as John Dykstra (he'd worked with Trumbull on *Silent Running*) who was overall supervisor of the visual effects in *Star Wars*, and instructed them to devise new and alternative ways of producing *2001*-style effects.

To achieve this Dykstra and his team had to design and build new equipment from scratch, such as the "motion-control camera". Basically, this is a camera whose movements are controlled by a computer system which enables the camera to make exactly the same movement over and over again. Whereas in *2001* the effects camera remained fixed while the model slowly passed by it several times in order to combine the various image components on the film, in *Star Wars* the model remained stationary and the *camera* moved . . .

This system allowed a greater degree of flexibility and freedom than Kubrick's. Instead of the camera having to remain in a fixed point in space it could become part of the action which increased the visual excitement of the model shots. But in one area Dykstra was obliged to use a conventional system; not having the time to produce mattes by hand (i.e., rotascoping) he had no choice but to use the blue screen automatic matting process. Even so he and his technicians made various improvements in the system, including the use of a specially designed $1 million optical printer which could achieve a better degree of resolution than any printer built before. Matte-lines *are* visible at times in

Star Wars but the quality of the blue-screen work is undeniably very high.

Star Wars suddenly made everyone special effects conscious, and close on its heels came another sf blockbuster that also depended on effects for much of its impact. This was *Close Encounters of the Third Kind*, which differed from *Star Wars* in that it was set on earth and therefore had effects shots that required a different kind of realism, such as highly detailed miniatures of landscapes and urban areas. Many of the effects in *Close Encounters* are of the type that are not recognized by the audience as *being* effects shots. But, of course, it also featured many of the attention-drawing type of effects, most obviously in its spectacular climax when the giant Mother Ship appears.

The effects in *Close Encounters* were supervised by Douglas Trumbull and he later set up an effects facility similar to George Lucas's Industrial Light and Magic operation, calling it the Entertainment Effects Group. Another such effects facility is Apogee Effects, which is run by John Dykstra.

After working on *Close Encounters* Trumbull supervised the effects on *Star Trek – the Motion Picture* and then his company became involved with one of the most impressive sf movies of the 1980s – *Blade Runner*. Trumbull, his partner Richard Yuricich, who is one of the top matte artists, and their staff had the job of creating the future Los Angeles, complete with vast buildings and flying cars, where the film is set. Apart from Yuricich's elaborate and very convincing matte paintings a great amount of model work was required which took nearly a year to shoot and cost $700,000. One of the biggest miniatures was the one built for the film's opening aerial shots of the cityscape. Yet, even though it seems to stretch for ever on the screen the miniature was only 13 feet deep and 18 feet wide. And only the model buildings in the foreground were constructed in any detail, the ones in the rear simply consisted of rows of brass silhouettes in diminishing scale to force the perspective and hence fool the camera, and the human eye ...

To shoot the models of the flying cars – called Spinners – Trumbull and team utilized the motion control camera techniques developed by Dykstra for *Star Wars* but instead of shooting the models against a blue screen Trumbull used a background of illuminated smoke (actually emulsified oil). First the computer-controlled camera made a pass by the model suspended against the "smoke" background and then the same pass was made again without the smoke in order to create a high contrast matte. When the shots of the models were matted into the footage of the miniature cityscape, also photographed using "smoke", the result was a much more textured composite shot than usual, with none of the hard edges of blue screen model shots.

After his work on *Blade Runner*, Trumbull returned to directing again and made the ill-fated, and disappointing, *Brainstorm*. Since then he has been concentrating on developing and promoting a new projection technique which he's called Showscan. Its main feature is that it runs 70 mm film through both camera and projector at 60 frames per second instead of the customary 24 frames per second. Trumbull claims that the image on the screen when projected at this speed is much more realistic than conventionally projected film images. He plans to make a feature film with Showscan as well as to use it to simulate space travel at exhibitions and theme parks.

Apart from new developments in optical effects the boom in sf films has also lead to developments in the art of make-up due to the increasing need for more grotesque and convincing aliens. In fact, in some cases make-up techniques have become so complicated that the dividing line between make-up and special effects has become blurred.

Typical of this situation were the "make-up effects" in John Carpenter's version of *The Thing*. They involved full-scale puppets and manikins operated by a maze of off-camera pneumatic and hydraulic tubes plus complicated electronic systems. The young make-up supervisor, Rob Bottin (who was only 22 at that time), had a team of 35 technicians assisting him on the movie, some of whom just concentrated on one small aspect of the project, like making a fake eye blink realistically.

The work of Carlo Rambaldi – doyen of the creature creators – is also nearer to special effects than make-up. Rambaldi, an Italian sculptor and painter, had worked in the Italian film industry for decades but was unknown in Hollywood until he worked on the 1977 version of *King Kong*. His full-sized mechanical ape for that picture was hardly impressive, apart from its size (all it could do was grimace and shrug) but the alien he built for *Close Encounters* was much more successful.

His next alien was very different – the monster in *Alien* (which he built from a design by H. R. Giger) – but he returned to the benign variety for Spielberg's *E.T.* where he helped create the most successful (in terms of box office receipts) movie alien to date. Actually there were six different ETs; three life-sized, working models which cost around $1,500,000 to build as well as separate head and torso sections used for close-ups. (There was also a suit worn by a midget for some long shots.)

The mechanical ETs were manipulated by a series of hydraulic and pneumatic cables in much the same way as Bottin's manikins in *The Thing* – different cables controlled different features on ET's "face", such as eye movement, wrinkling of the brow, opening and closing of the mouth, etc. The three working models, with their steel and aluminium skeletons overlaid with "muscles" made of polyurethane and foam rubber and covered with carefully painted latex "skins", each specialized in a different function. One for example, was good at moving its arms and hands, another was best at cute eye-rolling and so on.

But for all the technical improvements in this field, which is really puppetry, the real frontier in special effects "state of the art" (to use that embarrassing term) is in the area of computer-generated visual effects. Illustrations and designs by artists are digitized and encoded into a computer which is programmed to bring the illustrations to "life" by giving them movement, colour, weight and a three-dimensional shape. Three films to date have made extensive use of this process: *Tron*, *The Last Starfighter* and *2010: Odyssey Two*, and in all three films the same company, Digital Productions, supplied the computer animation.

In *Tron* the system was used to create an abstract setting – supposedly a world within a computer – and though the animations had more depth than conventional cartoon animation, it was hardly realistic. But with *The Last Starfighter* it was decided to use the computer animation to create realistic space ships as an alternative to the usual method of photographing miniatures. Though the process is expensive and involves the use of a Cray supercomputer (one second of animation requires several trillion computer calculations to map all the data points from one frame to new positions in the next; each frame takes up to three minutes to create on the computer) Digital Productions claim that their work costs only half as much as a similar amount of footage generated by ILM's motion camera control methods.

However, impressive as the "model" animation is in *The Last Starfighter* there is still a "cartoon" quality to it. It is also rather bland and lacking in texture compared to conventional model animation (just compare the sequence where a spaceship flies through a tunnel in an asteroid with the similar sequence in *The Empire Strikes Back*).

Computer animation was used more sparingly, and successfully, in *2010*, where it created shots of Jupiter (based on artist enhanced photographs taken by *Voyager*) and the scenes of the black monoliths replicating and changing shape.

It would seem that the system has built-in limitations but its adherents claim that the sky is literally the limit with computer-simulated effects, saying that one day it will be possible to simulate photo-realistic *living* things, including people, as well as objects. As unlikely as that may seem one must admit that the process is still in its early stages and already it's made remarkable progress. It is possible that by the end of the century computer simulation will have rendered all the other special effects processes described in this article completely obsolete.

Then again the idea that everything in a feature film, including actors, might be one day generated entirely within a computer sounds like pure science fiction.

Glossary of Special Effects Terms

Back-projection Also known as rear projection, this is the system by which background footage is projected on to a translucent screen from the rear while the actors are filmed in front of it. The projector and camera are synchronized and the result is to combine the two image components on the one frame. It is one of the simplest of the *travelling matte* systems.

Blue-screen process The most commonly used of the *travelling matte* (q.v.) systems. It involves the actors, models or whatever being filmed in front of an illuminated blue screen. The colour negative then undergoes a series of printings to produce a strip of film which is transparent within the outline of the actors etc., and opaque in the surrounding area. From this a counter-matte can be printed which is the reverse: opaque within the outline of the actors but transparent in the surrounding area. These mattes are then used in an optical printer to combine the footage of the actors (or whatever) with the separately photographed background footage on to a duplicate negative.

Front-projection This, as the term suggests, is the reverse of back projection. It is achieved by positioning a projector and camera at right angles to each other with a half-silvered mirror placed between them at a 45 degree angle. The camera is directly facing a screen covered with reflective 3M material, in front of which the actors are positioned. The image from the projector is bounced off the mirror and on to the screen and photographed by the camera through the 2-way mirror. As the 3M screen reflects the light back in a straight line the actors' shadows are exactly masked by their bodies. One of the advantages this system has over back projection is that the image on the screen is much brighter and therefore looks more realistic. Stanley Kubrick was the first-film maker to seriously exploit the system – in *2001: A Space Odyssey* – but the idea was patented as far back as 1942.

Hanging miniatures A technique by which models are suspended close to the camera to create the illusion, via forced perspective, that they are full-sized structures being photographed from a distance. The technique was used extensively in the silent era and in the 1930s but then went out of fashion, though some effects men still occasionally use it today.

Mattes Anything which is used to obscure part of an image being photographed in order to combine another image component on to the same frame of film. Mattes are produced in a variety of ways – some extremely complicated, some very simple. For example, an actor standing in front of scenery being projected on to a back projection screen is creating a matte with his own body.

Mechanical effects Also known as *physical effects* or *floor effects*, these include such effects as explosions, bullet holes, fires, collapsing buildings, car crashes, etc., and often involve the participation of stunt people.

Miniatures Also known as *models*, these can range from miniature buildings to spaceships. Some miniatures are quite large – model battleships, for example, have been built to over 50 feet in length, and the model of the spaceship *Discovery* in *2001* was 54 feet long.

Model animation This term covers a wide variety of techniques. It can apply to stop-motion model animation (see **Stop-motion photography**) or the animation of model spaceships. There are many ways to make a model move, or make it *seem* to move, from pulling it along on wires or with built-in motors, to moving the camera while the model remains stationary (the latter technique has been perfected by George Lucas's technicians and is called "motion control").

Optical printer The most important tool in the creation of modern visual effects. The simplest description of an optical printer is that it consists of a film projector facing a process camera. The projector contains the master positive and the camera contains a dupe negative. The obvious use of a printer is to make copies and indeed some printers are designed to perform just that function, but by adding various attachments, such as high precision lenses, and manipulating the projector in different ways, optical printers can create all manner of visual effects – from simple things like speeded-up action and "freeze frames" to the combination of a large number of separately filmed visual elements on to one dupe negative. Printers for complicated effects work can cost up to $1,000,000 to build.

Shuftan process Invented by the German cameraman Eugene Shuftan in 1923, this was a way of combining, by means of mirrors, shots of actors with shots of miniature. For example, to make it appear that an actor was standing in the doorway of a model house a mirror would be positioned between the model and the camera at an angle of 45 degrees. Then all the reflective material would be removed from the mirror except in the area of the model's doorway. Reflected into this area would be the actor standing in a full-sized doorway elsewhere on the set, thus actor and model would be combined. This is just one way in which the process could be used. It was very popular with film-makers in the 1920s and 1930s but isn't used very much now.

Stop-motion photography The process by which inanimate objects are made to seem animate by the camera. Involves the use of a movie camera which exposes just a single frame of film when activated. The operator then moves the object or model in front of the camera into a new position and exposes another frame of film. The process is complicated and time-consuming and the results not always very realistic. The most famous film using stop-motion was, of course, *King Kong*.

Travelling mattes Mattes that change shape from frame to frame. The simplest example is an actor walking by either a back or front projection screen – his body acts as a "travelling matte", blocking off the background footage in a different area from frame to frame. A more complicated way of producing travelling mattes is the *blue screen process* (described above) but the most laborious and time-consuming method of all involves hand-drawn mattes. For example, the only way of removing the wires that supported actor Christopher Reeve in the *Superman* films was to paint them out by hand on every frame of film in which they appeared.

All-Time Rental Figures for Sf Films

These figures are taken from *Variety*'s 1985 listing of all-time rental figures for the US–Canada Market and may be (approximately) doubled to get an idea of worldwide rental figures. I have given two placings for each film, the first an overall placing (for *all* films), the second a placing as far as sf films included in this book are concerned. (Figures are to nearest $1000.)

1	1 *E.T.*	209,977	261	40 *Tron*	16,704
2	2 *Star Wars*	193,500	274	41 *The Twilight Zone*	16,000
3	3 *Return Of The Jedi*	165,500	276	42 *Live & Let Die*	15,900
4	4 *The Empire Strikes Back*	141,600	287	43 *Flash Gordon*	15,404
6	5 *Ghostbusters*	127,000	297	44 *Planet Of The Apes*	15,000
7	6 *Raiders Of The Lost Ark*	115,598	306	45 *Blade Runner*	14,800
8	7 *Indiana Jones & Temple Of Doom*	109,000	317	46 *Coma*	14,500
			317	46 *The Warriors*	14,500
13	8 *Superman*	82,800	335	48 *Dune*	14,000
14	9 *Close Encounters Of The 3rd Kind*	82,750	339	49 *Conan The Destroyer*	13,707
			336	50 *Altered States*	12,500
16	10 *Gremlins*	78,500	369	51 *The Last Starfighter*	12,418
22	11 *Superman II*	65,100	375	52 *Quest For Fire*	12,250
30	12 *Star Trek*	56,000	390	53 *Capricorn One*	12,000
61	13 *Alien*	40,300	421	54 *Mad Max II*	11,300
62	14 *Star Trek II*	40,000	422	55 *20,000 Leagues Under The Sea* (1954)	11,265
66	15 *Star Trek III*	39,000			
67	16 *Young Frankenstein*	38,823	425	56 *Buck Rogers In The 25th Century*	11,168
69	17 *War Games*	38,000			
71	18 *Poltergeist*	37,725	426	57 *Invasion Of The Body Snatchers* (1978)	11,133
73	19 *Superman III*	37,200			
76	20 *King Kong* (1976)	36,915	436	58 *Escape From New York*	10,900
87	21 *Octopussy*	34,024	443	59 *Heavy Metal*	10,648
90	22 *Moonraker*	33,934	455	60 *Son Of Flubber* (1963)	10,450
118	23 *Never Say Never Again*	28,000	464	61 *Island At The Top Of The World*	10,200
122	24 *Thunderball*	26,912			
132	25 *The Black Hole*	25,430	465	62 *Neverending Story*	10,100
135	26 *The China Syndrome*	25,342	469	63 *The Thing* (1982)	10,017
137	27 *The Rocky Horror Picture Show*	25,000	473	64 *Outland*	10,000
			473	64 *Starman*	10,000
137	27 *Firefox*	25,000	509	66 *The Incredible Shrinking Woman*	9,507
146	29 *The Spy Who Loved Me*	24,350			
147	30 *2001*	24,100	513	67 *Logan's Run*	9,500
154	31 *The Dark Crystal*	23,553	520	68 *The Man With The Golden Gun*	9,400
163	32 *Goldfinger*	22,981			
168	33 *Conan The Barbarian*	22,507	536	69 *On Her Majesty's Secret Service*	9,100
201	34 *2010*	20,000			
202	35 *Diamonds Are Forever*	19,717	542	70 *Rollerball*	9,050
207	36 *You Only Live Twice*	19,388	571	71 *Krull*	8,655
224	37 *Time Bandits*	18,950	575	72 *Beneath The Planet Of The Apes*	8,600
252	38 *A Clockwork Orange*	17,000			
252	38 *The Terminator*	17,000	590	73 *The Cat From Outer Space*	8,477

Select Bibliography

AMELIO, RALPH J., **Hal In The Classroom: Science Fiction Films** (1974); *Pflaum Publishing, Ohio.*

BAXTER, JOHN, **Science Fiction In The Cinema** (1970); *A. S. Barnes & Co., New York/A. Zwemmer Ltd, London.*

BROSNAN, JOHN, **Movie Magic: The Story Of Special Effects** (1976); *Plume Books, New York/MacDonald, London.* **Future Tense: The Cinema Of Science Fiction** (1978); *MacDonald & Jane, London.*

CULTHANE, JOHN, **Special Effects In The Movies: How They Do It** (1981); *Ballantine, New York.*

FRANK, ALAN, **Sci-Fi Now** (1978); *Octopus, London.*

GIFFORD, DENIS, **Science Fiction Film** (1971); *Studio Vista/Dutton, London.*

HARDY, PHIL (ed.), **Science Fiction: The Aurum Film Encyclopaedia** (1984); *Aurum, London.*

HARRYHAUSEN, RAY, **Film Fantasy Scrapbook** (1981); *Tantivy Press, USA (Third Edition).*

JOHNSON, WILLIAM, (ed.), **Focus On The Science Fiction Film** (1972); *Prentice-Hall, Inc, USA.*

LEE, WALT, **Reference Guide To Fantastic Films; Science Fiction, Fantasy & Horror, Volume 1 (A–F)** (1972); *Chelsea-Lee Books, USA.* **Reference Guide To Fantastic Films; Science Fiction, Fantasy & Horror, Volume 2 (G–O)** (1973); *Chelsea-Lee Books, USA.* **Reference Guide To Fantastic Films; Science Fiction, Fantasy & Horror, Volume 3 (P–Z)** (1974); *Chelsea-Lee Books, USA.*

MANCHEL, FRANK, **Great Science Fiction Films** (1976); *Franklin Watts, New York and London.*

MENVILLE, DOUGLAS, **A Historical And Critical Survey Of The Science Fiction Film** (1975); *Arno Press, New York.*

MENVILLE, DOUGLAS and R. REGINALD, **Things To Come, An Illustrated History Of The Science Fiction Film** (1977); *Times Books, New York.*

NICHOLLS, PETER, **Fantastic Cinema** (1984); *Ebury Press, London.*

PARISH, JAMES ROBERT and PITTS, MICHAEL R., **The Great Science Fiction Pictures** (1977); *Scarecrow Press, New Jersey.*

PICKARD, ROY, **Science Fiction In The Movies: A–Z** (1978); *Frederik Muller, London.* **The Hamyln Book Of Horror & S.F. Movies Lists** (1983); *Hamlyn, UK.*

POHL, FREDERIK and POHL, FREDERIK IV, **Science Fiction Studies In Film** (1981); *Ace Books, Now York.*

ROVIN, JEFF, **A Pictorial History Of Science Fiction Films** (1975); *Citadel Press, USA.* **From The Land Beyond Beyond** (1977); *Berkly-Windhover Books, New York.*

SHIPMAN, DAVID, **A Pictorial History of Science Fiction Films** (1985); *Hamlyn, London.*

SOBCHACK, VIVIEN CAROL, **The Limits Of Infinity: The American Science Fiction Film** (1980); *A. S. Barnes & Co., New York/Yosselof, London.*

STRICK, PHILIP, **Science Fiction Movies** *(1976); Octopus Books, London.*

STRICKLAND, A. W. and ACKERMAN, FORREST J. **A Reference Guide To American Science Fiction Films, Volume 1** (1981); *USA.*

WARREN, BILL, **Keep Watching The Skies, Vol 1 (1950–1957)** (1982); *McFarland, USA.*

WILLIS, DONALD C., **Horror And Science Fiction Films: A Checklist** (1972); *Scarecrow Press, New Jersey.* **Horror And Science Fiction Films II** (1982); *Scarecrow Press, New Jersey.*